Theory of Shocks, COVID-19, and Normative Fundamentals for Policy Responses

Olga Ivanovna Pilipenko
The Russian Presidential Academy of National Economy and Public Administration, Russia

Zoya Andreevna Pilipenko
Bank of Russia, Russia

Andrey Igorevich Pilipenko
The Russian Presidential Academy of National Economy and Public Administration, Russia

A volume in the Advances in Finance, Accounting, and Economics (AFAE) Book Series

IGI Global
PUBLISHER of TIMELY KNOWLEDGE

Published in the United States of America by
IGI Global
Business Science Reference (an imprint of IGI Global)
701 E. Chocolate Avenue
Hershey PA, USA 17033
Tel: 717-533-8845
Fax: 717-533-8661
E-mail: cust@igi-global.com
Web site: http://www.igi-global.com

Library of Congress Cataloging-in-Publication Data

Names: Pilipenko, Olga Ivanovna, 1953- author. | Pilipenko, Zoya Andreevna, 1981- author. | Pilipenko, Andrey Igorevich, 1946- author.
Title: Theory of shocks, covid-19, and normative fundamentals for policy responses / by Olga Ivanovna Pilipenko, Zoya Andreevna Pilipenko, Andrey Igorevich Pilipenko.
Description: Hershey, PA : Business Science Reference, [2021] | Includes bibliographical references and index. | Summary: "This book examines the effect of shocks theory and self-development laws on economic systems"-- Provided by publisher.
Identifiers: LCCN 2019060093 (print) | LCCN 2019060094 (ebook) | ISBN 9781799843092 (hardcover) | ISBN 9781799852162 (paperback) | ISBN 9781799843108 (ebook)
Subjects: LCSH: Demand (Economic theory) | Economic development.
Classification: LCC HB801 .P495 2021 (print) | LCC HB801 (ebook) | DDC 338.5/4--dc23
LC record available at https://lccn.loc.gov/2019060093
LC ebook record available at https://lccn.loc.gov/2019060094

This book is published in the IGI Global book series Advances in Finance, Accounting, and Economics (AFAE) (ISSN: 2327-5677; eISSN: 2327-5685)

British Cataloguing in Publication Data
A Cataloguing in Publication record for this book is available from the British Library.

All work contributed to this book is new, previously-unpublished material. The views expressed in this book are those of the authors, but not necessarily of the publisher.

For electronic access to this publication, please contact: eresources@igi-global.com.

Advances in Finance, Accounting, and Economics (AFAE) Book Series

Ahmed Driouchi
Al Akhawayn University, Morocco

ISSN:2327-5677
EISSN:2327-5685

Mission

In our changing economic and business environment, it is important to consider the financial changes occurring internationally as well as within individual organizations and business environments. Understanding these changes as well as the factors that influence them is crucial in preparing for our financial future and ensuring economic sustainability and growth.

The **Advances in Finance, Accounting, and Economics (AFAE)** book series aims to publish comprehensive and informative titles in all areas of economics and economic theory, finance, and accounting to assist in advancing the available knowledge and providing for further research development in these dynamic fields.

Coverage

- Economic Theory
- Investments and Derivatives
- Development Economics
- Fiscal Policy
- Entrepreneurship in Accounting and Finance
- Applied Finance
- Economics Geography
- Labor Economics
- Auditing
- Finance and Accounting in SMEs

IGI Global is currently accepting manuscripts for publication within this series. To submit a proposal for a volume in this series, please contact our Acquisition Editors at acquisitions@igi-global.com or visit: https://www.igi-global.com/publish/.

The Advances in Finance, Accounting, and Economics (AFAE) Book Series (ISSN 2327-5677) is published by IGI Global, 701 E. Chocolate Avenue, Hershey, PA 17033-1240, USA, www.igi-global.com. This series is composed of titles available for purchase individually; each title is edited to be contextually exclusive from any other title within the series. For pricing and ordering information please visit https://www.igi-global.com/book-series/advances-finance-accounting-economics/73685. Postmaster: Send all address changes to above address.

Titles in this Series

For a list of additional titles in this series, please visit: www.igi-global.com/book-series

Money Laundering and Terrorism Financing in Global Financial Systems
Abdul Rafay (University of Management and Technology, Pakistan)
Business Science Reference • © 2021 • 374pp • H/C (ISBN: 9781799887584) • US $215.00

Financial Management and Risk Analysis Strategies for Business Sustainability
Joaquín Enríquez-Díaz (University of A Coruña, Spain) Laura Castro-Santos (University of A Coruña, Spain) and Félix Puime-Guillén (University of A Coruña, Spain)
Business Science Reference • © 2021 • 320pp • H/C (ISBN: 9781799876342) • US $215.00

Handbook of Research on Theory and Practice of Financial Crimes
Abdul Rafay (University of Management and Technology, Pakistan)
Business Science Reference • © 2021 • 650pp • H/C (ISBN: 9781799855675) • US $345.00

Comparative Research on Earnings Management, Corporate Governance, and Economic Value
Elisabete S. Vieira (University of Aveiro, Portugal) Mara Madaleno (University of Aveiro, Portugal) and Graça Azevedo (University of Aveiro, Portugal)
Business Science Reference • © 2021 • 433pp • H/C (ISBN: 9781799875963) • US $215.00

Examining the Intersection of Circular Economy, Forestry, and International Trade
Badri Narayanan Gopalakrishnan (University of Washington, USA) Taranjeet Duggal (Amity University, India) and Tavishi Tewary (Amity University, India)
Business Science Reference • © 2021 • 315pp • H/C (ISBN: 9781799849902) • US $195.00

Influence of FinTech on Management Transformation
Amira Sghari (Faculty of Economics and Management, University of Sfax, Tunisia) and Karim Mezghani (Al Imam Mohammad Ibn Saud Islamic University, Saudi Arabia & University of Sfax, Tunisia)
Business Science Reference • © 2021 • 273pp • H/C (ISBN: 9781799871101) • US $215.00

Handbook of Research on Institutional, Economic, and Social Impacts of Globalization and Liberalization
Yilmaz Bayar (Bandirma Onyedi Eylul University, Turkey)
Information Science Reference • © 2021 • 699pp • H/C (ISBN: 9781799844594) • US $445.00

Bridging Microeconomics and Macroeconomics and the Effects on Economic Development and Growth
Pantelis C. Kostis (National and Kapodistrian University of Athens, Greece)
Business Science Reference • © 2021 • 340pp • H/C (ISBN: 9781799849339) • US $195.00

IGI Global
PUBLISHER of TIMELY KNOWLEDGE

701 East Chocolate Avenue, Hershey, PA 17033, USA
Tel: 717-533-8845 x100 • Fax: 717-533-8661
E-Mail: cust@igi-global.com • www.igi-global.com

Dedicated to our parents:

Pilipenko Olga I., Klavdia and Ivan
Pilipenko Zoya A., Olga and Andrey
Pilipenko Andrey I., Nadezhda and Igor

Table of Contents

Preface viii

Acknowledgment xiv

Section 1
Theory of Shocks: Emerging Research

Chapter 1
Shocks vs. Impulse-Propagation Model of Economic Dynamics: The Look From the 2010s 1

Chapter 2
Methodological Approach to the Interpretation of the Essence of Shocks and Forms of Their Manifestation 29

Chapter 3
Shocks in the Economic Systems' Self-Organization 57

Chapter 4
Shocks and Operation of the Law of Denial of Negation: Dialectics of Self-Movement of the Economy in Statics and Dynamics 100

Chapter 5
Elevation of the Human Role in the Technology and Economy Interaction: Subjective Component of Shocks in the Dialectics of Systems' Self-Movement 135

Chapter 6
The Institutional Component of the Shock's Mechanism: Stabilization of the Economy at the Cost of Destabilization of Society 166

Chapter 7
Theory of Shocks About States in Static and Dynamic Economics 202

Section 2
Shocks Theory and Its Opportunities as Applied to Shock and Crisis Caused by the COVID-19 Pandemic

Chapter 8
COVID-19 Shock and Subsequent Crisis: How It Was 242

Chapter 9
COVID-19 Shock and Schumpeterian "Creative Destruction": Self-Enforcing Companies and Self-Development of the Future Dynamic Economy 272

Chapter 10
Nation State and Fighting the COVID-19 Pandemic Shock Who is Responsible? 314

Chapter 11
The State and the Construction of the Post-COVID-19 Future: What to Do? 345

Conclusion 389

About the Authors 393

Index 395

Preface

The motivation for undertaking the shocks' theory project came to the authors in the first half of the 1990s parallel to the process of the scientific work on problems of specifics of self-development of different national economic systems (compared to Russia). The authors came across the phenomenon of shocks, which was mentioned quite often in the literature on economic crises. But the authors did not find a fundamental explanation of either the factors realizing shocks, or the functions they perform in the self-movement of economic systems. Surprising for the authors became the fact that as early as the beginning of the 20th century, such famous scientists as R. Frisch (1929, 1933, 1992), E. Slutsky (1927a, 1927b, 1937a, 1937b), and Irma and Frank Adelman (1959) were engaged in shocks' (impulses') issues. Acquaintance with their works convinces the authors that the phenomenon of shocks refers to a system-forming problem that cannot be studied without dialectical ideas about the economy as a systemic integrity, without understanding the mechanism of its self-movement, without objective and subjective factors that mediate the action of dialectical laws in which shocks fulfill certain function. And here the fascination with philosophy played its fundamental role: the authors' search for the appropriate method of scientific research led them to the principles of dialectical logic.

The formation of the theoretical design of the authors took a lot of time, but was accompanied by an amazing feeling of touching the "great": problems, ideas, personalities in science, brilliant foresights. As a result, in the heads of the authors there arose an organically combining structure of a complex economic system, which was capable of developing, rebuilding itself, and being present as integrity at the same time both in a stationary state and in a changing one. In different years, the authors defended their doctoral dissertations, in which some of the above problems developed. But in practice, they faced the realization of shocks in the late 1990s in Russia, and then a series of shocks in countries and regions all over the Globe and the shock of 2007 and the global financial crisis of 2008-2009, as well as the last ones, connected with the coronavirus pandemic of 2020.

This book is not simple. It was created in "creative delight" from the fact that suddenly "truths" were discovered, deeply hidden in phenomena and processes. Much was inspired by the geniuses of the past and present who anticipated the distant future: G.W.F. Hegel (1892), K. Marx and F. Engels (1955-1974), A.A. Bogdanov (1934), J. M. Keynes (1936), Joseph A. Schumpeter (1949), representatives of the Austrian theoretical school, D. North (1981, 1996), Ludwig H. von Mises (1998), Ragnar Frisch (1933), E.E. Slutsky (1927a, 1927b, 1937a), and many other brilliant researchers. Working with the legacy of these giants led the authors to the idea of the need for a consistent analysis of the states of economic integrity from the philosophical standpoint on the foundation of the dialectics of systems self-movement. The choice of dialectical logic as a methodological approach to building the foundations of shocks' theory in itself turned out to be the great luck. But it was preceded by a major good luck associated with the actual choice of shocks as a research problem. From the very first steps, the authors realized the amazing multidimensionality of the phenomenon of shocks, which manifested itself in the definition of their essence and forms of manifestation, and in the mechanisms of implementation, taking into account their object, subjective, process and institutional components. The third luck was the deep integration of shocks into the "holy of holies" of the problems of self-movement of systemic integrities in the economy. Dialectical application of the tectological principles of A.A. Bogdanov to the organization of human-created systems in the economy, technology and society in connection with the shocks led the authors to the opportunity to see the simple in the complex and in the very complex. This confirms the truth that the great A. Einstein expressed in the following words: "*For, in reality, things happen in exactly the opposite way. It is only the theory which decides what can be observed*"! (The Einstein-Heisenberg discussion, 1926).

Obeying the dialectical logic of cognition, the authors naturally came to the formation of a hypothesis about the embeddedness of shocks into the mechanism of implementation of dialectical laws. On that basis, a model was constructed for the formation of systemic integrity in the economy in the simplest processes of differentiation and integration of human economic activity (labor), of its results and of organizations in the process of their endless complication. The dialectical approach to the interpretation of the interaction of shocks with the structure of system integrity made it possible to prove that shocks manifest themselves in different ways in the process of self-organization of a static system and of its self-development in a dynamic state. At the same time, destroying individual structural ties in a static economy at the stage of its self-organization or its entire structure during a "jump" into an uncertain dynamic future, shocks fulfill the mission of strengthening systemic integrity. As it turned out, it is in this capacity that shocks mediate turning points in the implementation of the action of the dialectical laws of self-movement of systems in the conditions of unity and struggle of opposites, the transition of quantitative changes into qualitative ones and denial of negation.

A complete revelation for the authors was the phenomenon of subjectivization of all structural ties in the economic system as it built a hierarchy of structural levels, which, on the one hand, increased the number of causal relationships, seemingly strengthening the stability of the entire system, and on the other hand, aggravated its fragility. And this dialectic of self-organization of economic systems organically fits shocks that are realized with the direct participation of economic agents. In this case, dialectical logic forced the authors to consider a person as a polysyllabic phenomenon, since by participating in market transactions, mediating their shock destruction, a person realizes the values, norms of behavior and principles of attitude towards his partners that he acquired in society. All further complication of the studied categories began to be predetermined by the idea of Emile Durkheim (1895) that Homo Sapiens is always and to the same extent also Homo Socius. This is how the understanding gradually came that the objectively operating organizational mechanism presented by A.A. Bogdanov (1934) by positive and negative selection, could quite adequately settle the dialectical contradictions of systemic integrities created by man, if they were represented only by their object component. However, the subjective component of all the processes of self-movement of systems in the economy turns shocks into an objective reality, without which it is impossible to "break" non-working structural connections (at the stage of self-organization) of systems or destroy the systemic structure as a whole that has exhausted its potential (at the stage of its self-development).

The authors are aware that a whole layer of problems awaits their further research, which is associated with the mechanism for the implementation of shocks and the behavior of the state, as well as with the institutional component of shock mediation of the dialectical laws of self-movement of systemic integrity in technology, economy and society. This will take time.

And today, a book on the positive and normative foundations of shocks' theory stopped researchers at the most interesting place, when they realized that shocks, as an objectively operating mechanism for the implementation of turning points in the action of dialectical laws, would always accompany a person in any area of his life. Without delving into the nuances of proving fundamental changes that accompany the dialectic of the interaction of systemic integrity in technology, economy and society, the authors are confident that the principle of human-centrism should become the dominant priority in theoretical research and in practical actions in the constructing the post-covid reality.

By the way, this was also proved by the applied part of the book related to the pandemic shock of COVID-19, in which the logic of understanding the development of events and factors of uncertainties of post-coronavirus reality was built.

And the logic turns out to be simple: the specificity of the technological revolution 4.0 in the unimaginable organizational diversity of its embodiment predetermines the need for the presence of critical mass of creative personalities; there will be no intellectually autonomous individuals, there will be no new technological base; there will be no new technological base, there will be no dynamic economy. At the same time, the epoch-making mission of forming a new structure of the post-covid dynamic economy lies with self-sufficient companies that are ready for the Schumpeterian creative destruction. This conclusion of the authors is based on the fact that the above mentioned companies, through the mechanism of downwards causation, structure themselves from the inside, and with the help of the mechanism of upwards causation, they objectively structure the external environment of their functioning both in the economy and in society. But it should be emphasized that it is the nation state that determines the choice of society of its future: between the architecting a dynamic economy for overall good or returning into Groundhog Day with the static economy as before the COVID-19 pandemic. The last scenario is the lost opportunities for future progress, but, unfortunately, this will only be obvious to future generations and only in comparison with dynamic societies. *Following Arthur C. Clarke, it is safe to say that the COVID-19 pandemic marked the "Childhood's End" of humanity. Now the main thing is that people realize this truth and immediately choose a great future.*

The structure of the book reproduces the above logic of the authors' reasoning.

Chapter 1 is dedicated to reviewing propagation problems and impulse problems in dynamic economics, submitted by R. Frisch in works such as (1) 'Propagation problems and impulse problems in dynamic economics'. In: *Economic Essays in Honour of Gustav Cassel.* (1933). London: Allen and Unwin, and (2) 'Statics and dynamics theory in economic'. *Structural Change and Economic Dynamics.* ([1929]; 1992). Vol. 3, No. 2, 1992. Translated by Peter Thomas from the original Norwegian article which appeared in *Nationaløkonomisk Tidsskrift,* Vol. 67.

In addition, the chapter presents the position of E.E. Slutsky about the summation of random causes as the source of cyclic process, which were described in his following works: (1) Slutsky, E. (1927b). 'The summation of random causes as the source of cyclic processes'. *The Questions of Conjuncture.* Vol. 3, No. 1. PP. 34-64. (Moscow: Conjuncture Institute of Moscow); (2) Slutsky, E. ([1927], 1937), 'The Summation of Random Causes as the Source of Cyclic Processes' (in Russian), in Problems of Economic Conditions, The Conjuncture Institute, Moscow, Vol.3, No.1; revised English version in *Econometrica,* Vol. 5, No 2, pp. 105-146; and (3) Slutsky, E. (1937). 'The summation of random causes as the source of cyclic processes'. *Econometrica.* Vol. 5. Issue 2. Apr. PP. 105–146.

In addition, the authors described the specifics of the bold experiment with the Klein—Goldberger model held by Irma and Frank Adelman. Based on the results of considering the essence of the concepts presented in connection with shocks and static and dynamic changes in the economy, the authors of the book built their logic of forming the foundations of shocks' theory.

Chapter 2 is devoted to the substantiation of the methodological approach to the interpretation of the essence of shocks and forms of their manifestation. For these purposes, the authors give their interpretation of modern well-established ideas about the phenomenon of shock as "a thing in itself". Its essence is manifested in the fact that the frequent use of shocks in publications does not bring readers closer to understanding this phenomenon. The interpretation of shocks based on the dialectical approach allows the authors to formulate the hypothesis of the objective embeddedness of shocks into the economic system's structure. The chapter ends with the identification of forms of shocks' manifestation in various markets as a result of a marginal gap between base and market prices of objects of exchange.

Chapter 3 examines the process component of the shocks phenomenon in connection with the self-organization of economic systems. The structuring of the chapter material started with dialectics of specialized economic activities' cooperation, which made it possible to determine market exchange as a sphere of shocks' realization. A difference was made in the impact of shocks on the structure of the economic system at the stage of its self-organization under the conditions of the law of unity and struggle of opposites and during the transition of quantitative changes into qualitative changes. The implementation of the mechanism of shock destruction of structural ties was demonstrated theoretically by the example of the destruction of the vertical structural ties of the system and practically by the example of the shock in the American market of unsecured mortgage loans in 2007 and the subsequent global financial crisis of 2008-2009.

Chapter 4 is devoted to the peculiarities of the implementation of the shock mechanism in the context of mediating the turning point in action of the law of denial of negation. It is about the imputation of the shock mechanism in dialectics of self-development of the economy during its transition from a static state to a dynamic one. The difference in the implementation of a shock effect on the structural links of a self-organizing and self-developing system is proved. The authors substantiate the need to analyze the interaction of the integrity of society with the economic system during its transition to the stage of self-development.

In Chapter 5, the authors demonstrate the elevation of the human role in the context of a dynamic change in a self-developing economic system. The multidimensionality of this process is shown, which is associated with the need to study the tendencies of subjectivization in the interaction of technology and a person, taking into account his education, in the process of replacing the monetary equivalent with trust in financial transactions as a vertical structural hierarchy is formed at the stage of transition of quantitative changes to qualitative ones in the self-organization of economic systems. The brilliant guesses of J.M. Keynes (1936, 1937, 1939) and the arguments of H.P. Minsky (1957, 1985, 1992, 2008) in support of the "propensity of the market economy to instability" are considered. As a result, a proof is formulated that the subjective factor predetermines the endogeneity of the mechanism of shocks adjustment of structural fragility.

Chapter 6 is devoted to the substantiation of the institutional component of the shock's mechanism, which manifests itself in the fact that at the stage of self-development of the economic system. It is the violation of the integrity of society that predetermines the destruction of the structure of the economic system under the influence of the law of denial of negation. In parallel, conditions are formulated for the transformation of further theoretical research due to their human-centrism.

Chapter 7 deals with the theory of shocks in the context of the missions of the state in the economic system at the stage of its statics and dynamics. The institutional component of the mechanism of destruction of structural ties in a static economy at the stage of self-organization and the violation of the dialectics of the economy and society during the shock's destruction of the entire structure of the economic system during its jump to the stage of self-development are substantiated. The paramount importance of the restoration of the dialectics of society and the economic system by the state in its dynamic status, with a critical mass of humans with the quality of intellectual autonomousness, and with human-centrism as the dominant principle of organization is proved.

Chapter 8 provides an insight into the implementation of the COVID-19 shock and subsequent crisis development. There are considered two waves of the COVID-19 pandemic as well as there is analyzed the failure of the national public healthcare systems in the categories of missed opportunities. The rise of human factors is seen through a tough imperative set by the COVID-19 pandemic shock to the state: the safeguarding lives and livelihoods of people. The result of the chapter is the option, formulated by the authors, of the state's choice of a post-covid future: the architecting a dynamic economy for overall good or returning into Groundhog Days with the static economy as before the COVID-19 pandemic.

In Chapter 9 COVID-19 shock is interpreted in the context of the Schumpeterian "creative destruction" that could be implemented by self-enforcing companies in self-development of the future dynamic economy. The interpretation of large companies in the context of their ability to structure the future at the stage of self-development of the economic system is predetermined by their mechanism of self-movement. Self-organizing companies are capable to mediate the downwards causation process, and their self-development is associated with the upwards causation process.

In Chapter 10, the authors substantiate the need to change the functions of the state in the context of the transition from fiscal mechanisms of fighting a humanitarian catastrophe ex post to the priority of a human-centric policy of preventing it ex ante. Only in this context do the authors see the possibility of increasing governments' efficiency and their new functions after the COVID-19 pandemic.

Chapter 11 claims to be the normative aspect of the theory of shocks in connection with the justification of the state's behavior in the conditions of self-development of the economy and the restoration of the dialectics of the economic system and society, the dominance of human-centrism and the formation of high-quality education and healthcare system. In addition, the state should rethink the mission of large self-sufficient companies as the main drivers of architecting the post-coronavirus dynamic economy, which is characterized by self-development, by a dynamic state and by the complete uncertainty of the way it could be implemented.

In Conclusion the authors give an overview of the foundations of their theory of shocks in its positive and normative aspects and the future of its future development.

REFERENCES

Adelman, I. (1959). The dynamic properties of the Klein-Goldberger model. *Econometrica.*

Bogdanov, A. A. (1934). Tectology or General Organizational Science. Academic Press.

Clarke, A. C. (1990). *Childhood's End.* Pan Books Ltd.

Durkheim, E. (1895). *The Rules of Sociological Method.* Sage Publications.

Frisch, R. (1933). Propagation problems and impulse problems in dynamic economics. In *Economic Essays in Honour of Gustav Cassel.* Allen and Unwin.

Frisch, R. (1992). Statics and dynamics theory in economic. Structural Change and Economic Dynamics, 3(2). (Original publication 1929)

Hegel, G. W. F. (1892). The science of logics. In The Logic of Hegel (2nd ed.). Oxford University Press.

Holton, G. (2004). *Werner Heisenberg and Albert Einstein*. Working paper, Department of Physics, Harvard University. http://nrs.harvard.edu/urn-3:HUL.InstRepos:37852648

Keynes, J. M. (1936). *The General Theory of Employment? Interest and Money. The Selected Works*. Harcourt, Brace and Company.

Keynes, J. M. (1937). The "ex ante" theory of the rate of interest. *Economic Journal (London)*, *46*(186), 241. doi:10.2307/2225525

Keynes, J. M. (1939). The process of capital formation. *Economic Journal (London)*, *49*(195).

Marx, K., & Engels, F. (1955-1974). *Coll. Cit.* (2nd ed.). Moscow: Political Literature Publishing House.

Minsky, H. P. (1957). Central banking and monetary market changes. *The Quarterly Journal of Economics*, *71*(2), 171. doi:10.2307/1883812

Minsky, H. P. (1985). The financial instability hypothesis: a restatement. In P. Arestis & T. Skouras (Eds.), *Post-Keynesian Economic Theory: A Challenge Neoclassical Economics*. Wheatsheaf.

Minsky, H. P. (1992). Profits, deficits and instability: A policy discussion. In D. B. Paradimitriou (Ed.), *Profits, Deficits and Instability*. Macmillan. doi:10.1007/978-1-349-11786-4_2

Minsky, H. P. (2008). *Stabilizing an Unstable Economy*. McGraw-Hill.

Mises, L. H. E. v. (1998). *Human Action: A Treatise on Economics*. Yale University Press.

North, D. (1996). *Institutions, Institutional Change and Economic Performance*. Cambridge University Press.

North, D. C. (1981). *Structure and Change in Economic History*. W. W. Norton & Co.

Schumpeter, J. A. (1949). The Theory of Economic Development: An Inquiry into Profits, Capital, Credit, Interest, and the Business Cycle. Harvard University Press.

Slutsky, E. (1927b). The summation of random causes as the source of cyclic processes. In The Questions of Conjuncture. Conjuncture Institute of Moscow.

Slutsky, E. (1937). The summation of random causes as the source of cyclic processes. Econometrica, 5(2), 105–146. doi:10.2307/1907241

Slutsky, E. (1927a). The Summation of Random Causes as the Source of Cyclic Processes (in Russian). In Problems of Economic Conditions. The Conjuncture Institute.

Slutsky, E. E. (1927a). The accumulation of accidental causes as the source of cyclic processes. In *Problems of Economic Conditions*. Conjuncture Institute publishing house.

Acknowledgment

Any research problem is able to unite creative individuals and motivate them to implement a joint project. For its successful start and completion, many conditions are necessary, but the main thing for the researchers of the foundations of the theory of shocks turned out to be the fundamental theoretical base of the co-authors, the complementarity of their knowledge and the insatiable desire to "learn the still unknown".

The theoretical foundation was laid by the university education of the participants in the shock theory project. Deep knowledge in the field of philosophy, economics and finance is the result of painstaking teaching and research work of the creative team of the Department of Economics of Foreign Countries and Foreign Economic Relations of the Faculty of Economics of Lomonosov's Moscow State University under the guidance of Professor V.P. Kolesov. The functions of the thinking tank of this department were performed by Prof. M.V. Kulakov, Prof. M.N. Osmova, Prof. V.F. Zhelezova, Prof. E.A. Kasatkina, Prof. E.K. Mazurova, Prof. S.V. Penkina, and etc. The fundamental approach of the authors of the book to the unknown phenomenon of shocks, the choice of dialectical logics as the basis for structuring systemic categories is undoubtedly the merit of the patriarchs of science from Lomonosov's Moscow State University. By the way, the very choice of shocks as the main research problem of this book, its authors owe it to this team. About 10 years ago they very actively discussed the phenomenon of shocks as the topic of the doctoral dissertation of one of the authors of the book, which was successfully defended in the same team.

Mathematical modeling of economic and social phenomena in the book was based on the university specialization of one of the authors of the book in physical and mathematical sciences and his in-depth immersion in physical and chemical phenomena as a graduate student of the Institute of Physical Chemistry of the USSR Academy of Sciences. The preparation of a dissertation in physical and mathematical sciences took place with the participation of the author in fundamental research of sorption processes under the guidance of leading scientists: Academician M.M. Dubinin, Prof. V.V. Serpinsky, Prof. A.M. Voloshchuk.

Further work of the authors of the book at various Russian universities in Bryansk, Kursk and Moscow led to the unifying them research problem related to the formation of intellectually autonomous individuals and their socialization. Immersion in the treasury of pedagogical sciences, created by Soviet and Russian scientists-educators, and the deepening of the global crisis in education led one of the authors of the book to prepare and defend a doctoral dissertation in pedagogy at the Russian Academy of Education. It was in it that the foundations of the theory of psychological and cognitive barriers in learning were formulated, which were formed in scientific discussions with Prof. Yu.I. Dik, Prof. A.A. Pinsky, Corresponding Member of Russian Academy of Pedagogical Sciences V.I. Slobodchikov, Academician V.G. Razumovsky.

A huge gratitude should be expressed to all the people who inspired the future authors of this book, believed in their scientific potential and constantly generated their confidence in the success of the research projects undertaken. It is about such bright personalities as Prof. V.D. Sukhov, Prof. N.Ya. Gvozdareva, Prof. B.I. Gvozdarev, Prof. I.M. Aren, Prof. E.I. Evseenko, Prof. Yu.V. Shishkov, Prof. A.Ya. Eljanov, Prof. N.M. Klemeniev, Prof. G.B. Polyak, Prof. V.A. Polovnikov, Prof. V.A. Shvandar, et al.

By the time of the first foreign publications, three participants in a research project related to shock theory had a total of more than 250 publications. Bruno S. Sergi (an instructor on the Economics of Emerging Markets and the Political Economy of Russia and China at Harvard University) became the first foreign editor to include 5 works of authors in his two books and the journal. The first book was published in the USA by IGI Global, and the second one in the UK by Emerald Publishing Ltd. Magdalena Ziolo (Associate Professor, University of Szczecin, Poland), who regularly included chapters prepared by the authors in her books published in the USA by IGI Global, gave them the great creative perspective and the opportunity to diversify the topics of their publications.

It was Bruno S. Sergi and Magdalena Ziolo who inspired the authors to participate in the preparation of an application for a book for IGI Global, which invited potential authors to cooperate in connection with the 30th anniversary of its activity. The authors consider this contact with the IGI Global team to be predetermined from above. The authors did not expect to meet such a creative approach and thoughtful work of the entire IGI Global team. First of all, the authors express their deepest gratitude to Ms. Jan Travers, Director of Intellectual Property & Contracts of IGI Global, to Melissa Wagner, Editorial Director, Ms. Crystal Moyer, Assistant Development Editor, and Maria Rohde, Book Development Coordinator. Without their sincere empathy and desire to improve the content of the monograph, the authors would hardly have reached the stage of its publication.

Of particular note is the IGI Global's selection of reviewers for potential authors' manuscripts evaluation. In the case of this book, it was the reviewers with their depth of knowledge, scientific erudition and sincere desire to help, who initiated the authors to perform significant work on correcting the manuscript.

Section 1
Theory of Shocks: Emerging Research

Chapter 1
Shocks vs. Impulse-Propagation Model of Economic Dynamics:
The Look From the 2010s

ABSTRACT

Ragnar Frisch, the Nobel prizer in economics, drew attention to two phenomena: propagation problems and impulse problems in dynamic economics. His deep scientific contribution relates to the interpretation of business cycle transformed under the influence of impulses (shocks). But some terminological misunderstandings arose. One of them forced the authors to focus on the phenomenon of systems' self-movement: their self-organization in statics and their self-development in dynamics. Another one relates to exogenous nature of impulses (shocks) that forced the authors to prove the endogenous embeddedness of shocks into the mechanisms of dialectical laws implementation. Eugen Slutsky demonstrated the stochastic approach as to random fluctuations as a source of cyclical processes in the economy. The confusion in the concepts of cycles and waves predetermines the need to create a wave theory of systemic self-organization (Chapter 2). Modern shocks theory develops a new approach which makes it possible to eliminate misconceptions of past theories.

INTRODUCTION

It is about ten years since the onset of the global financial crisis, but some fundamental questions connected with it remain open. A misunderstanding of some aspects related to the global financial crisis of 2007–2009 and of subsequent slowdown of the global economic growth forced the authors to focus on the study of the nature of financial shock, which served as a trigger in multiplying the phenomenon of the breakdown of the structural transnational relations in the late 2000s. The need for a systemic interpretation of the phenomenon of shock (impulse) in the context of the self-development laws of national economies was generated by ideas that remained outside the attention of theorists for many decades.

DOI: 10.4018/978-1-7998-4309-2.ch001

Back in 1933, Ragnar Frisch (1933) in his famous work "Propagation problems and impulse problems in dynamic economics" substantiated the "impulsive-propagation" approach to modeling the macroeconomic business cycle. In addition, at the beginning of the last century, such coryphaeus of Russian science as N.D. Kondratieff (1922; 1935), E.E. Slutsky (1927a, 1927b, 1937) and other representatives of the famous Kondratyev's Conjuncture Institute (Moscow), linked economic shocks with the most important areas of research. So, in particular, Ragnar Frisch (1933) was one of the first to question the acceptability of deterministic models for explaining economic cycles. He substantiated the hypothesis that it was precisely random effects - "impulses" (or shocks – as they are called today) on the economic system - that served as the beginning of a cyclical model of its reaction to external influence. In the late 50s of the last century Irma and Frank Adelman (1959) tested the impulse-propagation approach in the empirical studies of economic fluctuations. It turned out that the amplitude and duration of economic cycles caused by simulated external impulses, surprisingly exactly repeated those that actually took place in the United States. The results showed the evidence that investigation of shocks as key elements of the impulse model of cyclical economic development is very important for understanding of the contemporary world economy's development as well as its future cycles.

Having deeply worked out the theoretical positions of the above-mentioned authors, we considered it necessary to highlight those phenomena that remained outside the attention of these researchers or were not thoroughly worked out. They can be briefly summarized as follows.

1. The concepts of impulse in general, its essence and forms of manifestation, as well as ideas about the mechanism of its implementation and impact on the economy as a structural integrity have not been substantiated.
2. There is no theoretical description of the interaction of impulses and self-propulsion mechanisms of economic systems.
3. A vague concept of shocks is given, which does not allow to define them theoretically, neither from the point of view of phenomenology, nor from the standpoint of the mechanism of their generation and manifestation, nor in relation to crises. This largely predetermined the emergence of the phenomenon of shocks today as a thing-in-itself.

These and other provisions of the above scientists are discussed in detail in paragraphs 1.1 - 1.3, and are also detailed and commented on from the standpoint of the shocks theory developed in this book in the paragraph 1.4.

1.1. 'Propagation Problems and Impulse Problems in Dynamic Economics' Treated by R. Frisch

The authors retained in the chapter the logic of the research of R. Frisch, according to which he distinguished two fundamental problems: first, the *propagation* problem; second, the *impulse* problem. Moreover the propagation problem was connected with the structural properties of the swinging system. It is about the character of the swings started in some initial situation. The merit of R. Frisch lies in the fact that he initially sought to consider the swinging system of economy as a dynamic process that predetermines a causal relationship between developing events. He writes that it is from the standpoint of the dynamic theory it should be explained how one situation grows out of the foregoing. At the beginning of the last century, such a statement about the need for a dynamic approach to explaining the swinging system of the economy contrary to the system of Walrasian equations can be called a real scientific challenge. At the same time, R. Frisch believes that 'in one respect, however, must the dynamic system be similar to the Walrasian: it must be determinate'.

It should be noted that the beginning of the scientific study of the authors in the formation of the basics of shock theory began precisely with the allocation of the dynamic characteristics of the economic system. And the position of R. Frisch that economic phenomena should be understood on the principle of "how one situation grows out of the foregoing" led the authors to formulate a systemically important goals for shocks' theory: to determine the dynamic characteristics of the economic system as an integrity, to distinguish its perpetual mechanism of self-development, also subject to dynamic changes, and to understand the place and functions of shocks in these complex structures. By choosing the principles of dialectical logic as the main ones, the authors became able to coordinate those causal relationships in their design both with regard to the movement of the economic system through the stages of its self-development and to the self-organization of the structure of the system, which is based on building causal relationships between hierarchical levels of exchange.

A lot of thoughts were caused with the following reasoning of R. Frisch (1933):

1. «The most important feature of the free oscillations is that the length of the cycles and the tendency towards dampening are determined by the intrinsic structure of the swinging system, while the intensity (the amplitude) of the fluctuations ***is determined primarily by the exterior impulse***» (Frisch, (1933), p.171);
2. "The propagation problem is the problem of explaining by the structural properties of the swinging system what ***the character of the swings would be in case the system was started in some initial situation***" (Frisch, (1933), P.171).

These thoughts of R. Frisch became the starting point in an in-depth study of the dialectics of the interaction of philosophical categories of a system and its structure as applied to a complex economy. The authors' arguments were based on the fact that both production and consumption, on the one hand, and the integrated unity of differentiated types of activity and the exchange of its results, incorporating them, on the other hand, could not depend on «the character of the swings in case the system was started» and "be determined primarily by the exterior impulse". The system of the economy in essence should be self-developing, i.e. capable of constantly reproducing itself, constantly changing itself, correcting itself, generating its additional segments, as well as rebuilding them. This is predetermined by its constituent economic entities, which constantly consume, initiating production to meet their needs for constant growth. And for this it is not necessary to assume the presence of some initial push. Indeed, the possibility of such an infinite self-development of the economic system is associated not with external impulses, but with its inherent mechanism internally built into it, which ensures this endless process of its changes. Apparently R. Frisch, speaking about dynamic changes in the economy, had in mind precisely this fact. But the traditional at that time technology for analyzing long-term changes in the economy connected its dynamics not with the mechanisms of breaking cycles and of changing oscillations, but with the mechanism of their propagation (implementation). And this made scientists fall into the Procrustean bed of analysis of the business cycle. This fact is confirmed by the ideas of R. Frisch about this "dynamics" of economic phenomena, expressed graphically by him on Fig. 1.

Figure 1. The ideas of R. Frisch about "dynamics" of economic phenomena
Source: Frisch, Ragnar. (1933). 'Propagation problems and impulse problems in dynamic economics'. In: Economic Essays in Honour of Gustav Cassel. London: Allen and Unwin, Fig. I, p. 174.

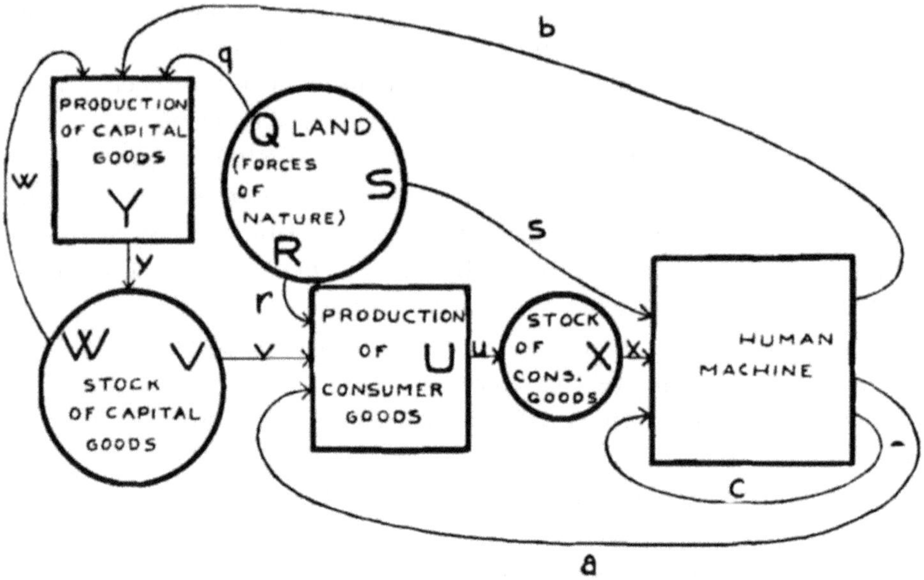

Relevant R. Frisch' explanations for this figure (Fig. 1) are given below.

"The notation is chosen such that capital letters indicate stocks and small letters flows. For instance, ***R*** means that part of land (or other forces of nature) which is engaged in the production of consumer goods, ***r*** is the services rendered by ***R*** per unit time. Similarly ***V*** is the stock of capital goods engaged in the production of consumer goods and ***v*** the services rendered by this stock per unit time. Further, ***a*** is labour (manual or mental) entering into the production of consumer goods, so that the total input in the production of consumer goods is $r + v + a$.

The complete macro-dynamic problem, as I conceive of it, consists in describing as realistically as possible the kind of relations that exist between the various magnitudes in the Tableau Economique exhibited in Fig. I, and from the nature of these relations to explain the movements, cyclical or otherwise, of the system." (Frisch, (1933), PP.173-174)

R. Frisch's logic described by his approach to the analysis of the dynamics of the system in his understanding made it possible to formulate a contradiction between the statics and the dynamics of economic changes. The authors give the following reasoning of R. Frisch (1933, P. 174): «This analysis, in order to be complete, must show exactly what sort of fluctuations are to be expected, how the length of the cycles will be determined from the nature of the dynamic connection between the variables in the Tableau Economique, how the damping exponents, if any, may be derived, etc.»

The authors drew attention to the fact that R. Frisch, modelling "dynamic" economics (in his understanding), relied on a deterministic system of differential equations. However, realizing that the real economic system is not subject to deterministic laws, R. Frisch believed in the future to use «an interesting synthesis between the stochastical point of view and the point of view of rigidly determined dynamical laws» in the description of the dynamic system. Since these wishes were not realized, the authors were forced to take the path of identifying philosophical ideas about the laws of self-development of dynamic systems in the economy (Chapter 4 of this book). Model of the dialectic of self-development of the economy as a complex system at its main stages using dynamic sets is presented in Fig. 2 (Fig.7 from Chapter 4 of this book).

As soon as a more or less satisfactory result was obtained, the authors became able to formulate the main contradiction, which did not allow R. Frisch and other brilliant theorists to go beyond the study of a stationary balanced state of the system, which is typical for it at the first stage of infinite economic dynamics. It is about the stage of unity and struggle of opposites. It is at this stage of self-development of economic systems that changes take place in them in the form of oscillatory movements. As for the two other stages, the oscillatory economic changes on them are not amenable to rigorous mathematical description, since they take on a stochastic character. As for the third stage of the system's self-development, it is generally difficult to describe it mathematically, since the economy faces a multivariance of the directions of further self-development.

It should be noted that R. Frisch himself admitted that oscillatory changes in the economy "...are just the essential problems in business cycle analysis. In order to attack these problems on a macro-dynamic basis so as to explain the movement of the system taken in its entirety, we must deliberately disregard a considerable amount of the details of the picture. We may perhaps start by throwing all kinds of production into one variable, all consumption into another, and so on, imagining that the notions "production," "consumption," and so on,' can be measured by some sort of total indices."

R. Frisch throughout the work tries to go beyond the stationary state of the system, describing, however, its oscillatory changes. His attention in the first part of the work to the "fundamental propagation problem" testifies to his desire to find mechanisms that can break these oscillatory movements of economic phenomena. So, for example, he writes «....it is rather in production than in consumption we ought to look for the factors that can explain the turning-point of the cycle» (Frisch, (1933), P. 177). If he realized this intention, then he would really be able to move from scientific foresights to the formation of a dynamic theory of complex economic systems. However this did not happen. Nevertheless, R. Frisch systematically introduced the propagation problem, practically realizing all the developments that were being conducted at that time in the study of the dynamic aspects of economic systems (see ***basic mathematical model of R. Frisch*** (1933, Part 4) below).

1.1.1. Basic Mathematical Model of R. Frisch (1933, Part 4. 'A Macro-Dynamic System Giving Rise to Oscillations')

Let y_t be the quantity of capital goods whose production is *started* at the point of time ***t***. We shall call y_t the "capital starting" or the "production starting," and we shall assume that this magnitude is determined by an equation of the form

$$y = mx + \mu \frac{dx}{dt} \qquad (1)^1$$

Figure 2. General model of interaction of self-organization and of self-development mechanisms of economic systems: shocks in the mechanisms of implementation of dialectical laws
Source: Chapter 4 of this book, Figure 7.

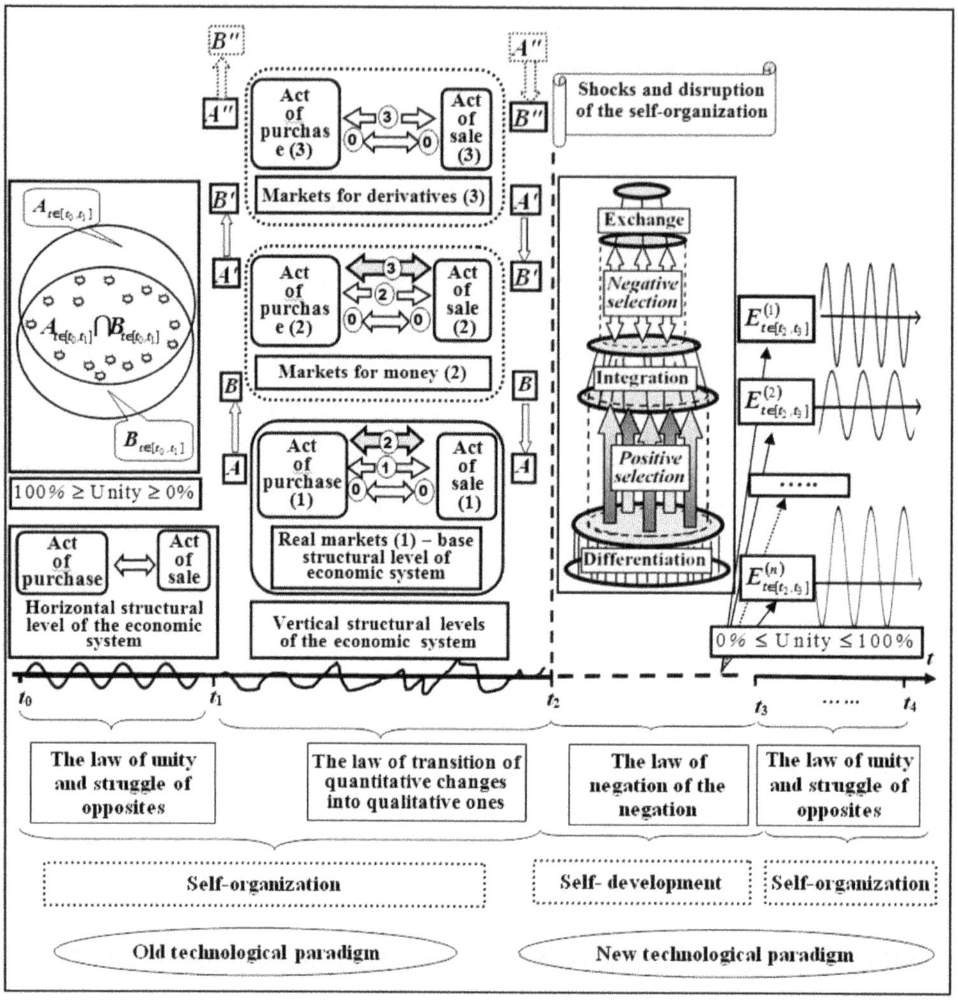

A capital object whose production is started at a certain moment will necessitate a certain production activity during the following time in order to complete the object. The productive activity needed in the period following the starting of the object will, as a rule, vary in a certain fashion which we may, as a first approximation, consider as given by the technical conditions of the production. Let D_τ be the amount of production activity needed at the point of time $t + \tau$ in order to carry on the production of a unit of capital goods started at the point of time t. The function D_τ we shall call the "advancement function."

This being so, the amount of production work that will be going on at the moment t will be

$$z_t = \int_{\tau=0}^{\infty} D_\tau y_{t-\tau} d\tau \quad (2)^2$$

The magnitude z_t we shall call "the carry-on-activity" at the point of time t. In the formula of the *encaisse desiree* it is now z that will occur instead of y, so that the consumption equation will be

$$\frac{dx}{dt} = c - \lambda\left(rx + sz\right) \tag{3}$$ [3]

where c, λ, r and s are constants.

Now back to the equation (1):

$$y = mx + \mu\frac{dx}{dt} \tag{1}$$

where m and μ are constants. The constant m expresses the wear and tear on capital goods caused directly and indirectly by the production of one unit of consumption, and μ expresses the size of capital stock that is needed directly and indirectly in order to produce one unit of consumption per year.

(2), (3) and (1) form now a determinate system in the three variables x, y and z.

If the carry-on function D_τ is given, the above system may be solved. If D_τ is given only in numerical form, the system has to be solved numerically, taking for granted a certain set of initial conditions. If D_τ is given as a simple mathematical expression, the system may under certain conditions be solved in explicit form. As an example we shall assume

$$D_\tau = \begin{cases} 1/\varepsilon, & 0 < \tau < \varepsilon \\ 0, & \tau \geq \varepsilon \end{cases} \tag{4}$$ [4]

where ε is a technically given constant. This simply means that a given element of capital starting will cause a certain constant amount of carry-on-activity per unit time over the ε units of time following the starting, and that in this point the object is finished, so that no further carry-on-activity is needed. This is obviously a simplified assumption, but may perhaps be taken as a first approximation.

In this case we get from (1) by differentiating with respect to time

$$\varepsilon\frac{dz}{dt} = y_t - y_{t-\varepsilon} \tag{5}$$ [5]

For certain purposes it will be convenient to differentiate also the equation (3) in order to get rid of the constant term, which gives

$$\frac{d^2x}{dt^2} = -\lambda\left(r\frac{dx}{dt} + s\frac{dz}{dt}\right) \tag{6}$$ [6]

Equation (6) actually introduces into consideration the maintaining oscillations in the macro-dynamic system.

In this case we get from (2) by differentiating with respect to time (5)

For certain purposes it will be convenient to differentiate also the equation (2) in order to get rid of the constant term, which gives (5)

The three equations to be considered now are (3), (1) and (5) (or possibly (6) may replace (3)). This is a mixed system of differential and difference equations. It is therefore to be expected that the solution will depend, not only on the initial conditions of the system in a given *point* of time, as initial conditions we shall have to consider the shape of the curve over a whole interval of length $\boldsymbol{\varepsilon}$.

The remarkable insights of R. Frisch allowed the authors to come closer to understanding the self-organization of market structures. It's about money and credit markets. He wrote that it is necessary to consider «the need for cash on hand, is made up of two parts: cash needed for the transaction of consumer goods and producer goods respectively» (Frisch, (1933), P.179). "We simply assume that, as the activity and consequently the need for cash increases, there is created a *tension* which counteracts a further expansion' (Frisch, (1933), P.179). However, R. Frisch viewed money solely in the context of ensuring the expansion of the purchasing power of economic agents. Nevertheless, this conjecture is of great importance, since it allowed the authors to evaluate the importance of money as means of exchange and as financial income-earning asset.

In addition, R. Frisch (Frisch, (1933), P.172) focused on the behavioral aspect in the micro-dynamic analysis: "When we approach the study of business cycle with the intention of carrying through an analysis that is truly dynamic and determinate in the above sense, we are naturally led to distinguish between two types of analyses: the micro-dynamic and the macro-dynamic types. The micro-dynamic analysis is an analysis by which we try to explain in some detail the behavior of a certain section of the huge economic mechanism, taking for granted that certain general parameters are given".

This aspect gave rise to the authors to introduce into the theory of shocks a subjective factor, which turned out to be, perhaps, determining in the structure of its categories. Having revealed the general contours of self-movement of all the economic complexity, the authors set a goal to trace the behavior of economic agents that make up dialectical pairs in exchange. Of primary interest are the factors, motives and consequences of both their adequate (rational) activity (with the dominance of unity of goals, trust and collective actions), and their inadequate (antisocial, irrational, opportunistic) behavior.

But, undoubtedly, the greatest food for the mind was given by R. Frisch' interpretation of the second fundamental *impulse* problem of his essay.

First of all, R. Frisch was interested in the problem of the *mechanism* by which such irregular fluctuations may be transformed into cycles. And the authors fully reproduce Frisch's conclusion on this subject (Frisch, (1933), P. 202-203). "Thus, by connecting the two ideas: (1) the continuous solution of a determinate dynamic system and (2) the discontinuous shocks intervening and supplying the energy that may maintain the swings – we get a theoretical setup which seems to furnish a rational interpretation of those movements which we have been accustomed to see in our statistical time data. The solution of the determinate dynamic system only furnishes a part of the explanation: it determines the *weight system* to be used in the cumulation of the erratic shocks. The other and equally important part of the explanation lies in the elucidation of the general laws governing the effect produced by linear operations performed on erratic shocks".

As a result, R. Frisch (1933, P. 203) formulated the idea of impulses (shocks) as follows: "The idea of erratic shocks represents one very essential aspect of the impulse problem in economic cycle analysis, but probably it does not contain the whole explanation. There is also present another source of energy operating in a more continuous fashion and being more intimately connected with the permanent evolution in human societies. The nature of this influence may perhaps be best exhibited by interpreting it in the light of Schumpeter's theory of the innovations and their role in the cyclical movement of economic life. Schumpeter has emphasized the influence of new ideas, new initiatives, the discovery of new technical procedures, new financial organizations, etc., on the course of the cycle. He insists in particular on the fact that these new ideas accumulate in a more or less continuous fashion, but are put into practical application on a larger scale only during certain phases of the cycle. It is like a force that is released during these phases, and this force is the source of energy that maintains the oscillations. This idea is also very similar to an idea developed by the Norwegian economist, Einar Einarsen (*Gode og daarlige tider,* Oslo, 1904). In mathematical language one could perhaps say that one introduces here the idea of an auto-maintained oscillation".

The shocks in the interpretation of R. Frisch do not fit into the theoretical constructions that were already substantiated by the authors of this book in relation to the self-developing system of a complex economy and the self-organizing mechanism of its self-development. The main thing that did not suit the authors was that the brilliant scientists mentioned by R. Frisch, as well as he himself considered the impulses that he called in Part 6 (Frisch, (1933), P. 203) of his work ("The innovations as a factor in maintaining oscillations") shocks, as external (internal) irregular impacts on economic phenomena. In other words, they linked them to ensuring and maintaining the oscillatory trajectory of economic changes.

The authors initially went the other way. They first built the fundamental construction of a self-developing economy, a self-organizing mechanism for its self-development based on the principles of dialectical logic and taking into account the philosophical laws of self-development. After that, it was impossible to superficially consider shocks as a phenomenon that arises from time to time and may or may not affect economic integrity and its structure.

Such a superficial interpretation of shocks did not fit into the theoretical design of the authors, so it was necessary to deal with the phenomenon of shocks fundamentally, relying on all possible studies, both of the present and of the past. As a result, the authors radically diverged from R. Frisch in the interpretation of shocks as factors affecting economic phenomena, processes, etc. In-depth studies of this phenomenon led the authors to the conclusion that shocks occupy a strong place in the dialectic of the movement of a self-developing system. Moreover, they turned out to be connected with its structure, and more precisely with the exchange of economic activity and its results as a mechanism for the self-development of economic integrity. In this case, shocks should be associated with the mechanism of breaking structural bonds, which begins to act as the formation of both objective and subjective conditions. Moreover, shocks mediate the movement of the system from the transition from quantitative to qualitative changes in the infinite dynamics of economic changes to a new stage of their denial of denial.

1.2. "The Summation of Random Causes as the Source of Cyclic Process" by E.E. Slutsky

The authors substantiate the reasons for their interest in the phenomenon of "shock" and the many questions that it raises, which were ignored by theorists and practitioners, either because of the seeming insignificance of the "shock problem" or the difficulty in determining the factor (moment) with which it was advisable to associate a shock's effect. The global financial crisis of 2008 did not clarify the problem with shocks, but only fuelled the authors' interest in understanding this phenomenon, which was paid attention to at the beginning of the last century by such famous scientists as R. Frisch (1933), and E.E. Slutsky (1927a, 1927b, 1937). They were the first to interpret impulses (shocks) in connection with the processes of dynamic changes in the economy.

At the same time, R. Frisch relied on all the research results of his colleagues, including the works of E.E. Slutsky. The authors give literally his reasoning about the scientific results of a number of scientists. R. Frisch (1933, P. 198) wrote the following: "Neither Knutt Wicksell nor Johan Akerman had taken up to a closer mathematical study the *mechanism* by which such irregular fluctuations may be transformed into cycles. This problem was attacked independently of each other by Eugen Slutsky (*The Summation of Random Causes as the Source of Cyclic Processes*, vol. iii, no. 1, Conjuncture Institute of Moscow, 1927. (Russian with English summary) and G. Udny Yule (*On a Method of Investigating Periodicity in Disturbed Series, Trans. Royal Society,* London, A, vol. 226, 1927)."

And then R. Frisch (1933, P. 199) wrote: "Slutsky studied experimentally the series obtained by performing iterated differences and summations on random drawings (lottery drawings, etc.). Yule only used second order differences, but tried to interpret the random impulses concretely as shocks hitting an oscillating pendulum. By the experimental numerical work done by these authors, particularly by Slutsky, it was definitely established that some sort of swings will be produced by the accumulation of erratic influences, but the exact and general law telling us what *sort* of cycles that a given kind of accumulation will create was not discovered. Later certain mathematical results which are of interest in connection with this problem were given by Norbert Wiener (*Generalized Harmonic Analysis, Acta Mathematica*, 1930)".

Since 1925 Johan Akerman, who in his doctorial dissertation discussed the fact that small fluctuations may be able to generate larger ones. In 1927 E.E. Slutsky took up to a closer mathematical study of the *mechanism* by which irregular fluctuations might be transformed into cycles. By the experimental numerical works by Slutsky (1927a, 1927b, 1937), it was definitely established that some sort of swings will be produced by the accumulation of erratic influences. But the exact and general law telling us what *sort* of cycles that a given kind of accumulation will create was not discovered.

Nevertheless, this problem was attacked by E.E. Slutsky (1927a, 1927b, 1937) (Fig. 3.4). Empirically, he revealed the following. For random waves, there are three "areas" with rules changing around some critical points, after which a new picture is formed. In a space where two "regions" of random waves overlap, the empirical series is subordinate to the compound rule, formed by adding both rules that belong to the corresponding "regions". E.E. Slutsky (1937) expressed a new hypothesis. In his opinion, a preliminary expression of the features of this quasi-regularity of random waves can be, for example, as follows. The addition of random causes generates a cyclic series, which tends to imitate, over a more or less significant number of waves, a harmonic series composed of a relatively small number of sinusoids. After a more or less significant portion of a series (sometimes spanning several full periods), each "mode" is upset, and the transition to another "mode" occurs either gradually or sharply near certain critical points.

E.E. Slutsky (1937) defined the following sequence of presentation of material.

1. *Key points.* The subject of this work was to show a) that cyclic, i.e. wave-like processes can occur due to the addition of mutually independent random causes, and b) that these random waves can demonstrate a certain correctness, which is an imitation, to a greater or lesser extent, of strictly periodic oscillations.

2. *Addition of random causes.* Suppose $\ldots, x_{i-1}, x_i, x_{i+1}, \ldots$ are a number of mutually independent random causes. Then, denoting for E the mathematical expectation and and assuming, for simplicity, $Ex_i = 0;\ Ex_i^2 = \sigma_x^2 = const$, we must have: $E(x_i, x_j)=0;\ i>j$.

The following is a transition to a series of consequences of independent random causes.

$$x_i^{(1)} = \sum_{k=0}^{n-1} \alpha_k^{(1)} x_{i-k}, x_i^{(2)} = \sum_{k=0}^{n-1} \alpha_k^{(2)} x_{i-k}^{(1)}, \ldots, x_i^{(s)} = y_i = \sum_{k=0}^{n-1} \alpha_k^{(s)} x_{i-k}^{(s-1)} = \sum_{k=0}^{n-1} A_k^{(s)} x_{i-k},$$

where $x_i^{(1)}, x_i^{(2)}, \ldots, x_i^{(s)}$ – *consequences* of the 1st, 2nd, ..., s-th order, $\alpha_k^{(1)}, \alpha_k^{(2)}, \ldots, \alpha_k^{(s)}$ – *partial,* and $A_k^{(s)}$ – *total weights.* If n = 2, and all $\alpha_k^{(j)} = 1$, we have $A_k^{(s)} = C_s^k$, whence approximately (for s even):

$$y_i = x_i^{(s)} = D \sum_{k=0}^{s} \alpha_k^{(s)} x_{i-k}^{(s-1)} = D \sum_{k=0}^{s} x_{i-k} \Phi\left(\frac{k - s/2}{\sqrt{s/4}} \right),$$

where D is constant, but $\Phi(u) = \frac{1}{\sqrt{2\pi}} \exp\left(\frac{-u^2}{2} \right)$ – Gauss-Laplace law.

A similar result can be obtained for any n, if all $\alpha_k^{(j)} = 1$

3. *Serial correlations.*

For a random series of causes $\ldots, x_{i-1}, x_i, x_{i+1}, \ldots$ and some of their consequences $y_i = \sum_{k=0}^{n-1} A_k^{(s)} x_{i-k}$ it becomes easy to find $\sigma_y^2 = Ey_i^2 = \sigma_x^2 \sum_{k=0}^{n-1} A_k^2$ and $E\left(y_i, y_{i+y}\right) = \sigma_x^2 \sum_{k=0}^{(n-1)-t} A_k A_{k+t}$. Hence the correlation coefficient between y_i and y_{i+t} is $r_t = \frac{\sigma_x^2 \sum_{k=0}^{(n-1)-t} A_k A_{k+t}}{\sum_{k=0}^{n-1} A_k^2}$.

From the point of view of the authors, E.E. Slutsky explores not deterministic, but stochastic relationships between variables. In this case, strict causal relationships give way to correlation and autocorrelation. The integral effect of adding independent random causes is the so-called random waves. E.E. Slutsky (1927a) compared relevant empirical models with empirical correlation functions, and also performed a Fourier-analysis.

Below authors give examples of illustrations as examples of proof of the approximate correctness of random waves.

4. *Further tasks.*

It is necessary to study the oscillating series, taken from statistical data, and to subject them to comparative study in conjunction with artificial models (artificial models). This analysis, which, as far as E.E. Slutsky (1927b) could hope, would appear in the near future and would be based on the study of theoretical and empirical periodograms (series). Then it would become possible to obtain even more evidence of the ability of random waves to simulate the correct harmonic oscillations (Fig. 4).

Figure 3. English market index in 1855-1877 (solid line) and model I (points 20-145) (dashed line)
Source: Slutsky E.E. (1927a). 'The accumulation of accidental causes as the source of cyclic processes', In: Problems of Economic Conditions. Moscow: Conjuncture Institute publishing house, Fig.3.

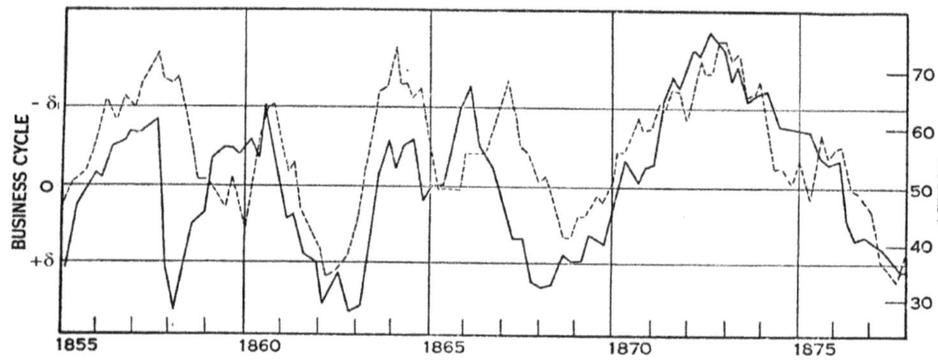

Figure 4. The first 100 terms in the model **IVb** *and* **IVc**
Source: Slutsky E.E. (1927a). 'The accumulation of accidental causes as the source of cyclic processes'. In: Problems of Economic Conditions. Moscow: Conjuncture Institute publishing house. Fig. 4

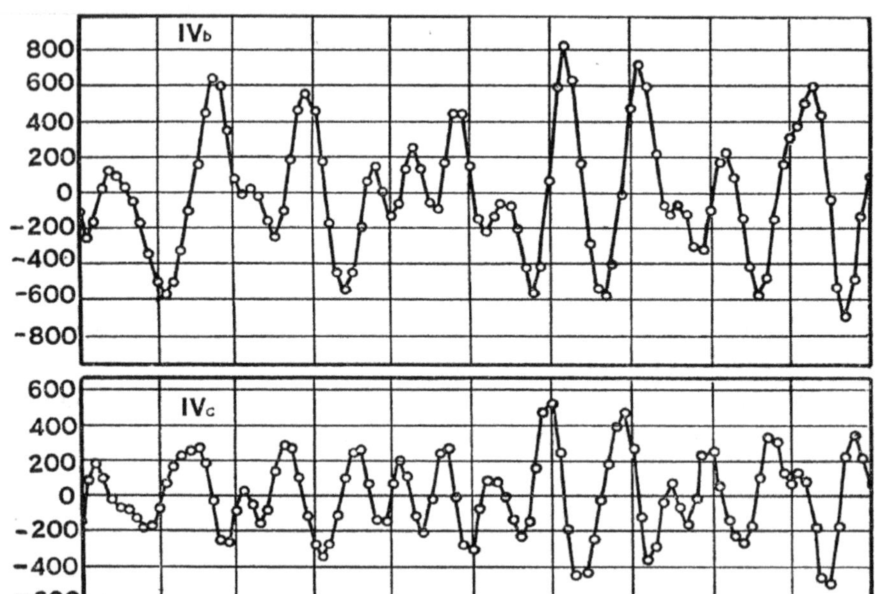

Results obtained by R. Frisch (1933), E.E. Slutsky (1927a, 1927b, 1933) and by other scientists, did not allow the authors of this book to find answers to fundamental theoretical questions regarding the phenomenon of shocks, the authors were forced to build their own logic of research, which allowed them to ultimately structure the foundations of shocks theory. First, the authors settled on the priority of the dialectical method of research, and turned out to be right, because it was dialectics, that were masterfully realized by the classics (G.W.F. Hegel, 1892; K. Marx, and F. Engels, 1955-1974) in their researches determined the sequence of solution of problems related to the theoretical understanding of shocks. Secondly, this method gave the authors a completely unique chance to delve into the problems of dynamic changes in economic systems and highlight their stages, predetermined by the dialectical laws of unity and struggle of opposites, the transition of quantity into quality and negation of negation.

In this context, the phenomenon of shock should be investigated through the prism of such a dialectical unity of statics and dynamics in changes in the state of the economy. The absence of the foundations of economics acceptable to economic theory in the aggregate of its static and dynamic states complicated the structuring of theoretical approaches to understanding the phenomenon of shocks. The authors were forced to proceed from the fact that if shocks are present in real life, then their interpretation should be related to their place (positioning) both in dynamic and in static changes in the economy. In this case, one should single out an extremely deep thought by J.A. Schumpeter (1961) that the content of any economic changes is predetermined by causal relationships.

Subsequently, the authors proved that either the stationary nature of the phenomenon of the economic system or its dynamic changes in the process of self-development depends on the specifics of their functioning. If the causes and effects change places in the course of changes, then the phenomenon constantly returns to its starting point. This is a circular (cyclic) movement, during which the balance, stability, stationarity of the phenomenon is ensured. Everything is the same in economics. The development and self-development of a phenomenon is an irreversible movement from cause to effect, a movement in one direction, without returning to the starting point, i.e. irreversible one.

Anticipating the conclusions substantiated in Chapters 2-4, it is advisable to note that a deeper understanding of the mechanism of self-organization and self-development of a complex economy allows the authors to deepen the idea of shocks in the direction of their greater specification:

1. the association of shocks with the mechanism of breaking continuity in the trajectory of economic changes in the economic system as it transitions from the stage of accumulation of qualitative changes (at the stage of self-organization of the economy) to the stage of its denial of negation can be attributed to their essence;
2. the essence of the mechanism for the realization of shocks is associated with their embeddedness as an indispensable element in the universal mechanism of the self-movement of a complex economy that is endless in time;
3. shocks implement a mechanism for breaking structural ties in economic integrity, represented by the exchange of economic activity and its results at the stage of self-organization of the economic system;
4. at the same time, shocks are capable of destroying both the vertical and horizontal structural levels of a static economy when they mediate its jump from the static stage to the dynamic stage, from self-organization to self-development;
5. If we consider shocks as intermediaries in the implementation of turning points in the operation of dialectical laws, then in the unity and struggle of opposites and in the transition of quantitative

changes to qualitative ones, the cause-and-effect relationships of the structural levels of exchange are broken with the active participation of subjective factors. In this context the shocks themselves are realized as a multilevel phenomenon, represented by the object and subjective components and realizing their action in the process of self-movement of systemic integrity in the economy.

In Chapter 5, the authors formed a dialectical picture of the subjectivization of shocks as a mechanism for breaking structural bonds in exchange at the stage of transition of the economic system from the stage of transition of quantitative changes to qualitative ones at the stage of denying the denial of their infinite self-movement (Fig. 2).

So, in the process of studying the fundamental processes of self-movement of complex economic systems, the authors proved that shocks are unlawfully associated with factors affecting macro-dynamic fluctuations according to R. Frisch (1933) and E. Slutsky (1927a, 1927b, 1937). According to the authors, the shock and global financial crisis of 2007-2009 as well as the shock of the COVID pandemic of 2020 confirmed their findings that shocks should be understood differently. Shocks act as the subjective mechanism of the destruction of structural ties in the exchange of economic activity results that is predetermined by the realization of the effect of a crowd of irrationally thinking participants in market transactions. In addition, shocks have a destructive effect on individual structural links of a self-organizing economy, but they can completely destroy the structure of the system, mediating its jump from statics and dynamics. This is happening today in front of our eyes amid the coronavirus pandemic.

1.3. Irma and Frank Adelman and their Bold Experiment with the Klein—Goldberger Model

Irma Adelman made both conceptual and policy breakthroughs throughout her career. Early in her career, her research emphasis was more methodological, addressing dynamic and stochastic processes. Her classic paper of 1959, mentioned above, resulted from a pioneering simulation that confirmed Ragnar Frisch's theory of business cycles, in which basically stable economies are driven through cycles by random shocks (Bodkin Ronald G. (Ed.), (1991), P. 73).

Irma Adelman and Frank Adelman explored the question of how well the Klein-Goldberger Model succeeded in reproducing the business cycle. The time paths associated with shocks of type I and II are shown in Fig. 5, and 6 (Bodkin Ronald G. (Ed.), (1991), P. 75).

In their now classic study, the Adelmans (I959) particularly investigated the issues as to whether this model 'really offers an endogenous explanation of a persistent cyclical process", 'whether the system is stable when subjected to single exogenous shocks, what oscillations (if any) accompany the return to the equilibrium path, and what is the response of the model to repeated external and internal shocks'. In dealing with these issues, they proceeded as follows.

First, the model was simplified by deleting insignificant coefficients." and the equations for import demand and the two interest rates. Second, the least squares trends for most of the exogenous variables were specified. Third, the observed 1952 values for the remaining 22 endogenous variables including taxes were inserted as initial conditions. And finally the time paths of the endogenous variables of the entire non-linear model (with taxes endogenous) were traced, year by year, for the next 100 years to the year 2052.

Figure 5. The first simulation, when the system was exposed to distinct types of random impulses: in shocks of type I, random shocks were superimposed on the extrapolated values of the exogenous variables
Source: Adelman I., and F. Adelman (1959), Fig. 1 chapter 3(Selected time paths under Type I impulse)

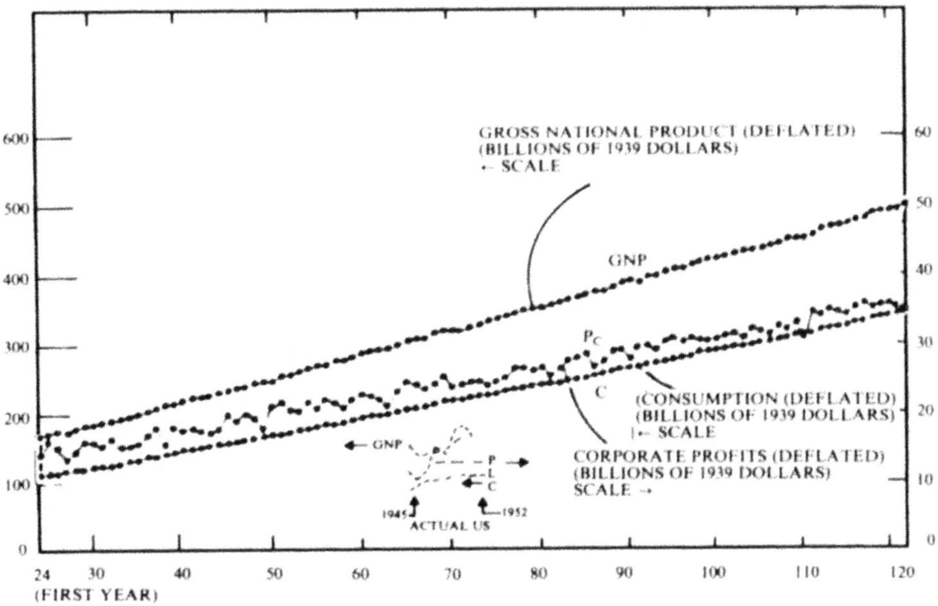

Figure 6. The second simulation, when the system was exposed to distinct types of random impulses: in shocks of type II, random errors were introduced into each of the estimated equations making the system stochastic
Source: Adelman I., and F. Adelman, (1959), Fig. 2 chapter 3 (Selected time paths under Type II impulse)

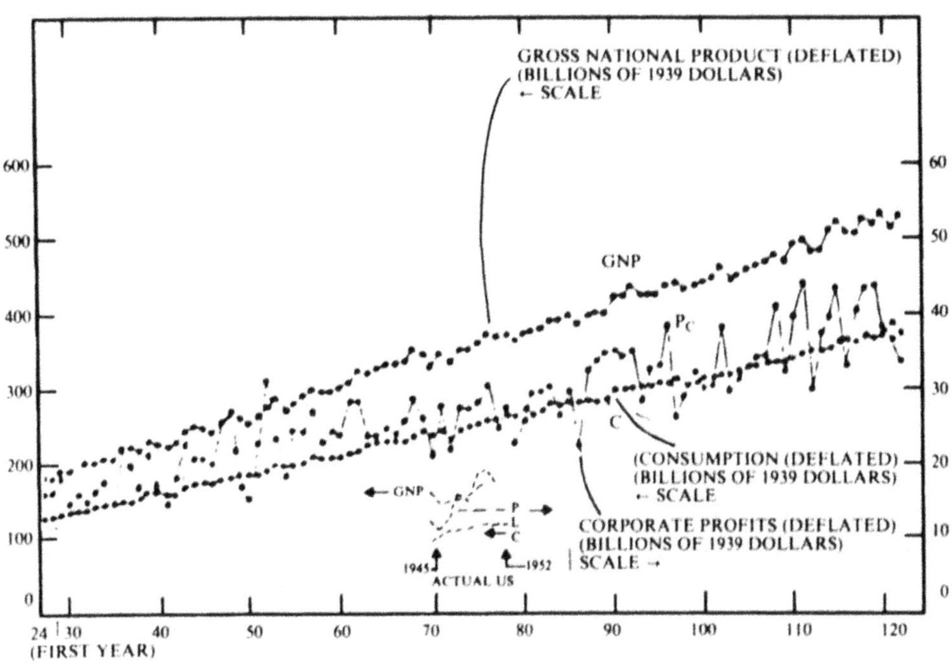

The first solution corresponded to the deterministic version of the model with no additional external constraints or shocks. The model exhibited unrealistic stability by producing fluctuations that were excessively damped. The issues raised at the beginning of the study were decided unequivocally, and the Adelmans observed, 'After a brief "settling down" period, the system is quite monotonic and essentially linear. There is no hint whatever of any internally generated business cycle, and, indeed, even in the first few years, the shock of start-up is not sufficient to induce more than a single turning-point in any variable' (p. 602). Under ordinary conditions, with great stability of the external environment, the model was clearly non-oscillatory in nature (Bodkin Ronald G. (Ed.), (1991), P. 74).

In the second simulation, the system was subjected to a severe and sudden shock in terms of reduction in the government expenditures. The resulting time paths of the variables indicate that, after having been thrown into deep depression, the system recovered in four to five years and settled back to its long-run stable path. Once again, the system was stable in a deterministic environment. In the next two simulations, the system was exposed to distinct types of random impulses: in shocks of type I (Fig. 5), random shocks were superimposed on the extrapolated values of the exogenous variables, and in shocks of type II (Fig. 6), random errors were introduced into each of the estimated equations making the system stochastic. The magnitude of these shocks or errors was obtained by random drawings from the appropriate probability distributions, namely a normal distribution having zero mean and variance corresponding to the variance of the residuals in the observed sample.

The model did generate three- to four-year cycles but their average amplitude was unrealistically small. Finally, the simulation with shocks of type II imposed on the estimated equations told a very different story. Not only did it generate three- to four-year cycles but the overall properties of these cycles appeared to be reasonably realistic. The time paths are shown in chapter 3 Figure 2 (Bodkin Ronald G. (Ed.), (1991), P. 76).

The Adelmans (1959) investigated further the cyclical properties of the time paths generated with shocks of type II by applying the techniques developed at the National Bureau of Economic Research (NBER) for the analysis of business cycles. They found a startling correspondence between the business cycle produced by the Klein Goldberger Model and the four-year post-Second-World-War cycles in the US economy. The average expansion of Klein-Goldberger cycles covered 2.6 years, its average contraction only 1.5. The observed figures for the United States economy were 2.1 and 1.8 years, respectively. Similarly, in the cycle produced by the Klein-Goldberger Model, 51 per cent of the individual series had maxima coincident with an upper turning-point of the business activity and 52 per cent had minima coincident with a reference trough. The corresponding figures for the US economy were 58 per cent and 52 per cent respectively. This analysis led the Adelmans to the following conclusion about the cyclical properties of the Klein-Goldberger Model (Ronald G. Bodkin (Ed.), 1991), P. 74).

All in all, it would appear that there is a remarkable correspondence between the characteristics of fluctuations generated by the superposition of random shocks upon the Klein-Goldberger system and those of the business cycles which actually occur in the United States economy.

The resemblance is not restricted to qualitative parallelism, but is, indeed, quantitative, in the sense that the duration of the cycle, the relative length of the expansion and contraction phases, and the degree of clustering of peaks and troughs arc all in numerical agreement (within the accuracy of measurement) with empirical evidence, (pp. 614-16) (Bodkin Ronald G. (Ed.), (1991), P. 75).

Finally, their overall observations on the dynamic properties of the model were summarized in part: "... our investigation into the dynamic nature of the econometric model of Klein and Goldberger suggests that their equations do not offer an immediate explanation of an internally generated cyclical process. For, in the absence of perturbations, the time paths of the economic variables are monotonic and essentially linear in character. Furthermore, the behavior of the model is remarkably stable, as evidenced by the fact that the solution resumes its unperturbed equilibrium growth trend even after a strong exogenous disturbance ...". On the other hand, when random shocks of a realistic order of magnitude are superimposed upon the original form of the Klein Goldberger equations, the cyclical fluctuations which result are remarkably similar to those described by the NBER as characterizing the United States economy. The average duration of a cycle, the mean length of the expansion and contraction phases, and the degree of clustering of individual peaks and troughs around reference dates all agree with the corresponding data for the United States economy ... All in all, it would appear that the shocked Klein-Goldberger model approximates the behavior of the United States economy rather well, (pp.619-20) (Bodkin Ronald G. (Ed.), (1991), P. 76).

Bodkin Ronald G. (1991) concluded by noting that Howrey (1968; Howrey, et al., 1974) had studied the dynamic properties of the Klein-Goldberger Model by an alternative technique, namely spectral analysis in general and a study of the spectrum matrix of the endogenous variables in particular. He found that the dynamic properties of the model are considerably altered when one passes from the model variant with exogenous taxes to that with endogenous taxes. Bodkin Ronald G. (1991) noted that Klein (1969) estimated several variants of an updated version of the Klein-Goldberger, in connection with a study of the properties of several simultaneous equations estimators (Bodkin Ronald G. (Ed.), (1991), P. 76).

As later researchers noted, and with which Klein himself agreed, the Klein-Goldberger model alone did not directly explain the internal processes that generated the cycle. In order for this model to reproduce fluctuations in the US economy, in its equations should have been random disturbances with realistic amplitude of deviations from the general trend are included.

1.4. The Look from the 2010s: the Logic of Forming the Foundations of Shocks' Theory

The methods of economic dynamics are given an important place in the methodology of modern economic theory. A significant contribution to its development was made by Dr. Ragnar Frisch with his deepest understanding of the features of self-movement of economic systems. It was he who formed a new type of economic thinking, developing the theory of economic dynamics based on the comparison of dynamic models of mechanics as a branch of physics and dynamic processes in economic systems. These ideas has become very popular these days, as the method of dynamic analysis has established itself as the most realistic method of analyzing the behavior of an economy or certain economic variables over the time.

Nevertheless, here it is appropriate to pay attention to the accepted terminology. Analysis, which considers the relationship between relevant variables, the values of which relate to different points in time, are usually defined as dynamic analysis or economic dynamics. In this case, it is advisable to turn to the origins of mathematical modeling of dynamic phenomena, in particular, fluctuations in economic reality.

It should be emphasized once again that it was R. Frisch's studies that for many years laid the foundation for the development of theoretical and empirical ideas about dynamic laws, in particular cyclical processes, in economic systems, both in the national and global aspects. They stimulated numerous and fruitful discussions, continuing today, about the mechanisms that generate certain economic cycles, as well as a number of deep studies of the historical development of scientific thought in the field of cyclical problems of the economy (Qin, D., at al., 2001; Escañuela, 2016; Singh, 1997).

At the same time, it should be noted that the authors of this book were faced with the fact that already pioneering theoretical works gave rise to a number of terminological misunderstandings, to which Ragnar Frisch had already drawn attention (Frisch, ((1929) 1992)). But they continue to stretch like a train to the present time

And, meanwhile, if for the analysis of these problems we rely on a methodology based on the foundation of the laws of dialectics, it is possible to see what is impossible even to imagine within the framework of already established theoretical concepts. How not to remember the words of A. Einstein: "We cannot solve our problems with the same thinking we used when we created them." (Einstein, 1993).

Many researchers have drawn attention to this. Valerie A. Ramey's chapter "Macroeconomic Shocks and Their Propagation," published in NBER Working Papers 21978 introduces the trend in economic thought from the 1920s to the 1990s. Unfortunately, the fundamental research of Ragnar Frisch, E.E. Slutsky was not continued by modern researchers. This conclusion can be reached based on the reasoning of Valerie A. Ramey. In particular, she states the following fact: "The 1980s witnessed two important innovations that fundamentally changed the direction of the research." Let's note the main thing here: "Sims' (1980a) paper "Macroeconomics and Reality" revolutionized the study of systems driven by random impulses by introducing vector auto-regressions (VARs). Sims' VARs made the link between innovations to a linear system and macroeconomic shocks. Using his method, it became easier to talk about identification assumptions, impulse response functions, and to do innovation accounting using forecast error decompositions." (Ramey, 2016).

Thus, the dialectical potential of the heralds of a new theoretical approach in economic theory did not receive its due. But we are talking about dialectics, which allowed Ragnar Frisch to single out dialectical pairs: "static law - dynamic law", "Propagation Problems - Impulse Problems", which allowed further deepening the theoretical understanding of the problems of statics and dynamics in the self-movement of economic systems (Frisch, ((1929) 1992; Frisch, 1933). We should also mention the synergetics of Evgeny Slutsky in the opposition: "randomness - regularity", "stochastics - determinism", "random events - cyclical oscillations" (Slutsky, ((1927), 1937); Slutsky, 1937).

The text below follows the logic of the authors highlighting the noteworthy ideas of Ragnar Frisch and E. Slutsky and the subsequent theoretical analysis of the authors of this book "as the look from the 2010s".

1. In terms of the dialectical approach developed by the authors, which logically follows from the gaps in theoretical studies of the phenomena of dialectical laws in economics, shocks, dynamic models, it should be emphasized that methods of economic dynamics occupy an important place in the methodology of modern economics. This state of affairs is the greatest discovery and merit of Dr. Ragnar Frisch. It was he who formed a new type of economic thinking, developing the theory of economic dynamics based on the comparison of dynamic models of mechanics as a branch of physics and dynamic processes in economic systems.

He described this idea as follows. "The idea is: if quantitative phenomenon A is of a given magnitude, then quantitative phenomenon B will be of such and such a magnitude. Or, more generally: if the constellation within phenomenon-complex A is such and such, then the constellation within phenomenon-complex B will be such and such. Thus, the static law is a law which can be formulated without introducing the notion of time in a specific form. The observed variations are not variations with regard to time, but variations with regard to certain alternatives. In this sense ***the static law is timeless*** (highlighted by the authors)." (Frisch, ((1929) 1992), p. 391).

From the point of view of the authors of this book, a self-moving mechanism operates in the economic system. A static economy obeys the dialectical laws of self-organization: the unity and struggle of opposites and the transition from quantity to quality. These laws determine the complication of the structural integrity of the economic system and unfold in time. As for the self-development of the system in its dynamic state, its self-movement in this state is regulated by the law of denial of negation. Moreover, shocks mediate turning points in the operation of all dialectical laws, being organically built into their mechanism. Thus, following dialectical logic allows one to disagree with the conclusion of Ragnar Frisch that "the static law is timeless", since it contradicts reality. The static state of the economy cannot last forever, since the self-organization of the system is replaced by its self-development, and so on ad infinitum. Therefore, everything in this world is transient, but it is this state that is eternal.

2. From R. Frisch point of view: "The dynamic law, on the other hand, is a law whose aim is to describe how a situation changes from one point in time to the next. The situations that are compared by the dynamic law are, in contrast to the static law, not alternative situations (as in the static law) but successive situations. In the static law the compared situations are equivalent alternatives. In the dynamic law we add a new principle by which the situations are ordered in a certain succession, namely the time succession. It is precisely this chronological principle and the comparison between one situation and the following which is the essential point in the dynamic analysis." (Frisch, ((1929) 1992), 391-392).

Based on the logic of the presentation of the authors' position in paragraph 1, the self-movement of the system and its dynamics are different things. By adding time, we only emphasize the self-movement of the system, and not its dynamics. On the other hand, the chronological principle can accompany a dynamic / time series of values of an indicator of economic reality. Of course, this circumstance does not give grounds to call the economy dynamic.

As for the dynamic law, it is advisable to designate the physical source of this concept, namely. The dynamic law as the basic law of dynamics in physics (in the science of mechanics) is Newton's second law: in the inertial frame of reference, the vector sum of all forces (not equal to zero) $\vec{R} = \sum_{i=1}^{n} \vec{F}_i$, applied to a body of mass m, causes its acceleration $\bar{a}$

$$\vec{a} = \frac{\vec{R}(t)}{m}, \tag{1}$$

directed along the vector sum of $\vec{R}$, proportional to its modulus $|\vec{R}|$ and inversely proportional to body mass m. If the vector equality to design the coordinate axis OX, directed along the vector $\vec{R}$, we can represent law (1) in scalar form (2)

$$a = \frac{R(t)}{m}. \tag{2}$$

Since acceleration is the second derivative of the coordinate of a material point $x(t)$ with respect to time, Newton's second law of dynamics can be represented in differential form (3)

$$\frac{d^2x(t)}{dt^2} = \frac{R(t)}{m}. \tag{3}$$

And from here it is a stone's throw to oscillatory motion in various systems, in general, and, in particular, oscillatory processes observed in the economy (oscillations of economic variables). It is interesting that Ragnar Frisch, apparently focusing on the specific level of mathematical training of economists, correctly encoded the meaning of analytical expressions (1) - (3) in his next statement. "So far, I have not mentioned the distinction between kinematics and dynamics. If one were to take into account this distinction, we would have the following scheme of analysis. First, we have statics, in which variations as regards time are absent. Second, we have a part of the analysis in which such variations occur. The latter in turn falls into two parts, namely kinematics and dynamics (in the strict sense). Dynamics (in the strict sense) are based on the notion of force. In kinematics this notion is absent. In the following I shall not go into the distinction between kinematics and dynamics (in the strict sense). What, in the following, will be called dynamics (in economics) is the entire non-static part of the analysis. In those parts of economic theory in which it is possible to define a notion of force, it will also be possible to subdivide this non-static part of the theory into a kinematic part and a part which is (in a more restricted sense) dynamic." (Frisch, ((1929) 1992), p. 393).

3. Ragnar Frisch wrote: "It should be realized that according to the viewpoint applied here, the distinction between statics and dynamics refers to the analytical method, not to the nature of the phenomena. We may thus speak of static or dynamic analysis, but not of a static or dynamic phenomenon. Phenomena as such are neither static nor dynamic. On the other hand, phenomena as such may be stationary or evolutionary" (Frisch, ((1929) 1992), p. 392).

This phrase contains remarkably precise wording. However, this correct position of Ragnar Frisch is violated in the wording of the title in Frisch's "Propagation Problems and Impulse Problems in Dynamic Economics". As a result, "dynamic economics" takes on the meaning of some kind of *pseudo-term*.

Indeed, the title of Dr. Ragnar Frisch "Propagation problems and impulse problems ***in dynamic economics***" informs the reader about that ***dynamic economics*** is considered. Perhaps Ragnar Frisch believed that a dynamic model of fluctuations in an economic system automatically characterizes the system itself as dynamic. However, this is not true. So, in systems of the most diverse nature, for example, mechanical, electromagnetic, chemical, thermodynamic, economic and other oscillations are observed. Consequently, it is about the presence of analogies between oscillatory phenomena in these systems. In this context, in the theory of oscillations, one generally speaks of a dynamical system. A dynamical system is called dynamic because its state at any moment of time t must be uniquely determined by its state at some previous moment of time t_0. The behavior of a dynamic system can be described by differential, integral or finite-difference equations. In this sense, a dynamical system is only a mathematical model of the investigated real system. And any real system, firstly, is always subject to some uncontrollable influences (fluctuations), and secondly, its initial state cannot be determined with acceptable accuracy. For this reason alone, a real system cannot be called dynamic. In the process of the self-movement, it can be in both static (self-organization) and dynamic (self-development) states (Chapters 3 - 5).

4. It is advisable to once again refer to the title of Frisch's work "**Propagation problems and impulse problems in dynamic economics**" in order to consider another important aspect of the **Propagation Problems** identified by R. Frisch: the excitation and propagation of **waves** in the real market (in related segments of the real market). In the course of this process, endogenous shocks built into the self-organization mechanism can be realized (Chapters 3 –7).

The authors consider the self-organization mechanism as a source of excitement, in particular, harmonic oscillations in a specific market segment, their transmission to related segments and, as a result, the emergence of a wave form of self-movement in the market environment (Chapter 2). The basis of the developed approach is the following model concepts: self-organization of structural links launches the mechanism of excitation of harmonic oscillations and their transmission in the market environment in the form of a wave process. Its mechanical counterpart gives this model a visual. Let's highlight the mechanical aspect. If a part of any medium is brought into oscillatory motion, then these oscillations, in the presence of bonding forces between the particles of the medium, will be transmitted to other parts, will propagate, i.e. there will be a wave form of motion - waves will propagate.

It is logical to assume that a similar phenomenon is inherent in the economic environment. In particular, the authors consider the self-organization mechanism as an internal source of excitation of harmonic oscillations in a specific market segment, their transmission to related segments and, as a result, the emergence of a wave form of self-movement in the market environment. The mathematical model of wave propagation in the economic environment is proposed in Chapter 2. (see the equation (21)).

5. Eugen Slutsky was one of the pioneers of the theory of stochastic processes. His idea that random shocks can generate regular oscillations of the economic variables is important and seminal. (Slutsky, ((1927), 1937), pp. 105-146; Slutsky, (1937), pp. 105-146.

According to the authors, confusion arises again in the concepts of **cycles and wa**ves on the example of the pioneering work of Eugen Slutsky. The undoubted merit of E. Slutsky is that he significantly expanded the scope of the traditional thinking of economists, demonstrating the possibilities of the stochastic approach and proving that the sum of random fluctuations can be a source of cyclical processes in the economy. At the same time, it should be noted that the terminology used by him was distinguished by a certain dualism "cycle-wave". This can be clearly seen from the fragments below from the original texts of his famous work. Wrong term "**waves**" is highlighted by the authors.

E. Slutsky wrote: "Thus we are led to our basic problem: is it possible that a definite structure of a connection between random fluctuations could form them into a system of more or less **regular waves**?" (Slutsky, E. (1937). p. 106)

"What is the mechanism of causality which, decade after decade reproduces the same **sinusoidal wave** which rises and falls on the surface of the social ocean with the regularity of day and night? What means of explanation, however, would be left to us if we decided to give up the hypothesis of the superposition of **regular waves** complicated only by purely random components? The presence of **waves** of definite orders, the long waves embracing decades, shorter cycles from approximately five to ten years in length, and finally the very short waves, will always remain a fact begging for explanation. The approximate regularity of the periods is sometimes so distinctly apparent that it, also, cannot be passed by without notice." (Slutsky, E. (1937). p. 107)

"Thus, in short, the **undulatory character** of the processes and the approximate regularity of the **waves** are the two facts for which we shall try to find a possible source in random causes combining themselves in their common effect." (Slutsky, E. (1937). p. 107)

"Generally speaking, **the theory of chance waves** is almost entirely a matter of the future. For the sake of this future theory one cannot be too lavish with experiments: it is experiment that shows us totally unexpected facts, thus pointing out problems which otherwise would hardly fall within the field of the investigator." (Slutsky, E. (1937). p. 107)

"Our models, representing several sets of experiments, give an inductive proof of our first thesis, namely, that the summation of random causes may be the source of cyclic, or **undulatory processes**." (Slutsky, E. (1937). p. 114)

"It is, however, not difficult to determine the reason why it must be so inevitably. We shall first observe a series of independent values of a random variable. If, for the sake of simplicity, we assume that the distribution of probabilities does not change, then, for the entire series, there will exist a certain horizontal level such that the probabilities of obtaining a value either above or below it would be equal." (Slutsky, E. (1937). p. 115)

"Let us designate as a ***half-wave*** a portion of the series in which the deviation does not change sign. Thus, for 1000 numbers of the third basic series we find 540 **half-waves** (instead of the theoretically expected 500). Taking from this number the first 512 **half-waves** we find among them a number of **half-waves** of the length 1,2, etc." (Slutsky, E. (1937). p. 115)

"Let us again examine Model II (Figure 2). In many places there are, apparently, **large waves** with massive outlines as well as **smaller waves lying**, as it were, over them; sometimes these are detached from them, sometimes they are almost completely merged into them. For example, at the beginning of Figure 2, **three waves** of nearly equal length are apparent, that is, from the first to the third minimum, from the third to the fifth, and from the fifth to the sixth. Upon **these waves** smaller ones can be seen having also approximately equal dimensions. A careful examination of the graphs of our models will disclose to the reader a number of places where the approximate equality of the length of the **waves** is readily apparent. If we had a much shorter series, such as a series offered by the ordinary statistics of economic life with its **small number of waves**, we should be tempted to consider the sequence as strictly periodic, that is, as composed of a few regular harmonic fluctuations complicated by some insignificant casual fluctuations." (Slutsky, E. (1937). pp. 120 - 121)

"It is known, of course, that practically any given curve can be represented by a sum of a series of sinusoids provided a large enough number of terms is taken. It is not for every empirical series, however, that we can obtain such a significant correspondence and such a sharply expressed periodicity with a comparatively small number of harmonics. The approximately **regular waves** which were apparent even in the crude series are much more distinct now when they are isolated by deducting the sum of the first five harmonics. Of course, we cannot assert that the rest of Model II would follow the same periodicity, but, for our purposes, it is sufficient that successive waves should maintain an approximate equality of length for six periods. This hardly can be considered to be a chance occurrence; the explanation of such an effect must be found in the mechanism of the connection of the random values." (Slutsky, E. (1937). pp. 121 - 122).

"The deviations from the sum of six harmonics are plotted in Figure 10 together with the corresponding fluent curves. These curves are obtained **as interference waves of two sinusoids** with equal amplitudes and approximately equal periods. In other words, such a curve can be represented as the product of two sinusoids or as a sinusoid with an amplitude also changing along a sinusoid. These bending sinusoids separate on the graph the regions which place our empirical series in a definite regime." (Slutsky, E. (1937). p. 122).

Based on the analysis of the above text, the authors believe that it is impossible to: (1) treat cycles as waves; (2) propagate wave characteristics to cyclic fluctuations; (3) talk about wave interference in the case of addition of harmonic oscillations, (4) replace the concept of the oscillation period with the concept of wave length. The time series of sums of random variables, ingeniously constructed by E.

Slutsky, is characterized only by a time parameter, and the propagation of, for example, a plane wave is characterized not only by time, but also by the coordinate (Chapter 2).

6. According to R. Frisch, "If a cyclical variation is analyzed from the point of view of a free oscillation, we have to distinguish between two fundamental problems: first, the *propagation* problem; second, the *impulse* problem. The propagation problem is the problem of explaining by the structural properties of the swinging system what the character of the swings would be in case the system was started in some initial situation." (Frisch, (1933), p. 171).

However, this requirement is violated in chapter «5. Erratic Shocks as a Source of Energy in Maintaining Oscillations». In the text of this chapter R. Frisch wrote: "Consider for simplicity an oscillating pendulum whose movement is hampered by friction. If $\boldsymbol{y}$ denotes the deviation of the pendulum from its vertical position, the equation governing the movement of the pendulum will be

$$\frac{d^2y}{dt^2}+2\beta\frac{dy}{dt}+\left(\alpha^2+\beta^2\right)y=0 \tag{1}$$

where $\frac{dy}{dt}$ and $\frac{d^2y}{dt^2}$ are the first and second derivatives of $\boldsymbol{y}$ with respect to time, and $\boldsymbol{\beta}$ and $\boldsymbol{\alpha}$ are positive constant, $\boldsymbol{\beta}$ expressing the strength of the friction." (Frisch, (1933), p. 199).

Frisch's requirements regarding the resolution of the propagation problem are grossly violated here.

First, the equation of damped oscillations (1) contains an error, which is corrected in the equation ($_*$).

Secondly, $\boldsymbol{\beta}$ don't expressing the strength of the friction.

Thirdly, if we say only that $\boldsymbol{\alpha}$ is a positive constant, it actually means that its role in the dynamic process (1) remains unknown.

Thus the equation of free oscillations of the pendulum relative to the equilibrium position in the presence of medium resistance has the form ($_*$)

$$\frac{d^2y}{dt^2}+2\beta\frac{dy}{dt}+\alpha^2y=0, \tag{$_*$}$$

where a positive constant $\boldsymbol{\alpha}$ – circular frequency at which oscillations would occur in the absence of damping (cyclic frequency of natural oscillations); a positive constant $\boldsymbol{\beta}$ – damping coefficient of oscillations, which determines the rate of their damping.

The authors of this book have provided a detailed rationale in Chapter 2 (equation (8)). They also develop ideas about the structure of the economic environment in which the oscillator functions ($_*$), in other words propagation problems are resolved.

7. From the point of view of Valerie A. Ramey, "insights of Eugen Slutsky, George Udny Yule, Ragnar Frisch shifted the focus of research from developing mechanisms to support a metronomic view of business cycles, in which each boom created conditions leading to the next bust, to a search for the sources of the random shocks. Since then economists have offered numerous candidates for these "random causes," such as crop failures, wars, technological innovation, animal spirits, government actions, and commodity shocks." (Ramey, (2016), p. 3).

Then the authors of this book have a question: Why shocks may not be what they seem to be? R. Frisch wrote in Chapter 5 titled "Erratic Shocks as a Source of Energy in Maintaining Oscillations". One way which I believe is particularly fruitful and promising is to study what would become of the solution of a determinate dynamic system if it were exposed to a stream of erratic shocks that constantly upsets the continuous evolution, and by so doing introduces into the system the energy necessary to maintain the swings." (The constructive role of shocks seems to be justified!) (Frisch, (1933), p. 197).

From the point of view of the authors, according to this conclusion Frisch's own macrodynamic analysis moved into the forefront of research. It was based upon a vision of a mechanical system in damped regular motion exposed to erratic shocks. Analytical dynamics proved to be useful and possible without being closely related to the core general equilibrium theory.

Frisch considered shocks as a necessary reinvigoration element of the oscillatory system based on lags, accelerator and limiting factors, so a way to maintain the swing. He tried to interpret the random impulses concretely as shocks hitting an oscillating pendulum or the discontinuous shocks intervening and supplying the energy that minght maintain the swings.

R. Frisch further stated: "Thus, by connecting the two ideas: (1) the continuous solution of a determinate dynamic system and (2) the discontinuous shocks intervening and supplying the energy that may maintain the swings – we get a theoretical setup which seems to furnish a rational interpretation of those movements which we have been accustomed to see in our statistical time data. The solution of the determinate dynamic system only furnishes a part of the explanation: it determines the *weight system* to be used in the cumulation of the erratic shocks. The other and equally important part of the explanation lies in the elucidation of the general laws governing the effect produced by linear operations performed on erratic shocks." (Frisch, (1933), pp. 202-203).

So the following interesting question arises: How were external impulses smoothly transformed into external erratic shocks? The last question could be concretized as follows: how could the random causes of Slutsky be smoothly transformed into external chaotic shocks?

The authors summarize all the above as follows: (1) R. Frisch considers impulses as external influences (exogenous impulses). (2) N. Kaldor treats shocks as endogenous impulses, since they appear as a result of nonlinear relationships (Kaldor, (1939), pp. 549-552). (3) Further, a new filling of the concept of impulse gradually deepens by shifting from impulses to shocks. Thus, the initial concepts, due to the presence of elements of uncertainty in them, are blurred: both impulse and shock exist as Immanuel Kant's the **thing-in-itself**. The intrigue of the situation under discussion also lies in the fact that external (exogenous) impulses-shocks, which, following Ragnar Frisch and the established tradition, affect national economic integrity, in the global economy turn into endogenous impulses. And in a situation of lockdown due to the COVID-19 pandemic, the role of external shocks is generally minimized. But economic oscillators have not "frozen". Thus, an explanation for the phenomenon of shock should be sought in the dialectics of the processes of self-movement of economic integrity: at the stages of a static economy and the mechanisms of self-organization and at the stage of a dynamic economy and the mechanisms of self-development (Chapters 2 – 7). However, in economic science, as far as the authors know, researchers avoid a consistent analysis of the states of economic integrity from the philosophical standpoint of the dialectics of systems self-movement. Meanwhile, such a (dialectical) approach opens up ample opportunities for studying the patterns of self-movement of economic systems. It is especially valuable that this approach reveals the internal (endogenous) mechanism of the ripening of shocks in the economic system at the turning points of the dialectical laws' operation.

Based on the above, the authors built the logic of forming the foundations of shocks' theory.

First, it was necessary to define the concept of shocks: to find out the essence of the shock phenomenon and describe the forms of its manifestation.

Second, it was necessary to ask a question about the mechanism of the ripening of shocks, of their implementation and of impact on the economy. The philosophical approach to the study of shocks as a complex phenomenon implied the allocation of that component of the economic system, which was more susceptible to the shock effect.

Third, interpreting the systemic integrity in the economy, taking into account its subjective, object and process components, the authors had to follow dialectical logic in relation to the study of shocks as a complex phenomenon in the dialectical unity of the object, subjective and process components.

Fourth, the selection of the process component of the phenomenon of shocks should predetermine the need for their interpretation in accordance with the process component of the economic system itself.

Fifthly, on this basis, the economic system should appear as a self-moving integrity, which differs in the mechanisms of its self-movement. In this context, the combination of the mechanism of action of shocks, on the one hand, and the mechanisms of self-movement of economic systems under the influence of the dialectical laws of unity and struggle of opposites, the transition of quantitative changes into qualitative ones and the denial of negation, on the other hand, turned out to be extremely promising.

Sixth, the dialectical logic of the authors' research should have led them to analyze the object component of the mechanism for the realization of shocks and to compare its action with the action of universal mechanisms of positive and negative selection of forms of organization of human activity. The interaction of these processes, regulating the complication of systemic integrity as to their object component, should have deepened the theoretical understanding of the phenomenon of shocks.

Seventh, it was logical to consider the mechanism for the realization of shocks in the context of their subjective component. The conclusions reached by the authors turned out to be extremely relevant from the point of view of understanding the essence of the shock destruction of structural ties caused by the COVID-19 pandemic in 2020.

In fact, in this form, the authors initially formulated a working model for the study of shocks, conditioned by the need to follow dialectical logic. The results obtained exceeded the most optimistic expectations of the authors (the results are presented in the conclusion to the book).

CONCLUSION

The material described above represents the logic of the work of remarkable scientists on the complicated problem of identifying the patterns of functioning of complex dynamic systems in the economy. The merit of Ragnar Frisch is the formulation of the fundamental theoretical problem associated with the laws of development of complex dynamic systems in the economy. He presented a systemic vision of this problem, dividing it into two fundamental ones: the first one was connected with the propagation problem; and the second one - with the impulse problem. He managed to make a deep scientific contribution to the study of those problems.

In parallel with Ragnar Frisch, E.E. Slutsky worked on the problem of the functioning of macro-dynamic systems in the framework of the theory of random waves. Thus, E.E. Slutsky was among the first to doubt the adequacy of determinist models to explain economic cycles. He validated a hypothesis pointing out that the random effects – "impulses" (or "shocks") – on economic system launched the cyclical response (reaction) to the external influence. He deepened the stochastic approach to describing the macro-dynamic characteristics of complex systems, exploring the effect of the summation of random causes as the source of cyclic process.

Applied aspect of those scientific researches of R. Frisch and E. Slutsky was realized by Irma Adelman and Frank Adelman. At the end of the 1950s impulse transmission approach was tested in the empirical research of economic fluctuations by I. and F. Adelman. Analyzing the influence of random shocks with the help of Klein-Goldberger model, they proved that the amplitude and duration of cycles generated by modeled external impulses showed striking resemblance to the actual observations. The model applied by the scientists in their experiment was exposed to the effects of random shocks: the resulting fluctuations of business activity repeated the US economic dynamics, structured according to the data of National Bureau of Economic Research.

Their results confirmed scientific foresights and hypotheses of R. Frisch (1933) and of E. Slutsky (1927a, 1927b, 1937). All their findings provide some evidence for the hypothesis that the cyclical model of development of any economic system means its adjustment to new conditions caused by external impulses (shocks). To reinforce the findings, some results associated with other theoretical investigations and analytical researches are presented.

Thus, the brilliant researches of these remarkable scientists of the past give an idea of the future possible direction of investigation in the framework of the theoretical developments of the authors of this book.

REFERENCES

Adelman, I. (1959, Oct.). The dynamic properties of the Klein-Goldberger model. *Econometrica*.

Akerman, J. (1928). *Det ekonomiska livets rytmik* (Doctoral dissertation). Lund.

Bodkin Ronald, G. (Ed.). (1991). *A History of Macroeconometric Model-Building. American Econometric Models of the 1950s*. Edward Elgar Publishing.

EinsteinA. (1993). *Quotes*. https://www.brainyquote.com/quotes/albert_einstein_121993

Escañuela, R. I. (2016). *Randomness, Determinism and Undecidability in the Economic Cycle Theory*. MPRA Paper No. 75488. https://mpra.ub.uni-muenchen.de/75488/9/MPRA_paper_75488.pdf

Frisch, R. (1933). Propagation problems and impulse problems in dynamic economics. In *Economic Essays in Honour of Gustav Cassel*. Allen and Unwin.

Frisch, R. (1992). Statics and dynamics theory in economic. Structural Change and Economic Dynamics, 3(2). (Original publication 1929)

Hegel, G. W. F. (1892). The science of logics. In The Logic of Hegel (2nd ed.). Oxford University Press.

Howrey, E.P. (1968). A spectrum analysis of the long swing hypothesis. *Scandinavian Economic Review, 9*(2), 228-52.

Howrey, E.P., Klein, L.R., & McCarthy, M.A. (1974). Notes on testing the predictive performance of econometric models. *International Economic Review, 15*, 366-83.

Kaldor, N. (1939). Welfare propositions of economics and interpersonal comparisons of utility. *Economic Journal (London), 49*(195), 549–552. doi:10.2307/2224835

Klein, L. R. (1969, September). Econometric model building for growth projections. *Business Economics (Cleveland, Ohio), 4*(4), 45–50.

Kondratieff, N. D. (1935). The long waves in economic life. The Review of Economic Statistics, 17(6), 105-115. doi:10.2307/1928486

Kondratiev, N. D. (1922). *The World Economy and its Conjuncture During and After the War*. Conjuncture Institute Publisher.

Marx, K., & Engels, F. (1955-1974). *Coll. Cit.* (2nd ed.). Moscow: Political Literature Publishing House.

Qin, D., & Gilbert, C. (2001). The error term in the history of time series econometrics. *Econometric Theory, 17*(2), 424–450. doi:10.1017/S0266466601172063

Ramey, V. A. (2016). *Macroeconomic Shocks and Their Propagation*. National Bureau of Economic Research. Working Paper 21978. http://www.nber.org/ papers/w21978

Schumpeter, J. A. (1961). *The Theory of Economic Development*. Oxford Univ. Press.

Singh, J. (1997). *Methodology of Economics: Economic Statics and Dynamics*. https://www.economicsdiscussion.net/essays/economics/methodology-of-economics-economic-statics-and-dynamics/1097

Slutsky, E. (1927b). The summation of random causes as the source of cyclic processes. In The Questions of Conjuncture. Conjuncture Institute of Moscow.

Slutsky, E. (1937). The Summation of Random Causes as the Source of Cyclic Processes (in Russian). In Problems of Economic Conditions. The Conjuncture Institute. (Original publication 1927)

Slutsky, E. (1937). The summation of random causes as the source of cyclic processes. Econometrica, 5(2), 105–146. doi:10.2307/1907241

Slutsky, E. E. (1927a). The accumulation of accidental causes as the source of cyclic processes. In *Problems of Economic Conditions*. Conjuncture Institute publishing house.

Udny, Y. G. (1927). *On a method of investigating periodicity* (Vol. 226; D. Series, Trans.). Royal Society.

Wiener, N. (1930). *Generalized Harmonic Analysis* (Doctoral dissertation). Acta Mathematica.

ENDNOTES

1 Equation (I) from: Frisch, Ragnar. (1933). 'Propagation problems and impulse problems in dynamic economics'. In: *Economic Essays in Honour of Gustav Cassel*. London: Allen and Unwin, P. 177.

2 Equation (I) from: Frisch, Ragnar. (1933). 'Propagation problems and impulse problems in dynamic economics'. In: *Economic Essays in Honour of Gustav Cassel*. London: Allen and Unwin, P. 182.

3 Equation (2) from: Frisch, Ragnar. (1933). 'Propagation problems and impulse problems in dynamic economics'. In: *Economic Essays in Honour of Gustav Cassel*. London: Allen and Unwin, P. 182.

4 Equation (3) from: Frisch, Ragnar. (1933). 'Propagation problems and impulse problems in dynamic economics'. In: *Economic Essays in Honour of Gustav Cassel*. London: Allen and Unwin, P. 182.

5 Equation (4) from: Frisch, Ragnar. (1933). 'Propagation problems and impulse problems in dynamic economics'. In: *Economic Essays in Honour of Gustav Cassel*. London: Allen and Unwin, P. 182.

6 Equation (5) from: Frisch, Ragnar. (1933). 'Propagation problems and impulse problems in dynamic economics'. In: *Economic Essays in Honour of Gustav Cassel*. London: Allen and Unwin, P. 182.

Chapter 2
Methodological Approach to the Interpretation of the Essence of Shocks and Forms of Their Manifestation

ABSTRACT

Research methodology of shocks is based on the dialectic of interaction of such categories as system, structure, integrity, exchange, as well as two main forms of organizing economic activity – its specialization and cooperation. The dialectic of interaction of differentiation and integration with the exchange of economic activity and its results makes it possible to highlight the structure of the system. Structural connections are formed through the exchange and predetermine the system's integrity. Thus, if shocks have a strong negative impact on the system, they apparently violate its integrity and, consequently, its structure. Outwardly, shocks manifest as a marginal gap between market and base prices of traded goods, services, or any other assets. Structural disruptions are mediated by either sellers or buyers in the marketplace. The authors formulate a hypothesis about the embeddedness of shocks in the mechanism of self-movement of system.

INTRODUCTION

Recent events related to the coronavirus pandemic have confirmed the urgent need to rethink the patterns of self-movement of human-made economic systems, as well as the role of shocks in it. The words "shock" or "shocks" have long become common in modern literature (Calomiris, 2011; Calomiris, 2009; Boyd, et al., 2004; Acharya, et al., 2011; Calomiris, et al., 2016; Kovacevich, 2014; etc.), but have not yet been treated as the subject of theoretical research. Nevertheless, back in the first half of the last century, the shock phenomenon attracted the attention of such famous researchers as R. Frisch (1933), E. Slutsky (1937) as well as Irma Adelman and Frank Adelman (1959).

DOI: 10.4018/978-1-7998-4309-2.ch002

A series of famous crises in the last century (Kindleberger, et al., 2005), including the Great Depression (Galbraith, 1997), global financial crisis of 2008-2009, as well as the crisis caused by the COVID-19 pandemic in 2020 had certain unity. The authors were able to establish that all of the above crises described in numerous books (Reinhart, et al., 2009; Kindleberger, et al., 2011; Bitros, 2015; Burenin, 2017), were preceded by shocks. These shocks were reflected in the minds of ordinary people by incomprehensible (and therefore causing great anxiety) violations of the usual order of phenomena associated with the effect of chaos in the economy, in the field of finance, credit, money, in society, etc. Moreover, these violations turned out to be very significant for people acting as households, consumers, producers, assets owners, officials, so on and so forth, since shocks radically changed their standard of living, material well-being, life prospects, opportunities for social lifting, and etc. All these subjective feelings of people were a reflection of the objective changes that took place and are happening in the economic systems created by mankind.

Such famous scientists as R. Frisch (1933) and E. Slutsky (1927, 1937) were the first to interpret impulses in connection with the processes of dynamic changes in the economy. Having not found answers to fundamental theoretical questions regarding the phenomenon of shocks, the authors were forced to build their own logic of research, which allowed them to ultimately structure the foundations of shocks theory. First, the authors focused on the priority of the dialectical method of research, and they turned out to be right, since it was dialectics that allowed the classics to obtain important results (Hegel, 1892; Marx, and Engels, 1955-1974) in their works, determined the sequence of problems' solution related to the theoretical understanding of shocks. Second, this method gave the authors a completely unique chance to delve into the problems of static and dynamic changes in economic systems and highlight their stages, predetermined by the dialectical laws of unity and struggle of opposites, of the transition of quantitative changes into qualitative ones and of negation of negation. This methodological approach made it possible to understand the causes of instantaneous fundamental or shock changes in economic systems accompanied by subsequent crises. In addition, that logic helped to determine the role (place, function) of shocks in the implementation of the objective dialectical laws of self-movement of economic systems.

Systemic reproduction of dialectical method in the study of the phenomenon of "shocks" allowed the authors to substantiate the foundations of the theory of shocks. Dialectics made it possible to determine the sequence of theoretical reasoning at scientific understanding of the phenomenon of shocks. It became as follows. (1) If shocks preceding subsequent crises are their indispensable attribute, then the economic (financial) system should have segments exposed to shocks that generate subsequent crises (Chapter 2.1). (2) These segments of the system must predetermine its stability, a fundamental quality of integrity, the violation of which turns into shock and crisis. Such a place in the system is occupied by its structure, the role of which in the economy is played by exchange. Then shock is essentially a mechanism, or rather, a trigger, to the rupture of structural ties in the market exchange (Chapter 2.2). (3) Shock disruption of exchange or structural ties between buyers and sellers in the market is externally manifested as a price gap between the market price and the base price of the traded asset (Chapter 2.3). It gave the authors reason to call all shocks as price ones, and to associate their differences with the quality (specificity) of the traded product (asset). In this regard, the authors consider it correct to identify the essence of shocks with their ability to break the structural ties in market exchange, and the form of their manifestation – with the gap between market and base prices for a traded asset in a specific market for goods, services or assets.

2.1. Modern Well-Established Ideas about the Phenomenon of Shock as "a Thing in Itself"

In numerous publications of foreign and Russian authors on economic and financial crises "shock(s)" have become common words, the essence of which is supposed intuitively clear. After examining publications in which shocks were mentioned with different frequencies and in various interpretations, the authors of this book highlighted the books written by Charles P. Kindleberger (1996), as well as by him in collaboration with Robert Z. Aliber (2005). Those publications were typical in the context of the use of the word "shock (s)" when describing the manifold crises in economic history. The above books are distinguished by its encyclopedic coverage of the financial crises phenomena in connection with chain letters, financial bubbles, pyramid schemes, Ponzi finance, and manias as somewhat overlapping terms, as well as «shock(s)», that accompanied the economic crises since the beginning of XVII century until the end of XX. Moreover, Charles P. Kindleberger, and Robert Z. Aliber (2005) highlighted and studied the following famous financial bubbles: the Dutch Tulip Bulb Bubble in 1636; the South Sea Bubble in 1720; the Mississippi Bubble in 1720; the late 1920s stock price bubble in 1927–1929; the surge in bank loans to Mexico and other developing countries in the 1970s; the bubble in real estate and stocks in Japan in 1985–1989; the 1985–1989 bubble in real estate and stocks in Finland, Norway and Sweden; the bubble in real estate and stocks in Thailand, Malaysia, Indonesia and several other Asian countries in 1992–1997; the surge in foreign investment in Mexico in 1990–1993; the bubble in over-the-counter stocks in the United States in 1995–2000. In describing the above, the authors quite often mentioned "shocks", but did not give a deep theoretical interpretation of that phenomenon. So, speaking of the nature of the outside, exogenous shocks, those authors identified them with a trigger of the mania in different historical settings including the onset and the end of the war, a series of good and bad harvests, the opening of new markets and new natural resources as well as the development of different innovations – the railroads, electricity, email, and etc. Charles P. Kindleberger and Robert Z. Aliber (2005) interpreted the phenomenon of "mania" by emphasizing its irrationality; and of the "financial bubble" as a sign that some values would eventually burst. But they abstracted from the characteristics of shocks. Obviously, for this reason, "shocks" are absent in the titles of the chapters of their books, although in their texts 'shocks' are widely used to describe shocks' effects on the economy, which change horizons, expectations, the possibility of obtaining estimated profits and the behavior of economic agents.

All Charles P. Kindelberger' contemporaries did the same: mentioning the "shocks" in the texts of their publications, they, however, did not delve into the essence and forms of manifestation of this phenomenon. This conclusion is based on the fact that in the titles of publications cited by Charles P. Kindlberger and Robert Z. Aliber in their books, the word "shock (s)" is missing, although this word is often used in their texts. O. Blanchard (2003, 2009) gave some semblance of an explanation for the widespread use of the word "shock (s)" in literature and of the absence of their strictly scientific interpretation as follows. From his viewpoint, in each particular case, it is difficult to determine exactly what should be treated as a shock, which violated the stable state of the economic system, since that violation was preceded by the whole series of events that ultimately caused it. Really, in this whole series of events it was necessary to highlight the one that actually generates a landslide gap in cause-and-effect relations in the market.

Thus, the authors of this book were confronted the fact of expanding the boundaries of the use of the word "shock(s)" in theoretical and practical literature on crises issues by the end of the 1990s and the absence of any systemic understanding of this phenomenon. The farther, the more difficult it became to understand the phenomenon of "shock", since it began to be used quite widely in scientific researches with various adjectives as price shocks, currency shocks, public debt shocks, liquidity shocks, shock's therapy, and etc. (Hatzius, et al., 2010; Suter, 1992; Hakro, et al., 2014; Alom, 2012; Bahi, 2015; Rostam, 2017). Gradually, shock terminology began to be used as the titles of the publications as well (Christiano, et al., 1999; Gilchrist, et al., 2009; Bems, et al., 2019; Easterly, et al., 2000; Hausmann, et al., 1996; etc.).

Shocks have appeared to be not easy phenomenon. A number of analytical works were devoted to its theoretical understanding, in which skillfully developed models of interactions in financial markets were presented (Christiano, et al., 1999; Hatzius, et al., 2010; Evans, 2009a; Evans, 2009b; Evans, 2009c). Nevertheless, as there was no understanding of the essence of the shocks, so it does not exist today. As a result over the years of national and global shocks' existence, the theoretical and practical puzzle associated with them has formed. But until now this phenomenon has remained not cognized (Yankov, et.al., 2009; Bems, et al., 2019; Easterly, et al., 2000; World Bank, May 2020; Mutuku, 2012; Lalanne, 2014; IMF, August 2020).

The category of "shock(s)" appeared even in educational literature on macroeconomics in conjunction with the non-price determinants. The latter were connected with supply and demand shocks, which in turn, generated corresponding shifts of either the aggregate demand curve or of the aggregate supply curve. As a result, these curves intersected at a new point, predetermining the changed macroeconomic equilibrium (McConnell, et al., 2008; Brue, et al., 2013; Sachs, et al., 1993). Thus, a static understanding of economic phenomena, including shocks, has taken root.

The global financial crisis of 2008-2009 as well as the COVID-19 pandemic shock added new unresolved fundamental problems. In 2009 William White (2009), the former BIS chief economist, wrote: "…the latest global economic crisis (of 2008-2009) has proven that simplifying assumptions dictated by a static perception of economic reality in modern macroeconomics cast doubt on its understanding of real events and dynamic processes in it". Joseph A. Schumpeter (1949) noted that the development (self-development) of economic system meant its dynamics. Over a century ago J. B. Clark (2007) insisted on the need to separate statics and dynamics in the processes of economic changes. At the beginning of the last century N.D. Kondratiev (1984) emphasized that dynamic economic changes significantly differ from their stationary, static (circular) state. W. White (2009) substantiated a misunderstanding of the patterns of maturing of the large-scale global and economic crisis of 2008-2009 by the fact that a static (equilibrium) paradigm prevailed in macroeconomic theory. Laurence H. Summers (2014a, 2014b) from the Harvard University supported this idea in 2013 at the IMF conference. He emphasized that within the framework of the previous "equilibrium paradigm" it is impossible to understand either the phenomenon of slowdown in the growth of developed economies or the factors initiating it. In other words, the absence of a dynamic paradigm in economic theory predetermined a misunderstanding of the changes in the economy in the categories of macroeconomic equilibrium or circulation. It does not allow to predict the shocks as well as the probability of crises maturing similar to the one occurred in 2008-2009 (Mankiw, 2006).

This circumstance has increased the significance of the problem of shocks, highlighting its new slice, associated with their ability to block the mechanism of "effective markets". These trends emerged in 2007 as the shock rupture of structural ties in the US unsecured mortgage market began to spread rapidly across national borders to the entire global financial space (Wolf, 2019; IMF, July 2019). So the first global financial shock in the recent history destroyed the idea of the automatic restoration of macroeconomic equilibrium in the post-shock period. On the contrary, it turned out to be a "starting button" that launched a mechanism of multiplying financial and economic imbalances in interconnected national economic systems.

Thus, the global financial crisis of 2008-2009 and the shock that caused it in the American unsecured mortgage market, and even more so the shock from COVID-19, increased the importance of developing theoretical approaches to understanding the phenomenon of shock. Despite this, the status of "a thing in itself" was entrenched for this phenomenon, the nature, functions and forms of manifestation of which failed to be cognized (Pilipenko, et al., 2016; Pilipenko, et al., 2018; Pilipenko, 2020; Pilipenko, 2021).

And, meanwhile, in the course of the study of shocks, they turned out to be associated with a whole range of problems, including the most complex interactions between static economic systems and dynamic ones in the context of dialectics of their self-organization and self-development, not to mention the objective integration of shocks and subsequent crises into these processes. All this puts the authors of this book in a paradoxical situation because, on the one hand, they agree with the conclusions of such brilliant theorists of the past as R. Frisch, E. Slutsky, the Adelmans, John Bates Clark, Thomas C. Leonard (2003) and Joseph A. Schumpeter, but on the other hand, certain one-sidedness (limitation) of offered judgments now becomes evident, and therefore it is impossible to share viewpoints of those theorists in full. Only an adequate methodological basis and strict adherence to dialectical logic allowed the authors to consistently build the foundations of the theory of shocks, integrating it into the theory of self-movement of systemic integrity in the economics.

2.2. Essence of Shocks: A Hypothesis of the Objective Embeddedness of Shocks into the Economic System's Structure

Shocks and crises are frequent phenomenon in recent economic history. Moreover, they not only significantly slowed down the rate of economic growth, but often threw economic systems far back. The data below (Fig. 1) suggests that in 2020 the COVID-19 pandemic shock and the subsequent Great Lockdown caused the annual global GDP rate to fall to -3%. This is 30 times the loss to the global economy in 2009 due to the shock on the US unsecured mortgage credit market and to the subsequent global financial crisis of 2008-2009.

In total the "Great Lockdown" losses are tentatively estimated at $ 9 trillion, which is equivalent to the GDP of Japan and Germany combined (Fig. 2). Otherwise, the global economy will suffer such losses if the coronavirus infection is defeated in the second half of 2020. Otherwise, the global GDP could drop by an additional 3% in 2020. If the COVID-19 pandemic persists in 2021, the global economy will lose another 8% of GDP compared to the IMF baseline scenario in April 2020.

For the first time since the Great Depression, the economic downturn due to the COVID-19 shock will affect all groups of countries of the world: developed economies, with emerging market and developing countries (Fig. 3,4,5). The divergence in income prospects between advanced economies and emerging and developing economies (excluding China) triggered by this pandemic is projected to worsen. The IMF experts are upgrading their forecast for advanced economies for 2020 to -5.8 percent, for emerging market and developing countries (excluding China) to -5.7 percent.

Such destructive consequences of shocks make theoretical studies devoted to shocks, their essence and functions, as well as the reasons for their ripening and the mechanisms of their impact on national and global economies extremely relevant. Moreover, the recurrence in general of "scenarios" of shocks and further development of crises in new and recent economic history suggests that there are fundamental reasons for such a development of events. If they are adequately understood, it would be possible to avoid huge economic losses in the future by preventing a shock slowdown in economic growth rates or a "rollback" of the economy back.

Figure 1. The fall in real GDP amid the 2020 "Great Self-Isolation" caused by COVID-19 and as a result of the 2008-2009 global financial crisis
Source: IMF (2020). World Economic Outlook April 14

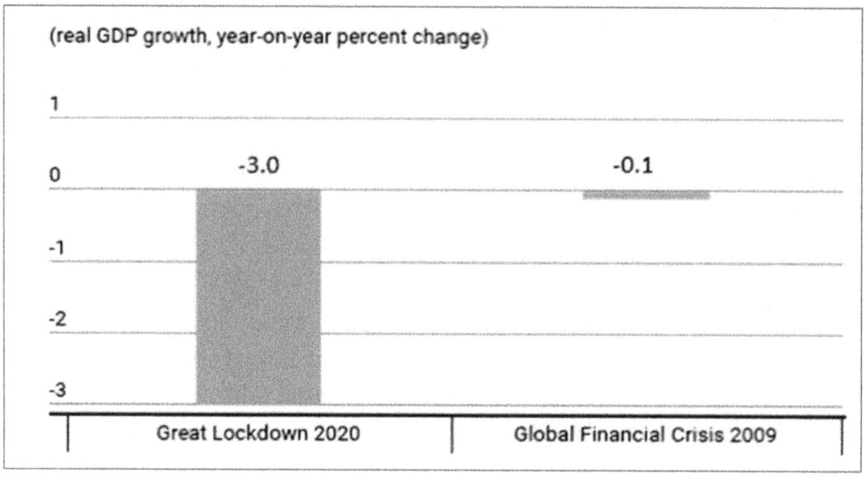

Figure 2. The dynamics of global GDP in the conditions of the "Great Lockdown " in 2020
Source: IMF (2020). World Economic Outlook April 14.

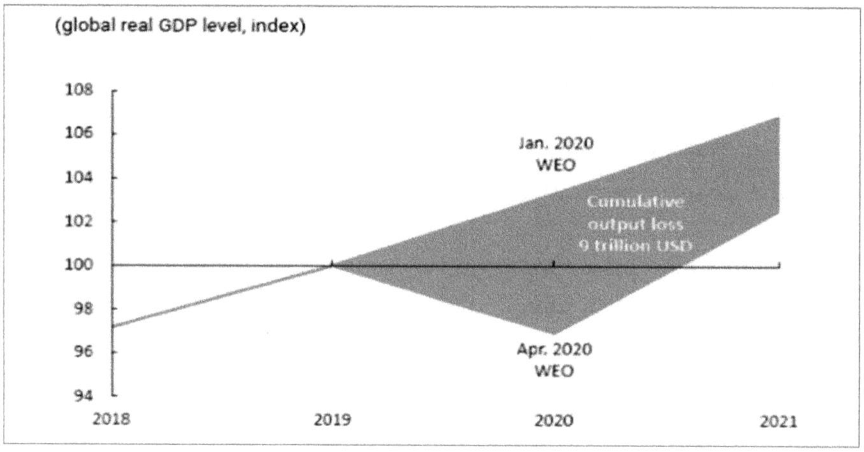

From a philosophical point of view, the repetition of certain phenomena makes it possible to assume that they are associated with objectively operating mechanisms within the framework of systemic integrity. In this context, shocks are invariably accompanied by blocking the ability of the economic system to instantly restore its original equilibrium state. And the crisis following the shock accompanies the economic recovery up to the growth rates' increase. To prove the validity of these conclusions and to identify the essence and forms of shocks' realization, it was necessary to determine the methodological principles of their study. They were structured taking into account the provisions substantiated by the creators and developers of such theoretical concepts as general systems theory (H. Hacken, 1977), synergetics (Ludwig von Bertalanffy, 1968), tectology (A.A. Bogdanov, 1934), the catastrophe theory (V.I. Arnold, 1975, 1979; J. Guckenheimer, 1973; E.C. Zeeman, 1977; R. Thom, 1969; 1974; and etc.), theory of large cycles of economic conjuncture (N.D. Kondratiev, 1984), as well as the modern theory of complexity economics (W. Brian Arthur, 1999; Arthur, et al., 1997; Anderson, et al., 1988; Hausmann, et al., 1996), etc.

Figure 3. Economic recession in all countries of the world in 2020 in comparison with the global financial crisis of 2008-2009.
Source: IMF (2020). World Economic Outlook April 14.

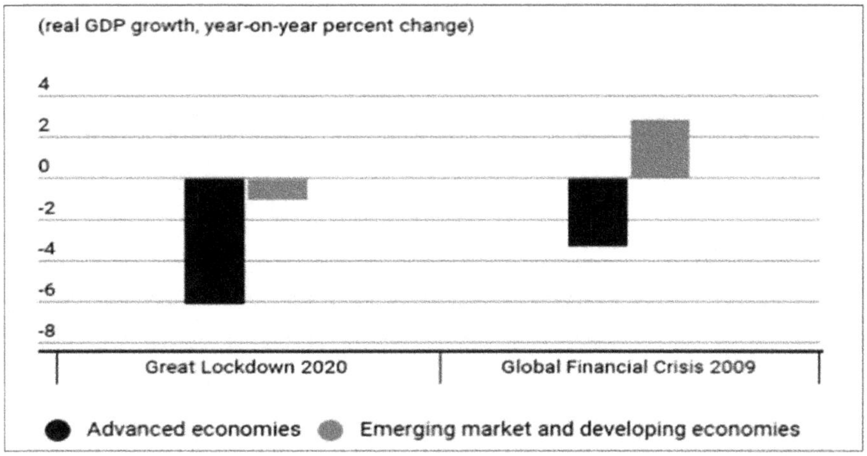

Figure 4. Upgraded IMF forecasts for advanced economies and China, but a downgrade for emerging markets and developing economies (year-on-year percent change)
Source: IMF (2020). World Economic Outlook. October.

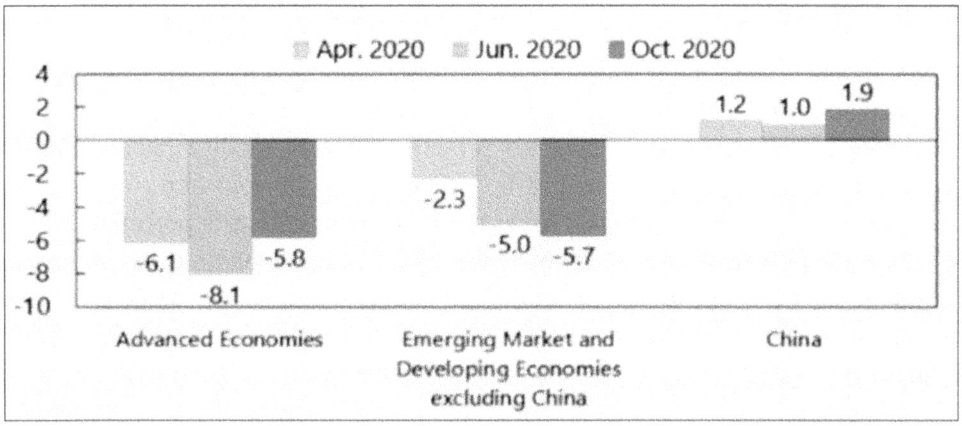

Deepening into the problem of shocks, the authors developed a hypothesis about their objective embedding in the mechanisms of self-movement of economic systems. To prove it, there were involved philosophical principles of knowledge (B.M. Kedrov, 1963; A.P. Sheptulin, 1957; A.A. Zinoviev, 1960) and the logic of materialist dialectics, which is associated with the names of prominent representatives of the German philosophy - Immanuel Kant (1781); Friedrich Wilhelm Joseph von Schelling (1993), and Georg Wilhelm Friedrich Hegel (1892, 1967 as well as the findings of such brilliant thinkers as K. Marx (1995); Vladimir I. Vernadsky (1967), Ludwig Heinrich Edler von Mises (1998), Friedrich August von Hayek (1991), Fernand Braudel (1981), and etc. All the above theoretical developments allowed the authors of this book to construct their own methodological approach, implemented in the foundations of shock theory, which is consistent with the laws of self-movement of the economy as a systemic integrity. That is why the study of the mechanisms for the implementation of these laws in the economy became paramount.

Figure 5. Latest World Economic Outlook growth projections (percent change), 2019-2021
Source: IMF (2020). World Economic Outlook. October.

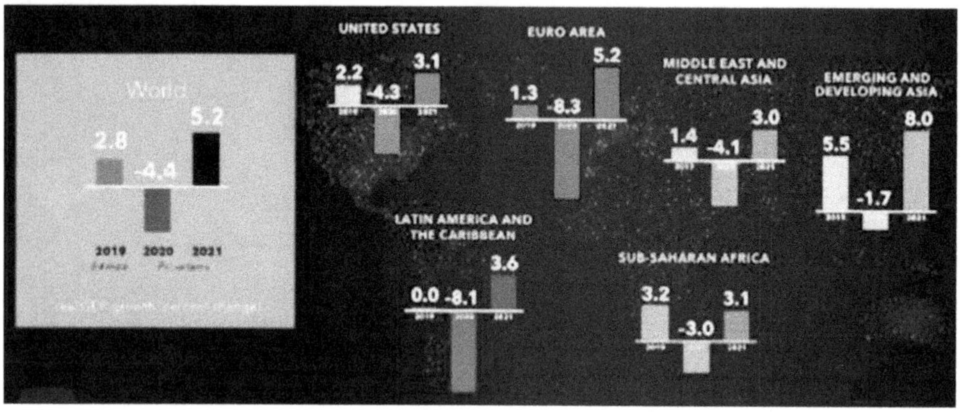

So, any system created by man is in the process of its constant complication, implementing its ability to self-movement. Systems' transition from simple to more complex organizations occurs both by increasing the number of elements and by strengthening the relationships between them. As a result the interactions of some elements with each other become more and more stable. The dominance of the internal interactions of the elements of the system generates its new property of integrity, which is implemented through the ability to independently provide systemic stability and equilibrium. In other words as a result of strengthening or weakening the interaction of elements of the system their qualities changes. In the case of progressive changes, the system integrity acquires a potential that significantly exceeds the sum of the potentials of its constituent elements. At the same time, the elementary components of the system inevitably abandon some of their inherent properties, and objectively acquire others that are aimed at strengthening the system integrity that integrates them. With the acquisition of the property of integrity, the system ceases to be a summative organization and turns into an organic one. Thus the systemic integrity is ensured by the internal interconnections of the elements of the system due to their stability, constant repeatability and immutability. It is these relationships in the system that represents its structure, that provides its property of integrity. If the system partially or completely loses this property, failures occur in its functioning, which are manifested in the deterioration of growth rates (for example, in the economy). For this, the structural elements that ensure the integrity of the system must also be characterized by constancy, stability and balance. Consequently, in the case of shocks that externally manifest themselves as failures in the economy it is necessary to identify the dialectics of their interaction with the structure of the system, which ensures its integrity. And this means that the phenomena of shocks must be philosophically interpreted in the context of the complication of the structural connections of the system integrity and the laws of its self-movement.

From a philosophical point of view, the structure of the system embodies "the principle, method, law of the connection of elements within the systemic whole" (Sheptulin, 1975, 1978). In other words, the quality of systemic integrity is predetermined by the structural links of the system. And in the process of their self-movement, dialectical laws are implemented, being predetermined by the norms inherent in structural connections. The importance of this provision is related to the fact that it allows one to come closer to understanding of what quality should be the shock's impact on the systemic integrity so that the system itself or some of its segments could collapse. If structural connections in an integral system implement the action of dialectical laws that ensure its self-movement, then the phenomenon of shocks must be theoretically interpreted in connection with the rupture of structural ties and violation of the integrity of the system. However, shock's breaking structural ties is not an easy action, since they can be destroyed, and this will affect the dialectical laws that govern them only if this result is objectively predetermined by the state of the system. It is logical in this context to conclude that if the shock's rupture of structural ties is objectively predetermined, then this is a consequence of the action of the dialectical laws themselves. With this approach, shocks should act as a mechanism for these laws' implementation in conditions objectively formed for this. The provisions substantiated above allow the authors to formulate a hypothesis about the embeddedness of shocks into the mechanism of complicating the structure of the economic system with the quality of integrity. Then the shock's rupture of structural ties, which negatively affects the mechanism for ensuring the stability, equilibrium and balance of economic integrity, occurs as a result of the accumulation of objective conditions for this. This explains the fact why the formation of the theory of shocks by the authors was carried out in parallel with the philosophical understanding of the specifics of the structural connections of the system, the laws of its self-movement and the quality of systemic integrity.

Considering all of the above, it is advisable to concretize the conclusions obtained in relation to the specifics of structural ties in the economy. The economic system is a set of many types of diverse economic activities of people. The basis of the economic activity of people is work, which can be characterized according to Karl Marx (1995), as the labor process of interaction between man and nature. All human-created economic organizations are the result of the interaction of two main forms of economic (labor) activity – of its specialization (division, differentiation) and cooperation (association, integration). According to A.A. Bogdanov (1934), economic activity changes from elementary to its most complex forms in the process of interaction of its simplest acts, represented by "differentiation - integration". Integration (unification, cooperation) needs diversity, which is possible to unite, as well as differentiation needs the consistency of the manifestation of properties as functions, otherwise they lose their expedient character for the system as a whole. At the same time, integration not only "harmonizes" functional properties in the process of their implementation, but also limits the differentiation of the system, i.e. reduces the possibility of separation within its framework. As such, these forms of organizing economic activity structure the economic system. In the process of labor (work) differentiation positive selection of types of economic activities is carried out ensuring their complication and increasing the diversity of economic organizations. As such, specialization of economic activities generates more and more complications for them. As for the integration of economic activity, it mediates negative selection, since it simplifies the possibilities of differentiation and removes from them everything that is fragile, discordant, and contradictory. As a result, integration brings homogeneity, consistency and orderliness to economic activity.

It is difficult to disagree with A.A. Bogdanov (1934) in the fact that these two forms of organization of economic activity dialectically complement each other, and, thus, objectively organize economic reality. It is in the process of their interaction and mutual struggle that existing connections become more complicated, new ones are generated, and their positive and negative selection takes place. As a result, some of these connections turn into structural ones, and they ensure the integrity of the economic system.

The structure of the economic system is directly related to the phenomenon of exchange. This is due to the fact that the division (specialization, differentiation) of labor necessitates the appearance of exchange, as well as its cooperation (integration, unification) genetically and functionally contains exchange. The relative independence and opposition of the phenomena of division and cooperation of economic activity makes them mobile forms of its organization, reacting to any impact. As for the market exchange, it implements the method of internal interconnection of these two forms of organizing economic activity. It is in the process of mediation of exchange that the structural links that ensure the integrity of the economic system stand out and become constantly repeated. The division and cooperation of economic activity dialectically interact exclusively through exchange, which, in turn, is conditioned by them. In this case, exchange serves as a necessary condition for the differentiation and integration of economic activity, since the unification of coexisting labor is impossible without communication with each other.

In general, the categories of division and cooperation of labor are interrelated aspects of a single process of joint economic activity. At any given moment, these forms of organization of economic activity are mutually dependent on each other in such a way that they could be called the abscissa and ordinate of the economic curve describing the systemic integrity. Exchange is an internal moment of the organization of economic activity and is characterized by stability, conservatism in relation to changes in its forms. It is these properties of exchange that make it related to structural connections in the system. The interaction of the categories described above is presented by the authors in Fig. 6 in a vertical section of the model of organizing economic activity. Judging by Fig. 6, the differentiation of economic activity realizes a positive selection of its specialized types, increasing their diversity. Integration, using various types of specialized labor, realizes their negative selection, generates connections between them and coordinates the forms of their manifestation. That is why the results of the integration are significantly inferior in scale to the variety of differentiated types of economic activities

A.A. Bogdanov compared the processes of differentiation and integration with a universal regulatory mechanism in all spheres of human activity. From his point of view, the differentiation of human activity (positive selection), "by complicating the forms, increases the heterogeneity of being, delivers material for it that is ever increasing". As for its integration (negative selection), it, "simplifying this material, eliminating from it all fragile, discordant, contradictory, introducing homogeneity and consistency in its connections, orders the latter. Complementing each other, both processes spontaneously organize the world" (Bogdanov, 1934).

However, the relationships that arise within the framework of the economic system as a result of integration and differentiation of economic activity, not all become structural, i.e. constantly repetitive, stable and balanced. Such a quality of interaction can arise only within the framework of dialectical pairs, which are predetermined by the dialectics of unity and struggle of opposites (Chapter 3). Moreover, they are mediated by exchange, which transforms into structural only a part of the links that have arisen within the framework of the integration association of differentiated types of activity. That is why in Fig. 6 the scale of exchange is much smaller than both the area of the figure describing the integration and the area of the figure representing the differentiation. However, the importance of exchange for the economic system as the integrity lies in the fact that it is the exchange that regulates the behavior of structural links, aiming them at strengthening the stability and equilibrium of the entire system. Dialectical laws of self-movement of systemic integrity in the economy are implemented through the exchange of economic activity and of its results. It is about the laws of unity and struggle of opposites, of the transition of quantitative changes into qualitative ones and of the negation of negation (Chapters 3, 4).

Figure 6. Model representation of the interaction of differentiation and integration as forms of organizing economic activity and their essence, represented by the exchange of economic activity and its results
Source: the authors' development

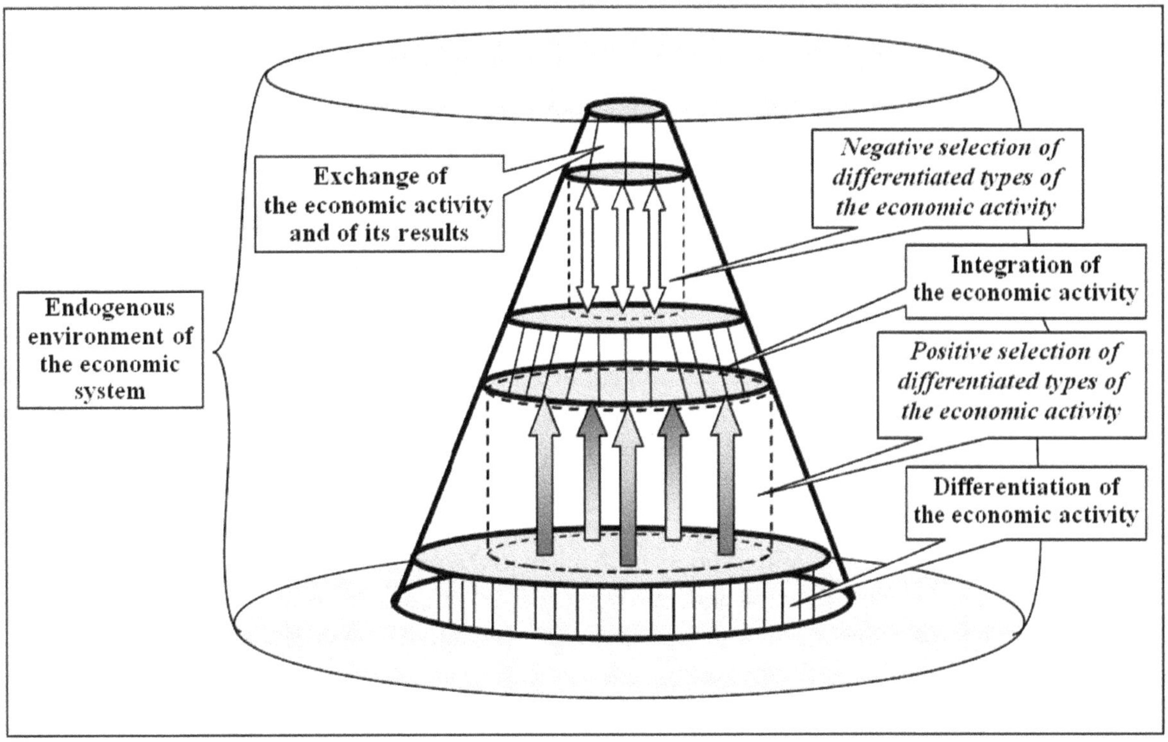

Now it becomes possible to summarize the preliminary results of the study of the relationship between the categories of the system and the shocks that affect its structure.

1. Shocks can make a major impact on the functioning of an economic system only if they disrupt the structural links that mediate the exchange of economic activity and its results.
2. The structure of any systemic integrity ensures its stability, equilibrium and balance because it is immune to changing forms of organization of economic activity therefore the implementation of a shock rupture becomes possible only if necessary and sufficient conditions ripen to block the interaction of dialectical pairs.
3. It follows that the conditions of a shock rupture of structural ties, which are predetermined by the dialectical laws are in full accordance with these laws' operation. Otherwise, the integrity of the system could not be shocked.

4. As a result, the authors, in the first approximation, specify the hypothesis of the embeddedness of shocks into the mechanism of structural ties' performing, or rather of dialectical laws' action mediated by the structure of the economic system.

So, the structure of systemic integrity in economics mediates the action of dialectical laws (Chapter 3, 4), ensuring its self-movement. In this context, the essence of shocks is manifested in their ability to break the structural ties of the economic system that mediate market exchange. The realization of this ability of shocks is possible only if they are objectively built into the structure of economic systems.

2.3. Forms of Shocks' Manifestation in Various Markets: Marginal Gap between Base and Market Prices for Exchanged Products

Singling out exchange as the basis for the formation and complication of structural ties, it is necessary to clarify that for this part of the study it is quite sufficient to specify exchange as a set of markets in which various goods are exchanged. So, shocks as a mechanism for breaking the structural relationships of dialectical pairs can occur at any market where various objects of exchange are traded. Thus, each market or its segment provides the exchange (trade) of specific goods, and therefore can be named depending on the specifics of the goods: milk market, crude oil market, etc. It is in this connection that shocks are often associated with the market for a specific product, where the shock's rupture of structural ties has occurred. That is why many theoretical and applied works devoted to crisis phenomena in certain markets determine shocks depending on the specific market in which the shock mechanism of breaking structural ties was realized. And it seems perfectly justified. However, it should be noted that the external manifestation of the shock mechanism in a certain market in the process of destruction of its structure or market exchange is only the tip of a giant "iceberg" of invisible qualities of the shock phenomenon. All the variety of manifestations of the shock mechanism in the markets of various goods, services and other assets are united by one common feature (characteristic). This is due to the fact that, regardless of the specific market, the shock mechanism of rupture of structural ties is implemented in the form of a breakaway (rebound) of the limit values of market prices for a traded object from their base prices. This means that shocks can occur in different markets, but their essence remains unchanged and manifests itself in the maximum price jump up or their extreme fall down.

And already at this stage of entering the problem of shocks, taking into account the conclusions obtained in Chapter 2.2, it becomes possible to interpret the shock impact on the structure of the market exchange as its visible manifestation in the form of a price gap. The fact is that the structure of the economic system, as its most conservative characteristic, changes in the last turn and, as such, predetermines its stability and integrity. In this case, it is about only one structural level of systemic integrity, represented by the market exchange of a certain specific utility. In this market, the structural interactions that mediate the functioning of dialectical pairs are torn apart by shocks which manifest itself in the form of a marginal rise in prices or their landslide fall. In any market such a price reaction can be generated by the marginal discrepancy (gap, mismatch) between the supply of goods and the demand for them, i.e. non-equilibrium exchange of its object component from the point of view of structural imbalance. Then prices react to this imbalance quite predictably: when the demand for goods falls, prices fall, and vice versa: when it rises, prices rise. However, the resulting price gap must reach certain limit values for them and overcome them, causing a collapse of the market structure as a result of a shock rupture of structural ties. Moreover, structural ties strengthen the integrity of the system by stabilizing market exchange before prices reach their limit values. As soon as market prices become prohibitive, structural ties under the influence of shock collapse and the structure ceases to provide the integrity of the entire system. Thus, the marginal mismatch of the prices for the traded asset triggers the shock mechanism of destruction of the market structure.

If considering only the object component of the structural links mediating the exchange of utilities by dialectical pairs, then understanding the shock effect is difficult. Questions arise related to why, or in what case, structures become able to restore the integrity of systemic formations in the form of a market, and in which cases not. It should be noted that comprehensive answers to these questions will be substantiated in Chapter 3. But it is already becoming clear that for a deep understanding of shocks, all categories associated with them must be considered in the process of complicating the structural links of the system (Chapters 3 and 4), as well as in the interaction of their object and subjective components (Chapters 5 and 6). In this point it is necessary to provide a logical justification for the need to move from objects of exchange as an object component of structural links to a subjective one, which will bring closer to understanding the causes of shocks and their functions in the mechanism of self-movement of economic (market) structural integrity.

The fact is that if structural links were predetermined by object content, then the market structure would function according to mechanistic principles that would not be difficult to understand and correct in order to prevent the occurrence of shocks. Hypothetically speaking, it is possible to consider the case of market imbalance, proceeding from the analysis of only its object component and make the following conclusions. If the supply of goods exceeds their demand, then it will be satisfied at the market price, and when all the goods are sold, then sales will stop until a good of similar utility appears in this market. In the opposite situation, the goods will simply remain unsold until prices balance their supply and demand. This explains the need for a separate study of changes in structural ties, taking into account their object component, and then from the point of view of subjects owning assets, sellers and buyers of goods, as well as direct participants in structural ties as representatives of dialectical pairs. So, in the case of determining unity of shocks, diverse in terms of the object of exchange, it is necessary to appeal not only (and maybe not so much) to the dialectics of the interaction of acts of purchase and of sale, of sold and of purchased goods, but to the behavior of sellers and buyers on the market. This aspect will be considered only in connection with the price forms of manifestation of various market shocks, since the procedural aspects of the shock mechanism will be considered in the context of the self-organization of economic systems in Chapter 3, and in connection with its self-development – in Chapter 4.

So, shocks as a mechanism for breaking structural ties in the market of certain tangible or intangible assets cannot be understood without including into consideration the behavior of dialectically interconnected participants of the goods exchange on a particular market. The main attention in the analysis of the subjective component of structural ties regarding the exchange of goods should be devoted to assessing the equivalence of transactions from the point of view of their subjects. If taking into account that structural ties are formed by participants in the exchange of goods, which are dialectically related to each other, then the main thing in understanding equilibrium, stability of structural ties should be attributed to the mutual coincidence or non-coincidence of the interests of the participants in the exchange of goods. This order of structural interactions of partners in a dialectical pair is due to the operation of the law of unity and struggle of opposites. If unity prevails over the opposing (conflicting) interests of the participants, then their exchange operations will strengthen the integrity of the market structure and ensure its balance. In this case, prices do not reach their limit values either with growth or with a fall, and the structure without hindrance, both by its object and its subjective components, strengthens the integrity of the whole system. As soon as the opposites of the participants in a dialectical pair of exchange transactions begin to replace their unity, the order of the connection of elements changes: instead of the law of unity and struggle of opposites, the law of transition of quantitative changes in structural ties into their qualitatively new state begins to operate. And the quality of the structural ties of the subjects of the transaction changes as the accumulation of irreconcilable contradictions between them, requiring changes in the mechanisms of stabilization of systemic integrity. It is this state of market structures that explains price volatility, which goes beyond the limit states for a particular market in comparison with the base value of the traded object (Arnold, 1975, 1979).

Overcoming the price limit for a specific market is a prerequisite for a shock rupture of structural ties in it. In other words mechanism of the shock breaking the structural relationships in the market starts operating as soon as the traded asset' price fluctuations overcome the marginal levels for each specific market (Arnold, 1975, 1979; Bak, 1996; Thom, 1969, 1974; Taleb, 2007, 2012). The main participants in the shock destruction of the structure are the subjects of transactions, i.e. subjective component of market exchange mediating structural links in the market. The main reason for the price of a traded asset to reach its limit values is the hype behavior of either sellers or buyers as participants in dialectical pairs. Their aggressive behavior, far from normal, on both the demand and supply sides, turns into a market dominant that destroys the objectively necessary coordination of structural ties. So, the irrational behavior of market participants causes either a jump of the prices of the traded asset, or their drop compared to the base price. This abnormality in the behavior of the partners in the deal compared with the conservative norm is predetermined by the fact that they do not want to give up their positions on prices. The explanation for this lies in the fact that the partners in the transaction are driven not by a single goal of stabilizing the situation, but by deepening contradictions, pursuing individual goals of enrichment at the expense of the partner, despite the impending crisis for all.

Outwardly, their irrational behavior is manifested in the increasing amplitude of price fluctuations around the underlying base value of asset (Shiller, 2004). All this suggests that the shock mechanism of rupture of structural ties and violation of system integrity refers to an objective and subjective phenomenon that is organically integrated into the mechanism of self-structuring of the economic system. In this sense, all shocks known in history are the same in that they are externally manifested in the overcoming by the market price of an asset of the limit values for a particular market, causing the shock's effect as multiplying structural breaks downs (Haken, 1977) due to the gap between the market price of the asset and its real (base) value. In this context, it can be argued that the shock effect on the structural ties, destroying system integrity is realized through the hype behavior of one group of participants of dialectical ties, turning into the dominant of market relations and demonstrating irrational behavior of participants either on the demand side or on the supply one. Anticipating the conclusions that will be substantiated in other chapters, the multiplier effect that accompanies shocks should be mentioned. In other words, shocks within certain limits can be viewed as triggers that generate a series of shock effects across all interconnected market structures. Indeed, the multiplying mechanism in the process of implementing the destructive impact of shocks is carried out, as a rule, as follows: speculation, monetary expansion, rising asset prices, then their sharp decline, the rush of economic agents to convert the value of assets into "real" money. As a result, one of participants of the dialectic pair begins to constantly upset the balance of dialectic relations in the market, irrationally increasing demand or supply, the market price of the asset gradually or stepwise rises or falls in comparison with its base value, causing a split-effect.

EMPIRICAL EVIDENCE

The phenomenon of the multiplying effect of the shocks' impact can be given a mathematical interpretation (Pilipenko, et al., 2016). For this purpose it is reasonable to imagine the appearance of the higher yielding assets on the stock market, which attract attention of the rational economic agent. Rather high income paid for the period τ and the possibility to increase the investment till the level of m for the relatively small forecast horizon attracts new participants whose behavior gradually begins to differ from rational.

Expansion of the economic agents allows principals-issuers increase securities issue, more and more coming off their financial security. In other words, the behavior of principals also acquires the character of irrationality. Let the number of economic agents whose behavior is characterized as irrational one because they do not analyze the real availability of securities and real terms possible interest payments by issuers without loss of economic self-sufficiency, grow exponentially with denominator q. Hence, cash inflow to issuers of securities data obeys the same geometric progression. This means that during the period n irrational economic agents acquire securities for the sum of $q^{n-1}m$.

If the behavior of principals was more rational, they could estimate the limiting moment (n – period number τ) since which resource inflow would be completely paid as interest income. Really, the condition under which some financial receipts remain to principals after interest income is paid to economic agents, can be written down, for example, as follows

$$q^{n-1}m - rm\sum_{i=1}^{n-2} q^i > 0, \qquad (1)$$

where r – the interest rate for the period τ.

Applying the formula for the sum of members of a geometrical progression

$$\sum_{i=1}^{n-2} q^i = \frac{q^{n-1}-1}{q-1},$$

let's transform an inequality (1) to a kind

$$q^{n-1}m - rm\frac{q^{n-1}-1}{q-1} > 0. \qquad (2)$$

As $q^{n-1} > 1$, it is possible to present an inequality (2) as follows

$$\frac{1}{q^{n-1}-1} > \frac{r}{q-1} - 1. \qquad (3)$$

The left part of an inequality (3) is always positive. The sign on the right part depends on the parity between sizes q and r. Obviously, two cases are possible. If $r<(q-1)$ the inequality (3) is carried out at any

$\boldsymbol{n}$, i.e. the sum of monetary receipts increases. If $r>(q-1)$ at enough big $\boldsymbol{n}$ the inequality (3) is not carried out and there can come the moment when it is not enough financial receipts even for interest payment.

The rational economic agent and the principal could easily estimate the moment of crisis of the tendency as to money resources growth to their falling. Really, in conditions when $r>(q-1)$, the following restriction can be received from an inequality (3) that makes sense as below

$$q^{n-1} < \frac{r}{r-q+1}. \tag{4}$$

Taking the logarithm of an inequality (4), we will come to the following estimation of the moment of tendencies change

$$n_{\lim} = 1 + \frac{\ln\left(\frac{r}{r-q+1}\right)}{\ln q}, \tag{5}$$

where $n_{\lim}$ – marginal number of the periods of financial operation with participation of irrational economic agents.

Even such a simple scheme throughout the several following periods makes it possible to describe the exchange operations of the given principal on the stock market, for example, in connection with its shock destruction.

If we generalize the behavior of all participants of purchase and sale transactions on the market for a traded asset, then the consistency and inconsistency of relations between them regarding the exchange is manifested in the form of fluctuations of market prices around the base value of the traded product. It is reasonable to offer the following scheme for describing the whole price fluctuations in the market of a particular asset.

If any economic unity is considered as a system then it should have keep its stability because of fluctuation' changes of its internal structural connections. These oscillations provide system's dynamic equilibrium under the influence of the symmetry law. The simplest or monochromatic fluctuations of the economic systems' structural connections could be described with the help of trigonometric functions "sine" or "cosine" from any argument, linearly dependent on time. In particular, the harmonic oscillatory process is described by the law of "sine":

$$q(t) = Q_0 \sin(\omega_0 t + \varphi_0), \tag{6}$$

where $q(t)$ – deviation of same characteristic of interest to us q (for example, the price of the traded product) of fluctuating system (the market of the given utility as a whole) from the equilibrium position (for example, average value) at the moment of time t;

Q_0 – amplitude of oscillation or maximum deviation of the system (prices for the goods of the same utility) from the equilibrium position;

$(\omega_0 t + \varphi_0)$ – function argument "sine", representing of the development phase of the fluctuation process at the current time t;

ω_0 – the so-called cyclic or circular frequency of natural oscillations of the system, connected with the period of natural oscillations T_0, by the correlation $\omega_0 = \frac{2\pi}{T_0}$;

φ_0 – starting phase of fluctuations or phase value $(\omega_0 t + \varphi_0)$ of sinusoidal oscillation at the time $t = 0$.

Following the accepted designations in the fluctuations theory, square ω_0^2 of the circular frequency of natural system fluctuations is determined as the ratio of system's adaptive properties (structural interrelations, markets, national economic as a whole) k to its inertial properties m, i.e. $\omega_0^2 = \frac{k}{m}$. Based on these representations, the authors propose to consider value k as the conditional internal static rigidity of the economic system in terms of its oscillatory properties as the quasi-elastic medium.

If the natural fluctuations take place in the system without losses, then the linear oscillator equation is ordinary differential equation of the second order and it can be presented in the form

$$\frac{d^2 q}{dt^2} + \omega_0^2 q = 0. \qquad (7)$$

Such an oscillator is accepted to call harmonic, because the function (6) becomes the solution of the given differential equation. The equations of the type (6) and (7), as well as (8) and (9) (see below) are usually called equations of dynamics or dynamic models of the investigated reality. However, this does not mean at all that this reality, in the case of the economic system, is a dynamic system. Fig. 7 offers the graphical interpretation of the system' natural harmonic oscillations for the case: amplitude of oscillation $Q_0 = 3$, starting phase $\varphi_0 = \pi/12$.

Figure 7. The schedule of the stable economic system with the model harmonic oscillations according to the low $q(\omega_0 t) = 3\sin\left(\omega_0 t + \pi/12\right)$, *where the axis of abscissa is graduated with dimensionless units* $\omega_0 t$.
Source: the authors' development

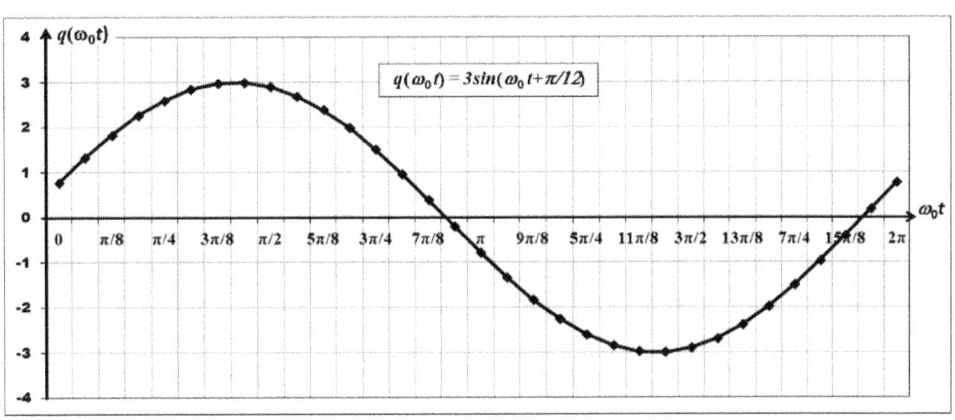

In fact the authors have got the schedule of any economic integrity' functioning in the case of stable dynamic equilibrium, meaning that no shock can destroy the system's structural relations. It is possible to judge about the oscillation' stability of the system' structural relations dealing with the so-called phase portrait of the oscillatory system, which displays the dynamic properties of the model, given, for example, in the form of a linear oscillator (7).

Let the shock generate cyclical fluctuations inside the given economic system. It should be noted, that some elements (structural relations) of the system will be able "to resist" the influence of the external impulse in the sense that R. Frisch (1933) put into it (Chapter 1). As a result dynamic model will differ from the linear oscillator (7) as to the term that takes into account the damping of system natural oscillations

$$\frac{d^2q}{dt^2}+2\beta\frac{dq}{dt}+\omega_0^2 q=0. \tag{8}$$

This describes the damped (non-harmonic) oscillations, where ω_0 – circular frequency at which oscillations would occur in the absence of damping (cyclic frequency of natural oscillations); β – damping coefficient of oscillations, which determines the rate of their damping

The solution of the equation (8) could be presented in the following form

$$q(t)=Q_0 e^{-\beta t}\cos\left(\sqrt{\omega_0^2-\beta^2}\,t+\varphi_0\right), \tag{9}$$

or in the form

$$q(\omega t)=Q_0\exp\left(-\frac{\beta}{\omega}\omega t\right)\cos\left(\omega t+\varphi_0\right), \tag{9'}$$

where $\omega\equiv\sqrt{\omega_0^2-\beta^2}$ – circular frequency of the damped oscillations with the period $T=\frac{2\pi}{\omega}$; quantity $Q_0 e^{-\beta t}$ – "amplitude" of the damped oscillations, rapidly diminishing by exponential law.

Fig. 8 offers the graphical interpretation of the system's damped (non-harmonic) oscillations in the form (9) for the case: amplitude of oscillation – Q_0 = 3.0, starting phase – φ_0 = 0, natural harmonic frequency of the system fluctuations – ω_0 = 2.094395; shock's characteristics of the permanent non-periodic impact to the economic system – β = 0.375 (or β = 0.750); frequency of damped oscillations – ω = 2.060 (or ω = 1.956). Note that when β = 0.750 then significant attenuation of the amplitude of oscillation takes place in the period of fluctuations – T.

So Fig. 8 is the graphic interpretation of the economic system's structural connections break down, when they become marginal under the influence of the shock.

Obviously, ordinary differential equation (8) could be applied to any part of the economic system of any level, starting from the national economy and finishing with the global one. Only meaning of parameters of appropriate differential equations can change. In a broad sense, these equations are usually called linear oscillators. This term is implied to the systems, which realize small fluctuations round the equilibrium point.

Figure 8. The schedule of the attenuation of the system' own fluctuations for the model situations ***q(t)****=3exp(-0.375****t****)cos(2.060****t****) and* ***q(t)****=3exp(-0.375****t****)cos(1.956****t****)*
Source: the authors' development

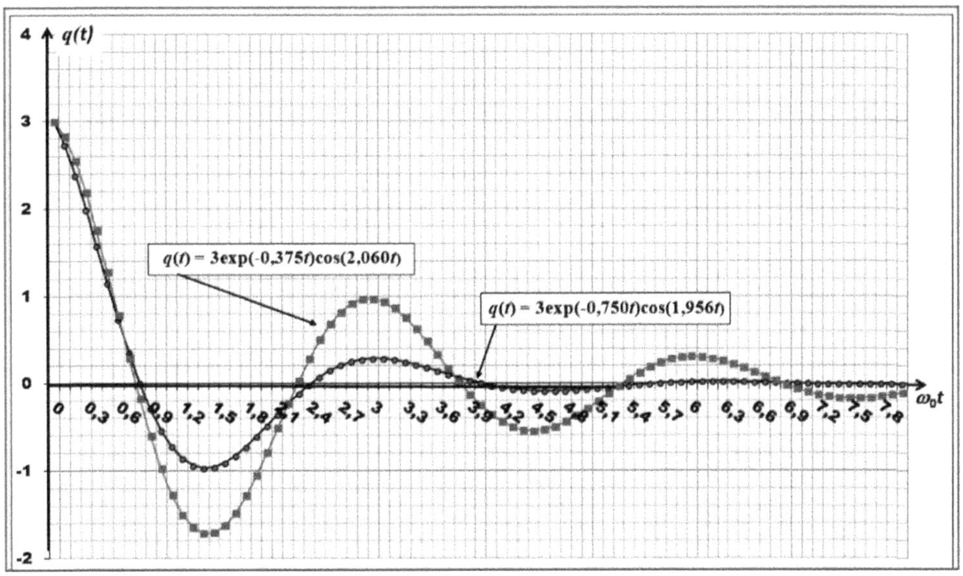

Nevertheless, it is necessary to take into account that under the shock influence there could be several different scenarios of the economic system development. If the structural connections' fluctuations (or the elements changes) of the system are coherent (in the case of the same frequency of their oscillations or constant phase difference), then system' structural connections (or elements) could change (1) in anti-phase; (2) fall behind or be in advance of one another regarding their wave fluctuations; (3) coincide or differ in amplitude of their fluctuations.

The formulated remarks require the development of wave ideas about the propagation of oscillations in the economic system. As far as authors know the mechanism of the wave form of propagation of oscillations within the economic system has not yet been presented in economic studies. It is advisable to single out in the economic system some economic units (subsystems) that maintain stability (their own and of the system as a whole) due to oscillatory changes in their internal structural relationships. The authors propose to consider the totality of such economic units with the presence of internal structural links as a quasi-elastic medium. In this case (and only in this case) it can be the propagation of oscillations with a certain finite speed in the form of a wave. The point is that the structural links of the economic system correspond to each other, and therefore quasi-elastic oscillations are sequentially excited in them near the equilibrium state. In other words, the self-movement of the system is realized in the wave form. Of course, these waves propagate at a finite speed.

The easiest way would be to consider this problem very briefly, but succinctly on the basis of theoretical concepts developed in the methods of mathematical physics [Jeffreys, et al., 1966; Stone, et al., 2009; Landa, 1997; Bagrov, et al., 2012]. For clarity of the developed concepts, it is advisable to proceed from a mechanical model of oscillations in a system of coupled oscillators. A system of coupled oscillators, in which they are ordered so that each of the oscillators is connected only with two neighboring ones (maybe, with the exception of two extreme ones), is called a chain of oscillators. As an example, consider a linear chain of homogeneous or identical mechanical pendulums connected by springs (Fig. 9).

Figure 9. The chain of N + 2 connected identical oscillators
Source: the authors' development

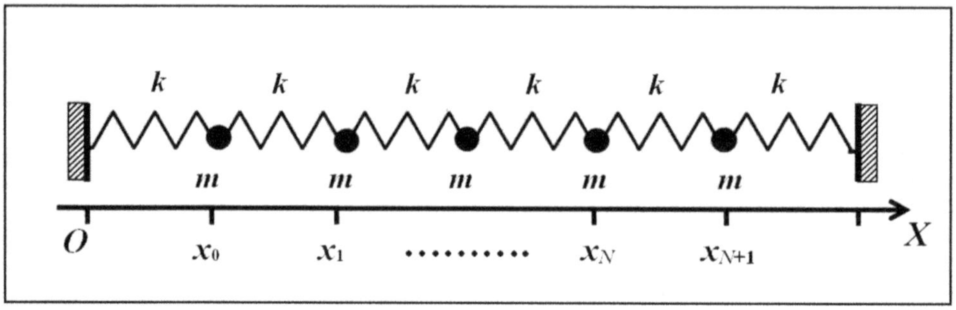

The masses of the pendulums (***m***) are the same, and the coefficients of stiffness of the springs (***k***) are the same. All pendulums are located at the same distance from each other. For simplicity, it is advisable to consider $N+2$ oscillators, the coordinates of which are given by the conditions (10)

x_i, where i – oscillator number, $i = 0, 1, \ldots, i-1, i, i+1, \ldots N, N+1$. (10)

The authors proceed from the assumption that the extreme oscillators numbered $i = 0$ and $i = N+1$ are fixed in the equilibrium position. This condition is very important, since it cuts off the widespread idea that only external influences (impulses) excite fluctuations in economic systems. The endogenous nature of the oscillations is presented in the mathematical model of reconciliation of interests in Chapter 4, in equations (1) – (13).

To construct a dynamic model of a chain of identical oscillators, the authors introduce the notation: x_i the deviation of the oscillator with number i from the equilibrium state. As a result the following equations of motion can be written.

$$\begin{cases} x_0 = 0 \\ \dfrac{d^2 x_i}{dt^2} + \omega_0^2 x_i = \dfrac{k}{m}\left(x_{i-1} - 2x_i + x_{i+1}\right), i = 1, 2, \ldots, N. \\ x_{N+1} = 0 \end{cases} \quad (11)$$

where ***k*** – is the coefficient of quasi-elasticity of the medium of coupled economic oscillators; ***m*** – measure of inertness of the environment.

Since the authors are interested only in the fundamental aspect of the issue of the formation and propagation of waves in economic, technological and social systems, the search for a solution to the dynamic model (11) is not yet included in the task. The development of ideas about the formation and propagation of the wave form of motion presupposes the transition from model (11) to a one-dimensional continuous isotropic medium (an integral economic system as a quasi-elastic medium) in a chain of oscillators (economic units with internal connections). If oscillations are excited in such a medium in any oscillator, then, due to the interaction between the oscillators of the chain, the propagation of oscillations from the oscillator to the oscillator with a certain finite velocity v will arise. The process of propagation of disturbances in such an elastic (quasi-elastic) medium is called ***a wave*** or ***an elastic (quasi-elastic) wave.*** In this case, the propagation of perturbations of the states of the oscillators occurs, but the oscillators themselves perform small oscillations near their equilibrium positions. There is a huge variety of physical, chemical, economic and other processes that cause waves. However, their formation is based on a general principle. So, if at some point $M(x_1)$ on the coordinate axis OX at the time point t_1 the oscillator has come to an excited state, then the propagating disturbance after a certain time interval, Δt will reach the point $M(x_2)$, and

$$\Delta t = \frac{x_2 - x_1}{v} \text{ or else } x_2 = x_1 + v\Delta t.$$

In other words, the oscillations of the oscillator at the point x_2 will begin with a time delay by the value Δt. Since in the considered model, the wave disturbance propagates along the OX axis, it is customary to speak of a ***plane wave***. This means that its wave surfaces (planes) are perpendicular to this axis.

In the general case, the equation of a harmonic plane wave propagating in a conservative medium along the positive direction of the OX axis has the form

$$\xi(x,t) = A\cos\left[\omega\left(t - \frac{x}{v}\right)\right], \tag{12}$$

while moving in the negative direction

$$\xi(x,t) = A\cos\left[\omega\left(t + \frac{x}{v}\right)\right]. \tag{13}$$

From equations (12) - (13) it follows that $\xi(x, t)$ is not only a periodic function of the time t, but also a periodic function of the x coordinate.

Based on the model concepts of a harmonic plane wave (12) - (13), it is easy to obtain a generalized expression for the waves. It is about differential equations in partial derivatives, which relate in time and space changes in the functions that characterize the wave.

First, the authors obtained ***the simplest wave equation***. To do this, they introduced the designation of the plane wave phase in the equation (12)

$$\varphi = \omega t - \omega \frac{x}{v} \tag{14}$$

Taking into account the dependence $\xi = \xi\,[\varphi\,(x, t)]$ this equality has been differentiated (***a***) in time t and (***b***) in the coordinate x:

$$(\boldsymbol{a})\quad \frac{\partial \xi}{\partial t} = \frac{\partial \xi}{\partial \varphi}\frac{\partial \varphi}{\partial t} = \frac{\partial \xi}{\partial \varphi}\cdot \omega \tag{15}$$

$$(\boldsymbol{b})\quad \frac{\partial \xi}{\partial x} = \frac{\partial \xi}{\partial \varphi}\frac{\partial \varphi}{\partial x} = \frac{\partial \xi}{\partial \varphi}\cdot\left(-\frac{\omega}{v}\right). \tag{16}$$

Comparison of expressions (15) and (16) makes it possible to obtain the equation

$$\frac{\partial \xi}{\partial x} = -\frac{1}{v}\frac{\partial \xi}{\partial t} \tag{17}$$

If we introduce the phase φ for equation (13) in a similar way, and then execute items (*a*) and (*b*), then it becomes possible to get an equation similar to (17) only with the «+» sign on the right side. As a result, it becomes possible to write down the simplest first-order wave equation in partial derivatives (18)

$$\frac{\partial \xi}{\partial x} = \mp\frac{1}{v}\frac{\partial \xi}{\partial t}, \tag{18}$$

in which, depending on the positive or negative motion of the wave along the ***OX*** axis, the sign is chosen as «–» or «+» respectively.

It is easy to obtain an equation that will be valid not only for a wave of any direction, but also for a superposition of these waves. To do this, it should be necessary to differentiate expressions (15) and (16) again in time t (19) and in coordinate x (20) respectively:

$$\frac{\partial^2 \xi}{\partial t^2} = \frac{\partial^2 \xi}{\partial \varphi^2}\frac{\partial \varphi}{\partial t}\cdot \omega = \frac{\partial^2 \xi}{\partial \varphi^2}\cdot \omega^2, \tag{19}$$

$$\frac{\partial^2 \xi}{\partial x^2} = \frac{\partial^2 \xi}{\partial \varphi^2}\frac{\partial \varphi}{\partial x}\cdot\left(-\frac{\omega}{v}\right) = \frac{\partial^2 \xi}{\partial \varphi^2}\cdot\frac{\omega^2}{v^2}. \tag{20}$$

Comparing expressions (19) and (20), we arrive at a one-dimensional wave equation of the second order in partial derivatives (21)

$$\frac{\partial^2 \xi}{\partial x^2} = \frac{1}{v^2}\frac{\partial^2 \xi}{\partial t^2}. \tag{21}$$

Thus, relying on a mechanical model of a chain of oscillators, the authors showed that in an integral economic system as a quasi-elastic medium in a chain of economic oscillators (economic units with internal connections) a wave form of disturbance transmission along the chain of economic oscillators. The authors extended the wave equations (18) and (21) to this process.

In fact, the above models give an idea of the self-movement of systemic integrity in the economy, the complication mechanism of which is endogenously inherent in it, due to structural links that are organized as a result of positive and negative selection of multiple types of economic activity. In other words, examining shocks in the context of the self-movement of systemic integrities and expressing a hypothesis about the embeddedness of shocks into the mechanism of self-movement of economic systems, the authors supplement it with a statement about its endogeneity. And shocks, in order to break the structural ties of the systemic integrity and implement the operation of the dialectical laws of its self-movement, must be embedded into this endogeneis mechanism internally inherent in the structure of the system. Otherwise, the economic system would be deprived of the ability for self-movement and for changes without shocks' adjustments of structural ties and subsequent crises needed for their restoration. But all these phenomena are present…

CONCLUSION

A series of famous crises in the last century (Kindleberger, et al., 2005), including the Great Depression (Galbraith, 1997), global financial crisis of 2007-2009, as well as the crisis caused by the COVID-19 pandemic in 2020 have certain commonality. The authors were able to establish that all the above crises described in numerous books (Reinhart, et al., 2009; Kindleberger, et al., 2011; Bitros, 2015; Burenin, 2017], were preceded by shocks. Moreover, the economic losses that they caused at different times were significant. But as for the shock associated with the COVID-19 pandemic, human and material losses have reached unprecedented levels in 2020. And the beginning of 2021 does not allow making optimistic forecasts.

A huge number of publications devoted to all kinds of crises and shocks have shown that there are no theoretical developments among them that make it possible to understand the essence and forms of manifestation of shocks. All the above predetermined the scientific interest of the authors to form the foundations of the theory of shocks. Dialectical logic made it possible to determine the sequence of tasks to be solved aimed at theoretical understanding of the phenomenon of shocks. The authors managed to identify the very segment of the economic system that predetermines its stability, the fundamental quality of integrity, the violation of which turns into shocks and crises. It is about structure of the economic system represented by the market exchange. Exchange mediating the structural relationships between sellers and buyers as dialectical pair of economic agents, itself contains contradictions. They are resolved through shock breaks in the structural ties of the economic system.

However, it is very difficult to destroy the structure of the system, since structural connections mediate the interaction of dialectical pairs under the influence of dialectical laws of the unity and struggle of opposites, of the transition of quantitative changes into qualitative ones, and of the denial of negation. Hence it follows that any shock destruction of structural ties is the implementation of the above-mentioned laws of system's self-movement. In Chapters 3 and 4, the authors will prove that shocks can destroy structural bonds, since they are embedded into the mechanisms of self-organization and self-development of the economic system. This is precisely the essence of the shock mechanism of destruction of the structural links of the system.

As for the forms of manifestation of shocks, they are associated with the transaction of buying and selling goods, services, as well as any other assets. Therefore any shock as for its form is a price one connected with the gap between the market price and the basic value of the tradable product. Marginal jump or drop of the market price is accompanied by the speculative behavior of the participants of the market transactions. But a simple violation of market supply and demand is quickly corrected by the mechanism of structural self-organization, until prices go beyond their margin. And the main actors in these prices' manifestation of shocks are participants of market transactions (Chapter 5).

So examining shocks in the context of the self-movement of systemic integrities and expressing a hypothesis about the embeddedness of shocks into the mechanism of self-movement of economic systems, the authors supplement it with a statement about its endogeneity. And shocks, in order to break the structural ties of the systemic integrity and implement the operation of the dialectical laws of its self-movement, must be embedded into this endogeneis mechanism internally inherent in the structure of the system.

REFERENCES

Acharya, V. V., Adler, B., & Richardson, M. (2011). *A proposal to resolve the distress of large and complex financial institutions.* New York University Stern School of Business Working Paper.

Adelman & Adelman. (1959, Oct.). The dynamic properties of the Klein-Goldberger model. *Econometrica.*

Alom, M. F. (2012). *Volatility and Spillover Effects of Oil and Food Price Shocks.* Lambert Academic Publishing.

Anderson, K., Arrow, J., & Pines, D. (Eds.). (1988). *The Economy as an Evolving Complex System.* Addison-Wesley.

Arnold, V. I. (1975). Critical points of smooth functions. *Proc. of International Congress of Mathematicians, 1*, 19-40.

Arnold, V. I. (1979). Catastrophe theory. *Nature*, (10), 54–63.

Arthur, W. B. (1999). Complexity and the economy. *Science, 284*, 107-109.

Arthur, W. B., Durlauf, S. N., & Lane, D. A. (Eds.). (1997). *The Economy as an Evolving Complex System II.* Addison-Wesley.

Bagrov, V. G., Belov, V. V., Zadorozhnyi, V. N., & Trifonov, A. Y. (2012). Methods of Mathematical Physics. Tomsk: TPU Publishing House.

Bahi, D. R. (2015). *Energy Price Shocks and Macroeconomics Performance.* RFF Press.

Bak, P. (1996). *How Nature Works: the Science of Self-Organized Criticality.* Copernicus Books. doi:10.1007/978-1-4757-5426-1

Bems, R., Caselli, F., Grigoli, F., & Gruss, B. (2019). *Gains from anchoring inflation expectations: evidence from the taper tantrum shock.* IMF Working Paper, WP/19/75.

Bitros, G. C. (2015). Thinking ahead of the next big crash. Cato Journal, 35(1), 67-93.

Blanchard, O. (2003). Macroeconomics (3rd ed.). Pearson Education Inc.

Blanchard, O. (2009). *Macroeconomics* (5th ed.). MIT.

Bogdanov, A. A. (1934). Tectology or General Organizational Science. Academic Press.

Boyd, J. H., De Nicoló, G., & Smith, B. (2004). Crises in competitive versus monopolistic banking systems. *Journal of Money, Credit and Banking*, *36*(3b), 487–506. doi:10.1353/mcb.2004.0041

Braudel, F. (1981). *Civilization & Capitalism: 15th–18th Century. The Structure of Everyday Life: The Limits of the Possible*. William Collins Sons & Co Ltd.

Brue, S. L., McConnell, C. R., & Flynn, S. M. (2013). Essentials of Economics (3rd ed.). McGraw-Hill.

Burenin, A. N. (2017). On the inevitability of economic crises in the modern market economy. Ekonomicheskaya Politika, 12(5), 8-21.

Calomiris, C. W. (2009). The subprime turmoil: What's old, what's new, and what's next. *Journal of Structured Finance, 15,* 6-52.

Calomiris, Ch. W. (2011). Banking crises and the rules of the game. In G. Wood, T. Mills, & N. Crafts (Eds.), *Monetary and Banking History: Essays in Honour of Forrest Capie* (pp. 88–132). Routledge. PP.

Calomiris, C. W., & Stephen, H. H. (2016). Fragile by design: the political origins of banking crises and scarce credit. Ekonomicheskaya Politika, 11(4), 7-34.

Christiano, L. J., Eichenbaum, M., & Evans, C. L. (1999). Monetary policy shocks: what have we learned and to what end? In J. B. Taylor & M. Woodford (Eds.), Handbook of Macroeconomics. Elsevier. doi:10.1016/S1574-0048(99)01005-8

Clark, J. B. (2007). *Essentials of Economic Theory: As Applied to Modern Problems of Industry and Public Policy*. Ludwig von Mises Institute.

Easterly, W., Islam, R., & Stiglitz, J. E. (2000). *Shaken and Stirred: Explaining Growth Volatility. Macroeconomic Paradigms for Less Developed Countries*. World Bank. Retrieved from: http://www.worldbank.org/research/growth/ growth%20volatility%20jan%202000.html

Evans, C. L. (2009a). *The international financial crisis: asset price exuberance and macroprudential regulation.* Remarks given at the 2009 International Banking Conference on September 24, 2009, Chicago, IL. Available at: http://www.chicagofed.org/webpages/ publications/speeches/2009/09.24_IBC_speech.cfm

Evans, C. L. (2009b). *Should monetary policy prevent bubbles?* Remarks given at the Asset Price Bubbles and Monetary Policy Conference on November 13, 2009, Paris, France. Available at: http://www.chicagofed.org/webpages/publications/speeches/2009/11.13_BoF_ speech. cfm

Evans, C. L. (2009c). *Too-big-to-fail: a problem too big to ignore.* Remarks given at the European Economics and Financial Center on July 1, 2009, London, UK. Available at: https://www.chicagofed.org/webpages/publications/speeches/2009/07.01_EEFC_Speech.cfm

Frisch, R. (1933). Propagation problems and impulse problems in dynamic economics. In *Economic Essays in Honour of Gustav Cassel*. Allen and Unwin.

Galbraith, J. K. (1997). The Great Crash, 1929. New York: Houghton Mifflin Company.

Gilchrist, Yankov, & Zakrajsek. (2009, May). Credit market shocks and economic fluctuations: evidence from corporate bond and stock markets. *Journal of Monetary Economics*.

Guckenheimer, J. (1973). Bifurcation and catastrophe. Proc. International Sympos. In M. Peixoto (Ed.), *Dynamical Systems*. Academic Press.

Haken, H. (1977). *Synergetics. An Introduction*. Springer-Verlag.

Hakro, A. N., & Omezine, A. M. (2014). *Oil Price Shocks and Macroeconomic Fundamentals of Oman Economy*. Lambert Academic Publishing.

HatziusJ.HooperP.MishkinF.SchoenholtzK. L.WatsonM. W. (2010). *Financial conditions indexes: a fresh look after the financial crisis.* NBER Working Paper Series, 16150. Retrieved from: https://www.nber.org/papers/w16150

Hausmann, R., & Gavin, M. (1996). *Securing stability and growth in a shock prone region: the policy challenge for Latin America.* Inter-American Development Bank. Working Paper. No. 315. Office of the Chief Economist.

Hayek, F. A. v. (1991). *The Trend of Economic Thinking: Essays on Political Economists and Economic History.* Chicago: University of Chicago Press.

Hegel, G. W. F. (1892). The science of logics. In The Logic of Hegel (2nd ed.). Oxford University Press.

Hegel, G. W. F. (1967). *Hegel's Philosophy of Rights* (T. M. Knox, Trans.). Oxford University Press.

IMF. (2019). *World Economic Outlook. Growth Slowdown, Precarious Recovery.* Washington, DC: IMF.

IMF. (2020). External stress and the international investment position. In External Sector Report: Global Imbalances and the COVID-19 Crisis. Washington, DC: IMF.

Jeffreys, H., & Jeffreys, B. S. (1966). *Methods of Mathematical Physics*. Cambridge University Press.

Kant, I. (1781). *Critic der Reinen Vernunft*. Verlegts Johann Friedrich Hartknoch.

Kedrov, B. M. (1963). *The Unity of Dialectics*. Logics and Theory of Cognition.

Kindleberger, C. P. (1996). *Manias, Panics and Crashes. A History of Financial Crises*. John Willey&Sons, Inc.

Kindleberger, C. P., & Aliber, R. Z. (2005). *Manias, Panics, and Crashes: A History of Financial Crises* (5th ed.). John Wiley & Sons, Inc., Hoboken. doi:10.1057/9780230628045

Kindleberger, Ch. P., & Aliber, R. Z. (2011). *Manias, Panics, and Crashes: A History of Financial Crises*. Palgrave Macmillan.

Kondratiev, N. D. (1984). The Long Wave Cycle (G. Daniels, Tran.). New York: Richardson and Snyder.

Kovacevich, R. (2014). The financial crisis: why the conventional wisdom has it all wrong. Cato Journal, 34(3), 541-556.

Lalanne, C. (2014). Mechanical Vibration and Shock Analysis (3rd ed.). Wiley.

Landa, P. S. (1997). 'Universality of oscillation theory laws. types and role of mathematical models'. *Journal of Discrete Dynamics in Nature and Society*, *1*(2), 99–110. doi:10.1155/S1026022697000113

Leonard, T. C. (2003). A certain rude honesty: John Bates Clark as a pioneering neoclassical economist. *History of Political Economy*, *35*(3), 3. doi:10.1215/00182702-35-3-521

Mankiw, G. (2006). *The macroeconomist as scientist and engineer.* NBER Working Paper No. 12349.

Marx, K. (1995). *Capital: A New Abridgement.* Oxford University Press.

Marx, K., & Engels, F. (1955-1974). *Coll. Cit.* (2nd ed.). Moscow: Political Literature Publishing House.

McConnell, C., & Brue, S. (2008). *Economics* (17th ed.). McGraw-Hill.

Mises, L. H. E. v. (1998). *Human Action: A Treatise on Economics.* Yale University Press.

Mutuku, C. (2012). *Monetary and Fiscal Policy Shocks: VAR Econometrics.* Lambert Academic Publishing.

Pilipenko, Z. (2016). Impulse transmission model of macroeconomic cycle within the framework of the theory of shocks: aspect of economic security. In *Dependability Engineering and Complex Systems: Advances in Intelligent Systems and Computing* (Vol. 470). Springer International Publishing. doi:10.1007/978-3-319-39639-2_32

Pilipenko, Z. (2020). Shocks' theory: financial mechanism of economic systems'destabilization. In Social, Economic, and Environmental Impacts Between Sustainable Financial Systems and Financial Markets. IGI Global.

Pilipenko, Z. (2021). COVID-19 pandemic shock: success of business in human-centric socio-economic system. In M. Ziolo (Ed.), *Adapting and Mitigating Environmental, Social, and Governance Risk in Business.* IGI Global. doi:10.4018/978-1-7998-6788-3.ch008

Pilipenko, Z. A., & Pilipenko, A. I. (2018). Shocks in global economy: impulse model of macroeconomic cycle. In B. S. Sergi, F. Fidanoski, M. Ziolo, & V. Naumovski (Eds.), *Regaining Global Stability After the Financial Crisis.* IGI Global. doi:10.4018/978-1-5225-4026-7.ch012

Reinhart, C. M., & Rogoff, K. S. (2009). *This Time Is Different. Eight Centuries of Financial Folly.* Princeton University Press.

Rostam, B. (2017). *Stock Markets and Oil Price Shocks.* Lambert Academic Publishing.

Sachs, J. D., & Larrain, F. B. (1993). *Macroeconomics in the Global Economy.* Prentice Hall.

Schelling, F. W. J. v. (1993). *System of Transcendental Idealism.* University of Virginia Press.

Schumpeter, J. A. (1949). *The Theory of Economic Development: An Inquiry into Profits, Capital, Credit, Interest, and the Business Cycle.* Harvard University Press.

Sheptulin, A. P. (1975). Dialectics of the Special and of the General. Krasnoyarsk.

Sheptulin, A. P. (1978). *Marxist-Leninist Philosophy*. Progress Publishers.

Shiller, R. (2004). *Irrational Exuberance* (2nd ed.). Princeton University Press.

Slutsky, E. (1937). The summation of random causes as the source of cyclic processes. Econometrica, 5(2), 105–146.

Slutsky, E. E. (1927). The summation of random causes as the source of cyclic processes. In Questions of Conjuncture. Conjuncture Institute of Moscow.

Stone, M., & Goldbart, P. M. (2009). *Mathematics for Physics*. Cambridge University Press. doi:10.1017/CBO9780511627040

Summers, L. H. (2014a). Reflections on the new secular stagnation hypothesis. In T. Coen & R. Baldwin (Eds.), *Secular Stagnation: Facts, Causes, and Cures*. Centre for Economic Policy Research.

Summers, L. H. (2014b). U.S. economic prospects: secular stagnation, hysteresis, and the zero lower bound. Business Economics, 49(2), 65–73.

Suter, C. (1992). *Debt Cycles in the World-Economy. Foreign Loans, Financial Crises, and Debt Settlements, 1820-1990*. Westview Press, Inc.

Taleb, N. N. (2007). The Black Swan: The Impact of the Highly Improbable. New York: The Random House Publishing Group.

Taleb, N. N. (2012). *Antifragile: Things That Gain from Disorder (Incerto)*. The Random House Publishing Group.

Thom, R. (1969). Topological models in biology. *Topology, 8,* 313-36.

Thom, R. (1974). Catastrophe theory: its present state and future perspectives. Dynamical Systems-Warwick, 468, 366–372.

Vernadsky, W. (1998). *The Biosphere*. Springer-Verlag.

von Bertalanffy, L. (1968). General System Theory: Foundations, Development, Applications. University of Alberta.

White, W. (2009). Modern macroeconomics is on the wrong track. Finance & Development, 46(4), 15-18.

Wolf, M. (2019). Today and tomorrow: to meet future challenges, the IMF must have strong backing from its members. *A Quarterly Publication of the International Monetary Fund, 56*(2).

World Bank. (2020). *The COVID-19 Pandemic: Shocks to Education and Policy Responses*. World Bank.

Yankov & Zakrajsek. (2009, May). Credit market shocks and economic fluctuations: evidence from corporate bond and stock markets. *Journal of Monetary Economics*.

Zeeman, E. C. (1977). *Catastrophe Theory: Selected Papers. 1972–1977*. Addison-Wesley.

Zinoviev, A. A. (1960). *Philosophical problems of multivalued logic*. USSR Academy of Sciences.

Chapter 3
Shocks in the Economic Systems' Self-Organization

ABSTRACT

The logic of understanding the phenomenon of shocks predetermines the need to deepen the understanding of the embeddedness into the mechanism of self-organization of the economic system under the influence of dialectical laws of unity and struggle of opposites and of the transition of quantitative changes to qualitative ones. Shocks are called to mediate the action of the dialectical laws realizing the possibility of systems' further self-movement. If the mechanisms of positive and negative selection failed to promptly "reject" the structural links that destroy the system's integrity, shocks perform this function at the turning points of dialectical laws. All stages of crises following shocks are aimed at restoring the existing structure by destroying unemployed links, restoring the "working" structural ties, and forming new links instead of the destroyed ones. At the end of the crises, hypothetically, the system should restore its integrity.

INTRODUCTION

The formation of an economic system as integrity covers a long period of time. This process is accompanied by the complication of the two main forms of organizing economic activity – its differentiation (specialization, disintegration), and integration (cooperation, association) as well as their interaction. The fundamental significance of these phenomena is due to the fact that they generate conditions for the transformation of the economic system into integrity. This quality is predetermined by the structural interrelationships of dialectical pairs of objects, subjects, processes and phenomena. Having become dialectically connected, all of them mediate the action of the dialectical laws of economic systems' self-movement. At the stage of self-organization of systems, such laws are the unity and struggle of opposites and of the transition of quantitative changes into qualitative ones. This logic leads the authors to the conclusion that shocks can cause great damage to the economic system only if they are embedded into the structure of system integrity, which mediates the mechanism for implementing dialectical laws. In other words, shocks are capable of destroying the system structural ties only if they are embedded into

DOI: 10.4018/978-1-7998-4309-2.ch003

the mechanism for implementing the dialectical laws of unity and struggle of opposites and of the transition of quantitative changes into qualitative ones. Only in this context it becomes possible to understand such serious disruptions of the shocks' impact on the functioning of economic systems, their different duration and difficulties of eliminating the consequences of the crises generated by them.

Research has shown that the shock's mechanism within the framework of the law of unity and struggle of opposites has its own specificity in comparison with its mediation of other dialectical laws. In the case of unity and struggle of opposites, the mechanism of shocks destroys the horizontal basic structural level of systemic integrity that arises in the exchange of material goods and services, i.e. in real markets. The specificity of horizontal structural links is due to the fact that they mediate the interactions of dialectical pairs that combine themselves their causes and effects. Moreover, the authors came to the conclusion that shocks mediate a turning point in the dialectic of the law of unity and struggle of opposites, i.e. the transition of the dialectical pair from the dominance of the unity of interests to the priority of their contradictions. As a result, the shock destroys the horizontal structural ties, and the crisis that follows it restores the broken cause-and-effect relationships, destroying old or generating new structural ties based on the unity of interests of the subjects of dialectical pairs at the horizontal level. Thus, at the end of the crisis, system integrity should be restored.

However, the self-organization of the system is realized not only under the influence of the law of unity and struggle of opposites, but also under the law of the transition of quantitative changes into qualitative ones. In the latter case, the self-organization of the system realizes its ability to self-structure in the process of generating vertical structural levels in the image and likeness of the basic level. This occurs as a result of the substitution of unity in horizontally located dialectical pairs with opposites of their interests and their further quantitative growth in the direction of the vertical superstructure above the horizontal level. This means that horizontal causal relationships are broken, and structural levels-causes give rise to structural levels-consequences in the form of money markets, then derivatives markets, and then many other markets of financial products to solve the problems of downstream structures. The law of the transition of quantitative changes into qualitative ones regulates the self-organization of the structural links of the system in the process of generating and functioning of the vertical structural hierarchy, when causes and effects in the interaction of dialectical pairs are broken and placed vertically. In the same way, the shock's destruction of vertical structural dependencies mediates a turning point in the operation of the law of transition of quantitative changes into qualitative ones, when the accumulated quantity necessarily predetermines a new quality of structural links. As a result, the crisis following the shock is intended to restore the chain of vertical dialectical pairs destroyed by the shocks, the causes and consequences of which are violated vertically. Thus, the problem becomes more complicated, and crises become more protracted when shocks destroy structural links not only at the horizontal level, but also in financial markets located along the vertical structural hierarchy.

All theoretical conclusions were obtained as a result of a study of the historical features of the formation of market relations in the process of integration and differentiation of the economic activity of people in the process formation of systemic integrities in the economy. As a result it became obvious that the structural connections of an integral system not only mediate exchange, but also predetermine the mechanism of its self-organization. The self-organizing system is constantly changing, usually becoming more and more complex. But this happens up to certain limits, which are dictated by capabilities of system's structure. At the same time, the structure itself, in order to preserve the qualitative certainty and integrity of the system, is forced to self-structure.

The whole process of complicating the exchange is accompanied by the problem of mismatching interests of the subjects of transactions. It is they who define the turning point in the transition from unity to opposites in structural interactions at the horizontal structural level of the system. As for the law of the transition of quantitative changes into qualitative ones, this limit is associated with changes in structural ties in connection with the increase to a certain marginal level of transactions with deferred payment, when the acts of purchase and sale are torn apart in time and space. The specificity of this gap is due not so much to the absence of money in general as a universal equivalent in exchange, but to the absence of money in the function of a mean of payment (as one-time intermediary in the exchange) at the disposal of one of the participants in a particular market transaction. Deferred payment transactions are mediated by money as a means of payment in transactions between borrowers and creditors.

If imagining the process of complicating the exchange in the context of appearing the money as a means of exchange and a means of payment then it has a long history associated with the interaction of processes of differentiation and integration of economic activities. Such transactions mediate the process of structuring the vertical levels of the structure, which are subordinated to solving the problems of temporal and spatial discontinuities in transactions for the sale and purchase of material goods and services at the basic horizontal level of the system. The problem of the smooth implementation of transactions with deferred payment in the exchange became of a fundamental character, but could not be solved in the course of implementing the law of unity and struggle of opposites. This is due to the fact that the current situation presupposed a break in the causal relationships of dialectical pairs (represented by individual partners, or firms, segments of economic activity or regions of the national economy), which at the horizontal level were locked in themselves.

The replacement of horizontal causal relationships with vertical ones was mediated by the formation of dialectical ties between market participants, which began to mediate the self-movement not so much in the form of material goods and services (horizontally), but in the form of money in their function as a means of payment (vertically). The scale of market operations began to expand rapidly. They involved both the subjects of the real markets as well as the participants of the money market and of the market for financial derivatives. In this subordination of exchange levels, the reason for the formation of structural links connected with the exchange of money as means of payment was the real market. Naturally, the problems of the asymmetry of transactions of material goods and services were aggravated, since they began to depend on the equilibrium of the exchange of funds in the money market, which arose as a result of unresolved problems in the real market. In this case, acts of sale and purchase of material goods and services, as well as money as a means of payment, complicated the structural ties, which made their shock breaks more destructive and the crises – much longer in restoring the structural integrity of the system.

The logic of this chapter assumes first an analysis of the processes of formation of systemic integrity in the economy (Chapter 3.1), then the conditions for the formation of its ability to self-organization under the influence of the dialectical laws of unity and struggle of opposites (Chapter 3.2.) and the transition of quantitative changes into qualitative ones (Chapter 3.3). The main attention is paid to the formation of the limiting states of structural ties in economic systems in the process of their self-organization as well as to the mechanisms for the realization of breaks in the action of the dialectical laws of unity and struggle of opposites and of transition of quantitative changes to qualitative ones, mediated by shocks. The chapter ends (Chapter 3.4) with a description of the shock and the global financial crisis of 2007-2009 in terms of self-organization of systemic integrity.

3.1. Dialectics of Specialized Economic Activities' Cooperation: Market Exchange as a Sphere of Shocks' Realization

The theoretical concept of the interdependence of system's categories in the context of their objects and subjects (Chapter 2) is the fundamentals for the in-depth study of shocks phenomena in the process of systemic changes, complication and organizational transformation. This step is necessary to identify the role (functions) of shocks in the mechanism of self-movement of economic systems, taking into account their process component. In this case, it becomes possible to confirm or refute the validity of the hypothesis of the authors of this book connected with the embeddedness of shocks into the mechanism of systems' self-organization. For these purposes, the authors resorted to a philosophical interpretation of the peculiarities of interaction between the categories of specialization, integration and exchange in the process of their changes.

The specificity of the relationship between the cooperation of economic activity and its differentiation is due to the fact that they represent a dialectical pair, the change of which is regulated by the dialectics of the unity and opposition of the phenomena that form it. Indeed, neither cooperation nor differentiation can realize their potentials for the growth of economic performance without interaction with each other. And, nevertheless, from the point of view of the content of economic activity, these forms of its organization are not compatible. Following the logic of the reasoning of Karl Marx (1995), labor acts as the content of economic activity, which is differentiated depending on specific labor, specific objects and means of labor, specifics of production processes, the skills of workers, as well as the final results (specific utility). In such a concrete embodiment, it is impossible to integrate the results of specialized labor, which acts as coexisting labor. However, all the divided types of concrete labor and the utilities produced with their help are completely meaningless if they are not combined in the process of producing utility ready for consumption, and even more so if the latter are not brought to a specific consumer in the process of exchange. As a result, on the one hand, the disconnected forms of organizing economic activity cooperate to create results ready for consumption, and on the other hand, to bring specific utilities to the consumer. Thus, another dialectical pair appears which is represented by concrete labor in differentiated economic activity, and in abstract labor conditioned by its cooperation. They are as united in their opposites as differentiated and integrated economic activity. The functioning of these dialectical pairs of phenomena becomes possible only if the contradictions inherent in them are resolved through exchange. It is the market exchange that is prepared for the function of mediating the movement of the results of concrete labor, on the one hand, and abstract labor, on the other, in exchange between representatives of another dialectical pair - sellers and buyers as subjects of exchange.

Karl Marx (1995) made a fundamental contribution to the study of these dialectical phenomena and to the understanding of the conditions for the unification of "non-combinable" phenomena. It was he who considered the stability of phenomena in the economy through the prism of their content, due to the interconnections of dialectically single and opposite pairs of objects, subjects and processes. This interpretation of the above phenomena is consistent with the philosophical ideas of the great theoreticians of the past: G.W.F Hegel (1892), Immanuel Kant (1781), Friedrich Wilhelm Joseph von Schelling (1993), K. Marx, and F. Engels (1955-1974. Vol. 25. Part II). They substantiated that any form of phenomenon has its own content, and any content has a form of its manifestation. So the exchange of economic activity and of its results resolves the contradiction between integration and specialization of economic activity, between concrete and abstract labor, between its results, as the embodiment of concrete and of abstract labor simultaneously. In other words, exchange is based on the interaction of opposite phenomena, since it embodies what unites them. The criterion of the complexity of exchange also predetermines the integrity of the economic system (Arthur, 1999), as a unity in diversity (cooperation of specialized types of economic activity), which has been formed over a long time, starting from natural distribution of utilities to exchange not mediated by an equivalent, and then mediated by money, from personified exchange to modern non-personalized one. According to K. Marx (1995), exchange does not create divisions of spheres of production, but establishes a connection between spheres that are already different, and turns them into more or less dependent on each other branches of total social production.

The authors identified a number of stages in the process of formation and complication of exchange, each of which is predetermined by a special combination of differentiation and integration of labor as the basis of economic activity. The starting point in the formation of exchange as a stable phenomenon was the emergence of surplus products as the results of labor in comparison with the individual needs for them among the subjects of economic activity themselves. Using the dialectical approach of Karl Marx, it is advisable to consider potential objects of exchange from the point of view of their qualities of commensurability and incommensurability, which must be resolved between potential sellers of these surpluses and their buyers. In this case, it is advisable to present the surplus of the produced product intended for exchange in the categories of K. Marx, who called it a commodity as a result of labor intended for exchange. From his point of view, the commodity, as a product of labor for the purpose of its exchange, is a contradictory category. This logically follows from the fact that it is the result of both concrete and abstract labor. As a result, on the one hand, as the embodiment of concrete labor, the commodity must satisfy certain human needs and serve for consumption, and on the other hand, as the embodiment of abstract labor, it must be able to exchange in accordance with the abstract labor expended on it, i.e. possess value, as K. Marx defined it. In modern exchange, use value as the ability of a thing to satisfy human needs is objectively replaced by utility, as a subjective assessment by the consumer of the qualities of the acquired thing. As for the value (cost) of the goods, for the convenience of further reasoning, it will be associated with its ability to exchange.

With this interpretation, the commodity becomes the excellent example of the dialectical unity of opposites. Indeed, being the embodiment of concrete labor, all objects of exchange are qualitatively heterogeneous and quantitatively incommensurable, which makes them, in principle, incapable of exchange. But at the same time, all the results of concrete labor contain what unites them. It is about the expenditure of human energy, labor costs, which can be expressed in hours of working time or in money. And in this context, as lumps of human energy, as the costs of abstract labor, all goods are qualitatively homogeneous and quantitatively commensurate, and therefore are able to exchange. The accumulation of such fundamental changes in exchange presupposes a long path of its formation, and in parallel with it, of the system capable of self-organization. Everything explains the lack of an adequate tool for resolving the dialectical contradiction inherent in the product, which predetermined its long search.

It all started with the appearance of a surplus of labor results in comparison with what is needed for domestic consumption. Under the conditions of the emergence of human society and economic activity itself, not so much the division (specialization, differentiation) of labor, as natural conditions and differences in natural factors played a decisive role in the sporadic emergence of surplus labor results. They were the ones who mediated *simple or casual exchange* of goods. It was the first result of the positive and negative selection of economic activity, which was embodied in the organization of an unstable exchange, since the surplus of labor results has not yet become a permanent phenomenon. As a result, the random exchange did not cause difficulties, since it was forced: what surplus products of labor were offered for exchange, such were exchanged. In such a situation, the exchange could take place either regardless of the usefulness of the exchanged product, or their owners refused to exchange. In the latter case, each seller was left with his product, receiving nothing in return. This situation slowed down the formation of a stable market exchange and hindered economic progress.

With the deepening of the first and second social division of labor, the efficiency of economic activity began to be influenced not only by natural conditions, but also by the specialization of instruments of labor in the working process. According to A. Smith (1776), as soon as the division of labor is established everywhere, only a very small fraction of the needs of each person can be satisfied with the products of their own labor. He satisfies a much larger part of them by exchanging the commodity surplus of the products of his labor, which remains after satisfying his needs, for the surplus product of the labor of other people, which he needs. In other words, with an increase in the productivity of economic activity, the amount of surplus labor began to grow, their diversity increased, i.e. the need for a constant exchange of diverse surplus labor increased significantly. Moreover, the absence of constant exchange began to significantly slow down the progress (complication) of people's economic activity.

As a result, the dialectics of positive and negative selection predetermined the emergence of an *entire (full) or enlarged* form of organization of exchange (by analogy with the full or expanded form of value called by K. Marx). It was at this stage of the complication of exchange that the main problems of its organization were formed: the discrepancy between the acts of purchase and sale in time and space, as well as the absence of an equivalent commodity acceptable for all in exchange. From that moment on, all subsequent forms of organizing exchange in the process of its complication were subordinated to the solution of these problems, which are inherent in the dialectical contradiction of the product itself: between its utility and the ability to exchange, between its qualitative heterogeneity and quantitative commensurability. And taking into account the subjective component of the exchange, to this contradiction it could be added the dialectics of unity and contradictions in the relationship between sellers and buyers.

The main problem of the full or enlarged form of organization of exchange is that it is fundamentally impossible to exchange surplus products according to their usefulness, as the results of concrete labor. In this capacity, they are qualitatively heterogeneous and quantitatively incomparable. As a result, the participants of exchange, in principle, could not agree on their equivalent exchange. This also reveals the dialectics of the properties of the commodity: the seller is not interested in the utility of the commodity he sells, which serves only as a condition for him to exchange for another commodity, which is the target utility for him. But, as a buyer, he is interested in acquiring a specific utility. In other words, each participant in the exchange acts in two hypostases: as a seller of one utility (embodied in his product) and as a buyer of another utility (embodied in the purchased product). At the same time, the seller is interested in his own product as a criterion of equivalence in exchange, but when he becomes a buyer, he acquires a product that is valuable to him as a utility.

Thus, the entire or enlarged form of organization of exchange could not mediate the sale and purchase of specific products. Exchanges of products as utilities could not resolve the dialectical contradictions inherent in the commodity, as utility and as the ability to be exchanged, as well as in the participant of exchange, as a seller and as a buyer at the same time. Indeed, in order to satisfy his needs, the seller first seeks the goods he needs as utility, and then tries to exchange the product of his own labor as the mean of exchange. Due to the incompatibility and lack of an objective basis for achieving equivalence in the exchange of goods as the embodiment of concrete labor, the acts of purchase and sale ceased to coincide in time and space, and the exchange was objectively divided into two - sale and subsequent purchase. Moreover, if the seller found a buyer for his product, then the acquisition of the goods he needed as utility, as a rule, became an insoluble task. The exchange took place only if the estimates of the usefulness of the exchanged goods were confirmed by both the seller and the buyer. Otherwise the exchange did not take place. Actually, such a primitive scheme conceals a prototype of future shock breaks of structural ties in modern economic systems. So, in the conditions of the full or enlarged form of organization of exchange, the gap between acts of sale and purchase of goods as utility was predetermined by the discrepancy between the assessments of the equivalence of these transactions as perceived by sellers and buyers. The radical solution to this problem was associated with the search for an equivalent product that would mediate the acts of sale and purchase in the exchange of goods.

As a result of positive and negative selection of economic activity the third form of organization of exchange emerged. It is characterized by the appearance of a prototype of the mediating product-equivalent. To the authors' mind F. Braudel (1981. Vol. 2. P. 126) quite accurately expressed the essence of the complication of exchange, describing the movement of goods both as utilities and as equivalents in exchange: «...this reciprocity to any movement from A to B corresponded to a certain return movement from B to A, no matter how complex and tortuous it is». The authors, following Karl Marx, called the third stage of complication of the exchange of goods as the *universal (overall)* form of its organization. At the same time, it should be stipulated that K. Marx associated the new qualities of exchange with the forms of the value of a commodity, bearing in mind the cost of labor for its production. In other words, he was interested in these stages, rather, in connection with the peculiarities of the raising a certain quality of the commodity - its ability to be exchanged. The authors of this book focus on the formation of structural links in exchange, which, under certain conditions could be ruptured by the shock in future. That is why taking the definitions that K. Marx gave to the changed forms of value the authors extended them to the forms of organizing exchange as a whole.

So, within the framework of the universal (overall) form of organization of exchange, acts of purchase and sale have become stable phenomena in certain periods of time and in certain territories where markets were located. This was due to the fact that more or less stable equivalent goods appeared which suited both sellers and buyers as an intermediary in exchange. With its appearance, the contradiction of the commodity as a unity of utility and equivalence, as well as a subject acting both as a seller and a buyer, was resolved. The main problem of this stage of the organization of exchange was associated with the instability of the role of the equivalent commodity or with the lack of a universally recognized quality of the universal equivalent in any market. At this stage, a variety of goods acted in this capacity, which as a rule was in high demand due to their temporary shortage. In addition, the equivalent goods varied depending on the territorial location of a particular market. The problems of a multiplicity of equivalent goods were also associated with the inconvenience of their storage, with inadequate quantitative ratios in exchange, etc.

Below is a model of the universal form of exchange of goods in the conditions of the appearance of an equivalent product that changes depending on time and territorial location of the market (Fig. 1). In Fig. 1 the sequence of acts of exchange is shown, corresponding to the chain of preference for utilities in exchange in the coordinates of the spatial (axis $\boldsymbol{Ox}$) and temporal (axis $\boldsymbol{Ot}$) localization of the goods. Here, the chain of preference for utilities in exchange, in particular, means that it is desirable to exchange the product $\mathbf{T}_1$, spatially related to the coordinate $\boldsymbol{x} = 1$, for the product $\mathbf{T}_3$, spatially localized at the coordinate $\boldsymbol{x} = 3$. At the same time, in the exchange process, product $\mathbf{T}_4$ must take position $\boldsymbol{x} = 3$, and product $\mathbf{T}_n$ – position $\boldsymbol{x} = 4$. This entire multi-step process can be started because there is a preference for placing commodity $\mathbf{T}_1$ at position $\boldsymbol{x} = 2$ n in exchange for the $\mathbf{T}_{eq}$ commodity equivalent located there.

Figure 1. Spatial-temporal distribution of acts of goods' exchange with a universal product-equivalent in full or expanded form of exchange organization
Source: the authors' development

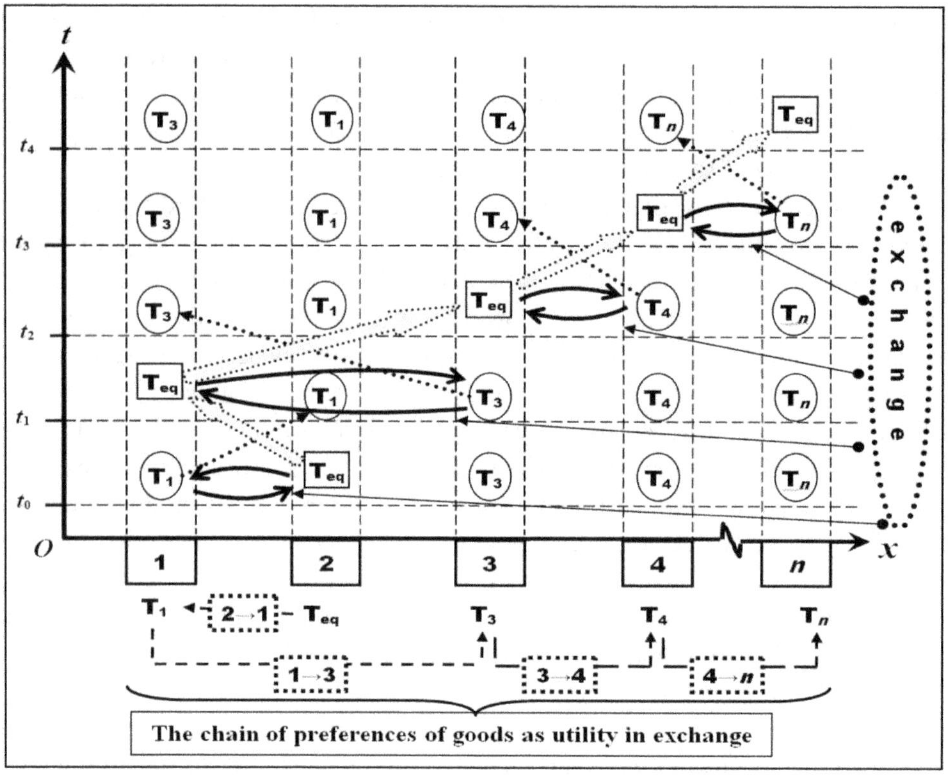

The fourth stage in the complication of exchange was the *money form* of its organization, when everywhere and regardless of the period of time, the equivalent commodity became universal. The equivalent status performed by this product suited all participants in the exchange, since it was convenient as its intermediary. It was this commodity that came to be called money. The definition of money was given by many theorists, but, unfortunately, there is still no universally accepted one. In this book, money is associated with a commodity, which, according to Karl Marx, performs the functions of a universal equivalent. Ludwig von Mises (1998) defined a medium of exchange as a commodity that people acquire not for their own consumption and use in production activities, but with the intention of exchanging it later for those goods that they wish to use for consumption or production.

The monetary form of exchange takes an important place in the generation of structural links in the economic system and in the formation of its quality of integrity. In fact, with the advent of money as a universal equivalent, the mechanisms of positive and negative selection generated dialectical pairs of subjects, objects, processes and other phenomena. It is they, in their unity of opposites that ensure equilibrium and stability of the economy as integrity. But the most important thing is that with the emergence of the monetary form of organizing exchange, the economic system acquires the ability of self-organization, thanks to the emergence of a structure and its inherent self-structuring mechanism.

3.2. The Economic System and its Ability to Self-Organization: Shocks in the Dialectical Law of Unity and Struggle of Opposites

Due to the appearance of money as a universal equivalent, the dialectical interconnections of the subjects of exchange become stable, equilibrium, constant. Such a quality of interaction of dialectical pairs generates the structure of the system, which is functionally designed to ensure its stability, qualitative definiteness and immunity to changes. At the same time, both the system and the structure change, although the latter is the least prone to variability. As a whole, the multiplication of changes is due to the interaction of causes and effects that are inherent in dialectical pairs of objects, subjects, processes and phenomena interacting within the system itself. Actually, their contradictory interaction lies at the basis of the system's inherent self-movement mechanism, which the authors identify with its self-organization. In other words, with the emergence of money as a stable equivalent in exchange, the economic system acquires an internal mechanism of self-movement generated by the interconnections of dialectical pairs as its structure.

This mechanism of self-organization of the system operates as follows. It implements the dialectics of the processes of differentiation and integration of economic activity, as well as its positive and negative selection. Endless self-movement inside the economic system is set by the multiplicity of differentiated types of activity, or rather by the growth of specialized, unrelated its elements. These processes are predetermined by a positive selection mechanism (Chapter 2, Fig. 6). The greater this diversity, the more progress economic activity can achieve. However, for objective reasons, not all specialized types of labor and elements may be in demand at any given time. In other words, not all of them can be required to generate structural links between them, which fulfill the mission of strengthening systemic integrity. It is about integration as a manifestation of self-movement of the system through a negative selection of differentiated types of economic activity (or specialized elements). And this, in fact, is the realization at any given moment of time of the potential for progressive changes in the system by means of its complication. The dependence here is direct: the more numerous the specialized elements (types of economic activity) and the more diverse the organizational forms of their integration, the greater the potential for self-movement is realized by the economic system and vice versa.

The final point necessary for understanding the mechanism of self-organization of the system is the choice of those interconnections of dialectical pairs, represented by integration and differentiation, which are most effectively able to ensure the stability of the economic system as integrity. In this case, the formation of a structure from the interaction of dialectical pairs and its stable state is provided by the exchange. Exchange mediates the structural connections of dialectical pairs by the movement of goods as utilities - the results of concrete labor that can be exchanged, since they simultaneously embody abstract labor. In addition to the object component, exchange has the subjects' component, since sellers and buyers of goods participate in it and embody the unity of opposites. All these interactions are the basis of structural connections that predetermine their changes and complication in the process of self-structuring and self-organization in connection with the tendencies to change inherent in the systemic integrity.

This provision is extremely important. It makes it possible to understand that it is very problematic to imagine the ability of shocks to destroy or negatively affect a self-organizing system, the integrity of which is predetermined by numerous structural connections. Such a possibility arises only if the shocks are integrated into the structure of the system and themselves mediate the implementation of the principles of its self-organization. Dialectical logic makes it possible to deepen the understanding of the validity of the hypothesis of the embeddedness of shocks into the mechanism of dialectical laws. The fact is that, in theory, if there is an objectively operating mechanism of self-organization in the economy, which is implemented in the process of dialectical interaction of positive and negative selection of forms of organizing economic activity aimed at strengthening systemic integrity then no other mechanisms are needed. If not for one BUT.

In all processes of self-organization of economic systems, there are subjects' and objects' components. The objects' component is adequately regulated by the mechanisms of positive and negative selection. But the subjects' component is represented by human behavior and is due to criteria that are far from economic values. Moreover, the more complex the economic system becomes, the more the behavior of the economic subject is predetermined by the value ideas generated by the society. As a result, it is the subjects' component of exchange that can hinder the optimization of organizational selection mechanisms that clearly weakens the integrity of the system. It is for these cases that the dialectical laws regulating the complication of the system at the stage of its self-organization provide for an additional (safety) mechanism of shocks, which is capable of instantly destroying structural ties that weaken the integrity of the system. It is another matter that in addition to the "non-working" connections in the system, other interconnections connected with them, quite effective, will be destroyed along the chain. But in any case, from the point of view of dialectics, this means a greater or lesser "rollback" of the system back, which depends on the importance of structural links that occupy a certain place either in the basic structure of real markets, or in the vertical structural hierarchy of money markets and financial markets. (Chapter 3.3). During a crisis (including all its stages) generated by a shock, the system "rejects" ineffective structural connections and the process of self-organization continues due to the complication of its structure.

In this context, it should be noted that one and the same system in its endless self-movement realizes its ability to self-organization, being in statics, and its ability to self-development, in its dynamics (Chapter 4). Until the potential for self-organization is exhausted, the system uses the possibilities of static complication (self-organization) under the influence of the laws of unity and struggle of opposites and of the transition from quantity to quality. If the possibilities of self-organization (self-structuring) have been exhausted, then shocks solve the problem of not repairing structural connections, but transforming a static economy into a dynamic one through the leap into a new reality. Then the restoration of the structural links of a static economy in the course of a crisis after a shock, in fact, realizes a return to "Groundhog Day" or to the period of self-organization with its constantly repeating reversible processes. And the shock that mediates the leap of the system from a static to a dynamic state generates a crisis, during which a completely different structure of the system with irreversible connections must be built, which is fundamentally different from its static past (Chapters 4, 6, 8, 11).

The formation of a static economic system was accompanied by the complication of exchange (from simple or casual to monetary one), the emergence of dialectical pairs in exchange and the strengthening of structural ties between them. As a result, the economic system acquired the ability to self-organize due to a structure that provides systemic integrity in a static state. Although the structure of the system is much more conservative than the system, it also has to change (become more complex) in order to maintain the integrity of the increasingly complex system. These objective processes are regulated by the action of the dialectical laws of unity and struggle of opposites and of the transition of quantitative changes into qualitative ones. These laws of self-organization of system integrity are mediated by stable, constantly renewable structural interactions, which create their internal order, norms, or laws of systemic changes. In other words, they can only be destroyed by an objectively embedded mechanism that, under certain circumstances, mediates the implementation of dialectical laws that prevent the destruction of the integrity of the system. The shock mechanism mediates this kind of manifestation of the dialectical laws of self-movement of the system, if the organizational mechanisms of positive and negative selection could not achieve this in time. Therefore, shocks, rejecting structural links that destroy the integrity of the system, no matter how paradoxical it may sound, are aimed at their further strengthening. Such a manifestation of shocks is possible only under conditions of maturation both the necessary and sufficient conditions for the destruction of structural ties in the economic system.

The fact is that the number of structural connections increases, they begin to intertwine both horizontally and vertically of the system, so shocks cannot point-wise "reject" the "non-working" ones. The latter, in any case, along the chain of cause-and-effect relationships, negatively affect other relationships. The dialectic of this phenomenon lies in the fact that crises following shocks are aimed at restoring structural ties (which strengthen integrity), at destroying (those of them that undermine the integrity of the system), at forming new ties (capable of replacing old, ineffective ones). It is in this context that it becomes clear why shocks, on the one hand, destroy structural ties, and on the other hand, contribute to their strengthening and the integrity of the entire system in the future.

Below is the sequence of the formation of horizontal levels of structural links in the economic system. As the complexity (Arthur, 1999, 2013) of exchange mediated by money, a basic horizontal structural level in the economic system begins to form (Fig. 2). It is this structural level that ensures the exchange of material goods and services in real markets. The peculiarity of its self-structuring lies in the fact that it is regulated by the action of the dialectical law of unity and struggle of opposites. Initially appearing in connection with the exchange of goods, horizontal structural ties mediated the relationship of dialectically related buyers and sellers, who were equivalent in their desire to acquire the desired utility. And the quality of the utility of the goods was certain: they were the results of concrete economic activity in the form of material goods and material services. It should be emphasized that these structural connections are horizontal in this construction and will be the same in any other, since the cause-and-effect relationships of the participants in dialectical pairs are concentrated inside only in their interactions. Consequently, the potentially possible shock rupture of these ties is solved either by the restoration of ties between them, or by the generation of new ties by the subjects. But in any case, cause and effect are concentrated within the framework of the dialectical pairs themselves and their participants.

The shock rupture of these ties may be due to the fact that the exchange did not resolve the contradictions between the possible set of differentiated types of economic activity ready for cooperation and the forms of their integration formations that were to arise. But for some reason, they didn't occur. It turned out that the dialectical pair disintegrated, and it not only did not recover, but no new one emerged either. Some segment of the real market "sank". And if the relationships in the exchange were not renewed, then that threatened the integrity of the system because there were unsold products and those who wanted to buy them, but the exchange did not occur. If the number of such unfulfilled transactions increases to a critical one, then shocks break inactive structural ties, and in the subsequent crisis period dialectical pairs are restored, in fact, as well as structural ties along the horizontal of the economic system. All this further strengthens its integrity.

The specific action of the law of unity and struggle of opposites in the course of the complication of the economic system at the stage of its self-organization is illustrated below. It should first be emphasized that all objects, subjects, processes and phenomena in the system, connected by dialectical ties, are constantly changing, as a rule, becoming more complex, and the structure of the system with all these changes is designed to ensure its stability, equivalence and integrity. This can only be achieved by strengthening (or forming) those structural bonds that are capable of this, and destroy those of them that have lost such ability. The dialectical law of unity and struggle of opposites regulates these changes along the horizontal of the systemic integrity, realizing a strict order as a sequence of ongoing changes. And in the implementation of this law, shocks and crises have a very definite place. This will be understandable by the differentiation of the operation of the law of unity and the struggle of opposites at two stages of the formation of horizontal structural ties in the economic system: in the process of the formation of dialectical unity and in the period of its violation under the influence of the struggle of opposites. At the same time, in order to understand the turning point in the operation of dialectical laws, it is necessary to distinguish between the objects' and subjects' components, which are objectively interconnected. The fact is that if the equilibrium in exchange is easy to observe by the equivalence of the demand for a product and the supply of a product in quantitative and price parameters, then the internal spring of their changes is often ignored. And, meanwhile, it is hardly possible to understand the operation of dialectical laws without taking into account the paramount importance of the subjects' component of exchange.

Figure 2. Model concept of the formation of the horizontal level of structural ties in the economic system at the stage of its self-organization under the influence of the dialectical law of unity and struggle of opposites
Source: the authors' development

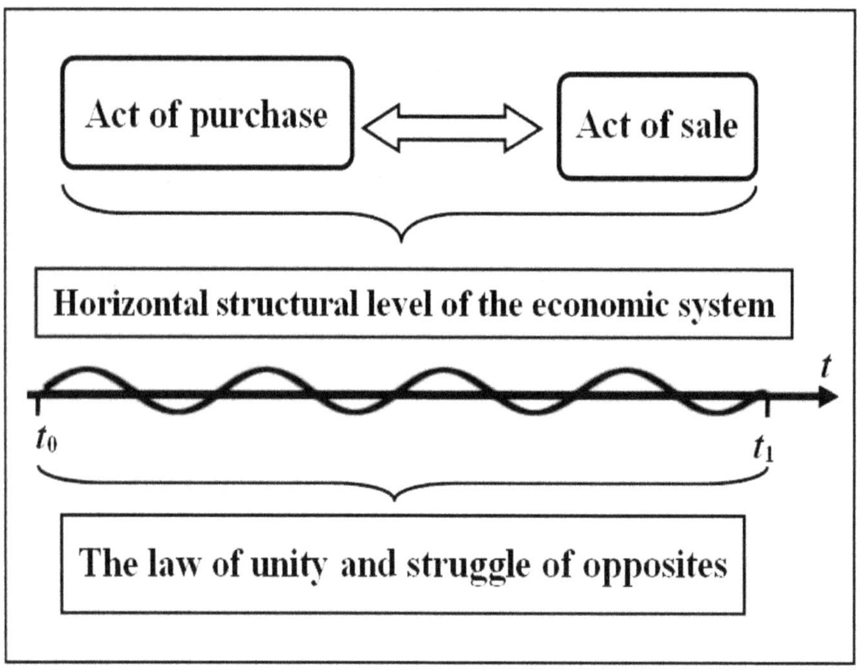

The formation of the monetary form of organizing exchange was preceded by several transitional forms of it, which changed in an effort to find a criterion for the exchange of specific goods to be equivalent only in connection with the subjects' presence of purchase and sale. It was they who were not satisfied with the subjective parameters of evaluating various goods in exchange for each other. And this was the main obstacle to the progress of all economic activity. Thus, the search for an equivalent commodity in exchange was initiated by the fact that sellers and buyers could not agree on the equivalence of the exchanged products with specific utility. And the exchange got up. The appearance of money as a universal equivalent solved that subjects' problem, since buyers and sellers agreed on equivalence in exchange in terms of the equivalence of time (or its monetary equivalent) spent on the production of different goods, taking into account the complexity of specific labor.

It seems that with the advent of the monetary form of exchange, the subjects' problem connected with the equivalence of goods in exchange has been solved. However, this is not the case, since the price of a commodity, as a monetary expression of labor costs for its production, always includes and will include a subjective aspect. Indeed, if the seller or the buyer are not satisfied with the market price of the product, then they will not exchange it. In other words, the exchange participant will buy or sell the goods only if the price suits him, or rather, if it is mutually agreed by the two sides of the dialectical pair in exchange. And this agreement is predetermined by many circumstances, which may be associated not only with economic factors. So the exchange will take place if the market price of the product suits both the seller of this product and its buyer. It is about such an equivalent exchange, equilibrium price and equilibrium in the market, which mediate the relationship of dialectical pairs and the structure of systemic integrity.

If using the model of dynamical sets that are self-affiliated within the framework of the theory of sets with self-affiliation (Mirimanoff, D., 1917; Chechulin, V.L., 2012), then a model arises that makes it possible to reflect the turning point in the operation of the law of unity and struggle of opposites, from the point of view of its subjects' component. This model representation allows interpreting the interaction of participants in dialectical pairs in the process of forming unity and struggle of opposites in their structural connections. In this example, the change in the segments of the intersection of dynamic sets illustrates how the structural connections of dialectically related exchange participants change. It should be noted that it is about the formation of horizontal structural links that mediate the exchange of material goods and services at the stage of self-organization of the system. As long as the subjects are satisfied with the parameters of the exchange of goods, their interests vary from 100% coincidence to 50% (Fig. 3). Under this condition, the stability of transactions is strengthened, and they are constantly repeated. Harmony of interests of sellers and buyers predetermines unity in comparison with opposites in the dialectic of the law of unity and struggle of opposites. And the structure unhindered ensures the integrity of the system. In the above diagram (Fig. 3) such a state is described by a white arrow with parameters 0.

However, the most volatile component of the economic system is associated with the permanent process of deepening specialization and the generation of diverse forms of organizing differentiated economic activity (positive selection). This transformation of labor should be objectively accompanied by integration through the formation of cooperation of its differentiated types (negative selection). If contradictions arise between integration and differentiation as forms of organization of economic activity, then they are removed (solved) by forming dialectical pairs and structural links between them. This process is regulated by the law of unity and struggle of opposites and is implemented in strengthening the integrity of the system if the dynamic sets representing the coordination of the interests of participants in dynamic pairs coincide within the range from 100% to 50% (Fig. 3).

However, the forms of organization of the interaction of dialectical pairs are also constantly changing, this happens in the process of self-organization of the system and of structural connections. It is no coincidence that in the operation of the law of unity and struggle of opposites, a turning point is indicated - from unity to opposites. This indicates that as the horizontally located structural connections of dialectical pairs become more complex, the opposites of the participants in the exchange replace their unity. At the same time, it is the subjects' factor that predetermines the reduction of segments of the intersection of dynamic sets from 50% coincidence of interests of participants of exchange to 0% (Fig. 4). In this case, differentiation takes over, i.e. dialectical pairs disintegrate, separate, unconnected elements are released, their number increases. This negatively affects the stability of the system as a whole, and the structure is designed to provide system integrity at all costs.

Figure 3. Dominance of the unity of interests of subjects of dialectical pairs, mediated by horizontal structural ties in the economic system under the influence of the law of unity and struggle of opposites
Source: the authors' development

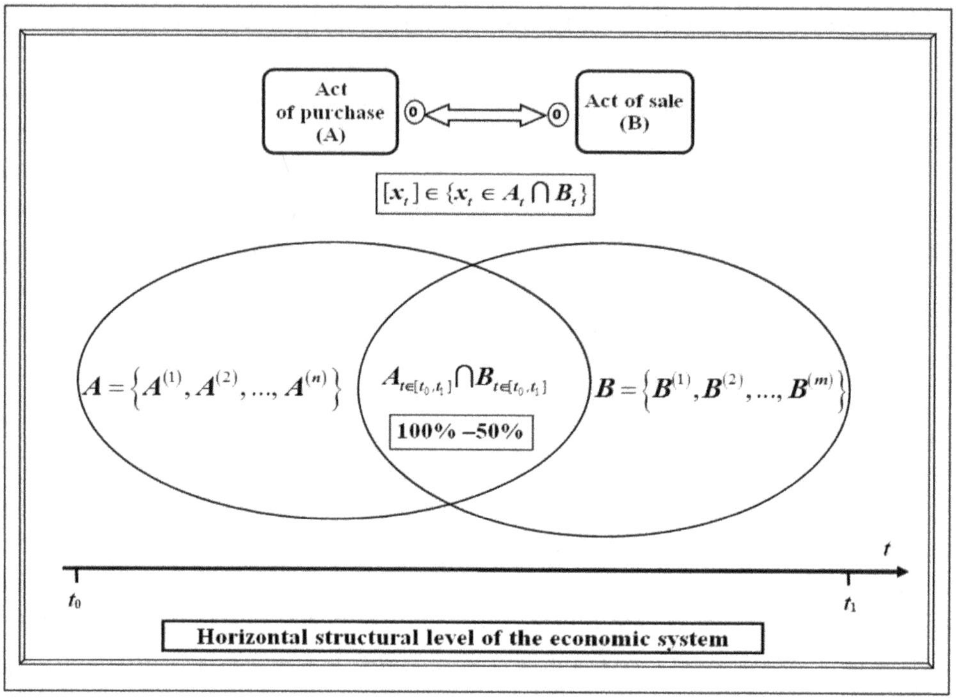

If the dialectic of positive and negative selection of new dialectical pairs does not work and does not strengthen the integrity of the system, then a shock mechanism comes into play, which is built into the action of the law of unity and struggle of opposites at the turning point (transition from the priority of unity to the dominance of opposites). In Fig. 4 the situation with a shock rupture of structural ties is represented by broken relationships between acts of purchase and sale with number 1. In the course of the crisis following the shock, horizontal structural ties are restored with greater or lesser efficiency, mediating the exchange of material goods and services. In any case, after a shock, there can be three main scenarios: restoration of old structural links, if they are able to strengthen the integrity of the system; destruction of structural links that can no longer strengthen the integrity of the system; and creating new ones that will perform the same system function. It is in this context that the authors see the objectivity of the hypothesis that shocks are embedded into the mechanism for realizing the dialectical law of unity and struggle of opposites.

If shocks were not embedded into the self-organization mechanism of the systemic integrity as well as of the dialectical laws' implementation, they could hardly have such a serious impact on the system, let alone break structural ties. In order for shocks to cause serious harm to the economic system, the necessary and sufficient conditions for breaking the structural ties, which are predetermined by the law of their self-movement, must mature. At the horizontal level of the structure of the system, it is about the dialectics of the law of unity and the struggle of opposites. And the exchange in this case is implemented in real markets, represented by the market for investment goods and for consumer goods, as well as for the labor.

Figure 4. Dominance of opposites of interests of subjects of dialectical pairs and a shock rupture of horizontal structural ties in the economic system under the influence of the law of unity and struggle of opposites
Source: the authors' development

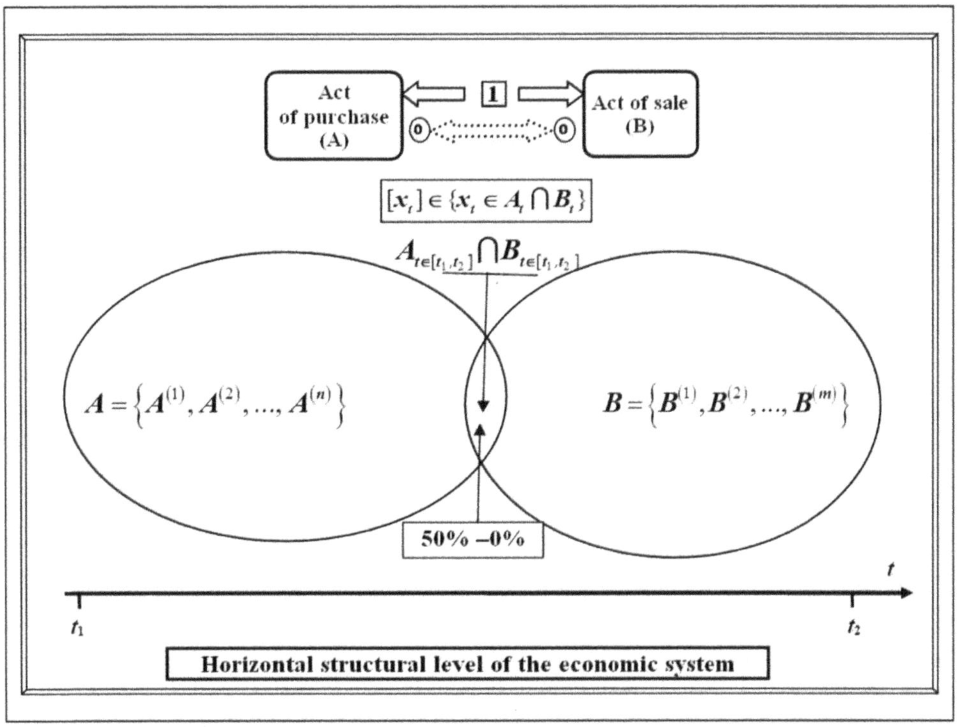

3.3. Self-Organization of Economic Systems and Dialectics of Transition of Quantitative Changes into Qualitative ones: Shock Destruction of Vertical Structural Levels

Now it is advisable to ask the question of how the actions of the dialectical laws of unity and struggle of opposites and the transition of quantitative changes into qualitative ones are combined, and how they complement each other. The authors' reasoning obeys the following logic. First, the law of the unity and struggle of opposites regulates the self-organization of the system in terms of the complication of its horizontal structural links mediating exchange in real markets; and the law of the transition of quantitative changes into qualitative ones predetermines the self-organization of the system integrity in the context of the formation of its structural connections in the form of a vertical hierarchy of structures. Second, the law of unity and struggle of opposites regulates structural connections in dialectical pairs that combine cause-and-effect relationships within their own framework; and the law of the transition from quantity to quality extends to structural connections, the dialectics of which builds causal relationships between dialectical pairs at different structural levels. The economic implications of these phenomena will be described in Chapters 4 and 5. And, third, if the basic structural level in the system dominates, represented by real markets, which are subordinate in their self-organization to the action of the law of unity and struggle of opposites, then the system has not exhausted its potential for self-organization; if a vertical hierarchy of markets is built, dialectically related to each other according to the principle of vertical division of causes and effects, then the potential for self-organization is approaching exhaustion. In essence, this means that a static economy has exhausted its possibilities of self-organization due to the complication of its horizontal and vertical structural links. It must take advantage of the possibilities of a dynamic economy, the potential of self-movement of which is associated with self-development on a new technological base, with new elements and with the forms of their organization (Chapter 4).

As for the first and second remarks, their explanation should be associated with the phenomenon of the growth of opposites in the interests of participants in dialectical pairs at the basic level of real markets under the influence of the law of unity and struggle of opposites. It is about the substitution of integration as negative selection, which manifests itself in the formation of dialectical pairs and structural connections between them, with differentiation as positive selection. The latter is manifested in an increase in the variety of unrelated types of economic activity, subjects involved in them, as well as of the results of their work. Why does their appearance not end with the formation of dialectical pairs on the same horizontal base level of real markets? Why do they cease to be the object of the influence of the law of unity and struggle of opposites and begin to be regulated by the law of the transition of quantitative changes into qualitative ones? The answers to these two questions are rooted in the specifics of those types of economic activity that increase in quantity, but have nothing to do with the exchange of material goods and services.

If all dialectical pairs disintegrated and subjects of exchange and objects of exchange would appear in their place, which are associated with material goods and services, then the number of dialectical pairs and horizontal structural connections that mediate the exchange of material goods and services would increase. In fact, the dominance of opposites in dialectical pairs at the horizontal level in connection with the exchange of material goods was largely predetermined by the emergence of a fundamental problem of the imbalance of exchange in the real market in connection with the growth of transactions with deferred payment. The search for a solution to this problem has begun to multiply the variety of types of specialized activities that have nothing to do with the exchange of material goods and services. Moreover, transactions in real markets, mediated by horizontal structural ties, began to be broken down into transactions with material goods and transactions with money under the obligation to return them after a certain period of time. Thus, cause and effect, closed within dialectical pairs participating in the exchange of real goods at the horizontal level of the system, began to be divided vertically between participants in real markets and participants in money markets. It is in this context it becomes understandable the operation of the law of the transition of quantitative changes into qualitative ones at its stage of increasing quantitative changes.

In other words, the increase in subjects, objects and specialized types of activity in a sphere not related to material goods could not fall under the influence of the law of unity and struggle of opposites and be regulated by increasing horizontal structural ties. The mechanism of positive selection strengthened the tendency of differentiation of subjects, objects and specialized types of activity in the sphere that was associated with transactions with money. And it was in this regard that there appear other terms of exchange, participation of the subjects of the transaction and the rules for supporting transactions with money and obligations under them. In other words, the mechanism of positive selection formed new participants of structural ties beyond the boundaries of real markets in order to solve problems of the real markets. Such a transitional state of dialectical pairs participating in transactions both on one structural level and another one was regulated by the law of the transition of quantitative changes into qualitative as well as by mechanisms of positive and negative selections. Quantitative changes served as a form of implementing differentiation processes in the context of the emergence of new subjects and objects of exchange, new types of specialized activities. As for qualitative changes they were associated with the emergence of structural links between them as a result of the mechanism of negative selection operating.

As a result the new structural level was generated. It was connected with the exchange of money between new dialectical pairs and was formed above the real markets. It was served the exchange of banking loans, bonds, stock and of martgage loans. In other words, the markets for money were formed under the law of transition of quantitative changes into qualitative ones. The relationships between structural levels, represented by real markets and markets for money, were built according to the subordination principle of causes and effects located vertically. Markets for money generated the first vertically located structural level of the economic system, which first solved the problem of securing transactions with deferred payment in real markets, and then turned into a self-sufficient ones represented by its own dialectical pairs. If each dialectical pair at the horizontal structural level combined cause and effect inside itself, the relationships between vertically located structural levels, represented by real markets and markets for money, were built according to the subordination principle of causes and effects located vertically.

Fig. 5 presents the basic diagram of the implementation of the process of self-organization of systemic integrity in the economy with the participation of both horizontal and vertical structural levels. Fig. 5 deepens model concepts of generating a vertical hierarchy of structural levels of an economic system in the process of its self-organization (at the stage $t_1 - t_2$ in Chapter 4, Fig. 7). The logic of the formation of a vertical hierarchy of structural levels is predetermined by the needs of their basic horizontal level. The latter mediates the functioning of real markets, represented by the market for consumer (material) goods and services, the market for investment goods, and by the market for labor. Arrows with index **0** show equilibrium in these markets, therefore, the unity of interests of the participants prevails over their opposite. However, as transactions with deferred payment increase, there is a need for intermediary transactions related to lending borrowers against their obligations to repay debt. The problem of transactions with real goods with delayed payment is depicted by a dashed arrow with index **1** (Fig. 5). The increase in this kind of transactions to a critical level is the reason for the formation of a vertical structural level represented by money markets. This dependence is depicted by dashed lines with an arrow with index **1** to square **A** - the reason for the formation of a new level - consequence, represented with square **B**. The dashed line with index **2**, which returns to the level of real markets, solves the problem of credit support for transactions with material goods and services and restores the broken equivalence in transactions with deferred payment. It is in this connection that all vertical structural levels arise, realizing the causal subordination of higher levels to the solution of problems of lower structural levels. In Fig. 5 this logic has been replicated in the interconnections between money markets and financial derivatives markets.

As the volume of exchange transactions in real markets grows, the number of transactions with deferred payment increases, which is associated with a persistent lack of money at a particular moment to close the transaction. This predetermines the demand for money as a means of exchange and the desire of people to acquire it in order to increase their cash balances. The dynamics of the demand for money and of their supply affects the exchange relations of money, on the one hand, and of goods, on the other. The increase in the number of market transactions with deferred payment predetermines structural changes in the exchange itself. Thus, first the mechanism of positive selection of the types of transactions with money comes into play, and then does the mechanism of their negative selection that are regulated by the law of transition of quantitative changes into qualitative ones. As a result, an additional level of structural ties arises vertically, serving transactions with money as a means of payment.

Figure 5. A model of the formation of vertical structural levels of the system in the process of its self-organization according to the principle of their causal relationship
Source: the author's development

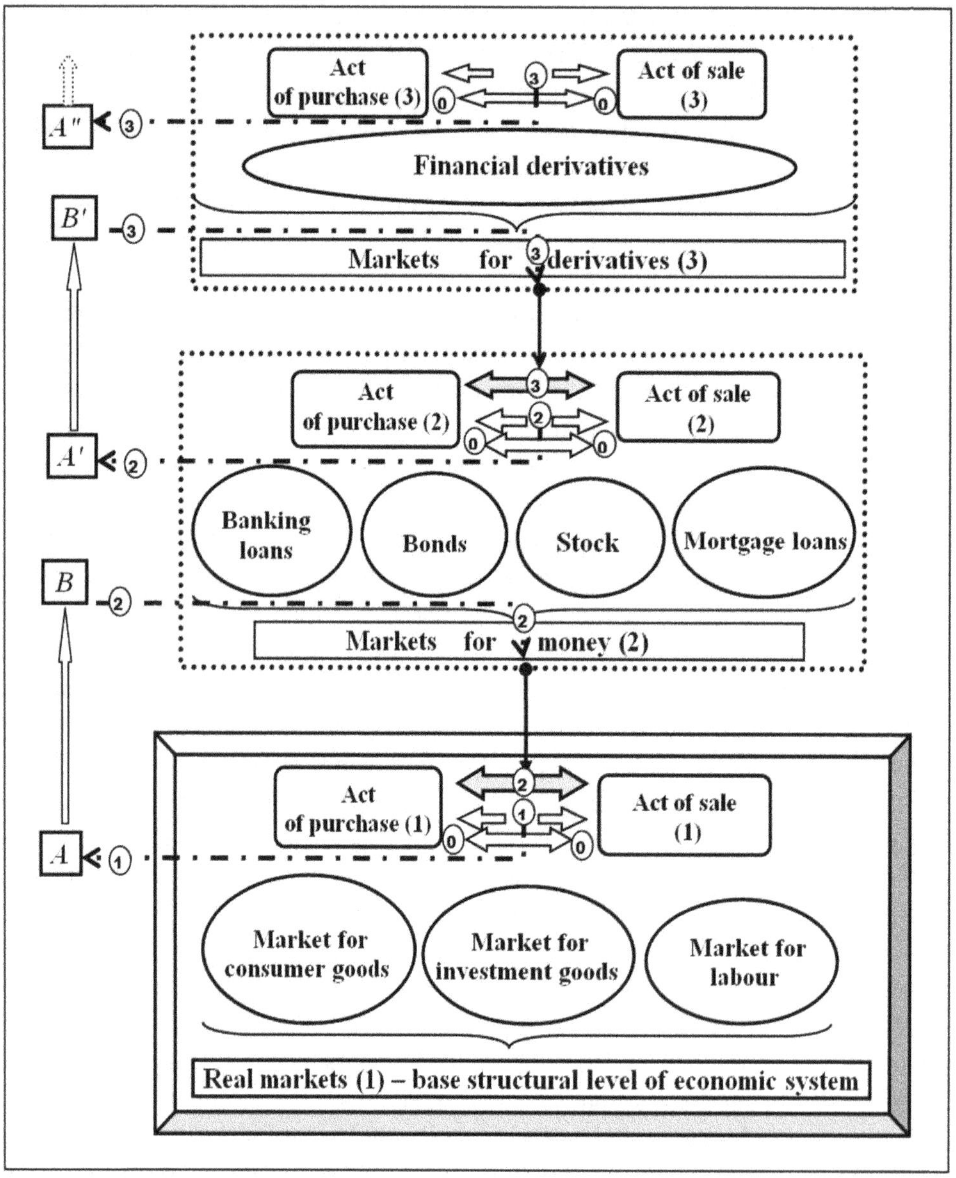

Until this level is formed as a set of dialectical pairs mediating their own structural connections in exchange, the complication of the markets for money is predetermined by the structural level - cause, i.e. the real markets. However, as a result of the operation of the law of the transition of quantitative changes into the qualitative ones money market becomes completely self-sufficient: dialectical pairs and their structural connections at this level begin to be regulated by the law of unity and struggle of opposites. At the same time, a specific feature arises in the interaction of the structural level-cause, represented by real markets, and the structural level-effect in the composition of such money markets as the credit market, the bond and stock market, and the real estate market (Taleb, 2007, 2012). All structural levels dialectically interact with each other vertically. Thus, each of them is governed by the law of unity and struggle of opposites horizontally and, at the same time, by the law of the transition of quantitative changes into qualitative changes along the vertical. In this case, money in the cash balance of an individual or a firm is freely replaced by substitutes for money, without causing an imbalance in exchange. But for this, all participants in transactions must precisely comply with the terms of payments, ensure material security of solvency and be ready to pay for their obligations. Only in this case, money substitutes can completely replace money in the cash balance of an individual or a firm and ensure equilibrium at all levels of the structural hierarchy. Under these conditions, the entire structural hierarchy of systemic integrity becomes more and more fragile (Taleb, 2012).

So the traditional money market began to be structured into the market for banking loans, market for bonds, the stock market and the market for mortgage loans (Bootle, 2009). All these markets initially served real markets with money, resolving those dialectical contradictions that arose in them due to the lack of money for exchange. The emergence of the markets for money as new structural level of exchange, which has arisen as a result of significant problems of lack of money in real markets, is a demonstration of the process of self-organization of the economic system on the example of structuring the exchange of economic activity and of its results in general. And as demand for money in this quality grows, a dialectic contradiction arises in the money markets themselves. It is connected with the money markets' limits in organizing a new quality of transactions. As a result these dialectical contradictions are resolved by creating new markets for financial products that become specialized in transactions with money as income-earning assets (Santomero, 1996).

Thus, financial markets in the process of self-organization of exchange acquire self-sufficiency, their own importance for the structure as well as for the economy as a whole. Thus the emergence of its own dialectical problems negatively affects economic and exchange processes, which objectively necessitates the need for self-organization of a new structural level in the hierarchy of exchange aimed at solving them. And this process is objectively predetermined to constant repetition: first, it will be aimed at solving the dialectical contradictions of the previous level - the cause, and then it will acquire its own significance for the stability of the exchange as a whole and will become the cause in its hierarchical dependencies. Later, the need to resolve its own problems, which threaten to break the ties between the acts of purchase and sale, will lead to self-organization of a new structural level - consequence, subordinated to the solution of dialectical contradictions of the structural level - cause. This is the logical model of the formation of the structural hierarchy of the exchange of economic activity and its results, depending on the causal subordination of the higher structural levels of the exchange hierarchy to the lower levels (Fig. 5).

Bearing in mind that all self-organizational processes in the system are based on the tendencies of division and unification of various types of economic activity, in this context, the law of the transition of quantitative changes into qualitative changes makes it possible to overcome the limits of complexity (Arthur, 1999, 2013) (bottlenecks) of negative selection implemented by integration (exchange) and action of the law of unity and struggle of opposites. Indeed, in fact, the replacement of unity in the horizontal structural connections of dialectical pairs with opposites means an increase in quantitative changes in the relationships of their participants in the process of positive selection (differentiation). The action of this mechanism brings the organization of structural links to a certain limit of complexity, when the system can lose the quality of integrity, and the mechanism of negative selection of those structural links that, within the framework of dialectical pairs, can preserve and strengthen it comes into force (consonant thoughts are present in Taleb, 2012). Moreover, the achievement of any limits of complexity is accompanied by the readiness of the shock mechanism to break the structural links that destroy the integrity of the system, and to strengthen it through updated structural links. This is how the transition from the dominance of unity to its replacement by opposites is carried out, as well as from quantitative changes to the new qualitative ones. At the same time, horizontal structural ties begin to generate relationships outside the horizontal level by superstructuring them along the vertical of the system as a result of replacing one dialectical law (of unity and struggle of opposites) with another (of transition of quantity to quality). In essence, it is about replacing the mechanism of negative selection (integration) with the mechanism of positive selection (differentiation) and vice versa. This happens in conditions when the horizontal level of structural ties loses its ability to provide stability, equilibrium, and integrity of a constantly changing system. In this case, the law of the unity and struggle of opposites is replaced by the law of the transition of quantitative changes into qualitative ones.

From the point of view of the state of structural relationships that ensure the integrity of the system, the emergence of structural levels-consequences, designed to solve the problem of balancing the levels-reasons that generated them, the conclusion is ambiguous. On the one hand, the emergence of new structural links and the complication of the structure of the system due to the generation of its new vertical segments should strengthen the integrity of the system. This is due to the fact that, all other things being equal, the more structural links, the more stable the system. However, on the other hand, in the conditions of the coincidence in time of the acts of purchase and sale and the simultaneous exchange of goods and money, the causes and consequences of their imbalance were concentrated in the dialectical pairs themselves, located at the same level. Problems arose but they could be resolved by the exchange participants themselves without any third party. With the separation of causes and effects in solving the problems of exchange between the structural levels of the system, the difficulties of one level began to depend on the possibilities of their elimination on the part of a higher level. This made the structural level-cause dependent on stability at the structural level-effect. As a result, the system as integrity, in which structural ties have increased, acquired additional sources of strengthening its integrity. But at the same time, the entire system has become more fragile, since the problems of one structural level, firstly, predetermine the imbalance at other levels, and, secondly, the solution of the imbalance problems presupposes an integrated approach associated with the return of symmetry at all levels interconnected according to the principle of cause and effect (Taleb, 2007, 2012).

As a result, if the mechanism of positive selection, which predetermines an increase in quantitative changes during the formation of additional structural levels, comes into conflict with the mechanism of negative selection in terms of strengthening their new quality based on the coincidence of interests of participants in exchange transactions in the range from 100% to 50%, shocks will destroy destabilizing system integrity structural links. And the crises following the shocks implement the typical scenario of restoring working structural links, eliminating those that are not working and creating new ones capable of ensuring the stability of the system in the process of its self-organization. And this will be repeated every time the system reaches the next limit of complexity generating vertical structural levels. Then, structural ties will be severed in a shock manner and the crisis will begin to realize its typical phases. This is essentially a process of self-organization, which could be associated with Groundhog Day with one important caveat: it is not about the transition of the system from a static state to a dynamic one through the law of denial of negation and its mediating shock.

Typical scenario for such shock destruction is described in Fig. 6. Lower structural levels, represented by dialectical pairs exchanging a traded asset, face a problem (for example, a lack of money or, conversely, the need to invest in a profitable asset). In vertical hierarchy of structural levels any higher structure is designed to solve the problems of a lower level. As long as this subordination remains, the self-organization of the structural ties of the economic system strengthens its integrity (the left panel of Fig. 6). However, the rush demand or supply of an asset as a subjective component of the shock triggers it (the right panel of Fig. 6) and, under certain circumstances, structural relationships begin to break through the chain of mutual relationships (Pilipenko, 2020, 2021). The structural levels-causes and structural levels-consequences change places and instead of strengthening the integrity of the economic system, they multiply the breakdown of ties and weaken the integrity of the entire system.

In other words, shocks arise at the turning point of the operation of the laws of unity and struggle of opposites and of the transition of quantity to quality, i.e. at the moment when the mechanisms of positive and negative selection come into conflict. Then the upper level, undergoing a shock rupture of structural ties, causes their rupture at lower levels. This is how the horizontal and vertical structural relationships collapse, which is restored at the stages of the crisis due to structural ties generation that can strengthen the stability of the system. So the shock destruction of structural ties today is a condition for the restoration of their working counterparts for the purpose of continuing the processes of self-organization in the future.

So the dialectics of the market exchange complication is understandable only when it is considered as the process of continuous formation of its new properties due to the changing relations of the participants of exchange, to the emergence of its new objects and to the structural interdependencies of various segments of market exchange and of their interacting levels. And the degree of shock's destruction depends on the structural level of exchange, which ceases to fulfill its function of restoring the integrity of a lower level, on its place in the hierarchical structure of exchange, on its significance for the economic system as a whole.

Most likely, this is what Didier Sornette (2003) had in mind when he wrote, that «...in complex systems, it has been found that the organization of spatial and temporal correlations do not stem, in general, from a nucleation phase diffusing across the system. Such ruptures involve interactions between structures at many different scales». So, the dialectical interaction of the laws of unity and struggle of opposites and of the transition of quantitative changes to qualitative ones is predetermined by the resulting effect of positive and negative selection of organizational forms of economic activities. As a result of such complex interactions, both the basic structural level and the hierarchy of the structural levels of the system are formed. The complication of the structure of a self-organizing system is aimed at strengthening its qualitative certainty and integrity. It is necessary to agree with W. Brian Arthur (2013) that a fundamental characteristic of an economic system as an integrity is its ability to create and recreate its own structures to strengthen its integrity. However, all organizational changes in the structure have their limits of complexity associated with both the marginal level of its diversity (differentiation) and the marginal level of its uniformity (integration). Upon reaching these margins, structures lose their ability to provide integrity, stability and equilibrium of the system. These metamorphoses are due to the dialectical connection between structure and system as the essence and form of the phenomenon.

Indeed, self-organizing economic integrity is constantly becoming more complex due to the emergence of new forms of organization of economic activity and new structural ties (Arthur, 1999). And in these conditions, it is the structure that is called upon to maintain the integrity of such a rapidly changing system. But form and essence, according to G.W.F. Hegel (1892), are identical and should be taken as

Figure 6. Model of shock's realization in the process of self-organization of structural links, built as a vertical hierarchy of structural levels-causes and structural levels-consequences in case of strengthening the integrity of the economic system (the left panel) and in case of their shock's destruction (the right panel)
Note: **A (A', A")** *stands for* **CAUSES;** **B (B', B")** *stands for* **CONSEQUENCE**
Source: the author's development

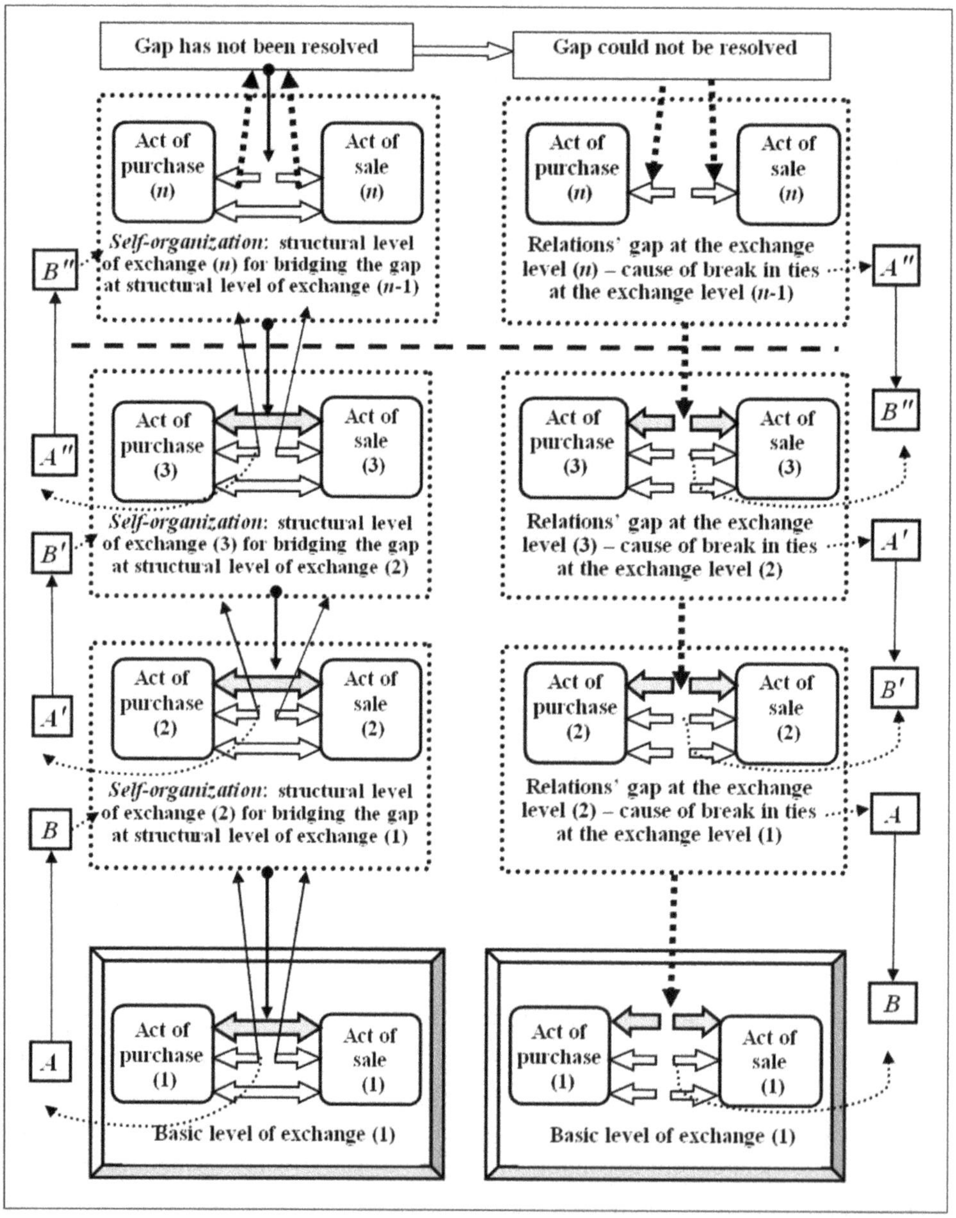

two sides of the same coin. That is why self-organization is realized through constant reproduction and complication of both the structure (essence) of the system and the systemic forms of its manifestation in different types of formations and at different stages (structural levels) of organization (complexity). According to A.A. Bogdanov (1934), all these phenomena in their mutual interweaving and mutual struggle, in their permanent changes, form a universal process of self-organization, infinitely dividing systemic components, and endlessly uniting them into various forms of systemic integrities.

Considering all of the above, the authors consider it expedient to interpret the laws of unity and struggle of opposites and of the transition of quantity into quality as a kind of dialectical phenomenon. Indeed, the law of unity and struggle of opposites acts first, resolving contradictions and forming structural links along the horizontal of the economic system. When the margin is reached in the self-organization of the system due to horizontal structural ties and the law of unity and struggle of opposites cannot overcome it, the law of the transition of quantity into a new quality comes into play. The shock mechanism, in its turn, mediates a turning point in the operation of each of these laws, as well as the transition from the priority of one of them to the priority of another. In other words, shocks are objectively embedded into the mechanism of action of these laws and perform the function of destroying "non-working" structural ties that threaten the integrity of the economic system, first, at the turning point of transformation of unity into opposites (diversity wins uniformity) and, second, at the margin of transformation of quantitative changes into new qualities (diversity can destroy integrity, and it is necessary to maintain uniformity).

In other words, a deeper understanding of the self-organization of a complex economy allows the authors to deepen the idea of shocks as to their greater specification:

1. shocks are embedded as indispensable elements in the universal mechanism of complex economy's movement at the stage of self-organization;
2. shocks' mechanism is realized in breaking of structural ties of the economic system, represented by the exchange of economic activity and of its results;
3. breaking the structural hierarchy of the system shocks cause crises of different depth in economic systems, depending on the position of the destroyed chains in the structure of cause-and-effect relationships of the system and their impact on its integrity;
4. the mechanism of shock destruction of structural links should be interpreted in the interaction of its three components: object, subjective and process ones. Moreover, under the conditions of the law of double negation, understanding the subjective component in the mechanism of shocks acquires paramount importance (Chapter 4).

In general, shocks, according to the authors, relate to the fundamental characteristics of systems capability to self-organization, since they mediate turning points in the operation of the dialectical laws of unity and struggle of opposites and the transition of quantitative changes into qualitative ones. In Chapter 4, the authors will demonstrate this ability of shocks when implementing the law of denial of negation in the process of self-development of a dynamic economy. Already at this stage of the study, it becomes obvious that self-organizing systems have the endogenous mechanism of their own self-movement, which is provided by the dialectics of positive and negative selections, by dialectical pairs, realizing by their structural connections the norms dictated by dialectical laws of unity and struggle of opposites and of the transition of quantitative changes into qualitative ones. Moreover, the authors' understanding shocks allow them to get closer to the answer to the question of how the economy is shaping itself and changing structurally to infinity. From the point of view of Joseph A. Schumpeter (1949), this phenomenon is one of the most important of all phenomena that economists seek to explain.

3.4. Shocks and Crises in Economic Systems at the Stage of Their Self-Organization: the Example of the Global Financial Crisis of 2007-2009

The application of the theory of shocks to the interpretation of shocks in national economies at the stage of self-organization is still awaiting publication. Apparently, the significance of shocks' theory in its positive and normative parts is difficult to overestimate. The authors have attempted to provide a theoretical interpretation of only one global financial shock 2007-2009. The undoubted uniqueness of this global financial crisis and the shock that preceded it is determined by the specifics of the self-organization of the economic systems that experienced them. By 2007, structurally complex economic systems already developed in most countries of the world under the influence of dialectical laws (of unity and struggle of opposites and of the transition of quantitative changes to qualitative ones). The vertical hierarchy of structural levels of markets for money and of financial markets was formed not only in national economies, but also in the globe. As a result, the shock destruction of the hierarchy of structural levels swept the global structural chains of interconnections of the financial markets of the countries of the world.

But it all started in the American financial market. In 2007, a separate segment began to form in the American financial market, where specific financial products were traded. Those financial products appeared because the national subprime risky loans were packed into the asset-backed securities. They represented part of the collateralized debt obligations (CDO) that were rated and sold to investors of different nationality. The emergence of these new segments of financial markets was caused by the need to resolve dialectical contradictions that arose at the lower structural levels of financial markets. The latter could not provide an exchange of risky subprime loans. To solve that problem, the new vertical structural level of exchange was formed, represented by the new structured finance products, dialectical pairs of participants and of their steadily repeating relationships. Thus, a causal subordination of the below and above located structural levels of the American financial markets was formed in order that a higher vertical level would solve the problems of a lower vertical level.

The new financial product had its own specifics. The phenomenon of the structured finance normally entails aggregating multiple underlying risks (such as market and credit risks) by pooling instruments subject to those risks (for example, bonds, loans, or mortgage-backed securities). The resulting cash flows are divided into "tranches" or slices and paid to different holders (Kodres, 2008). Payouts from the pool are paid to the holders of these tranches in a specific order, starting with the "senior" tranches (least risky) and working down through various levels to the "equity" tranche (most risky) (Fig. 7).

If some of the expected cash flows into the pool are not forthcoming (for instance, because some loans default), then, after a cash flow buffer is depleted, the equity tranche holders are the first to absorb payment shortfalls. If payments in the pool are reduced further, the next set of tranche holders (the "mezzanine" tranche) does not receive full payment. Typically, the super senior tranches and the senior tranches at the top of the capital structure are constructed so that they qualify for AAA credit ratings, meaning there should be a very low probability of their not receiving promised payments. Until July 2007, when the financial shock hit, the growth in structured credit finance products had been exponential. For example, issuance of selected structured credit products in the United States and Europe grew from $500 billion in 2000 to $2.6 trillion in 2007.

Figure 7. The self-organization of the vertical structural levels of the economic system: formation of the financial market of highly complex structured credit products
Source: Kodres, Laura. (2008). Crises of confidence...and a lot more. Finance & Development. A Quarterly Publication of the International Monetary Fund. June. Vol. 45. No. 2. PP. 9-13

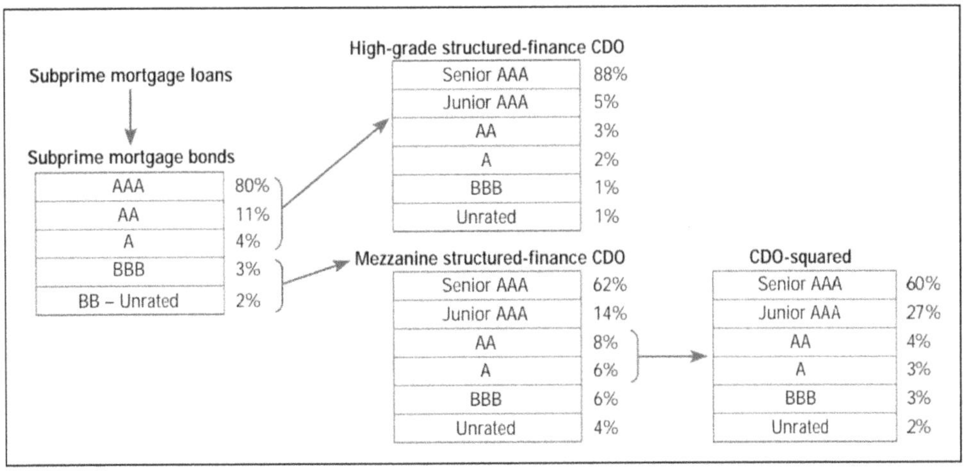

Actually on the eve of the crisis banks were estimated to have $740 billion of net subprime exposure, mostly held by U.S. banks (53 percent), with the remainder held by European (41 percent), Asian (5 percent), and Canadian (1 percent) banks (International Monetary Fund, April 2008). In terms of composition, U.S. banks (together with government-sponsored enterprises) held a greater proportion of overall exposure to the subprime market through unsecuritized subprime loans and asset-backed securities (ABS) collateralized debt obligations (CDOs) compared with European banks. But as for European banks they held a greater proportion of their exposure to the subprime market via ABS. The banks were assumed to hold the most senior tranches.

Thus, the object component of structural self-organization was strengthened by the subjects' component of vertical structural links, which ultimately predetermined the growing gap between the base and market price of that financial product in the structured finance market. Quite quickly, a turning point was reached in the operation of the law of unity and struggle of opposites in the exchange of highly complex structured credit products, which was accompanied by the agiotage behavior of agents in the market. In theory, the interaction of positive and negative selection mechanisms could "block" ineffective structural connections. And that would have occurred if it were not for the subjects' component of the self-organization mechanism. Built on the hierarchy of structured financial product tranches, that market was initially prone to structural collapse due to orientation to "Ponzi-lending" model described by H.P. Minsky (2008) (Chapter 5.3). The same idea was confirmed by other researchers, using a slightly different argumentation. B. Bernanke (1983) substantiated a "credit view" on the causes of financial instability that could be summed up with Schumpeter's words of "reckless lending. Regression models of systemic banking crises confirmed the main findings of G. Kaminsky and K. Reinhart (1999), M. Shularik and A. Taylor (2012) that overlending was a key factor of financial instability.

Nevertheless, it should be emphasized that it is possible to understand the true reason for the increasing fragility of vertical structural ties only if it could be understood the dialectics of the relationship between the object and subjects' components of the self-organization mechanism of static economic systems.

It should be borne in mind that the significance of the behavioral aspect of systemic self-organization increases as the vertical of the structural hierarchy of national systems increases (Chapters 5, 6). In the considered case of the shock on the American market for unsecured mortgage loans in 2007, only the shock mechanism could block the market-destroying behavior of exchange subjects of highly complex structured credit products. Moreover, the crisis following the shock, its duration and depth were largely predetermined by the developed transnational structural ties. Within 10 years before the start of the global crisis 2007-2009 structural ties concerning the exchange of highly complex structured credit products had acquired the quality of global ones. That made national economic systems even more fragile, since their vertical structural links were embedded according to the principle of cause-and-effect relationships not only into the vertical of national financial markets, but also into the global vertical structural chains. However, in addition to this, the fragility of self-organizing national systems had increased as a result of the inclusion in the circulation of national financial markets of such objects as highly complex structured credit products, which were issued by financial institutions of other countries and were determined by the rules of circulation developed in other national financial systems. In other words, the conditions for the emergence of shocks were predetermined not only by structural links near their limits, but also by the behavioral aspects of national subjects of exchange, as well as factors that are outside the static national economic systems at the stage of their self-organization.

It was precisely the price shock on the U.S. subprime unsecured mortgage loan market that triggered the global financial crisis in 2007. In essence, it was a break of the structural relationships, serving the exchange of highly complex structured credit products in the financial markets. Moreover, outwardly, that took the form of a shock violation of confidence between participants of dialectical pairs exchanging highly complex structured financial instruments (Fig. 8) for monetary liquidity (Chapter 5.2).

Figure 8. Self-organization of the vertical structural ties on the financial markets: the growth of exchange of highly complex structured financial instruments

Note: CDOs = collateralized debt obligations; ABSs = asset-backed securities, including auto, credit card, etc., and excluding MBSs; and MBSs = mortgage-backed securities, excluding U.S. agency MBSs.

Source: Inside MBS & ABS; JPMorgan Chase & Co.; and European Securitization Forum, Laura Kodres (2008).

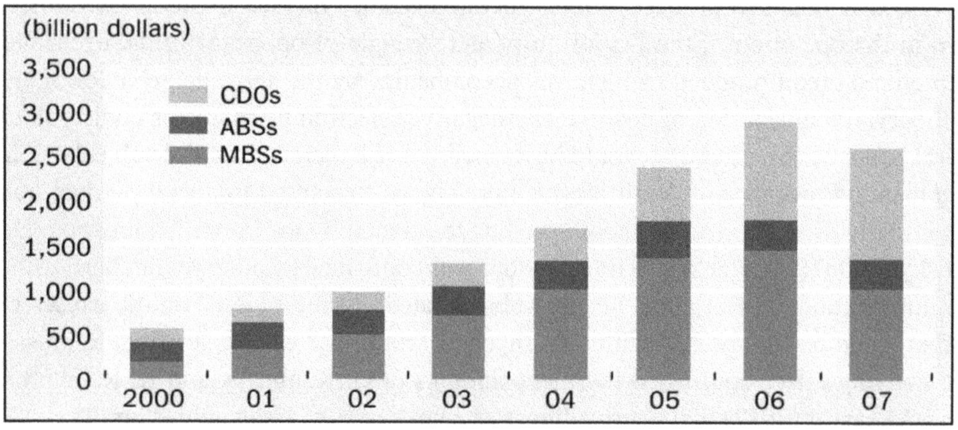

Low nominal interest rates, ample liquidity, low financial market volatility, and a general feeling of complacency encouraged many types of investors to take on more risk. The lengthy period of benign financial market conditions was expected to continue, global growth had been robust, and the previous excesses of the dot-com bubble seemed in the distant past. In short, the behavioral aspect of structural self-organization became apparent as many became convinced of the consolidation of the new paradigm of financial markets. The resulting situation clearly demonstrated the overlapping of the trends of increasing demand for complexly structured financial instruments, supported by the concentration of the necessary financial resources for their payment, and an increase in the supply of the required exchange objects. All that testified to the approach of those markets to their marginal state, which manifested itself in the maximum gap of the market price of the tradable asset – financial instruments and subprime mortgages loans – and its base value. And in accordance with the theory of shocks, the marginal state of market relations means the formation of necessary and sufficient conditions for a shock rupture of structural relations that undermine economic integrity. In the above case, it was about the market of unsecured mortgage loans, which was difficult and multivariate integrated into the system of interrelated and interdependent segments of diverse financial markets. As a result when confidence deteriorated, many holders of shorter-term asset-backed commercial paper (ABCP) that was backed by illiquid structured credit products cashed out of their holdings shortened the maturity they were willing to accept, or demanded higher yields. That tendency had been exacerbated as suspicions had become increasing that credit products held were based on unsecured subprime mortgages. As banks became unsure of their own liquidity needs, they hoarded liquidity, further exacerbating interbank market illiquidity.

So, the dialectical ties at the upper structural levels of the hierarchy of exchange represented by financial markets became predominantly transnational. That could be judged by the structure of losses, differentiated in Table 1. Based on average loss estimates of 15 percent for unsecuritized mortgage loans, 30 percent on ABS, and 60 percent on ABS CDOs as described above, potential losses of U.S. banks ($144 billion) were likely to be similar to those borne by European banks ($121 billion) (Table 1). Losses of Asian banks were likely to be less than one-tenth of losses in Europe. More than half of the aggregate subprime-related loss would likely come from exposure to CDOs, while the remainder was expected to come from ABS, unsecuritized subprime loans, and losses on off-balance-sheet liquidity lines. In particular, potential losses on off-balance-sheet conduit and structured investment vehicles (SIV) liquidity lines could result in $40 billion of losses globally ($27 billion for European banks and $13 billion of losses for U.S. banks). Those estimates were based on the assumption of an average loss of 5 percent on liquidity lines to off-balance-sheet conduits and SIVs. The 5 percent loss assumption was based on losses on a typical asset composition for conduits and SIVs. Losses on conduit assets were assumed to pass directly to the liquidity line, but losses on SIV assets were assumed to be mostly absorbed by the junior notes, given their funding structures (International Monetary Fund, April 2008).

Conduits and SIVs were weighted by their market proportions – 90 percent and 10 percent of the total, respectively – and it was assumed that all liquidity lines eventually got called (Table 1). One of the important questions emerged from the above, was, according to Randall Dodd, and Paul Mills (2008), how those losses could spread to other parts of the global financial system like an epidemic of an invisible virus infecting many people and communities. Really the financial crisis spread the losses to intermediaries in one non-transparent market but the last raised concerns about liquidity and solvency elsewhere (Dodd, 2007). However, a decade after the price shock of 2007, the process of self-organization of the exchange in the American market for unsecured mortgage loans was characterized by an increase of the international structural ties served, for example, by commercial banks (International Monetary Fund, April 2019) (Fig. 9).

Table 1. Global bank losses as of March 2008 (in billion U.S. dollars)

Country/Region	Total Reported Losses	Estimated Losses on U.S. Subprime/ Alt-A Loans	Estimated Losses on ABS	Estimated Losses on CDOs	Estimated Losses on Conduits/ SIVs	Total Estimated Subprime-Related Losses	Remaining Subprime-Related Losses Expected
Europe	**80**	**16**	**27**	**53**	**27**	**123**	**43**
Of which:							
United Kingdom	19	16	1	12	11	40	22
Switzerland	23	0	7	15	1	23	0
Scandinavia	0	0	0	0	1	1	**1**
Euro area	33	0	10	20	15	45	12
Unallocated	5	0	9	6	0	14	9
United States	95	29	12	90	13	144	49
Asia excluding Japan	1	0	3	0	0	4	3
Of which: China	1	0	3	0	0	3	2
Japan	10	0	5	5	0	10	0
Asia	11	0	9	5	0	13	3
Canada	7	0	2	5	0	7	0
Gulf Cooperation Council	1	0	1	1	0	1	0
Total	**193**	**44**	**50**	**153**	**40**	**288**	**95**

Note: Bank allocation to asset-backed securities (ABS) in Table 1 includes estimated losses on ABS and conduits/SIVs. CDO = collateralized debt obligation; SIV = structured investment vehicles.

Sources: Goldman Sachs; UBS; IMF staff estimates, IMF (April, 2008)

Figure 9. Global systemically important banks' global market share by asset or activity, 2016 (or latest) (Percent; US dollars)

Source: IMF (2017). Global Financial Stability Report: Is Growth at Risk? October. Washington, DC: International Monetary Fund

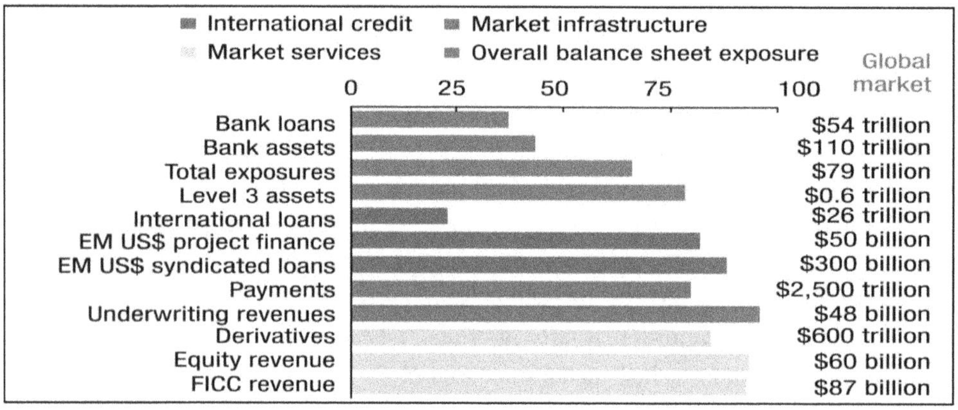

Although finance is generally believed to contribute to long-term economic growth, recent studies have shown that the growth benefits start declining when aggregate leverage is high (IMF, 2017). The experience from the global financial crisis of 2007-2009 showed that increases in private sector credit, including household debt, might have raised the likelihood of a financial - crisis and could lead to lower growth. As a result the basis for such a collapsing chain (Menzie, et al., 2002; Forbes, 2001; Pedroni, 1999] disruption of interrelations in the interacting segments of the financial market could be predetermined by the marginal levels of insecurity of financial transactions, such as, for example, in the case of exchange of structured financial products for unsecured loans received from banks. Such a dual non-equivalence of exchange, with the participation of dialectical pairs in the segment of structured financial products of the financial markets, in fact explained the phenomenon of the constant presence of shock mechanisms as realization of an unbearable propensity to instability (Minsky, 1992). According to Fig.9 the financial shocks on a global scale, including countries and numerous market segments, have so far left many unanswered questions about global financial stability, minimization of the likelihood of recurring financial shocks of this kind and, of course, mechanisms to eliminate possible causes of the future financial shocks (or rather price shocks in financial markets) (Dodd, and et al., 2008; Rajan, 2010).

The continuing urgency of all the problems mentioned above is confirmed by the opinions of experts expressed both during the global financial crisis (2007-2009) and ten years later (Perez, 2009; Reinhart, and Rogoff, 2009; Beneš, and et al., 2009; IMF, 2009; Hatzius, and et al., 2010, and etc.). The results of a decade researches since the t global financial crisis of 2007-2009 devoted to the self-organization of national and global economies, to the role of financial intermediaries, including the nature and forms of manifestation of financial shocks, can be summed up with the words of Valerie Cerra (2018, P. 4), Assistant Director in the IMF's Institute for Capacity Development: "....During the past decade, a lot of good work has been done to incorporate financial frictions into our economic models.... Some economists also underestimated the role of the financial sector before the crisis." It means that ten years after the last global financial crisis not all the questions about it have been answered. According to V. Cerra [2018, P. 4]: "We still don't understand very well why transitory shocks from the financial sector or elsewhere can lead to a persistent fall in productivity, employment, and investment." The following researchers are of the same opinion: M. Schularick, and A. Taylor (2012); R. Sahay, M. Cihak, P. N'Diaye, A. Barajas, R. Bi, D. Ayala, Y. Gao, A. Kyobe, L. Nguyen, C. Saborowski, K. Svirydzenka, and S. R. Yousefi (2015); P. O'Sullivan, Nigel F. B. Allington, Mark Esposito (2015); V. Cerra, and S.C. Saxena (2017); B. Sergi, F. Fidanoski, M. Zioło, and V. Naumovski (2018); M. Zioło (2019), and etc.

As for the Fed's actions in the United States, they fit well into the authors' notion that shocks immediately "reject" structural ties that destroy the integrity of the system, and crises are subordinated to the task of restoring a structure that would provide self-organization no less effectively than in the pre-shock period of economic system's self-organization. So the Fed acted in full accordance with this scenario. First, it used standard and then non-standard measures aimed at restoring the structural integrity of the system. A large-scale injection of additional liquidity into the economy became a standard measure. This was supported by the maximum possible reduction in the nominal base interest rate for an indefinite period. Since mid-2008, the federal funds rate were in the range from 0 to 0.25 percent, that was, in a small positive near zero. However, the crisis that gripped the US economy turned out to be so strong that those actions by the Fed were not enough. The market was provided with additional liquidity, but high risks blocked the issuance of new loans, including for the real sector of the economy. This was due to the fact that the rupture of structural ties that initially engulfed financial markets spread to real markets.

The housing construction market fell into stagnation. Due to the credit crunch, industrial production began to fall. In 2008 alone, the Dow Jones Industrial Average fell from 12,000 to 8,000 points, and US GDP in Q4 2008 decreased by 3.8% (in annual terms). As soon as the rupture of financial ties generated the same effect in real markets, the US monetary authorities resorted to a non-standard, unprecedented solution. It consisted in the fact that the state bought out "bad" assets, which were mediated by structural ties that destroy the stability of the market and of the economy, in order to remove them from the market exchange. Already such actions of the US government proved the fact that the shock of 2007 and the subsequent crisis of 2008-2009 signalled the exhaustion of the potential for self-organization. Since the usual shocks and subsequent crises "discarded" non-working structural links and then new economic growth followed, since the potential for self-organization of a static economy was not yet exhausted. And in the event of a price shock in the financial market for unsecured mortgages and the ensuing crisis, it became clear that things were going differently. No coincidence, September 18, 2008 Ben S. Bernanke said in his address to Congress: "...without a comprehensive financial bailout plan by Monday, we could lose the entire economy"(Bernanke, 2008). In October 2008, the US and EU authorities took on coordinated commitments to recapitalize banks (to buy back their shares). They also pledged to guarantee or buy back their remaining toxic (non-risk-based) assets worth $ 14 trillion. In other words, the state undertook the historic mission of restoring the structure of the economy to restore its integrity. This is precisely the task that the so-called "Paulson plan" was fulfilling to create the TARP program for the buyback of distressed assets worth $ 700 billion. It was followed by Barack Obama's law on measures to stimulate the economy in the amount of $ 787 billion, and the Fed spent $ 600 billion for the same purpose (Kostyuk, 2014). Those measures made it possible to carry out a large-scale redemption by the state of illiquid assets of banks and other financial institutions.

In this way, non-functioning structural ties were discarded, which threatened the stability of the entire economic system. And only after that did the national economic systems begin to return to economic growth. However, not everything turned out to be so simple. In the developed countries of the world, although the growth rates were above zero, they were significantly inferior to the indicators of the late XX and early XXI centuries. This indirectly proves the validity of the authors' conclusion that the economic systems of developed countries with rather complex horizontal and vertical structural ties have come to the point of exhaustion of the potential of self-organization for static economies. That is why, in order to restore the structural integrity of their systems, states were forced to take unprecedented steps to buy out "toxic" assets, blocking market segments and structural ties that destroyed the integrity of the economic system.

A model representation of the dialectical contradiction, at the solution of which the shock of 2007 and the subsequent crisis of 2008-2009 were aimed in the national economic systems is shown in Fig. 10.

So, the law of the transition of quantitative changes into qualitative ones mediates the action of the mechanisms of positive selection of differentiated types of economic (financial) activity and of negative selection in the context of structuring the links between them. But not all potential types of organization of economic activity at any given moment can be implemented and therefore not all of its results can serve as the basis for the exchange, for formation of dialectical pairs of sellers and buyers and of self-organization processes to resolve their contradictions. These conclusions are made on the basis of the presence of structural links within the national system, and their focus solely on ensuring its integrity. In other words, if we abstract from the potential opportunity to obtain a macroeconomic effect, then any interactions of participants in dialectical pairs of different nationalities across national borders should be regarded negatively, from the point of view of the integrity of each of the national economies. In 2007 the price shock occurred in the American market for highly complex structured credit products. And this in itself testified to the limiting state of the static US economy in terms of its potential for self-organization.

Figure 10. The specific of the economic system's self-development at the stage of transition of quantitative changes to qualitative ones: the dialectical contradiction between the national endogenous environment and the exchange of both national and transnational structural ties
Source: the authors' development

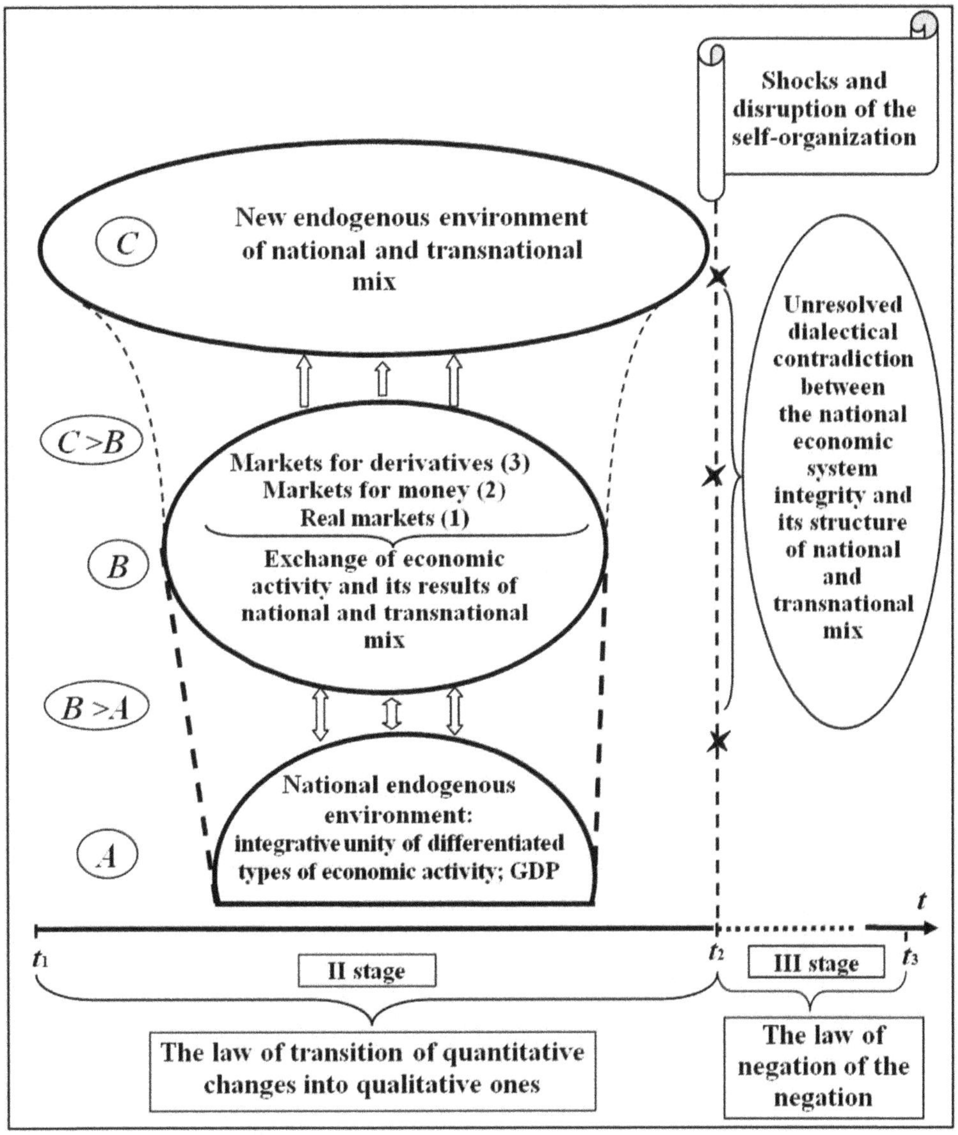

However, structural interrelationships regarding the exchange of highly complex structured credit products increased the problems of this segment of the American financial market due to the presence of participants of dialectical pairs separated by national boundaries. It turns out that the causal relationships lined up not only along the vertical of the structural ties of the US national economy, but also included vertical structural ties with subjects of different nationalities. As a result, the total volume of transactions in the financial market due to transactions with highly complex structured credit products in each of the participating countries significantly exceeded the level of their national GDP. In this regard, the scale of exchange is significantly inferior to the volumes of the endogenous environment of the economic system, under the influence of which its structure changes, i.e. exchange as a mechanism for self-development of the economic system. However, the financial shock of 2007 in the American unsecured mortgage market and the subsequent global financial crisis, the end of which date back to 2009, adjusted the idea of exchange, given the scale of transnational financial markets. Moreover, "trust" as a guarantor of obligations under transactions of speculative players of different nationalities did not allow optimal rejection of structural ties using mechanisms of positive and negative selection. The shock to the American market for the highly complex structured credit products was inevitable. And it testified that the static economy, as exemplified by the developed countries of the world, exhausted its potential for self-organization (i.e., self-movement because of complication of structural ties) and conditions began to ripen for systems to jump at the stage of self-development. In fact, this was fully confirmed by the shock caused by the COVID-19 pandemic in 2020.

Moreover from the moment of the financial shock in 2007 to the present, the scale of exchange only at the structural level of transnational financial markets has significantly exceeded their material base in terms of GDP of any country in the world. From the theoretical point of view, this means that exchange as a structure of the economic system has become able to mediate significantly more structural links that can be generated by their foundation - any complex economic system within its national borders. So the structure of the economic system responsible for its integrity, and stability, comes into contradiction with the system as an integrative unity of differentiated types of economic activities.

According to the form of manifestation, this can be expressed (Fig. 10) by comparing the exchange, which includes the totality of real markets, money markets and markets for financial products, with their material basis - the totality of all types of activities within national borders that generate the result that becomes the object of exchange. In 2007-2009, according to the logic of the authors, the shock break of structural relations in exchange, starting from the upper structural levels of its hierarchy, was supposed to mediate the jump of national economies from the stage of transition of quantitative changes to their new quality to the stage of their denial of their denial. In Fig. 10 this jump after the "gap" of continuity in the infinite dynamics of economic changes is marked in italics. As a result, the structural links of exchange were to be restored in accordance with the new base of the endogenous environment of economic systems (Chapter 4). Thus, theoretically at the new stage the law of denial of denial predetermines the need for restoration of dialectical interaction between an unprecedented in scale exchange on its material base.

And since the volume of transactions in global financial markets has long gone beyond the horizontal and vertical structural levels of national systems, then a new theoretical layer of unknown unknowns appears. It is advisable to list only some of them. First, in national systemic integrities, the formation of both horizontal and vertical structural levels is regulated by the laws of the unity and struggle of opposites and of the transition of quantitative changes into qualitative ones. What is the logic behind generating the horizontal structural level of global real and financial markets, what problems does their functioning solve? How are the effects of the complication of global structural links between their national participants distributed? Second, the construction of vertical structural levels in national economic systems obeys the logic of cause-and-effect relationships, according to which the higher structural levels solve the problems of the lower ones. How does this system interact in the context of the intertwining of global and national causal relationships in connection with the exchange of financial assets? Third, on what basis are non-functioning structural ties that are dangerous to the integrity of the global economy "rejected"? And how does this affect national systemic integrity? All these problems await their researchers.

EMPIRICAL EVIDENCE

Financial markets are complex organizations with their own economic and institutional structures that play a critical role in determining how prices are established, or "discovered." These factors also shape markets are complex organizations with - the stability and orderliness of the marketplace. The architecture of over the counter (OTC) markets helps explain why CDOs (which divide the risk of the underlying assets into several slices, each of which is sold separately) and other structured securities faced problems during the last crisis. Credit derivatives, commercial paper, municipal bonds, and securitized student loans were traded on OTC markets, which were liquid and functioned well during normal times (Dodd, et al., 2008). But they failed to demonstrate resilience to market disturbances and had become illiquid and dysfunctional. That led to two serious complications: the inability to value one's holdings and the inability to trade them. More problems occurred when the securities were distributed and traded.

The vulnerability of leveraged, or thinly capitalized, investment positions and the illiquidity of many structured credit markets were exposed when trading was disrupted in a host of other markets—subprime-linked MBSs, CDOs, asset-backed commercial paper (ABCP), and credit derivatives (Dodd, 2007). High degrees of leverage, in which investors borrowed heavily or used derivatives to increase returns to capital, made investment strategies vulnerable to large market price movements. Mortgage originators, broker-dealers, hedge funds, and the structured investment vehicles (SIVs) banks maintained off their balance sheets were highly leveraged. The principal risk management strategy was to plan to trade rapidly out of a loss-making position. But such a strategy, which relies on markets remaining liquid, failed when markets rapidly became illiquid. It is a challenge to any financial market when trading becomes one-sided—with everyone trying to sell or to buy. But some markets have proved to be more reliably liquid than others.

Below there is the authors' model of presenting the situation of the formation of a price shock in the financial market, when the market price of an asset maximally detaches from its base price, forming the marginal gap between them. Let the market price of the financial instrument being traded be - $Price_{Market}$, and its base price - $Value_{Base}$. For greater clarity of the graphic image of this dependence, it is advisable to assume that the base prices are a linear function of time with an angular coefficient k

$$Value_{Base}(t) = k \times Value_{Base} t ,$$

or more compact equation

$$V_B(t) = kV_B t. \tag{1}$$

Market prices will be interpreted as a non-linear function of the base price

$$Price_{Market} = f\left(Value_{Base}(t)\right),$$

or in a compact form

$$P_M = f(V_B(t)). \quad (2)$$

As a non-harmonic oscillator that generates fluctuations (spread or separation) of market prices near the base price, it has been chosen the second-order differential equation of Euler (Leonhard Euler) in the form

$$\frac{d^2P_M}{dV_B^2} + b_1\frac{dP_M}{dV_B} + b_0P_M = 0. \quad (3)$$

Relations (1) and (3) specify the model being developed:

$$\left.\begin{aligned} &\frac{d^2P_M}{dV_B^2} + b_1\frac{dP_M}{dV_B} + b_0P_M = 0 \\ &V_B(t) = kV_Bt \end{aligned}\right\}. \quad (4)$$

To construct the corresponding graphs, it should be obtained an analytical solution of the Euler' equation, i.e. to identify consistent pattern (2).

The general solution of the differential equation (3) is conveniently represented as:

$$_M(V_B) = CV^{\rho}\, sin\left[q\,ln(V_B) + A\right], \quad (5)$$

where A, C = const, ρ and q non-harmonic parameters.

In the oscillatory process (5) the constant C – is the amplitude at zero value of the parameter ρ ($\rho = 0$). In general, the parameter ρ does not accept a zero value. In this case, the multiplier V^{ρ} essentially plays the role of a non-linear multiplier of the process of dispersion of market prices. The constant A can be considered as the initial phase of the oscillations. The multiplier $qln(V_B)$ represents a phase of oscillation that changes non-linearly with time.

For simplicity and clarity of calculations, it is advisable to assume that $C = 2$; $A = 0$; $\rho = 1/2$; $q = 5$. The results of the relevant calculations are presented in Figure.11.

Here, for more informative and comparative elements of the model (4), two dependencies are combined: (1) $V_B(t)=kV_Bt$, where $k = 0.5$, in the axes tOV_B; and in the axes V_BOP_M solution (5) is presented taking into account the accepted numerical values of parameters

$$_M(V_B) = 2V^{\frac{1}{2}}\, sin\left[5\,ln(V_B)\right].$$

Figure 11. Model idea of the mechanism of maturing price shocks in the financial market based on Euler' differential equation
Source: developed by the authors

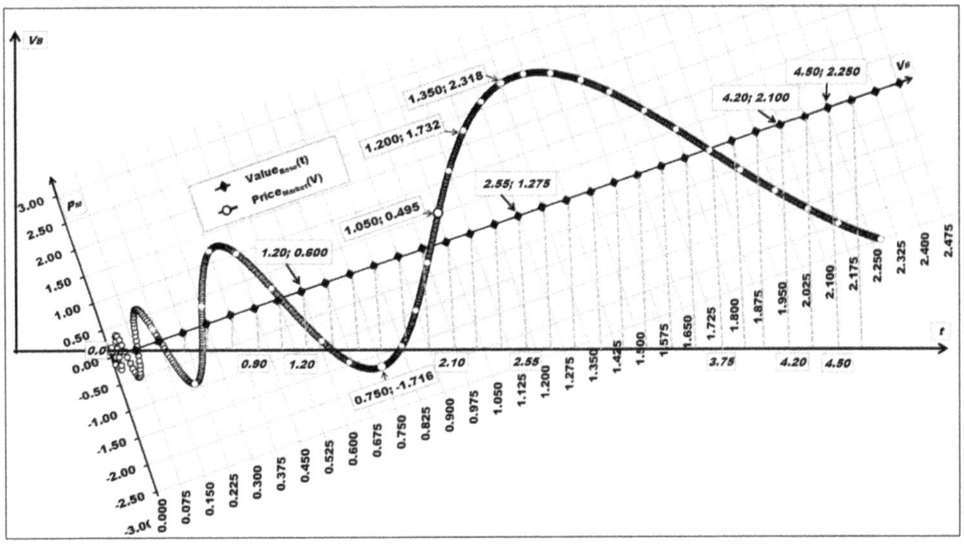

To match the elements of the two graphs, data labels are also applied – coordinates of some points.

As it is known, real market price fluctuations are far from harmonious. As far as the authors know, modifications of the Euler' differential equation have not been considered as non-harmonic oscillator of price modeling in the financial market. As it turned out, the results obtained in the framework of model (4) adequately describe the dynamics of market prices in the direction of maturing price shocks.

Hence, if the economic agents on the markets begin increasing purchases or sales of tradable assets regardless of their real cost, it is possible to prove that upon reaching the bifurcation point (marginal divergence of market prices of assets and their real value) any economic system loses its stability because of the breakdown of its structural connections (Pilipenko, and et al., 2018). The confidence multiplier (Shiller, 2004) leads either to increase or to decrease of demand (in direct proportion to the trust) for a particular asset. Finally, the initial increase in demand, pushing the market to a certain margin, finishes causing the shocks' break of structural ties in markets.

So, such a rapid spread of the price shock, first in the US market of unsecured mortgage loans, and then in other segments of the global financial market can theoretically be explained by the fact that there has been a shock break of dialectical relations in the interacting segments of the global financial markets. In 2007 the shock's discontinuity in the development of the US unsecured mortgage loans market was due to the combination of unsecured obligations from both the seller and the buyer of complex structured financial instruments. On the one hand, issuers of structured financial instruments had come a long way to deprive their market analogs of material security, but at the same time to achieve a high level of leverage and of capital gains. On this thorny path, the number of participants grew, starting with organizations that originally issued mortgage loans, broker-dealers, and ending with hedge funds and companies that traded structured investments that were not registered in banks' balance sheets. On the other hand, the buyers of these complexly structured financial instruments presented an increasing demand for them, paying cash based on loans, less and less secured by tangible assets.

More than 10 years have passed since the crisis of 2007–2008 in the global financial markets, which was initiated by a price shock in the US market of unsecured mortgage loans. And 2019 marks the formation of new segments of macroeconomic instability that are linked to the global financial debt market, including sovereigns (Tabarraei, and et al., 2019), firms, nonbank financial institutions and households. For example, the level of corporate debt has been rising around the world, and there is a weak tail of companies with high leverage and weak earnings prospects. There are growing signs that this credit cycle may be maturing, and risks of an economic slowdown are rising. The most highly indebted companies could be vulnerable to such a shock.

As to emerging markets their fundamentals are stronger and policy frameworks generally more resilient than in the past, some countries have low reserves, high leverage, or high foreign currency exposures that could make them more vulnerable to capital flow pressures. Furthermore, in Europe, fiscal challenges in some countries have reignited worries about the sovereign bank nexus as a potentially powerful amplification mechanism in economies with more indebted sovereigns. Finally, housing markets in many advanced and emerging markets are at risk (International Monetary Fund. April, 2019). In sum, these rising financial vulnerabilities point to elevated medium-term risks to financial stability. Yet there is more debt than ever in the global financial system (Fig. 12).

The combined global debt of governments, nonfinancial corporations, and households has grown by US$72 trillion since the end of 2007 (Fig. 12) (Rajan, 2010). The increase is smaller but still pronounced when measured relative to GDP. From 2008 to mid-2017, global government debt more than doubled, reaching US$60 trillion. Among Organisation for Economic Co-operation and Development countries, government debt now exceeds annual GDP in Japan, Greece, Italy, Portugal, Belgium, France, Spain, and the United Kingdom (McKinsey Global Institute, 2017; World Economic Outlook, October, 2018). High levels of government debt have set the stage for pitched battles over spending priorities well into the future. Public debt across all emerging economies is more modest, at 46 percent of GDP on average compared with 105 percent in advanced economies.

As to corporate indebtedness, an extended period of historically low interest rates has enabled companies around the world to take on cheap debt. Global nonfinancial corporate debt, including bonds and loans, has more than doubled over the past decade to hit US$66 trillion in mid-2017. This nearly matches the increase in government debt over the same period. In a departure from the past, two-thirds of the growth in corporate debt has come from developing countries. This poses a potential risk, particularly when that debt is in foreign currencies (International Monetary Fund, April, 2019). The growth of corporate debt in developing countries poses a risk, particularly as interest rates rise and when that debt is denominated in foreign currencies. If the local currency depreciates, companies might be caught in a vicious cycle that makes repaying or refinancing their debt difficult. Over the next five years, a record amount of corporate bonds worldwide will come due, and annual refinancing needs will hit US$1.6 trillion to US$2.1 trillion (McKinsey Global Institute, June 2018). Given that interest rates are rising and some borrowers already have shaky finances, it is reasonable to expect probability of price shocks in the years ahead.

Unsustainable household debt in advanced economies was at the core of the 2008 financial crisis. It also made the subsequent recession deeper, since households were forced to reduce consumption to pay down debt. Ben S. Bernanke pointed to the "global savings glut" generated by China and other countries with large current account surpluses as a factor driving interest rates lower and fueling the real-estate bubble (Bernanke, 2005). Because much of this capital surplus was invested in US Treasuries and other government bonds, it put downward pressure on interest rates. This led to portfolio reallocation and,

Figure 12. Global debt has continued to swell since the crises but has remained stable relative to world GDP since 2014

Note: Total debt outstanding in US$ trillion, constant H1 2017 exchange rate, includes household, nonfinancial corporate, and government debt; excludes debt of the financial sector. Estimated bottom up using data for 43 countries from Bank for International Settlements (BIS) and data for eight countries from McKinsey's Country Debt Database.
Figures may not sum to 100% because of rounding.
Source: Bank for International Settlements (BIS); McKinsey Country Debt Database; McKinsey Global Institute (2018).

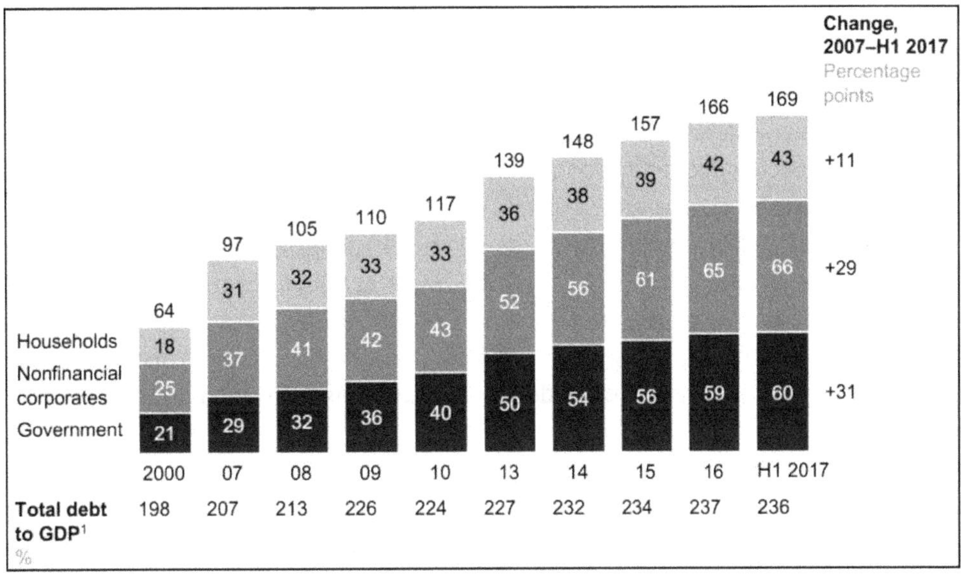

ultimately, a credit bubble. Today, this pressure has subsided—and with it, the risk that countries will be hit with shock if foreign capital suddenly pulls out.

The above is a possible scenario for creating conditions for a price shock in the global financial debt market. A necessary and sufficient condition for a shocks' break of structural relationships will be the threat of illiquidity in one of the segments of this market and the multiplication of distrust of sellers and buyers of financial instruments. And an objective condition for the realization of price shocks can be marginal levels of material insecurity of market transactions for the sales of debts in the global financial market.

The world is full of other unknowns. High-speed trading by algorithms can cause "flash shocks." Over the past decade, investors have poured almost US$3 trillion into passive exchange-traded products. But their outsized popularity might create volatility and make capital markets less efficient, as there are fewer investors examining the fundamentals of companies and industries. Crypto-currencies are growing in popularity, reaching bubble-like conditions in the case of Bit-coin, and their implications for monetary policy and financial stability is unclear. And looming over everything are heightened geopolitical tensions, with potential flash points now spanning the globe and nationalist movements questioning institutions, long-standing relationships, and the concept of free trade (International Monetary Fund, April 2019). All the above confirms the hypothesis of H.P. Minsky (2008) on the immanent instability of a market economy, predetermined by the state of its financial segments, which in every moment create the conditions for the shocks' break of system's integrities structure (Chapter 5.3).

The global economy is becoming more and more integrated, facilitating the spread of shocks, crises, recessions, uncertainty, and risks. The worldwide economic system is undergoing a series of transformations that subject the future to considerable uncertainty, economic and financial shocks, and unpredictability. Shocks affect the economic system, breaking its structural relationships that arise as a result of the interaction of dialectic pairs' of participants - sellers and buyers. The market exchange resolves the dialectical contradiction of economic entities by realizing the desire of one participant to sell the utility (any tradable asset), and of the other one - to buy it. As such, the exchange, mediated with money (or its modern substitutes), forms the integrity of the economic system, ensuring the smooth transformation of goods created in the society into money and vice versa.

So, complex economic systems with the quality of integrity have an inherent self-propelling mechanism. If self-movement occurs due to the complication of the structural organization of the system in the process of forming the base level represented by real markets and building vertical levels above them from the money and financial product markets, then it is about self-organization. The self-organizing system is complicated due to the generation of new structural levels at which reversible processes mediated by dialectical pairs in the exchange are realized. Such self-organization of systemic wholes is governed by the dialectical laws of the unity and struggle of opposites and the transition of quantitative changes into qualitative ones, into which shocks are embedded as a mechanism for mediating the "turning points" in the laws' action.

The price shock in the US market for unsecured mortgage loans in 2007 was also aimed at discarding structural ties that destroy the stability of the market structure. However, the subsequent global financial crisis of 2008-2009 forced to pay attention to its depth and duration of the post-shock economic recovery. Such consequences, together with the damping rates of economic growth, can be interpreted only in the context of the exhaustion, primarily by the developed countries of the world, of the potential for self-organization through the complication of the structures of their economic systems. Consequently, systemic integrity approaches the limit in self-movement, when its mechanism must radically change due to irreversible processes and the mechanism of self-development of dynamic systems (Chapter 4). And the shock of COVID-19 confirmed those findings of the authors.

CONCLUSION

The problems considered above are subordinated to the goal of deepening the understanding of the process component (along with the objects' and the subjects' ones) of the self-organization mechanism of the systemic integrity in the economy. This aspect of the study made it possible to prove the validity of the hypothesis expressed by the authors about the embeddedness of shocks in the internal mechanism of self-organization of economic systems. Allocation of exchange as their main structure-forming characteristic made it possible to single out dialectical pairs and structural interactions mediating them, the complication of which predetermines the mechanism of self-organization of systems in statics. Thus, the interconnections of participants in economic systems that have arisen as a result of the integration of specialized types of activity are intended to become structural ones. As a result the economy acquires the quality of systemic integrity and its own mechanism of self-structuring or self-organization. In other words, with the emergence of a structure, the economic system becomes self-organizing, i.e. capable of self-movement due to the complication of its structure (structural connections). Moreover, the presence of its own mechanism of system self-movement indicates that it does not need external factors to initiate its changes. Moreover, the specificity of the self-organization mechanism of the economic system is associated with structural interactions within the framework of dialectical pairs.

Historically, as monetary forms of settlements for transactions with real goods and services expanded the horizontal level of structural interactions between participants of dialectical pairs emerged. At the horizontal level, these structural relationships are determined by cause-and-effect relationships, which are concentrated within a dialectical pair. Their complication is regulated by the dialectical law of the unity and struggle of opposites. As for shocks, they mediate the action of this law at its turning point from the dominance of the unity of interests of the participants of dialectical pairs to the dominance of their opposites. As a result, the shock eliminates the non-working structural ties, destroying them, and the subsequent crisis generates new structural ties instead of destroyed ones or at restoring old ones that are still quite effective in terms of strengthening the integrity of the system. This happens if the mechanisms of positive and negative selection of economic activities have not previously rejected non-working structural connections that violate the integrity of the system.

Further change in the mechanism of self-organization of the economic system occurs due to the formation of vertical structural links based on the causal relationships of dialectical pairs. In this case the system self-organization is governed by the law of the transition of quantitative changes into qualitative ones. And again, shocks mediate this law at its margin, when quantitative changes accumulate, and the new quality of the structure cannot be realized, since the mechanism of negative selection has not worked. Shocks instantly discard structural ties that threaten the integrity of the economic system. Thus, the mechanism of self-organization of static economic systems is based on direct and feedback links of dialectical pairs, reversible processes of their complication, and predetermined by the structuring of internal interactions of dialectical pairs and by the action of two dialectical laws of unity and struggle of opposites and of the transition of quantitative changes into qualitative ones. All this deepens the authors' proofs of the hypothesis that shocks are embedded into the mechanism of self-organization of the economic system due to their mediation of the turning points in the two above mentioned dialectical laws' action. So the shock ruptures the structural ties only if the mechanisms of positive and negative selection have not previously rejected them dealing with the objects' component of systemic integrity.

The proof of the validity of the authors' reasoning is the consideration of the example of the shock of 2007 and the global financial crisis of 2008-2009. The epicenter of the global financial crisis was really the housing market. Households were borrowing more than they could afford. And it started the process of fueling housing-price increases. These houses are worth a lot, so they have an asset. But the problem started when housing prices stopped growing and instead started declining. And suddenly a lot of households found that they had a lot of debt.

But what made the 2008 financial crisis so globally devastating was that there were a lot of complex, opaque derivative securities that had been built on top of these underlying mortgage assets. So the subprime mortgage market in the US was pretty small. It was not more than maybe 10 percent of all US mortgages. Yet banks had taken these mortgages, pulled them together, and created something called asset-backed securities. Then they took those and pooled them together again. And so they built trillions and trillions of dollars of financial instruments whose value was riding on those mortgages being repaid. When a few households started defaulting on mortgages, the pain went far beyond those households and the banks that originated them to all these investors around the world.

Moreover, it arose as a result of the material insecurity of the structured asset offered by the seller, as well as due to the material insecurity of the loans that provided cash to their buyers. In this situation, the real separation of market prices from their base value in this market was mediated by the mutual exchange of unsecured tangible assets. Thus, the Ponzi-relations (according to H. Minsky, 2008) have developed for both participants of the dialectical pairs in exchange in the financial markets. But as soon as the confidence of the participants (sellers and buyers) of the market exchange was replaced by mutual distrust, a shock break became inevitable. This is understandable, since the principal risk management strategy in such transactions is to trade rapidly out of a loss-making position. As soon as there are signs of illiquid market, the number of sales increases, which means the beginning of the end. So the shock of 2007 testified that the static economy, as exemplified by the developed countries of the world, exhausted its potential for self-organization (i.e., self-movement because of complication of structural ties) and conditions began to ripen for systems to jump to the stage of self-development. That finding was fully confirmed by the shock caused by the COVID-19 pandemic in 2020.

REFERENCES

Arthur, W. B. (1999). Complexity and the economy. *Science*, *284*, 107-109.

Arthur, W. B. (2013). *Complexity economics: a different framework for economic thought.* Santa Fe Institute Working Paper: 2013-04-012.

Arthur, W. B. (2014). *Complexity Economics*. Oxford University Press.

Beneš, J., Ötker-Robe, İ., & Vávra, D. (2009). *Modeling with macro-financial linkages: credit and policy shocks in emerging markets.* IMF Working Paper, WP/09/123.

Bernanke, B. S. (1983) Nonmonetary effects of the financial crises in the propagation of the Great Depression. *American Economic Review*, *73*(3).

Bernanke, B. S. (2005). *The global savings glue and the US current account deficit.* Remarks at the Sandridge Lecture, Virginia Association of Economists.

Bernanke, B. S. (2008, Oct. 1). Article. *New York Times*.

Bogdanov, A. A. (1934). Tectology or General Organizational Science. Academic Press.

Bootle, R. (2009). *The Trouble with Markets: Saving Capitalism from Itself.* Nicholas Brealey Publishing.

Braudel, F. (1981). *Civilization & Capitalism: 15th–18th Century. The Structure of Everyday Life: The Limits of the Possible*. William Collins Sons & Co Ltd.

Cerra, V. (2018). The global financial crises: 10 years on, why many still feel the pain. IMF Research Perspectives, 19(1).

Cerra, V., & Saxena, S. C. (2017). *Booms, crises, and recoveries: a new paradigm of the business cycle and its policy implications.* IMF Working Paper, WP/17/250.

Chechulin, V. L. (2012). *Set Theory with Self-affiliation (foundation and some applications)* (2nd ed.). Perm State University.

Dodd, Randall. (2007). Subprime: tentacles of a crisis, *Finance & Development*, *44*, 15–19.

Forbes, K. J. (2001). *Are trade linkages important determinants of country vulnerability to crises?* NBER Working Papers. 8194. National Bureau of Economic Research, Inc.

HatziusJ.HooperP.MishkinF.SchoenholtzK. L.WatsonM. W. (2010). *Financial conditions indexes: a fresh look after the financial crisis.* NBER Working Paper Series, 16150. Retrieved from: https://www.nber.org/papers/w16150

Hegel, G. W. F. (1892). The science of logics. In The Logic of Hegel (2nd ed.). Oxford University Press.

IMF. (2009). *Staff Team from the Fiscal Affairs Department of IMF.* International Monetary Fund.

IMF. (2017). Global Financial Stability Report: Is Growth at Risk? Washington, DC: International Monetary Fund.

International Monetary Fund. (2008). *Global Financial Stability Report: Containing Systemic Risks and Restoring Financial Soundness.* Washington, DC: IMF.

International Monetary Fund. (2019). *Global Financial Stability Report: Vulnerabilities in a Maturing Credit Cycle.* Washington, DC: IMF.

Kaminsky, G., & Reinhart, C. (1999). The twin crises: The causes of banking and balance-of-payments problems. *American Economic Review, 89*(3).

Kant, I. (1781). *Critic der Reinen Vernunft.* Verlegts Johann Friedrich Hartknoch.

Kostyuk, V. N. (2014). Unbalanced behavior of financial markets. Proceedings of Russian Academy of Sciences Institute of Systems Analysis, 64(1), 36-44.

Laura, K. (2008). Crises of confidence…and a lot more. Finance & Development, 45(2), 9-13.

Marx, K. (1995). *Capital: A New Abridgement.* Oxford University Press.

Marx, K., & Engels, F. (1955-1974). *Coll. Cit.* (2nd ed.). Moscow: Political Literature Publishing House.

McKinsey Global Institute. (2017). *The New Dynamics of Financial Globalization.* McKinsey Global Institute.

McKinsey Global Institute. (2018). *Rising corporate debt: peril or promise*? Discussion Paper. McKinsey & Company.

Menzie & Forbes. (2002). A decomposition of global linkages in financial markets. In *Global Linkages Preconference.* International Monetary Fund.

Minsky, H. P. (1992). Profits, deficits and instability: A policy discussion. In D. B. Paradimitriou (Ed.), *Profits, Deficits and Instability.* Macmillan. doi:10.1007/978-1-349-11786-4_2

Minsky, H. P. (2008). *Stabilizing an Unstable Economy.* McGraw-Hill.

Mirimanoff, D. (1917). Les antinomies de Russel et de Burali-Forti et le probleme fundamental de la théorie des ensembles. *L'Enseygnement Mathematiques, 19*, 37–52.

Mises, L. H. E. v. (1998). *Human Action: A Treatise on Economics.* Yale University Press.

O'Sullivan, P., Allington, N. F. B., & Esposito, M. (Eds.). (2015). *The Philosophy, Politics and Economics of Finance in the 21st Century. From Hubris to Disgrace* (1st ed.). University of Cambridge. doi:10.4324/9780203797723

Pedroni, P. (1999). Critical values for cointegration tests in heterogeneous panels with multiple regressors. *Oxford Bulletin of Economics and Statistics, 61*(4, supp.), 653–670. doi:10.1111/1468-0084.61.s1.14

Perez, C. (2009). The double bubble at the turn of the century: technological roots and structural implications. *Cambridge Journal of Economics, 33*(4), 779–805.

Pilipenko, A., & Pilipenko, Z. (2018). Shocks in global economy: Impulse model of macroeconomic cycle. In B.S. Sergi, F. Fidanoski, M. Zioło, & V. Naumovski (Eds.), Regaining Global Stability After the Financial Crisis. IGI Global.

Pilipenko, Z. (2020). Shocks' theory: financial mechanism of economic systems' destabilization. In Social, Economic, and Environmental Impacts Between Sustainable Financial Systems and Financial Markets. IGI Global.

Pilipenko, Z. (2021). COVID-19 pandemic shock: success of business in a human-centric socio-economic system. In Z. Magdalena (Ed.), *Adapting and Mitigating Environmental, Social, and Governance Risk in Business*. IGI Global. doi:10.4018/978-1-7998-6788-3.ch008

Rajan, R. G. (2010). *Fault Lines: How Hidden Fractures Still Threaten the World Economy*. Princeton University Press.

Randall, D., & Mills, P. (2008). Outbreak: U.S. subprime contagion. Finance & Development, 45(2), 14-18.

Reinhart, C. M., & Rogoff, K. S. (2009). *This Time is Different. Eight Centuries of Financial Folly*. Princeton University Press.

Sahay, R., Cihak, M., N'Diaye, P., Barajas, A., Bi, R., Ayala, D., Gao, Y., Kyobe, A., Nguyen, L., Saborowski, C., Svirydzenka, K., & Yousefi, S. R. (2015). *Rethinking financial deepening: stability and growth in emerging markets*. IMF Staff Discussion Note, SDN/15/08.

SantomeroA. (1996). The Regulatory and Public Policy Agenda for Effective Intermediation in Post Socialist Economies. https://ssrn.com/abstract=7913

Schelling, F. W. J. v. (1993). *System of Transcendental Idealism*. University of Virginia Press.

Schinasi, G. J. (2006). *Safeguarding Financial Stability: Theory and Practice*. IMF.

Schularick, M., & Taylor, A. (2012). Credit booms gone bust: monetary policy, leverage cycles, and financial crises, 1870–2008. *American Economic Review, 102*.

Schumpeter, J. A. (1949). The Theory of Economic Development: An Inquiry into Profits, Capital, Credit, Interest, and the Business Cycle. Harvard University Press.

Sergi, B. S., Fidanoski, F., Zioło, M., & Naumovski, V. (Eds.). (2018). Regaining Global Stability After the Financial Crisis. IGI Global. doi:10.4018/978-1-5225-4026-7

Shiller, R. (2004). *Irrational Exuberance* (2nd ed.). Princeton University Press.

Smith, A. (1776). *The Nature and Causes of the Wealth of Nations*. W. Strahan and T. Cadell. The Federalist Papers Project. Retrieved from: www.thefederalistpapers.org

Sornette, D. (2003). *Why Stock Markets Crash: Critical Events in Complex Financial Systems*. Princeton University Press.

Tabarraei, H. R., Rouabah, A., & Pierrard, O. (2019). *Sovereigns and financial intermediaries spillovers*. IMF Working Paper, WP/19/43.

Taleb, N. N. (2007). The Black Swan: The Impact of the Highly Improbable. New York: The Random House Publishing Group.

Taleb, N. N. (2012). *Antifragile: Things That Gain from Disorder (Incerto)*. The Random House Publishing Group.

World Economic Outlook. (2018). *Challenges to Steady Growth*. Washington, DC: IMF.

Zioło, M. (Ed.). (2019). *Social, Economic, and Environmental Impacts Between Sustainable Financial Systems and Financial Markets*. IGI Global.

Chapter 4
Shocks and Operation of the Law of Denial of Negation:
Dialectics of Self-Movement of the Economy in Statics and Dynamics

ABSTRACT

The long history of complication of static economy objectively leads it to exhaustion of self-organization potential and to the point of no return – a leap into dynamic state with self-development mechanism. In the new quality, the dynamic economy is regulated by the dialectical law of negation of negation with new functions of shocks in its operation. As for self-organizing systems, shocks are determined to destroy the structural links that weaken systemic integrity. In order, the static system could jump into a dynamic state, shocks realize the first negation, destroying the vertical hierarchy of structural links, and as for the second negation, shocks destroy basic structural level as well. The epochal task is associated with construction of new dynamic systemic integrity on the modern technological base by forming new structure since the previous structural hierarchy has been completely destroyed by shocks embedded into the dialectical law of double negation.

INTRODUCTION

The authors associate the deepening of ideas about the mechanisms of self-movement of systems created by man with the need to identify the main factors that predetermine the formation of the technological paradigm of material production and the design of structural links of the economic system on its basis. These aspects are of particular importance for understanding the processes of self-development in the economy. In fact, the technology and organizational capabilities of its implementation in various spheres of the economy (as well as other spheres of human life) realize the potential of scientific and technological progress. In this context, it is advisable to present all forms of organizing economic activity on a technological basis in connection with the implementation of their structural potential. Considering the category of "economy" as an example, it should be emphasized that each national economic system

DOI: 10.4018/978-1-7998-4309-2.ch004

implements it taking into account its own capabilities. That is why there is no any national economy similar to each other in terms of realizing the possibilities of new technologies and forms of its implementation in economic and other spheres of human activity. Consequently, having dealt with the theoretical model of the combination of the main factors of production on the dominant technological base at any given moment, it is possible, with a deep analysis of the specific features of each national economy, to answer the question of why the performance of the economy is higher in one country and lower in another. Moreover, in this analysis it is necessary to highlight two aspects related to (1) the technological paradigm (and the implementation of the potential inherent in it) and to (2) the mechanisms of organizing technological processes in connection with full implementation of the self-development potential. According to the further presentation of the content of the chapter, the authors put forward the following provisions, which will be further substantiated using dialectical logic.

First, the technological base is formed by the large-scale implementation of scientific and technical discoveries and technological innovations (especially in the field of power plants) in all production processes. On this basis, an organizational mechanism for constructing integration associations of differentiated economic activity is being implemented. In other words, first a new technological paradigm must be formed, and by this time the economic system must have generated dialectically complex elements that are capable of realizing the potential of the new technological revolution. At the same time, dialectically complex structures of the system (Chapter 9) are formed during a long process of self-organizing a static economy, accompanying its complex systemic changes associated with the organization of its both horizontal and vertical structural levels. And only with the maturation of a new technological paradigm (technological revolution) and the exhaustion of the potential for self-organization, shocks mediate the jump of a static system from the stage of self-organization to the stage of self-development (Chapters 6 and 8). Thus, without a new technological paradigm and without the formation of dialectically complex elementary structures in the process of self-organization of a static system, there cannot be a dynamic economy and a mechanism for its self-development (Chapter 11). The technological base for a dynamic economy is of fundamental importance, since it generates much larger-scale opportunities for the integration of differentiated types of economic activity, which is realized in a higher quality of economic effect. It should be especially noted that as a result of the action of the dialectical law of negation of negation, shocks destroy the structure of a static economy. Therefore, the new technological paradigm will always raise the question of the drivers of the structuring process for the new dynamic economy (Chapter 4.1). That is why the outcome of the self-organizing economy, associated with the maturation of dialectically complex elementary structures in a static system, plays such an important role. It is their mission that will include the formation of structural links of a dynamic system in the process of its self-development on the base of the technological revolution 4.0.

Second, under any circumstances, the self-development of a dynamic system must certainly be preceded by a stage of self-organization of a static economy on the previous technological base. Its potential must be performed in the process of static systems' complication, i.e. growth of quantitative changes due to internal organizational restructures in the process of forming, first, the horizontal level of structural links, and then – the vertical structural hierarchy. The exhaustion of the potential of a static economy is manifested in the form of a damping of economic growth rates on the existing technological foundation. But this happens gradually as the organizational capabilities are exhausted, which are predetermined by the complication of horizontal structural links and the structural hierarchy of levels-causes and levels-effects. A self-organizing system in its static state is regulated by the dialectical laws of unity and struggle of opposites and of the transition of quantitative changes into qualitative ones.

Such a destructive effect of shocks on economic systems is explained by the fact that they are embedded into the mechanism of their self-organization and mediate the action of dialectical laws at their turning point from the unity of interests of participants in dialectical pairs to their opposites, as well as from the accumulation of quantitative changes in the structure of the system to their implementation in qualitatively new forms of organization. Moreover, an external sign of the exhaustion of the potential for self-organization of economic systems is a slowdown in the growth of the economic effect after the shocks' outburst and post-crisis economic rebuilding as well as after the restoration of the structure that strengthens the integrity of the system.

As soon as the possibilities of self-organization of a static economy due to complicating its structure are exhausted, the self-movement of the system does not stop. Shocks are capable of not only destroying selectively those structural links that destroy the integrity of a static economy they are capable of completely destroying the structure of a static economy, realizing the law of denial of negation. In fact, in this case, shocks destroy both the structural levels-causes and structural levels-consequences of the self-organizing economy, thereby breaking the continuity of its self-movement in a static state. After the destruction of the structure, the system, as it were, passes the point of no return, finding itself at the beginning of the stage of its self-development, when there is present a completely new technological paradigm as well as the most complex dialectically organized elements. "Very little" remains to be done: these dialectically complex elements, which were formed in a static system in the process of its self-organization, should spread a new technological paradigm into all spheres of human activity and build new structural connections on its basis.

Having received a new structure, the system will complete the stage of self-development and organically move to a new ("already well-known") stage of its self-organization on a new technological base and with new drivers of all further complications. The self-development of the economic system itself begins with the introduction of a new technological paradigm into all spheres of society's life (including the technology itself and the economy). In fact, at the stage of self-development, the number of objects, subjects, processes and phenomena with their multivariate specialization grows as a result of their positive selection. It will be replaced by negative selection, which will generate dialectical pairs of objects, subjects, processes and phenomena on the new technological paradigm. Those connections that will turn into constantly repeating and stable ones will form the structure of the system (by the way, in any sphere of human activity) and generate its ability to self-organize. This is the general logics of the dialectics of complex systems created by man, which are capable of self-movement, changing its hypostases - from static to dynamic and so on ad infinitum.

The authors connect the turning point of such fundamental changes in economic (technological and social) systems with the shock of the COVID-19 pandemic and the uncertainty of the post-covid future, which is associated with the beginning of the stage of self-development of the economy (at least in the case of the developed countries of the world). It is no coincidence that many experts express the idea of an unconditional cardinal difference between the future reality and the current situation (De Smet, et al., 2021). Indeed, the state of the economy of developed countries and the rapid implementation by firms of the results of the 4th technological revolution during the COVID-19 pandemic indicate the presence of a new technological paradigm and of the exhaustion of the possibilities of self-organization of static economies. In this regard, it is logical to assume that the post-covid reality ("New Normal") is nothing more than the beginning of the transformation of a static economy into a dynamic one with a completely uncertain scenario of the initial phase of its self-development.

A number of new trends have appeared that predetermine the specifics of the period of self-development of the modern economy in terms of its near future. First, the formation of the energy component of the new technological base will be accompanied by the replacement of energy with a huge emission of CO2 into the atmosphere by green, waste-free energy. This is one of the fundamental characteristics of the new technological paradigm. It is her penetration into all spheres of human life that will provide its main component. Second, the defining characteristic of the technological revolution 4.0 will be the digitalization of all spheres of human life. It will determine the self-development of the economic system, and then the possibilities of using its potential through organizational tools. Third, the process of adaptation of all national socio-economic systems to the specifics of the stage of self-development will not be linear, it will be long, depending on many conditions, factors, circumstances, and so on of national and global character. Fourth, the most important aspect of the self-development of national economic systems, according to the authors, is the priority of reorganizing the interaction between the technological system, economy and society within the country. This problem is fundamental, since only recently has it begun to gain importance due to the societal crisis caused by the COVID-19 pandemic. In this regard, it will be necessary to understand that in the new conditions, the problems in the economy and technology in the context of the formation of a new technological base and self-development of systems have social roots. According to the authors, at the stage of self-development between systems there is an absolute dialectical relationship, which can be expressed as follows: what is the degree of integrity of society such are the rates of technical and economic progress. This is a completely new reality, which has been objectively ripening, perhaps, over the last century. Proof of this is the growing hostility of society towards such manifestations of its structural imbalance as a huge polarization of incomes of the population, corruption in state authorities, a significant scale of shadow business and, by the way, a crisis in the education system. However, theoretically, all these imbalances are still separate, unrelated, cells of the fundamental puzzle. The authors of the theory of shocks tried to organically link all the disparate parts together to solve the puzzle and to get an opportunity to approach the holy of holies of the mechanism of self-movement of all human-created systemic integrities.

Taking into account all of the above, the content of the chapter is structured as follows: first, the features of the progress of technology as a separate phenomenon (Chapter 4.1) are considered, then interrelationships of the mechanisms of self-organization and of self-development of the economy in statics and dynamics are analyzed (Chapter 4.2), and, finally, the factors of self-development of a dynamic economy in interaction with technology and society as a whole are substantiated (Chapter 4.3). The results obtained make it possible to substantiate the choice of the future reality that humanity should make out from two alternatives: either regression according to the type of "secular stagnation" within the framework of the former self-organization of a static economy, or progress and construction of a self-developing dynamic socio-economic system, which today is characterized by complete uncertainty.

4.1. The Role of the Technological Paradigm in the Mechanisms of Self-Organization and Self-Development of Economics: in Statics and in Dynamics

The new technological paradigm predetermines the point of "no return" separating the self-development of economic systems from their self-organization. In this regard, it is advisable to determine the patterns of complication of the technologies themselves. The beginning of these transformations lies in human labor as a way of interaction between the human and the nature. The creation of tools was subordinated to the goal of first facilitating, and then increasing the effectiveness of the labor activity. And this meant an increase in the degree of satisfaction of people's needs. Thus, technological progress has served, serves and will serve the desire of people to facilitate their work and make it more productive for the purpose of maximizing human utility (Mokyr, 2005).

Initially, the human himself opposed nature and interacted with it. But with the development of labor activity and the growth of its technological equipment, it was labor and technology that began to mediate the relationship between the man and the nature. It is no coincidence that philosophers interpret labor as the most important type of human social activity, which acts as its genetically starting point. In fact, human labor is a material process of exchange of matter, energy and information between a person and the natural environment. As a result, these relationships were divided into two components: (1) "Human – Labor (+ technology)" and (2) "Labor (+ technology) – Nature". The technological equipment of labor changed the quality of this interaction. While man was creating the most primitive tools of labor, he strove to adapt to natural conditions (Marx, 1995; Bogdanov, 1934). However, gradually, as its technological equipment grew, labor as a process of interaction between the man and the nature acquired structural qualities: (a) it became typical for a person, (в) it became a recurring phenomenon, (c) and it began to be distinguished by stability and stability. Thanks to these changes, the man has become increasingly persistent in adapting the conditions of nature to his needs. The fundamental reason for such "aggressive" behavior is the human desire to expand the sphere of his life (to settle the natural environment), aiming at maximizing his utility (meeting his needs).

This is due to the fact that in conditions of limited human energy (human resources, labor), the goal of maximizing utility can be achieved exclusively by increasing the productivity (efficiency) of human labor. According to S. Lem (1964, p. 66), "... a person must build between himself and the nature the whole chain of links, in which each subsequent link will be an amplifier of his capabilities more powerful than the previous". Technological support of human labor (economic) activity serves as the basis for the growth of its efficiency. This determines the subordination of progress in the field of technology and economics. The higher the rate of technological progress the more, all other things being equal, the effectiveness of human economic activity. Moreover, technological progress is interpreted in the context of the growing capabilities of humanity to achieve its goals.

Technological progress is realized in the process of complication of tools and means of labor, as well as technologies for organizing operations. At the first stage of technological evolution, the formation of new technologies was carried out purely empirically, by the method of numerous trial and error by obsessed experimenters who, as a rule, could not explain the nature and possibilities of using their engineering developments (Mokyr, 2005, 2009). In fact, until the 18th century, many outstanding inventions were made without a scientific basis to prove them: engineering was not supported by mechanics, iron production developed without metallurgy, agriculture without soil science, mining without geology, hydropower without hydraulics, dye production without organic chemistry, and medicine without microbiology and immunology. The second stage of technological progress is associated with the emergence and development of theoretical developments, which became the starting point for experimenters in the field of technology development. Theoretical knowledge as discoveries or progress in the material world is integrated into the technological process, during which the deliberately dead-end directions of experiments are cut off and a significant leap forward is provided because of time saving and the achievement of an effect in all spheres of human life. According to S. Lem (1964, p. 11), knowledge of a human brought him to the stage of exiting the empirical state of technology development in conditions when, in essence, the possibilities of technological progress predetermined exclusively by patience and perseverance, insights and glimpses of intuition of practitioners, had been exhausted. Moreover, theoretical knowledge, as a rule, significantly outstripped the technological developments of practical engineers. S. Lem (S. Lem, (1964), P. 115) noted that if the growth of the theory stopped, then the "reserves" already accumulated by it would be enough to further improve the technology for a century ahead. In the middle of the 19th century, the growth of technology on the globe was about 6% per year, but the needs of a significant part of humanity were not met. In the twentieth century, this gap deepened even more as the quality of technological progress changed. It follows that any slowdown in technological progress predetermines not just socioeconomic stagnation, but the beginning of regression. At the same time, this gigantic technological leap in the progress of the human community was accompanied by a build-up of huge problems, in which one should look for the origins of the current global economic slowdown, global geo-natural disasters, multiplying anti-social phenomena, etc.

The authors believe that the stages of technological progress are associated with the self-organization and with the self-development of technological systems. And all technological revolutions known in history are a change in the stages of self-organization and self-development of technological systems, implementing much more diverse options for the specialization of technological capabilities, their integration and combination. Self-development in this case is associated with a leap due to the emergence of a new technological paradigm, with breakthroughs in theory and in technological solutions of the problems set in the past. But after the stage of self-development, the stage of self-organization begins, associated with the multidimensional organizational use of the capabilities of the new technology until the potential of the existing technological paradigm is completely exhausted.

But since the technology was initially subordinated to the goal of maximizing the economic effect for the goals of mankind, the authors are interested in the relationship between changes in the technological paradigm itself and the forms of organizing technological solutions with the mechanisms of self-organization and self-development of economic systems. To this end, the authors set themselves the goal of identifying a component of technological breakthroughs proper in technological evolution as the implementation of discoveries in theoretical knowledge as well as a component of changes in the organizational forms of new technologies usage.

To highlight the organizational component of technological progress, the authors used the classification that was proposed by P. De Latil (1958) in the middle of the last century. He based it on the presence of effectors, which, from the point of view of the authors, it is advisable to associate with certain thresholds of complexity (organization) in the complication of technologies. The first effectors, according to P. De Latil (1958), were *determined* ones. These include highly specialized technologies, either simple tools of labor, or more complex devices, or tools that are directly related to the environment. Their main characteristic is predetermined by the fact that they do not mediate (implement) feedbacks (for example, an automatic fire alarm). In other words, the evolution of technology begins with the creation of unrelated accelerated specialized technological devices that directly interact with nature and do not have the ability to provide feedback.

The second stage of technological evolution is associated, according to P. De Latil (1958), with the emergence of *organized effectors*. It is about technological devices that can be built into technological chains. P. De Latil (1958) concretized them in technologies such as (1) automata with built-in determinants that predetermine their action (such as automatic regulators, for example, in steam engines), (2) automata with a variable purpose of action (programmable from the outside, for example, electronic machines), and (3) self-programming automata (systems capable of self-organization such as animals and humans). It is about the formation in technological devices of the ability to serve as an intermediary in direct and feedback connections in the technological chain.

P. De Latil (1958) associated the following organizational changes in technologies with the capability of technology to self-change to achieve a specific goal. Technological systems with such a quality become more complex in such a way that they acquire the ability to change their own organization like a living biological species in the process of natural evolution. It makes it possible to see the mechanism of self-organization as a set of interconnections of technological systems, in particular, with a person which is manifested in their stability, constant renewability, the ability to be generated by initiating a person to change relationships for a stable homeostatic state of technological systems. Technological systems of this quality are capable of transmitting direct and feedback links and perceive them along technological chains. As a result, there are mechanisms for ensuring a steady state of the entire technological base and restoring homeostasis in the relationship "Human – (Labor and Technology) – Human". In fact, it is about the formation of relationships (reversibility of relationships) in technological systems, which prove the formation of mechanisms of their self-organization at certain stages of organization of technological components. In other words, with their appearance, technologies will function on the basis of forward and backward connections that ensure a constant repetition of an unchanging cycle, a stationary state of the system, and the reversibility of processes and operations. So technologies in the process of their evolution acquire the ability to self-organize.

P. De Latil (1958) fantasized about the next stage of organizational changes in the process of complication of technological systems. He assumed their absolute limitlessness in the choice of not only methods of organization, but also of materials and raw materials for their own creation. Indeed, as the technology becomes more complex, links appear in it (stages, elements of labor tools, phenomena, etc.), organized according to the principle of interdependence. In this case, one exists only because the other coexists with it, interacts with it, i.e. one functions, conditioning the functioning of the other and vice versa. Why are not dialectical pairs? In other words, at a certain stage of the complication of technologies in their functioning will certainly appear probabilistic or deterministic regularity. The latter can be associated with the appearance of the property of self-organization or its individual signs in them. S. Lem (1964, p. 216) wrote about this: "If the parts of the future machine are formed according to a certain principle (organization), then a new meaning will appear in the system itself." Indeed, the essence of this statement reveals the content of the process of complication of any integrity. According to William Ross Ashby (1972), a simple machine, integrating into a technological system, begins to behave in such a way that its internal state, as well as interaction along the technological chain, unambiguously determine the subsequent state within the framework of the algorithm for increasing the complexity of structural links. In other words, a machine created by a man should be characterized by its internal and definite external state, and constantly reproducible interdependencies are the basis of the constancy, integrity of the formed technological system.

The infinite generation of elements and mechanisms of their organization in the interweaving of processes of differentiation and integration (as mechanisms that spontaneously organize the world, according to A.A. Bogdanov (1934) may be associated with the future of humanity itself, as well as technological progress in the interests of the human. It is a person who associates with technology his goal of maximizing utility both in the economy and in society. It is a human who, forming systems in technology, in the economy and society, establishes relationships with nature, adapting it to his needs. But it is precisely a man who is given to understand that limit as a violation of his homeostatic state in interaction with nature, which he must restore for his own good. And a person will do this with the help of technological systems created by him for these purposes, capable of mediating direct and feedback connections in technological chains. Only such dialectics of interrelationships between man, technology and nature makes it possible to interpret the phenomenon of self-movement of human society through its own self-organization and self-development as an irreversible process, infinite in time. In other words, breakthroughs in theoretical knowledge, their implementation in the complication of technological systems and the emergence on this basis of their newest organizational complexes is only a means of complicating the systems created by man in the economy and society. If considering the organizational component of technological progress and the self-organization of the economic system, then it is the organizational capabilities that can bring both the technological system and the static economy to the exhaustion of their potential capabilities on the existing technological base. The exhausted technological base of a self-organizing economic system serves as an objective prerequisite for a shock discontinuity in the complication of self-organizing systems as an implementation of the law of negation of negation.

So, if we associate technological progress, in fact, like any process of self-movement of system integrity, with the process of complicating technologies, then it is realized either through the emergence of new elements, parts, complexes, or through an increase in the variety of forms of their organization through positive (specialization) and negative (integration) their selection. Moreover, new and newest specialized technologies can be formed on the basis of a combination (integration) of existing technologies. Joseph A. Schumpeter (1949, 1954) called such a combination the key driving force of the "development" process. At the same time, special attention should be paid to the interconnection of the "new combination of means of production" (technologies) and new energy sources that bring them into action. It is this complex of interacting technologies that predetermines (or potentially carries in itself) the emergence of a new technological paradigm that denies the old industrial base. The appearance of qualitatively new system components generates the latest technological capabilities for numerous ways of organizing them both in the technological base itself and in the economic system oriented towards it. Here it is already about irreversible processes that are associated with the complication of both technological systems and the economy, but already in the form of self-development. In fact, the sequence of discontinuity in the evolution of the previous self-organization is synchronized both at the level of technology and economics. And the self-development of the system begins and ends with the restructuring of the technological base and the introduction of a new technological paradigm, new technologies and ways of organizing interaction both in the technology itself and in the economy. This is the essence of the self-development of economic systems. It is in this sense that all known technological paradigms are named in honor of that element of its new structure, which could make it possible to unite other technological elements, parts, complexes, processes, etc. in a new way, giving impetus to the irreversible self-development of technology and the economy based on it.

Over the decades, technology has become more sophisticated, demonstrating a phenomenal ability to combine and separate its elements, parts, complexes, processes, and also generate (emerge) their new conglomerates or integrative complexes of specialized technologies (Perez, 2002; Arthur, 2009, 2013). It was in the course of their diverse organizational transformations that from time to time such technological structures arose, which were called steam, electrical, chemical, and digital. With certain methods of integration, they became generally available and, moreover, many times increased the potential of their multivariate forms of organization, not only in technology and in the economy, but in all spheres of human activity. Actually, such complex opportunities, introduced by a specific form of technology "packaging", are called not just technological, but industrial revolutions, capable of cascading not only the technological base, but the economy. In the view of W.B. Arthur (2009; 2013), new technologies give rise to new technologies: when computers appeared, they "demanded", or generated, a demand for new data storage technologies, computer languages, computing algorithms, semiconductor switches.

New technologies make possible the existence of the newest technologies: the emergence of vacuum tubes made possible, or "ensured" the existence of new technologies such as radio transmission and reception of signals, broadcast, relay circuits, the first computing operations and radars. And those new technologies, in turn, required and provided the following new technologies.

The first industrial revolution (1760-1840) was associated with the transition to machine production and its factory organization (Fig. 1).

Figure 1. Industrial revolutions and unprecedented rise in economic growth fueled by innovation
Source: Data of McKinsey and Company. Retrieved from: McKinsey.com

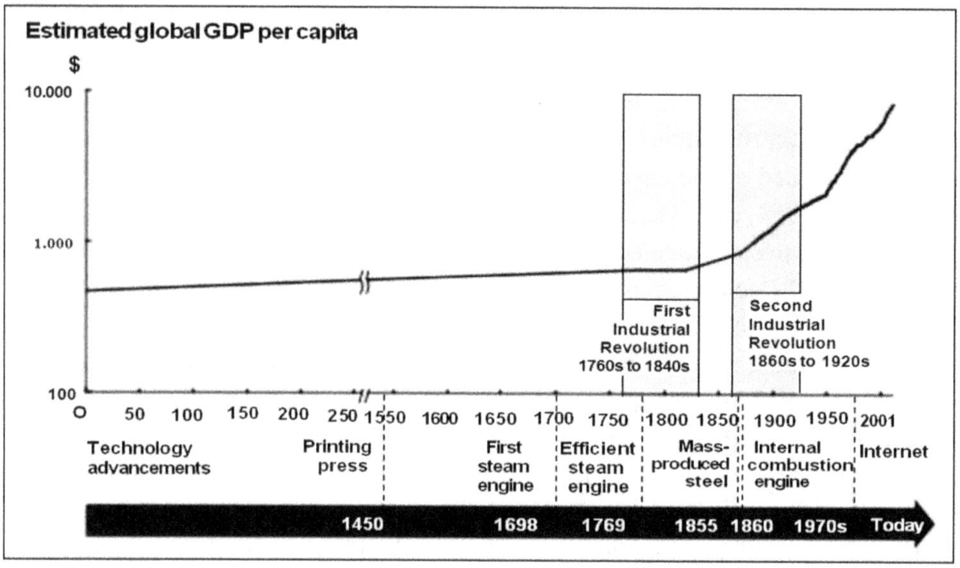

Its starting mechanism was the construction of railways and the invention of the steam engine, which contributed to the development of mechanical production (Schwab, 2016; Schwab, et al., 2020). The second revolution was implemented by mass production on the necessary technological base. The possibilities of its conveyor organization were realized thanks to the introduction of electricity. Usually its beginning is associated with the end of the 19th century, and the end with the beginning of the 20th century. The third technological revolution begins in the 1970s and is associated with the appearance of the first programmable logistics controller, and with further automation based on electronics and information technology.

At the turn of the 21st century, technological conditions began to form for the deployment of the fourth industrial revolution. They are associated with the possibility of forming cyber-physical systems that connect real objects with information processes or virtual objects through information networks and the Internet. The contours of the future technological paradigm are associated with such new elements and processes as autonomous robots, Big Data, augmented reality, additive manufacturing, cloud computing, cybersecurity, the Internet of things, integration systems, modeling, etc. K. Schwab (Schwab, 2016; Schwab, et al., 2020) believes that the future contours of the industrial revolution are generated by the modern possibilities of technological breakthroughs. The new technological paradigm connected with the industrial (technological) revolution 4.0 makes it possible to introduce the following: (1)

cyber-physical systems into production, develop cloud technologies that blur the line between physical, digital and biological spheres; (2) the emergence of diverse new areas of human activity due to cloud technologies, BIG Data, crowdsourcing, biotechnology, self-driving cars, the possibility of introducing 3D printing in medicine and other sectors of the economy; (3) Bitcoin cryptocurrencies and Blockchain technology, which will significantly transform the field of finance.

In principle, digital technologies based on hardware, software and networks are not new, but by 2020-2030 they will be more and more improved and their ability to integrate will increase. And their introduction into all spheres of human activity can push a radical transformation of national communities and even the entire global economy. Based on these circumstances, MIT professors Eric Brinyolfsson and Andrew McAfee called this period "the second machine age" (Brynjolfsson, et al., 2014). However, the fourth industrial revolution is not only about interconnected intelligent machines and systems. It realizes the unprecedented potential of generating further breakthroughs in a wide variety of areas of human activity: from decoding information recorded in human genes to nanotechnology, from renewable energy resources to quantum computing. The integration potential of these technologies in the context of their interaction between physical, digital and biological systems predetermines the fundamental characteristic of the fourth industrial revolution (technological revolution 4.0) in comparison with all previous technological (industrial) revolutions.

From the point of view of Klaus Schwab (2016), the fourth industrial (technological) revolution is distinguished by the following three features.

1. *Velocity*. Contrary to the previous industrial revolutions, this one is evolving at an exponential rather than linear pace. This is the result of the multifaceted, deeply interconnected world we live in and the fact that new technology begets newer and ever more capable technology.
2. *The breadth and depth* predetermined by the digital revolution and the endless variety of combinations of various technologies that cause unprecedented changes in paradigms in the economy, business, society, in each individual. According to Klaus Schwab (2016), the fourth industrial revolution is not only changing the "what" and the "how" of doing things but also "who" we are.
3. *The systems impact* of this revolution is manifested in the fact that it involves the transformation of entire systems, across (and within) countries, companies, industries and society as a whole.

According to M. Piore, and C. F. Sabel (1984), at certain points in history, one industrial paradigm begins to significantly limit the other, which determines the emergence of "industrial divides" or turning points. From the authors' point of view, it is about the limits of complexity that arise in the self-organization of the structure of a technological system as a manifestation of the regressiveness of the previous technological paradigm. It is the new technological paradigm that creates the objective conditions for interrupting the continuous process of self-organization of a static economy, which has also passed the optimum point, forming a vertical hierarchy of structural levels according to the principle of causation. So, with technological (industrial) revolutions, the stage of self-development of technological systems begins due to the emergence of new elements (parts, processes), scientific discoveries (breakthroughs) in technology, as well as unlimited possibilities of their organization in the context of integration, differentiation, combination and distribution in all areas human activity.

In fact, the "technological revolution" marks a change in the technological paradigm due to the exhaustion of its possibilities, which manifests itself in a steady slowdown in the growth rate of labor productivity, economic effect and company profits. So, in the late 2000s - early 2010s, i.e. on the eve of the technological revolution 4.0 in most developed countries, the potential for further productivity growth in the current economic and technological order turned out to be close to exhaustion. Productivity growth rates in developed countries began to decline significantly in the 1970s. Since 2011, the values of this indicator began to fluctuate within limits not exceeding 1% per year (this is more than half as much compared to the periods 1990-2000, 2000-2007 and 2007-2013) (Fig. 2, 3).

Figure 2. Dynamics of economic productivity growth rates in the G-7 countries, 1973-2013
Source: Data base of OECD and of the Russian Center for Strategic Research

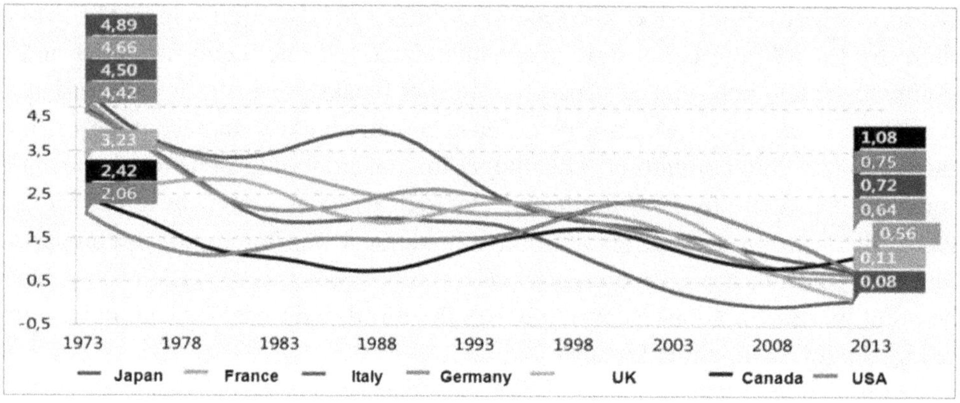

Figure 3. Annual growth rates of labor productivity in some developed countries (GDP per 1 hour employed in %, on average for the period)
Source: The future of productivity — preliminary version (2015). OECD. P. 83.

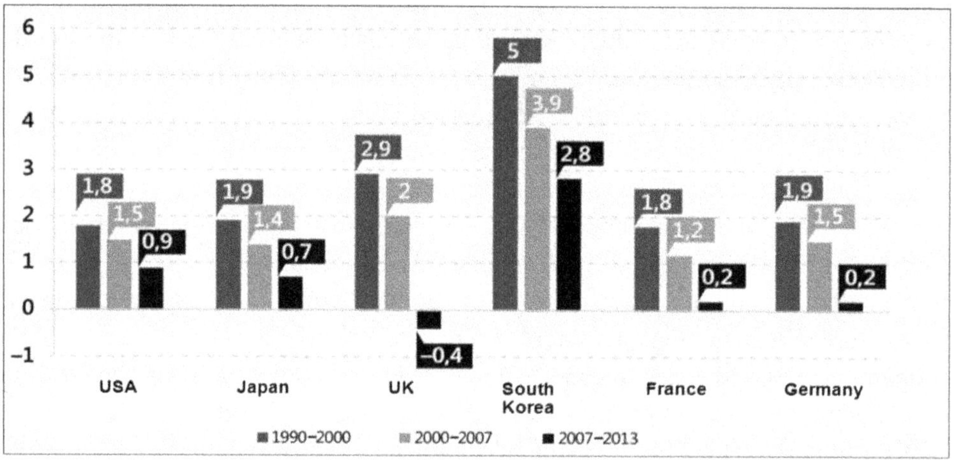

The growth of productivity in the manufacturing industry, which acts as a system customer and consumer of the products of innovative technological industries, has dropped especially significantly. In fact, it is about the fact that traditional production technologies in most sectors have approached the "ceiling" of productivity, beyond which the return on investment in their development drops sharply. In the United States, one can see that a fivefold increase in fixed capital investment over the period 1980-

2015 did not lead to a similar increase in productivity (Fig. 4). Productivity in industries that do not use advanced technology has increased by even less than 50%. Traditional technologies also began to approach the limits of productivity and efficiency in non-industrial sectors of the economy: agriculture, transport, energy, healthcare, education and the social sphere in general.

Figure 4. US industrial productivity, 1980-2015 (1980 = 100)
Source: Brookings Institution data

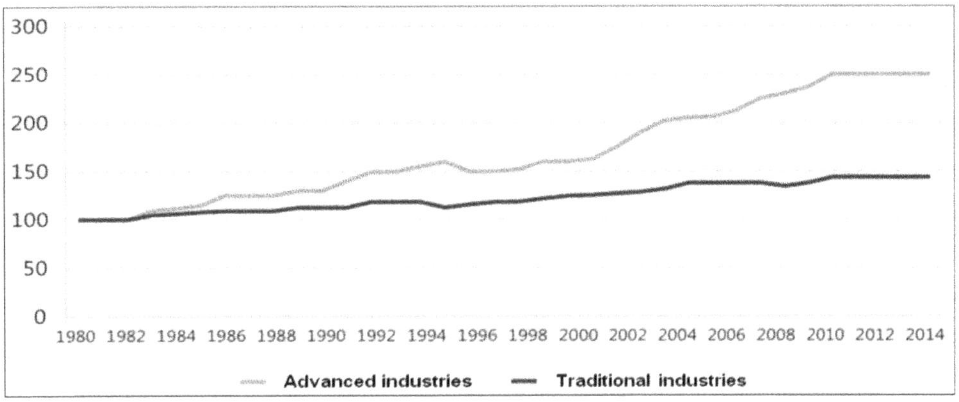

Thus, in the 2010s, it became obvious that the previous technological paradigm had exhausted its potentialities and the orientation towards it of industrial production even in the developed countries of the world became very costly for national communities. As for the economic effect from the introduction of such opportunities of the 4th technological revolution as "end-to-end" technological processes for all types of industries in the form of automation, robotization and intellectualization, it is impressive (Fig. 5 – 6).

Figure 5. The dependence of economic growth on the use of advanced production technologies (the contribution of technologies to the projected economic growth, %)
Source: Moskowitz, Sanford L. (2009). The Advanced Materials Revolution: Technology and Economic Growth in the Age of Globalization. Canada: John Wiley & Sons, Inc.

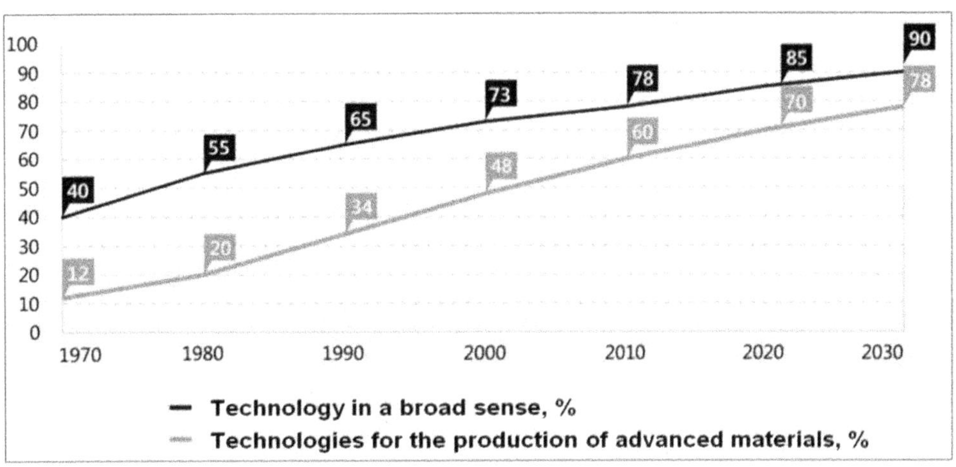

Figure 6. The projected economic impact of technology in 2025
Source: McKinsey & Company. (2019). What technologies will change life, business and the global economy? McKinsey.com

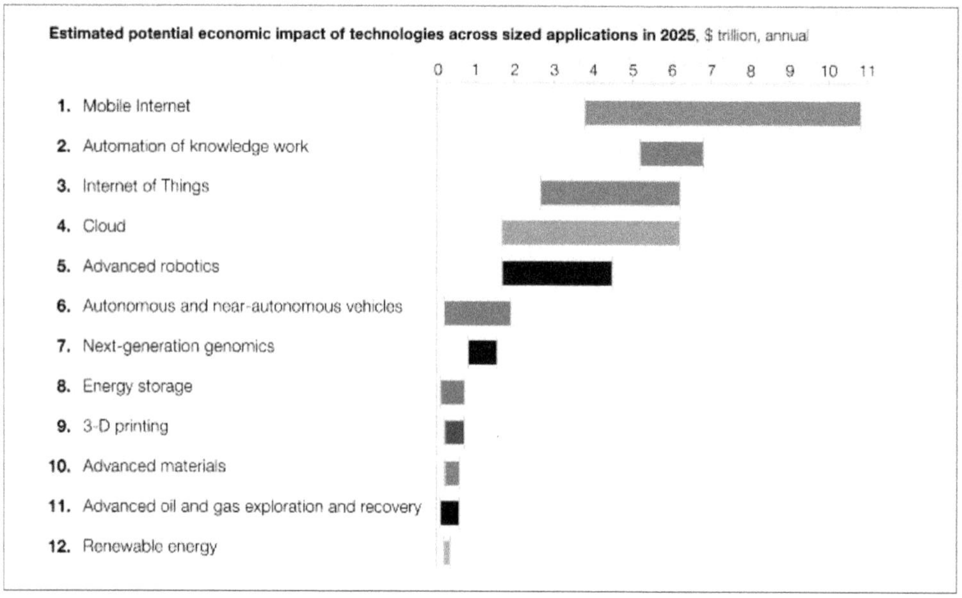

In July 2019, consultancy McKinsey released a report on technologies that could change lives, businesses and the global economy in the coming years, including mobile internet, self-driving cars and cutting-edge genomics. According to forecasts of its analysts, by 2025 the potential economic effect from the introduction of such technologies will be about $ 14-33 trillion [McKinsey, 2019]. From the point of view of C. Freeman and C. Perez (1988), the central role in obtaining such an effect is assigned to load-bearing products and industrial sectors, which contribute to the entire system and are universal technologies that increase efficiency. And the sustained recovery is not the result of technical innovation in one or more industries, but rather the diffusion of a new technical and economic paradigm from several leading sectors into the rest of the economy, and especially in the industries producing capital goods and related services.

Actually, the mechanism of multiplication of new technologies and the process of forming and improving various forms of their organization determines the macroeconomic effect that can be obtained. In other words, this effect can only be achieved if these arrays of technologies are adapted within the economy; encountered in industry, coupled with business processes that already exist and give rise to new lines of business, new incentives, new available processes and small corruptions in the form of small firms, few of which go further to become large firms. So it is about the formation of interaction between elements, processes and systems in technology and economics, which characterizes their dynamics at the stage of self-development. However, for this it is necessary to interrupt the continuity of the stage of self-organization and cross the point of "no return" in the direction of an indefinite future - the dynamics at the stage of self-development of all human-made systems.

According to W.B. Arthur (2009), a new technology in the form of technological complexes generates incessant waves of disturbance, causing new disturbances in technology and in human activities' spheres. As a result, the processes of self-organization of structures of system integrity in technology and the economy associated with it become more intensive and accelerated. This is due to the fact that the multiplication of technological innovations constantly at an accelerated pace upsets the equilibrium state of systems, and the self-organizing structure, which is responsible for their integrity and stability, is forced to form structural links in an accelerated mode in order to restore their equilibrium. At the same time, the peculiarity of the new technological revolution 4.0 is predetermined by the fact that the technological foundation introduced by it carries the potential capabilities of much more diverse forms of organization (in the form of complexes with different options for combining integration and disintegration). This is due to the fact that those dialectically interacting structural complexes that have developed under the previous technological paradigm at the stage of its self-organization are complex in themselves. And it is they that predetermine the possibility of successful self-development as a result of the "leap" of the economic system and the beginning of the formation of a new technological paradigm, brought about by the 4th technological revolution.

However, in order for the new paradigm to become the technological basis of the economy in the future, and all spheres of human activity to be ready to reorganize taking into account all the latest technological advances, it should be formed the necessary social economic conditions (Payor, et al., 1984). It is about the political choice of various economic actors (firms, trade unions, national governments), about the distribution of financial resources, about the level of education, etc. (Boyer, 1986). Thus, the triumph of the latest technological and industrial paradigm depends on the state of society, or rather its readiness to take advantage of the fantastic opportunities of the 4th technological revolution.

4.2. The Law of Denial of Negation and the Shock Break of Continuity of Static Economics' Self-Organization: the Stage of Self-Development

It should be emphasized that only a static economy can function on an unchanged technological base, a distinctive characteristic of which is an increase in the efficiency of economic activity by optimizing the forms of its organization due to mechanisms of positive and negative selection. At the same time, a self-organizing system strengthens its quality of integrity due to structural links that are formed at its horizontal and vertical levels. Dialectical pairs bring stability, constant repetition and stability to exchange in the static economic system. They also determine the main characteristics of a static economy, self-organizing due to direct and reverse structural links, their cyclical repetition, i.e. the reversibility of the processes and phenomena occurring in it. And these features apply to all spheres of human activity, including economics and technology in their static state.

As a result, a self-organizing static economy is only a manifestation of one of its essences. During the period of self-development, the economy becomes dynamic, characterized by the irreversibility of phenomena, processes, subjects, objects, elements and structural connections. Becoming self-developing, the system turns into non-equilibrium, unstable, capable of realizing in future any alternative that opens up in front of it in connection with the almost limitless potential of the new technological paradigm. The quality of self-organization, on the contrary, makes it possible for a static economic system to strengthen its integrity, stability, and equilibrium position by building up structural ties based on reversible processes, relationships, dependencies and phenomena. In this situation, the static economy changes, becoming more complex quantitatively and keeping its integrity quality unchanged on the formed technological base. In contrast, a dynamic economy is an economy in which shocks have destroyed the old structure, and the new structure has not yet formed. Its new quality will be different from that of a static system, since its technological base, elements in technology and economics, which will be structured as a result of positive and negative selection, will be qualitatively different. By the way, this is precisely why the future of self-development of the economy is characterized by complete uncertainty. This phenomenon became apparent due to the coronavirus pandemic in 2020.

The problems of the dialectic of a static and dynamic economy are significant. More than a century ago J.B. Clark (Clark, 2007) drew attention to those phenomena. He wrote that "the distinction between principles of economic statics and of economic dynamics was not clear". That idea was shared by J.A. Schumpeter (1949), who in his famous book "Theory of Economic Development" linked the development (self-development) of the economy only with those changes that were not implemented in the form of a cycle, of a systematic repetition of events and of their oscillatory movements around a certain center. These thoughts apply equally to any field of human activity, regardless of whether it is technology, economics, social relations, formal institutions or the structure of human values and the behavior of subjects in society. This conclusion, predetermined by the logic of the dialectical research method, turned out to be identical to the one, formulated by W.B. Arthur in 2013. From his view point, equilibrium economics is a special case of non-equilibrium and therefore complexity economics is economics done in a more general way. Such an economy perpetually invents itself, creating novel structures and possibilities for exploitation, and permanently being open to response (Arthur, 2013).

Thus, the most important characteristic of the state of equilibrium of the system is the constant cyclically repeated cause and effect relationships, when each partner in the dialectic pair both depends on and predetermines his relationship with the second participant in the exchange. Actually, changes in the economy in statics are described by static indicators such as the magnitude of annual GDP, its growth rate in percent, annual GDP per capita in current prices and in percent. In accordance with John Bates Clark (2007), the world from which change is excluded is unreal, but the static laws which can be most clearly discerned by mentally creating such a world are absolutely real. Thus, being static in its equilibrium state, the system, quantitatively changing, remains unchanged in its quality to a certain limit (Arnold, 1975, 1979; Bak, 1996; Thom, 1974). Further research allowed the authors to confirm the above conclusions of the great economists and to connect the self-development of economic systems with processes of qualitative changes in which the causes and effects of phenomena could not be interchanged. Thus, the foundation was formed for the philosophical justification of the laws of dialectics in economics, which manifest themselves in the process of complication of systems in various spheres of human activity, in the organic unity of their statics and dynamics. In this regard, the following words of John Bates Clark (2007) deserve attention. He wrote that the economic theory of this time succeeded in formulating principles of economic statics and a fragment or two of a science of economic dynamics. In this regard the distinction between the two divisions of the science is not clear.

The mechanism of self-evolvement is inherent to any to any systemic integrity having formed in the process of human activity. This is largely due to the fact that, in contrast to the summative system, in an organic system capable of self-movement, the internal connections of its elements prevail over their external connections. As these ties are strengthened, the system builds up its potential significantly exceeding the sum of the potentials of its constituent elements. The progress of such a system is associated with its complication, either due to the addition of additional elements, or due to additional structural relations. Moreover, these processes are taking place permanently. It is these systems that are capable of endless self-movement, thanks to their inherent endogenously built-in mechanisms of self-organization and self-development. Being static, systems are permanently changing due to the constant self-organization of their structural connections mediating the interaction of dialectical pairs under the influence of dialectical laws of unity and struggle of opposites and the transition of quantitative changes into qualitative ones.

As for the self-development of the system, which is associated with its swing into a qualitatively new technological paradigm, this metamorphosis occurs under the influence of the law of negation of negation, which begins to act as a result of the shock's destruction of both the vertical and horizontal structures of the static economy. The irreversibility of such a fundamental transformation of a static economy into a dynamic one implements the mechanism of self-development of the system, subject to the transition to the latest technological paradigm. The leading drivers of these transformations become dialectically complex elements, capable of generating structural interactions from the simplest to more and more complex. Moreover, if the self-organization of systems limits their organizational capabilities to the potential of the existing technological base, then a dynamic system at the beginning of its self-development chooses its future from a variety of vectors of possible progress, which are predetermined by a much more powerful technological paradigm in comparison with the past.

In modern conditions, the quality of the 4th technological revolution predetermines the mechanism of self-development of human-created systems, which depends on a person with the qualities of intellectual autonomousness (Pilipenko, et al., 2021) (Chapter 5). This is due to the fact that the number of elements (processes, stages, links, participants, etc.) is growing both in technology and in the economy, their combinations become more diverse in the universal processes of their positive and negative selection. And all these connections are mediated by people. Consequently, for each national economic system, the prospects for self-development will depend on the presence of a critical mass of intellectually autonomous persons. Only under this condition can the national system realize bizarre combinations of differentiation and integration of human activity in any of its spheres using a new technological paradigm. As a result, the more fully static economies take advantage of the capabilities of the old technological paradigm, the more leap forward (with all other conditions) it can make as a self-developing economy. Taking into account the specifics of the modern technological paradigm associated with a person in a self-developing economy, it should be emphasized that even if all national economies have the opportunity to take advantage of the results of the 4th technological revolution, the future they constructed on this new technological base will be completely different. Already at this stage of the study, a fundamental question can be raised about which factor will play a key role in transforming a static economy into a dynamic one and how to make the most positive use of the opportunities provided by the shock caused by the COVID-19 pandemic.

The authors' emphasis on the technological base when characterizing self-development, for example, of the economic system, is explained by their desire to emphasize the subordination of the dynamics of all systemic integrity in all spheres of human activity. At the same time, the fact of the priority and paramount importance of self-organization and self-development of systemic integrity in technology is indisputable. If the structural basis of reversible phenomena in technology has not exhausted its potential, then systems subordinate to it, for example, in the economy, in the institutional environment, etc., cannot count on the implementation of self-development. This is due to the fact that they have not yet exhausted the potential of structural complication in the process of self-organization. Only upon reaching the threshold of complexity by technological systems, all the systemic integrity in the economy and other spheres predetermined by them, can realize their own self-development. In this sense, both the double negation, and the irreversible "leap" of the system into an indefinite future with the mechanism of self-development, and the self-organization of its structure, as reversible changes at each of its stages, should be considered dialectically. In this sense, the dialectical idea of repetition of all the stages of systemic self-movement is an essential moment of any self-development as well as of any self-organization, due to action of dialectical laws. This position is associated with ideas of G.W.F. Hegel (1892) that matter is both divisible and continuous, and at the same time it is neither one nor the other. In the understanding of G.W.F. Hegel (1892), none of the definitions concerning the categories of continuity and discreteness, taken separately, is true, but only their unity is true. In any case the process of self-movement of economic systems in connection with self-organization and self-development should be interpreted as a dialectical process, which is the unity of discontinuous and continuous, relative rest and constant change, the transition of quantitative changes into qualitative ones and back through jumps or discontinuities (Fig. 7).

This dialectic concept of G.W.F. Hegel (1892) suggests that self-organization and self-development are characteristic of the objective world. These characteristics are inherent in all systemic integrities. With this approach, self-development should be understood as endless changes in the system as a whole, including certain stages, which are mediated by a mechanism inherent in the system itself. In other words, it is only about changes in the "left to itself" system integrity in the economy, society or technology and not about the impact of external impulses on it. The last conclusion refers to the mechanism of self-organization, which is realized due to the ability of the system to reproduce its structures and similar structural levels to ensure its integrity. The mechanism of self-development is more difficult to implement, since it involves the coordination of the stages of self-movement, at least of two systems - technological and economic, not to mention society. The formation of a new technological paradigm is predetermined by theoretical discoveries and the latest technological solutions based on them. But since the technological system is created by man and is subordinated, ultimately, to the achievement of his goals, it also goes through the stages of self-organization and self-development, implementing the action of dialectical laws. Moreover, the mechanisms built into them predetermine the self-movement of the system integrity in technology as well. But the technological system is subordinate to the economic system, initially acting as a means of achieving human economic goals (Chapter 5.1). If a person mediates the structural connections of both systems and largely predetermines the dialectically complex elements as necessary components of the self-developing systems then it should be concluded that (1) the technological paradigm of the economy becomes one of the fundamentals of its self-development; (2) dialectically complex elements preserved after the shock disruption of the self-organization of the economy belong to the second component of the mechanism of systemic self-development; and (3) together they predetermine the content of the endogenous mechanism of the system's self-development inherent in it. In this context, technology and all its changes should be interpreted as an internal component of the self-development mechanism of the economy.

However, in reality it is rather an idea, which over time has become apparent to many researchers. As a result over the last twenty-five years, a different approach to economics has been slowly birthing, and slowly growing as the science of complexity economics (Arthur, 2013). In these studies, complexity economics is treated as an economic system that is not necessarily in equilibrium. Moreover, in the endless process of its changes, the economy as a system of complexity is basically being in a state of disequilibrium. And then the statics (balance, equilibrium) of the system becomes a special case of its state in the process of its infinite changes. Nevertheless, any state of the system's integrity represents its dialectical unity of static and dynamic representations (states, forms).

The transition from the accumulation of quantitative changes and the formation of a new quality to the stage of double negation by the system has the main quality of its discrete nature, of disrupt continuity in the process of the system's self-organization. In this case, it is about the vector of changes of complex economics (complexity economics), or rather about choosing one of the many alternatives of the new direction of the system's self-development upon reaching the threshold of complexity. In this context, denial (double negation) is interpreted by G.W.F. Hegel (1892) as a moment of connection in the endless process of self-movement of the system. The new state of the economic system keeps everything positive from the old one, but becomes richer in content, and in this status it, in its turn, becomes the starting point for the further self-evolvement.

Fig. 7 shows a model of interaction of the above construction, which connects such dialectically interrelated categories as static economy and dynamic one, self-organization of a static economy and self-development of a dynamic economy. Moreover, at the stage of self-organization, the structural ties of the economy are governed by two dialectical laws, at the turning point of which a shock mechanism of destruction of structural ties can arise to strengthen the integrity of the system. When the system passes from the stage of self-organization to the stage of self-development, the shock mechanism realizes the action of the law of denial of negation. Moreover, the economy, being both static and dynamic, is subject to constant changes (complication). The integrity of a static system is ensured by its structure, represented by the structural connections of dialectical pairs at the horizontal and vertical levels.

In Fig. 7 the law of unity and struggle of opposites operates in a time interval $t_0 - t_1$, in which the structure at the horizontal level ensures the self-organization of an integral system. At this time stage, its specificity is predetermined by the priority importance of maintaining the consensus of interests of the subjects of the dialectical pair participating in the exchange. As shown in Fig. 7, the change in this consensus predetermines the relationship between the unity and struggle of opposites of the participants' interests in structural ties, which is represented by intersecting segments of dynamic sets. Theoretically, they range from 100% coincidence of interests of dialectically related participants to zero, since in the process of complicating the economic system, their unity is replaced by opposites. This is the subjective essence of structural changes aimed at ensuring systemic integrity. The shock rupture of all fragile structural ties that hinder its strengthening is the key to stabilizing the system. If the law of unity and struggle of opposites at the stage $t_0 - t_1$ of the action of the self-organization mechanism has exhausted its possibilities, it is replaced by the law of the transition of quantitative changes into qualitative ones. This is shown in Fig. 7, which illustrates the impact of this law on the self-organization mechanism at the stage $t_1 - t_2$.

So, as the complexity of the self-organizing economic system, structural ties, in which opposites of interests of the participants prevail and their quantitative diversity grows, cannot ensure its integrity. Under the influence of the law of transition of quantitative changes into qualitative ones, the horizontal structure of the system generates additional vertically located structural levels that allow maintaining the integrity of the entire system. Fig. 7 shows that the basic structural level represented by real markets are forced to generate vertical structural levels, first in the form of markets for money, and then financial markets. The separation of causes and effects between these levels under the influence of the law of transition of quantitative changes into qualitative ones, on the one hand, strengthens the integrity of the system, on the other hand, makes this process multi-step one, and the system itself becomes fragile.

Shocks realize their function of destroying ineffective structural ties at the limit of their complexity under the influence of the laws of unity and struggle of opposites and the transition from quantity to a new quality under the conditions of self-organization of the economic system. Moreover, the accelerated growth of the vertical structural hierarchy in the system indicates the "beginning of the end" of the process of self-organization itself. And this is explained by the fact that the more complex the vertical hierarchy of structural levels, the more fragile self-organizing systems become, the more likely the shock destruction of the "weakest structural link" is. Indeed, as soon as the higher structural level-consequence ceases to solve the problems of the lower level-cause, conditions are created for the inclusion of a shock mechanism of non-functioning structural links destruction and the subsequent crisis. In accordance with

Figure 7. General model of interaction of self-organization and of self-development mechanisms of economic systems: shocks in the mechanisms of implementation of dialectical laws
Source: the authors' development

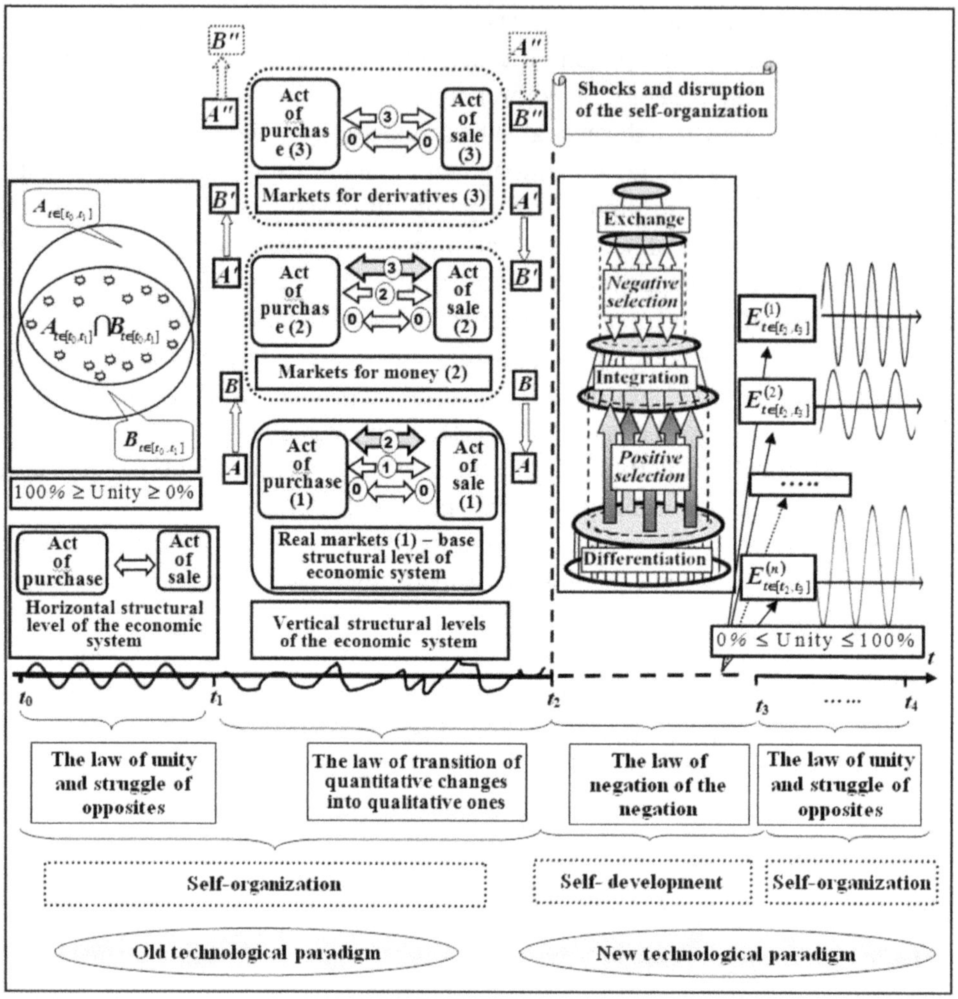

this logic, the authors hypothesized that shocks are embedded into the mechanisms mediating the action of all dialectical laws.

So, in the time interval $t_2 - t_3$ (Fig. 7) the process of self-organization of the system, its structure, designed to strengthen its integrity, and the operation of the laws of unity and struggle of opposites and of the transition of quantitative changes into qualitative ones begins to approach the exhaustion of the organizational possibilities of structural ties and the potential of the old technological paradigm. And it is not just about the economic system and its national and global forms of organization (although this too). The main thing is the lack of opportunities to reconcile the existing principles of structural changes and self-organization of the economic system, technological system and society (Chapters 5, 6). Fig. 7 presents the situation with a shock break in the continuity of the previous evolution of the system at the stage of its self-organization. The dashed line limits the time interval (which can be of different duration), within which the structure of the future system integrity will be formed on the newest technological paradigm. Moreover, in the time interval $t_2 - t_3$ the law of double negation is realized shock's destruction of structural levels-effects, and structural levels-causes (the second negation), as well as the basic level of structure represented by real markets (the first negation). And with the destruction of the structure of a self-organizing system, the action of the dialectical laws of unity and struggle of opposites and the transition of quantitative changes to qualitative ones ceases.

And it is this period that is associated with the self-development of the economy in its dynamic state. At the same time, the principles on which the integrity of new systems and the structures serving them will be built will differ in the specifics of their implementation. However, as for the sequence of forms of their implementation in the context of the sequence of stages of self-organization and self-development, the dialectics of interaction of the laws regulating them and the shock mechanisms built into them, everything remains unchanged. All this must be understood with a small amendment, which is fundamental: the efficiency of the economy, social consensus and the degree of implementation of technological progress during the period of self-development will depend on the adequacy of mankind's choice of the principles of coordinating intersystem interactions (between the economy, society and the technological foundation). In any case, this will be a step forward in the progressive self-movement of mankind, but its quantitative parameters will depend on many circumstances, which are conditionally summarized in three scenarios for the implementation of self-organization of system integrity ($E^{(1)}$, $E^{(2)}$,..., $E^{(n)}$) at its first stage - actions in the time frame $t_3 - t_4$.

All the above allows the authors to represent the self-movement of the system as a dialectical unity of such opposites as variability and immutability, as statics and dynamics, as self-organization and self-development. From the point of view of R. Bootle (2009, P. 88), it is paradoxical that the basic models of perfect markets are completely static, yet the very essence of the market economy in practice is change. The economic growth the market system produces creates change – and the market system is good at adapting to change that occurs from this or other sources. This idea was brilliantly expressed by J. Robinson (1980), that as soon as the researchers realized that the economy exists in time, and that history moves in one direction, from an irreversible past to an unknown future, the concept of equilibrium objectively has become necessary to be recognized as insolvent.

EMPIRICAL EVIDENCE

To prove the embeddedness of mechanisms of self-organization and self-development of the economic system into its structure, the conditionality of all processes of self-movement of static and dynamic economy, taking into account the priority of the subjects' component the authors built a dynamic model for reconciling the interests of the dialectical buyer-seller pair using the example of implementing the law of unity and struggle of opposites.

Let $N_1(t)$ be the number of participants in the dynamic set $A_{[t_0,\, t_1]}$, expressing the sphere of interests of the members of this set as buyers. Accordingly, $N_2(t)$ is the number of participants in the dynamic set $B_{[t_0,\, t_1]}$, expressing the corresponding sphere of opposing interests as sellers. Horizontal structural level of the economic system under the action of the law of unity and struggle of opposites reflects the process of self-organization in the direction of strengthening the integrity of the system. The intersection of dynamic sets $A_{t\in[t_0,t_1]} \cap B_{t\in[t_0,t_1]}$ corresponds to the unity of interests of the participants in the dialectical *buyer-seller* pair in the market of goods and services. In the simplest case, the intrigue of the law of unity and struggle of opposites is determined by the phenomenon of the mathematical Lotka–Volterra model (Lotka, 1920, 1925; Volterra, 1926, 1931).

In this semantic field, the following system of ordinary differential equations of the first order appears, solved with respect to the derivative (1)

$$\left.\begin{aligned}\frac{dN_1}{dt} &= \varepsilon_1 N_1 - \alpha_1 N_1 N_2 \\ \frac{dN_2}{dt} &= -\varepsilon_2 N_2 + \alpha_2 N_1 N_2\end{aligned}\right\}. \tag{1}$$

It should be noted that this model is aggregated, since it does not consider individual elements of dynamic sets $A_{[t_0,\, t_1]}$ and $B_{[t_0,\, t_1]}$ in the time interval $t\in[t_0, t_1]$. It only describes their combined behavior. Thus, in the first equation of system (1) the term $\varepsilon_1 N_1$ takes into account the growth of the sphere of interests of the participants in the set $A_{[t_0,\, t_1]}$. Here ε_1 is the positive growth rate of interests due to the appearance of new representatives of the set $A_{[t_0,\, t_1]}$. On the other hand, the term $-\alpha_1 N_1 N_2$ characterizes a decrease in their sphere of interests due to the growth of opposites that predetermine the behavior of the participants in the set $B_{[t_0,\, t_1]}$, for example, in connection with the search for another market for the sale of their goods and services. s for the dynamics of the interest of the participants in the set $B_{[t_0,\, t_1]}$, it decreases when the seller reorients to another market segment, where more profitable options for the sale of his goods appear. This process is described by the first term of the second equation $-\varepsilon_2 N_2$. Accordingly, an increase in interest can be associated with an increase in the mutual interest of the buyer and the seller, which takes into account the term $\alpha_2 N_1 N_2$.

In order to simplify the model, we will also assume that the coefficients in the system of equations (1) do not depend on which part of the dynamical sets $A_{[t_0,\, t_1]}$ and $B_{[t_0,\, t_1]}$ are going to take into account. In this case, one speaks of spatially homogeneous sets. Moreover, these coefficients are positive constants.

Further, since the authors are interested in the parity of interests of participants in dialectical pairs, it is necessary to investigate the equilibrium solution of the system of differential equations (1). In this case, the rates of change of the quantities $N_1(t)$ and $N_2(t)$ become zero. In other words, the derivatives on the left-hand sides of system (1) disappear, and we arrive at the system of algebraic equations (2)

$$\left.\begin{aligned}N_1\left(\varepsilon_1 - \alpha_1 N_2\right) = 0 \\ -N_2\left(\varepsilon_2 - \alpha_2 N_1\right) = 0\end{aligned}\right\}. \tag{2}$$

Obviously, system (2) has two groups of solutions.

The first group of solutions expresses the necessary and sufficient condition for the unity of interests of the dialectical ***buyer-seller*** pair

$$\left.\begin{aligned} N_2^0 &= \frac{\varepsilon_1}{\alpha_1} \\ N_1^0 &= \frac{\varepsilon_2}{\alpha_2} \end{aligned}\right\}. \tag{3}$$

In this case, the intersection of dynamic sets reaches the maximum value $A_{t\in[t_0,t_1]} \bigcap B_{t\in[t_0,t_1]} = max$ (i.e. *Unity* = 100%), which corresponds to the state of equilibrium. Of course, it is about the dynamic equilibrium of the intersection of dynamical sets. This means the presence of small fluctuations of interests among the participants of the dialectical pair. Taking into account small deviations from the equilibrium state, the system of solutions (3) should be rewritten as (4)

$$\left.\begin{aligned} N_1(t) &= \frac{\varepsilon_2}{\alpha_2} + n_1(t) \\ N_2(t) &= \frac{\varepsilon_1}{\alpha_1} + n_2(t) \end{aligned}\right\}, \tag{4}$$

where the variables $n_1(t)$ and $n_2(t)$ should be considered sufficiently small in comparison, respectively, with the variables $N_1(t)$ и $N_2(t)$. In other words, they are of the first order of smallness compared to $N_1(t)$ и $N_2(t)$. Note also that the rates of change of variables $n_1(t)$ и $n_2(t)$, in other words, their derivatives are respectively equal to the time derivatives of the variables $N_1(t)$ and $N_2(t)$.

Under these conditions, substitution of expressions (4) into the system of equations (1), after performing a number of transformations, leads to the system of equations (5)

$$\left.\begin{aligned} \frac{dn_1}{dt} &= -\varepsilon_2 \frac{\alpha_1}{\alpha_2} n_2 \\ \frac{dn_2}{dt} &= \varepsilon_1 \frac{\alpha_2}{\alpha_1} n_1 \end{aligned}\right\}. \tag{5}$$

Let's find out what information this dynamic system carries. To do this, we differentiate in time, for example, the first equation of system (5). In the resulting expression, we substitute the value of the first derivative of the variable n_2 from the second equation of the system. As a result, we get an equation that can be considered as a harmonic oscillator (6)

$$\frac{d^2 n_1}{dt^2} + \varepsilon_1 \varepsilon_2 n_1 = 0. \tag{6}$$

Indeed, since the coefficients ε_1 and ε_2 are positive, we can introduce the notation $\omega_0^2 = \varepsilon_1 \varepsilon_2$. As a result, we get the well-known equation of a harmonic (or linear) oscillator performing free oscillations (7)

$$\frac{d^2 n_1}{dt^2} + \omega_0^2 n_1 = 0, \tag{7}$$

where $\omega_0 = \frac{2\pi}{T}$ – cyclic natural frequency of a linear oscillator, and T – period of such fluctuations. Obviously the numerical value of ω_0 is determined by the ratio $\omega_0 = \sqrt{\varepsilon_1 \varepsilon_2}$.

Now it is easy to find the period T of harmonic oscillations in matching the mutual interests of the dialectical *buyer-seller* pair:

$$T = \frac{2\pi}{\omega_0} \Rightarrow T = \frac{2\pi}{\sqrt{\varepsilon_1 \varepsilon_2}} \tag{8}$$

Thus, the parity of interests of the buyer-seller system performs free harmonic oscillations near the equilibrium state, the period of which is inversely proportional to the square root of the product of the growth-loss factors of each component of the dialectical pair.

It is important to note that the obtained result (7) or (8) is methodologically very important. He objectively points out that the excitation of harmonic oscillations in the economic system does not need an external impulse, as it was commonly believed, starting from work of R. Frish (1933) and subsequent works. It is the endogenous factors that are primarily responsible for the formation of oscillators in economic, technological and social systems. Thus, it is shown how the first group of solutions of system (2) ensures the coordination (parity) of interests within the framework of the law of unity and struggle of opposites.

The second group of solutions to system (2), at first glance, seems to be quite trivial (9)

$$N_1=0; N_2=0. \tag{9}$$

However, this decision has deep methodological meaning. Namely, it testifies to that stage of the law of unity and struggle of opposites, when the intersection of dynamic sets is an empty set $A_{t\in[t_0,t_1]} \cap B_{t\in[t_0,t_1]} = \varnothing$ (i.e. *Unity* = 0%). In other words, there are no common interests, opposite interests prevail. But this means that the law of unity and struggle of opposites at the horizontal structural level of the economic system at the moment t_1 has exhausted itself. The law of the transition from quantity to quality comes into force.

It is advisable to provide a graphical illustration of the dynamic model (6) or (7). As is known, the general solution of the second-order linear differential equation (7) has the form (10)

$$n_1(t) = C_1 \cos(\omega t) + C_2 \sin(\omega t), \tag{10}$$

and the general solution of equation (6) can be represented as

$$n_1(t) = C_1 \cos\left(\sqrt{\varepsilon_1 \varepsilon_2} t\right) + C_2 \sin\left(\sqrt{\varepsilon_1 \varepsilon_2} t\right), \tag{11}$$

where C_1 and C_2 are arbitrary constants whose value is easy to calculate.

Let at the moment $t = 0$ the parity of interests of the buyer-seller system is in an equilibrium state, i.e. $n_1(0) = 0$. Hence it follows that $C_1 = 0$. On the other hand, the system goes through the equilibrium state with maximum speed, i.e. derivative of equality (11)

$$\frac{dn_1}{dt} = C_2\sqrt{\varepsilon_1\varepsilon_2}\,cos\left(\sqrt{\varepsilon_1\varepsilon_2}\,t\right) \tag{12}$$

at $t = 0$ has the greatest value. In order to simplify the calculation of the constant C_2 let's say that $\varepsilon_1 = \varepsilon_2 = 1$, and the value of the derivative is taken to be 0.25. Under these conditions $C_2 = 0.25$ is the vibration amplitude. Let us denote the vibration amplitude as C.

In Fig. 8 expressions (11) and (12) are presented as functions of dimensionless time, where the amplitude takes on the value $C = 0.25$

$$n_1\left(\frac{t}{T}\right) = C\,sin\left(2\pi\frac{t}{T}\right) \text{ and } \frac{dn_1}{dt} = C\,cos\left(2\pi\frac{t}{T}\right) \tag{13}$$

Fig. 8 clearly illustrates the properties of the system of equations (13). So, the displacement from the equilibrium position and the speed of the linear oscillator change according to the harmonic law. In this case, the speed is ahead of the phase displacement by one fourth of the oscillation period. To complete the picture, it is necessary to construct a phase trajectory determined by the equations (13). It is shown in Fig. 9 and, as is easy to see, is symmetric about the coordinate axes n_1 and $\frac{dn_1}{dt}$.

Note that the original system of dynamic equations (1), which is adequate to the Lotka – Volterra model, does not possess such a symmetry property for phase trajectories. So, the model representation of the role of the subjective component on the example of the implementation of the law of unity and struggle of opposites (Fig. 8-9) demonstrates the presence of an internally built-in mechanism of self-organization and of self-development, inherent in systemic integrity in both the economy and technology (society is no exception).

Figure 8. Harmonic fluctuations of the parity of interests of the buyer-seller and the rate of change of the parity of interests with amplitude **C** *= 0.25 for the case* $\varepsilon_1 = \varepsilon_2 = 1$ *and dimensionless time*
Source: the authors' development

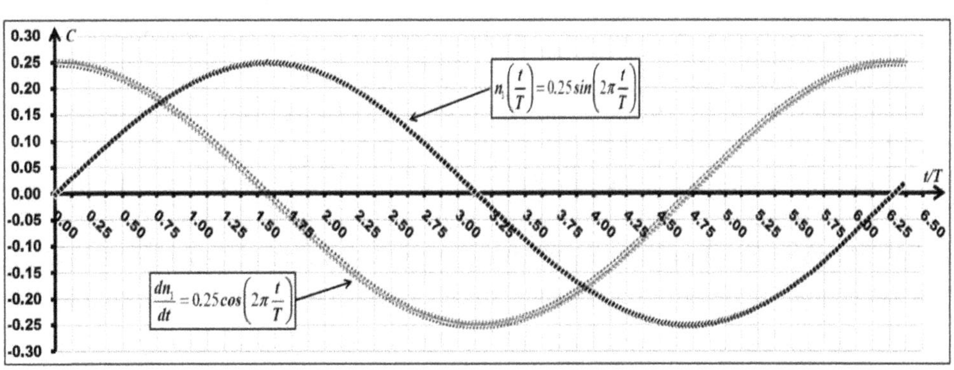

Figure 9. Phase trajectory (phase portrait) of the system of equations (13) on the plane $\left(n_1, \frac{dn_1}{dt}\right)$ *at* $\varepsilon_1 = \varepsilon_2 = 1$
Source:the authors' development

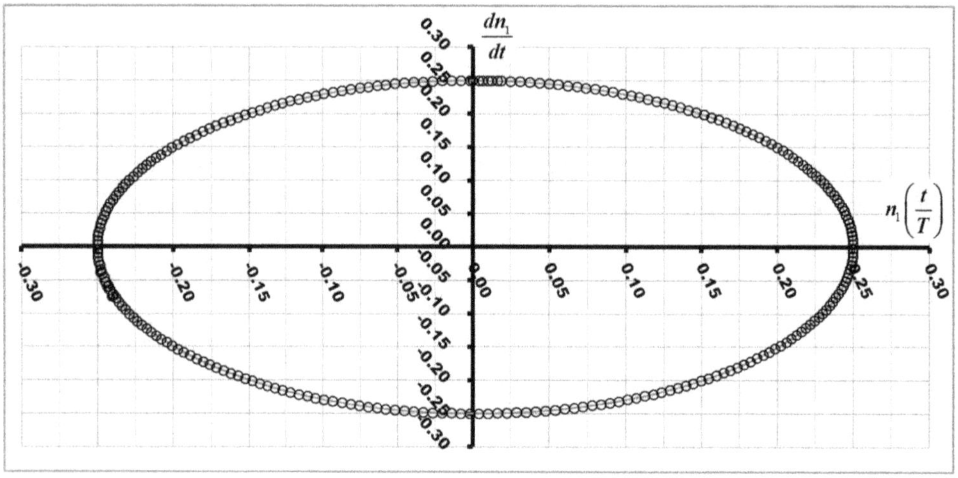

Self-movement of systemic integrities is largely predetermined by the interests (their coincidence or divergence) of the participants in structural ties both in the conditions of self-organization and at the stage of self-development. As shown above, the authors consider the mechanisms of self-organization and self-development as an internal source of excitation of harmonic oscillations in a specific segment of any market, which are transmitted through structural links to other market segments. This demonstrates the wave form of self-movement of economic integrities in the process of complicating the structure.

It should be noted that the mathematical model developed by the authors can be adequately applied to obtain similar assessments of unity and opposites, quantity and quality, convergence and divergence of interests of dialectically related objects, subjects, processes and phenomena in the case of coordinated interaction of technological, economic systems, as well as society, or differentiation and integration of types of human activity in the interaction of mechanisms of their positive and negative selection, etc.

4.3. Violation of the Societal Integrity: Obstacles to Technological Progress and Economic System's Self-Development

So, the process component of the mechanisms of self-organization and self-development of a dialectically complex system with the quality of integrity is presented above, and the embeddedness of shocks in its structure is proved. However, as for the mechanism of self-development of the economic system, it has certain features. First, it is realized as a result of the shock mediation of the law of negation of negation, as a result of which the self-organizing system's structural levels-causes and structural levels-consequences are destroyed. Second, the jump of a static system from the stage of self-organization to the stage of self-development into a new dynamic state should be preceded by the emergence of a new technological paradigm, which has a unique element composition and organizational capabilities of the latest technological solutions. Third, the mechanism of self-development is mediated by the actions of dialectically complex elements of the economic system that were formed at the stage of its previous self-organization. Moreover, this mechanism of self-development of the future systemic integrity is implemented in the process of mediation by complex structures in the form of leading national companies that have mechanisms for the formation of upwards and downwards causal relationships. Thanks to this mechanism of causation, companies are able to structure their new internal organization in accordance with the requirements of technological progress and the changed situation in the economy. And through the upwards causation mechanism, companies have the ability to structure the external environment of their functioning (chapters 9.1, 11.2, 11.3). In this case, we are talking about building new structural ties in accordance with the dynamic state of economic system. In other words, the self-development of the economic system is predetermined not so much by its internal organizational state, as by the consistency with the quantitative and qualitative parameters of the systemic integrities of technology and society.

One of the most important problems of the self-development of the economic system becomes understanding the main driver of all structural changes in technology, economy and society. In modern conditions, the role of such a driver can only be played by a subject as a participant of the formation of new organizational structures. It should be noted that in the case of self-organization of the economic system, the significance of the subjects' aspect faded into the background due to the predetermination of structural changes with the object component of structural ties. This subordination of the objects' and of subjects' principles in the structuring processes was especially evident at the basic horizontal level represented by real markets. Only as the vertical structural levels were built, the subordination of the objects' and subjects' components changed towards the priority of the latter. However, this fact remained outside the attention of the state and people making political decisions during the period of self-organization, which ultimately led to an underestimation of the role of social integrity for progress of technology and the economy. And meanwhile, replacement of money equivalents (or monetary substitutes) with a trust equivalent in transactions with financial assets along the vertical of the structural hierarchy actually objectified the role of the subjective factor, the importance of which increased already at the final stage of self-organization of economic systems. And in the conditions of self-development of the economic system, the subject of structural ties turns into the factor of its dynamics of paramount importance.

Actually, the most serious modern problem is connected with the subject as a driver in the processes of structuring the post-COVID-19 reality. To put into action all the upcoming epoch-making changes, a person must possess the qualities of an intellectually autonomous personality, capable of "assembling" a dynamic system from complex elements both in technology, in the economy, and in society (Chapters 5.2, 6.3, 8.3, 9.2, 10.2, 11.1). With this approach, both self-development and the subsequent self-organization of future technological, economic and social systems are predetermined by the central place of a person in all systemic transformations. This fact confirms the validity of the conclusion about the endogenous mechanisms of self-movement inherent in all the systems indicated above. And the central place of a person in mediating these mechanisms in the future poses the problem of reorientation to human-centricity in all organizational processes (instead of the currently dominant capital-centricity). If the introduction of a new technological paradigm into all systemic transformations becomes an integral condition for the self-development of the economic system, then it is logical to consider technology (technological progress, technological revolution) as an endogenous factor that predetermines this mechanism. Joel Mokyr (2005, 2009) does not question the importance of technology as a determinant of self-development of the dynamic economy.

A person as a driver of self-development processes of dynamic systems should be considered not just as human or intellectual capital, which is a factor of material production. It is necessary to take into account the fact that a person, in addition to the hypostasis of an economic agent, is an individual with his own desires and reluctances, positive and negative assessments that can significantly adjust his behavior not only in the economy, but also in society. If a person mediates the self-development of not only the economic system, but also in technologies and society, then the dialectical subordination of these processes largely depends on him as a human being with his own value ideas about what is good and what is bad. And in the current conditions of the formed dialectic of the interaction of all interconnected systems within the national framework, the value orientations of a person can play a decisive role in coordinating their organizational transformations.

This problem is not only of theoretical importance. Today, in the process of exponential growth of the possibilities of the 4th technological revolution, mankind may enter a strip of accelerated progress in all spheres of human life, and may miss this chance as well. The conditions under which a chain reaction of technoevolution, self-development of the economy and social progress will begin, depends on the state of society, or rather on the position of a person in it. Klaus Schwab (2016) associated this phenomenon with the capability of the technological revolution 4.0 to return the "human capabilities to a man". The meaning of the latter is associated with a return to the human phenomenon from the point of view of a philosophical understanding of the main mission of a human, his functions and of the purpose of the society he created. The self-development of systems is designed to create conditions for the realization of the inexhaustible possibilities of a person, since without a person, his creativity it is not possible to realize the self-development of system integrity in the future. Without transformation of an economic subject into an intellectually autonomous person, it is very problematic to achieve unhindered multiplication of technological progress and endless self-movement of human-created systems in the economy and society. In other words, in modern conditions, technoevolution and self-development of the economy depend on the degree of intersection of interests (motivation, preferences) of the individual and society, of the individual and the economy, of the individual and technology. So, objectively, the conditions for the implementation of the law of denial of negation in economics depend on the priority of a person in the context of his role in the mechanisms of further complication of the systems created by him. The following is the proof of the last statement.

As for technoevolution, no more than 10% of all humanity is involved in the creation of new theoretical knowledge. And this number of especially gifted people, capable of creating and discovering new things in theoretical knowledge, has so far been quite enough to ensure the unhindered development of engineering thought and the creation of new technologies for a century ahead. However, the technological revolutions of the past and the technological revolution 4.0 are different. The modern technological revolution has all the necessary characteristics for implementation into the economy and society as a new technological paradigm, with hitherto unseen opportunities. The integrative potential of the latest technologies makes it possible to design bizarre complexes of physical, digital and biological systems, increasing many times the diverse capabilities of a person. It is about new complex components in technology, about the most diverse ways of integrating them with each other, about the possibilities of creating hitherto non-existent configurations of technological chains with the quality of self-organization. However, the most important obstacle on this path is a person who must be able to generate new forms of technology organization in the technological system itself, as well as adapt them to the organizational mechanisms of positive and negative selection in economic activity, and most importantly, to the construction of other communication systems in society.

In other words, it is about a person as an intellectually autonomous person [Pilipenko, et al., 2019; Pilipenko, 2020], capable of working in uncertain conditions when atypical problems arise, analyzing the causes of their occurrence and finding non-trivial effective solutions from their potential diversity. Based on this, the authors believe that the main obstacle to the cascade self-organization of technology and economics is the state of society and the critical mass of people in society in terms of their education, and readiness to pursue the interests of society. The priority is for a creative personality, which still needs to be formed, which must be adequate to the current conditions of the technological revolution and a dynamic economy. In this context, the problem of education is ancient and eternal.

Many experts describe this, highlight the main reasons for the decline in the quality of knowledge and justify the need for their compliance with new and newest technologies (Romer, 1986; UNESCO, 2016; UNESCO, 2016a). However, in 2018, in its World Development Report, the World Bank (World Bank, 2018) formulated a disappointing conclusion that the education system was in a state of crisis. Following dialectical logic, the authors tried to highlight the essence of the problem of the ineffectiveness of the educational process, taking into account more and more advanced methods of presenting material, more and more skillful teaching technologies, etc.

But the learning crisis due to the COVID-19 pandemic, according to the World Bank (World Bank, 2020) manifests itself in the following: (1) 258 million children and youth of primary- and secondary-school age are out of school; (2) ... the Learning Poverty rate in low- and middle-income countries was 53 percent; (3) … the crisis was not equally distributed: the most disadvantaged children and youth had the worst access to schooling, highest dropout rates, and the largest learning deficits; (4) the world was already far off track for meeting Sustainable Development Goal 4.

In the context of the current crisis state of the education system in the world, the emergence of a "lost generation" as well as of generation of the precariat (Precariat, 2020; World Economic Forum, 2021) due to the COVID-19 pandemic, the end of which is still difficult to predict, the most important strategic goal of any society becomes the generation (debugging, restructuring) of a modern education system. And society can and must fulfill this mission. Moreover, these forms of manifestation of the learning crisis rather reflect the crisis of youth socialization both in education and in professional activity. The economy should provide material support for the education of intellectually autonomous people, and the technological system should provide modern technological means for this. However, education is only one component of technological and economic progress in the context of an adequate human personality with the qualities of intellectual autonomousness. It is about a person as a human capable of self-organization and self-development (Pilipenko, et al., 2021). Consequently, the problems of self-development of the economic system are not solved by simply introducing a new technological paradigm without creating a high quality education system in society (and by society itself!). It should be available to everyone, regardless of social status, religion and gender. And this education system should be aimed at the formation of a self-organizing and self-developing human. The country that would rethink and implement the priority of education in its self-development will be the first on the path of accelerated progress and not only in the field of technology.

A person with the qualities of intellectual autonomousness will be capable to design and technologically ensure the integration of successive interconnections, thus generating an almost unlimited multiplication of a positive effect from one sphere of his life to another. However, in order to acquire these qualities, he must acquire the ability for self-organization and self-development while still in the education system. The authors came to the conclusion that self-organization of a person is associated with his ability to overcome psychologist-cognitive barriers (PCB), which are formed in the learning process, and self-development is predetermined by his effective socialization in society (Pilipenko, 2021). Today, adequate socialization of an intellectually autonomous personality is a fundamental problem that has come out on top in connection with the societal crisis caused by the COVID-19 pandemic.

Since the mid-2010s, the problems of socialization of individuals (comparable in meaning with the category of "inclusion") have begun to be actively discussed as at the macro-level (WEF, 2015, 2016, 2017, 2018; Breen, 2016) and at the level of companies (Dixon-Fyle, et al., 2020). At the same time, the mechanism of socialization or inclusion of individuals in the economic and social systems as a whole differs significantly from inclusion of employees into companies' teams. Running a little ahead, it should be emphasized that in the current conditions of the coronavirus, the processes of socialization at the firm level ultimately predetermine the features of socialization at the macro level. The features of such socialization at the firm level are predetermined by the quality of diversity of employees, which, in turn, is the result of their education. It is about the ability or inability of individuals at the end of their learning to reflect, self-reflect and, most importantly, to transcend. Without going deep into the characteristics of the specific mechanism of inclusion (Chapters 5.1, 9.3), it should be noted that it is largely due to the experience acquired by the individual at the end of the educational process from the following list: (1) experience of cognitive activity, recorded in the form of knowledge (cognitive component); (2) experience in the implementation of known methods of activity in the form of the ability to act according to a model (operational component); (3) experience of creative activity - in the form of the ability to make effective decisions in problem situations (creative component); (4) experience in the implementation of emotional-value relationships - in the form of personal orientations (motivational-orientational component). The acquisition by a student of a certain set of experiences as a result of education serves as the basis for diversity in society (Chapter 5.1).

It is logical that education, in the context of preparing an intellectually autonomous personality capable of self-development, performs the function of ensuring the dominance of human-centric principles in the organization of a new post-COVID-19 social reality. And its main creator is a self-developing person who can fully realize his subjectivity only in society. And the quality of an intellectually autonomous personality allows him to socialize (self-develop in society) consciously, since his success is predetermined by his individual ability to overcome PCBs both in education and in social reality. For such an individual, the digitalization of society does not threaten with the loss of a job, since he is able to create cyber-human systems that involve people and machines and combine the wisdom of humans with the capabilities of technology for the greater good (Malone, 2018).

It means that upon graduation, individuals capable of self-development objectively need socialization (integration, inclusion into the various structures of society), since it mediates their self-development. In other words, in the human-centric system, education has a special mission - to create conditions for the formation of a critical mass of individuals with the qualities of intellectual autonomousness, capable of adequately socializing and self-developing for the purpose of ensuring societal integrity and social progress. Thus, it is only as a result of education that a person develops dialectically interconnected abilities for reflection and for transcending, which predetermine his socialization. In this interpretation, education becomes a necessary condition for constructing the future post-COVID-19 reality in the form of a human-centric system, and socialization becomes its sufficient condition. In this process, a self-developing personality structures his inner subjectivity in the process of his self-organization, and objectifies it outwardly through transcending.

It is logical to assume in this regard that it is possible to ensure the self-development of systems in technology, economy and society only in case of overcoming gap between a person's ability to self-reflection and his ability to transcend, i.e. between the self-organization of his inner subjectivity and self-development as a manifestation of his individuality (selfhood) outside in the form of intellectual autonomousness. And this problem can be solved only if the integrity of society and personality is restored as a dialectical unity in diversity. If an individual has not acquired the ability to transcend in education then his socialization into the structure of society does not strengthen it (at best, does not change). In such a state, society is ready for a quick break of its structural relationships due to extreme conditions, since only a self-developing personality with a high ability to transcend is capable of quickly solving extraordinary problems of implementing the law of double negation in the process of turning a static economy into a dynamic one and generating an irreversible process of its self-development. The human capable to creativity can be considered as a driver of technological progress and self-development of economic systems only if he fully shares the norms of behavior and life of people in society. Only if a person as a creator perceives freedom “as a conscious need”, society will be able to avoid the massive “Perelman effect”. This is about the outstanding Russian young mathematics – G.Ya. Perelmane, who brilliantly proved the Poincaré conjecture, which was not solved for 100 years and refused all public confessions and active professional activities for the benefit of society due to considerations of a subjective nature. And this is not an isolated example. So on 10.12.2020, the news feed brought the message that after Braxit, about 10,000 university professors left the UK as a result of disagreement with the government’s decision to isolate from the continental part of Europe.

The COVID-19 pandemic has proven that, oddly enough, the weakest link in the chain of centuries-old self-movement of human society is a person who himself becomes more complex in the process of growing up under the influence of the mechanism of his own self-organization (primarily due to education), and then and the mechanism of self-development. But those who make decisions at the state level are far from this problem. And the boomerang returns: in education at the stage of self-organization of a person, society “creates” from him a future member, and after receiving education at the stage of self-development, this very person will adapt society to its requirements. The COVID-19 pandemic has revealed the rejection by the growing number of citizens of the order that has developed in society. This was evident in their street protests against government measures in the fight against coronavirus. It turns out that society tried to prepare its members to strengthen society, and they, going into adulthood, completely deny the established norms of behavior, destroying the unity of society.

Thus, the conditions for the self-development of the economy in its dynamics change priorities: social preferences (norms of behavior) replace economic criteria of efficiency (not everything that is effective from an economic point of view, effective for the unity of society);; the social system predetermines economic and technologically possible solutions for implementation; a person as a bearer of intelligence and creativity comes to the fore in social and economic progress in comparison with the owners of financial assets and capital. It is about replacing the capital-centric principles of organization with human-centric ones both in the economy and in society.

In the context of the modern 4th technological revolution, the problems of self-organization and self-development of a person came to the fore. And this is critically important, since today humanity has two alternatives: either put man at the forefront and take all measures so that the subject-creator begins to structure a promising future; or do not change anything and each time return to unsolved problems that predetermine stagnation and regression. The latter option brings mankind closer to the catastrophe of its own, of society and of the entire eco-natural system, which nurtured a person as its child. But in any case progressive trends will prevail, but time will be lost and it will be much more difficult to start all over again with the participation of those generations whose parents lost the chance for a better life, first because of the pandemic, and then because of the short-sightedness of political decision-makers.

The most important thing is that it should not become too late, as environmental problems grow to catastrophic proportions.

Returning to the specifics of the new technological base, corresponding to a dynamic economy in the conditions of its self-development, it is advisable to emphasize that an intellectually autonomous person becomes a necessary and sufficient condition for socio-economic progress. In other words, the theoretical interpretation of the subjects' and process components of the self-organization and self-development of systemic integrity in technology and economics led the authors to the conclusion that it is the subjects' component that was originally inherent in all these processes and its priority is absolute. As a result, without interpreting the role, functions, behavior and motivation of a person (subject, individual), it is impossible to deeply understand either static or dynamic economics, not to mention technological progress, especially in its modern form of the 4th technological revolution.

CONCLUSION

So, the law of negation of negation begins to operate when the laws of unity and struggle of opposites and the transition of quantitative changes into qualitative ones cannot solve the problems of further self-movement of the system, since the potential for self-organization of a static economy has been exhausted. Realizing the negation of the negation of the previous structural hierarchy of a static economy, shocks interrupt the continuity of the previous period of self-organization of the system, which means its qualitative leap to the beginning of a new path of formation of structural ties, but already from the interaction of elements, much more complex, because of their dialectical content. In this context, the law of denial of negation implements the denial of both causes and effects, both vertical structural levels and horizontal, both dialectically related subjects and objects, both structure and systemic integrity. It is this stage of self-movement of the system that represents its dynamics, i.e. its own self-development.

In this chapter, the authors deliberately highlight the subjects' component, which was initially decisive in the mechanisms of complication of technological systems. But this became obvious in the modern conditions of the 4th technological revolution due to the fact that its specific features of the embodiment of the technological paradigm within the framework of a dynamic economy objectively predetermine the participation of a person with special qualities of an intellectually autonomous personality and of an adequately socialized one. The first is due to the educational system through which society prepares such human beings, and the second is a consequence of the self-development of these individuals, realizing their ability to transcendence only in a society that meets its value preferences. As a result, the modern stage of technological progress can be realized only under the condition that its main driver - a person accepts the norms of behavior accepted in society and feels his "freedom" in it as a conscious need. In other words, the objective process of technology complication has brought society to a limit that clearly distinguishes its main participant and the means of acquiring the corresponding quality of an intellectually autonomous personality.

Before the coronavirus pandemic, the role of man in technological progress was important and also varied depending on his quality of education, but his participation was not limited to the formation of a new technological paradigm within a still static economy. In the past it was about the replication of already understandable engineering solutions in various spheres of human activity, which was structured in the direction of complication using understandable organizational mechanisms of positive and negative selection. The 4th technological revolution is just beginning with the formation of a new technological paradigm on which complex technological complexes will be built and technological chains that will realize the potential of the latest technological solutions. For the most part, these engineering solutions do not exist in practice, and their deployment requires not just workers, but such specialists who are capable of creativity, non-trivial thinking, taking the risks of unsuccessful searches for "truth" and obtaining the final result.

And this is just the beginning. The law of denial of negation by means of a shock mechanism destroys the structure of a static economy, giving rise to complete uncertainty in relation to a dynamic economy and, in fact, with the very stage of its self-development. Only an intellectually autonomous person can minimize uncertainty in the dynamics of the economic system. So, the COVID-19 pandemic clearly marked a change in drivers in the further self-movement of the human community. Capital, or rather the owners of financial assets, cannot cope with this task. To form a new technological base, build on it a new dynamic economy, without resorting to the best creative practice, which does not exist in nature, can only be a critical mass of intellectually autonomous individuals who, by their actions in the professional sphere, can minimize the uncertainty with which experts associate the post-covid future.

However, all the previous economic history testifies to the fact that practitioners and politicians were looking for and are looking for the causes of "financial bubbles" and economic crises exclusively in the sphere of economics. This mindset still prevails in the third wave of the coronavirus pandemic in 2021, as political leaders believe in a panacea for economic solutions to all social problems. It is about fiscal subsidies of the governments, adequate regulation of the money market from behave the central banks and so on. But all imbalances in the economy are nothing more than an extrapolation of the effect of the destruction of the unity of society, the divergence of the value concepts of people and the society in which they live. And this became obvious in the context of an economic lockdown and an increase in anti-government protests in an environment when the state is trying in every possible way to cope with the consequences of the COVID-19 pandemic.

REFERENCES

Arnold, V. I. (1975). Critical points of smooth functions. *Proc. of International Congress of Mathematicians*, 1, 19-40.

Arnold, V.I. (1979). Catastrophe theory. *Nature*, *10*, 54-63.

Arthur, W. B. (2009). *The Nature of Technology: What it Is and How it Evolves.* Free Press.

Arthur, W. B. (2013). *Complexity economics: a different framework for economic thought.* Santa Fe Institute Working Paper. 2013-04-012.

Ashby, W. R. (1972). *Introduction to Cybernetics*. Chapman & Hall.

Bak, P. (1996). *How Nature Works: the Science of Self-Organized Criticality*. Copernicus Books. doi:10.1007/978-1-4757-5426-1

Bogdanov, A. A. (1934). *Tectology or General Organizational Science*. Conjuncture Institute publishing house.

Bootle, R. (2009). *The Trouble with Markets: Saving Capitalism from Itself.* Nicholas Brealey Publishing.

Boyer, R. (1986). *La Theorie de la Regulation. Una Analyse Critique*. Editions la Decouverte.

Breen, K. (2016). *Why does inclusive growth matter?* The World Economic Forum.

Brynjolfsson, E., & McAfee, A. (2014). *The Second Machine Age: Work, Progress, and Prosperity in a Time of Brilliant Technologies*. W. W. Norton & Company.

Clark, J. B. (2007). *Essentials of Economic Theory: As Applied to Modern Problems of Industry and Public Policy*. Ludwig von Mises Institute.

De Latil, P. (1958). Sztuczne Myslenie. Academic Press.

De Smet, Gagnon, & Mygatt. (2021). *Organizing for the future: Nine keys to becoming a future-ready company*. McKinsey.com.

Dixon-Fyle, Hunt, Dolan, & Prince. (2020). *Diversity wins: How inclusion matters*. McKinsey & Company.

Freeman, C., & Perez, C. (1988). Structural crisis of adjustment, business cycles and investment behavior. In G. Dosi (Ed.), *Technical Change and Economic Theory*. Frances Pinter.

Frisch, R. (1933). Propagation problems and impulse problems in dynamic economics. In *Economic Essays in Honour of Gustav Cassel*. Allen and Unwin.

Hegel, G. W. F. (1892). The science of logics. In The Logic of Hegel (2nd ed.). Oxford University Press.

Lem, S. (1964). Summa Technologiae. Academic Press.

Lotka, A. J. (1920). Analytical note on certain rhythmic relations in organic systems. *Proceedings of the National Academy of Sciences of the United States of America*, *6*(7), 410–415. doi:10.1073/pnas.6.7.410 PMID:16576509

Lotka, A. J. (1925). *Elements of Physical Biology*. Williams & Wilkins.

Malone, T. W. (2018). *Superminds. The Surprising Power of People and Computers Thinking Together*. Little, Brown Spark.

Marx, K. (1995). *Capital: A New Abridgement*. Oxford University Press.

McKinsey. (2019). *What technologies will change life, business and the global economy?* McKinsey.com.

Mokyr, J. (2005). The intellectual origins of modern economic growth. *Journal of Economic History*, *65*(2), 285 – 351.

Mokyr, J. (2009). The Enlightened Economy. Yale University Press.

Moskowitz, S. L. (2009). *The Advanced Materials Revolution: Technology and Economic Growth in the Age of Globalization*. John Wiley & Sons, Inc.

Perez, C. (2002). *Technological Revolutions and Financial Capital: The Dynamics of Bubbles and Golden Ages*. E. Elgar. doi:10.4337/9781781005323

Pilipenko, A. I. (2020). Education and theory of psychological and cognitive barriers: human capital as driver of stable economic growth. In Social, Economic, and Environmental Impacts Between Sustainable Financial Systems and Financial Markets. IGI Global. doi:10.4018/978-1-7998-1033-9.ch011

Pilipenko, A. I., Pilipenko, O. I., & Pilipenko, Z. A. (2019). Education and inclusive development: puzzle of low-learning equilibrium. In B. S. Sergi (Ed.), *Modeling Economic Growth in Contemporary Russia* (pp. 163–198). Emerald Publishing Limited. doi:10.1108/978-1-78973-265-820191006

Pilipenko, A. I., Pilipenko, Z. A., & Pilipenko, O. I. (2021). Rebuilding a stronger business in the uncertain post-covid-19 future: factor of intellectually autonomous and adequately socialized employees. In Adapting and Mitigating Environmental, Social, and Governance Risk in Business. IGI Global.

Piore, M., & Sabel, C. F. (1984). *The Second Industrial Divide: Possibilities for Prosperity*. Basic Books.

Precariat: The emergence of a new class (collective monograph). (2020). The Russian Academy of Sciences. Institute of Sociology. Federal Center of Theoretical and Applied Sociology.

Robinson, J. (1980). Time in economic theory. Kyklos, 33(2), 219–29.

Romer, P. M. (1986, October). Increasing returns and long-run growth. *Journal of Political Economy*, *94*(5), 1002–1037. doi:10.1086/261420

Schumpeter, J. A. (1949). The Theory of Economic Development: An Inquiry into Profits, Capital, Credit, Interest, and the Business Cycle. Harvard University Press.

Schumpeter, J. A. (1954). *History of Economic Analysis*. Allen and Unwin.

Schwab, K. (2016). *The Fourth Industrial Revolution*. Geneva: World Economic Forum.

Schwab, K., & Malleret, T. (2020). *COVID-19's legacy: This is how to get the Great Reset right. In Sustainable Development Impact Summit*. WEF.

The Economist. (2020). *Covid-19 and the crisis for higher education*. Report. London: The Economist Intelligence Unit Limited.

Thom, R. (1974). Catastrophe theory: its present state and future perspectives. Dynamical Systems-Warwick, 468, 366–372.

UNESCO. (2016). *Education for People and Planet: Creating Sustainable Futures for All*. Global Education Monitoring Report 2016, Paris: UNESCO Publishing. Retrieved from: https://unesdoc.unesco.org/images/0024/002457/245752e.pdf

UNESCO. (2016a). *Contemporary learning crisis: education' failure in "creating sustainable future for all". In The Global Education Monitoring Report* (2nd ed.). UNESCO Publishing.

Volterra, V. (1926). Fluctuations in the abundance of a species considered mathematically. Nature, 118, 558–560.

Volterra, V. (1931). *Leçons sur la Théorie Mathématique de la Lutte pour la Vie*. Gauthier-Villars.

WEF. (2018). *The Inclusive Growth and Development Report*. The World Economic Forum.

World Bank. (2018). *World Development Report 2018: Learning to Realize Education's Promise*. World Bank.

World Bank. (2020). *The COVID-19 pandemic: shocks to education and policy responses.* World Bank Report.

World Economic Forum. (2021). *Global Gender Gap Report 2021*. Insight Report. WEF.

Chapter 5
Elevation of the Human Role in the Technology and Economy Interaction:
Subjective Component of Shocks in the Dialectics of Systems' Self-Movement

ABSTRACT

The peculiarities of the formation of the technological paradigm led the authors to the idea of the organic involvement of a person in the processes that mediate technical progress, the self-structuring of systemic integrity in the economy, since this is consistent with his own goal of expanding the sphere of his life and the means of achieving it. A human acts in several fundamental roles, creating new technological solutions, acting as an economic subject and integrating into social interactions. At the stage of self-organization of the economy, human trust gradually replaces the monetary equivalent or its substitutes in vertical structural ties, making the systemic integrity fragile, predetermined with the propensity of the market economy to instability. At the stage of self-development, it is a person who is destined to implement the achievements of the technological revolution 4.0 and form the latest technological base for a dynamic economy of the post-coronavirus future.

INTRODUCTION

The promotion of a person to the first place in the study of the phenomenon of shocks was dictated by the completion of the positive part of the theory of shocks, which objectively led to the need to answer the question about the reasons for the imputation (endogeneity) of shocks in the mechanism of self-movement of the economy and about the typicality of the stages of self-movement of systemic integrity in technology and society. An in-depth study of the mechanisms of self-movement of technology allowed the authors to establish the subordination of self-movement of technological and economic systems as

DOI: 10.4018/978-1-7998-4309-2.ch005

human goals to satisfy their needs and as the means of achieving them. As a result, it turned out that a person is objectively at the crossroads of all intersystem connections, mediating the interaction of technology, economy, and society. In this capacity, a person mediates structural changes in all these systems, changing, in turn, under their influence. As human needs expressed in economic parameters, are replaced by non-material needs, the subordination of society and the economy changes, as well as the implementation of the potential of technological revolutions as a means of achieving the spiritualized value needs of a person. As a result, the future of humanity begins to be seen, which Karl Marx presented as the transition of humanity from the "kingdom of necessity" to the "kingdom of freedom." And in this context, all the prerequisites for the self-movement of systemic integrities are determined by man. That is why human mediation of all structural changes predetermines their imputation as mechanisms of self-movement of human-created systems.

It is this idea that the authors developed when substantiating the endogeneity of the technological factor of self-movement of the economic system, presenting a model of interaction between technology and humans (Chapter 5.1). And presenting the person himself as a complex phenomenon, the authors identified the mechanisms of his self-movement, which implement the self-organization of a person, primarily in education, as well as his self-development - in socialization to society. In the first case, the education (and, of course, health care) of a person becomes of paramount importance, with whom skills gap and skills mismatch are associated today. All of the above predetermines the fact of human integration into the system formation of technological systems and the endogeneity of the technological factor (progress, revolution) of the self-movement of the economic integrities.

The next confirmation of the conclusions of the authors about the intrinsic complex systems created by man, their own mechanisms of self-organization and self-development, is the subjectivization of the vertical structural links of self-organizing economic systems (Chapter 5.2). In modern economies all the stages of market exchange processes are uniquely related to money. Being separated in time and space, acts of purchase and sale more and more involve elements of participant's trust. Financial markets, mediating the relations of participants in the exchange of assets, are actually built on the relationship of the trust of participants in the sale and purchase under conditions of growing uncertainty that is difficult to adequately evaluate. In this sense the main uncertainty factor is connected with the problem whether an economic exchange of full contracted value actually occurs (Schinasi, 2006). In essence, financial market is mediating the temporary exchange of the finality-of-payment services of fiat money for a promise that involves uncertainty about human trust (Schinasi, 2006, P. 33; Kindleberger, 1996, P. 21). So human trust plays an essential role in financial market as the latter offers the superior store-of-value services compared with the fiat money facilitating inter-temporal exchange. So financial market operates with trust as a fragile human emotion and as a result becomes subject to instability under certain conditions when according to Garry J. Schinasi (2006, P. 40) "too much finance is created on too little trust". This situation is adequately explained by the dialectic of self-movement of economic systems at the stage of their self-organization under the influence of the law of transition of quantitative changes into qualitative ones. It is the reproduction of vertical structural ties for the purpose of strengthening the integrity of the economic system, mediated by a person that ultimately structures the cause-and-effect relationships of dialectical pairs vertically, increasing the overall systemic fragility.

Such a steady tendency towards the growth of the significance of the subjects' component of self-organization processes indicates the endogeneity of all structure formations, since they are mediated by man. It is no coincidence that the transaction partners themselves mediate shocks in the market, predetermining the situation, when the market price of an asset deviates as much as possible from its base price. This increases uncertainty and risks, which generates conditions for a potential shock break of dialectical relations in the financial market and its interrelated segments. And this mechanism of shocks realization acquires behavioral content, i.e. becomes subjective in the essence.

In addition, the promotion of the human factor to the first place in understanding the mechanisms of self-movement of a static and dynamic economy was evidenced by the increasing frequency of shocks in a variety of markets, accompanied by increasingly protracted crises since the end of the twentieth century. In this regard, the developments of such theoretical geniuses as J.M. Keynes and H.P. Minsky, which are still relevant today, are admired (Chapter 5.3). Even in the last century, they identified the essence of the fragility of the market economy, which H.P. Minsky connected with the "propensity of the market economy to instability". Although they did not describe this property using the principles of dialectical logic, but in this quality singled out by them, the self-movement of economic systems is seen, which are based on market exchange, and, consequently, on the structural ties. It is their function that predetermines the constancy of changes in the market economy, and the strengthening of ties due to the differentiation of cause-and-effect relationships along the vertical leads to an increase in the fragility of the system and its susceptibility to shocks that are designed to fight against its fragility.

5.1. Human and his Education in Technological Progress: Arguments in Favor of the Endogeneity of the Technological Factor of Self-Movement of the Economic System

Initially man acted as a generator of the complication of technology, economy and society. This is due to the fact that he had to build an integral chain between himself and nature, in which each of the links became an amplifier of his capabilities, providing a greater effect. As for technological evolution, its starting point was the primitive tools of labor created by man, which, hundreds of thousands of years later, acquired their modern embodiment in self-organizing technological systems. Man participated in technological progress in order to facilitate his labor as a process of his interaction with nature. As a result, labor productivity and the degree of satisfaction of human needs increased. The initial interaction between man and nature, as technology was introduced into the labor process, began to bifurcate into the following two: (1) «Human - Labor (Technology)» and (2) «Labor (Technology) - Nature».

In this process of self-movement of technologies from primitive to more and more self-organizing, a person created a mechanism for influencing himself, which subsequently began to initiate a change in the person himself. C. Goldin, and L. Katz (2008, P. 121) formulated the question of why those technological changes led to an increase in the complementarity among human skill, capital, and technology. This question can be answered by following the logic justified by the authors of this book, according to which technological progress is realized only through human participation. Moreover, as technological progress accelerates, the quality of the human education is more and more predetermined by technological changes. By the way, the converse is also true. Fig. 1 shows a chain of interdependencies mediated by a person who acts as a transmitter, first of the direct and then of the reverse effect of structures on each other during the transition of technology from one stage of complication to another.

Fig. 1 demonstrates a key link in the chain of phenomena accompanying technological progress. To understand the above provision, it is advisable to present the relationship of the phenomena accompanying the stages of the endless process of technology complication in the following form: (1) Human → Technology → Human'; (2) Human'→ Technology → Human''; (3) Human''→ Technology → Human''' and so on. The main link turns out to be a Human, since it is he who, at the "input" into the technologically transformed labor process (Human - Technology) generates a change in technology, and at the "output" (Technology – Human') he himself is exposed to it. This predetermines all stages of technological progress, which the authors divide into four main ones: Stage 1 - a set of highly specialized, unrelated technologies; Stage 2 - fragile chains of integrated specialized technologies; Stage 3 - self-organizing technological structures, united horizontally; Stage 4 - self-organizing technological structures united in vertical structural hierarchies. The dots between the stages of technological evolution - … represent the transition from one of them to another.

Moreover, judging by Fig. 1, the duration of the transition depends on a person's readiness to generate a new round of technology complication. In other words, the more adequate the level of education of a person in terms of the ability to adequately use theoretical knowledge, the faster technological progress will be realized. This idea was also emphasized by Joel Mokyr (Mokyr, 2005), who advocated the correlation between technological progress and "the growth of useful knowledge». In this sense, the quality of a person's education should be correlated with the requirements of technology, based on a specific stage of its complication (both at the entrance to each stage, and at the exit from it). It is the human who carries out the transmission of both negative and positive effects, multiplying it along all the links of interconnected systemic integrities.

So, all the processes of complication of technological structures are mediated by direct human participation. And this is extremely important, because to interpret the progress of technology as an objective process of its complication, then it begins and ends with a change in the quality of education of a person who stands at the "output" of technology from the previous stage of its complication and at the "input" into its new stage.

Figure 1. Human mediation of transitions from stage to stage in the process of technology complication
Source: the authors' development

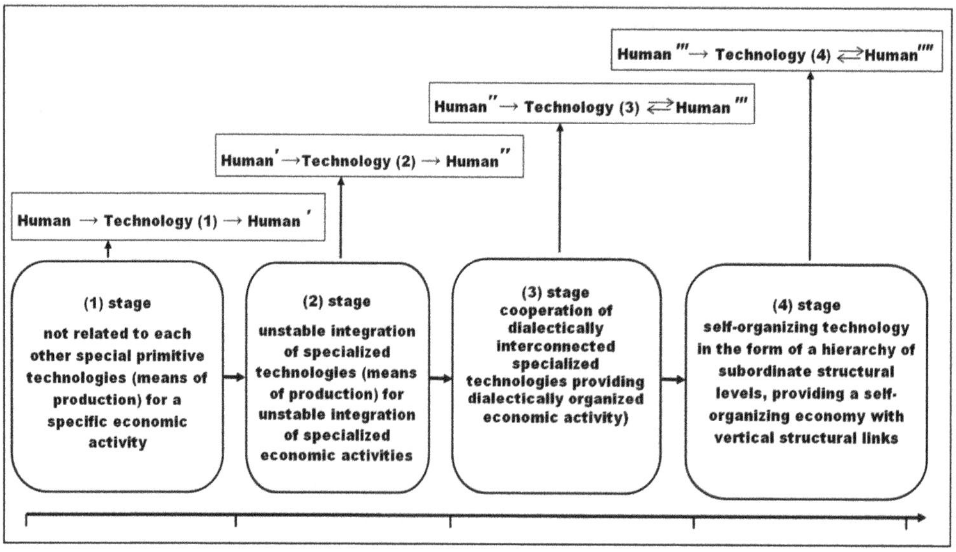

As a result, if a human education does not meet the requirements of a self-organizing technology at its various stages of complication, then rapid technological progress will not happen. This idea is confirmed by Paul M. Romer (Romer, 1988), who defines knowledge as an endogenous source of socio-economic progress. Knowledge of a human in their universal understanding is formed in the process of education and is accumulated in society as intellectual capital. It is in this capacity that it becomes the most important endogenous factor of both technological and socio-economic progress. In this regard, education is of paramount importance, which is called upon in modern conditions to form a human with the qualities of an intellectually autonomous personality. Only a professional of this level will be able to freely service all the processes of complication of technology, both at the stages of its self-organization and in the conditions of the formation of a new technological paradigm, realizing the potential of the technological revolution 4.0. In other words, a human becomes a generator of new technological solutions, a transmitter of impulses from one level of interconnection to another, and the main participant in structural self-organization in technological systems.

As for education, then, on the one hand, the level of requirements for a human's education depends on the stage of technological progress. But, on the other hand, the anticipation by education of the vector of future scientific and technical changes turns the education system and the intellectual capital formed in it into the main endogenous factor of future changes in all spheres of human activity. Based on the logical structure justified above, technological progress is realized only with human participation, provided a certain level of his education, adequate to the requirements of a particular stage of technological changes. This logic of reasoning is implemented by the authors in Fig. 2.

Evolving technology changes (as a rule, increases) the requirements for a human's education. That is why ***Human*** when entering the first stage of the evolution of technology differs from ***Human'*** when leaving it. In this case ***Human'*** reflects the growth in demand from technology for a person with a higher level of knowledge that should be formed in the education system. Ideally, the highly educated ***Human'*** at the "entrance" to the second stage of self-organization of technology should correspond to the demand for ***Human'***, which the technology broadcasts to education at the end of the first stage of its evolution. That is why the demand for ***Human'*** on the part of technology at the first stage of its complication corresponds to the supply of ***Human'*** from the side of education at the "entrance" to its second stage. And so it is repeated at all stages of technological progress.

It's just that in the first case ***Human'*** as the desired intellectual capital realizes the demand from the technology at the end of the first stage of its self-organization, and when ***Human'*** enters its second stage, it generates the beginning of the next stage. As a result, the more adequately the education system correlates the demand for an educated person with his supply, the faster technological progress will be realized. Moreover, such a dialectical relationship between education and technology remains at all stages of its self-organization, proving the paramount importance of the subject factor in all organizational changes of the technological system.

Thus, Fig. 2 presents the logic of understanding human-mediated interdependencies in the process of technological evolution, taking into account the role of education in all forms of its organizational changes. All of the above allowed the authors to conclude that the process of technology complication is mediated by a person, whose role becomes more and more significant as the demand for his quality of education grows. A person contributes to an ever more complete realization of the potential capabilities of technology if the level of his education is adequate to the requirements of technological progress at a particular stage. On this basis, the authors conclude that a person, mediating all the processes of system formation in different spheres of his activity, actually predetermines the endogeneity of the mechanism that ensures both self-organization and self-development of all systemic integrities created by him.

All the above allows the authors to concretize the following features of the mutual influence of a person and his education, on the one hand, and changes in technologies at various stages of their complication, on the other.

Figure 2. The role of education in technological progress
Source: the authors' development

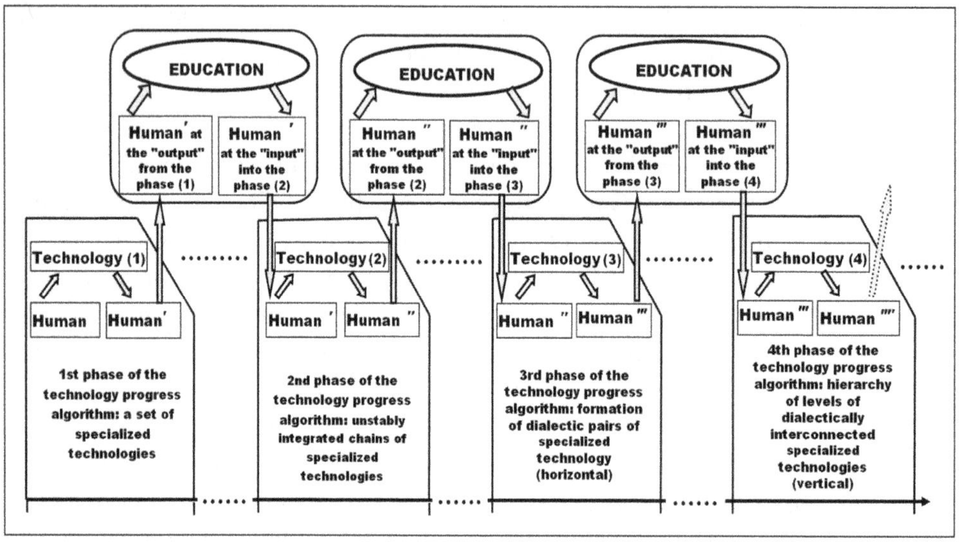

1. In the ideal case of continuous technological progress, education should generate such qualities of an educated person that would allow him to realize the next stage of self-organization of technology.
2. If the quality of a person's education (the level of his theoretical knowledge, according to P. M. Romer (1988) corresponds to the previous stage of self-organization of technology, then this will lead to an objective inhibition of the time spent on the next stage. Moreover, education is able to provide such a step forward in the pace of technological progress only if the student in the educational process learns to independently overcome psychological and cognitive barriers (PCB) on the way of assimilating and applying knowledge. Subject to deep theoretical knowledge of students, they are quite capable of functioning in a professional environment as intellectually autonomous persons. In fact, education provides such a person with theoretical knowledge, with the ability to adapt them in an uncertain environment as a result of the acquisition of skills to overcome numerous PCBs, and the generation of new models of their application is within the power of any creative personality.
3. Taking into account the historical fact that the integration of science into the technological process greatly accelerates its progress, education should focus on the formation of a self-developing individual capable of intellectual autonomy in the face of the uncertainty of large-scale manifestations of the technological revolution 4.0. However, this can be achieved only if such a person is adequately socialized.

4. The education system is a public institution, therefore, it is society and its attitudes in relation to the formation of a self-developing person that are priority to achieve the quality of human capital in terms of its education and specific requirements from technological structures. At one time, S. Lem (1964) defined the importance of education as an objective gradient of technological and socio-economic progress.

However, in order to deepen the understanding of the objectivity of the process of increasing the significance of the subjective component in the process of complicating system integrity in all spheres of human life, starting with technology, it is necessary to make the following remarks. The role of a human and of his qualities, formed in the education system, has an enduring high importance. However, at the stages of self-organization of technologies on the basis of the existing technological paradigm, the role of professionals is reduced to replicating technological solutions in all possible links of technology, economy and society. This is due to the fact that at this stage organizational decisions are of paramount importance in terms of optimizing the mechanisms of positive and negative selection within any systems created by man. In other words, in the context of the implementation of the laws of unity and struggle of opposites and of the transition of quantitative changes to qualitative ones complication of any systems occurs due to the structuring of relationships in the system. It is also about the fact that in the event of a shock break, professionals must quickly restore working connections, replace the destroyed ineffective ones, or form their combinations for the purpose of strengthening system integrity. The first place among the tasks of an educated specialist is the task of optimal replication of technological experience, differentiated by spheres of human activity, a combination of technological solutions and their repetition, repetition and repetition.

As for the operation of the law of denial of negation and the shock "discontinuity" of the previous evolution of a static economy, it is about the complete destruction of the old structure, which should not be restored, but should be replaced with a completely new one. Moreover, if the structure is destroyed, then the point of no return of the system has been passed. And this irreversibility in the context of the implementation of progressive changes in society is of great importance in relation to the implementation of the law of denial of negation. Self-development of a new dynamic system can be ensured only if it transitions to a new technological paradigm. In this case an educated person faces a variety of problems that have not yet been resolved in practice. It is about ways of structuring a new technology as a new paradigm that provides the dynamics of the technological system itself, as well as the implementation of its organizational capabilities. This requires professionals with the qualities of intellectual autonomousness. And if their number does not reach a critical mass of specialists, then technological progress will slow down at best, and at worst – all systems are doomed to stagnate and compete with old obsolete technological structures. Moreover, the outcome may be technological regression (Yaremenko, 1997), which will cause both economic slowdown and social disorder. And in this case, it is quite certain that a person's education and the formation of his qualities of an intellectually autonomous personality are an uncontested condition for the dynamics of all systems, including technological progress.

Only those who are creative, intellectually autonomous are able to provide the dynamics of all systems, which today are spoken about only in terms of "the future will differ from the present," "the New Normal is coming," "the future is absolutely uncertain," etc. (WEF, July 2020; WEF, January 2020; McKinsey & Company, August 2020; McKinsey & Company, September 2020). But it should not be forgotten that under these conditions the role of the subject is elevated, because it is he who is capable to gradually minimize this uncertainty. This is largely due to the fact that the new 4th technological revolution has prepared all the conditions for the formation of a new technological paradigm. It will be based on flexible, high-performance production of customized products as opposed to mass standardized products. The unification of technological chains is ensured by their automation and robotization based on "breakthrough" technologies and "radical" innovations. Moreover, the entire technological process is distinguished by its intellectualization. The basis of the industrial structure should be high-tech industries based on scientific knowledge and innovative technologies. As a result, the speed will increase, the accuracy, flexibility, and complexity of technological complexes will grow in comparison with those that were typical for the previous technological paradigm.

The specificity of the new technology lies in the fact that it not only acts as a one-time disturbance of the equilibrium, but is a constant generator of more and more new technologies that themselves generate and require the next technologies. Thus, W.B. Arthur (2009) described the specifics of self-organization of a new technological paradigm. Modern technology is becoming more complex in the form of incessant waves of disturbances that cause new disturbances that operate in parallel in technology and in the economy and in their various areas. These processes are based on the implementation and realization of the potential of innovative designs (products) and advanced technologies, the use of which causes a large-scale transformation of the production, technological and social spheres. In other words, the need for the technologies themselves is increasing, i.e. at any moment of time there is an open network of opportunities for involving the next technologies and mechanisms. According to W.B. Arthur (1999), they can set in motion a sequence of events that never ends, since each of them can initiate a cascade of subsequent events. The algorithm may be simple, but once run it generates diverse, complex, infinitely new behavior.

New technologies often come into "play" in groups (Perez, 2002; Arthur, 2009): technologies are incoherently formed on the basis of one or two former central technologies, subsequently making up for the lack of required subtechnologies. These arrays of technologies are not adapted within the economy; rather, they are encountered in industry, combined with business processes that already exist and generate new lines of business, new incentives, new available processes and small irruptions in the form of small firms, few of which go further to become large firms (Freeman, et al., 1988; Perez, 2009).

If abstracting from the objects' and processes' components of all these phenomena, then the main subject on which the prospect of technological progress and the future of the economic system and society depend is a human (Solow, 1957). It is about a person capable of constructing the future, possessing the qualities of intellectual autonomousness. Considering the main relationships shown in Fig. 2, then the fact of an endogenous source of self-movement of all systemic integrity becomes obvious. It is the intellectually autonomous personality that mediates the self-organizing structural process of the emergence of new technologies, their penetration into the economy through the prism of creating and recreating mutually supportive complexes that form the endogenous environment of a complex economic system, which predetermines the mechanism of its self-development.

It should be noted the great merit of W.B. Arthur, (2009) who laid the foundations for the theory of complex economics and examined the structure of the process of emergence of technologies and their implementation in the economy (Arthur, 2013a, 2013b, 2014). However, the subjective side of the self-structuring of technological systems remained outside his research.

Although it is difficult to quantify the contributions of education to economic growth, C. Goldin, and L. Katz (Goldin, et al., 2008) emphasize that they are bound to have been quite large. As for the relationship between human capital and technological progress - the creation and adoption of new technologies - it is useful to note that it operates at least through three channels (Acemoglu, et al., 2012). *First*, the human capital and access to education of the most talented individuals in society is probably the most important factor underpinning technological progress. *Second*, the human capital of the individuals may influence the pace of technological change both because of human capital externalities and because it changes the incentives for overall technological progress (as many technologies may not be profitable without the requisite skills from the workforce). *Third,* accordingly, the educational level of human capital of the professionals potentially affects the direction of technological progress (Acemoglu, 1998).

In addition, a highly educated person is important because of the high premium for his quick adaptation (World Bank, 2018). To thrive in today's innovation-driven economy workers need a different mix of skills than in the past. The shift in skill demand has exposed a problem in skill supply: more than a third of global companies reported difficulties filling open positions in 2014, owing to shortages of people with key skills (Manpower Group, 2014; Boston Consulting Group, 2017). And only the shock caused by the COVID-19 pandemic put everything in its place, putting a human in first place in all processes of system formation both in the economy and in society. The modern societal crisis made it clear that further progress in technology and in the socio-economic sphere depends only on a human. Moreover, a person's education becomes a kind of synchronizer of transformation processes in systemic integrities. Today it should be noted that if by the beginning of the 19th century the interaction between knowledge "what" (propositional) and knowledge "how" (prescriptive) became much closer, then at the beginning of the 21st century the problem of "who" arose with gigantic significance.

5.2. Subjective Essence of Self-Organizing Economic Structure: Substitution of Money for Human "Trust" as an Equivalent in Market Exchange and Increasing Fragility of Systemic Integrities

As mentioned above, the process of raising the role of the subjective component of the self-organization mechanism of economic systems, with all its subordination to the object and process components became obvious already during the formation of a vertical hierarchy of structural links that mediate transactions in the money and financial product markets. The subjective component took on a specific form of trust in mediating transactions with financial assets as financial markets separated from their material basis, represented by real markets and material production proper. As a result of such a gap and the transformation of money and financial derivatives markets into self-sufficient structures, the subjective factor has become the main factor inflating financial bubbles with its irrational behavior. However, the behavioral manifestations of the subjective component of structural ties and the mechanism for implementing shocks did not alert the financial authorities and the state and did not force them to look for the true reason for the elevation of the role of the subject of transactions with financial assets. And, meanwhile, the impact on the participants of transactions in financial markets by economic levers did not give a result, did not lead to a rapid restoration of market equilibrium. And the shock rupture of vertical structural ties caused more and more prolonged periods of crises, during which structural interactions were restored. At the same time, the subject component turned into the main factor of imbalance in the markets and the generation of shock breaks in structural ties, first in national, and then in global markets.

The deepening of the problems of restoring structural ties after their shock rupture was associated with human, which, on the one hand, was an economic subject, and on the other hand, a representative of society, with its own individual ideas about justice, norms of behavior and social values. Thus, gradually, as money was replaced by trust as an equivalent in market transactions, the problems of the economy (market equilibrium) shifted to the social sphere. The state of the integrity of society gradually began to predetermine the possibility of shocks and agiotage (irrational) behavior of the subjects of market transactions in the economy.

Chapter 3 demonstrated how the emergence of money in mediating transactions of purchase and sale of material goods and services in real markets marked a significant leap in the formation of a complex economy as a systemic integrity capable of self-organization. The structure of the system ensured its stability, as well as equilibrium, despite its rapid changes. It should be noted that the situation in the economy repeated the one described above in relation to the complication of technology. A human stood at the origins of the formation of systemic integrities, which at the stage of formation of dialectical pairs acquired structural stability. But with the emergence of the quality of self-organization, the principles governing it came to the fore, and a human was forced to obey dialectical laws so as not to destroy the systemic integrity he created. It should be emphasized that the structural connections embodying the dialectics of their object and subjective components, more and more appeared on the surface of phenomena as a mediator in the movement of objects of exchange. And a person, as a subject of structural interactions, went into the "shadow", being replaced by object and process forms of their organization. This is especially evident in the structural connections that mediate the interaction of dialectical pairs at the horizontal structural level of the system. And, meanwhile, the well-visible forms of manifestation of objects' (exchanged material and intangible goods and services) and process components of the mechanism of self-organization of economic systems (positive and negative selection of economic activities) only veiled the essential reason for emerging imbalances in various markets and shock breaks of structural ties in them.

While real markets were provided with full-fledged money, or with their substitutes, really backed with gold reserves of central banks, the object component of structural ties predetermined the equivalence of market transactions of subjects participating in exchange transactions. The replacement of the objects' component of market exchange with "trust" as their subjects' analogue occurred gradually as the number of transactions with deferred payment increased. In fact, it was about the self-organization of the economy due to the complication of structural ties and the formation of vertical structural levels serving transactions with money and with financial instruments. In parallel with the growth of the volume of such transactions, their security was increasingly detached from tangible assets and replaced by the obligations of the parties to the transaction based on "trust". Thus, the formation of a vertical hierarchy of structural ties in the economy was accompanied by the replacement of money by "trust" as their subjective analogue.

Such a radical change in the quality of the intermediary in the exchange entailed serious problems for the market economy in the context of maintaining its equilibrium, and stable state. While national central banks officially guarantee on behalf of the state the status of paper money as a universal equivalent with all functions of a means of exchange, of payment and of saving, the stability of market exchange can be regulated by the monetary instruments of their influence on the market. However, the process of subjectivization of structural ties in the form of replacing money or material security of obligations with "trust" in real markets, as well as in the markets of money and financial instruments, began to accelerate as the volume of transactions with money and with financial instruments grew. The faster the material security of obligations in market transactions was replaced, the more important became the intangible equivalent – "trust" as a tool for ensuring equilibrium in market exchanges.

It is this situation that has already predetermined the need to theoretically rethink the reasons, the role and patterns of changes in the subjective component of structural ties in the economy, as well as the possibility of its regulation in order to ensure the stability of the entire system of markets. Actually, from that moment on, a situation began to form, predetermining the rise in the importance of the subjective component of structural ties in the economy to maintain their balance. The behavior of partners in market transactions began to be predetermined by their personal assessment of the need to fulfill obligations under a transaction based on trust, and to trust or not trust the borrower, focusing only on faith in his decency. In other words, theorists-economists have lost sight of the rubicon of optimization in the systemic organization of structural ties at the moment when the material security of obligations is replaced by "trust". And, meanwhile, such a subjectivization of structural ties, or rather the replacement of their object component by its subjective one, has led to an elevation of the role of individual in ensuring economic stability as a guarantor of the balance of purchase and sale transactions. The new parity of dialectically interconnected subjective and object components of structural ties predetermined the need to look for the causes of imbalance in the economy outside. Indeed, the true causes and ways to resolve them have moved from economics and finance to society. This is explained by the fact that the phenomenon of "trust" is associated with the value attitudes of a person, and not with his motivation as an economic subject.

Understanding the essence of the phenomenon of subjectivization of structural ties in the economy was complicated by the fact that it manifested itself in the financial markets, which had many segments that mediate the acts of buying and selling money and their many substitutes, credit resources, securities and various financial instruments, including modern financial innovations such as bit-coins and crypto-currencies. Moreover, the process of subjectivization was veiled by the fact that initially the financial markets served the exchange of goods, services and other tangible assets in the situation when acts of sale and purchase did not coincide in time and space. As the demand for money as the means of payment function was constantly growing, the scale of financial markets functionally designed to serve this demand was also expanding. The scale of financial operations gradually increased. At the same time, it grew in parallel with the number of players aimed at speculative operations with financial assets. As a result, a dialectic leap took place in the self-organization of the financial markets and their new quality was formed. If initially the money market was formed to solve the problems of a shortage of means of payment in real markets, and the financial asset market – to solve the problems of a lack of money in the money market, then due to the law of the transition of quantitative changes to qualitative changes, these markets turned into self-sufficient. In other words, each of these markets acquired its own structure based on dialectical pairs, whose relations began to be regulated by the law of unity and struggle of opposites.

Financial markets, mediating the relations of participants in the exchange of assets, are actually built on the relationship of the trust of participants in the sale and purchase under conditions of growing uncertainty that is difficult to adequately evaluate to the participants of the transactions. In other words, the stability of financial markets objectively depended on the fulfillment of obligations by partners on financial transactions and their refusal from opportunistic behavior. In this sense the main uncertainty factor is connected with the problem whether an economic exchange of full contracted value actually occurs (Schinasi, 2006). In essence, financial market becomes mediating the temporary exchange of the finality-of-payment services of fiat money for a promise that involves uncertainty about human trust (Schinasi, 2006; Kindleberger, 1993; Kindleberger, et al., 2005). So human trust plays an essential role in financial market as the latter offers the superior store-of-value services compared with the fiat money facilitating inter-temporal exchange. The financial markets operate with trust as with a fragile human emotion and as a result become subject to instability under conditions when opportunistic actors begin to deliberately destroy the market, acting as a critical mass either as buyers or sellers in the market. If imaging the financial asset market conditionally in the form of a commercial bank, which functions only on the basis of investor confidence in it, and it - in borrowers, then the violation of this trust will unambiguously lead to the simultaneous appearance of all investors or the declaration of all borrowers of the bank bankrupts. No market can withstand such imbalances. This situation is realized when the market price of an asset deviates as much as possible from its base price. This increases uncertainty and risks, which generates conditions for a potential shock break of dialectical relations in the financial market and its interrelated segments. And this mechanism of shocks realization acquires behavioral content, i.e. becomes subjective in the essence.

According to G.J. Schinasi, (2006), the macroeconomic sustainability takes place if all the financial market's segments are capable, first, to efficiently and smoothly facilitate the inter-temporal allocation of resources from savers to investors as well as economic resources in general; second, to reasonably assess price and to relatively well manage forward looking financial risks; and, third, to comfortably absorb financial and real economic surprises and shocks. If any of these key functions is not been properly executed, the economic system as integrity becomes less and less stable down to its shock destruction. The core of concept of the gradual instability reintroduction in financial markets is connected with the inter-temporal contracts that voluntarily and gradually reintroduce uncertainty and risks about human trust. Financial markets can create potentially superior near-fiat-money substitutes as stores of value (in the form of bank credit, for example), but do it successfully only to the extent that uncertainty about trust can be properly priced and risk-managed.

To structure all of the above in the context of the theory of shocks it is necessary to build the following logical reasoning. The state of structural (financial) relations of the participants of dialectical pairs will be stable until the price fluctuations of the traded asset overcome their marginal level. This happens through the agitated behavior of one group of participants of dialectical relations which turn to become a dominant of market relations and demonstrate the irrational behavior of partners of a transaction, either on the side of demand for an asset or on the side of its supply. As a result the amplitude of fluctuations of asset prices around its base value increases, regardless of the exchange object or the specifics of speculation with them. Exactly the aggressive behavior of one group of participants on the market (either on the demand-side or on the supply-side) determines the assets' price jump over its marginal level (the whole society could not afford to pay for the good at such a speculative price) (Pilipenko, 2012; Pilipenko, et al., 2018). This phenomenon is confirmed by G. Akerlof and R. Shiller, (2004) introducing "the confidence' multiplier" that works because of the existence of several rounds of the expenditure' circle.

As a result, structural interactions in the economic system as a whole have become more complex as their vertical structures emerged and interactions between them based on cause-and-effect relationships. Already, these organizational changes made the economic system fragile, prone to failures at the slightest violation of the cause-effect relationships in its vertical hierarchy. This in itself predetermined more and more frequent shock destruction of structural bonds. But to these objective reasons for the growth of instability in systemic integrity were added subjective grounds associated with the tendency of the subjects of market transactions to opportunistic manifestations of their personal values under the slogan "to get rich at any cost". And with an increase in the importance of "trust" as a subjective basis for the equivalence of transactions in financial markets, the fragility of economic systems was additionally conditioned by the disunity of society, an increase in its conflict onset. Thus, the separation of interests and values of citizens and society increased the susceptibility of the economic system to shock destructions of its structure. The essence of this problem is definitely expressed in words "too much finance is created on too little trust" (Schinasi, 2006, P. 40).

EMPIRICAL EVIDENCE

The material below proves that on the eve of the COVID-19 pandemic, financial authorities regulated stability in financial markets using monetary leverage, abstracting from the subject component of structural ties that mediate transactions with financial assets. It should be noted that money in the cash balances of an individual or company can be replaced by substitutes of money, without causing an imbalance in the exchange. For this purpose, a certain amount of money must be paid and redeemed upon presentation (Gurley, et al., 1968). At the same time, there should not be the slightest doubt about the solvency of the debtor and his readiness to pay for his obligations. Then all parties to the transaction must strictly observe the following characteristics: terms of payment, secured solvency and willingness of the debtor to pay his obligations. Only in this case, money substitutes can completely replace the money in balance sheets of individuals and companies. However, if at least one of the above conditions is violated in the market for money, an imbalance arises and it can affect the real markets (Mises, 1996).

To illustrate the problem of accumulation of dialectical contradictions in the money market, the authors used an example of the Russian Federation and the simple equation, called the money multiplier (***M*** = ***mB***), where ***m*** is represented as $\frac{1+{}^{C}\!/_{D}}{{}^{C}\!/_{D}+{}^{R}\!/_{D}}$.

It establishes a relationship (an identity if these parameters are fixed) between central bank money *B* held as bank reserves by the banking system and the money supply ***M***. According to this equation, the money stock (***M***) is equal to high-powered money or the monetary base (***B***) times the money multiplier (***m***).

$$M=\left[\frac{1+\frac{C}{D}}{\frac{C}{D}+\frac{R}{D}}\right]B,$$

where ***C/D*** is the currency to deposit ratio of the public, and ***R/D*** is the cash (or reserves) to deposit ratio of the banks.

(1) At first there should be necessary to compare the dynamics of money stock (***M***) and monetary base (***B***) at current prices. ***M*** parameter will be represented by the monetary aggregate called broad money or **M2X** monetary aggregate. It includes total amount of cash in circulation outside the banking system, funds of Russian Federation residents (non-financial and financial organisations (excluding banks) and households) in settlement, current and other on-demand accounts (including bank card accounts), time deposits and other types of deposits in the banking system denominated in the currency of the Russian Federation or a foreign currency, interest accrued on them and deposit and savings certificates in the currency of the Russian Federation issued by credit institutions. As to parameter ***B***, it will be presented by the broad monetary base, including cash in circulation (outside of the Central Bank of the Russian Federation) and the total funds of credit institutions in the Central Bank of Russia accounts and bonds. If the money stock (***M***) is divided into the monetary base (***B***) then it will be the following: ***M* / *B* = *m*.** On the left side of this equation, there is the ratio ***M*** to ***B*.**

Based on the dialectic of the development of the money market in the process of self-organization of the exchange as a whole, it is necessary to ensure the coordination of the interests of buyers and sellers in the markets for money. This will avoid structural imbalance in the hierarchy of exchange. For these purposes, national mega-regulators in money markets set price fluctuation limits to balance them. This is aimed at ensuring that the money market maintains its potential to successfully solve the problems of real markets in centrally established indicators. For example, the Central Bank of Russia defines the marginal levels of certain indicators for the ensuring equilibrium on the market for money. It deals with the ***M*** to ***B*** ratio through the prism of the elasticity of the money supply (in this case, functions) to monetary base (in this case, the argument) changes (in accordance with the generally accepted formula of point elasticity).

Given the changes elasticity of the parameter ***M*** to the parameter ***B***, their maximum values are recorded in the periods of 01.05.2012 – 01.09.2012 (the economic growth stage); of 01.01.2009 – 01.05.2009 (the economic crises stage) and of 01.01.2015 – 01.05.2015 (the economic stagnation stage). All other periods are characterized by more or less stable ratios of changes of ***M*** to ***B***. From the latter it follows that the marginal levels of ***M*** and ***B*** are hardly suitable as the mega-regulator indicators of the equilibrium of the market for money.

(2) It was noted above that the specificity of the self-organization of exchange as a mechanism of self-development of the economic system is connected with the fact that the hierarchy of structural levels is generated by lower levels for the purpose of resolving their own dialectic contradictions. However, the money market, having arisen as a result of persistent problems of their lack in real markets, is gradually becoming self-sufficient in terms of the appearance of its own dialectic problems. The latter begin to stably inhibit the exchange as a whole and the development of the economic system. It is about the exchange of money as of financial income-earning assets and about the emergence of structured financial products as new objects of exchange. That is why equilibrium in the money market cannot be considered outside the banking system. It is the latter that institutionally ensures the functioning of the money market, and then their exchange as financial assets.

As a result the stability of the market for money is primarily determined by the equilibrium of the banking system. In this regard, it is advisable to analyze the dynamics of elasticity coefficients, connecting the parameters of the numerator of the money multiplier coefficient as well as of its denominator. Moreover, the numerator of the multiplication coefficient demonstrates the possibilities of deposit expansion, and the denominator shows the credit expansion potential. As to the numerator of the money multiplier coefficient the aim is to define the marginal levels of ***C*** and ***D*** parameters through their correlation being transformed in the elasticity equation. According to the last it could be possible to determine the reaction of ***C*** (*total amount of cash in circulation*) under the influence of the parameter ***D*** *(deposits included into the broad monetary base)* change per unit according to the generally accepted formula of point elasticity (Fig. 3).

In this case it becomes of the great interest the dynamics of elasticity coefficient values of the ***C*** and ***D*** parameters in comparison with the same tendencies as to the elasticity of the money supply to monetary base changes for the analyzed periods (Fig. 4). It should be noted that the elasticity of parameters ***C*** and ***D*** is more significant (than ***M*** and ***B***), since it is consistently estimated at 10 or more and shows growth at the points of "discontinuity" or macroeconomic gaps. This confirms the jump in the coefficient of ***C*** to ***D*** elasticity in the period of the spread of the global crisis outside of Russia – 05.01.2008, and in the period of its spread in Russia – 01.01.2009 – 01.05.2009. Moreover, the value of these coefficients increased by 2.5-3 times. Another jump was recorded 01.01.2015 in the midst of economic stagnation in Russia. Thus, the maximum values of the coefficient of ***C*** to ***D*** elasticity could be taken as an indicator of the appearance of signs of the economic system slipping into a state of imbalance.

Figure 3. Dynamics of elasticity of the money supply to monetary base changes and GDP growth rates in Russia for the period of 2008-2018 (January-September)
Source: calculated by the authors according to the Bank of Russia data

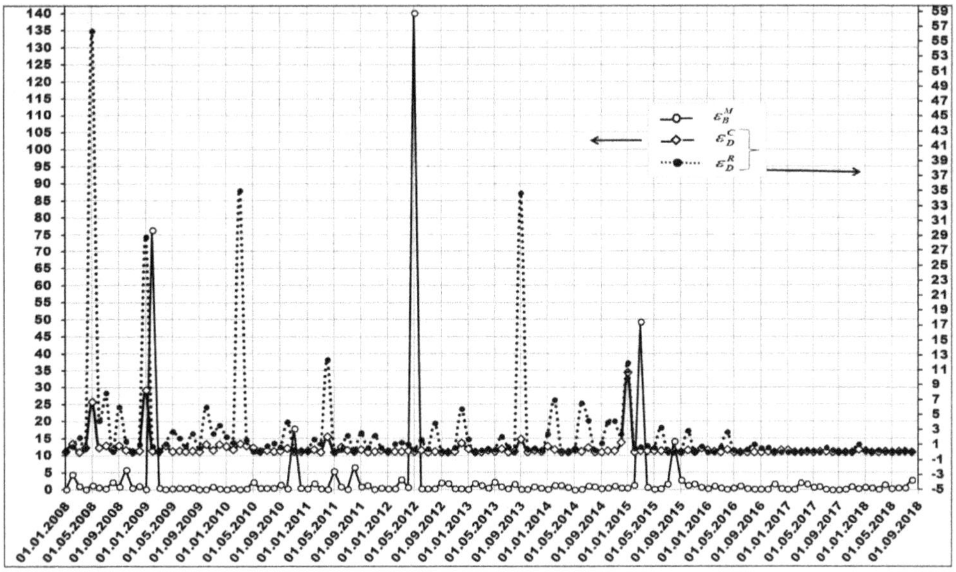

Figure 4. Dynamics of the multiplier **m** *as well as of GDP growth rates in Russia for the period of 2008-2018 (January-September)*
Source: calculated by the authors according to the Bank of Russia data

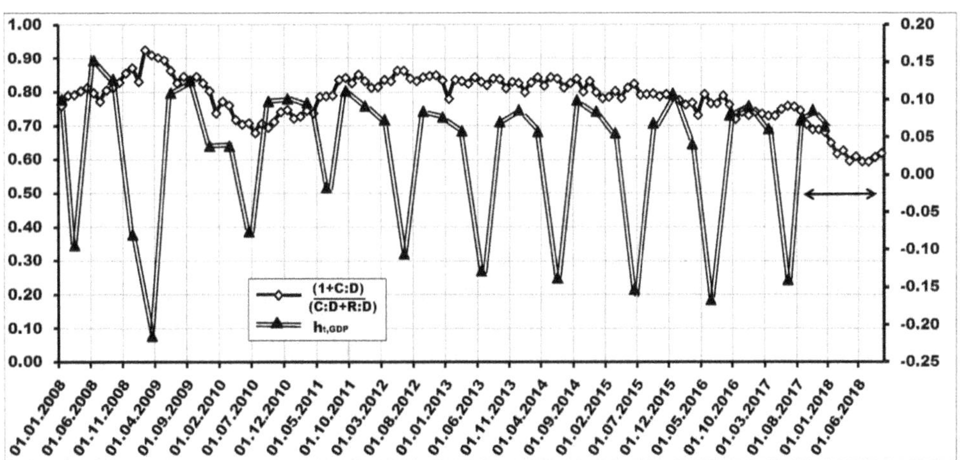

(3) The last step is aiming at reviewing through the elasticity correlations the ratio of reserves ***R*** (as the difference between ***B*** and ***C***) to deposits ***D*** in the denominator of the formula for the coefficient of money multiplier. The latter demonstrates the most significant volatility compared to the above indicators (coefficient of ***M*** to ***B*** elasticity as well as coefficient of ***C*** to ***D*** elasticity). The latter is very important because this indicator (in the denominator of the money multiplier equation - ***R / D***) contains reserves as a regulatory instrument in the hands of the central bank. So, in the process of self-organization of

exchange real markets generate the new structural level serving money exchange as an intermediary in real markets. And, in its turn, money markets form new markets that mediate the exchange of money as income-generating assets.

Given the content of Fig. 5, the authors clarify the role of the basic structural level in the model in Fig. 4. It consists in ensuring equilibrium in real markets (of consumer and investment goods and of the market for labor) and in resolving their dialectical contradictions by generating new structural levels in exchange.

Then the second structural level arises in the process of self-organization of exchange as a mechanism of self-development of the economy as a whole. It is initially organized in the form of money markets aimed at solving the problems of a lack of means of exchange in transactions in real markets. This is how self-organization of exchange manifests itself when a higher level of money markets, including the bank credit market, market for bonds, stock market and real estate market, are subordinate to solving dialectic problems of the basic level of exchange - real markets. However, as they develop, the latter acquire their own significance and autonomy, generating a new quality of money as the financial income-earning assets. And as demand for money in this quality grows, a dialectic contradiction arises in the money markets themselves. It is connected with the money markets' limits in organizing a new quality of transactions. As a result these dialectical contradictions are resolved by creating new markets for financial products that become specialized in transactions with money as income-earning assets (Santomero, 1996).

The existence of money as a financial asset gives each spending unit the opportunity to spend more or less than its income. It opens the way to lending by savers and borrowing by investors. It permits a more efficient allocation of spending to output in the complex economy. It turns out that money as the financial income-earning asset permits the reallocation of income among spenders and allows some potential spenders to pit their spending options against others. In other words, the new structural level of exchange in the form of a money markets begin gradually solving not only the problems of real markets, but also other problems associated with the placement and use of financial assets as a whole in the self-evolving economy.

*Figure 5. Dynamics of the numerator **(1+D/C)** and denominator **(1+R/C)** of the money multiplier equation as well as of the inflation **(j_t)** in Russia for the period of 2008-2018 (January-September)*
Source: calculated by the authors according to the Bank of Russia data

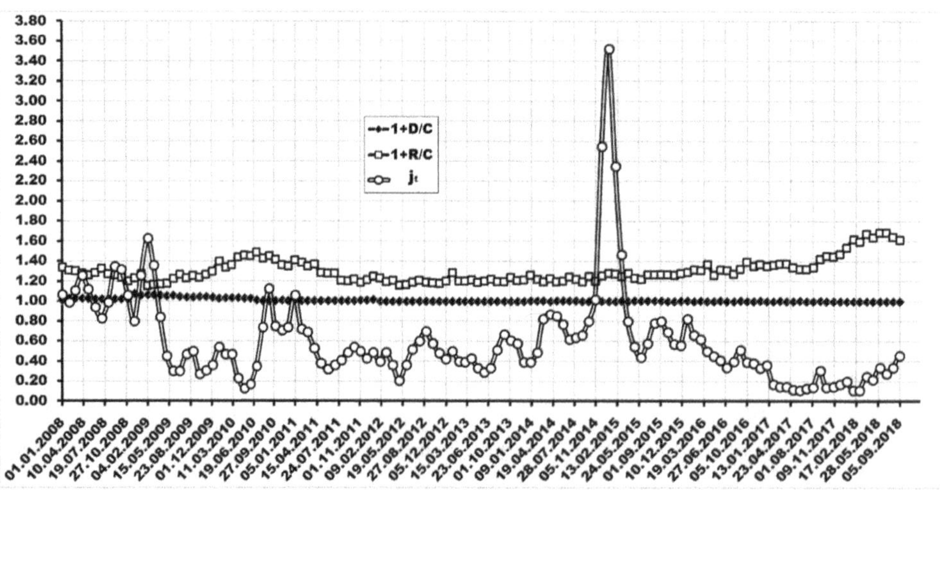

This was objectively predetermined by the fact that the expenses of economic agents began stably consisting only part of the income received by them. As a result, the share of deferred demand began to grow steadily in both absolute and relative terms, and its nomination in money led to the generation of their new quality to serve income-earning assets. The implementation of this new property of money predetermined the emergence of a new structural level of exchange in the process of its self-organization - financial markets in which various financial products began to be traded as a means of providing income-earning assets. The problem, as J.M. Keynes (1936) so brilliantly exposed, is that in a money economy, people do not experience the increase in desired savings as an increased desire, or need, to invest. Admittedly, the act of saving results in an increased flow of money into financial balances. So the increased supply of finance is met by an increased demand for finance. Moreover, currently the financial markets themselves in the process of self-organization of exchange generate their new segments, which, for example, in the case of markets of financial futures and of options are mainly markets for intermediaries rather than individuals or firms.

5.3. J.M. Keynes and H.P. Minsky on the "Propensity of the Market Economy to Instability": Subjective Factor of the Endogenous Mechanism of Shocks' Adjustment of Structural Fragility

The formation of the hierarchical structure of the market exchange in the process of systemic self-organization essentially represents the construction of a mechanism for ensuring the stability of the exchange itself as a guarantor of the integrity and stability of the economic system as a whole. However balanced estate of the complex economics is only an instant in an endless process of structural changes. They predetermine the gradual accumulation of their quantity, which will inevitably cause a new quality at the stage of transition of quantitative changes in the economy as a complex system to its new quality. Moreover, this stage ends with the shock's interruption of the "continuous" process of self-organization and with the jump of the system into the uncertainty of its dynamic state under the low of negation of negation.

The process of self-movement of exchange has its own specifics dictated by three dialectic laws of the economic system's complication. As to the specifics of self-organization of exchange at the stage of transition of quantitative changes to their new quality they could be described as follows. First, from the point of view of quantitative indicators, the modern exchange of economic activity and of its results is expanding at a galloping pace. Moreover, this happens not so much due to the expansion of real markets, although they grow at current prices, but rather through a spasmodic growth of financial markets. It is about the vertical structural levels of exchange represented by the markets where financial products and the income-earning assets are traded. This fact is confirmed by many authors. So, according to Franklin Allen, and Anthony M. Santomero (1996), financial markets such as the stock and bond markets have grown in size using nearly any metric, such as the value of companies listed or any other conceivable measure of their importance. In the 1970s and 1980s there has been extensive financial innovation accelerating. This includes the introduction of new financial products, such as various mortgage backed securities and other securitized assets, as well as derivative instruments such as swaps and complex options. These have all had a virtual explosion in volume. At the same time, new markets for financial futures, options and other derivative securities have appeared and become major markets.

Donald A. MacKenzie (2006) noted that in 1970 the market for financial derivatives in the United States and elsewhere was very small by today's standards (there are no reliable figures for its total size), and to trade many of today's derivatives, such as the Merc's S&P 500 futures, would have been illegal. By 1987, derivatives played a central role in the U.S. financial system. Derivatives markets were also beginning to emerge around the world. By June 2004, derivatives contracts totalling $273 trillion (roughly $43,000 for every human being on earth) were outstanding worldwide (MacKenzie, 2006). According to the Bank for International Settlements (2004, P. 10, Table A2) this figure includes the sum of the total notional amounts of exchange traded and over-the-counter derivatives contracts at the end of June 2004. Even after serious correction, derivatives remain a major economic activity. The Bank for International Settlements estimated the total gross credit exposure (Bank for International Settlements, 2003, P. 5) in respect to derivatives of the sixty or so largest participants in the over-the-counter (direct, institution-to-institution) market at the end of June 2004 as $1.48 trillion, roughly equivalent to the annual output of the French economy. As for exchange-traded derivatives contracts they had a total notional amount at the end of June 2004 of nearly $53 trillion. As a result there has been a dramatic change in the weight of financial services in the economy. The sector accounted for less than 3% of the US economy in 1950, 3½% in 1960, and still only 4% in 1970. But in 2007, on the eve of the Great Implosion, the sector's share had risen to about 8% (Markowitz, 1959, P. 288; Levy, and Markowitz, 1979). In the 1970s, the share of the financial sector in US domestic corporate profits was about 20%, but in 2002 it exceeded 40% (Black, et al., 1974; Bodie, et al., 1995).

From here follows the second conclusion, connected with the fact that such quantitative changes in the structural hierarchy of market exchange have given it a new quality. Such a grandiose volume of financial transactions could not have 100% material security. In other words, the vast majority of financial obligations of participants in transactions with derivatives were unsecured ones, now called "financial bubbles". However, following dialectical logic, the authors argue that financial transactions without material support should have been based on the substitute of the latter, which is connected with the subjective factor - human trust. The latter represents one of the main features of contemporary financial markets. However, the human trust of subjects of market transactions does not have a monetary value and is associated with other categories, including formal and informal institutions.

The specificity of structural connections in modern financial markets (both national and global ones) is the exchange of tradable assets for obligations to pay for the transaction with delay. Over time, the increasing transactions with financial assets are reoriented to unsecured liabilities. Under the new conditions, the cause-effect relationships between the levels of the vertical hierarchy of exchange can radically change, and turn into a house of cards, which is capable to be destroyed, starting from its upper floors to the lower ones. D. Sornette (2003) noted, that the origin of crashes is much more subtle than often thought, as it is constructed progressively by the market as a whole, as a self-organizing process (Fig. 6). The fundamental economic changes that took place on the eve of the price shock in the American market for unsecured mortgages in 2007 can be summarized as follows. Before the last global financial crisis, a situation was distinguished by a huge, ever-growing gap between the size of finances that ensure the redistribution of GDP and the volume of GDP itself. Moreover, if considering the hierarchy of structural levels of exchange, then it is increasingly taking the form of an inverted funnel: its lower levels, represented by real markets, are inferior in magnitude to the integrative unity of differentiated activities (as endogenous environment) (Fig. 6).

Figure 6. The result of self-organization of exchange at the stage of self-development of the complex economic system: the formation of a dialectical contradiction between the national *endogenous environment (integrative unity of differentiated types if economic activity) the structural hierarchy of* national *and* transnational *markets*
Source: the authors' development

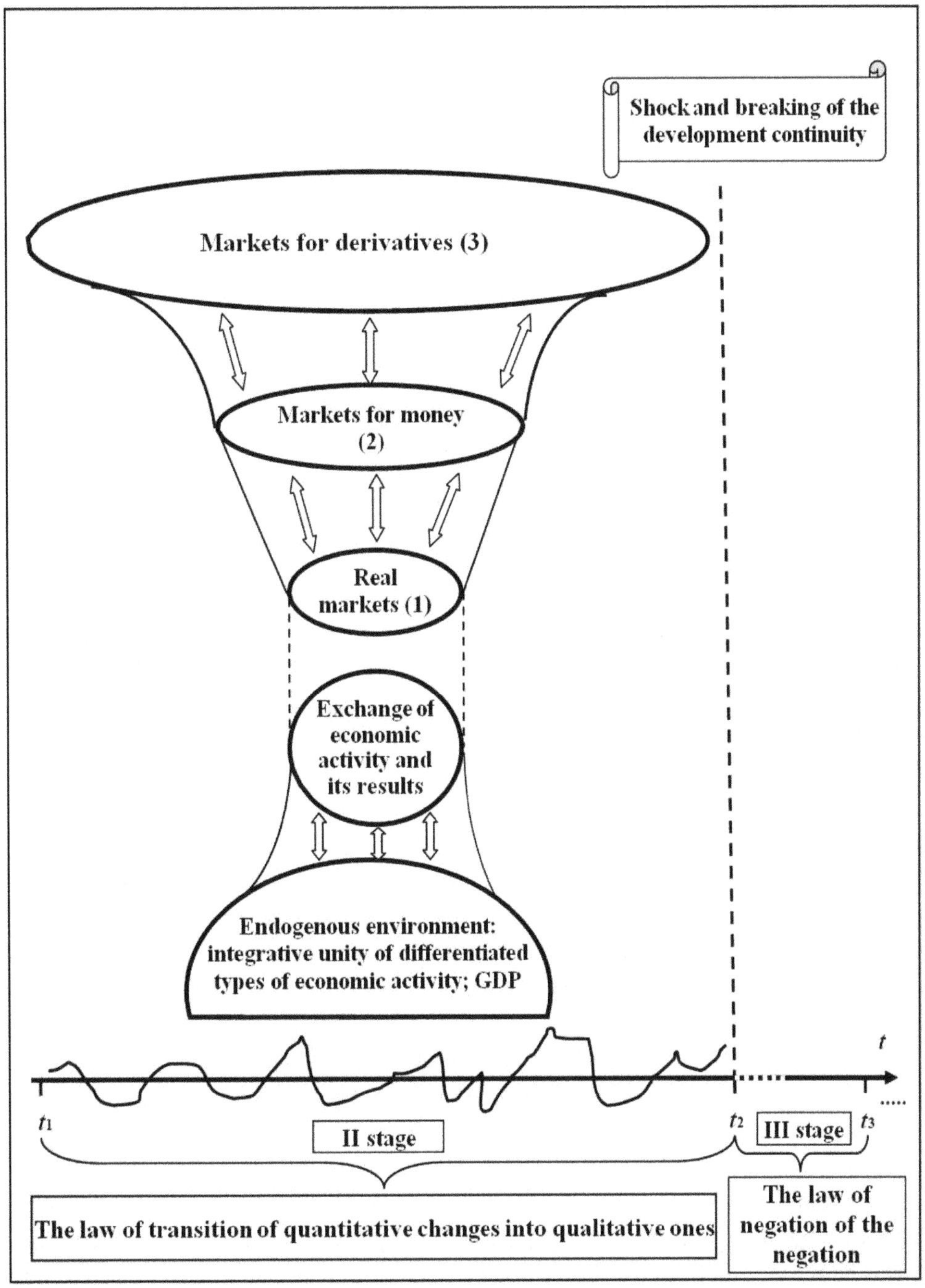

As for the next structural level of exchange represented by the money market, it has already exceeded the volumes of the real market as a whole. But financial markets, which are still in a constant process of self-organization, mediating the exchange of financial products, are transnational in scope. In other words, their scale far exceeds the GDP of any country in the world, including the United States. In other words, the process of self-organization of exchange as a mechanism for the self-development of economic systems, limited by the national framework, mediates their accumulation of quantitative changes, which make their new qualitative manifestations obvious (Bootle, 2009, P. 11) linked these changes on the eve of the global financial crisis of 2008-2009 with the dominance of the "Ponzi-lending" model (Minsky, 1985).

That predetermined the growth of debt financing in financial markets. For example, investors borrowed billions to invest in hedge funds, the latter borrowed billions more to invest in assets. So the whole financial system was a gigantic inverted pyramid of debt, resting on a tiny base of capital as well as of national GDP. It is about a rapidly growing gap between the endogenous environment of the national system, formed as a result of the interaction of differentiation and integration of economic activity within national borders, on the one hand, and the structure of the system, represented by the exchange of national and transnational economic activity and its results, on the other hand, which performs functions of the system's self-development mechanism. In the process of self-organization of exchange, its multi-level hierarchy was formed, including the highest level represented by numerous financial products' markets. The latter turned out to be able to mediate national and transnational structural ties, many times surpassing the material base (integration unity of differentiated types of economic activity) of any country in the world.

The weakest link in the structural hierarchy of exchange is its highest levels, represented by markets of (complex) financial products. It should be emphasized that the causal relationships of structural levels of exchange, built from bottom to top, strengthen the stability of the entire exchange system and the integrity of the economic system. However, if the causes and effects change places, and the financial chains of the dependencies of the exchange hierarchy begin to orient themselves from top to bottom, then the shock mechanism comes into effect. Under its influence, the existing dependencies between structural levels of exchange, between interconnected national and global markets, are being destroyed. In this case, not only the integrity of national economies, but also the global economic complex is endangered.

It is possible to restore balance, but specific forecasts in the conditions of complete uncertainty of the future are an ungrateful thing. From the point of view of dialectic logic, the authors determine the unconditional need to restore the dialectic interdependence between the endogenous environment and the exchange of new quality, which includes its most "problematic" level presented by the structured financial products market. Obvious to the authors is the fact that not a single national economy in its local framework can restore this relationship. According to the authors, this is exactly what Didier Sornette had in mind (Sornette, 2003), when he wrote that in that sense, the true cause of a crash could be termed a systemic instability.

Back in the last century, remarkable insights into the systemic imbalance of complex economic systems were made by J.M. Keynes (1937). Based on them H.P. Minsky (1957) formulated his own financial instability hypothesis, substantiating the idea of systemic instability of the capitalist (market) economy. It was he who formulated the dialectical paradox, according to which economic stability could be destabilizing. I. Rozmainsky (2015, PP. 120-143) reduced Minsky's main idea to the following three main points: (1) decision-making under uncertainty; (2) the cyclical nature of the capitalist production process; and (3) financial relations of the developed market economy (Minsky, 1985). From viewpoint of H.P. Minsky (1985), any market economy operates in the uncertain environment, because its future is fundamentally unknowable. At the same time, it is based on private ownership of production assets and functions largely due to the peculiarities of investing in these assets. Lack of reserves to meet the firms' investment demand (Keynes, 1937; 1939) was satisfied by banking institutions with the help of financial innovations (Minsky,1985), such as repurchase agreements, certificates of deposit, euro-dollar loans, securitization, "off-balance sheet activities" (for example, the provision of credit lines). In this sense the frequency of shocks and subsequent economic and financial crises is generated by negative changes in the expectations of economic agents and the systematic inability of firms (borrowers) to repay their debts to the financial sector. During the business cycle there appears a decrease in the liquidity of the balance sheets of economic entities, which makes the private sector more and more fragile. The obtained results confirm the correctness of the Minsky's hypothesis related to the financial sphere, capable to permanently generate instability.

In fact, the process of strengthening the fragility of the financial system, especially in terms of financial product markets, is associated with a reduction in the material security of the obligations of participants in the transaction. The separation of the exchange from its material base has a long history and begins when the monetary reserve maintained by the debtor against the money put into circulation becomes less than the total amount of these substitutes. In this case, the amount of money substitutes in excess of the reserve is converted into instruments that are not secured. The bank may issue instruments having coverage, for example, in the case of a commodity loan. Then he gives a loan only from equity or from funds in accounts that clients have entrusted to him. However, the issuance of instruments that do not have material security increases the bank's credit resources beyond these limits. In this case, it is about a fiduciary loan, which is ensured by the release of instruments without material security. It is such financial instruments that increase money circulation and the volume of markets' transactions (Mises, 1996). As a result, as material security of financial transaction liabilities decreases, the human trust between their participants becomes a significant factor in the stability of financial markets.

This is exactly what H.P. Minsky, (1992, PP. 7-8) meant, insisting on different financing regimes of the market economy that could make it stable or unstable. The second theorem of the financial instability hypothesis of H.P. Minsky proves that periods of long-term prosperity make the economic system move from stable financial relations to unstable ones (according to Minsky's ***"stability is destabilizing"*** (Minsky, 1992, PP.7-8). H.P. Minsky actually described the process of separating financial transactions from their material security using the "Ponzi-lending" mechanism as an example, when unsecured loans generated new unsecured loans for the purpose of paying interest on previous transactions. Nevertheless, this is not the only mechanism that mediates the separation of the material basis, represented by the integration of differentiated types of activity, from the exchange of its results. Commercial banks, for example, are able to withdraw risky debts (loans) beyond the balance sheets of their organizations. At the same time, new participants, objects, processes, etc., are involved in the exchange, which accelerate the process of separation of the financial obligations of participants in dialectic pairs in exchange from their material security. The case in point is the securitization mechanism of significant unsecured financial liabilities, the assignment of certain (often high) ratings to them and, in fact, the transfer of the risks of financial losses to unprofessional participants in financial transactions.

In addition, it is advisable to mention those financial instruments that mediate transactions, the essence of which R. Bootle (2009) determined by the expression «Money for Nothing». In his opinion, even where this is not the case, there is a justification for so much apparently zero-sum activity in financial markets. That is that it confers gains for society because it increases "liquidity" – that is, it enables each of us, both individuals and businesses, to transact quickly and cheaply, or to get our money back, at short notice and without loss. So the emergence of markets naturally tends to generate market activity – much of it activity that wouldn't have been missed if it hadn't been possible. So this kind of evolution of the financial markets further contributes to the endogeneity of the money supply. If the firms resort to external financing, then new determinants of investment process are connected with "lender risk" and "borrower risk". With the increase of debt investment, these risks grow, which limits the amount of capital investment. All above predetermines the content of the financial instability hypothesis of H.P. Minsky (1985, PP. 289-290), connected with the ability of the market economy to endogenously generate a financial structure that is predisposed to shocks' break of vertical structural relations in self-organizing economy. From the point of view of H.P. Minsky (2008), an increase in the financial sector depth, regardless of the needs of the developing real sector of the economy, may cause a gap between financial operations and their material base that destabilizes the stable economy.

The problems of the relationship between the sphere of finance and the economy as a whole are discussed quite deeply and often. Many authors (Bernanke, 1983; Kaminsky, and Reinhart, 1999; Schularick, and Taylor, 2012; Dell'Ariccia, 2001; Rajan, 2005, 2010) paid serious attention to conditions that are created for the formation of financial bubbles, the systematic risks underestimation, for the increasing fragility of the financial system and susceptibility to the negative impact of shocks.

As for the authors' point of view, the main thing in characterizing the unstable state of exchange, which gradually loses its ability to ensure the integrity of the economic system as a whole, is the inherent ability to upset the balance of the economy as a complex system. W.B. Arthur (2014) noted that disequilibrium is a natural state of the economy, and therefore the economy was always open to reaction. This is because the disequilibrium originates endogenously in the economy. Structural relationships of the economic system are interdependent, interconnected and diverse. Such kind of the structural relationships' property allows a shock effect, implemented in one market segment, to be extended through cooperative links to the other dialectically interconnected market sectors and so on along the chain of cooperative dialectic interactions. This effect of the shock impact multiplication is carried out by structural connections throughout the entire economic system, since it acts as a dialectical unity, integrating all the diversity of its many elements and structural levels.

All the above confirms the hypothesis of H.P. Minsky (2008) on the immanent instability of a market economy, predetermined by the state of its financial segments, which in every moment create the conditions for the shocks' break of structural relationships. The specificity of structural connections in modern financial markets (both national and global ones) is the exchange of tradable assets for obligations to pay for the transaction with delay. Over time, the increasing transactions with financial assets are reoriented to unsecured liabilities.

Consequently, if the marginal state of structural relations on such segments of financial market causes their shock breakdown, then the exchange of the assets to be traded and the payments of obligations concerning these transactions will not occur. Thus, there is a replication of the structural qualities according to the hierarchy of relationships interconnecting systems of varying degrees of organization. As a result, the shock effect on the structure of one system, violating its integrity, objectively initiates the destruction of structural links in the system of a higher level of organization, which integrates the above system. The essence of the process of accumulating quantitative changes that predetermined a new quality and self-developing economic system and self-organizing structure of exchange is to expand the practice of concluding unsecured transactions in financial markets. Being a dialectical phenomenon, they, on the one hand, were predetermined by the economic system objectively striving for growth, and on the other hand, they became a threat to its integrity as its systemic conflict escalated.

The core of concept of the gradual instability reintroduction in financial markets is connected with the uncertainty generated by finance in the process of the assets exchange in which the acts of purchase and sale separate in time and localization. These inter-temporal contracts voluntarily and gradually re-introduce uncertainty and risks about human trust, that represent one of the main features of financial markets and the cause of financial instability' reintroduction (O'Sullivan, et al., 2015). Financial markets can create potentially superior near-fiat-money substitutes as stores of value (in the form of bank credit, for example), but do it successfully only to the extent that uncertainty about trust can be properly priced and risk-managed. Continuing this idea, the authors can hypothesize that, for certain reasons, financial markets have enormous potential, both for stabilizing the exchange as a whole as a mechanism of self-development of the economy, and for the shock destruction due to changes in the technology of using cause-effect dependencies in it hierarchical structure (Anderson, et al., 1988; Anderson, 1972) endless in time, is realized. Entering the stage of quantitative economic changes and of the formation of the new quality, the economic system self-organization turns out to become a process of self-destruction under the influence of shocks.

The formation of the hierarchical structure of the market exchange in the process of its self-organization essentially represents the construction of a mechanism for ensuring the stability of the exchange itself as a guarantor of the integrity and stability of the economic system as integrity. However balanced estate of the complex economics is only an instant in an endless process of economic changes. They predetermine the gradual accumulation of their quantity, which will inevitably cause a new quality at the stage of transition of quantitative changes in the economy as a complex system to its new quality. Moreover, this stage ends with the shock's interruption of the "continuous" process of self-development and with the jump of the system into the uncertainty of the negation of negation towards its dynamics.

CONCLUSION

The dialectical approach to the specifics of the processes of self-organization and self-development of the economic system made it possible to prove the fact that technological progress is embedded in this self-propelled mechanism and substantiate the importance of technological progress for a static and new technological paradigm for a dynamic economy. The technological basis of a self-organizing and self-developing economy led the authors to the idea of the organic involvement of a person in these processes, because he coordinated them with his own goal of expanding the sphere of activity and with a means of achieving it.

The process of technology complication is mediated by a person, whose role becomes more and more significant as the demand for the high skilled workers grows. A person contributes to an ever more complete realization of the potential capabilities of technology if the level of his education is adequate to the requirements of technological progress at a particular stage. On this basis, the authors conclude that a person, mediating all the processes of system's formation in different spheres of his activity, actually predetermines the endogeneity of the mechanism that ensures both self-organization and self-development of all systemic integrities created by him.

All the above makes it possible to concretize the following features of the mutual influence of a person and his education, on the one hand, and changes in technologies at various stages of their complication, on the other.

1. In the ideal case of continuous technological progress, education should generate such qualities of an educated person that would allow him to realize the next stage of self-organization of technology.
2. If the quality of a person's education corresponds to the previous stage of self-organization of technology, then this will lead to an objective inhibition of the time spent on the next stage.
3. Taking into account the historical fact that the integration of science into the technological process greatly accelerates its progress, education should focus on the formation of a self-developing individual capable of intellectual autonomy in the face of the uncertainty of large-scale manifestations of the technological revolution 4.0.
4. The education system is a public institution, therefore, it is society and its attitudes in relation to the formation of a self-developing person that are priority to achieve the quality of human capital in terms of its education and specific requirements from technological structures.

So the main factor on which the prospect of technological progress and the future of the economic system and society depend is a human. It is about a person capable of constructing the future, possessing the qualities of intellectual autonomousness. It is in this context that the objectivity of the existence of an endogenous source of self-movement of all systemic integrities becomes obvious.

The process of raising the role of the subjective component of the self-organization mechanism of economic systems is connected with the formation of vertical hierarchy of structural links that mediate transactions in the money and financial markets. While real markets were provided with full-fledged money, or with their substitutes, really backed with obligations of central banks, the objects' component of structural ties predetermined the equivalence of market transactions of subjects participating in exchange transactions. The replacement of the object component of market exchange with "trust" as their subjective analogue occurred gradually as the number of transactions with deferred payment increased. It was about the self-organization of the economy due to the complication of structural ties and the formation of vertical structural levels serving transactions with money and with financial instruments. In parallel with the growth of the volume of such transactions, their security was increasingly detached from tangible assets and replaced by the obligations of the parties to the transaction based on trust. In addition, a person acts in several roles, creating new technological solutions, realizing himself as an economic entity and as a representative of society. And, it turned out that by mediating all structural connections in all system integers, it predetermines their quality.

Such a radical change in the quality of the equivalent in market transactions entailed serious problems for the market economy in terms of maintaining its equilibrium and stability. It is in this connection that the emergence of shocks as a mechanism of breaking non-working structural ties in connection with the agiotage behavior of participants in speculative market transactions becomes understandable. Structural interactions in the economic system have become more complex because of their vertical hierarchical structure and cause-and-effect relationships between its levels. These organizational changes made the economic system fragile, prone to shocks' rupture at the slightest violation of the cause-effect vertical relationships. This in itself predetermined more and more frequent shock destruction of structural bonds.

Back in the last century J.M. Keynes and H.P. Minsky formulated their understanding of the objectively present predisposition of the capitalist economy to instability. H.P. Minsky formulated the dialectical paradox, according to which economic stability could be destabilizing. Its essence could be reduced to the following: (1) decision-making under uncertainty; (2) the cyclical nature of the capitalist production process; and (3) financial relations of the developed market economy. It means the larger the financial markets become and the faster they break away from their material basis, the more fragile the market structure of the economic system becomes. This means that the subjective factor of trust in exchange transactions becomes the main guarantor of the stability of the economic system. But subjective grounds of systemic stability in economy are dependent on the societal integrity. However, on the eve of the coronavirus pandemic, it became obvious that society is increasingly dominated by the tendency of the subjects of market transactions to opportunistic manifestations of their personal values under the slogan "get rich at any cost". And with the growing importance of "trust" as a subjective basis for the equivalence of transactions in financial markets, the fragility of economic systems was aggravated by the disunity of society, the strengthening of its conflict principle. Thus, the separation of interests and values of citizens and society increased the susceptibility of the economic system to shock destructions of its structure. Thus, the elevation of the role of man in all fundamental processes associated with the construction of a dynamic economy of the future, leads to an understanding of the main essential feature of the future reality - with human-centrism in all structural transformations.

REFERENCES

Acemoglu & Autor. (2012). What does human capital do? A review of Goldin and Katz's *The Race between Education and Technology. Journal of Economic Literature, 50*(2), 426–463.

Acemoglu, D. (1998). Why do new technologies complement skills? Directed technical change and wage inequality. *Quarterly Journal of Economics, 113*(4), 1055–89.

Allen, F., & Santomero, A. M. (1996). *The theory of financial intermediation.* Working Paper Series. University of Pennsylvania. The Wharton Financial Institutions Center.

Anderson, P. W. (1972). More is different. *Science, 177*(4047), 393–396. doi:10.1126cience.177.4047.393 PMID:17796623

Anderson, P. W., Arrow, K. J., & Pines, D. (Eds.). (1988). *The economy as an evolving complex system.* Addison-Wesley.

Arcand, J.L., Berkes, E., & Panizza, U. (2015). Too much finance? *Journal of Economic Growth, 20*(2).

Arthur, W. B. (2013a). *Complexity economics: a different framework for economic thought.* Santa Fe Institute Working Paper: 2013-04-012.

Arthur, W. B. (1999). Complexity and the Economy. Science, 284, 107–109.

Arthur, W. B. (2009). *The Nature of Technology: What it Is and How it Evolves.* Free Press.

Arthur, W. B. (2013b). Complexity economics: a different framework for economic thought. In *Complexity and the Economy.* Oxford University Press.

Arthur, W. B. (2014). *Complexity Economics.* Oxford University Press.

Bank for International Settlements. (2003). *OTC Derivatives Market Activity in the First Half of 2003*. www.bis.org

Bank for International Settlements. (2004). *Triennial and Semiannual Surveys on Positions in Global Over-the-Counter (OTC) Derivatives Markets at end-June 2004*. www.bis.org

Beck, T., Levine, R., & Loayza, N. (2000). Finance and the sources of growth. *Journal of Financial Economics*, *58*(1-2), 261–300. doi:10.1016/S0304-405X(00)00072-6

Beneš, J., Ötker-Robe, İ., & Vávra, D. (2009). *Modeling with macro-financial linkages: credit and policy shocks in emerging markets*. IMF Working Paper, WP/09/123.

Bernanke, B.S. (1983) Nonmonetary effects of the financial crises in the propagation of the Great Depression. *American Economic Review*, *73*(3).

Black, F., & Scholes, M. (1974). From Theory to a New Financial Product. *The Journal of Finance*, *29*(2), 399–412. doi:10.2307/2978810

Bodie, Z., & Merton, R. C. (1995). The Informational Role of Asset Prices: The Case of Implied Volatility. In *The Global Financial System: A Functional Perspective*. Harvard Business School Press.

Bootle, R. (2009). *The Trouble with Markets: Saving Capitalism from Itself*. Nicholas Brealey Publishing.

Boston Consulting Group. (2017). *Russia 2025: From Workforce to Talents*. Boston Consulting Group, October.

Chandavarkar, A. (2009). *The Unexplored Keynes and Other Essays: A Socio-Economic Miscellany*. Academic Foundation.

Dell'Ariccia, G. (2001). Asymmetric information and the structure of the banking industry. *European Economic Review*, *45*(10).

DeLong, J. B., & Summers, L. H. (2002). *The "New Economy": background, historical perspective, questions, and speculations*. Economic Policies for the Information Age.

Demirguc-Kunt, A., & Detragiache, E. (2002). Does deposit insurance increase banking system stability? An empirical investigation. *Journal of Monetary Economics*, *49*(7), 1373-1406.

Demirgüç-Kunt, A., Feyen, E., & Levine, R. (2013). The evolving importance of banks and securities markets. *The World Bank Economic Review*, *27*(3), 476–490. doi:10.1093/wber/lhs022

Dodd, R. (2007). Subprime: tentacles of a crisis. *Finance & Development*, *44*, 15–19.

Domac, I., & Peria, M. S. M. (2003). Banking crises and exchange rate regimes: is there a link? *Journal of International Economics, 61*(1), 41-72.

Eichengreen, B. (2014). Secular stagnation: a review of the issues. In Secular Stagnation: Facts, Causes, and Cures. London: Centre for Economic Policy Research (CEPR).

Forbes, K. (2001). *Are trade linkages important determinants of country vulnerability to crises*. NBER Working Paper, No. 8194.

Freeman, C., & Perez, C. (1988). Structural crisis of adjustment, business cycles and investment behaviour. In G. Dosi (Ed.), *Technical Change and Economic Theory*. Frances Pinter.

Goldin, C., & Katz, L. (2008). The Race between Education and Technology. Belknap Press for Harvard University Press.

Gurley, J. G., & Show, E. S. (1968). *Money in a Theory of Finance*. The Brookings Institution.

HatziusJ.HooperP.MishkinF.SchoenholtzK. L.WatsonM. W. (2010). *Financial conditions indexes: a fresh look after the financial crisis*. NBER Working Paper Series, 16150. Retrieved from: https://www.nber.org/papers/w16150

IMF. (2009). *Staff Team from the Fiscal Affairs Department of IMF*. International Monetary Fund.

IMF. (2017). Global Financial Stability Report: Is Growth at Risk? Washington, DC: International Monetary Fund.

International Monetary Fund (2008). *Global Financial Stability Report: Containing Systemic Risks and Restoring Financial Soundness*. Washington, DC: IMF.

International Monetary Fund (2019). *Global Financial Stability Report: Vulnerabilities in a Maturing Credit Cycle*. Washington, DC: IMF.

Kaminsky, G., & Reinhart, C. (1999). The twin crises: The causes of banking and balance-of-payments problems. *American Economic Review, 89*(3).

Keynes, J. M. (1936). *The General Theory of Employment? Interest and Money. The Selected Works*. Harcourt, Brace and Company.

Keynes, J. M. (1937). The "ex ante" theory of the rate of interest. *Economic Journal (London)*, *46*(186), 241. doi:10.2307/2225525

Keynes, J. M. (1939). The process of capital formation. *Economic Journal (London)*, *49*(195).

Kindleberger, C. P. (1996). *Manias, Panics and Crashes. A History of Financial Crises*. John Willey&Sons, Inc.

Kindleberger, C. P., & Aliber, R. Z. (2005). *Manias, Panics, and Crashes: A History of Financial Crises* (5th ed.). John Wiley & Sons, Inc., Hoboken. doi:10.1057/9780230628045

King, R. G., & Levine, R. (1993). Finance and growth: Schumpeter might be right. *The Quarterly Journal of Economics*, *108*(3), 717–737. doi:10.2307/2118406

Laura, K. (2008). Crises of confidence…and a lot more. Finance & Development, 45(2), 9-13.

Law, S. H., & Singh, N. (2014). Does too much finance harm economic growth? *Journal of Banking and Finance*, *41*.

Lem, S. (1964). Summa Technologiae. Academic Press.

Levine, R., Loayza, N., & Beck, T. (2000). Financial intermediation and growth: Causality and causes. *Journal of Monetary Economics*, *46*(1), 31–77. doi:10.1016/S0304-3932(00)00017-9

Levine, R., & Zervos, S. (1998). Stock markets, banks, and economic growth. *The American Economic Review*, *88*(3).

Levy & Markowitz. (1979). Approximating Expected Utility by a Function of Mean and Variance. *The American Economic Review*, *69*, 308–317.

Lipton, D. (2019). Shining a light: bringing money out of the shadows means improving governance. *Finance & Development, 56*(3), 4.

MacKenzie, D. (2006). An Engine, not a Camera: How Financial Models Shape Markets. The MIT Press.

Mamonov, M. (2017). *Long-term forecasting of the size and structure of the Russian financial sector.* The Bank of Russia's Working Paper Series, No. 20.

Mamonov, M., Akhmetov, R., Pankova, V., Pestova, A., Solntsev, O., & Deshko, A. (2018). *Search for optimal depth and structure of the financial sector in terms of economic growth, macroeconomic and financial stability.* Series of Economic Research Reports, The Central Bank of the Russian Federation, No. 3.

Manpower Group. (2014). *The Talent Shortage Continues: How the Ever Changing Role of HR Can Bridge the Gap*. Manpower Group.

Markowitz, H. M. (1959). *Portfolio Selection: Efficient Diversification of Investments.* Yale University Press.

Marx, K. (1995). *Capital: A New Abridgement.* Oxford University Press.

McKinsey & Company. (2020). *The Next Normal: The recovery will be digital.* McKinsey.com.

McKinsey & Company. (2020). *What now? Decisive actions to emerge stronger in the Next Normal.* McKinsey.com.

McKinsey Global Institute, (2017). *The New Dynamics of Financial Globalization*. McKinsey Global Institute.

McKinsey Global Institute, (2018). *How secure is the global financial system a decade after the crisis?* McKinsey Podcast. McKinsey Global Institute.

Menzie & Forbes. (2002). A decomposition of global linkages in financial markets. In *Global Linkages Preconference.* International Monetary Fund.

Minsky, H. P. (1957). Central banking and monetary market changes. *The Quarterly Journal of Economics*, *71*(2), 171. doi:10.2307/1883812

Minsky, H. P. (1985). The financial instability hypothesis: a restatement. In P. Arestis & T. Skouras (Eds.), *Post-Keynesian Economic Theory: A Challenge Neoclassical Economics*. Wheatsheaf.

Minsky, H. P. (1992). Profits, deficits and instability: A policy discussion. In D. B. Paradimitriou (Ed.), *Profits, Deficits and Instability*. Macmillan. doi:10.1007/978-1-349-11786-4_2

Minsky, H. P. (2008). *Stabilizing an Unstable Economy*. McGraw-Hill.

Mises, L. H. E. v. (1996). *Human Action. A Treatise of Economics* (3rd ed.). Chicago: Contemporary Books Inc.

Mokyr, J. (2005). The Intellectual Origins of Modern Economic Growth. *Journal of Economic History, 65*(2), 285–351.

O'Sullivan, P., Allington, N. F. B., & Esposito, M. (Eds.). (2015). *The Philosophy, Politics and Economics of Finance in the 21st Century. From Hubris to Disgrace* (1st ed.). University of Cambridge. doi:10.4324/9780203797723

Ono, S. (2012). *Financial development and economic growth: Evidence from Russia. In Europe-Asia Studies* (Vol. 64). Taylor & Francis Journals.

Papadimitriou, D. B., & Wray, L. R. (2008). Minsky's Stabilizing an Unstable Economy: Two Decades Later. In *Unstable Economy. McGrow-Hill.*

Pedroni, P. (1999). Critical values for cointegration tests in heterogeneous panels with multiple regressors. *Oxford Bulletin of Economics and Statistics, 61*(4), 653–670. doi:10.1111/1468-0084.61.s1.14

Perez, C. (2002). *Technological Revolutions and Financial Capital: The Dynamics of Bubbles and Golden Ages*. E. Elgar. doi:10.4337/9781781005323

Perez, C. (2009). The double bubble at the turn of the century: technological roots and structural implications. *Cambridge Journal of Economics, 33*(4), 779–805.

Pilipenko, A. I., & Pilipenko, Z. A. (2018). Shocks in global economy: impulse model of macroeconomic cycle. In B. S. Sergi, F. Fidanoski, M. Ziolo, & V. Naumovski (Eds.), *Regaining Global Stability After the Financial Crisis*. Advances in Finance, Accounting, and Economics. IGI Global. doi:10.4018/978-1-5225-4026-7.ch012

Pilipenko, Z. A. (2012). *Global Financial Shocks' Impact on the World Economy.* Abstract of the Doctoral Thesis in Economics. Moscow: M.V. Lomonosov' Moscow State University Press.

Rajan, R. G. (2005). Has financial development made the world riskier? *Proceedings. Economic Policy Symposium, Jackson Hole Issue*. 10.3386/w11728

Rajan, R. G. (2010). *Fault Lines: How Hidden Fractures Still Threaten the World Economy*. Princeton University Press.

Rajan, R. G. (2010). *Fault Lines: How Hidden Fractures Still Threaten the World Economy*. Princeton University Press.

Rajan, R. G., & Zingales, L. (1998). Financial dependence and growth. *The American Economic Review, 88*(3).

Randall, D., & Mills, P. (2008). Outbreak: U.S. subprime contagion. Finance & Development, 45(2), 14-18.

Reinhart, C. M., & Rogoff, K. S. (2009). *This Time is Different. Eight Centuries of Financial Folly*. Princeton University Press.

Rioja, F., & Valev, N. (2004). Does one size fit all?: A re-examination of the finance and growth relationship. *Journal of Development Economics*, *74*(2), 74. doi:10.1016/j.jdeveco.2003.06.006

Romer, P. M. (1988). Increasing returns and long-run growth. *The Journal of Political Economy, 94*(5), 1002-1037. http://links.jstor.org/sici?sici=0022-3808(198610)94:5<1002:IRALG>2.0.CO;2-C

Rozmainsky, I. V. (2015). Investor myopia and persistence of the global crisis: A Post-Keynesian view. *Montenegrin Journal of Economics*, *11*(1), 107–116.

Sahay, R., Cihak, M., N'Diaye, P., Barajas, A., Bi, R., Ayala, D., Gao, Y., Kyobe, A., Nguyen, L., Saborowski, C., Svirydzenka, K., & Yousefi, S.R. (2015). *Rethinking Financial Deepening: Stability and Growth in Emerging Markets,* IMF staff Discussion Note, SDN/15/08.

SantomeroA. (1996). *The Regulatory and Public Policy Agenda for Effective Intermediation in Post Socialist Economies*. https://ssrn.com/abstract=7913

Schinasi, G. J. (2006). *Safeguarding Financial Stability: Theory and Practice*. IMF.

Schinasi, G. J., Drees, B., & Lee, W. (1999). Managing global finance and risk. *IMF Finance & Development*, *36*(December).

Schinasi, G. J., & Smith, T. (2000). Portfolio diversification, leverage, and financial contagion. *IMF Staff Papers*, *47*.

Schularick, M., & Taylor, A. (2012). Credit booms gone bust: Monetary policy, leverage cycles, and financial crises, 1870–2008. *American Economic Review*, *102*.

Schwartz, A. J. (1986). Real and pseudo-financial crises. In F. Capie & G. E. Woods (Eds.), *Financial Crises and the World Banking System*. St. Martin's. doi:10.1007/978-1-349-06788-6_2

Sergi, B. S., Zioło, M., Fidanoski, M. F., & Naumovski, V. (Eds.). (2018). *Regaining Global Stability After the Financial Crisis*. IGI Global. doi:10.4018/978-1-5225-4026-7

Shiller, R. (2004). *Irrational Exuberance* (2nd ed.). Princeton University Press.

Skidelsky, R. (2009). *Keynes. The Return of the Master*. Public Affairs.

Sloman, D. (2005). Economics. Publishing House "Piter".

Solow, R. (1957). Technical Change and the Aggregate Production Function. Rev. Economics and Statistics, 39, 312–320.

Sornette, D. (2003). *Why Stock Markets Crash: Critical Events in Complex Financial Systems*. Princeton University Press.

Summers, L. H. (2014). Reflections on the 'New Secular Stagnation Hypothesis'. In Secular Stagnation: Facts, Causes, and Cures. Centre for Economic Policy Research (CEPR).

Tabarraei, H. R., Rouabah, A., & Pierrard, O. (2019). *Sovereigns and financial intermediaries spillovers*. IMF Working Paper, WP/19/43.

Thornton, H. (1802). *An Enquiry into the Nature and Effects of Paper Credit of Great Britain.* Augustus Kelley.

WEF. (2020). Taking the Pulse of the New Economy. *Chief Economists Outlook.*

WEF. (July 2020). Emerging Pathways towards a Post-COVID-19 Reset and Recovery. Chief Economists Outlook.

World Bank. (2018). *World Development Report 2018: Learning to Realize Education's Promise*. World Bank.

World Economic Outlook. (2018). *Challenges to Steady Growth.* Washington, DC: IMF.

Yaryomenko, Y. V. (1997). *Theory and Methodology of Research of a Multilevel Economy*. Moscow: Publishing House.

Zioło, M. (Ed.). (2019). *Social, Economic, and Environmental Impacts Between Sustainable Financial Systems and Financial Markets*. IGI Global.

Chapter 6
The Institutional Component of the Shock's Mechanism:
Stabilization of the Economy at the Cost of Destabilization of Society

ABSTRACT

In all objective processes of self-movement of systems, the subjective aspect associated with a person as a thinking creature is seen. This introduces a fundamental aspect of being aware of the actions of a creative person, who should feel freedom as a perceived necessity. So, society and its integrity come to the fore, which will predetermine the dialectic of interaction with the economy. It is this aspect of the state's activity that will make its way through a long thorny path, since it is preceded by the experience of the government in a capital-centric economy with the economic measure of all its successes. And the formation of a human-centric organization is a completely new sphere of nation states' activity. In these conditions, the state should be responsible for ensuring the integrity of systems, or rather for the institutionalization of their dialectical interaction and their adequate self-structuring in all spheres.

INTRODUCTION

The dialectic logic of the subordination of chapters is dictated by the need to consider first the features of self-movement of the economic system at the stage of its self-organization, and then at the stage of its self-development. In the course of researching the process component of the shock implementation mechanism, the authors encountered the peculiarities of integrating the object and subjective components into it. The object component was successfully described using the dialectic of exchange and changes in the goods that mediate it. However, the study by the authors of the mechanism of self-organization of structural ties only through the prism of material mediation of purchase and sale transactions made it possible to conclude that the self-structuring of the economic system in this case was driven by two universal organizational mechanisms of positive and negative selection (Chapters 3 and 4). However, this did not explain the shock phenomenon in any way. Following dialectical logic, the authors were

DOI: 10.4018/978-1-7998-4309-2.ch006

forced to look for a dialectical pair of the object component of the shock mechanism of mediating the laws of self-movement of systemic integrities in the economy, since only it could help find the place of the shock mechanism in the dialectic laws of their self-movement. Highlighting the subject component of market exchange and structural links of the economic system allowed the authors to highlight the difficult predictability of shocks. This was explained by their subjective component (mediation of the mechanism for the implementation of shocks by the subjects of market transactions), which acted as a dialectical pair with an object component. As a result, it is logical to assume that the self-organization of the object component of the structure of the economic system was regulated by positive and negative selection, and the subjective mediation of structural connections was regulated by the mechanism of shocks, rejecting non-working connections and thus strengthening the integrity of the system.

To be convinced of the validity of this conclusion, the authors were forced to investigate the subjective factor and determine the tendencies of its increase in importance at the stage of self-organization of the economic system and during the leap of the system to the stage of its self-development. In the first case, the rise of the subjective component was proved by the example of the formation of vertical structural ties in a self-organizing economy, the specificity of which was the gradual replacement of the monetary equivalent as an intermediary in financial transactions with subjective "trust". So the subjective component of the shock mechanism replaced the object component of the positive and negative selection of organizational forms in the economy (Chapter 5). This allowed the authors to explain the phenomenon of the embeddedness of the mechanism of shocks into the dialectical laws of unity and struggle of opposites, of the transition of quantitative changes into qualitative ones and of the denial of negation (Chapter 4). In the latter case, the subjective factor is considered in connection with the implementation of technological progress, which in this context cannot but be an endogenous factor in the self-movement of the economic system, especially at the stage of its self-development.

If to proceed from the authors' hypothesis about the embeddedness of shocks in the structural ties of economic systems, or rather in the order of implementation of dialectical laws, then the following proposition can be formulated. While economic systems are at the stage of self-organization, which is realized in the process of changing the system and complicating its structure, their imbalance arises objectively. It goes like this. The system, the structural links of which are based on the balance of interests of the participants in exchange transactions, is constantly becoming more complicated, since their moods change – from 100% coincidence of interests to 50% and from 50% to 0%. These changes are reflected in the action of dialectical laws – the unity and struggle of opposites and the transition from quantitative changes to qualitative ones. The turning point in the operation of these laws occurs at the moment when the interests of participants in market transactions begin to diverge (from 50% to 0% or from 0% to 50%) and turn into either a struggle of opposites (in the case of the law of unity and struggle of opposites) or an increase in quantitative changes (in the case of the transition of quantitative changes to qualitative ones). It is during these transitional moments in the state of structural connections that the importance of positive and negative selection procedures increases. If they are combined optimally, then the differentiation of objects and subjects of market transactions will not go beyond the organizational framework, and the integrity of the system will be preserved. Otherwise, the mechanisms built into these laws and implemented by the shock rupture of ineffective, unpromising structural ties from the point of view of returning the stability and equilibrium of the system are activated. Something similar was described by V. Arnold (1975, 1979) when he considered the limiting state of centripetal and centrifugal forces in a mathematical model (phase portrait) describing the equilibrium state of the system. If the mechanisms of positive and negative selection did not lead to an adequate organizational solution, a shock mechanism is triggered, restoring the integrity of the system at the stage of its self-organization. This is, in fact, the object and process components of shocks. As for their subjective component, the form of its implementation is associated with the "freedom" of a person to observe the norms of behavior accepted in the economy as a "perceived need".

Following this logic, the position of Chapter 6 becomes understandable, which is devoted to the mission of the subjective factor in the implementation of the above dialectical laws of self-movement of systemic integrity and in the action of the mechanism of shocks mediating these laws that arise at their turning point for the purpose of strengthening the structure of the system at the stage of its self-organization and for its destruction when the system leaps into the dynamic stage of its self-development. In this context, paragraph 6.1 is devoted to the problem of the subjective factor, which until recently was not considered in its multivalued integrity: both as Homo Sapiens and simultaneously to the same extent as both Homo Economicus and Homo Socius (Durkheim, 1895; Schwartz, et al., 2012; Weber, 1947). This lack of understanding of a person in his dialectical diversity is the ineffectiveness of the interaction of formal and informal institutions in the economy and the reason for the lack of understanding of the dialectics of their interaction with social institutions. That is why the phenomenon of stabilization of the economy at the cost of destabilization of society remains so stable, which predetermined such negative consequences of the destruction of national structures in connection with the COVID-19 pandemic (paragraph 6.1). Such a systemic mismatch between the economy and society has been investigated in conditions of self-organization under the influence of the law of unity and struggle of opposites (paragraph 6.2), of the transition of quantitative changes to qualitative ones (paragraph 6.3) and of double negation (paragraph 6.4).

6.1. Stabilization of the Economy at the Cost of Destabilization of Society: Formal Institutions in Economics vs. Social Institutions in Society

As the building of an increasingly complex vertical hierarchy of structural ties in national economies and the increasingly frequent repetition of shocks and subsequent global financial crises, the financial problem has come to the fore in ensuring the stability of the economy. Since the 2000s financial stability issue has become an increasingly significant objective in financial researches as well as in economic policymaking. More and more national central banks have been launching the projects devoted financial stability safeguarding. International organizations such as the International Monetary Fund (IMF), the Bank for International Settlements (BIS), and the World Bank did not become an exception. The scientific publications continued growing dealt with specific financial-stability problems, debating the special role of the government, the causes, consequences, the causes of emergence of financial crises (Bordo, et al., 2001) as well as their considerable costs (Lindgren, et al., 1996; Caprio, et al., 2010, Caprio, 2013; Hoggarth, and Saporta, 2001). Great interest was caused by the problem of assurance of stable and smoothly functioning financial and payments systems (Volcker, 1984) as well as of market sources of financial fragility and systematic risk (Acharya, et al., 2011; Allen and Gale, 2003, 2004; Bernardo and Welch, 2004). In fact, it was about finding mechanisms for institutionalizing the behavior of financial market participants that could adequately maintain their stability and prevent financial shocks in a timely manner. But instant problems, requiring solutions, were complicated and stresses arose within a poorly understood set of formal institutions on the global and national financial markets. So in spite of the important progress in understanding specific financial-stability issues the challenges of fundamental financial stability safeguarding problems have been and still are daunting. The contemporary version of this problem is further complicated by the COVID-19 pandemic shock, falling rates of economic growth and disintegration tendencies all over the world.

Thus, in fact, the problem of financial instability was not in any way associated with the state of society, although the behavioral aspect associated with the behavior of players with financial assets was highlighted in it. The essence of financial instability understanding should be preceded by the theoretical treatment of the category of finance that lacks a generally accepted and used framework. Finance predetermines the stability of the financial system, representing its structure as a set of persistent recurring interrelations of participants of transactions of assets' sales and purchases that do not coincide in time and space. In this interpretation the sellers and the buyers of the assets as well as acts of buying and selling that mediate the transfer of the asset and the monetary equivalent of the market value from one partner of the transaction to another, are dialectical couples whose sustainability depends on sustainability as the special quality of these relations. Being dialectically interconnected, sellers and the buyers of assets mutually assume and at the same time deny each other. So only the simultaneous existence of the seller and the buyer of the object of exchange, as well as of the acts of its purchase and sale, makes it possible to realize the exchange of assets for cash equivalents of their value with postponed payment on the part of the buyer or with postponed delivery of the asset by the seller. This quality of the dialectical connection between the seller and the buyer of the transaction causes uncertainty in their relations which generates greater or lesser risks of losses as a result of the assets exchange with differed maturity or delivery.

If finance means structural relations of partners of transactions with deferred payment or delivery they form the structure of the national financial system and, being stable, preserve its stability, but, being destroyed, predetermine its instability at the macroeconomic level. The main cause of the financial instability of economic system is connected with the marginal state of financial system, mediating the structural relationship between sellers and buyers of any asset in the transactions with differed maturity or delivery. The state of structural (financial) relations of the participants of dialectical pairs will be stable until the price fluctuations of the traded assets overcome their marginal level (of values). And even after theoretical breakthroughs of G. Akerlof and R. Shiller [Akerlof, et al., 2009; Shiller, 1984, 2002, 2004, 2015] the behavior of economic agents was in no way connected with their position as individuals in society. The reasoning was as follows. The breakdown of financial or structural relations between dialectically interrelated partners of transactions hinders the sale of products, the completion of production processes, the receipt of income and the acquisition of necessary goods and services by households, by firms and by the state (the public sector) that does not safeguard the financial stability of the economic system (Pilipenko, et al., 2018, PP. 245-246).

If all the financial relations could be defined as a structure of the economic system, then they represent the basis of the national financial system, which, as a whole, mediates the exchange of assets, with the acts of purchase and sale, separated in time and space. It is logical to assume that finance, forming the structural relations, predetermines financial stability or instability as a state of the economic system. And in these conditions, the stability of the economy began to be linked directly with the maintenance of financial stability. Although it has already been proven that it was the agiotage behavior of market actors that caused a shock rupture of structural ties in a particular market. In other words, the social roots of this behavior of the individual as an economic subject were completely ignored. Not even taken into account the fact that although in modern economies all the stages of assets exchange processes are uniquely related to money, but acts of purchase and sale, separated in time and localization, involve elements of participants trust. It should be taken into account that in such transactions money is used as a universally accepted means of payment because of the expectation and trust that will also be accepted by others. But finance can create potentially superior near-fiat-money substitutes as stores of value (in the form of bank credit, for example), but does it successfully only to the extent that uncertainty about trust can be properly priced and risk-managed. In essence, finance is a temporary exchange of the finality-of-payment services of fiat money for a promise, and this promise involves uncertainty about human trust (Schinasi, (2006), p. 33; Kindleberger, (1993), p. 21) that plays an essential role in the economic activity. Dealing with trust as fragile human emotion finance is intrinsically fragile and, therefore, subject to instability under certain conditions.

Taking the above into account it makes possible to treat the finance as the human promise to pay back fiat money to those willing to part with its services temporarily. In the developed modern societies some sort of social arrangements has been created – as to social and business conventions, financial institutions, financial markets – in order to provide liquidity and low risks as well as to facilitate any inter-temporal exchanges involving human promises and trust. Such social arrangements can be defined as the way any society resorts to minimize the uncertainty and risks (Shubik, 1999). If confidence in the trust underlying economic and financial transactions breaks down, the ability of markets and financial institutions to perform their basic pricing follows the same way. This breakdown means the threats of financial instability.

If the economic system is exposed to the uncertainty and risks then all the dialectically interrelated parts of the market transactions should do their best to minimize their negative influence. If the production costs are easily controlled and evaluated, as to transactional costs assessment it presents great difficulties. The finance as a process accompanied by the gradual reintroduction of the uncertainty and risks is connected with transactional costs that could be characterized as the price of the uncertainty and risks. The longer the inter-temporal gap between the acts of assets' sales and purchases the greater the importance of financial institutions (social arrangements) aimed at minimizing the transaction costs of finance. In this sense the finance as the process of the uncertainty and risks minimization is accompanied by the efforts of the sellers and the buyers to decrease positive transaction costs with the help of some social settlements (Coase, 1937, 1988). To settle this problem the organizations and institutions prove to be very useful (Menard, 2003). Modelling an efficient stable financial economy requires a complex mix of formal and informal institutions, as emphasized by D. North (1990). Market organizations are represented by the social settlements of the partners in different forms, but the institutions are defined as the behaviour rules, incentive and punishment mechanisms, settled by them. In this sense the core of institution as a category can be defined as a means of cooperative solution of the partners' problems appeared in the process of market exchange (North, 1987, 1990, 1997, 2005).

So the market exchange transactions institutionalization is realized in the form of contracts between the buyers and the sellers of any assets that minimize the market uncertainty and decrease risks of breaking down contract obligations of transactions' partners (Hodgson, 1988). So, the institutions can play a positive role when trust is solidly grounded, but may also hamper the financial stability and the development of financial transactions, when trust is absent or, even worse, when corruption and illegal activities push transaction costs towards price margin (Oleinik, (2007), Chapters II.2 and II.6). The formal institutions make much sense in preventing and guaranteeing security of transactions as well as transactors and of the centrality of the judicial system in safeguarding financial stability.

Formal institutions are precisely those structures that are designed to regulate the behavior of participants in market transactions. In other words, the generation of formal institutions by the state is a fact of recognizing the importance of the subject component of market exchanges and an attempt to regulate human behavior for the purpose of stabilizing the economic system. However, formal institutions are called upon to solve the behavioral problem in economics, abstracting from the fact that the roots of the irrational behavior of subjects are concentrated in society. Moreover, the prerequisites for their appearance and the functions that in this regard they must perform were determined by high transaction costs and high risks of the implementation of transactions. In other words, it is about the fact that a person can manifest himself in the economy in different markets both as a subject who strengthens the integrity of the system by his actions, and as a participant in the destruction of structural ties, which negatively affects the integrity of the system.

Expressing this idea in a chain of logical reasoning about the mechanisms of self-organization and self-development of the economy as an integrity, it is necessary to take into account this behavioral aspect in the context of the operation of all dialectical laws discussed above, and in connection with the state's desire to limit the destructive action of subjects with the help of formal institutions. Moreover, it turns out that formal institutions, in fact, should be aimed at regulating the subject component both during the period of self-organization of the economic system and during its self-development. And if the subjective component was previously inscribed by the authors into the structure of the system, which ensures its integrity, therefore, formal institutions also accompany structural connections. Moreover, their focus on their stability is quite obvious.

In the authors' concept, shocks are integrated into the mechanism for the implementation of dialectical laws and perform the function of instant destruction of structural ties in the market segment that poses the greatest threat to the stability of market exchange. Moreover, the object, subjective, and process components are involved in the implementation of shocks. If the state tries to exert a regulatory influence on the subjects, orienting them towards the observance of a socially significant order in market transactions, then one way or another, shocks should integrate the institutional aspect in the forms of their manifestation. Then shocks, destroying structural ties, thereby "encroach" on the formal institutions created by the state, rejecting them as ineffective along with structural ties and the objects and subjects of exchange participating in them. Thus, it is necessary to analyze formal institutions for their dialectics, reasons for change and inefficiency (Polterovich, 2010, North, 1987, 1990, 1997, 2005) understood by institutions as the "rules of the game" which, in the context of our reasoning, should strengthen exchange, structural ties and the integrity of the economic system. Thus, serving the subjective component of structural ties, formal institutions must also represent a dialectically complex structure. And, indeed, it manifests itself in the fact that they embody the dialectical unity of mechanisms for the implementation of incentives (in the case of compliance with certain "rules" by the subjects of transactions) and the implementation of restrictions (in case of non-observance of certain "rules" by the subjects of transactions). Moreover, the priority of these dialectically interacting mechanisms within the framework of formal institutions should objectively change depending on the prevalence of a specific dialectical law in the formation of structural ties, from the moment of breaks in these laws and the maturation of a certain quality of shocks (in the conditions of formation of horizontal or vertical ties, or when the system jumps from static state to dynamic).

It should be emphasized that formal institutions, as the interaction of motivation (incentives) and restrictions (punishments) for the subjects participating in structural connections in the exchange of various benefits, should mean what the state expects when institutionally accompanies their behavior in the economy. However, the individual's attitude to incentives and restrictions (formal institutions) in economic relationships is predetermined not by the economy, but by value concepts that arise in the social sphere as a result of self-organization and self-development of the individual. Formal institutions as a dialectic of motivation and punishment from the standpoint of the state and in the view of individual economic agents may not coincide. Moreover, the latter may come into conflict with formal institutions. In this situation, both the motivation mechanism and the punishment mechanism can give a negative result – the opportunistic (irrational) behavior of economic agents, which will destroy the structural connections of the system and its stability. It is important to note that in the context of the divergence of the positions of the state, represented by formal institutions, and the subject of market transactions, the implementation of the punishment mechanism will give a doubly negative result. If such conditions are formed and will apply to a critical mass of citizens, then no progress in technology and economy will be achieved.

The institutional aspect of structural ties and the mechanism of their shock destruction built into them are represented by the phenomenon of the dialectical pair "formal institutions - informal institutions». If formal institutions are constructed by society represented by the state, then informal institutions are created by subjects or their organizations as substitutes for formal institutions. By the way, the interaction of formal and informal institutions can be represented using the dynamic set model, which was already used in Chapter 3 (Fig. 3 and 4). Only their meaning will be somewhat different. If there is one dynamic set, represented by formal institutions, the implementation mechanism of which is 100% approved by economic agents, then there is no need for informal institutions (Fig. 1).

The situation in Fig. 1 can be called ideal, since there is a consensus in the economy. The stability of the economy is not threatened by the divergence of interests between the state and participants in market exchanges. However, more often formal and informal institutions substitute for each other if they are ineffective from the point of view of economic agents. If this substitution is expressed by the intersection of dynamic sets represented by formal and informal institutions, then as the sphere of their intersection increases from 0% to 50%, the efficiency of the replaced institution decreases (Fig. 2). Instead, the institution that replaces it strengthens its significance. In this case, two extreme situations are possible: if a formal institution is squeezed out, then the integrity of the system is under threat; if this happens with an informal institution, then, on the contrary, structural ties are strengthened. This interaction of formal and informal institutions, including the dialectics of the incentive and punishment mechanisms they contain, cannot be adequately understood based only on systemic categories associated with the economy. This is due to the fact that the formation of individual (subjective) ideas about the adequacy of the norms of behavior in the economy occurs in society, or rather, when a person's abilities for self-organization and self-development are realized.

In other words, the reasons for the ineffectiveness of formal institutions, in terms of the individual's observance of the rules of behavior in market transactions, lie not in the economy, but in society. It turns out that the state is trying to regulate the economic behavior of a market agent with tools of an economic nature, although it is predetermined by a person's position in society. More precisely, it is about its integrity, predetermined by adequate mechanisms of human transcending into society, outwardly acting in the form of his socialization (Chapter 11.2).

In Fig. 3 the substantiation of the fundamental reason for the inefficiency of formal institutions in the economy due to the orientation of their mechanisms of encouragement and punishment on the economic person is given. However, the rational or irrational (opportunistic) behavior of an individual in the economy is based on social roots, which are predetermined by his self-organization and self-development, primarily in society (Chapters 4.1 and 5.1). It turns out that it is the position of the individual in society that predetermines the manifestation of his individualized values in behavior as an economic subject.

It is in this sense that the person as human capital is associated with social capital, which in one or another combination integrates the individual-oriented and socially-oriented values of individuals (Schwab,

Figure 1. The dominance of formal institutions in market exchanges (from 100% to 50% of the total volume) predetermines the possibility of their replacement by informal institutions (in volumes from 0% to 50%)
Source: the authors' development

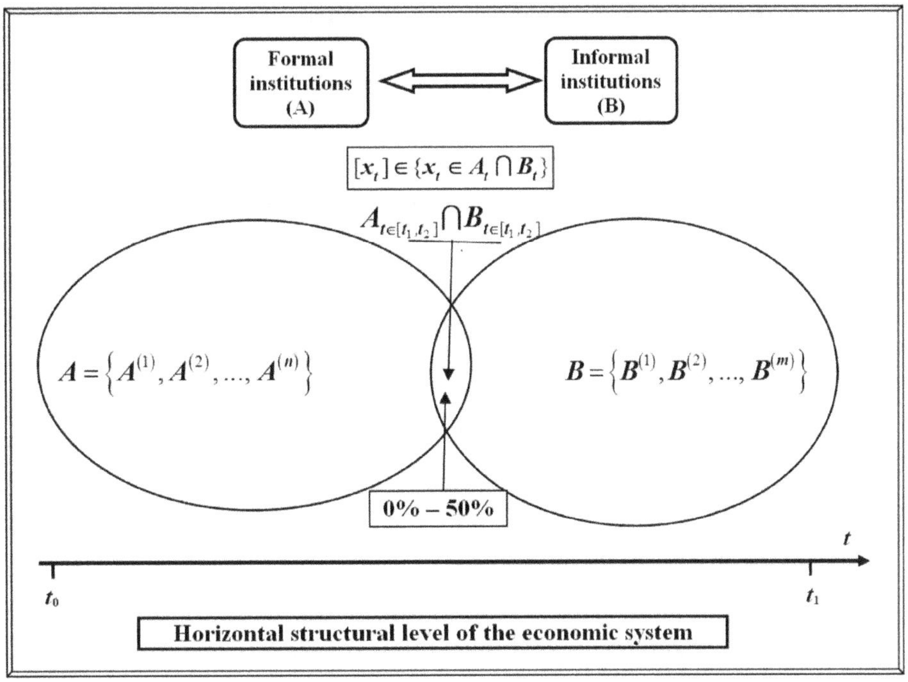

Figure 2. Replacement of formal institutions (50% to 0%) by informal institutions (from 50% to 100%) as ineffective from the standpoint of market entities.
Source: the authors' development

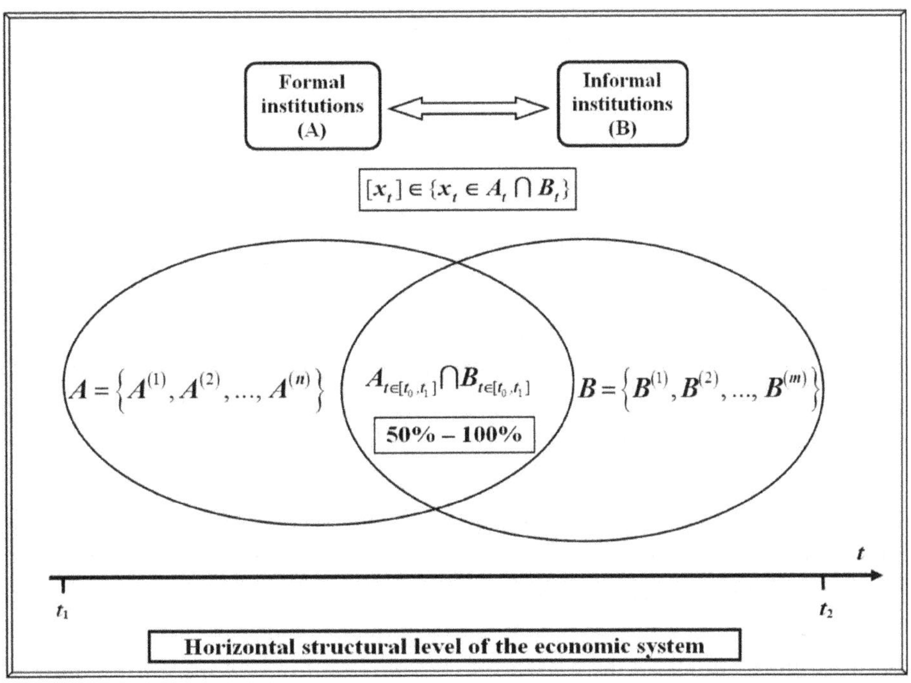

2016). And in this context, the society, at the stage of learning of individuals, should create the necessary conditions for the formation, both in the current and in the future, of socially oriented values in the form of attitudes and values. The graduate realizes his "failure" from the point of view of educational results acquisition. This negative post-educational feeling of a young individual as a carrier of human capital forms the basis of its individually-oriented values in relations with society as well as with economic system (including financial markets). They objectively predetermine his focus on opportunistic behavior in life at best with zero result ("win-lose") and at worst with negative result for all participants of social exchange. The more "unsuccessful" graduates of schools, the more modest will be the economic progress of the society, the less stable will be the social environment, as well as economics and finance.

Only an appropriately formed human capital is able to realize a new stage of technological and socio-economic progress. According to the author, this scenario can be realized only if there is adequate institutional support for an individual vital activity, in particular, in the process of his education and further implementation of his learning output in the profession. The theory of basic values of S. H. Schwartz (1994, 2012), as well as the developments of his followers (Magun, et al., 2015, 2015a) allow the author to link the fact that an individual forms his human capital with confessing certain values as desired cross-situational goals as guiding principles in his life (Schwartz, et al., 2012). To understand the value orientations of carriers of human capital, one should use the oppositely related pairs of value categories identified by S. Schwarz (1994) at the first level as follows: Saving vs Openness to changes; Self-affirmation vs Caring for people and nature. V. Magun, M. Rudnev and P. Schmidt (Magun, et al., 2015b) add to this structure the additional two pairs of broader second-level value categories: Individualistic orientation vs Social orientation and Self-defense vs Growth.

To understand the moment of generating conditions for the implementation of the subjective mechanism of shock, all of the above is of great importance. This is due to the fact that a person is a dialectically complex, controversial subject of economic activity. It contains genetically dialectical pairs of feelings, sensations, ideas, etc. (Fig. 3). In accordance with the Keynesian concept, any person makes serious investment decisions, relying on faith. But trust is easily replaced by distrust a positive assessment of the future is replaced by a negative, etc. But trust is easily replaced by distrust a positive assessment of the future is replaced by a negative one, etc. In fact, the dialectic of the relationship between rational and irrational principles manifests itself first in the psychological settings of a person, and then in his behavior.

It is important to emphasize that under the influence of many factors of an endogenous and exogenous nature under conditions of complete uncertainty of economic factors, the agent himself gives a subjective assessment of the environment and the factors that determine its change in the future he makes decisions and chooses a behavior model in accordance with his psychological settings. It should be borne in mind that the choice by subjects of market relations of priorities due to rational or irrational preferences begins to have a fundamental impact on the dynamics of the economic system as the effect of the "crowd" increases, that is, increasing the number of players and the volume of their transactions in assets' markets to a critical mass. If the leading strategy of these groups of subjects of market exchange becomes a game either on the demand side or on the supply side of assets, then the equilibrium of the sale and purchase transactions is destroyed, the market prices of the assets come off further and further from their base price. As a result, at the structural levels of exchange, dialectically determined interconnections of subjects of market relations begin to crumble, the process of multiplying the break in structural ties in all interconnected markets begins.

Thus, the effect of a crowd of irrationally minded subjects of market relations realizes shocks as a mechanism for breaking them under the condition of a maximum price gap for a traded asset. For this

Figure 3. Value orientations predetermined by the integration of an individual into society, and their manifestation in his behavior as an economic entity in the economy and in financial markets
Source: the authors' development

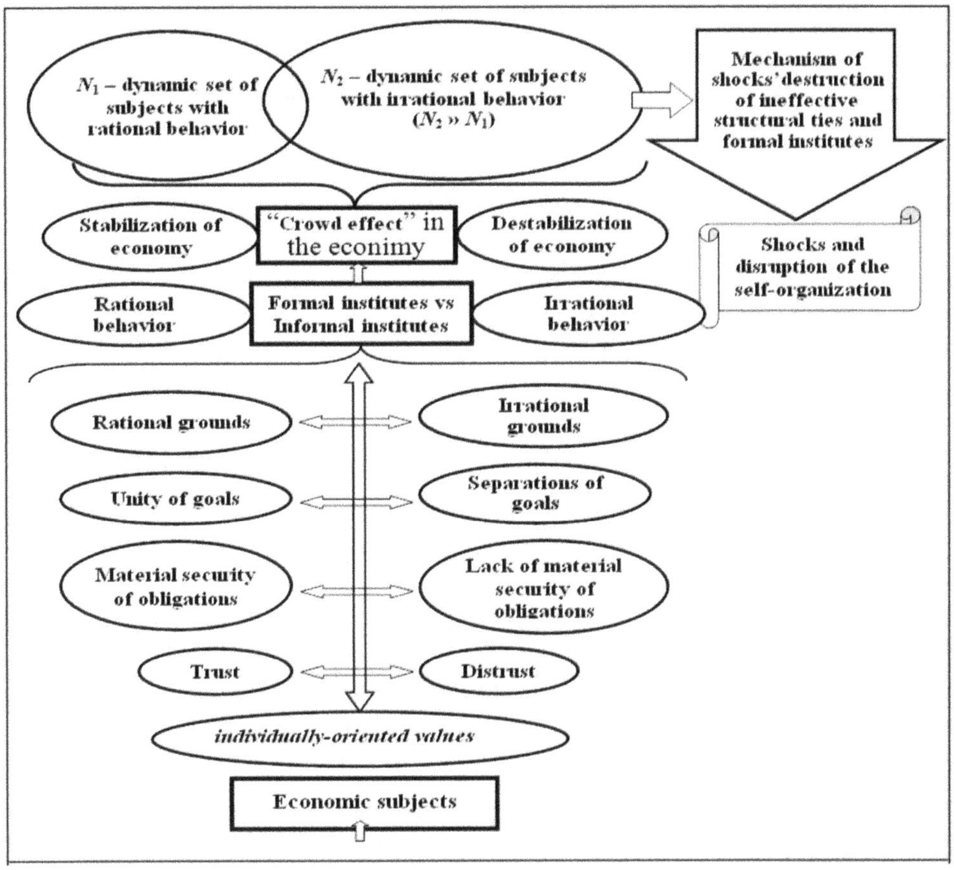

to happen, the subjects of market relations must be put by society in conditions that will force them to give preference to such psychological attitudes that will lead them to irrational behavior in the market.

As a result, it becomes possible to arrange the carriers of human capital on each of the above value axes, depending on their individual preferences. Then the latter can be estimated using the differences in the values of the corresponding value categories. While taking the "Individualistic Orientation – Social Orientation" value axis, then, according to V. Magun, M. Rudnev and P. Schmidt (2015b), each of the opposing values has a dual nature, which can be interpreted using the principle of social exchange (Homans, 1961; Gouldner, 1960). Then the formation and use of the human capital capable to become a driver of the social and economic progress under certain conditions is associated with the value orientations of its carriers as participants in social exchange.

Theoretically, there are two extreme options for the equivalent exchange of individuals with society, and, hence, two equilibrium states of its participants. First, it is about a socially oriented strategy of behavior of human capital carriers and, secondly, about individually oriented their values (Magun, et al., 2015; Magun, et al., 2015b). Two marginal cases of social exchange, in which these two opposite value orientations (located on opposite edges of the value axis) of individuals as carriers of human capital, are realized, provide participants with an equilibrium with a "zero amount" result (win-lose or lose-win). In other words, if a society benefits from individual, socially-oriented behavior, or an individual-oriented person benefits from the loss of society in return, the cumulative result is estimated to be zero at best, and at worst, to be absolute losses.

In any case, there will be no stable economic growth and sustainable social progress if it is achieved by subordinating the interests of some participants in the social exchange to the interests of others. Only in this way can one eliminate the opposition between the economic system and society. And formal institutions should be built on the foundation of the priority of the integrity of society and the predetermination of the individual's behavior in the economy from his state of agreement or disagreement with socially significant rules both in society and in the economy. In practice the result of social exchange with a "positive amount" (win-win) for carriers of human capital and for society as a whole is achieved only if their value orientations coincide. Such an outcome is possible only with adequate institutional support for the motivations (value orientations) of individuals who could serve the society with their human capital, subject to their interests and appropriate motivation. In other words, social exchange with a positive result (win-win) should be anticipated by appropriate institutional support for motivating individuals who form their human capital at the educational stage, and aimed at using it in order to stabilize economic growth at the stage of professional activity.

The evidence of the correctness of this statement is the events that occurred in 2007 on the market of unsecured mortgage loans in the USA. If at the same time trust collapses, then collectivism gives way to individual technologies of subjects for saving, and their rational behavior gives way to irrational ones. This behavior of partners in market transactions fills with different content causal relationships in the hierarchy of exchange: strengthening through the rational behavior of participants in dialectic couples, they begin to destroy their own interdependencies as the importance of irrational principles in their mass behavior is strengthened. These exchange characteristics are typical for a self-developing system at the stage of transition of quantitative changes to qualitative ones. How is forming conditions for the shocks carried out, and what role plays the transformation of the rational behavior of economic agents into irrational one? This question is not predetermined by simple curiosity, but by the constantly repeated "truth" about the difficulties to fix the moment of shock. In this case, it is about how to monitor the behavior of subjects of market transactions in order to have a clear idea of the generating process of the shock. It is necessary to specify at what point the breakdown of structural ties will necessarily occur through shock in its subjective form. The authors proceed from the fact that the dialectics of the interaction of entities of structural relations in the market is determined by their interaction within the framework of dialectic pairs of sellers and buyers. Moreover, their behavior is determined by the subjective choice of each individual between such internal motives as trust or mistrust, collectivism or individualism, rational principles or irrational ones. The choice of one of these internal attitudes as the guidelines of the subject determines the corresponding behavior, rational or irrational in essence. Moreover, it should be emphasized that such a difference should be made only in relation to the economic system and its structure – the exchange. If the behavior of an economic agent destroys the structural connections of the system, then it is irrational, and if it strengthens them, then there are rational goals in the actions of the subject. As for the individual himself, he subjectively chooses a rational behavior, from his point of view, because it allows him to achieve his personal goals. This is very important for understanding the subjective mechanism for the implementation of shocks, since it highlights the interaction of the subject and his economic environment as a serious problem. In case of shocks, rational behavior in the understanding of the subject may conflict with the irrationality of his behavior in terms of the integrity of the economic system. In other words, the choice of the irrational principle by the subject of economic activity is predetermined by his assessment of the attitude of the system to him. With this reasoning, the authors came to the conclusion that distrust, the preference for individual gain to the detriment of the stability of the entire system, and other selfish (opportunistic, irrational) attitudes of the subject reflect the influence on him of partners, the market, local and national communities, etc. And this means that in order to understand the stages of the self-development of the economy as a whole and the self-organizing levels of its exchange, it is necessary to analyze the factors that cause the effect of the crowd, which is realized with the irrational behavior of subjects.

To understand the moment of generating conditions for the implementation of the subjective mechanism of shock, all of the above is of great importance. This is due to the fact that a person is a dialectically complex, controversial subject of economic activity. It contains genetically dialectical pairs of feelings, sensations, ideas, etc. (Fig. 3). In accordance with the Keynesian concept, any person makes serious investment decisions, relying on faith. But trust is easily replaced by distrust a positive assessment of the future is replaced by a negative, etc. But trust is easily replaced by distrust a positive assessment of the future is replaced by a negative one, etc. In fact, the dialectic of the relationship between rational and irrational principles manifests itself first in the psychological settings of a person, and then in his behavior.

It is important to emphasize that under the influence of many factors of an endogenous and exogenous nature under conditions of complete uncertainty of economic factors, the agent himself gives a subjective assessment of the environment and the factors that determine its change in the future he makes decisions and chooses a behavior model in accordance with his psychological settings. It should be borne in mind that the choice by subjects of market relations of priorities due to rational or irrational preferences begins to have a fundamental impact on the dynamics of the economic system as the effect of the "crowd" increases, that is, increasing the number of players and the volume of their transactions in assets' markets to a critical mass. If the leading strategy of these groups of subjects of market exchange becomes a game either on the demand side or on the supply side of assets, then the equilibrium of the sale and purchase transactions is destroyed, the market prices of the assets come off further and further from their base price. As a result, at the structural levels of exchange, dialectically determined interconnections of subjects of market relations begin to crumble, the process of multiplying the break in structural ties in all interconnected markets begins. Thus, the effect of a crowd of irrationally minded subjects of market relations realizes shocks as a mechanism for breaking them under the condition of a maximum price gap for a traded asset. For this to happen, the subjects of market relations must be put by society in conditions that will force them to give preference to such psychological attitudes that will lead them to irrational behavior in the market.

Considering the price shock of 2007 in the U.S. market of unsecured mortgages, the crowd effect was initiated by those actors who appreciated the chance of acquiring real estate – the American dream, in the face of an almost ten-year rise in prices for it. Really during the 1990s the mortgage rates and unemployment rates were reduced and it played a significant role in the growth of the housing sector in the U.S. (Mason, and Rosner, 2007). As refinancing became easier, and cheaper, home ownership became merely another manageable asset in one's portfolio. As a result, real estate acquisition through mortgages began to increase at a clearly speculative pace (Fig. 4).

Judging by Fig. 4, everything that happened in the sphere of the U.S. home ownership in 1965-2007 fitted into the concept of "adventure of pure water", which was based on the "crowd effect" of irrationally minded entities, in terms of the stability of market exchange in general. However, it was appropriately institutionalized, which formed a specific financial market (of liars) in which financial organizations made loans to people who had no income, no jobs, and no assets. That practice was so ubiquitous that it attracted its own acronym, NINJA loans (no income, no job, and no assets loan is extended to a borrower who may have no ability to repay the loan).

In other words, the situation was generated by society, which created the conditions for the implementation of such a market situation. In such markets, real estate buyers could only miraculously repay their mortgage obligations lacking a stable background. However, this illusion, faith and positive expectations were predetermined by society, which initiated the euphoria of irrationally minded subjects (Mises, (1996), Part Four, Chapter XIV). Real estate buyers were not professionals in financial transactions and motivated their decisions with a "spontaneous determination" (Keynes, (1936), PP. 149-150; 161-162) to take advantage of a fabulous chance that may never arise again.

But the intermediaries that formalized their financial transactions in the market were professional financial institutions (banks, insurance companies, realtors, rating agencies, etc.). From the point of view

Figure 4. The U.S.: home ownership in 1965-2007
Source: Joseph R. Mason, and Joshua Rosner (2007).

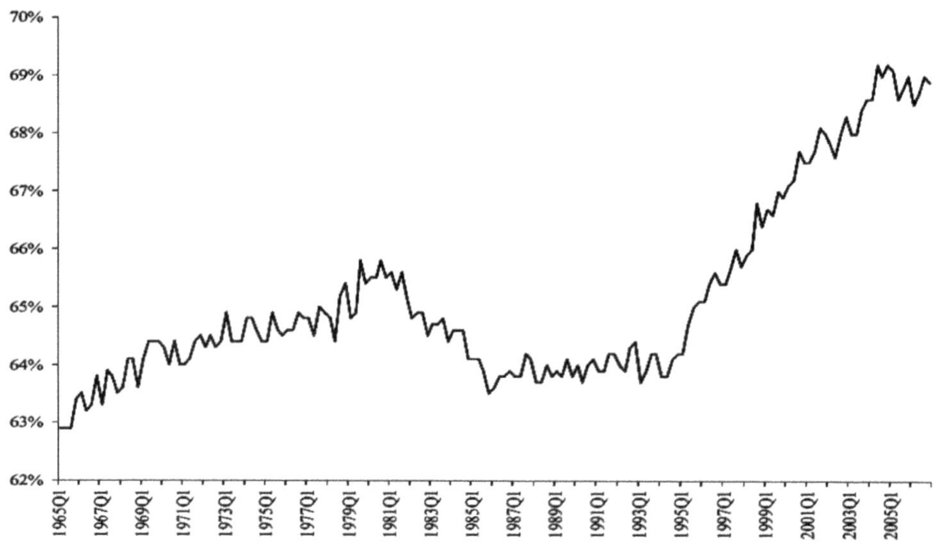

of a part of the low-income population, the decision to take a loan secured by constantly growing real estate prices and buy it immediately meant the approach of an "unattainable" future. A favorable prospect to pay off obligations in the future was pure illusion, which was based on the fabulous (irrational) ideas of the poor. Really homebuyers were usually expected to pay about 20 percent of the house's value that was a significant amount of money. But, the advance payments gave lenders the illusion that buyers had sufficient personal investment to pay off debt and to preserve the asset. According to the Fed data from 2000 to 2005 total mortgage equity withdrawal increased from $289 billion to over $900 billion. In the 1990s the dollar volume of mortgage refinancing ($3.37 trillion) exceeded the dollar volume of all mortgage originations in the 1980s ($2.93 trillion) (Mason, et al., 2007). The last two figures below demonstrate the shift to the irrational orientation in borrower behavior during the beginning of 2000s. Financial market professionals could not help but notice the irrational behavior of players in the real estate market and they well understood what could come of it. Consequently, they were also motivated by something to choose irrational behavior. And this something was predetermined by the calculation of fabulous profits on the market for NINJA loans. Meanwhile, the irrationality of their actions was predetermined by making profit at the expense of losses of other market players.

At the same time, professional financial intermediaries take advantage of real market trends that allow investors to get rich quickly when the market grows and save their money in a falling market. This is the psychological reaction of players to the behavior of the market itself. People tend to buy with an increase in the exchange rate and sell in response to its decline, which in itself is irrational. As a result, the exchange rate changes even more. George A. Akerlof, and Robert J. Shiller (2009; Shiller, 1984, 2002, 2004, 2015) called this phenomenon "price-to-price feedback". With its participation, a vicious circle is formed and self-maintains for a certain time. But this is nothing more than the realization of the effect of a crowd of irrationally minded players violating the market equilibrium with their behavior, since at first they massively buy assets, and then they are massively sold them. However, in the end, this leads to a jump in the market prices of the asset from their base level and the emergence of a "financial bubble". In other words, the irrational behavior of the subjects actually implements the conditions for the maturation of the shocks and for the subsequent mechanism of the collapse of the structural bonds. This is due to the fact that the "financial bubble" should burst, since the gap in the market prices of the asset from their base level is determined solely by the irrational expectations (illusions) of the subjects of their further increase. Rational principles of market relations cannot objectively provide such prices gap in financial markets.

The movement of asset prices affects people's confidence and the economy, forming a feedback "price-income-price". As a result, if stock prices rise, so does trust, people buy more, company earnings grow. This determines a further increase in stock prices, but not for long. With the reverse trend, everything happens the other way around. So in the U.S. low interest rates in 2003–2006 added to the incentives that had already been provided by government support for low-income housing and fuelled an extraordinary housing boom as well as increasing indebtedness. In addition the Fed reassured the economy that interest rates would stay low for a sustained period. The latter only pushed asset prices higher and increased financial sector risk taking. This irrational behavior of financial intermediaries became enormous in the U.S. real estate market in 2007. As a result, the volumes of high-risk (substandard) mortgage lending began to grow significantly: from 5% to about 20% of the mortgage market, i.e. up to $ 625 billion (Mason, and Rosner, 2007).

At the same time, new forms of irrational behavior in the financial asset market began to develop. It is about fraud tactics related to the sale of credit obligations, and the subsequent extraction of money received from creditors. They are later used to increase salaries, bonuses, corruption deals, high dividends and options, etc. As for the price shock of 2007 in the market of unsecured mortgage loans, banks irrationally oriented in their behavior used the technology of securitization of unsecured (risk debt) mortgage loans. The fraud of the buyers of these securities was that complex structured financial instruments were issued for the amount of unsecured mortgage loans and sold on the market. And the money received by banks for them actually testified to the transfer of all risks of unsecured debts to the buyers of these "fake" securities.

In addition to unsecured mortgages, the crowd effect extended to financial and non-financial organizations, the irrational behavior of which was manifested in the growth of abuses in financial transactions, which were invariably accompanied by violation of financial statements and the widespread use of fraudulent schemes. The objective circumstances of all these irrational phenomena are related to the fact that the main modern means of saving for the future are bonds, investments in pension funds and in life insurance. However, these assets are intangible and represent securities in which the promise of future payments is expressed. Their real value in most cases is in a sense unknowable in principle. Moreover, if the balance accounts are distorted, then the owners of shares or options for their purchase, for example, can make good money on the credulity of those who have trusted false accounting reports. The irrational behavior of stock sellers was manifested in the fact that at first they began to inflate the value of the shares, and then sell them to new owners expecting large dividends. However, the accounting reports of the companies were fake ones.

So, if in the dialectical unity of the subject and society the struggle of opposites prevails, and the latter, having achieved certain quantitative changes, pass into a new quality. And this means that in society, the dialectic of relations between subjects and society dictates the formation of structural levels along the vertical, mediating interaction in society on the principle of cause-and-effect relationships. If the unity of society is violated, the trust of partners in exchange transactions ceases to be an adequate equivalent to maintain the equilibrium of markets. This situation is aggravated by the pronounced opportunism of the behavior of the subjects in all spheres of their activity, including technology and economics. In this regard, the authors believe that all problems should be solved only in society, meaning the socialization of subjects into society.

6.2. Institutionalization of Structural Connections of Dialectical Pairs in the Conditions of the Law of Unity and Struggle of Opposites

The integrity of the economic system is predetermined by its structure, i.e. the exchange of economic entities with their activities and / or of its results. Moreover, in order to become a structure the interconnection of subjects of dialectic pairs must be stable, balanced and constantly renewed. The subjective aspect of exchange plays a significant role in disrupting its structural hierarchy and the stability of the economic system as a whole. Indeed, the subjects form dialectic pairs in exchange, and therefore their behavior either strengthens it if partners comply with the conditions institutionalized in market contracts, or destabilizes it in case of violation. In the latter case, this is manifested in the mass aggressive behavior of economic agents either on the demand side or on the supply side of the traded asset. The equivalence of acts of sale is violated and the dialectical equivalence of partners in market transactions comes to an end.

The behavior of participants in dialectical pairs in accordance with the stipulated conditions in market contracts, as a rule, is associated with its rational beginning. The stability of the exchange as a structure of the economic system is based on the rational behavior of the subjects, which implies the equivalence of relations between partners, the balance of exchange transactions. Consequently, the imbalance in the structural hierarchy of exchange is introduced by the irrational behavior of partners that violate their dialectical unity. The rational behavior of partners in the personalized exchange was determined by their long-term personal relationships, constantly repeating transactions and the stability of mutual contacts in a particular market. The feeling of trust of the participants in dialectic couples was reinforced institutionally by the inclusion in the transaction contracts of clauses on compliance with its conditions and on the existence of penalties in the case of their violation. Thus, the subjective sense of mutual trust of partners was ensured in real practice by institutions aimed at preventing their irrational behavior and cases of violation by the subjects of market transaction conditions. At the micro level of partners' relationships, these rules of their behavior were regulated by informal institutions, and at the state level - by formal ones. Thus, institutions strengthened the partners' subjective sense of trust, preventing the multiplication of irrational principles in their behavior. Indeed, in the case of the equivalence of the participants in dialectical pairs, the equivalence of their exchange operations, the rational beginning prevailed in their behavior. All this, together with trust, objectively ensured the stability of the exchange, as well as the balance of the economic system as a whole.

When replacing a personalized exchange with a non-personalized one, the significance of the factors of uncertainty and risks of violation of the agreements of transaction partners (in dialectic pairs) has increased many times. This increased the instability of the exchange and the inconsistency of the goals of partners in market transactions, which significantly increased the exchange costs, called transaction costs by R. Coase (1937) in his famous article 'The nature of the firm'. The growth of the latter began to significantly slow down economic growth and the subjects of market transactions began to introduce a mechanism for solving this problem, which took the form of (informal) institutions. From the authors' point of view, the aspect of relationships in market exchange turns out to be the most important, since it allows one to understand the emergence of trade-off between the coincidence of the interests of exchange partners on the stage of unity and struggle of the opposites of the endless dynamics of complex economic systems and their mismatch at its next stages.

Galloping growth in non-personalized exchange volumes was accompanied by an increase in the uncertainty of the future. Under these conditions, it is trust that becomes of the great importance for partners. And the institutions supported this trust, ensuring the rational behavior of subjects and the stabilization of exchange operations in dialectical pairs. Not by chance D. North (1987, 1990, 1997, 2005) identified the institutions (informal, in this case) with the "rules of the game", which were created by the subjects of market transactions to regulate their own behavior. In this case, it is about their collective desire to exclude any manifestations of irrational (opportunistic) actions. In essence, institutions were charged with the function of reducing uncertainty for decision-makers of market transactions, which was associated with ensuring the sustainability of long-term structural interactions of subjects of market transactions, matching their goals of minimizing transaction costs (exchange costs), understanding the priority of collective interests (actions) over individual ones in the implementation of mutually beneficial deals.

As the personalized exchange was crowded out the institutional function of the state became very important for the participants realizing the market transactions. D. North (1997) wrote that the emergence of non-personalized exchange and contractual relations meant the formation of the state. As a result, the reduction of the sphere of informal restrictions dominance in the conditions of personalized exchange was compensated for by the expansion of the influence of the formal institutions being created by the state in the process of the non-personalized exchange increase. Thus, the rational principles of behavior of subjects of market transactions were gradually strengthened. This was of great importance, since according to J. Commons (1931), it was a market transaction that accompanied (created, generated) an elementary relationship in the economy between sellers and buyers, including the alienation and acquisition by individuals of property rights and freedoms created by society. Moreover, from his point of view, a person's freedom may be accompanied by the loss of his own benefit and gaining of profit by the corresponding individual. In other words, it is about a dialectic pair of participants in market exchange, the equivalence of which is associated with the fact that each of the participants receives the desired utility as a result. The authors associate transactions in the categories of institutional theory with the exchange of economic activity and its results between economic agents operating autonomously (freely) in the market. The universal characteristic of any transaction and the rational behavior of interdependent agents is their joint interest in achieving the planned results. And the latter, in turn, directly depend on the coordination (coherence) of joint actions in the implementation of sales transactions.

It should be especially noted that for the theory of shocks, the most important is the aspect of relationships of market exchange between representatives of dialectical pairs. The main goal of the participants of the exchange is to maximize marginal utility, which is directly related to the reduction of rapidly growing transaction costs (exchange costs). A. Willis (1986) and D. North (1987) proved that market transactions are always accompanied by (transaction) costs. S.N.S. Chueng (1978) connected them with such costs, "the existence of which was impossible to imagine in the economy of Robinson Crusoe". K. Arrow (2012, 1962) singled out the macroeconomic content of transaction costs, identifying them with the "costs of maintaining economic systems in motion" by association with the concept of friction in physics (Breaden, et al., (1984), P. 166), which must be minimized for the purpose of ensuring the movement of the object.

If production costs are controlled and calculated by manufacturers quite easily, then the assessment of the transaction costs is very difficult. This is largely due to the fact that the structure of transaction costs is constantly changing and they include more and more new elements. And this requires new technologies, new structures and new mechanisms for their reduction. So, Y. Barzel (1982) expanded their composition due to "measurement costs", G.J. Stigler (1961) and P.G. Toumanoff (1984) added "information costs" to them. O. Williamson (1985) expanded the structure of transaction costs by taking into account "the costs of opportunistic behavior", but M. C Jensen and W. H. Meckling (1973) – by including "the costs of controlling the behavior of the executor (agent)" in them.

To reduce high transaction costs in general and each of their components individually, partners resort to various mechanisms to minimize them. As a result, as new elements of transaction costs appear in the market exchange, partners of market transactions develop "innovative" organizational forms of minimizing them. However, in conditions of rapid segmentation of modern markets, transaction costs, in principle, cannot be reset. In the future, more and more new elements will appear, as well as their numerous "mutations", which will initiate economic agents to create new informal institutions that ensure the implementation of market transactions with the lowest transaction costs. The variety of types of specialization and intersectoral cooperation in the organization of market exchange makes the set of informal institutions practically unlimited. It is in this context that it becomes clear why the subjects of market relationships in the face of individual entities and their many organizations become agents of the formation and change of informal institutions (at the micro level of the economic system). As a result, the rules by which they realize their market transactions become institutions that structure their behavior in order to ensure unhindered exchange. As for formal institutions, their formation and development is connected with the activities of the state and with laws and regulations adopted at the state level aimed at regulating the general rules of the game in a self-developing economy (Chapter 4).

Informal institutions were being steadily introduced, expanding their influence steadily, and generating new forms and organizations as exchange progressed. As a result, many generations of market transactions have perfected them, passing them from one of them to another. The authors connect the emergence of the ability of self-organization in exchange as a set of structural connections in the economic system with the long processes of institutionalization by economic entities of their rational behavior at the micro level of the system. According to the authors, this is crucial for understanding the role of the subjective factor in the self-organization of the structural hierarchy of exchange. Indeed, the process of the endless search for appropriate technologies to reduce transaction costs determines the self-organization of informal institutions. Moreover, they not only limit the behavior of economic agents, but also form a hierarchy of exchange with the quality of a self-organizing structure in a complex economic system.

Thus, the hierarchical exchange structure, built on the principle of causal dependence, when the higher level is predetermined to solve the dialectical problems of the lower level and so on to its upper segments, is only a mirror image of the structural hierarchy of informal institutions. However, one should pay attention to the fact that, by creating institutions that orient them towards rational behavior for the purpose of stabilizing the exchange, the subjects may just as well come into conflict with the laws of self-organization of exchange. This, in the final analysis, explains the subjectivization of the mechanism of shock breaking structural ties along the chain from top to bottom in the hierarchy of exchange at the moment when the irrational beginning becomes characteristic of the mass behavior of economic agents. And this characterizes already other stages of the infinite dynamics of economic changes following the stage of unity and struggle of opposites.

So, in essence, informal institutions are very stable, capable of self-organization and always aimed at the stability and sustainability of exchange, because they are based on the rational behavior of business entities. They are able to generate their new modifications, corresponding to new segments of the exchange, which often solve the problems of its basic level, which has caused them to life. Regarding the rules of behavior of subjects of market transactions, informal institutions are constantly in the process of self-organization, generating new rules for the behavior of participants in the market, adjusting existing ones and passing them from generation to generation. This explains the large "path-dependence" of the movement of economic structures in the case of exchange, which ensures the structure (integrity) of the system, while remaining resistant to the long-term effects of factors initiating various kinds of changes. But in any market with any subjects of market transactions, informal institutions include provisions that strengthen the structural hierarchy as a whole at the stage of unity and struggle of opposites in the dynamics of economic changes. It is a matter of binding rules of conduct for participants in the exchange that strengthen its stability, encourage bona fide transaction entities and punish those who act opportunistically. It is of such quality that informal institutions to a large extent ensure the process of self-organization of exchange, which only ultimately is capable of fulfilling the function of the mechanism of self-development of the economic system as a whole.

The resulting systemic construction of a complex economy with its inherent self-development mechanism is largely predetermined by the features of the formation and implementation of informal institutions. And if so, then the informal institutions themselves should initially possess qualities that are more or less adequately fixed in modern objectively existing structures in the economy. The incorporation of institutional canons of subjects' behavior into economic structures and the laws of their dynamic changes is carried out by transmitting from generation to generation of economic agents the awareness of the unconditional need for them to comply with rational foundations in market behavior. And in the consciousness of economic entities, this has become associated with strengthening the integrity of the economic system, with counteracting its destruction. For the same purposes, informal institutions provide for the implementation of mechanisms to encourage entities for conscientious behavior and compliance with the rules of market relations, on the one hand, and punishments for their irrational behavior, on the other.

As a result, the self-organization of the exchange of economic activity and its results, in fact, reproduces similar processes of dynamic changes of the informal institutions themselves. That is why exchange as a structure of a complex economic system predetermines its integrity, balance and stability over time, changing very slowly, preserving the inertia predetermined by the institutional support for the interaction of participants in dialectic pairs. Remaining on the principles of dialectical logic, the authors highlight the institutional (informal) aspect in the study of the problems of unresolved dialectical contradictions between the structure of the system, which today acquired the features of a mixed national and transnational, and its nationally isolated endogenous environment. The latter should be taken into account when studying the phenomenon of "secular stagnation" in national economic systems after a shock break in structural ties in 2007 in the market of unsecured US mortgages in the USA and the following global financial crisis. It is about objective processes that predetermine continuous economic changes and appropriate changes in informal institutions (Fig. 5).

So the exchange of economic activity and of its results as well as its institutional providing has its own stages of development, associated both with changes in the objects of exchange and in its subjects. Complication of the exchange occurs along the line of changing the already existing structural links between its participants in the dialectic pairs, of eliminating the outdated ones, and of forming new dialectic pairs. In other words, market exchange mediates the formation of structural links of the economic system and develops according to the laws of its self-organization. At the same time, the dialectic of the market exchange development is understandable only when it is considered as the process of continuous formation of its new properties due to the changing rules of behaviour of the economic agents, the emergence of its new objects and the structural interdependencies of various segments of market exchange and of their interacting levels. In the same way, accompanying the process of increasing the complexity of the hierarchy of exchange, new institutions emerge and resolve dialectic contradictions with existing ones, providing causal relationships between all structural levels of exchange. Institutions providing partner relations can strengthen the factors of rational behavior, as occurs at the stage of unity and struggle of opposites in the dynamics of economic systems. In this case, the behavior of sellers and buyers is rational, based on trust, and the coincidence of goals, lowering transaction costs determines the desire of transaction participants to close it in compliance with all obligations under the contract.

At the same time, material security for the obligations of partners trusting each other during the implementation of a market transaction plays an important role. It turns out that the stability of the economic system, the stationarity of its state and the stability of the exchange of the results of its activities is determined by trust, institutional providing of the rational grounds in the behavior of business entities and material support for their obligations under transactions. And such a state is characteristic of the bulk of market transactions in a system that is at the stage of unity and struggle of opposites.

From the philosophical point of view, this can be interpreted as follows. Unity will always triumph over contradictions in the motives of participants in transactions, if dialectically connected partners know that according to the terms of the transaction (in accordance with institutional settings) it will in any case be closed due to its material security from a possible "opportunistic" behavior of the subject (who wants to violate the conditions deals). In other words, the material security of market transaction' obligations, as well as informal institutions that regulate the rational behavior of exchange partners, help maintain confidence in the market environment. To a greater extent this is characteristic of real markets in which consumer goods, services, investment goods, and labor are traded.

K. J. Arrow (2012) expressed this thought as follows. "Virtually every commercial transaction has within itself an element of trust... It can be plausibly argued that much of the economic backwardness in the world can be explained by the lack of mutual confidence."Following dialectical logic, the authors determine that the stage of unity and struggle of opposites in the infinite dynamics of economic changes

Figure 5. Graphic model of self-organization of informal institutions, providing the process of self-organization of the exchange of economic activity and of its results at the stage of unity and struggle of opposites of complex economic dynamics
Source: the authors' development

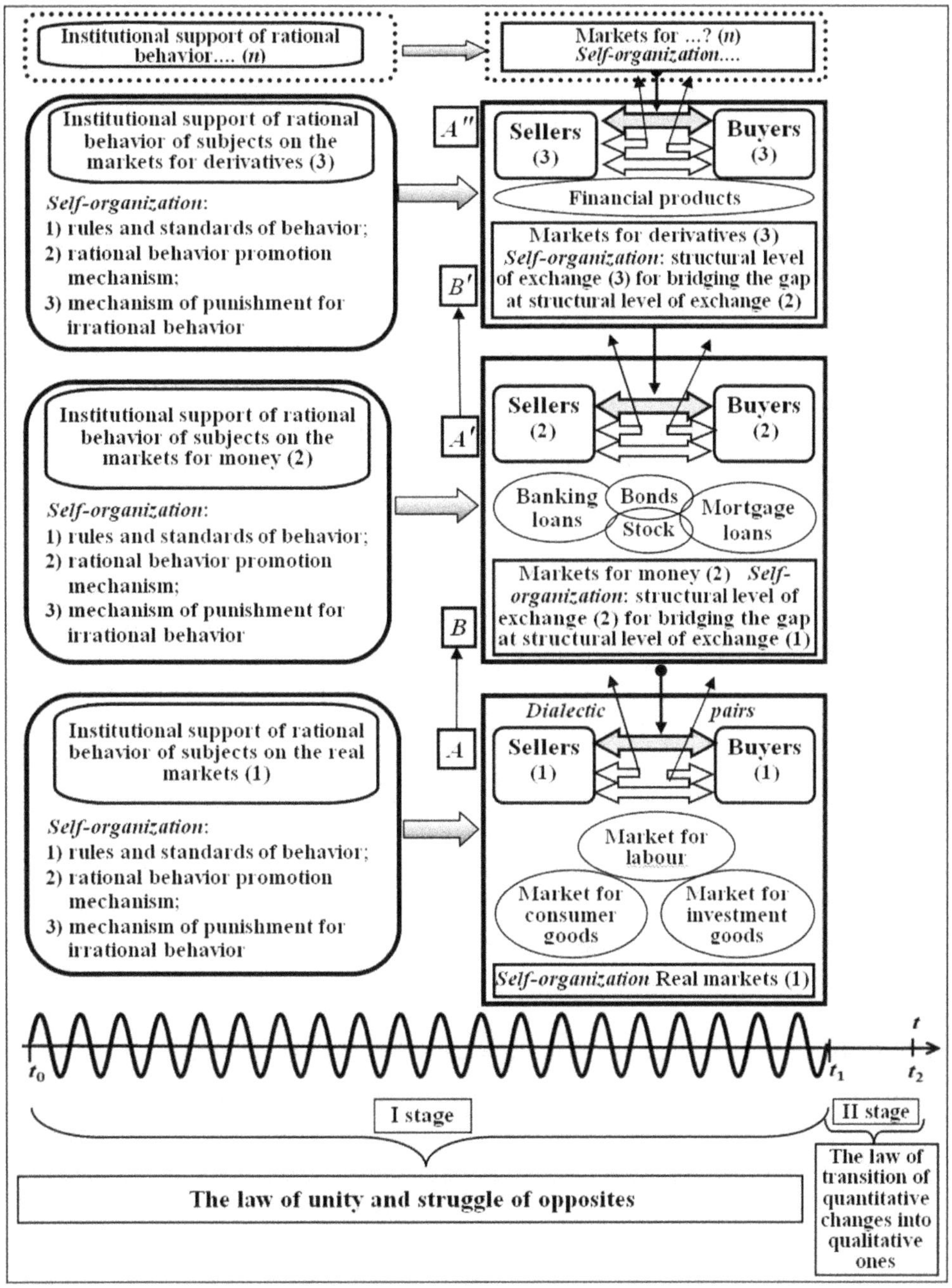

and the stationary state of the system are also predetermined by the crowd effect in the economic agents' behavior with rational intents' domination. It is it that predetermines the harmony of cause-effect dependencies in the self-organization of exchange as a structure of the system. The inclusion of the behavioral aspect into the theory of shocks allows the authors to define shocks not simply as a mechanism for breaking structural bonds in exchange, not just as its price form of manifestation, but as a mechanism which implementation is associated with the behavior of the bulk of market subjects. Moreover, this approach allows the authors to argue that shocks realize a turning point in the rational behavior of the critical mass of participants of market transactions and determine the substitution of rational principles with irrational goals in the behavior of the bulk of the players in financial markets. Moreover, such a shock transformation of human behavior is based on the substitution of trust with mistrust and the transformation of informal institutions, which guard rational grounds, into informal institutions, which ensure the triumph of the irrational principles.

It should be emphasized that the individual manifestation of trust or mistrust in the behavior of one person has little effect on the economic system. But as it turns into collective behavior of the masses, it begins to predetermine the characteristics of exchange and the state of the economic system at various stages of its economic dynamics. And in this context, price shock is the result of the collective behavior of a critical mass of participants in market transactions, dictated by the replacement of trust with distrust and of the rational principles with the irrational ones. Roger Brown (1986) wrote that economic agents were prone to antisocial (irrational) behavior, which often led to disruptions in the economy. In John K. Galbreith (1977) opinion, dishonesty (opportunism) of the behavior of economic agents may not formally go beyond the law, but with irrational (bad) motives, it can quickly spread in the economic system from time to time.

Now it should be clarified that under the influence of the law of unity and struggle of opposites, as well as the transition of quantity to quality, herd behavior is predetermined by rational principles before their turning points. As soon as unity is replaced by the opposite in horizontal structural relationships, and in place of quantitative changes, qualitative changes appear in vertical structural relationships - the prevailing behavior of the crowd becomes irrational. This is the effect of the subjective component of the shock mechanism of destruction of non-working structural ties that endanger the integrity of the economic system. As for the operation of the law of negation of negation, it should be emphasized that shocks destroy the basic structure of the entire static economy. In this situation, the irrational behavior of subjects does not manifest itself in any separate market, it realizes the leap of the economic system into a dynamic future, destroying the previous structural interaction between society and the economy. Actually, this is the main feature of the action of the subjective component of shocks as intermediaries in the operation of the law of double negation.

6.3. Institutionalization of Transition of Quantitative Changes in the Economy to its New Quality: Destabilization of Society due to the Divergence of Individual and Social Values

The possibilities for violating the rules of conduct by participants in dialectic pairs in exchange increase as the transactions' material security in money markets and financial product markets decreases. At the same time, this process of self-organization of exchange as a hierarchy of structural levels is invariably accompanied by their institutional support, which is still aimed at eliminating the opportunistic behavior of economic agents as participants in dialectic pairs mediating transactions with financial assets. The attribute of trust, which must necessarily be present in the exchange between participants in market transactions, remains unchanged. Only one thing disappears - the material providing of this trust. It is this feature that predetermines the stage of transition of quantitative changes in the economic system to their new quality, which is accompanied by the formation of structural relations of transaction subjects, based on trust, not supported by material assets.

From a philosophical point of view, this means that opposites in dialectical pairs begin to supplant their unity, and informal institutions created by people themselves begin to ensure the implementation of new rules of the market game. The latter is explained by the fact that it is possible to stop the chain reaction of structural link breaks only if the claims of one transaction partner are satisfied through the implementation of material support (pledged tangible assets) of the obligations of the other one. In conditions when trust is replaced by distrust, and irrational principles begin to dominate in comparison with rational ones, the motives of the behavior of dialectically related partners of market transactions change. This is determined by the fact that, being financially unsecured, the transaction (contrary to the agreements reached earlier) will in any case be closed at the end of the market contract. And the material fiasco of one of the partners in the deal, which is distinguished by irrational behavior (behaves opportunistically), destroys structural ties in this particular case, and not only. If other transactions connected with the last one also do not have material providing, then according to the principle of a chain reaction, the structural ties of their participants are destroyed starting with markets for financial products and money markets and finishing with real markets. The separation of the exchange from the material base begins when the cash reserve maintained by the debtor against the money put into circulation is less than the total amount of these substitutes. In this case, the amount of money substitutes in excess of the reserve is converted into instruments that do not have coverage. The issuance of non-covered instruments increases the bank's credit resources beyond these limits. In this case, it is about a fiduciary loan, built on trust. These very loans provide the release of tools that do not have coverage (material security). However, their increase leads to an increase in the volume of money circulation and transactions in all markets (Mises, 1996).

If at the same time trust collapses, then collectivism gives way to individual technologies of subjects for saving, and their rational behavior gives way to irrational ones. This behavior of partners in market transactions fills with different content causal relationships in the hierarchy of exchange: strengthening through the rational behavior of participants in dialectic couples, they begin to destroy their own interdependencies as the importance of irrational principles in their mass behavior is strengthened. These exchange characteristics are typical for a self-organising system at the stage of transition of quantitative changes to qualitative ones.

The following questions arise: how conditions for the shocks action are forming and what role the transformation of the rational behavior of economic agents into irrational one plays. These questions are not predetermined by simple curiosity, but by the constantly repeated "truth" about the difficulties to fix the moment of shock. In this case, it is about how to monitor the behavior of subjects of market transactions in order to have a clear idea of the generating process of the shock. It is necessary to specify at what point the breakdown of structural ties will necessarily occur through shock in its subjective form. The authors proceed from the fact that the dialectics of the interaction of entities of structural relations in the market is determined by their interaction within the framework of dialectic pairs of sellers and buyers. Moreover, their behavior is determined by the subjective choice of each individual between such internal motives as trust or mistrust, collectivism or individualism, rational principles or irrational ones. The choice of one of these internal attitudes as the guidelines of the subject determines the corresponding behavior, rational or irrational in essence. Moreover, it should be emphasized that such a difference should be made only in relation to the economic system and its structure – the exchange. If the behavior of an economic agent destroys the structural connections of the system, then it is irrational, and if it strengthens them, then there are rational goals in the actions of the subject. As for the individual himself, he subjectively chooses a rational behavior, from his point of view, because it allows him to achieve his personal goals. This is very important for understanding the subjective mechanism for the implementation of shocks, since it highlights the interaction of the subject and his economic environment as a serious problem. In case of shocks, rational behavior in the understanding of the subject may conflict with the irrationality of his behavior in terms of the integrity of the economic system. In other words, the choice of the irrational principle by the subject of economic activity is predetermined by his assessment of the attitude of the system to him. With this reasoning, the authors came to the conclusion that distrust, the preference for individual gain to the detriment of the stability of the entire system, and other selfish (opportunistic, irrational) attitudes of the subject reflect the influence on him of partners, the market, local and national communities, etc. And this means that in order to understand the stages of the self-movement of the economy as a whole and the self-organizing structural levels of its exchange, it is necessary to analyze the factors that cause the effect of the crowd, which is realized with the irrational behavior of subjects.

However, it is now becoming apparent that the specific state of society and its subjective reflection in the internal motives of the subjects living in it determines both their rational and their irrational behavior in mass manifestations. This also applies to informal institutions that are generated by the participants in market relations themselves. If society creates the individual's impression (illusion) of stability, progressive improvement of the economic situation, prospects for material well-being, etc., then the confidence that arises in him, faith in a happy future, joy for everyone, etc. and this leads to domination of the rational principles. As a result, structural exchange levels are strengthened, new markets are developing, the markets-causes generate the markets-consequences, which successively solve dialectic problems along a chain of vertical connections from bottom to top. This happens at the stage of unity and struggle of opposites. At the stage of the transition of the quantity of economic changes to their new quality, a situation actually arises as for the generation of circumstances in the system that determines an opposite orientation of the subjects. They refuse to believe in a happy future and make decisions that, in their opinion, can improve their own welfare, albeit at the expense of the losses of their partners. At the same time, subjects with such internal attitudes generate completely different informal institutions that provide the irrational behavior of the individuals from the point of view of interests of the integrity of society. According to George A. Akerlof, and Robert J. Shiller (2009), the effect of infection (the "virus" of irrationality) is realized in this way, and then the epidemic of irrationality covers a critical mass of economic agents. Thus, the necessary conditions are formed for a shock rupture of structural bonds in the exchange.

It is not possible to disagree with the outstanding scientist Ludwig von Mises [1996, Part Three, Chapter XII], who wrote that the world around us would be stable if all the circumstances of human life remained unchanged. However, constant changes are typical of the modern world there are no invariable points, relations, which could serve as a standard. The pretentious seriousness that statisticians demonstrate when calculating purchasing power and cost of living indices is hardly justified. Human activity itself is inherently prone to change. Since human activity exists, stability is a priori absent, only non-stop changes remain.

So, the replacement of rational behavior of subjects by irrational one occurs due to changes in their consciousness of certain psychological attitudes: trust gives way to distrust, confidence in the future changes to uncertainty, etc. For the steadiness of exchange and stability of the economy as a whole, this is of crucial importance. This is due to the fact that the behavior of the "crowd" (a critical mass of entities) can equally, in the case of rationality, strengthen the balance of the economic system and stabilize the exchange, and in the case of irrationality, - destroy everything. In good times, people are full of faith in future success, trust their partners, the market, the state, and act accordingly. But as soon as trust disappears, illusions evaporate, recklessness of actions becomes apparent. As a result, of the great importance become individual preferences of the subject, irrational attitudes orientation of behavior towards achieving personal preferences to the detriment of collective. Under these conditions, in a complex economic system, quantitative changes are intensifying, which predetermine the formation of its new quality.

To understand the moment of generating conditions for the implementation of the subjective mechanism of shock, all of the above is of great importance. This is due to the fact that a person is a dialectically complex, controversial subject of economic and social activities. It contains genetically dialectical pairs of feelings, sensations, ideas, etc. (Fig. 6). In accordance with the Keynesian concept (1936), any person makes serious investment decisions, relying on faith. But trust is easily replaced by distrust a positive assessment of the future is replaced by a negative, etc. But trust is easily replaced by distrust a positive assessment of the future is replaced by a negative one, etc. In fact, the dialectic of the relationship between rational and irrational principles manifests itself first in the psychological settings of a person, and then in his behavior.

It is important to emphasize that under the influence of many factors of an endogenous and exogenous nature under conditions of complete uncertainty of economic factors, the agent himself gives a subjective assessment of the environment and the factors that determine its change in the future he makes decisions and chooses a behavior model in accordance with his psychological settings. In this context, it is necessary to perceive a person as a creature capable of both self-organization and self-development (Chapter 11.1). It should be borne in mind that the choice by subjects of market relations of priorities due to rational or irrational preferences begins to have a fundamental impact on the dynamics of the economic system as the effect of the "crowd" increases, that is, increasing the number of players and the volume of their transactions in assets' markets to a critical mass. If the leading strategy of these groups of subjects of market exchange becomes a game either on the demand side or on the supply side of assets, then the equilibrium of the sale and purchase transactions is destroyed, the market prices of the assets come off further and further from their base price. As a result, at the structural levels of exchange, dialectically determined interconnections of subjects of market relations begin to crumble, the process of multiplying the break in structural ties in all interconnected markets begins. Thus, the effect of a crowd of irrationally minded subjects of market relations realizes shocks as a mechanism for breaking them under the condition of a maximum price gap for a traded asset. For this to happen, the subjects of market relations must be put by society in conditions that will force them to give preference to such psychological attitudes that will lead them to irrational behavior in the market.

R. Bootle (2009) wrote, that over the previous decade, clever investment bankers had invented a whole alphabet soup of new financial instruments: CMOs, CDOs, CDSs, and heaven knows what else (Chapter 3.4). They talked about a transformation in the financial world, mirroring the supposed transformation in the real world, thanks to new financial instruments and the advent of financial engineering. Never mind the technological revolution, this was a financial revolution. However, despite such financial progress, the algorithm for the movement of a self-organizing economic system remains unchanged, which involves its movement along the static and dynamic stages. The emergence of shocks is objective as a mechanism for breaking structural ties in exchange through the irrational behavior of the bulk of the players in the market for traded assets.

So from the view point of George A. Akerlof, and Robert J. Shiller (2009) economic changes largely depend on how the attitude towards the need to behave decently changes, and how many people behave in bad faith. During periods of mass spread of irrational behavior, it seems to the participants that everyone is doing this and everything will easily get away with. Such a process is part of the confidence multiplier mechanism: abuse generates even greater abuse. The spread of abuse and dishonesty is affected by the emergence of innovations in the financial sector and laws allowing them to be applied, although society may not immediately understand what their essence is. Over time the culture of encouraging or punishing dishonest behavior changes.

This, in fact, allowed the authors to deepen the idea of shocks, defining them as the subjective mechanism for breaking structural ties along the entire hierarchy of exchange along the entire chain, starting from its upper levels and ending with basic markets. At the same time, financial institutions mediate the irrational behavior of insolvent borrowers under unsecured mortgages. As a result, they actually turn into conductors of a "landslide" rupture of structural bonds along the entire chain of structural levels in the hierarchy of exchange, starting from the top to the lowest structural levels. As professionals, financial institutions also act irrationally, focusing on instantly receiving fabulous incomes due to the destruction of the entire exchange structure. At the same time, the entire chain of interaction of irrationally minded participants in real estate transactions, including financial intermediaries in the financial products market, was provided by informal institutions focusing on regional behavior of subjects. As a result, a critical mass of irrational players appeared on the financial field, who, for their own benefit, destroyed the existing causal relationships in exchange that ensured the integrity of the economic system.

Thus, formal institutions in the hands of the state are aimed at motivating the subjects of market transactions not to violate the requirements of contracts and to regulate their activities in such a way as not to destroy market structures. However, what can be observed in market economies suggests that formal and informal institutions conflict with each other. This results in the effect of a crowd of irrationally thinking players in financial markets in spite of the mechanisms of formal institutions. This proves the fact that formal institutions can regulate the behavior of a person as an economic subject only if they are based on his individual values, generated in the conditions of his transcending into society. If the mechanism of self-organization of a person in a society has led to a discrepancy between his internal beliefs and socially significant norms of behavior in society, then this conflict will be carried over to all other spheres of his life, including the economy. In other words, if the integrity of society is destroyed, then no formal institutions in the economy will help limit the irrational behavior of economic agents in the market. In this context, it becomes clear that informal institutions (institutional constraints) created by people will crowd out formal institutions in their function of strengthening the integrity of the economic system, and accelerate the multiplication of shock breaks along the entire chain of the structural hierarchy up to the horizontal structural level. This is how the institutional aspect manifests itself in the shock mechanism of the implementation of the dialectical law of the transition of quantitative changes into qualitative changes.

6.4. Shock's Performance of Double Negation in the Economy as a Solution to an Intersystem Conflict with Society: from the Priority of Economic Stabilization to the Priority of Social Integrity

Even more seriously, the institutional aspect, or rather the inconsistency, the rupture of the dialectical connection between formal and informal institutions in the economy and social institutions, manifests itself under the conditions of the law of denial of denial. The authors reason as follows. All organizational processes at the stage of self-organization of static systems and at the stage of their dynamics at the stage of self-development are reduced to two: differentiation (separation, disintegration) and integration (cooperation, unification). This pair of processes interacts dialectically through the mechanisms of positive selection and negative selection. The resultant of these processes is predetermined by the diversity of modern socio-economic systems within national boundaries. With their diversity and multiple differences, there is something that unites them. It is about the universal processes of organization, about the essence of the stages of self-organization and self-development, about the object and subjective components, about the functions of shocks in the mechanism of the implementation of dialectical laws of self-movement of systemic integrity. However, if the algorithms for self-movement of different countries are, in fact, universal, then the specific state of both the object and subjective components of these processes differ significantly.

Consequently, the prospect of self-development of national technological and socio-economic systems is completely ambiguous, which is predetermined for each of them in connection with the new reality caused by the shock of the COVID-19 pandemic. The institutional factor plays a huge role in these fundamental transformations, i.e. the quality of interaction between formal and informal institutions, the degree of disunity of society, the coordination of individual human values and socially significant norms of behavior in society, in the economy and in the technological sphere. Perhaps today we can confidently assert that the further perspective (the "New Normal", the Great Resert) of each country is decided not in the economy or technology, but in society. The speed of restoring the unity of society, and, consequently, restoring the dialectic of interrelationships between formal and informal institutions, directly predetermines the length of the "leap" that a national system can make in its dynamics at the stage of self-development.

Indeed, changing the order of cause-effect relationships in the structural hierarchy of the economic system turns the structure of the system into a house of cards when the collapse of its upper floors destroys all structures located below. An objective prerequisite is a significant excess of obligations on financial transactions of their material security. The trigger is the shock destruction of market ties as a result of the opportunistic behavior of economic agents, which leads to a marginal rebound in market prices for a traded asset from their base value. However, this outcome is predetermined by the mismatch of formal institutions in the economy and informal constraints, which are predetermined by individual values generated in society. In this regard, the authors define this situation as a violation of the dialectic of interaction between society and the individual, which takes the form of a mismatch between formal and informal institutions in the economy and social institutions. And this remark is fundamental. If to consider the modernity and the state of national systems during the second wave of the coronavirus pandemic, then the way out of it and the further construction of post-covid reality is predetermined by the understanding of the remark made.

By 2020, it became obvious that the conditions for the transition of countries, especially in the group of highly developed countries, to the stage of self-development were formed. The state shocked structural ties in the economy by announcing lockdowns. It became obvious that ordinary citizens did not accept the new norms of behavior in the majority of countries, which were urgently introduced by the nation states, representing the interests of the whole society and to protect this society. But even before the COVID-19 pandemic, there was a conflict between formal and informal institutions that were ready to confront each other. That is why the structural ties in the economy and in society were destroyed by the COVID-19 shock, and it became obvious that their restoration would take place in a new reality and already under new conditions. And the main quality of the new reality is characterized by complete uncertainty. In this regard, it becomes necessary to assess the vector of further movement. However, for each of the countries it will undoubtedly have its own specifics, since there are no "best practices" for such a transformation and will not be in the nearest future.

What other circumstances can be regarded as evidence that the current situation testifies to the results of the law of denial of negation: the end of the period of self-organization of a static economy and the beginning of the stage of self-development of a dynamic economy. First of all, it is about the new quality of technology as a result of the latest technological solutions in the framework of the technological revolution 4.0. A whole set of technological innovations, processes, opportunities for their further multiplication have already formed, capable of constructing a new technological paradigm, as the basis for the future self-organization of the economy, society, and the technological system itself. There can be no self-development of systems without such a new and promising technological basis. In addition, in order to understand the exhaustion of the former paradigm of self-organization of modern national economies, it is necessary to analyze the dynamics of indicators of economic performance – total factor productivity over the past decades. D. Sornett summed up the results of the last century, calling this period a "secular stagnation". In other words, the optimum of self-organization, which is determined by the moment of formation of horizontal structural ties in the economic system, has long been passed. And further continuation of static changes in the economy will not lead to dramatic shifts in its efficiency, regardless of the height of the vertical structural hierarchy. The authors once again emphasize that these arguments fit into the general model of self-movement of human-created systemic integers. Of course, each national system has its own position on this "spiral", based on the specific state of all factors that predetermine both self-organization and self-development, and even more the coordination of interests of subjects and society, formal institutions and informal restrictions.

If to evaluate the moment X in the context of a system jump into an uncertain future, namely, into a dynamic state, i.e. to the stage of self-development, then the conditions for the implementation of a new technological paradigm have already been formed, and in the late 1990s - 2010s the possibilities of a static economy in the process of its self-organization were exhausted. If so, what is the result of the operation of the law of negation of negation? (Chapter 4; Fig. 7)

First, the shock mechanism implemented this law by destroying the vertical levels of structure that arose as a consequence of solving the problems of structural levels-causes (first negation), and then structural links at the basic level of real markets (second negation). So far, in the conditions of the second wave of the pandemic, neither one nor the other has been restored in the countries of the world (with some exceptions). And all studies persistently link the future with a "New Normal", which is characterized by complete uncertainty.

Second, if the previous structural connections are destroyed, then the internal mechanism of self-movement of the system will be aimed at the formation of new connections, which in the future, in some part of them, will turn into structural. The dynamic state of the system is determined by the fact that it has only a set of technological innovations that can successfully become its technological basis and the basis for the formation of new connections both in technology and in the economy and society. Thus, the dynamics should be associated with the formation of a full-fledged technological paradigm and diverse future structural connections. Their configuration and specific embodiment in all spheres of human life is a complete uncertainty, both from the point of view of the general model and taking into account the specific embodiment in each country. In other words, dynamics is a period of trial and error in building the interaction of elements that were formed in the previous static economy and on which the construction of a new structure depends.

And now it should be dwelled on the third main point, which characterizes the specifics of the current state of economic systems. These are elements of a dynamic economy. It has no structural connections and they will arise by trial and error until some of them become structural, mediating the interaction of dialectical pairs. The elements of such a system are distinguished by a complex organization, structured from the inside as dialectical wholes. It is about large and largest companies capable for self-enforcing. Why should it be about them, and not about small organizational forms in the economy? The authors' arguments boil down to the following. It is the large and the largest, i.e. leading economic organizations, each in its own field of activity, are able to divide and grow. Moreover, they are able to create a variety of hybrid forms of organizational structures with other companies from other areas of human activity. In other words, they can change their configuration both vertically and horizontally, which is very important in conditions when there are no known winning practices and it is very important to experiment organizationally in order to take advantage of new technological solutions. In addition, it is they who carry in themselves, as in a dialectically unified organization, their inherent self-movement mechanism built into them. And their self-organization realizes this mechanism by structuring intra-firm interactions, and self-development – by splitting the existing structure into elements, or replacing some elements, or joining new elements (of other firms). It is in this way that a new structure will be formed in a new reality – an indefinite post-like future, mediating their functioning in a dynamic economy. In this scenario, self-enforcing companies are implementing the famous Schumpeterian "creative destruction" (Schumpeter, 1949).

Fourth, removing institutional barriers to these socio-economic dynamics becomes critical. And here it is also necessary to take into account the specifics of the interaction of formal and informal institutions in the economy, as well as with social institutions. Since there is still no integral economic and social system (all structural ties have been destroyed by shock in the process of implementing the dialectical law of denial of negation), there are no clearly understood wishes for formal institutions and the state in terms of companies' implementation of "creative destruction". If large and large companies become the main driver structuring the future reality, then their actions should be specified only in the direction of limiting the activity that is destructive for the socio-economic system. The main supporting structure of the future institutional reality is transferred to informal institutions in their relationship with social institutions. And this means that the speed of the self-development stage, the length of "that jump" - the progress that the economic system can achieve in the transition to its dynamics, as well as the new predetermination of formal institutions, depends on a person, or rather on the optimization of his own self-organization and self-development, and most importantly, the restoration of their dialectical connection with informal institutions, as well as the dialectic of interaction between the economy and society.

Fifth, based on the above, different perspectives become apparent for different socio-economic systems. And it's not a fact that only highly developed countries can take advantage of this chance. An accurate understanding of the essence of the processes that countries are implementing in the course of self-movement of their technological, economic and social systems will allow them to ensure a high rate of progress. The authors presented theoretically three possible options for the self-development of national systems, provided that the universal processes that predetermine their progress at the stage of self-development are understood. These are the following relationships and interdependencies:

1. differentiation of human activity, which is regulated by the mechanism of positive selection, dominates at the stage of self-development of human-created systems in conditions of complete uncertainty of future reality (future forms of organization and structural ties); the main drivers on this path are large and large companies, and the main actors are individuals with the qualities of intellectual autonomy; the leading institutions that determine the coincidence of the values of society and individuals are informal institutions developed by corporate structures; the role of formal institutions is minimized, since neither society, let alone the state, has decided on their mechanisms of motivation and punishment;
2. the integration of human activity, which is regulated by the mechanism of negative selection, participates in the selection of those organizational structures from a set of connections that can strengthen the integrity of the future system and will mediate the interaction of dialectical pairs; the contours of future reality are gradually emerging (future forms of organization and structural connections) (Chapter 11.1); the main drivers remain large and largest companies surrounded by a growing number of new, newest companies, taking into account the experience of their restructuring (Chapter 11.2), and the main actors remain the workforce, represented by individuals with the quality of intellectual autonomy; companies and individuals as teams begin to form, on the basis of the informal institutions they have developed, a network of formal institutions that dialectically interact with informal (Chapter 11.3); the role of formal institutions is gradually increasing, as the dialectic of interaction between society and the economic system is restored and the state begins to institutionalize the behavior of human-centric organizations that replace those based on capital-centrism.

As a result, taking into account the above, the authors identify three boundary scenarios (Fig. 6), as the basis for their numerous variations in relation to different national systems at the stage of their self-development.

The first scenario is realized in conditions when informal institutions have not become the basis for dialectical connections with formal institutions or their relationship is not optimal, i.e. they specify only a small part of the structural links without contradicting each other. In other words, the consequences of the societal crisis have not been completely eliminated and the integrity of society has not been restored. In this case, there is a slight coincidence of areas representing a variety of differentiated activities and their integrated organizations (by analogy with the models in Fig. 1 and 2). And, meanwhile, everything that remains outside the integration formations represents the potential of differentiated types of activity that could be integrated into specialized complexes that structurally strengthen the integrity of the system. But this did not happen due to the discrepancy between the mechanisms of informal and formal institutions, i.e. unresolved contradictions between individuals (firms) and society.

So the lack of dialectical interaction between formal and informal institutions predetermines the pace of progress in technology, and in the economy, and in society at the stage of self-development. The smaller the jump in the self-development of a dynamic system, the lower the potential for its self-organization in a static state, which will begin after the end of the dynamic changes in the integrity.

The second scenario (middle) scenario is more favorable for system integrity than the first. It is realized in conditions when all differentiated elements (activities) integrate, i.e. are implemented in structural relationships In fact, it turns out that the entire potential of specialization has been realized, since all connections of differentiated types of activity have become structural, mediating the dialectical pairs that have arisen.

Undoubtedly, this is an ideal option, in life it can become a reality only if all informal institutions and formal institutions were structured as dialectical pairs. For such a situation, the sphere of interests of individuals (firms) represented by informal institutions coincided completely with the public interests realized by formal institutions in the hands of the state. In other words, all informal institutions were specified by formal institutions. Such harmony of society, represented by the state and individuals (and companies), provides a dialectical relationship between the economy and society, and therefore, theoretically, the maximum progress as a "leap" of the dynamic system in its self-development.

The third scenario is most likely possible only in theory. It describes a situation where formal institutions are more progressive than informal institutions. And since institutions accompany and provide, together with the mechanism of negative selection, the structure of the future static economy during its transition to the stage of self-organization, the situation is as follows. Companies, due to certain circumstances, did not realize themselves in a variety of specialized activities and relationships generated on this basis. And the state and society have embodied significantly broader opportunities for the formation of structural ties. In this regard, formal institutions begin to define this broader perspective, expanding the possibilities of integration as negative selection to generate new structural ties. As a result, the state manifests itself as a more progressive structure than individuals and companies. And this situation is more related to the fantastic than to the real one.

CONCLUSION

This chapter describes the tendencies of the rise in the importance of the subject component in the mechanism of self-organization of economic systems under the conditions of the laws of unity and struggle of opposites and the transition of quantitative changes to qualitative ones. This problem was ignored by the state, which led to shocks that occurred in the late XX - early XXI centuries in connection with the frequent shocks and crises in the financial markets and other sectors of the economy. Since it is the subjects who mediate the shock ruptures of structural ties and their opportunism in relations with partners in transactions more and more definitely increases economic risks and transaction costs, society has made the state responsible for stabilizing the conditions for the implementation of market contracts by formal institutions.

As a result of the law of the transition of quantitative changes into qualitative ones, a vertical hierarchy of structural links was built, which, on the one hand, made the system more structured (and as a result of this stable), and, on the other hand, more fragile and dependent on the rupture of any link in this structural chain. And if we take into account that the basis of the structural constructions was "trust", which replaced the material support of financial transactions then this fragility was predetermined by the behavioral aspects of the subjects of exchange, whose value ideas could be fundamentally different. The authors see this very reason in the "inflation" of "financial bubbles".

The exchange of economic activity and of its results has its own stages of development, associated both with changes in the objects of exchange and in its subjects. Complication of the exchange occurs along the line of changing the already existing structural links between its participants in the dialectic pairs, of eliminating the outdated ones, and of forming new dialectic pairs. In other words, market exchange mediates the formation of structural links of the economic system and develops according to the laws of its self-organization. At the same time, the dialectic of the market exchange development is

Figure 6. Graphic model of destruction role of informal institutions, providing the process of self-destruction of the exchange of economic activity and of its results at the stage of negation of negation of complex economic dynamics
Source: the authors' development

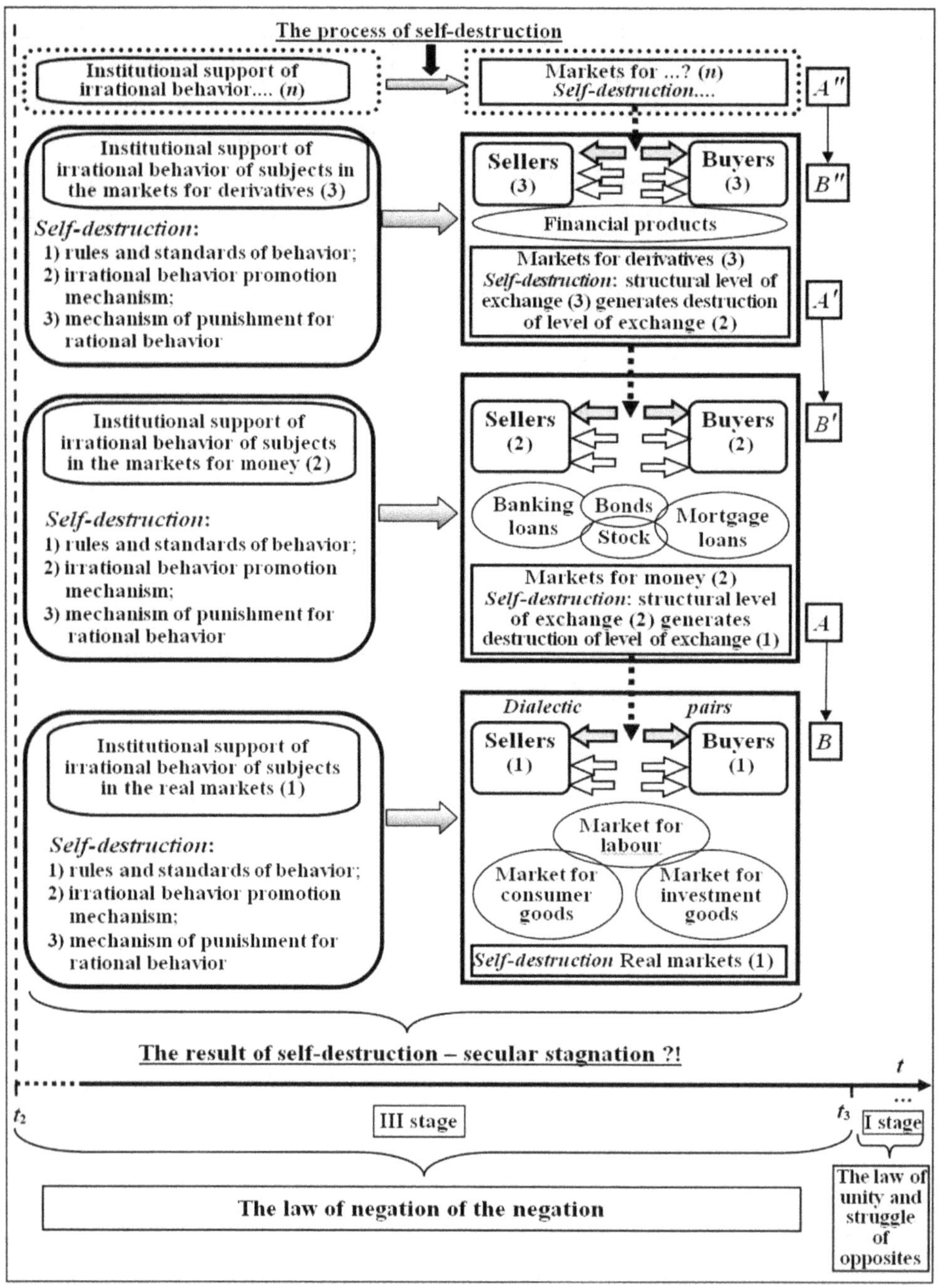

understandable only when it is considered as the process of continuous formation of its new properties due to the changing rules of behaviour of the economic agents, the emergence of its new objects and the structural interdependencies of various segments of market exchange and of their interacting levels. Likewise, accompanying the process of increasing the complexity of the hierarchy of exchange, new institutions emerge and resolve dialectic contradictions with existing ones, providing causal relationships between all structural levels of exchange.

In fact, informal institutions that regulate the behavior of participants in market transactions strengthen confidence in their relations. And this is important, because subjective relationships, the behavior of sellers and buyers, built on trust, in their signal the coincidence of the goals and intentions of the participants in the transaction to close it in compliance with all obligations under the contract. The factor that strengthens trust and ensures the stability of transactions built on trust is their material support. Thus, the subjective intentions of the participants in dialectic pairs are supported by material assets.

Not by chance, according to G.J. Schinasi (2006, p. 33) and C. Kindleberger (1993, p. 21), human trust plays an essential role in financial market as the latter offers the superior store-of-value services compared with the fiat money facilitating inter-temporal exchange. Financial markets, mediating the relations of participants in the exchange of assets, are actually built on the relationship of the trust of participants in the sale and purchase under conditions of growing uncertainty that is difficult to adequately evaluate to the participants of the transactions. Markets for money and financial products become operating with trust as a fragile human emotion and as a result becomes subject to instability under certain conditions when according to G.J. Schinasi (2006, P. 40) "too much finance is created on too little trust". The behavioral aspect of the dialectical dependencies of participants of market transactions gives a price form to the manifestation of shocks when the difference between the base and market prices of assets traded on the market reaches its maximum value. And this is due to the irresistible desire of economic agents to get a margin, which realizes the very price difference that accompanies the manifestation of shocks in any market.

Subjective components of market exchanges are represented in formal institutions by the dialectic of mechanisms of motivation and punishment of partners in transactions. In this regard, the system of formal institutions contains a fundamental contradiction due to the fact that they institutionalize the behavior of the subject as economic agents, without linking them with his individual value preferences acquired in society. As a result, the institutionalization of the individual's behavior in the economy for the purpose of stabilizing it without taking into account his dominant value preferences as a social being a priori leads to a violation of the dialectics of interaction between the economy and society, which aggravates the problems of integrity of both systems. Adapting the provisions of Emile Durkheim, (1895) and M. Weber (1947) to the problem of shocks in terms of the integration of intersystem mismatches at the stage of the jump of systems from a static state to a dynamic one, one should bear in mind the specific nature of man, into which his sociality is intertwined in an unusually difficult way. In other words Homo Sapiens is always and to the same extent Homo Economicus and Homo Socius. This fundamental position was confirmed by the shock caused by the COVID-19 pandemic and the subsequent societal crisis, which manifested itself in the loss of citizens' confidence in their state, which became one of the main obstacles in the fight against coronavirus infection and in the economic recovery. So, the shock leap of national economies from static to dynamics is predetermined not only by the exhaustion of the potential of their self-organization, but also by the violation of the dialectic of interaction between the economic system and society, not to mention the appearance of fantastic opportunities for the technological revolution 4.0 (Chapters 4.1 and 5.1). As a result, the self-development of systemic integrity will be accompanied by the restoration of the dialectic of interaction between society and the economy, provided that their new technological foundation is erected as the embodiment of the results of the technological revolution 4.0.

REFERENCES

Acharya, V. V., Adler, B., & Richardson, M. (2011). *A proposal to resolve the distress of large and complex financial institutions.* New York University Stern School of Business Working Paper.

Akerlof, G. A., & Shiller, R. J. (2009). *Animal Spirits: How Human Psychology Drives the Economy, and Why it Matters for Global Capitalism.* Princeton University Press.

Allen, F., & Gale, D. (2003). *Financial fragility, liquidity and asset prices.* Working Paper, 01-37-B, Wharton Financial Institutions Center.

Allen, F., & Gale, D. (2004). Financial fragility, liquidity, and asset prices. *Journal of the European Economic Association*, *2*(2), 1015–1048. doi:10.1162/JEEA.2004.2.6.1015

Arnold, V. I. (1975). Critical points of smooth functions. *Proc. of International Congress of Mathematicians*, 1, 19-40.

Arnold, V.I. (1979). Catastrophe theory. *Nature*, *10*, 54-63.

Arrow, K. J. (1962). The economic implications of learning by doing. Review of Economic Studies, 29(3), 155-173. doi:10.2307/2295952

Arrow, K. J. (2012). Social Choice and Individual Values. Yale University Press

Barzel, Y. (1982). Measurement costs and the organization of markets. *The Journal of Law & Economics*, *25*(1), 27–48. doi:10.1086/467005

Bernardo, A. E., & Ivo, W. (2004). Liquidity and financial market runs. *Quarterly Journal of Economics, 119*(1).

Bootle, R. (2009). *The Trouble with Markets: Saving Capitalism from Itself.* Nicholas Brealey Publishing.

Bordo, M., Eichengreen, B., Klingebiel, D., & Martinez-Peria, M. (2001). Is the crisis problem growing more severe? *Economic Policy*, *16*(April), 52–82. doi:10.1111/1468-0327.00070

Breaden, C. H., & Toumanoff, P. G. (1984). Transaction costs and economic institutions. In The Political Economy of Freedom: Essays in Honour of F. A. Hayek. Munchen.

Brown, R. (1986). *Social Psychology* (2nd ed.). Free Press.

Caprio, D'Apice, Ferri, & Puopolo. (2010). *Macro financial determinants of the great financial crisis: Implications for financial regulation.* Retrieved from: https://papers.ssrn.com/sol3/papers.cfm?abstract_id=1695335

Caprio, G., Jr. (2013). *Financial regulation after the crisis: did we get here, and how do we get out?* LSE Financial Markets Group Special Paper Series.

Chueng, S.N.S. (1978). *The Myth of Social Costs.* Academic Press.

Coase, R. H. (1937). The nature of the firm. *Economica, 4*(5).

Coase, R.H. (1988). The nature of the firm: origin, meaning, influence. *Journal of Law, Economics and Organization, 4.*

Commons, J. (1931). Industrial economics. *The American Economic Review, 21*(4).

Durkheim, E. (1895). *The Rules of Sociological Method.* Sage Publications.

Galbreith, J. K. (1977). *The Great Crash: 1929.* Houghton Mifflin.

Gouldner, A. (1960). The norm of reciprocity: A preliminary statement. *American Sociological Review, 25*(2), 161–178. doi:10.2307/2092623

Hodgson, G. M. (1988). *Economics and Institutions. A Manifesto for a Modern Institutional Economics.* Polity Press. doi:10.9783/9781512816952

Hoggarth & Saporta. (2001, June). Costs of banking system instability: some empirical evidence. *Financial Stability Review.*

Homans, G. (1961). *Social Behavior: Its Elementary Forms.* Harcourt Brace Jovanovich.

Jensen, M. C., & Meckling, W. H. (1973). Theory of the firm: Managerial behavior, agency costs, and ownership structure. *Journal of Financial Economics, 3*(5).

Keynes, J. M. (1936). *The General Theory of Employment. Interest and Money. The Selected Works.* Harcourt, Brace and Company.

Kindleberger, C. (1993). *A Financial History of Western Europe.* Oxford University Press.

Lindgren, C.-J., Garcia, G., & Saal, M. (1996). *Bank Soundness and Macroeconomic Policy.* IMF.

Magun, Rudnev, & Schmidt. (2015b). Russian basic human values through the lens of the European value types. *The Russian Public Opinion Herald Data. Analysis. Discussions, 3-4*(121), 74-93.

Magun, V., & Rudnev, M. (2015). Basic human values of the Russians: both different from and similar to other Europeans. In L. Harrison & E. G. Yasin (Eds.), *Culture Matters in Russia and Everywhere: Backdrop for the Russia-Ukraine Conflict.* Lexington Boo.

Magun, V., Rudnev, M., & Schmidt, P. (2015a). Within-and between-country value diversity in Europe: A typological approach. *European Sociological Review,* (August). Advance online publication. doi:10.1093/esr/jcv080

MasonJ. R.RosnerJ. (2007). *How Resilient Are Mortgage Backed Securities to Collateralized Debt Obligation Market Disruptions?* http://ssrn.com/abstract=1027472

MasonJ. R.RosnerJ. (2007). Where Did the Risk Go? How Misapplied Bond Ratings Cause Mortgage Backed Securities and Collateralized Debt Obligation Market Disruptions. https://ssrn.com/abstract=1027475 doi:10.2139srn.1027475

Menard, C. (2003). The economic of hybrid organization. *Journal of Institutional and Theoretical Economics.*

North, D. (1997). The process of economic change. *Research Paper* 128, World Institute for Development Economics Research Oleinik, A. (2007). In A. Oleinik (Ed.), *Institutional Economy*. INFRA-M.

North, D. (2005). *Understanding the Process of Economic Change*. Princeton University Press. doi:10.1515/9781400829484

North, D. C. (1987). Institutions, transaction costs, and economic growth. *Economic Inquiry*, *25*(3), 419–428. doi:10.1111/j.1465-7295.1987.tb00750.x

North, D. C. (1990). *Institutions, Institutional Change and Economic Performance*. Cambridge University Press. doi:10.1017/CBO9780511808678

Pilipenko, Z. A., & Pilipenko, A. I. (2018). Shocks in global economy: impulse model of macroeconomic cycle. In B. S. Sergi, F. Fidanoski, M. Ziołо, & V. Naumovski (Eds.), *Regaining Global Stability After the Financial Crisis*. Advances in Finance, Accounting, and Economics. IGI Global. doi:10.4018/978-1-5225-4026-7.ch012

Polterovich, V. M. (2010). The rise of general social analysis. Country Capital.

Schinasi, G. J. (2006). *Safeguarding Financial Stability: Theory and Practice*. IMF.

Schumpeter, J. A. (1949). The Theory of Economic Development: An Inquiry into Profits, Capital, Credit, Interest, and the Business Cycle. Harvard University Press.

Schwab, K. (2016). *The Fourth Industrial Revolution*. Geneva: World Economic Forum.

Schwartz, S. H. (1994). Are there universal aspects in the content and structure of values? *The Journal of Social Issues*, 50. doi:10.1111/j.1540-4560.1994.tb01196.x

Schwartz, S. H., Cieciuch, J., Vecchione, M., Davidov, E., Fischer, R., Beierlein, C., Ramos, A., Verkasalo, M., Lönnqvist, J.-E., Demirutku, K., Dirilen-Gumus, O., & Konty, M. (2012). Refining the theory of basic individual values. *Journal of Personality and Social Psychology*, *103*(4), 663–688. doi:10.1037/a0029393 PMID:22823292

Shiller, R. J. (2002). Bubbles, human judgement and expert opinion. *Financial Analysts Journal*, *58*(3), 18–26. doi:10.2469/faj.v58.n3.2535

ShillerR. J. (2004). *Household reaction to changes in housing wealth.* Cowles Foundation Discussion Paper No. 1459. https://ssrn.com/abstract=537343

Shiller, R. J. (2015). Irrational Exuberance (3rd ed.). Princeton University Press. doi:10.2307/j.ctt1287kz5

Shiller, R. J., Fischer, S., & Friedman, B. M. (1984). 'Stock prices and social dynamics'. *Brookings Papers on Economic Activity*, *2*(2), 457–498. doi:10.2307/2534436

Shubik, M. (1999). *Theory of Money and Financial Institutions.* MIT Press.

Sornette, D. (2003). *Why Stock Markets Crash: Critical Events in Complex Financial Systems*. Princeton University Press.

Stigler, G. J. (1961). The Economics of Information. *Journal of Political Economy, 69*(3), 213-225.

Volcker. (1984). Richard Freeman and Kathy Burdma. Volcker tells Reagan: 'Heads I win, tails you lose'. *EIR Economics, 11*(9).

von Mises, L. (1996). *Human Action: A Treatise on Economics* (4th rev. ed.). The Foundation for Economic Education, Inc., by Fox & Wilkes.

Weber, M. (1947). *The Theory of Social and Economic Organization*. Oxford University Press.

Williamson, O. E. (1985). *The Economic Institutions of Capitalism: Firms*. Markets, Relational Contracting.

Willis, R. (1986). Wage determinants: a survey and reinterpretation of human capital earnings. In O. Ashenfelter & R. Layard (Eds.), *Handbook of Labor Economics* (Vol. 1). North-Holland. doi:10.1016/S1573-4463(86)01013-1

Chapter 7
Theory of Shocks About States in Static and Dynamic Economics

ABSTRACT

The place of the state in the theory of shocks is predetermined by the increasing importance of the subjective component of the processes of self-movement of systemic integrities. The main problem is that the state formalizes the actions of subjects as economic agents, abstracting from social conditions that generate the individual values of a person implemented in the economy. So, the economic subject acquires its own individual values in a society with a sharp polarization of citizens' incomes, inequality of opportunities, a shrinking middle class, and an ineffective public healthcare system, as demonstrated by the coronavirus pandemic. As a result, a fundamental problem arises of the discrepancy between society and economy as well as formal and informal institutions that predetermine the opportunistic behavior of the economic subjects. Thus, the state persistently strives for financial stability in the economy, abstracting from the problems of social disunity.

INTRODUCTION

The state has a special role in the self-organization and self-development of systemic integrity in technology, economy and society. It is necessary to start with the fact that society initially made the state responsible for a number of functions, which R. Musgrave conditionally reduced to three main groups: (1) allocation of resources; (2) economic stabilization (subject to cost-effectiveness) and (3) (fair) redistribution of income (Musgrave, 1959). Their implementation was provided by formal institutions classified as public goods. These phenomena accompanied the process of self-organization of systemic wholes, which was distinguished by the dominance of the object component under the conditions of the law of unity and the struggle of opposites and an increase in the importance of the subjective component at the time of increasing quantitative changes to form their new quality. As for the state, throughout the static changes in technological, economic and social systems, its functions were financed from a part of the

DOI: 10.4018/978-1-7998-4309-2.ch007

GDP created in the economy. It is in this regard that the functions that somehow contributed to economic growth were paramount in terms of budget expenditures. It was about effective allocation of resources as well as about economic safeguarding (equilibrium). As for formal institutions, their focus on ensuring economic and financial stability was also seen as an unconditional imperative. Moreover, this approach to the role of the state in national systems remained unchanged, despite the transition from the formation of the basic structure of real markets to a structural hierarchy at the expense of money markets, financial markets, etc. In other words, if from the point of view of the object component of self-organization, the integrity of the economic system was strengthened by complementing the horizontal structure by building a vertical structural hierarchy, then the functions of the state remained unchanged. In other words, if, from a theoretical point of view, the structure objectively had to adjust to systemic changes in order to preserve its integrity, then the state, performing some semblance of structural functions, also had to change. However, it remained unchanged. This could not but affect negatively the state of the system as a whole. Economic balance and financial stability remained the priority of public policy, and this was the goal of formal institutions providing the functioning of real and financial markets. In other words, this conservatism of government actions objectively contributed to the shock destruction of structural ties as a result of the COVID-19 pandemic.

As the importance of the subjective component of self-organization processes increased, the fragility of the system increased not only due to the vertical separation of cause-and-effect relationships between different structural levels, but also due to the inflexibility of the state and of the formal institutions it created. In addition, as the vertical of the structural ties of the economic system increased the importance of the subjective component of self-organization processes in the process of replacing the material support of financial transactions with the subjective "trust" of partners in transactions. The state overlooked a significant point related to the fact that in the more frequent cases of shock ruptures of structural ties in the financial markets, it was the subjects who implemented shocks and gave a start to subsequent crises. And this meant that the state, in many respects, due to the non-adaptability of formal institutions, accelerated shock breaks, since neither the mechanisms of positive and negative selection, nor institutional instruments in the hands of the state were able to organizationally resolve the contradiction between the growing differentiation of financial transactions (objects, subjects, processes, etc. phenomena) and their integration in one form or another of dialectical relationships. However, the main reason for the unintentional participation of the state in generating shocks as a mechanism for the implementation of dialectical laws at the stage of self-organization of economic integrities was its lack of understanding of the need to establish dialectic interrelationships between formal and informal institutions as well as between the economy and t the society. Their conflict was based on abstraction of the state from the main essence of self-movement of systemic integrity, which can be expressed by the words "everything flows, everything changes". And, meanwhile, at the final stage of self-organization of the economy, the object component began to increasingly be replaced by its subjective component, the priority in relationships began to shift from the economy to society, from formal to informal institutions, from economic behavior to individual values that predetermined it. This multilevel conflict cannot be resolved within the framework of a static economy, entrenched formal institutions and the state with its focus on economic equilibrium and financial stability.

The COVID-19 pandemic only accelerated this process, and the objective law of denial of denial through a shock mechanism brought the end of the previous structure closer both in the form of the vertical hierarchy and in the form of the base level that gave rise to it. In the new conditions of self-development, there is no structure, and there is no need for the previous formal institutions, as well as in the form of the state that generated them. In complete uncertainty about the future dynamic economy, we can definitely assume that it will be formed by high skilled individuals and the largest self-enforcing firms – their employers. Informal institutions will be the main ones in ensuring their activities therefore the restoration of the integrity of society is becoming the main condition for rapid dynamics in the economy. And a person in such a new reality is needed as a creator with the quality of an intellectually autonomousness. And then the main problem of the dynamics of the economy, the integrity of society and the introduction of a new technological paradigm moves into the dialectic of self-organization and self-development of the person himself. Already today, it can be argued with certainty that his adequate specialization and integration in society will inevitably change the principles of organization of all systems – from capital-centric to human-centric.

The institutionalization of the function of ensuring social justice actually creates the basis for the implementation of the dialectical connection between formal and informal institutions, and through it the coordination of the processes of self-movement of the economy and society. However, this very foundation was not created in a society based on capital-centric principles of organization. As a result, informal institutions that came into conflict with formal institutions in society gradually corroded the integrity of the system, which, in the context of the shock caused by the COVID-19 pandemic, turned into a societal crisis as the main problem of further transformations.

Moreover, the economic and social lockdowns, introduced on an emergency basis by the nation states, in a shock manner destroyed structural ties in national economic and social systems. As a result, national governments faced a choice: either back to the restoration of destroyed structural ties, or move towards the dynamics and self-development of systems. And this means new functions of the state in society, the restoration of the dialectic of interaction between formal and informal institutions and the priority of human-centric principles of organization to restore the integrity of society. The state in this new reality will have to look for its new place, new functions and build new formal institutions in the interests of society, which will be constructed intellectually by autonomous individuals.

7.1. The State and the Integrity of Society: Formal Institutions and the Shock Destruction of a Static Economy

The focus of the modern state can be expressed with the words of the Russian philosopher N. Berdyaev: "The state does not exist to transform earthly life into paradise, but in order to prevent it from turning into hell" (V. Tanzi, 2011, P. 19). These problems should be investigated in connection with the role of the state to move society to the border with paradise, serving its interests and strengthening its integrity. At the same time, the concepts explaining the capabilities, potential and role of the state in society, including the economy, were constantly changing. According to J.M. Keynes (1936) the state is the only agent in society capable of working for the collective interest on a sufficient scale. Moreover, this is its duty – first to try to prevent a depression and then, if it occurs, to get the society out of it. As to financial markets huge uncertainty and long time horizons make them subject to wild swings of sentiment and herd behavior. Because of the importance of the financial markets for real economic activity, they cannot be left to their own devices. They require intervention, management, regulation, and restriction. After the 1980s the driving force became Milton Friedman (1962), who argued fervently that markets were rational and effective. From his viewpoint governments, by contrast, were inefficient and often irrational and could fall prey to corruption or be captured by group interests. As a result the Keynesian explanation for the Great Depression was that the last derived from a collapse of the confidence of investors, interacting with the peculiarities of a monetary economy. Friedman's explanation was based on policy failure.

The authors adhere to the contractual theory of the state (D. North, 1981, P. 22), according to which the state provides benefits to all members of the society as participants of the original treaty. In accordance with the theory of the social contract, the appearance of a state is viewed as an initial contract that recognizes the individual's rights to certain resources compared with the rights of other parties to the treaty in exchange for their refusal to claim other resources and the consent to respect other people's rights to them. Such interpretation determines the emergence of the state and its function of the arbitration party, which is designed to guarantee compliance with the terms of the original social contract. In fact, it is about the fundamental function of the state to form a system of formal institutions that provide the necessary rules for the behavior of participants in market transactions, incentive mechanisms and penalties for their violations.

The fundamental function of the state to create and improve the formal institutions necessary for a market economy is specifically subordinated to the goal of institutionalizing its priority functions: (1) allocation of resources; (2) economic stabilization (subject to cost-effectiveness) and (3) (fair) redistribution of income (Musgrave, 1959). Initially, R. Musgrave R. (1959) united the whole variety of specific responsibilities of the state to society in three above mentioned groups of functions. In his time he (Musgrave, 1998) described the forms of manifestation of the contradictoriness of specific duties of the state. Later they were structured in the form of a contradictory set called the "triangle dilemma". The theoretical paradox of this "triangle dilemma" is that the state in principle is not able to optimize the performance of all three main areas of its activities simultaneously, not to mention the implementation of their "efficiency" scheme. This is due to the fact that it is objectively impossible to realize at the same time three conflicting goals: effective allocation of resources in the society; social justice and macroeconomic stability. This explains the content of the paradox of the "triangle dilemma". Having the main functions of the state at the corners of the triangle, it is necessary to realize that only two of their three groups can be effectively realized simultaneously. Ensuring macroeconomic stability and social justice could be provided only if the principle of effective allocation of resources is abandoned, since horizontal equality is incompatible with the market (which should be the state's orientation) equality in the allocation of resources and property rights to them. The market is a dynamic equilibrium provided that the imbalances arise and permanently resolve, especially in the allocation of resources, including human capital. Similarly, the combination of the functions of economic efficiency and macroeconomic stability through the reduction of vertical imbalances (for the purpose of strengthening social justice) is possible only through increased horizontal inequality, i.e. social injustice.

The formal institutions proper were aimed at optimizing the implementation of all these functions of the state. The state's obligations to the society, structured into three groups of specific functions, manifest themselves in the form of budget expenditures. Since any expenses should be financed, in the case of public expenditures they are provided at the expense of the national income. The corresponding share of GDP and national income is redistributed through the mechanism of public finances in favor of the state, through which its functions are paid by the society. This mechanism allows to generate budget revenues of the state with the help of taxes, and to finance its budget expenditures in the process of fulfilling the functions defined by society. In his original state model D. North (1981) described this mechanism in the categories of mediation in exchange, when the state performs its functions to ensure, for example, "defense and justice", and society finances them by paying taxes to the budget incomes. As a result, the society as a whole wins, as these services are implemented by a specialized agency, whose functions are performed by the state. Such a delegation to the state of functions for the public goods and services production is predetermined by considerable economies of scale (Arrow, 1970). In this case, the state is charged with the function of a discriminating monopolist. It differentiates the population that pays taxes, into groups, and for each group it specifies property rights so as to maximize tax revenues of the state budget. As a result, the tasks assigned to the state are contradictory: the second task assumes a fully effective set of property rights in order to maximize the aggregate product of society. In this case, the first task leads to attempts to specify a set of fundamental rules that would allow the state to maximize his income (or maximize the monopoly rents of a group or class whose agent the state acts) (Alchian, 1984, P.6). Thus A. Alchian (1984) formulated the contradictoriness of state interests, caused by the contradictoriness of the state' essence as a subject and as an object of management. This quality is also manifested by the mechanism the GDP redistribution between the society and the state. It's about public finances that replace money in the exchange of public goods and services, real estate, financial assets between the state and society. In many ways, it is precisely the fact that society finances the functions of the state at its own expense (of the gross domestic product created in society) that predetermined the dominance of those expenditures (and of formal institutions) that, one way or another, stimulated the national economy. It is no coincidence that the problem of equilibrium in the economy, and before the COVID-19 pandemic, financial stability turned into a priority goal of the state and subordinated all the other above-mentioned functions of the state.

Specificity of finance in general, replacing money as a mechanism for mediating sales transactions, is associated with deferred payment for transactions in time and space (Pilipenko, et al. 2019). To ensure such transactions between them, the state is obliged to create rules for their behavior and penalties for their non-compliance with transaction participants. In other words, when the finance replaces money in payments with deferred maturity, the state as a subject of management creates formal institutions, dictating the rules of conduct that are binding on participants, encouraging their conscientious behavior and punishing them for their opportunism towards each other. The practitioners reasoned as follows. The society needs more of the markets to do what they are good at – incentivizing, signaling, and encouraging the best use of scarce resources, especially now in the fields of environmental protection, climate change, and public infrastructure usage. It is in this context that there has been a growing need to adapt formal institutions to the functioning of financial markets, which in various respects means an increased role of the government. But countries do not need more government they need to adjust the market economy as a whole. It is necessary to agree with R.P. Bootle (2009) that it is not the wrong regulation of a particular market, it is necessary to eliminate the practice of mismanaging the entire economy. The state should improve the quality and efficiency of its formal institutions in the sphere of economics and finance as a whole without expanding the scale of its impact on the market economy.

To this it should be added that on the eve of the COVID-19 pandemic, the effectiveness of the state and its formal institutions was assessed in the context of the state of the economy - whether GDP is growing or slowing down. All researchers of this problem are united in the opinion that the effective state formation is predetermined by the peculiarities of national economic systems and national communities (Pigou, 1924; Musgrave, 1959; Bator, 1960). However, the resolution of these particular problems must be preceded by an understanding of the fundamental problem related to a specific stage of self-movement of the economy (not to mention society). If it is about vertical structural ties in the economy, then the optimum in the self-movement of the economy has already been passed and this was reflected in the constant damping of economic growth. And in the context of a decline in GDP growth rates, growing budget expenditures naturally caused a budget deficit and an increase in public debt.

The state was unable to violate this fundamental tendency of self-organization of economic integrity at the stage of the law of transition of quantitative changes to qualitative changes. Another aspect, which also concerns the activities of the state, is associated with the inflexibility of formal institutions aimed at ensuring financial stability at any cost. It is about the absence of the dialectic of interaction between formal and informal institutions, since the state in its activities simply ignored individual values in the form of informal restrictions. Many aspects of this fundamental scientific problem, especially in the context of the state's functions on the different stages of the self-movement of the systemic integrities are far from understanding (Helpman, 2004).

Many years of research before the COVID-19 pandemic have made it possible to pass a verdict on the inefficiency of the state and of its formal institutions (Tanzi, et al., 1997, 2000; Angelopoupos, et al., 2008). In the new century specific forms of this phenomenon' manifestation have become (1) national states' inability to foresee the global crises emergence such as the latest one of 2007-2009, and to block quickly their devastating impact; (2) national governments inefficiency to change radically the modern slow down trend of economic dynamics and of aggregate factor productivity growth; (3) inadequate state performance of its function of an equitable income distribution in society, which has increased the income polarization of the richest and the poorest members of society; (4) and, finally, the helplessness of the state to compensate financial losses from the global economy's disintegration by activating the factors of inclusive development of its countries. Given the significant share of GDP redistributed by the state all over the world through budget channels (the taxation system and government expenditures), it should be recognized to a large extent responsible for the secular stagnation all over the Globe. This determines the paramount importance of an adequate theoretical understanding of the essence of the state as a phenomenon that is contradictory in its essence and has ample opportunities to institutionalize the self-organization and the self-development of the systemic integrity in the technology, economics and society.

By the way, this fundamental reason for generating shocks and the role of the state in it was demonstrated by the shock in the unsecured mortgage market in the American financial market back in 2007 and confirmed the shock of the COVID-19 pandemic in 2020. But on the surface of the phenomena, the inefficiency of the state was assessed by indirect indicators of the comparative rates of GDP growth and budget spending within the national framework. Statistical data showed that the effectiveness of the government's performance of the functions assigned to it and the provision of these budgetary expenditures by formal institutions became more and more ineffective, bringing less and less economic returns. This is evidenced by the data below, which was compiled before the onset of the COVID-19 pandemic.

The high growth rates of the global economy and its leading groups of countries have been in the past. In recent decades, the tendency has been rooted in slowing economic growth in all segments of the global economy (Fig. 1).

In 1970-1985 developed economies demonstrated an average 3% GDP growth per year; countries with average incomes and emerging markets - 4% and 6% respectively; and the annual growth rates for developing countries with low incomes were slightly higher than 4% in 2005-2010. The International Monetary Fund experts predict the economic development rates' decay all over the world in the perspective until 2020. The same opinion is shared by the World Bank experts.

As to the OECD (Guillemette, and Turner, 2018) baseline scenario with no institutional or policy changes, world trend real GDP growth declines from about 3½ per cent now to 2% in 2060, mainly due to a deceleration of large emerging economies as these continue to account for the bulk of world growth. India and China take up a rising share of world output as the world's economic centre of gravity shifts toward Asia.

Figure 1. Real GDP per Capita Growth, 1970–2020 (Percent)
Source: IMF. Fiscal Monitor (April 2018), P. 24.
Note: The dashed lines represent trends based on a Hodrick-Prescott filter.

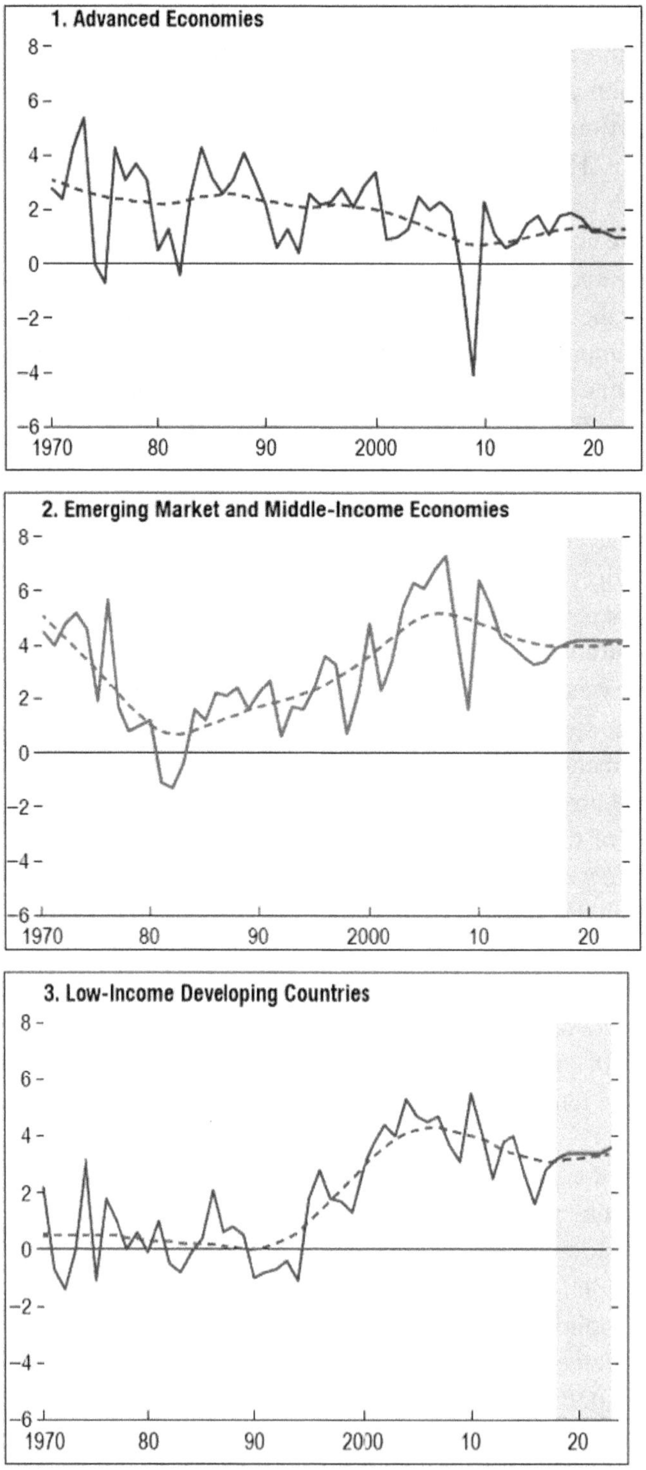

An interim summary of the discussions related to the problems of global development retardation can be summed up in the words of El. Helpman (2004), a specialist in economic growth issues. In his opinion, until now it has not been possible to understand the patterns of such a sustained downward dynamic, although it was possible to single out the forms of manifestation of inhibition processes of the global economy development and to describe them using statistical indicators. It was confirmed that the accumulation of physical and human capital is the most important factor determining the rate of economic growth of the countries all over the world. However, this only partially explains the deviations in per capita income and the rate of GDP growth (Aghion, et al., 2013). As for the institutional factors, they have an even more serious impact on the rate of accumulation of the main factors of production, and, consequently, on the economic dynamics, but their study has not been brought to an understanding of the laws of inhibition of the economic dynamics of modern communities (Helpman, 2004, P. 10).

In this connection, the question of the role of the state and state finances in these mechanisms of inhibition remains open. To answer this question, it is advisable to analyze statistical data, which allows to judge about the importance of the share of GDP that is redistributed by the state through the mechanism of public finances. First of all, we are talking about the dynamics of state budget revenues on the example of developed countries (Table 1).

Table 1. Advanced Economies: General Government Revenue, 2010–2020 (Percent of GDP)

Years	2010	2015	2018	2019	2020
Countries					
Australia	32.0	34.6	35.1	35.2	35.5
Austria	48.4	49.9	48.9	48.9	48.9
Belgium	49.3	51.3	50.4	50.1	49.9
Canada	38.4	39,8	39.4	39.5	39.5
Denmark	54.0	53,3	51.3	50.8	50.6
France	49.6	53,1	53,5	52,2	51.7
Germany	43.0	44.5	45.4	45.5	45.5
Italy	45.6	47,7	46.7	47.5	47.5
United Kingdom	35.3	35.6	36.7	36.7	36.6
United States	29.1	31.6	30.7	30.4	30.8
Global Average	34.9	36.5	36.3	36.1	36.4
G20 Advanced	33.7	35.7	35.4	35.3	35.5

Source: Composed by authors on the base of official data of IMF. Fiscal Monitor (October, 2018); IMF. Fiscal Monitor (April 2018), P. 111.

The authors will proceed from the fact that the developed countries of the world are somewhat ahead of the future of all other countries and show a long-term or medium-term outlook for the low-income developing countries, as well as for middle-income and emerging markets. Over the period of 2010-2020, as to the average for the world and for the developed countries of the G20 group, then their share of the national governments revenues of their budgets varies steadily around 34% of their GDP: in 2010 it averaged about 34%, and in 2020 it is projected at level of 35.5%. In other words, the states in the developed countries of the world redistribute through taxes 1/3 of their national GDP, and to this third they adjust the downward dynamics of GDP. At the same time, for 10 years period, the share of governments revenues is gradually increasing in all countries except Denmark (in 2010 it was 54%, and in 2020 - 50.6% of GDP). Even in the US, with the focus of fiscal policy on the priority of market principles, the corresponding share has increased, albeit slightly: from 29.1% of GDP to 30.8% accordingly. The budget revenues shares of GDP of such countries as Austria, Belgium, Denmark, France, Ital, are approaching to 50%. So judging by the share of budget revenues in GDP, the states play a crucial role in adjusting the dynamics of its countries' GDP in the long term. Other, no less effective instruments of public finance, which have a serious impact on macroeconomic dynamics, are government expenditures (Garcia-Escribano, et al., 2017). Judging by the data in Table 2, the national states of all countries all over the world redistribute an average of 40% of GDP by means of budgetary expenditures: in 2010 this figure was 42.6% of GDP, which was comparable to the average for the developed countries of the world - 42%.

As for the budget expenditures that ensure the state's fulfillment of its obligations to the society, the trend of their change from 2010 to 2020 has the opposite direction compared to the above described (Table 2).

Table.2. Advanced Economies: General Government Expenditure, 2010–2020 (Percent of GDP)

Years	2010	2015	2018	2019	2020
Countries					
Australia	37.1	37.4	36.8	36.3	35.7
Austria	52.8	51.0	49.2	49.0	49.1
Belgium	53.3	53.8	51.7	51.4	51.1
Canada	43.2	39,9	40.3	40.3	40.2
Denmark	56.7	54.8	52.1	51.3	50.9
France	56.4	56.7	55.9	55.3	53.7
Germany	47.3	43.9	44.0	43.8	43.8
Italy	49.9	50.3	48.2	48.4	47.8
United Kingdom	44.7	39.8	38.5	38.3	37.9
United States	40.0	35.2	36.0	36.3	37.9
Global Average	42.6	39.1	39.0	38.9	38.8
G20 Advanced	42.0	38.5	38.6	38.6	38.5

Source: Composed by authors on the base of official data of IMF. Fiscal Monitor (April, 2018), P. 112.

So, for the period from 2010 to 2020 the share of government spending in the GDP of the developed countries is decreasing: in Denmark - from 56.7 to 50.9% of GDP; in France - from 56.4 to 50.9% of GDP, in the USA - from 40.0 to 37.9% of GDP, respectively. Over 10 years before the COVID-19 pandemic, this indicator fell slightly, reaching in 2020 an average of 38.8% and 38.5%, respectively. Following the logic of the previous arguments, this allows us to assess the contribution of the state to the downward economic dynamics of the countries of the world at a level of 40% in terms of the state budgets expenditures. And in countries such as Austria, Belgium, Denmark, France, Italy, the share of the state's budget expenditures fluctuates around 50% of GDP, declining slightly for the period of 2010-2020. In the rest of the countries, this share is expected to decrease somewhat by the end of the analyzed period, remaining above 35% of GDP in the case of Australia and below 44% in Germany. In other words, if we consider the role of the state in the life of society on the developed countries' example, then their governments manage about a third of their countries' GDP through budget revenues and about 40% - in the process of performing their budgets expenditures.

In addition, states have the opportunity to influence the economic dynamics of their countries, financing the sustainable deficits of their budgets. External and / or domestic loans for current budgets deficit' financing reduce gross investments in the economy and increase the debts of future generations (Tables 3 and 4) (Checherita-Westphal, et al, 2012). Thus, public finances mediate an additional channel for the redistribution of GDP in favor of the state. Judging from the data in Table 3, in 2010-2020 practically all developed countries, with the exception of Germany, will maintain a negative balance of the consolidated budgets of their states.

Table 3. Advanced Economies: General Government Overall Balance, 2010–2020 (Percent of GDP)

Years	2010	2015	2018	2019	2020
Countries					
Australia	-5.1	-2.8	-1.7	-1.1	-0.1
Austria	-4.5	-1.1	-0.3	-0.2	-0.2
Belgium	-4.0	-2.5	-1.3	-1.3	-1.3
Canada	-4.7	-0.1	-0.8	-0.5	-0.3
Denmark	-2.7	-1.5	-1.5	-1.5	-1.5
France	-6.8	-3.6	-2.4	-3.1	-2.0
Germany	-4.2	+0.6	+1.5	+1.7	+1.6
Italy	-4.2	-2.6	-1.6	-0.9	-0.3
United Kingdom	-9.4	-4.3	-1.8	-1.5	-1.3
United States	-10.9	-3.5	-5.3	-5.9	-5.5
Global Average	-7.7	-2.6	-2.7	-2.8	-2.4
G20 Advanced	-8.4	-2.9	-3.2	-3.3	-2.9

Source: Composed by authors on the base of official data of IMF. Fiscal Monitor (April, 2018), P. 112.

However, the states intend to significantly reduce budget deficits: on average for the developed countries they will decrease from 8.4% of GDP in 2010 to 2.9% in 2020. Such a budget maneuver of the developed countries' states all over the world is explained by the significant size of the already accumulated consolidated net public debt, which on average in the global economy amounted to 69.6% of GDP in 2010 and is projected at 74.1% of GDP in 2020. The average indicators of the accumulated public debt of the developed countries are estimated at 75.7% and 80% of GDP for the period under review. Thus, the budget deficits of the developed countries and their current funding will lead, according to IMF experts, to the accumulation of public debt in 2020 to impressive proportions relative to GDP: from 16.1% in Germany, to 85% in Belgium and France and 114% - in Italy (Table 4). This raises the need to divert an increasing proportion of the national budgets expenditures for servicing the public

Table 4. Advanced Economies: General Government Net Debt, 2010–2020 (Percent of GDP)

Years	2010	2015	2018	2019	2020
Countries					
Australia	3.9	17.8	19.2	18.7	17.3
Austria	60.5	58.0	51.9	49.4	47.5
Belgium	88.4	93.1	88.6	87.1	85.7
Canada	26.8.0	27.7	27.4	26.6	25.7
Denmark	15.1	16.2	16.5	16.4	16.1
France	73.5	86.5	87.0	86.9	85.8
Germany	60.9	51.2	41.5	38.1	35.1
Italy	104.7	119.5	118.5	116.5	114.1
United Kingdom	68.4	79.6	79.6	79.6	79.6
United States	70.1	80.5	81.4	82.7	76.2
Global Average	69.6	75.7	75.0	74.5	74.1
G20 Advanced	75.7	81.0	80.6	80.4	80.0

Source: Composed by authors on the base of official data of IMF. Fiscal Monitor—Capitalizing on Good Times. Washington: IMF, April 2018. - P. 114.

debt, which means an additional redistribution of GDP in favor of the state and ineffective spending of budget funds, which negatively affects the dynamics of the national economies.

The OECD aggregate underlying primary deficit went from 4½ per cent of potential GDP in 2010 to ¼ per cent in 2016, and that of the euro area went from 1¾ to a 1½ per cent surplus over the same period. Public debt levels have nevertheless generally continued to increase over this period, rising by about 15 percentage points of GDP in both the OECD and euro area, and are now high by historical standards (Guillemette, et al., 2018, P. 37). But with interest rates having fallen to historically low levels, debt servicing has remained affordable. Experts are of the opinion that the precise confluence of factors behind this trend continues to be debated, but one hypothesis is that desired saving has been relatively stronger than desired investment, leading to a global saving glut (Bernanke, 2005; 2015). The decline in investment as of the early 2020s is driven largely by slowing employment and labour efficiency growth, so less capital investment is required to maintain a given capital-to-output ratio. As a result, the size of the budget deficit was considered as the current indicator of the inefficiency of public finance. And the total public debt relative to the national GDP was assessed by the cumulative (integral) indicator of their inefficiency (Table 4), since it is associated with the costs of future generations to pay for the results of ineffective work of the state in previous periods.

So, on the eve of the COVID-19 pandemic, formal institutions clearly did not ensure the effective functioning of the state at the stage of self-organization of national economic systems. This was manifested in a reduction in economic growth, in an increase in the budget deficit of countries of the world and an increase in public debt, which contributed to the build-up of structural imbalances and preparation of conditions for a shock rupture of structural ties. But the main problem of the state's inadequacy and the inefficiency of its formal institutions was still another. The priority of the economy and its integrity was absolute, and formal institutions were focused primarily on ensuring equilibrium in the economy and financial stability as its necessary condition. It was not about the object or subjective components of the self-organization process. The problem of their subordination came to the fore. Moreover, the line between static and dynamic economies has not yet been established in theory. Moreover, the practitioners did not speak about it. And since there are no theoretical ideas about the fundamental laws of self-movement of the economy and about its specific stages, it was problematic to single out the role of the state in relation to each of them. Before the COVID-19 pandemic, the established economy with its finances was considered as a given, governed by purely economic and financial levers specified through formal institutions. Neither a series of shocks nor subsequent crises changed anything in the perception of the state and its formal institutions. And now a humanitarian catastrophe broke out caused by the coronavirus pandemic and now practitioners are forced to face the fundamental issues of self-movement of systemic integrity, the role and functions of the state and of its formal institutions.

EMPIRICAL EVIDENCE

The fundamental reason for the constant imbalance of public finances is the impracticability at the same time of all without exception of the functions of the state, built according to the "dilemma of triangle" of R. Musgrave. In his investigations R.E. Wagner (Wagner, 1976) singled out the "redistribution" as a significant category, which allowed R. Musgrave (1998) to link it with the functions of the state and to structure them into three main groups according to the number of angles in its magic triangle. These are functions such as, (1) allocation of resources, (2) redistribution of income (implied to ensure equity in society) and (3) economic stabilization (in the context of economic efficiency). This triad does not specifically include the state functions of economic development and economic growth, although many modern governments increasingly declare them in the list of goals of their policies (Tanzi, 2011, PP. 159, 169). The first and third functions of the state, mentioned above, do not contradict each other and theoretically more or less successfully can be realized in its activity. However, the second function, related to the institutional maintenance of equity in the distribution of income in national societies, in principle cannot be successfully implemented simultaneously with the other two.

So the "dilemma of triangle" of R. Musgrave (1998) is based on the fact that conditionally all the basic functions of a state can be structured into three groups: (***A***) *allocative efficiency*, (***B***) *social equality (justice)*, (***C***) *macroeconomic stability* (Table 5). The simultaneous effective performance by the state of all these functions is in principle impossible. Below, the authors presented their version of the contradictory relationship of these state obligations. On practice ***A*** and ***C*** of the above-mentioned groups of functions of the state from the "dilemma of triangle" of R. Musgrave do not contradict each other and can theoretically more or less successfully be implemented almost simultaneously. As for the function of ensuring an equitable distribution of income (*social equality (justice)*) in national societies, it is difficult to implement simultaneously with the other two. And, moreover, it, as a rule, is implemented according to the residual principle in conditions of unfavourable macroeconomic dynamics and in the implementation of fiscal consolidation by national governments. Meanwhile, in the conditions of slowing economic growth in all countries of the world, social expenditures as the implementation of the state's function to ensure a fair distribution of income in society are directly related to the quality of human capital development (Cingano, 2014). And, the last one, according to the recognition of the leading theorists-economists in the conditions of fading rates of economic dynamics, can become a real productive force of society.

Table 5. "Dilemma of Triangle" of Musgrave as to the state basic functions

State basic functions (possible combinations of two functions from three)	*Explanation of the impossibility of simultaneously performing the third excluded function*
Ensuring (***C***) *macroeconomic stability* by reducing horizontal inequality. Improving (***B***) *social equality (justice)* by reducing horizontal inequality.	The state can realize both (***C*** and ***B***) functions only on condition of fiscal consolidation in the context of strengthening its tax base (due to the centralization of tax flows). However, the latter will lead to a decrease in revenues of lower budgets and will not allow for *allocative efficiency* (***A***).
Ensuring (***A***) *allocative efficiency* on the basis of strengthening the revenue autonomy of local budgets. Achieving (***C***) *macroeconomic stability* by reducing the vertical imbalance of the budget system.	Achieving (***A***) *allocative efficiency* on the basis of revenue autonomy will cause increasing (***B***) *social inequality* due to the horizontal inequality in the budget system. As a result, when (***C***) *macroeconomic stability* is achieved, (***B***) *social injustice* will increase.
Ensuring (***A***) *allocative efficiency* could be achieved by strengthening the revenue autonomy of local budgets. The same fiscal policy measures let the local governments ensure (***B***) *social justice*.	However, the implementation of these two functions ((1) *allocative efficiency and* (***B***) *social equality (justice)*) could be carried out by the state only if (***C***) *macroeconomic stability* is reduced.

Source: Composed by authors on the base of R. A. Musgrave's results (1959)

Taking into account all the above, the authors tried to give a mathematical solution of the "dilemma of triangle" of R. Musgrave. They proceed from the following considerations. The statistical nature of economic phenomena is ensured by the presence of a large number of dynamic links between elements of the economic system. Accumulating these dynamic relationships lead to statistical relationships in economic systems. One of the most important manifestations of such statistical laws is the phenomenologically announced Musgrave's position that it is impossible to simultaneously achieve the effectiveness of the three main groups of state functions (Musgrave, 1959). This phenomenon, by the way, is confirmed by the fundamental dilemma "*macroeconomic stability - social equality (justice)*", expressed by A.M. Okun (2015). It is about the futility of the state's desire to combine implementation of all the following functions: (***A***) *allocative efficiency*, (***B***) *social equality (justice)*, and (***C***) *macroeconomic stability*. It is the incompatibility of these functions of the state and the results of their implementation that explains the emergence of c (Fig. 2).

Analytically visual content of the "dilemma of triangle" phenomenon, discovered by R.A. Musgrave (1959), adequately reflects the principle (ratio) of uncertainty proposed by the authors

$$\Delta A \times \Delta B \times \Delta C \geq M, \quad (1)$$

where ***A, B*** and ***C*** represent the conjugate values, respectively, of the following groups of functions: (***A***) *allocative efficiency*, (***B***) *social equality (justice)*, and (***C***) *macroeconomic stability*. These values are subject to constraints, which, as R.A. Musgrave discovered, contain inevitable uncertainties. The scale of ΔA, ΔB and ΔC at their joint consideration is associated with the constant ***M***. For these purposes, a certain constant is introduced by analogy with the Planck constant in physics to estimate the Heisenberg uncertainty. The last parameter in the theory of state and public finance was named by the authors as the "Musgrave uncertainty principle" in connection with the recognition of his merits in studying the problems of effective state performance of state functions and the introduction of the "triangle dilemma" paradox. In this regard, the authors consider it very appropriate to call the proposed relation (1) the "Musgrave uncertainty principle", and the constant ***M*** - the "Musgrave constant"[1]

Figure 2. "Dilemma of triangle" of Musgrave as for the three basic functions of the state
Source: developed by the authors on the base of R. A. Musgrave's results (1959)

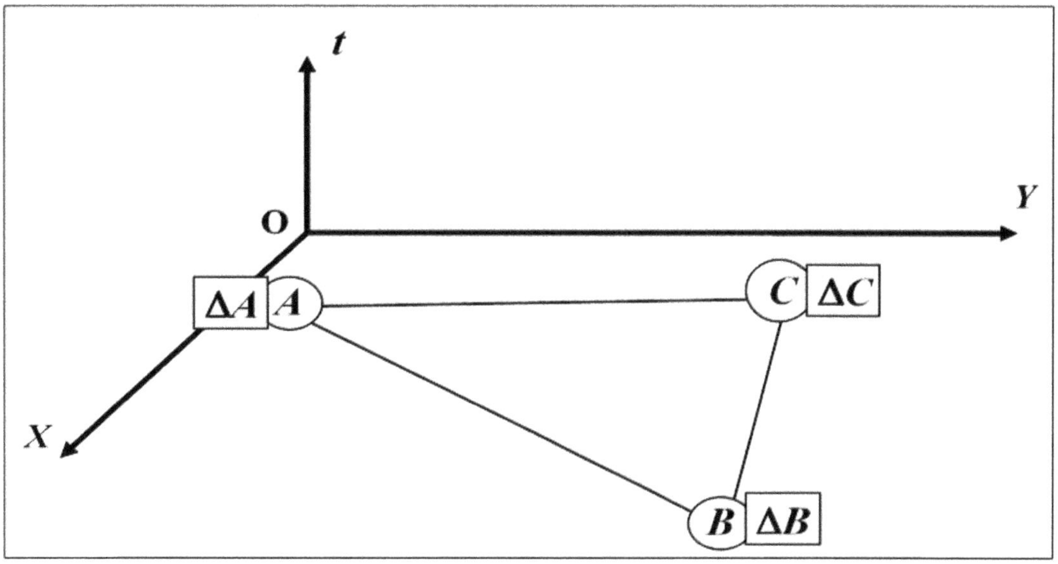

Following the Musgrave uncertainty principle, the fullest realization of the function group A and the function group B, means reducing (minimizing) the uncertainty (spread) of the values of ΔA and ΔB (i.e. $\Delta A \to 0$ и $\Delta B \to 0$). But in this case, in terms of the "dilemma of triangle", the group of functions C practically cannot be realized: $\Delta C \to \infty$. In other words, the choice of the most complete (best) intersection $A \cap B$, introduces a significant and uncertain variation in values of ΔC (i.e. $\Delta C \to \infty$)

Within the framework of relation (1), the case of small inaccuracies of ΔA and ΔB, i.e. at $\Delta A \to 0$ and $\Delta B \to 0$, in calculations of characteristics of A and B leads to complete uncertainty in calculating characteristic of C:

$$\Delta C \geq \left. \frac{M}{\Delta A \times \Delta B} \right|_{\substack{\Delta A \to 0 \\ \Delta B \to 0}} \to \infty \tag{2}$$

Analytically visual content of the phenomenon of the triangle dilemma, it is advisable to compare the corresponding graphic images. As mentioned above, Fig. 3 shows the graphical display of the Musgrave "triangle dilemma" phenomenon. Fig. 3 illustrates the graphical image of the authors' vision of the practical resolution of the triangle dilemma.

For an adequate resolution of the "triangle dilemma" (the effective implementation by the state of its basic functions), the authors propose a cyclic change in the combined groups of functions at certain intervals of time. Obviously, this also cyclically changes the corresponding groups of functions, characterized by complete uncertainty.

In the XOY coordinate plane at the vertices of the Musgrave triangle, the conjugate groups of functions of ***(A)*** *allocative efficiency*, ***(B)*** *social equality (justice)*, and ***(C)*** *macroeconomic stability* are placed, which inevitably are subject to constraints in the form of uncertainties of ΔA, ΔB and ΔC. The time axis **O*t*** is introduced for further consideration of modifications of triangles in the process of sequential resolution of the dilemma at different fixed points in time ***t***.

To achieve a balanced use of all groups of functions ***A, B,*** and ***C***, the authors propose the following scheme for resolving "the triangles dilemma" of Musgrave.

In the first stage (***t* = 1**) whenever possible, a complete realization of the group of functions ***A*** and the group of functions ***B*** is carried out, that is shown in Fig. 3 with double arrow between ***A*** and ***B***. Choosing the most complete intersection ***A*∩*B*** introduces significant uncertainty values of **Δ*C*** → ∞. In Fig. 3 this circumstance is represented by the symbol ***C*** in a black circle in combination with the symbol **Δ*C***. When achieving acceptable results in the first stage, the transition to the second stage (***t* = 2**). This transition is indicated by an arrow from ***t* = 1** to ***t* = 2**. At the second stage, a cyclic transition from a pair combination of groups of functions ***A*** and *B* to the selection of a new pair of groups of functions ***B*** and ***C*** is performed.

Figure 3. Resolving "The Triangle Dilemma" of Musgrave as for the state basic functions
Source: Composed by authors

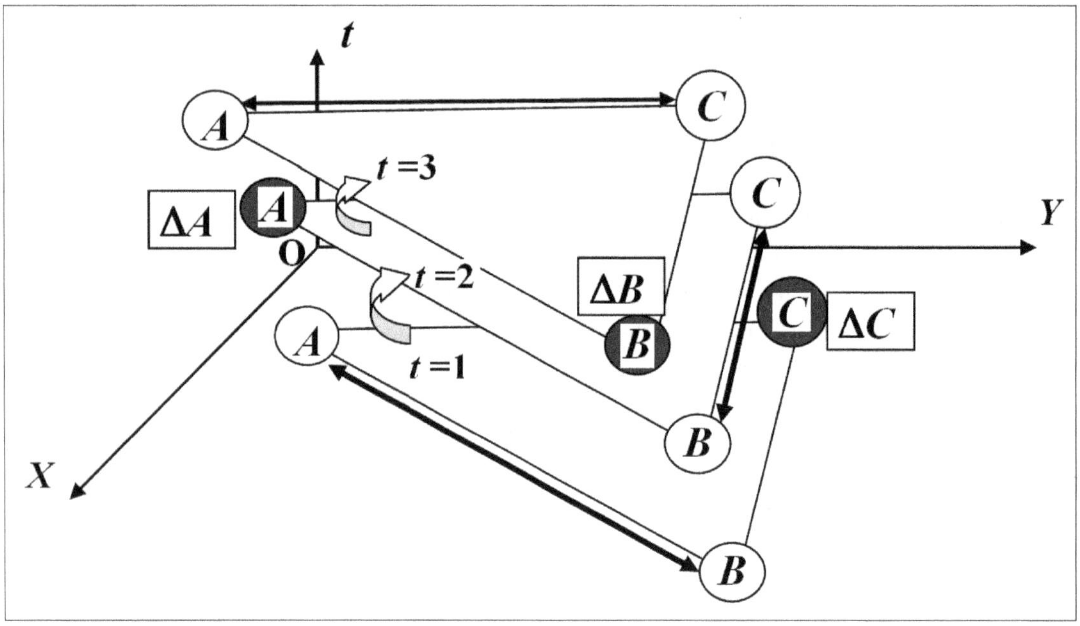

In Fig. 3 this selection is indicated by the corresponding arrow. In this case, the uncertainty of **Δ*C*** is removed, but instead, the uncertainty of **Δ*A*** appears, which is indicated in the same way as was done for the uncertainty of **Δ*C*** at the first stage. When a sufficiently complete realization of the combination of function group ***B*** and function group ***C*** is reached (due to the intersection of ***B*∩*C***), a new cyclic transition to the third stage (***t* = 3**) from the pair combination of function groups ***B*** and ***C*** to the choice of a new pair of function groups ***C*** and ***A*** (shown in Fig. 3 by a double arrow between ***C*** and ***A***). At this stage, the **Δ*A*** uncertainty is removed, but the uncertainty ***ΔB*** appears instead. Achieving an acceptable result at this stage means the possibility of a cyclical transition to a new stage, etc. The beginning and duration of the stages are fixed on the time axis **O*t***. The duration of the resolution of the "dilemma of triangle" of Musgrave could be significantly reduced if it was possible to start the multipliers' mechanism.

Thus, the comparison of the vectors of changes in the elasticity of GDP by income and by expenditure could be used to highlight those specific directions for spending budgets that give a real macroeconomic effect, that is, the fiscal multiplier in their case gives a value greater than zero. If, however, the item of budget expenditures is estimated by the fiscal multiplier at a level much greater than zero, then this direction of spending budget funds should increase. And its growth should be compensated by the reduction of inefficient expenditures from the point of view of macroeconomic returns. The conclusions confirm the results obtained by S. A. Vlasov, and E. B Deryugina (2018) in connection with fiscal multipliers and with the factors that determine their estimates. This could help to obtain the assessment of the degree of effectiveness of the state activity (implementation of state basic functions groups) in terms of safeguarding the public finance stability as well as the national economic growth as an indispensable condition for 'triangle dilemma' solution. In general, the overall effect of the budgetary measures implemented in the globe can be realized in providing 0.81% of the growth of the global economy with different contributions of tax and expenditure instruments: the fiscal multipliers used by the IMF for this estimate were 0.30.6 for state revenues, 0.51.8 for public investments, and 0.31.0 for other public expenditures (Spilimbergo, and et al., 2009).

In the course of recent research (Berg, et al., 2012; Berg, and Ostry, 2011a) it was found that, if the economic growth is considered in the long term, the dilemma between economic efficiency and social equality may disappear (Mazzucato, 2013,2018). In other words, ensuring sustainable growth lets the state to gradually solve the problem of social equality (justice). But these two goals, contradictory in their essence, which the state should pursue, at a certain ratio, can mutually ensure the achievement of each of them. According to the authors, the problem of the simultaneous impracticability of the three basic functions of the state could not be solved only in a short period.

In other words, if the state, even being unaware of the need to construct a dialectical interaction between formal and informal institutions, nevertheless optimized budget expenditures between all functions, including social justice, then the effect of the societal crisis as a result of the shock of the lockdown caused by the COVID-19 pandemic, could be avoided or mitigated. In the context of social tolerance, the success of the fight against coronavirus infection could be much more successful in most countries of the world.

7.2. The State and the Institutional Component of Shocks: Dialectics of the Economy and Society Interaction

Understanding the institutional component of the shock mechanism of impact on systemic integrity is based on the fact that the state, structuring the behavior of market agents through formal institutions in the economy, abstracts from the mechanisms for the formation of social institutions that are generated by individuals in society and which, in turn, have an impact on them. Even in the last century, a number of philosophers (Ward, 1903; Bunge, 1973; Bhaskar, 1975; Sellars, 1926) proposed a multilevel ontology, which does not contradict the authors' methodological approach, which is the basis for the interpretation of shocks in self-organizing and self-developing systems. If to apply the mechanism of structural self-organization to social institutions, habits and behavior of individuals in society, then the following subordination of formal institutions arises as a result of the action of the state and social institutions that structure the behavior of individuals, as the basis of informal institutions. At the same time, as the vertical structural levels of a self-organizing economy are formed and the importance of the subject component grows, an adequate understanding of the truth that it is individuals who form structures in the economy and society, which, in turn, structure the behavior of individuals themselves, becomes relevant.

Following this logic, the state is obliged to regulate the behavior of individuals as economic agents using formal institutions. However, if the state does not understand the patterns of the emergence of habits, behavior of individuals and social institutions as the basis of their informal analogues in the economy, then it will not be able to create effective formal institutions. And the events generated by the COVID-19 pandemic prove that the shock mechanism was brought to life, among other things, by a violation of the dialectic of interaction between formal and informal institutions, a lack of understanding of the driving motives behind the behavior of individuals in society and, undoubtedly, the ineffectiveness of government actions to strengthen financial stability in conditions when the structural integrity of society was destroyed.

And, meanwhile, the processes of self-organization and self-development of a person (Chapter 11) predetermine the mechanism of his self-creation, when the goals, intentions and inclinations of individuals affect the structural ties in society. At the same time, social institutions also have a reverse effect on individuals, adjusting their goals and preferences. According to A. Giddens, a structure is "recursively organized rules and resources" (Giddens, 1982. P. 35). Commenting on the theory of A. Giddens, I. Craib argued that structure and individual activity are thought of as "two sides of the same coin" (Craib, 1992; Hodgson, 1988). According to these scientists, considering social practices from one perspective, one can see actors and their actions; "if we look differently, we will see the structures they create". The structure of society is formed as a result of the interaction of subjects regarding the exchange of activities and other objects (information, for example). It is through structural interactions that individuals acquire "traces in memory", ideas or habits that arise as a result of repetitive actions. In other words, the constant interactions of individuals form the structure of society, which structures the behavior of individuals through social institutions. The quality of the integrity of the society in which individuals are socialized depends on their stability. Self-development of an individual occurs due to his inclusion in the structural ties of society, as well as the economy. If society does not correspond to the ideas of individuals, for example, about justice, then its ties with society cease to be structural, which destroys the integrity of society. At the same time, opportunism begins to prevail in the behavior of individuals both in society and in the economy, and social institutions (informal) and formal institutions cease to regulate their behavior.

On the eve of the COVID-19 pandemic, it is precisely this mismatch between formal and informal (predetermined by society) institutions that largely predetermined the shock fall of the economy and the deepest societal crisis in the countries of the world. The violation of the dialectic of formal and informal institutions in the economy was caused by a number of circumstances in society, which negatively affected the habits and behavior of citizens both in the economy and in society. Rising inequality and stagnating living standards in national economies have become the defining characteristic of modern conditions for correcting the behavior of individuals [N. Crafts, 2017]. Current mainstream growth projections for the United States and the European Union over the medium term represent a marked slowdown from growth rates in the decades prior to the global financial crisis of 2008-2009. Compared with 1995 to 2007, future US and European growth of real (after-inflation) GDP per person is expected to diminish by half, or even worse (Fig. 4). The income of only 27% of all people grew at a rate at par or above their countries' average (EBRD Transition Report 2016-2017). Only 44% of all people have experienced long-term income convergence with G7. As a result there appears a solid relationship between the wealth concentration, inequality, poverty and economic stagnation.

Social justice has traditionally been associated with the material base, which should be interpreted in terms of the well-being of citizens. The economic growth matters because it measures an important component of social progress—namely, economic welfare, or how much benefit members of society get from the way resources are used and allocated. And, meanwhile, in the modern world, phenomena were deepening that an ordinary citizen could assess as a violation of social justice, adjusting his behavior towards individualism, contrary to the accepted norms of behavior in society.

Social integrity is predetermined by equitable sharing of the benefits of increased prosperity, decent-paying jobs, equal employment and education opportunities, and improved access to and provision of health care and financial services. But national societies experience greater income disparity and higher poverty, and lag behind in access to key social services like health care and finance. There is of great necessity to strengthen the integrity of society not only because it is the morally right thing to do, but also because it is critical for ensuring further progress of the countries of the world at the stage of self-organization or at the stage of self-development of their national technological, economic and social systems.

During the 12 months to mid-2018, aggregate global wealth rose by USD 14.0 trillion to USD 317 trillion, representing a growth rate of 4.6% [Global Wealth Report, 2018]. This growth rate was lower than for calendar year 2017, but higher than the average growth rate in the post-2008 era, and a considerable improvement on the decline during 2014–15. It was also sufficient to outpace population growth, so that wealth per adult grew by 3.2%, raising global mean wealth to USD 63,100 per adult, a record high. But overall, over the past 30 years, median incomes increased a third less than the average income of the richest 10%. Moreover, in some countries the share of incomes at the very top has surged; in the United States, for example, the share of top 1% on total income has almost doubled from about 11% to 20% over the past three decades and almost half of all income growth over this period accrued to this group [Förster et al., 2014; Saez, 2018] (Fig. 5). Therefore, the economic influence of the middle class and its role as "centre of economic gravity" has weakened.

Thomas Piketty (Piketty, et al., 2016) became one of the first to attract attention to the investigation of the process of growing income gap between very rich and very poor strata of the population all over the world. Thanks in part to his publication, in part to the populist movements springing up in many countries nobody has been ignoring wealth inequality questions anymore. While the bottom half of adults collectively owns less than 1% of total wealth, the richest decile (top 10% of adults) owns 85% of global wealth, and the top percentile alone accounts for almost half of all household wealth (47%). The shares of the top 1% and top 10% in world wealth fell significantly between 2000 and 2008: the share of the top percentile, for instance, declined from 47% to 43%. However, the trend reversed after the financial crisis. The share of the top 10% was little affected. But in 2016 the share of the top 1% rose back above the level we estimate for 2000.

The trend in the share of the top 1% partly reflects the trend in the share of financial assets in the household portfolio, which fell during 2000–08 and then began to rise after the global financial crisis, raising the wealth of many of the richest countries, and of many of the richest people (Fig. 6). However, current findings reveal that the top 10% in the income distribution holds almost half of the total wealth, while the bottom 40% accounts for only 3%. The OECD has also documented that economic insecurity concerns a large group of the population: more than one in three people are economically vulnerable, meaning they lack the liquid financial assets needed to maintain a living standard at the poverty level for at least three months.

Figure 4. Percentiles of population with below-average income growth (1989-2016)
Note: Bars ranked by income decline (bottom to top).
Sources: World Bank Povcalnet, IMF, World Bank, UN, EBRD Transition Report 2016-2017 authors' calculations; EBRD Transition Report 2016-2017: Transition for all: equal opportunities in an unequal word.

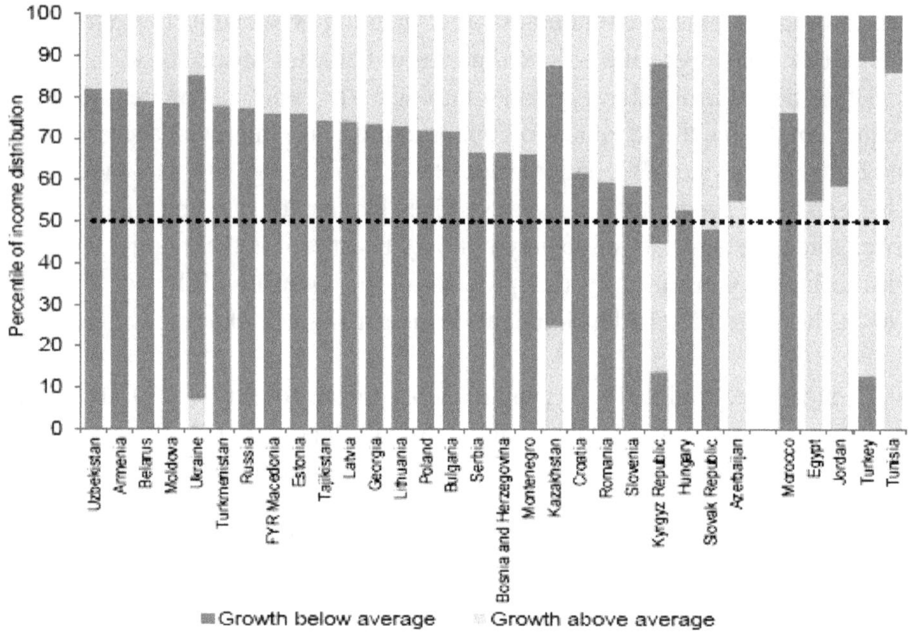

Social capability can be thought of as the incentive structures, such as regulation and taxation, that influence the investment and innovation decisions that allow businesses to effectively assimilate the technology developed by leaders (such as the United States) and to eliminate inefficiency. This context of scientific discussions of economists and financiers was typical, when the identification of trends and their causes in the economy took place outside of connection with the analysis of social institutions that structure the habits and behavior of individuals in society. Aside, there was the question of how social institutions structure the behavior of individuals and their economic preferences, and individuals adjust social and informal institutions. And sustainability of macroeconomic growth will be ensured only under the condition that informal institutions, in fact, determining the continuity of generations in the understanding of justice, will ensure high public confidence in the state and its social policy. In this interpretation the problem of the sustainable economic growth is strictly connected with the interdependence of formal and informal institutions.

There are many scientific researches, describing the negative influence of inequality on the economic performance (growth, employment, allocation). The authors' conceptual approach supports among others the view points of G.A. Marrero and J.G. Rodriguez (2010), D. Acemoglu, S. Naidu, P. Restrepo, and J.A. Robinson (2015), who consider bad quality of institutions as the main cause of all the latter problems.

G.A. Marrero and J.G. Rodriguez (2013) found robust evidence of the hypothesis that the impact of overall inequality on economic performance is ambiguous because the two main components of inequality may have opposite effects on economic growth: inequality of opportunity (IO) - negative and inequality of effort (IE) - positive. They carried out the empirical studies and obtained the following results:

Figure 5. Median incomes grew more slowly than top incomes. Real disposable income growth by income position, average for 17 OECD countries, 1985-2016 (1985 =100%)

Note: Unweighted average for 17 countries for which long-term data are available: Canada, Germany, Denmark, Finland, France, United Kingdom, Greece, Israel, Italy, Japan, Luxembourg, Mexico, Netherlands, Norway, New Zealand, Sweden and United States. Incomes are disposable incomes, corrected for household size.

Source: OECD (2019), Under Pressure: The Squeezed Middle Class, OECD Publishing, Paris. https://doi.org/10.1787/689afed1-en

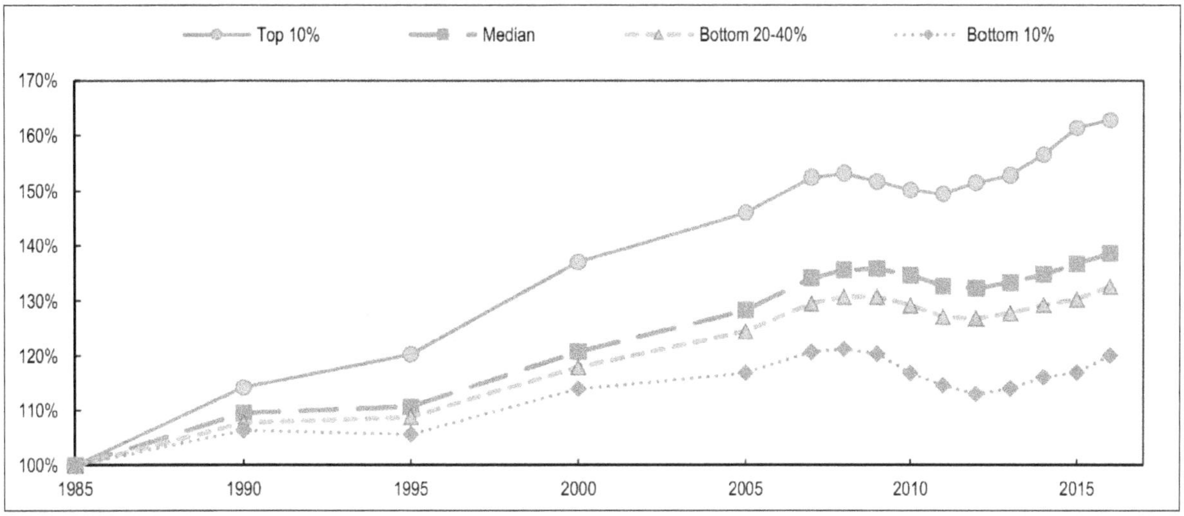

- Increasing IE by 1std raises 10-yrs growth in 2.3-4.1 p.p. (average was 20.2% per decade in 2000-2010), and 209-834 real US$/person (average was 14,363 US$/person in 2000-2010).
- Decreasing (lower-bound) IO by 1std raises 10-yrs growth in 1.1-1.7 p.p. and 124-229 real US$/person [Marrero, et al., 2015].

A variety of different channels via which inequality could affect growth have been suggested over the years. Some of them prove that income inequality is bad for the growth prospects of the poor but good for the rich. In this article the functions of institutions are investigated in connection with the relationship between intergenerational equity and macroeconomic growth sustainability, which are accompanied by institutions.

But the modern life is accompanied by the disappearance of personified relations which leads to multiplication of uncertainties, mistrust of partners and the increase of various risks. Institutions are deliberately created by partners for the purpose of reducing uncertainty and minimizing the risks of losses, including the economic ones. Consequently, the main function of the institutions that accompany partners relationship is the formation of the stable structure of interactions between partners in the process of exchange of any assets, because the discussion deals with the interrelation between equity' estimation in the opinion of the society and economic performance of the national integrity. If the institutions are called upon to introduce an element of stability in the interconnection of exchange partners they can be meaningfully defined as ways of cooperative solutions of the problems of the counter-agents cooperative "games".

Figure 6. Share of top 1% of wealth holders since 2007, selected countries, % of wealth
Source: James Davies, Rodrigo Lluberas and Anthony Shorrocks, Credit Suisse Global Wealth Databook 2018

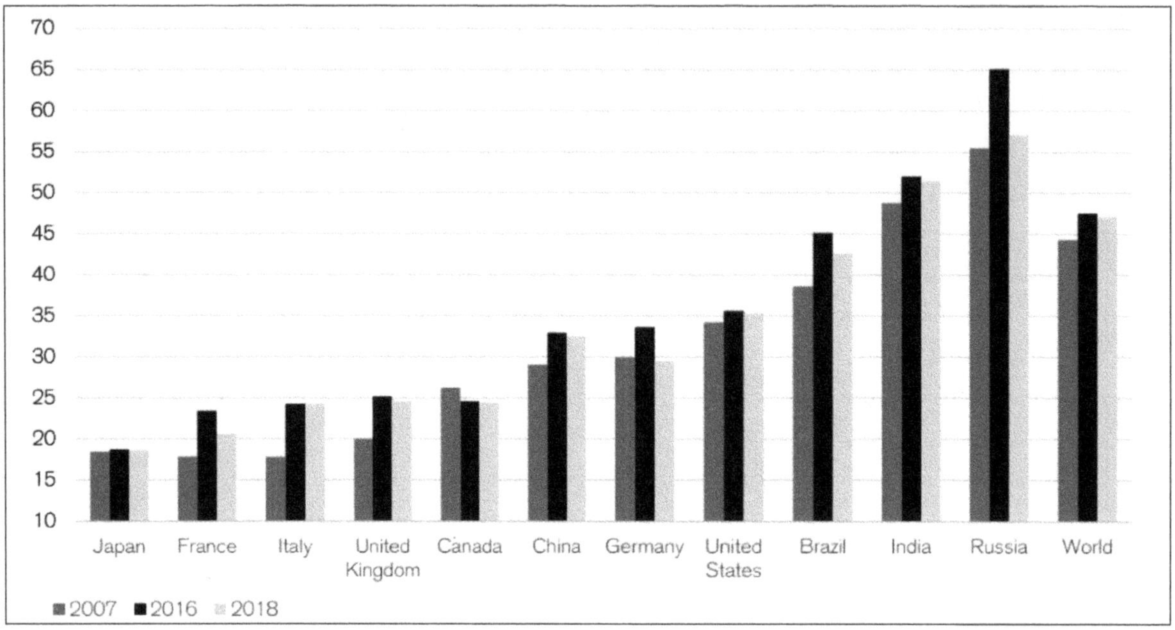

It is this quality of the institutions that D. North (1996) signaled out. His logical arguments are as follows: the institutions are formed as "rules of the game" or man-made restrictive frameworks for the relationships organization between people. They are aimed at reducing the uncertainty in the life with the help of establishing a stable (but not always effective) structure of interaction between economic agents. Then the subjects of economic interconnections presented by firms, state, individuals act as those who organize, realize and change the institutions and are the main players of their games following the rules, that make the institutions effective or not. Minimizing uncertainty and reducing the risks become the main functions of the institutions. In this context, they represent restrictive frameworks created by participants for themselves therefore they must also predetermine the structure of incentives for partners' interaction. Besides, the institutions act not only as constraints for society but at the same time as their opportunities. So the most important function of institutions is to solve the problems of cooperation in any sphere of socio-economic life (Coase, 1960).

The dialectic of interaction between formal and informal (social) institutions is manifested in the position of the middle class, which is a form of organization that provides a kind of social environment, space for action and habits. In this context, the middle class is an institutional organization that, given its stable position in society and in the economy, is capable of adequately providing the dialectic of formal and informal (social) institutions. A strong and prosperous middle class is crucial for any successful economy and cohesive society. In particular, middle classes generally invest heavily in their own education and that of their children, thus increasing current and future stock of human capital (Brown, et al., 2004; Pressman, 2007; Bassanini, et al., 2002). Human capital accumulation is therefore an important channel through which a strong middle class can support wellbeing and GDP per capita growth, as it boosts that share of population with secondary and tertiary education (Brueckner et al., 2017; OECD,

2003). Societies with a strong middle class have lower crime rates they enjoy higher levels of trust and life satisfaction, as well as greater political stability and good governance (OECD, 2019).

Overall, over the past 30 years, median incomes increased a third less than the average income of the richest 10%. Moreover, in some countries the share of incomes at the very top has surged; in the United States, for example, the share of top 1% on total income has almost doubled from about 11% to 20% over the past three decades and almost half of all income growth over this period accrued to this group (Förster, et al., 2014; Saez, 2018). Three decades ago, the aggregate income of all middle-income households was four times the aggregate income of upper income households, i.e. those with incomes above two times the national median; today, this ratio is less than three (Fig. 7). It has become more difficult for younger generations to make it to the middle class. This is because older generations are often better protected from changes in the labor market and from low-income risks than the newer generations. Since the baby boomer generation, the middle-income group has grown smaller with each successive generation (Fig. 8). The baby boom generation enjoyed more stable jobs during their working life than younger generations as well as well-developed pension systems.

Among middle-class households, there is now a *growing discontent with economic conditions.* In this context, the stagnation of middle-class living standards in OECD countries has been accompanied in recent years by the emergence of new forms of nationalism, isolationism, populism and protectionism. Nationalistic and anti-globalization sentiments can arise because a shrinking middle class produces disillusionment and damages political engagement, or turns voters towards anti-establishment and protectionist policies (Bettiza, 2010; Stiglitz, 2012). Political instability is an important channel through which a squeezed middle class may upset economic investment and growth (Alesina, et al., 1996). A rising sense of vulnerability, uncertainty, and anxiety has translated into increasing distrust towards global integration and public institutions (OECD, 2017).

Trust is not only essential for a well-functioning society; is also an important element for economic growth. Higher social trust reduces transaction costs and increases innovation (Gould, et al., 2016; Madland, 2015). Societies with a strong middle class experience higher levels of social trust but also better educational outcomes, lower crime incidence, better health outcomes and higher life satisfaction (Kelly, 2000; Lynch, et al., 1997; Thorson, 2014).

The middle class champions political stability and good governance. It prevents political polarization and promotes greater compromise within government. Middle classes also provide a solid basis to build a democratic state, not only by financing it through taxes but also demanding regulations, enforcement of contracts and the rule of law (Birdsall, 2016). So the middle class feels that the current socio-economic system is unfair: middle incomes have been growing much more slowly than higher incomes for more than three decades now. More and more people, especially among the lower end of middle-income households, feel that they contribute much more to the welfare state with taxes than they receive in return in form of benefits and services.

The OECD experts also found that children born to parents who did not complete secondary school have only a 15% chance of making it to university, compared to a 63% chance for children whose parents attended university. Health outcomes, and even life expectancy, are also heavily influenced by socio-economic background. These findings have prompted governments to take action to redress a situation that has become economically and politically unsustainable as it undermines public trust in policy and institution. R. Coase (1960) expressed the fundamental sense of this concept as follows: if the relationships of the partners are accompanied with the problems (which increase the transactional costs) it is the institution that is gaining importance. Then all the relationships in the society could be presented as the complex of very many institutions or as the whole institutional system. The latter is represented by a set of rules of partners' behavior, mechanisms of incentives' support and promotion as well as by a system of tools aimed at the punishing those breaking the rules.

Figure 7. Middle incomes are losing economic influence. Aggregate income share ratio between middle and upper income households, OECD average mid-1980s to mid-2010s

Note: Data refer to the aggregate income of all middle-income households as a ratio of the aggregate income of all upper-income households. "Middle income" households defined as households with income between 75% and two times the national median. "Upper income" households defined as households with income above two times the national median. OECD average comprises available data from Australia, Canada, Switzerland, Czech Republic, Denmark, Finland, France, Germany, United Kingdom, Hungary, Ireland, Italy, Luxembourg, Netherlands, Norway, Spain, Sweden, and United States. Incomes are disposable incomes, corrected for household size.

Source: OECD (2019), Under Pressure: The Squeezed Middle Class. Paris: OECD Publishing https://doi.org/10.1787/689afed1-en

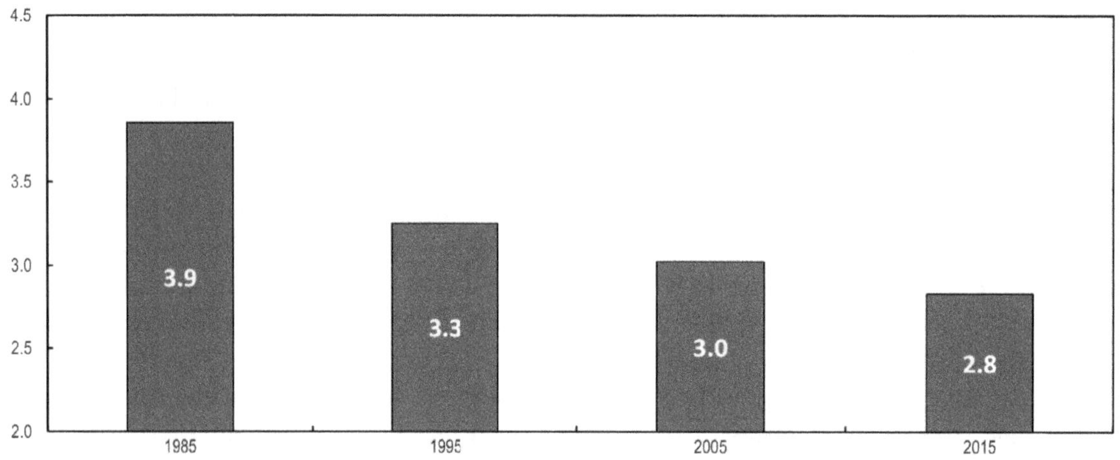

At the same time, the system of institutions is in fact a contradictory unity of formal and informal institutions that constantly conflict with each other, organizing human relations in all spheres of activity. Informal institutions (or complex of rules and restrictions) arise from information transmitted through social mechanisms and are part of the heritage, which is commonly called culture. R. Boyd, and P. J. Richerson (1985) defined the culture as a transfer through learning and imitation from one generation to other knowledge, values and other factors that influence the behavior. It is the cultural filter that provides continuity with the help of which informal solutions to the problems of cooperation, for example in market exchange, found in the past are transferred to the present and former informal constraints an important source of continuity in the process of long-term changes. As for formal institutions their existence, as a rule, is connected with the state (government), which formalizes informal institutions by giving them the power of laws and formal agreements.

The quality of economic and political institutions also plays a major role when it comes to explaining growth performance, as do the development of equity markets and demographic variables Inequality of opportunity also has implications for people's support for market reforms and democracy. The analysis in this chapter shows that inequality of opportunity can erode support for core economic and political reforms. However, inequality does not always hinder support for reforms. Indeed, it may actually strengthen it, provided that differences in income arise as a result of differences in effort, rather than individual circumstances such as gender or place of birth. This highlights the importance of implementing reforms, be it privatization or an overhaul of the tax system, in ways that are perceived to be fair and do not serve special interests. Public policies may need to specifically target access to education and employment by the most disadvantaged groups, helping to create a more inclusive society (EBRR. Transition Report 2016-2017).

Figure 8. Since the baby boomers generation, each new generation has seen its chances of belonging to the middle-income class fall. Share of population in middle-income households by generation and stage at the life cycle

Note: Silent generation: born before 1943, Baby boomers: born 1943-64, Generation X: born 1965-82, Millennials: born 1983-2002; Generation Z: born since 2003. The middle-income class comprises individuals in households with income between 75% and 200% of the median. OECD average based on data from OECD average comprises available data from Canada, Denmark, Finland, France, United Kingdom, Ireland, Italy, Luxembourg, Mexico, Netherlands, Norway, Spain, Sweden, and United States. Source: OECD Secretariat calculations based on data from LIS Data Center, expect EU-SILC for France (2014), Ireland (2014), Iceland (2014) and Sweden (2015).

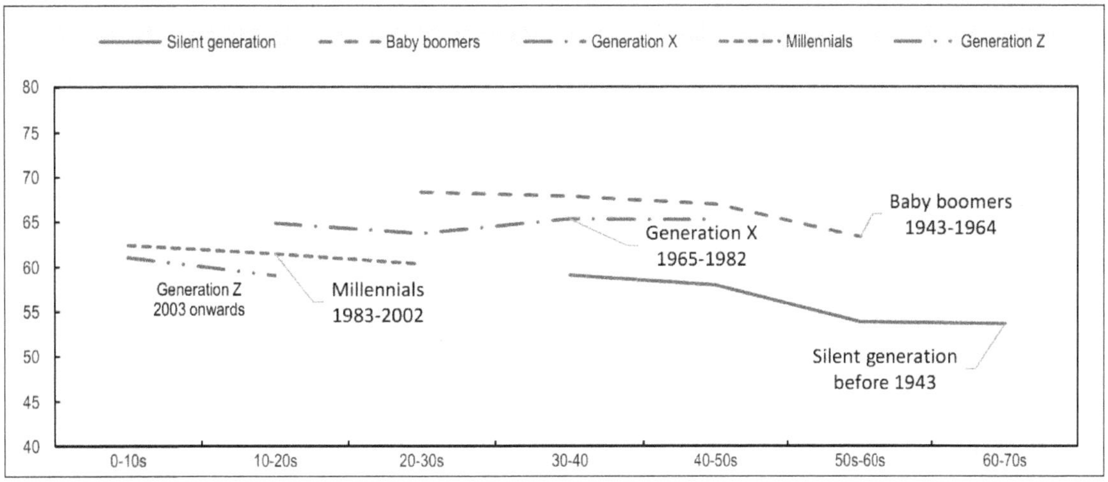

These negative interrelations should be broken through the weak link of the chain. This weakness is connected with the absence of the institutional base for equal opportunities for all the participants of society: to have education, good job, income that should not be limited by circumstances. The latter are predetermined by gender, race, place of birth, and / or parental background. If not then could appear inefficiency that prevents people from making the best use of their skills or from realizing their entrepreneurial ideas, and unfairness that may lead to the loss of confidence in the key economic and political institutions. The whole complex of these circumstances is capable to underpin societies and a market-based economic system. So only equal opportunities could have direct and indirect positive impact on economic equilibrium and social integrity (Fig. 9). According with Fig. 9 there appears strong evidence that inequality of opportunity (social institution) rather than income inequality (formal institution) matters. In fact, rise in inequality from (notionally) low levels means that only 44% personally experienced income convergence. This problem could be solved with the help of finance (including budgetary flows),

Figure 9. Dialectics of social (informal) institutions that ensure justice for individuals and formal institutions that structure their behavior as economic agents
Source: the authors' development on the base of data of the EBRR. Transition Report, 2016-2017

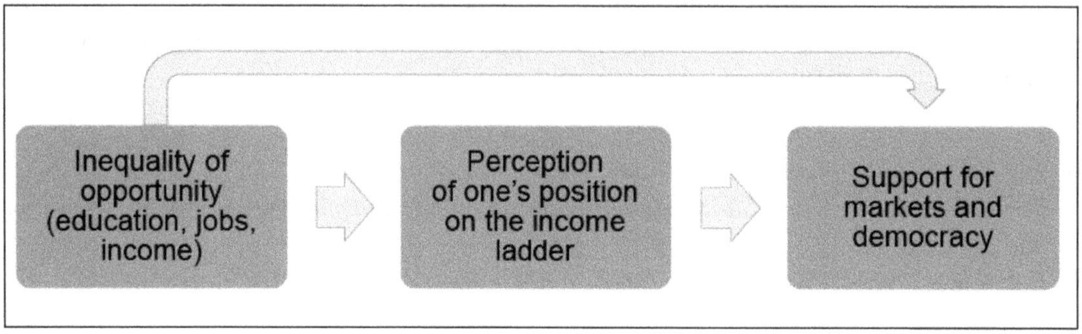

that realizes the redistribution of GDP, but a greater emphasis on improving equality of opportunity – as to education, financial inclusion and better connectivity – is even more imperative.

Moreover, the effectiveness of the state in carrying out its function of equitable distribution of incomes is the most important determinant of the duration of economic growth. It has been empirically proven that income inequality (*social inequality (injustice)*) is distinguished by the strength of its connection with the duration of the economic growth periods: a 10-percentile decrease in inequality (represented by a change in the Gini coefficient from 40 to 37) increases the expected duration of the growth periods by 50 percent (Berg, and Ostry, 2011b). Moreover, each direction of social expenditures should be calculated from the point of view of (1) the economic effect of scale and (2) a delay in the implementation of this effect. As a result, it will be possible to differentiate the increase in budget expenditures for the three groups of basic functions of the state, based on the need to obtain faster or the possibility of waiting for a delayed (time-postponed) economic effect. This is a short-term alternative choice between the impact of the state on economic growth and income distribution. In this case, the author's approach allows using the Musgrave's "uncertainty" method to determine how to proceed. As a result, in the long run, this choice of combined pairs of basic state functions can harmonize the goals of reducing inequality and of sustainable growth as two sides of a single coin.

Being more neutral with respect to the processes of inhibition of economic development, budget expenditures may be reduced, but the direction of such reduction should be evaluated from the point of view of forecasts of their impact on the trend of GDP change in the medium term. According to this logic, the rate of GDP growth can be indicated as a function (fiscal policy goal). At the same time, it is necessary to avoid extending short-term measures to the long-term (IMF, 2009).

The reaction of GDP to the change in the indicators of state revenues and expenditures corresponds to theoretical ideas. If we calculate the multiplier of government spending as a cumulative increase in GDP over three years after the increase in government spending in relation to the amount initially increased by government spending, the data, obtained in this chapter, correlates with the GDP elasticity coefficients for expenditures with adjustments by year. On average, for Russia this figure was 0.6 (i.e. with an increase in government spending by 1% of GDP, real GDP growth for the next three years will be 0.6%). These results can be compared with similar averaged IMF estimates (IMF WEO, 2008, PP.

159–196) for developed countries and economies in transition (Restrepo, et al., 2006; Blanchard, et al., 2002, PP. 1329–1368; Spilimbergo et al., 2008).

The results of the analysis of fiscal policy for its impact on GDP dynamics are in principle consistent with the IMF estimates (IMF, 2009a). In general, the overall effect of the budgetary measures implemented in the globe can be realized in providing 0.8-1% of the growth of the global economy with different contributions of tax and expenditure instruments: the fiscal multipliers used by the IMF for this estimate were 0.3-0.6 for state revenues, 0.5-1.8 for public investments and 0.3-1.0 for other public expenditures (Spilimbergo, et al, 2009). In any case, relying on the values of fiscal multipliers, it is necessary to determine the capital expenditures for infrastructure projects and social expenditures, for example, in terms of education, as those that produce a significant macroeconomic effect (in the case of education, with a lag of several years) but with a cumulative total.

The authors' identification of the institutional component of the shock mechanism of destruction of structural ties is indirectly confirmed by empirical studies of the sources of economic growth. The fact is that, based on standard production functions, they did not confirm the thesis about the decisive role of the accumulation of "physical capital". According to the calculations of E. Denison (1985), who first proposed methods of "calculating" economic growth, in the period 1929-1982 no more than 20% of the increase in US national income per employee can be "attributed" to the accumulation of real capital. The decisive role in this kind of calculations was played by the factor-indecomposable "remainder". E. Denison considered it a characteristic of the progress of knowledge, which includes "both technological progress and progress in our knowledge of management and organization" (Denison, 1985, P. 28). The same idea is confirmed by P. Romer (Romer, 1990), who singled out human capital, that is, the level of education and technical skills of workers, as the most important growth factor in this "remnant" of E. Denison. In the interpretation of the authors, it is about the implementation of the mechanism of self-organization of the individual, who, after his transcending into society, can really become the factor of the economic growth. However, this can be realized provided that significant BUTs are overcome on the way human self-development. These BUTs are predetermined by the institutional component of the processes of self-organization and self-development of systemic integrity in the economy and society. In other words, with the growing importance of the subjective component of all these processes, the problem of understanding the mechanisms of self-organization and self-development of a person moves to the first place. And these aspects are dialectically related to his habits, behavior, motivation, as well as social, informal and formal institutions.

In other words, in order for a person to act as a factor of socio-economic progress, the state must understand the interaction of institutional factors that regulate his behavior in society, in the economy, as well as in the context of the implementation of the technological revolution 4.0 (Greif, et al., 2004). It was through the institutional component of the shock mechanism that it became possible to understand the "remnant" of E. Denison in connection with the human potential, which can be used for the benefit of progress only if he considers it necessary for himself. The state, abstracting itself from the understanding of the institutional aspect as dialectics of formal and informal (social) institutions, turned out to be unable to realize its goal of ensuring financial stability as the basis of macroeconomic equilibrium in conditions of destruction of the integrity of society.

7.3. The State in a Dynamic Economy: Intellectually Autonomous Individuals and the Human-Centric Organization of Society

Based on the above, the authors come to the conclusion that there is an institutional component in the shock mechanism associated with the activities of the state. This is due to the fact that the state is called upon to perform structural functions in the economic system, ensuring its integrity in any given situation. Consequently, formal institutions are also focused on ensuring economic (financial) stability (market equilibrium), regardless of the state of the integrity of society and social (informal) institutions. In other words, for a static economy at the stage of self-organization, the problem of broken dialectics in the interaction of the economic system and society, as well as economic and social institutions is very relevant. Such an intersystem and institutional mismatch clearly affected the vertical structure of the economy during the transition of quantitative changes to qualitative changes. Ultimately, this largely predetermined the shock destruction of the structural ties of the economic system as the implementation of the law of denial of denial.

On the other hand, the process of reproduction of vertical structural levels in the economic system is accompanied by the rise in the importance of the subject component and its institutionalization. On this basis, the causal dependences of the subjects of market transactions and the institutions that regulate their behavior are among the factors that are directly and / or indirectly related to the shock mechanism of the realization of breaks in dialectical laws. At the stage of self-organization, shocks mediate the action of the laws of unity and struggle of opposites, and the transition of quantitative changes to qualitative ones. As for the shock leap of the economic system from the stage of self-organization to the stage of self-development, in this case, a double denial of its structural integrity, predetermined by both vertical structural levels and horizontal ones, is realized.

Latent accumulation of qualitative changes in self-organizing economies manifested itself in 2007 in connection with the shock in the US market for unsecured mortgage loans and the subsequent global financial crisis of 2008-2009. After the shock disruption of structural ties, the market mechanism could not automatically restore macroeconomic equilibrium. In essence, this meant that, for some reason, the structural links in the financial markets could not restore their integrity by reproducing their own kind. In other words, for some reason the mechanism of self-organization of economic systems failed. The authors believe that the reason lies in the fact that while the object component of structural interdependencies dominates, the self-organization mechanism (market mechanism) works flawlessly. But with the rise in the importance of the subject component (trust as an equivalent in financial transactions and minimization of their material support), the equilibrium in the economic system and the stability of financial markets began to be predetermined by non-economic parameters.

In this case, the behavior of economic agents was determined by social factors influencing individual habits, value orientations, and a tendency to opportunism in social interactions. Thus, economic (formal) institutions ceased to predetermine the norms of behavior of the subject, whose motivation was regulated by the society, or rather by the quality of its integrity. It is in this context that the authors identified the violation of the dialectics of the economy and society as an essential reason for generating conditions for the end of the period of self-organization of the economic system. The inconsistency in the interaction of economic (formal) and social institutions regarding the same subject - in one case as an economic agent, and in the other as a participant in social relationships - allows us to interpret it as an institutional component of the shock mechanism of rupture of structural ties. The latter is now directly related to the behavior of the state. In the case of the law of negation of negation, shocks broke the continuity of change in a static economy, marking the beginning of a new period of its self-development already in a dynamic state.

And the main problem that modern society has to solve in order to approach the post-like future is related to the restoration of the dialectic of economics and society. In this case, we are talking about the priority of restoring the integrity of society, about understanding the social reasons for the opportunistic behavior of a subject in the economy, about the need for a fundamental change in the principle of self-organization in the economy - from capital-centric to human-centric. And the main obstacle on this path is the state, which satisfactorily coped with the function of institutional support for the integrity of a static economy, regardless of the state of the integrity of society. But in the conditions of the system's leap into the complete uncertainty of its self-development, structural ties are destroyed due to the blocking actions of the state itself, their restoration should be dealt with by subjects who left society in a crisis state and not controlled by economic (formal) institutions. In extreme conditions, the state is forced not only to safeguarding lives and livelihoods, but also to generate urgently the best practices of its behavior in conditions when it faced a humanitarian catastrophe one-on-one.

For the state, the widely disseminated label "The New Normal" turns into a trap of misunderstanding the failure of the mechanism for automatic restoration of market equilibrium and objective predetermination under the slogan: «This time is different» (Reinhart, et al., 2009). In extreme conditions of the destruction of market equilibrium, the state, as a rule, resorted to various combinations of fiscal and monetary measures of influence on economic agents. However, the rise of the subject component as a priority in the mechanisms of self-development of economic systems predetermines the objective growth of the importance of the factors of consolidation of society and social institutions in the regulation of the behavior of subjects. In addition, the situation is aggravated by the fact that at the very end of the period of self-organization of economic systems, i.e. on the eve of the COVID-19 pandemic, the disrupted dialectic of economics and society manifested itself in numerous social problems. We are talking about a catastrophic polarization of the population in terms of income and wealth, a growing number of working poor, a shrinking middle class, social inequality in access to education and the health care system, gender inequality, etc.

In addition to a lack of understanding of the patterns of development of systemic integrity in the economy, society and technology, the state is faced with new conditions for ensuring the integrity of national socio-economic systems in the face of falling GDP, increasing unemployment, increasing budget deficits, increasing infections and deaths in connection with the second wave of the COVID-19 pandemic and increasing trends towards isolationism in the global economic space. Against this background, epoch-making opportunities arise to transfer the economy and society to the newest technological paradigm, which carries fantastic opportunities for socio-economic progress.

Only humans with his talents as well as resilient companies are able to realize these scenarios of the future after COVID-19. Moreover, in this tandem, a person must possess the qualities of intellectual autonomousness, allowing him to creatively adapt in an uncertain situation, forming innovative solutions that have no analogues. A big mistake, according to the authors, is the approach to a person as to human capital, which, regardless of the subjective beginning, accumulates like an ordinary capital asset. Namely, all other things being equal, capital when investing provides a certain increase, and in terms of compound interest, it is possible to calculate the corresponding result after a certain period of time. With such an interpretation, the state will not be able to realize those conditions, in particular, the need for a human-centric organization of economic activity, which can motivate a person to desire to accumulate knowledge and realize his unlimited intellectual potential for the good of society.

It is no coincidence that in recent years, more and more research has begun to describe the problem of creating and using quality employees or talents, on which future social and economic progress around the world depends (Cook. (Ed.), 2019; Winthrop, et al., 2016, P. 14; Neisser, et al., 1996). Thus, education as a necessary attribute of a talented employee came out on top. However, the traditional interpretation of education as an element of human capital on the part of the state, society, and firms has led the national education systems to a state that experts of the World Bank (WDR, 2018) assessed as a crisis. Indeed, the owner of capital assets himself looks for areas of profitable investment of his capital, becomes an investor at his own peril and risk, and in case of failure he himself bears all the financial risks. The loss of human capital only in the aspect of the inadequacy of the knowledge it acquired today turns into huge irreplaceable losses in the context of a humanitarian catastrophe: US$5T lost global GDP from lower labor productivity in 2017. OECD countries witnessed an average decrease in labor productivity due to skills mismatch of 6% only in 2016 (BCG, 2019). These figures of economic losses as a result of skills mismatch will be supplemented by an economic assessment of the loss of human lives in 2020 (Chapter 11.1), which objectively puts a person in the first place not as human capital, but as a self-developing person with the qualities of intellectual autonomy, on which future socio-economic progress and the realization of the potential of the 4th industrial revolution will depend.

If we conditionally estimate the period of study in the secondary education system at 9-12 years, then the loss of at least one young generation (X, Y, Z) turns into a 30-year period of socio-economic stagnation or regression. In this situation, the market mechanism for managing (distributing) human potential (capabilities) by the type of capital is in principle not acceptable. The validity of this conclusion of the authors is also confirmed by the fact that already from mid-2020 (at the end of the first wave of COVID-19) resilient companies were concerned about the current shortage of talents. In July-August 2020, 21% of CEOs surveyed identified talent risk as the greatest risk to growth today (KPMG, 2020). And the latest edition of the Boston Consulting Group (BCG, 2019), speaking in fact about the need for human-centrism in solving the problem of the skills mismatch, indirectly confirms the idea of the unacceptability of the state's market approach to solving the problem of the subject factor in the context of its interpretation as an exclusively economic entity or human capital. Boston Consulting Group experts attribute one of the reasons for the emergence of the skills mismatch today to the fact that the system for building human capital still uses an approach to training that was adopted in the twentieth century, with standardized education and centralized management of education and the labor market (Fig. 10). In other words, this education corresponded to the level of technological progress oriented towards industrial revolution 2.0, when the speed of the technology's distribution averaged 20 years. It was for this time that the skills formation system met the requirements of standard professions and standard mass education for all.

Currently, in the context of the introduction of a new technological paradigm, the destruction of fundamental structural ties due to the law of denial of negation, the action of which was accelerated by the COVID-19 pandemics, the spread of technological innovations has decreased to 3 years (Industry 4.0). Moreover, today and in the future, this trend will be determined by the use of cyber-physical systems. In conditions of full automation and digitalization of production, of formation of mega-cities and creation of customized products and services, the speed of the technology's distribution will clearly accelerate. According to Boston Consulting Group experts, during the implementation of the results of industrial revolutions 1.0, 2.0, 3.0 the skills formation system lags behind the needs of the economy and society (Fig. 10). However, at present, it is impossible to solve the problem of the skills mismatch without human-centrism in society and human-centric organization of activities in the economy. In this case, we are talking about the restoration of the dialectic of interaction between society and the economy in the context of one sphere - education, which is able to prepare a person with the qualities of intellectual autonomousness. This means that after receiving an education, such talents will be able to self-develop, since the approaches to knowledge and the ability to use it formed in their minds will generate their desire to acquire new information, structure it and, on this basis, construct new knowledge. It is this kind of knowledge that forms new knowledge that will allow highly qualified personnel to construct future reality in an uncertain environment based on the latest technological paradigm.

Figure 10. The basis of today's educational system dates back to the era of Industry 2.0
Note: Number of years from launch to mass distribution to 60% of households.
Source: BCG (2019). Mission Talent - Mass Uniqueness: A global challenge for one billion workers. Boston Consulting Group. August

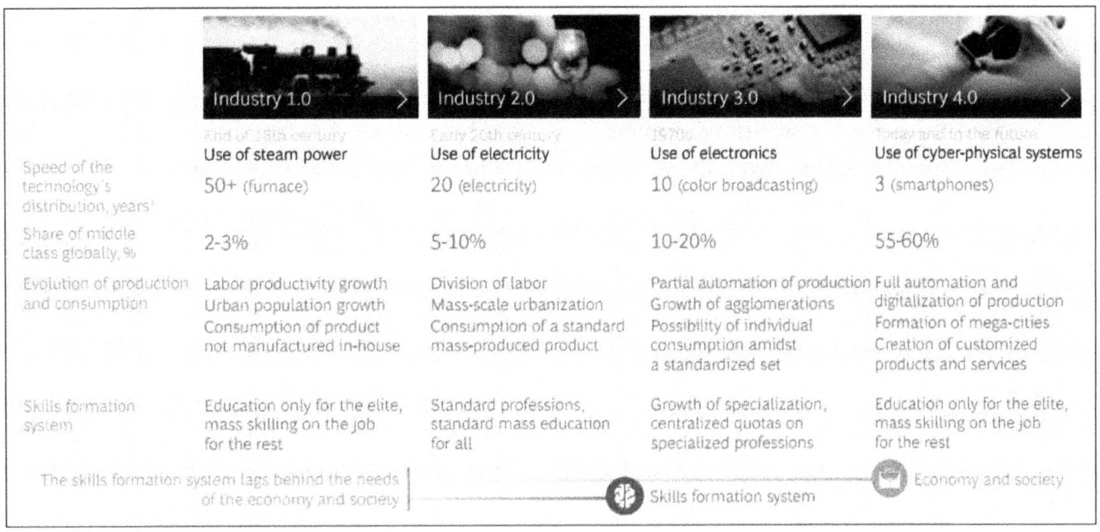

In this context, a person should be interpreted as a phenomenon that possesses known and unknown properties and qualities that, under certain conditions, can manifest themselves in society and be used for the benefit of social progress (Vernadsky, 1960; Vernadsky, 2018; Gumilev, 2012a; Gumilev, 2012b). To understand a person from the point of view of the possibilities of realizing his enormous potential in society, economy and technology is realistic only under the condition of understanding the laws of his self-organization (in the process of education) and his self-development (as a result of socialization / transcending into society). Dialectically interacting processes of self-organization and self-development in human psychology are regulated by its properties for reflection and transcendence. A person with this ability is a self-developing personality who easily adapts to a rapidly changing external environment, copes with non-trivial problems due to the growing uncertainty of future transformations in all spheres of human activity. In fact, it is about a self-developing personality, capable of being intellectually autonomous in professional activity and in life and not afraid of emerging problems, since he is able to overcome all psychological and cognitive barriers (PCBs), in whatever form they arise. As a result, he is objectively predisposed to change social reality, taking into account his ideas about justice, material well-being, value orientations in his behavior, etc.

In other words, with the growth of the dominant of a person's intellectual abilities in comparison with other capital assets, the dialectics of interaction between the individual and society, society and the economy also changes. Subject to the formation of a critical mass of intellectually autonomous persons, it is their individual values that become a priority in structuring post-covid reality (Arrow, 1963). Thus, with the beginning of the spread of a new technological paradigm, society is forced to change towards adapting the institutional environment to the requirements and value preferences of self-developing individuals. Education turns into a form of human existence, since it creates conditions for his self-development. It is in this respect that the new (or long forgotten) meaning of education is now associated with an increase of the "human being in the human". In this context, the technological revolution 4.0 returns humanity to fundamental questions such as "for whom progress is made", "who is in charge of all systems created by human", "who or what is the driver of all systemic complications in human activity", "who sets goals, who achieves them and who is the beneficiary of progressive changes" (Schwab, 2016; Cook, (ed.), 2019).

The priority goal of education in all human-centric systems created with the participation of a person is to create conditions for his self-development. As such, he will be able to dialectically integrate into society for the purposes of his own self-development. This is the mission of education in a complex community of people, especially in the context of the introduction of the latest technological paradigm.

In modern conditions, trends in the labor market in the Globe are characterized by the following data: today 85% of the global workforce are low- and mid-skilled workers; 13% will be global population growth by 2030; 1/3 of professions will change by 2035 due to automation and digitalization; 27% of new activities will emerge by 2022; 26% will be the share of Gen Z'ers in the total workforce by 2025 (BCG, 2019). In such a situation, education has a decisive role (if not to take into account the crucial role of an effective healthcare system) in self-organization and self-development of a person with the qualities of intellectual autonomy. This is the most difficult task, but only its solution will ensure the formation of a new technological paradigm as the basis for the dynamics of the socio-economic system after COVID-19. Human-centrism in this interpretation will assume that a person's knowledge in the process of mastering the methodology for overcoming PCB turns a talented person into a carrier of the highest qualifications, predisposed to creative activity. And only he, in the process of creation, will master new ideas and ways of their implementation in technology, in the economy and in society.

In fact, the prospects for the elimination of the skills mismatch depend on how society manages to create an education system that will provide people not only, maybe not so much with knowledge, as with the technology for their assimilation, overcoming difficulties along the way, and generating students' attitudes towards education as a normal way of being. In turn, taking into account the requirements of such individuals is necessary for the unlimited progress of society in the post-covid period. In fact, we are talking about human-centric principles of organizing all spheres of human activity.

The fundamental and global nature of industrial revolution 4.0 means it will become an integral part of all countries, economies, industries and people. This is largely predetermined by such a structural paradox as the complexity of the technological base, starting from which a new technological paradigm begins to form. At the same time, the orientation of socio-economic systems to a new technological base cannot be realized by one person, industry, region, the entire consolidated society must take part in it (Schwab, 2016).

What are the main functions of the state during the period of self-development of technology and socio-economic system? They are associated with the formation of conditions for adequate self-organization of individuals with the qualities of intellectual autonomy, as well as for their adequate socialization (Chapters 4.1, 5.1). In modern conditions of the destruction of structural ties, of GDP reduction, of the unresolved problems of protecting the health and physical survival of citizens in the context of the COVID-19 pandemic, etc. the state is forced to deal mainly with issues related to people. So the coronavirus shock in an instant brought a person to the first place as the purposes of the state and confronted him with a society of dissatisfied citizens acting opportunistically and unwilling to support the actions of the state in the fight against coronavirus infection.

Taking urgent measures in the fight against coronavirus infection, the state, nevertheless, remains with the same illusions, believing that re-building economics should safeguard the welfare of citizens, restore the integrity of the economic system and eliminate the consequences of the societal crisis. Actually, this is what is invested in the calls for the Great Reset (WEF, January 2021). In this case, the state can become one of the main obstacles to structuring the new economic and social reality. There are great fears that the state will only be forced to recognize the priority of man, the importance of social institutions for economic recovery and the need to institutionalize the process of replacing capital-centric forms of organization with human-centric ones both in the economy and in society.

CONCLUSION

The place of the state in the theory of shocks is due to the increasing importance of the subject component in the processes of self-organization and self-development of systemic integrity. The mechanisms of self-movement of systemic wholes are regulated by the action of the dialectical laws of unity and struggle of opposites, the transition of quantitative changes into qualitative ones and the denial of negation, and the state accompanies them with the institutionalization of the behavior of economic agents participating in market transactions. In this regard, the state reacts to shocks mediating a reversal of tendencies in these dialectical laws of self-movement of systems through formal institutions that structure the procedure for the implementation of exchange in both real and financial markets.

On the eve of the coronavirus pandemic, it became obvious that at the stage of self-organization of economic systems, the state ignored the problem of the dialectics of the economy and society, economic (formal) institutions and social institutions, which largely predetermined the shock mechanism for implementing the law of denial of denial. As a result during the COVID-19 pandemic it became obvious the following: (1) national states' inability to prevent the rapid spread of coronavirus infection; (2) national governments inefficiency to change radically the modern slow down trend of economic dynamics and of aggregate factor productivity growth due to the violation of dialectics in the interaction of society and economy; (3) inadequate state performance of its function of an equitable income distribution in society, which has increased the income polarization of the richest and the poorest members of society; (4) and, finally, the helplessness of the state to safeguard the lives and livelihoods as a result of economic and social lockdowns.

The study of the dynamics of development of national economies made it possible to state the fact of fundamental changes in the national economy' structural characteristics. Now they are associated not so much with the objective, easily modeled factors of its development, as with the subjective ones, difficult to be understood, but increasing in importance. The latter, in particular, deals with national existing pension system' quality, which directly links the elderly and young family members and predetermined informal institutions' quality, regulating the economic agents behavior in the society. These attributes are inherent in carriers of human capital, the formation of which as a key factor in the development of society can provide an adequate response to the technological challenges of the future. In other words, with the transformation of human capital into the leading driver of the new cycle of the economic spiral, subjective value judgments of equality and equity (including intergenerational one) predetermined by the attitude of society (represented by the state) to the citizen come out. This is due to the fact that human capital can serve the good of society voluntarily, realizing that this society suits it according to the parameters of equity and justice. Such fundamental changes in the structure of economic growth factors on a new technological base have returned both the state and society and citizens to the dilemma of preferences declared by A.M. Okun (2015): either social justice or economic growth. As a rule, the modern idea of social justice is connected with the state budget expenditures for the social needs of society, including the pension system, the health care system and the social protection of the disadvantaged. And hence the chronic government budget deficit, the rising cost of public debt and the greater problems of its financing in the context of falling economic growth rates. It seems that there is no alternative choice of the priority of state policy oriented to economic growth. Only the latter will make it possible to largely solve the problems of state financing of the social needs of society.

Before the COVID-19 pandemic ([Berg, et al., 2012; Berg, and Ostry, 2011a) it was found that, if the economic growth is considered in the long term, the dilemma between economic efficiency and social equality may disappear. In other words, ensuring sustainable growth lets the state to gradually solve the problem of social equality (justice). But these two goals, contradictory in their essence, which the state should pursue, at a certain ratio, can mutually ensure the achievement of each of them. According to the authors, the problem of the simultaneous impracticability of the three basic functions of the state could not be solved only in a short period. But the state ignores this possibility, apparently internally focusing on a simpler explanation of its irrational behavior in connection with the institutional ensuring of the fair distribution of income in society according to the residual principle. And in modern conditions, the implementation of this social function of the state is perhaps the most important in the problem solution of secular stagnation at the national level. The unresolved nature of this problem by the state, and the lack of appropriate formal institutions predetermine irrational psychological attitudes of business entities that give rise to the corresponding informal institutions. Moreover, the absence of appropriate formal institutions, the irrational behavior of the state, its unwillingness to stand guard over justice for citizens only aggravates the phenomenal tendency of the economic system to imbalance and to its shock manifestation. In this context subjects' irrational psychological attitudes are reinforced by the apparent inefficiency of the public finance in the context of their impact on the economic growth. In the case of growing economics, such a question may not arise. However, in conditions of secular stagnation, this problem becomes extremely urgent.

However, according to the authors, the state is not yet ready for a radical solution of the problem of the construction of the post-COVID-19 future, all the more for adequate institutionalization of the conditions for the formation of a critical mass of people capable of self-organization and self-development. In this regard, it is the state that can become the main obstacle to the rapid self-development of a dynamic economy. Meanwhile, only the formation of such personalities will make it possible to create the necessary reserves of intellectual capital within the national framework, which will make it possible to implement a new technological (technical-industrial) reality, to multiply on this basis new technological solutions in all spheres of human life and to "humanize" uncertainty in the form of a new social reality.

For these purposes, the state must skillfully institutionalize the dialectical relationship between externalization and objectification in relations with individuals for the purpose of their adequate socialization within the framework of the human-centric system it has created. At the same time, the state must take into account the peculiarity of transferring objectified social reality into the consciousness of an intellectually autonomous person. The point is that formal institutions must ensure the internalization of a person, which, in fact, makes him a social product capable of solving technological and socio-economic problems in connection with the latest technological revolution.

In connection with the above, education will ultimately be the touchstone on which in the near future the "voting" of national communities for rapid progress or latent stagnant marking time will be tested. This decision will not be easy, since the main opponent of progress will be the state, accustomed to act in the past. But such is the specificity of self-development of systems, which from a philosophical point of view means "interruption of continuity" for the sake of a jump into a dynamic future. It is not by chance that the peculiarities of the functioning of the human-centric socio-economic system are predetermined by the ability of intellectually autonomous individuals to construct, first of all, a new institutional reality. Only in this case it is possible to achieve the goal of accelerated implementation of the results of the 4th technological revolution and the transfer of the socio-economic structure of society to the new technological base.

As a result, the state, without creating the dialectical unity of formal institutions in the economy and social institutions in society, persistently sought financial stability in the economy, while destroying the integrity of society. This made it possible for the authors to blame the state for the inconsistency of formal (informal) institutions in the economy and social institutions, which formed the institutional component of the mechanism of shock destruction of structural ties under the conditions of action of the laws of self-movement of systemic integrity. Without the restoration of the dialectic of formal (informal) and social institutions, the state can only slow down the progress of technology, economy and society for as long as it will be in the dark that modern transformations are predetermined by the law of double negation. And this means that it is precisely the subjects that are destined for a special role in the dynamics of organizational structures at the stage of their self-development, provided that capital-centric principles are replaced by human-centric ones at all levels of system integrity. And in order to achieve this, it is necessary to restore the dialectic of society and economy, bringing social and economic institutions into dialectical correspondence.

The further deepening of the theory of shocks could be connected with considering the categories of "stocks" and "flows" in the context of the role of nation states in the processes of self-organization of systemic integrity in the economy and society and their self-development (Schoenman, 1966, Edmans, 2011). Even a surface glance at these problems reveals certain associations of "flows" in connection with the complication of the structure of a static economy, and "stocks" in the context of the formation of a new structure of a dynamic economy at the stage of its self-development. In the latter case, it is about a fundamental restructuring of everything that society has: stocks of capital, labor, technological knowledge, etc.

The future research could be inspired by the publications of M. Mazzucato (2013, 2018), who raises the problem of "public values", the creation of which is of a collective nature. This acquires special significance in the context of the construction of post-covid reality, the need to restore societal integrity, return citizens' trust in the state and awareness of the new role of the state in society as objective conditions for structuring a dynamic socio-economic system.

REFERENCES

Acemoglu, D., Naidu, S., Restrepo, P., & Robinson, J. A. (2015). Democracy, redistribution and inequality. In A. Atkinson & F. Bourguignon (Eds.), *Handbook of Income Distribution* (Vol. 2). North-Holland: Elsevier.

Aghion, P., & Kharroubi, E. (2013). *Cyclical macroeconomic policy, financial regulation and economic growth.* BIS Working Paper, 434. Basel, Switzerland: Bank for International Settlements.

Alchian, A. A. (1984). Specifity, specialization, and coalitions. *Journal of Institutional and Theoretical Economics, 140*(1), 6.

Alesina, A., & Perotti, R. (1996). Income distribution, political instability, and investment. *European Economic Review, 40*(6), 1203–1228. doi:10.1016/0014-2921(95)00030-5

Angelopoupos, Philippopoulos, & Tsionas. (2008). Does public sector efficiency matter? Revisiting the relation between fiscal size and economic growth in world sample. *Public Choice, 137*(1-2), 245-278.

Arrow, K. J. (1963). Social Choice and Individual Values. Cowles Foundation for Research in Economics at Yale University

Arrow, K. J. (1970). Political and economic evaluation of social effects and externalities. In J. Margolis (Ed.), *The Analysis of Public Output.* Columbia University Press.

Bassanini, A., & Scarpetta, S. (2002). Does human capital matter for growth in OECD countries? A pooled mean-group approach. *Economics Letters, 74*(3), 399–405. doi:10.1016/S0165-1765(01)00569-9

Bator, F. M. (1960). *The Question of Government Spending: Public Needs and Private Wants.* Harper and Brothers.

BCG. (2019). *Mission Talent - Mass Uniqueness: A Global Challenge for One Billion Workers.* BCG.

Berg & Ostry. (2011a). *Inequality and unsustainable growth: two sides of the same coin?* IMF Staff Discussion Note, 11/08.

Berg & Ostry. (2011b). Equality and efficiency. Is there a trade-off between the two or do they go hand by hand? *Finance & Development, 48*(3), 12-15.

Berg, A., Ostry, J. D., & Zettelmeyer, J. (2011). *What makes growth sustained?* EBRD Working Paper, No. 133.

Bernanke, B. (2005). *The Global Savings Glut and the U.S. Current Account Deficit.* Remarks at the Homer Jones Lecture.

Bernanke, B. (2015). *Why Are Interest Rates So Low, Part 3: The Global Savings Glut.* Ben Bernanke's Blog.

Bettiza, G. (2010). Re-examining soft power in the age of Obama. *The International Spectator. Italian Journal of International Affairs, 45*(4), 104-106.

Bhaskar, R. (1975). *A Realist Theory of Science.* Leeds Books.

Birdsall, N., Sabot, R., & Ross, D. (2016). *Inequality and Growth Reconsidered: Lessons from East Asia.* Working Papers id:8848, eSocialSciences.

Blanchard, O., & Perotti, P. (2002). An empirical characterization of the dynamic effects of changes in government spending and taxes on output. *The Quarterly Journal of Economics, 117*(4), 1329–1368. doi:10.1162/003355302320935043

Bootle, R. P. (2009). Redrawing. Rethinking the role of the state and markets. IMF. Finance & Development, 46(1), 34-35.

Boyd, R., & Richerson, P. J. (1985). *Culture and the Evolutionary Process.* University of Chicago Press.

Brown, D. S., & Hunter, W. (2004, September 1). Democracy and human capital formation: Education spending in Latin America, 1980 to 1997. *Comparative Political Studies, 37*(7), 842–864. doi:10.1177/0010414004266870

Brueckner, M., Dabla-Norris, E., Gradstein, M., & Lederman, D. (2017). *The rise of the middle class and economic growth in ASEAN.* Policy Research Working Paper. World Bank.

Bunge, M. A. (1973). *Method, Model and Matter.* Reidel. doi:10.1007/978-94-010-2519-5

Checherita-Westphal, C., & Rother, P. (2012). The impact of high government debt on economic growth and its channels: An empirical investigation for the Euro Area. *European Economic Review, 56*(7), 1392–1405. doi:10.1016/j.euroecorev.2012.06.007

Cingano, F. (2014). *Trends in income inequality and its impact on economic growth.* OECD Social, Employment, and Migration Working Papers, No. 163.

Coase, R. H. (1960). The problem of social cost. *The Journal of Law & Economics, 3*(3), 1–44. doi:10.1086/466560

Cook Justin, W. (Ed.). (2019). Sustainability, Human Well-Being, and the Future of Education. Palgrave Macmillan doi:10.1007/978-3-319-78580-6

Crafts, N. (2017). Whither economic growth? Finance & Development, 54(1).

Craib, I. (1992). *Anthony Giddens* (Vol. L). Routledge.

Denison, E. (1985). *Trends in American Economic Growth. 1929-1982.* The Brookings Institution.

Edmans, A. (2011). Short-term termination without deterring long-term investment: A theory of debt and buyout. *Journal of Financial Economics.* Retrieved from: www.elsevier.com/locate/jfec

Förster, M., Llena-Nozal, A., & Nafilyan, V. (2014). *Trends in top incomes and their taxation in OECD countries.* OECD Social, Employment and Migration Working Papers, No. 159. doi:10.1787/1815199X

Friedman, M. (1962). *Capitalism and Freedom.* Chicago University Press.

Garcia-Escribano, M., & Liu, C. Y. (2017). *Expenditure assessment tool (EAT). In Fiscal Affairs Department Technical Notes and Manuals.* International Monetary Fund.

Garcia-Escribano, M., & Liu, C. Y. (2017). *Expenditure assessment tool (EAT). In Fiscal Affairs Department Technical Notes and Manuals*. International Monetary Fund.

Giddens, A. (1982). *Profiles and Critiques in Social Theory*. Macmillan. doi:10.1007/978-1-349-86056-2

Global Wealth Report. (2018). Credit Suisse Research Institute.

Gould & Hijzen. (2016). *Growing Apart, Losing Trust? The Impact of Inequality on Social Capital.* IMF Working Paper. WP/16/176.

Greif, A., & David, D. L. (2004). A theory of endogenous institutional change. American Political Science Review, 98(4), 633-352.

Gumilev, L. N. (2012a). *Ethnosphere: History of People and History of Nature*. Eksmo Publishing House.

Gumilev, L. N. (2012b). *Ethnogenesis and the Earth's Biosphere*. Eksmo Publishing House.

Helpman, E. (2004). The Mystery of Economic Growth. Harvard University Press.

Hodgson, G. M. (1988). *Economics and Institutions. A Manifesto for a Modern Institutional Economics*. Polity Press. doi:10.9783/9781512816952

IMF WEO. (2008). *Financial Stress. Downturns, and Recoveries*. IMF.

IMF WEO. (2009). *Sustaining the Recovery*. IMF.

Kelly, M. (2000). Inequality and crime. *The Review of Economics and Statistics*, *82*(4), 530–539. doi:10.1162/003465300559028

Keynes, J. M. (1936). *The General Theory of Employment, Interest and Money*. McMillan.

KPMG. (2020). CEO Outlook. COVID-19 Special Edition. KPMG.

Lynch, J. W., & Kaplan, G. A. (1997, July 1). Understanding how inequality in the distribution of income affects health. *Journal of Health Psychology*, *2*(3), 297–314. doi:10.1177/135910539700200303 PMID:22013024

Marrero & Rodríguez. (2015). Inequality of opportunity and economic performance. In *Economic Mobility Conference.* Federal Reserve System Community Development Research.

Marrero, G. A., & Rodríguez, J. G. (2010). *Inequality of opportunity and growth.* ECINEQ. Society for the Study of Economic Inequality. Working Paper Series. ECINEQ WP 2010-154.

Marrero, G. A., & Rodríguez, J. G. (2013). 'Inequality of opportunity and growth. *Journal of Development Economics*, *104*, 107–122. doi:10.1016/j.jdeveco.2013.05.004

Mazzucato, M. (2013). *The Entrepreneurial State: Debunking Public vs. Private Sector Myths*. Anthem Press.

Mazzucato, M. (2018). *The Value of Everything: Making and Taking in the Global Economy.* Penguin Random House.

Musgrave, R. (1959). *The Theory of Public Finance*. McGrow-Hill.

Musgrave, R. (1998). The role of the state in the fiscal theory. In P. B. Sorensen (Ed.), *Public Finance in a Changing World* (pp. 35–50). Macmillan.

Neisser, Boodoo, & Jr, Bouchard., Boykin, Brody, Ceci, & Halpern. (1996). Intelligence: Knowns and unknowns. *The American Psychologist, 51*(2).

North, D. (1996). *Institutions, Institutional Change and Economic Performance.* Cambridge University Press.

North, D. C. (1981). *Structure and Change in Economic History.* W. W. Norton & Co.

OECD. (2003). Education at a Glance. In *OECD Indicators 2003.* OECD.

OECD. (2017). *Education at a Glance. OECD Indicators 2017.* OECD.

OECD. (2019). *Under Pressure: The Squeezed Middle Class.* OECD Publishing. doi:10.1787/689afed1-

Okun, A. M. (2015). *Equality and Efficiency: The Big Tradeoff.* Brookings Institution Press.

Pigou, A. (1924). *The Economics of Welfare* (2nd ed.). McMillan.

Piketty, T., Saez, E., & Zucman, G. (2016). *Distributional national accounts: methods and estimates for the United States.* NBER Working Paper Series, No. 22945.

Pilipenko, A. I., Pilipenko, O. I., & Pilipenko, Z. A. (2019). Education and inclusive development: puzzle of low-learning equilibrium. In B. S. Sergi (Ed.), *Modeling Economic Growth in Contemporary Russia* (pp. 163–198). Emerald Publishing Limited. doi:10.1108/978-1-78973-265-820191006

Pressman, S. (2007). The decline of the middle class: an international perspective. *Journal of Economic Issues, 41*(1).

Reinhart, C., & Kenneth, S. R. (2009). This Time Is Different: Eight centuries of financial folly. Princeton University Press.

Restrepo, J., & Rincon, R. (2006). *Identifying fiscal policy shocks in Chile and Colombia.* Central Bank of Chile Working Paper, No. 370.

Romer, P. M. (1990). Endogenous technological change. *Journal of Political Economy, 98*(5), S71-S102.

Saez, E. (2018). *Striking it Richer: the Evolution of Top Incomes in the United States.* UC Berkeley. doi:10.4324/9780429494468-9

Schoenman, J. C. (1966). An Analog of Short-term Economic Change. Stockholm Economic Studies.

Schwab, K. (2016). *The Fourth Industrial Revolution.* Geneva: World Economic Forum.

Sellars, R. W. (1926). *The Principles and Problems of Philosophy.* Macmillan.

Spilimbergo, A., Symansky, S., Blanchard, O., & Cottarelli, C. (2008). Fiscal Policy for the Crisis. IMF. Staff Position Note 08/01, International Monetary Fund.

Spilimbergo, A., Symansky, S., & Schindler, M. (2009). *Fiscal multipliers.* IMF Staff Position Note, No. 11. Retrieved from http://www.imf.org/external/pubs/ft/spn/ 2009/spn0911.pdf

Stiglitz, J. E. (2012). *The Price of Inequality: How Today's Divided Society Endangers Our Future*. W.W. Norton and Company.

Tanzi & Schuknecht. (1997). Reconsidering the fiscal role of government: the international perspective. *American Economic Review, 87*(May), 164-168.

Tanzi & Schuknecht. (2000). *Public Spending in the 20th Century*. Syndicate of the Press of the University of Cambridge.

Tanzi, V. (2011). *Government versus Markets: The Changing Economic Role of the State*. Syndicate of the Press of the University of Cambridge.

Thorson, K. (2014). Facing an uncertain reception: Young citizens and political interaction on Facebook. *Information Communication and Society, 17*(2).

Transition Report, E. B. R. D. (2016). *Transition for all: Equal Opportunities in an Unequal World*. October. EBRD.

Vernadsky, W. I. (1960). Biosphere. In Selected works. Moscow: Academic Press.

Vernadsky, W. I. (2018). *Philosophy of Science. In Selected Works*. Youwright Publisher.

Vlasov, S. A., & Deryugina, E. B. (2018). Fiscal multipliers in Russia. *Journal of the New Economic Association, 38*(2), 104-119.

Wagner, R.E. (1976). Revenue structure: fiscal illusion and budgetary choice. *Public Choice, 25*(Spring), 45-61.

Ward, L. F. (1903). *Pure Sociology: A Treatise on the Origin and Spontaneous Development of Society*. Macmillan. doi:10.2307/1412722

WDR. (2018). *World Development Report 2018: Learning to Realize Education's Promise*. World Bank.

Winthrop, R., & McGivney, E. (2016). Skills for a Changing World: Advancing Quality Learning for Vibrant Societies Washington, DC: Center for Universal Education, Brookings Institution.

ENDNOTE

1 Relation (1) echoes Werner Heisenberg's uncertainty principle, which resolves the dialectical contradiction of wave-particle duality in physics.

Section 2

Shocks Theory and Its Opportunities as Applied to Shock and Crisis Caused by the COVID-19 Pandemic

Chapter 8
COVID-19 Shock and Subsequent Crisis:
How It Was

ABSTRACT

The COVID-19 pandemic has wreaked havoc on national socioeconomic systems, causing the deepest economic downturn since the Great Depression. The rapid spread of coronavirus infection around the world revealed the absolute unpreparedness of national health systems to block fatal disease. The COVID-19 shock revealed a phenomenal paradox: an economy focused on meeting the needs of people, subordinated their desires, value orientations to economic goals. Macroeconomic equilibrium and financial stability have become publicly recognized social priorities, which violated the dialectic of society and the economy interaction. The post-shock societal crisis raised fundamental questions of what kind of society was built and what post-coronavirus reality should be. Following the shocks' theory findings, the contours of uncertain post-COVID future will be associated with new technological paradigm of the self-developing economy and society, the restoration of social integrity as a basis of constructing future economy, and the replacement of capital-centrism by human-centrism in all organizational structures.

INTRODUCTION

The rapid spread of coronavirus infection in 2020 across countries and continents was a real shock for the entire global community. The ecosystem posed before humanity the fundamental problem of saving human lives, which affected not only all countries of the world, but also global organizations such as the World Health Organization (WHO), the International Monetary Fund (IMF), the World Bank, the Organization for Economic Cooperation and Development (OECD), etc. Having first manifested itself in December 2019 in the Chinese province of Hubei, already in mid-March 2020, the coronavirus infection acquired all the signs of a pandemic. It was accompanied by an exponential increase of people who infected COVID-19 and died from this infection. The COVID-19 virus, which spread so rapidly across

DOI: 10.4018/978-1-7998-4309-2.ch008

countries, affected all spheres of human activity. Rising coronavirus human deaths called into question national health systems' ability to withstand COVID-19 pandemic. In total, from the beginning of the pandemic to the end of 2020, more than 76 million people were infected, and more than 1.6 million died. According to Johns Hopkins University, as of 21.12.2020 a sad anti-rating for cases of coronavirus infected and deaths by countries was as follows: US – 17.8 million and 0.3 million accordingly; India – 10 million and 0.14 million; Brazil – 7.2 and 0.18; Russia – 2.9 and 0.05; France – 2.5 and 0.06; United Kingdom – 2.04 and 0.06 accordingly; and etc. From December 24, 2020 to January 6, 2021, Italy announced a nationwide lockdown similar to that of March 2020. In Switzerland, restaurants were closed for a month since December 22, 2020. In Slovakia, a ban on leaving home without a vital necessity came into force. In Austria, on New Year's Eve, it was forbidden to go out and launch fireworks. In London and the southeast of Britain, the highest, fourth tier of restrictions was imposed since December and promised Christmas breaks were lifted.

The enormous loss of life and unprecedented restrictive measures indicated, inter alia, that virtually all national health systems failed to adapt quickly to the extreme conditions of fighting against an unknown infection that threatened human lives. The high mortality rate from the coronavirus COVID-19 raised a lot of questions to the institution of the state, the most important function of which is to protect the life and health of its citizens. In the fight against the coronavirus pandemic, formal institutions created by the state to ensure effective interaction between society and the state, the individual and society, citizens and the state turned out to be ineffective.

The scale of the economic challenge created by the COVID-19 pandemic has not been faced in the global economy in nearly a century since the Great Depression (Cheng, et al., 2020). The specificity of the COVID-19 shock is due to the fact that it generated a whole series of crises, from societal and economic, to the one of food and of public healthcare system. Uncertainty has intensified, which has become a hallmark of post-COVID-19 reality (Okamoto, 2020). As a result, 2020 divided the history of humankind into the period before and after the COVID-19 pandemic. The words "this time is different" spoken by C.V. Reinhart and K.S. Rogoff became relevant again (Reinhart, et al., 2009). Already in April 2020, it became obvious that under the new conditions society would be significantly different from that before COVID-19. This was unanimous both political leaders and practitioners, both businessmen and ordinary citizens. It is no coincidence that the top leadership of countries in which the peak of the population's disease in the first wave of coronavirus was passed, as well as representatives of international organizations, began to seriously think about what the new world should be like after COVID-19. And it is not only about protecting the health of citizens in extreme conditions of pandemics, reducing unemployment and increasing real incomes of citizens. The most important for future national communities are the problems of restoring the integrity of society, restructuring the relationships between the state, society, business, households and individuals, taking into account fundamental changes in the self-awareness of citizens and in their assessments of the quality of formal institutions that structure interaction in the economy. The uncertainty of the future economic, social, political world after the pandemic and the role of the state in it was expressed by the Dean of the Faculty of Economics of Lomonosov's Moscow State University Professor A. Auzan with the words of Douglas North: «The court has retired for deliberation and has not yet returned» (RBC, 2020). In this chapter, the authors substantiate their answers to the above questions, proceeding from the foundation of the theory of shocks.

Taking into account all of the above, the structure of the chapter assumes, first, consideration of the features of the spread of two waves of the COVID-19 pandemic across the countries of the world and the justification of the economic assessment of the negative consequences of the humanitarian catastrophe in the context of missed opportunities (Chapter 8.1); second, interpretation of COVID-19 pandemic shock through the prism of the hardest imperative faced by nation states: safeguarding lives and livelihoods of citizens (Chapter 8.2); and, third, highlighting the most important negative consequences of the COVID-19 shock associated with the deepening societal crisis, the most acute manifestation of which was the loss of citizens their confidence (trust) in their states (Chapter 8.3).

8.1. Two Waves of the COVID-19 Pandemic: The Failure of National Public Healthcare Systems and Economic Assessment of Missed Opportunities

Below is the dynamics of the total cases of COVID-19 infection as of 11.01.2020. Rising human losses due to deaths of those infected with coronavirus (Fig..1) have questioned the ability of national health systems to withstand the COVID-19 pandemic. In addition, the increase in the incidence of the world's population is compared with the dynamics of the daily COVID-19 Case Fatality Rate (CFR). Thus, the daily COVID-19 CFR is approaching 2% globally and converging across regions (Fig. 2). The apparent ineffectiveness of national health systems in the fight against the deadly COVID-19 virus that suddenly appeared and quickly spread throughout the world has many explanations. Leaving aside the financial aspect of ensuring a highly effective public health system, one can assess its state according to the experts of the Economist Intelligence Unit and Johns Hopkins Center for Health Security. It was they who, at the end of October 2019, released the fundamental work "Global Health Security Index (2019). Building Collective Action and Accountability ", i.e. a month before the first cases of coronavirus infection appeared in China in the province of Hubei.

Judging by the overall finding, at the end of 2019, the state of the national health systems in general was clearly unsatisfactory. The experts of the Economist Intelligence Unit as well as of Johns Hopkins Center for Health Security expressed this opinion with the following words: «National health security is fundamentally weak around the world.

No country is fully prepared for epidemics or pandemics, and every country has important gaps to address. Collectively, international preparedness is weak. Many countries do not show evidence of the health security capacities and capabilities that are needed to prevent, detect, and respond to significant infectious disease outbreaks» (Global Health Security Index, 2019).

Experts assessed the state of the national health systems of 195 countries and found that the average overall GHS Index score assessed is 40.2 of a possible score of 100. Regarding the state of health in the 60 high-income countries, than the average GHS Index score is 51.9. If to take a group of 116 high- and middle-income countries, than the average GHS Index do not score above 50 of a possible score of 100. Moreover, this index assesses the state of the health care system in the country according to indicators such as abilities to prevent, detect, and respond to health emergencies; severe gaps in health systems; vulnerabilities to political, socioeconomic, and environmental risks confound outbreak preparedness and response; and a lack of adherence to international norms. It should be noted that the GHS Index scoring system includes three tiers. Countries that score between 0 and 33.3 are in the bottom tier (also called "low scores"), countries that score between 33.4 and 66.6 are in the middle tier (also called "moderate scores"), and countries that score between 66.7 and 100 are in the upper or "top" tier (also called "high scores").

As for prevention, less than 7% of countries score in the highest tier for the ability to prevent the emergence or release of pathogens. In regard to detection and reporting only 19% of countries receive top marks for detection and reporting. By indicator of «rapid response» fewer than 5% of countries scored in the highest tier for their ability to rapidly respond to and mitigate the spread of an epidemic. The average score for health system indicators is 26.4 of 100, making it the lowest-scoring category. And as to risk environment than only 23% of countries score in the top tier for indicators related to their political system and government effectiveness. Eventually there is little evidence that most countries have tested important health security capacities or shown that they would be functional in a crisis (Fig. 3).

Figure 1. Dynamics of the total cases of COVID-19 infection as of 11.01.2020
Source: COVID-19: Briefing materials. (2020). Global Health and Crisis Response. Update: October 30. McKinsey & Company. McKinsey.com
Notes: 1. Increasing: > 10% increase in cumulative incremental cases over last 7 days, compared to incremental cases over last 8-14 days; stabilizing: -10% ~10%; if difference in incremental cumulative cases over last 7 days vs 8-14 days is less than 100, stabilizing; 2. Includes Puerto Rico and US Virgin Islands; 3. All remaining European countries, including Russia; 4. Includes Japan, Singapore, and South Korea; 5. All remaining Asian countries, not including Russia; 6. Includes European territories in the Caribbean.

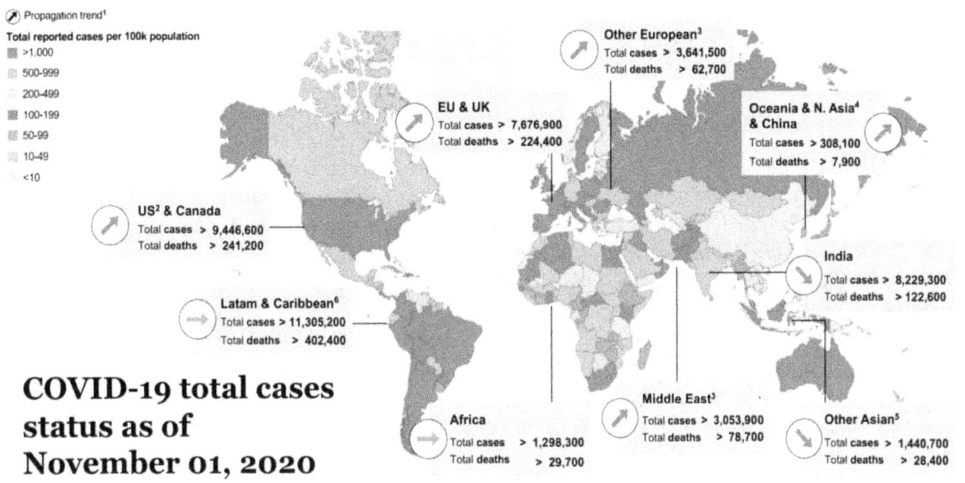

However, even these more than modest results turned out to be far from assessing the real state of affairs in the health care system of the countries of the world in the case of the COVID-19 pandemic. The situation at the end of December 2020 indicates that the countries that took the first lines in the GHS Index were the most vulnerable in the fight against coronavirus infection. It has become apparent that one health is a key to preventing pathogens from spreading from animals to humans. Today, nearly two-thirds of known pathogens and three quarters of newly emerging pathogens are zoonotic—meaning they spread from animals to humans (Taylor, et al., 2001). This dangerous trend toward disease spillover from animals to humans can be traced to a host of modern-day factors, including increased human encroachment on wildlife territory, land-use changes that increase the rate of human-wildlife and wildlife-livestock interface, and climate change. Human, animal, and environmental health are intertwined and must be effectively addressed together to prevent the spread of infectious disease.

In accordance with Global Health approach, the results of the Global Health Security (GHS) Index are not encouraging (Global Health Security Index, 2019):

- Fewer than 30% of countries demonstrate the existence of mechanisms for sharing data among relevant ministries for human, animal, and wildlife surveillance.
- Fewer than 8% of countries demonstrate a cross-ministerial department, agency, or similar unit dedicated to zoonotic disease.
- Only 51% of countries offer field epidemiological training programs that explicitly include animal health professionals, although a much larger number (80%) offer an applied epidemiological training program.

Meanwhile, the loss of health and life of people cannot be compared with the preventive financial expenditures for ensuring a high level of national health care. The COVID-19 pandemic becomes an unwelcome reminder of just how much health matters for individuals, society and the global economy. However, in recent years, a focus on rising healthcare costs, especially in mature economies, has dominated the policy debate, whereas health as an investment for economic return has largely been absent from the discussion. Better health promotes economic growth by expanding the labor force and by boosting productivity while also delivering immense social benefits.

Figure 2. Dynamics of the daily COVID-19 Case Fatality Rate (CFR) as of 01.11.2020
Notes: 1. Daily CFR is calculated with a 13 day lag from cases to deaths (e.g. CFR for April 1, 2020 = deaths on April 14, 2020/cases on April 1, 2020), uses 7 days moving average for cases and deaths to account for reporting differences; 2. Includes Puerto Rico and US Virgin Islands; 3. Includes European territories in the Caribbean; 4. All remaining European countries, including Russia; 5. All remaining Asian countries, not including Russia
Source: COVID-19: Briefing materials. (2020). Global Health and Crisis Response. Update: October 30. McKinsey & Company. McKinsey.com

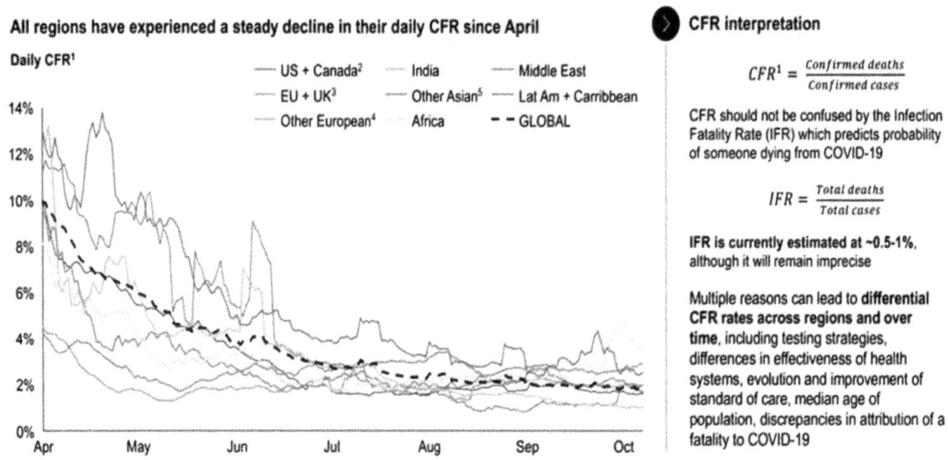

Over the past century improved hygiene, better nutrition, antibiotics, vaccines and new technologies have contributed to tremendous progress in global health (Fig. 4). Experts of the McKinsey Global Institute estimate that about one-third of economic growth in advanced economies in the past century could be attributed to improvements in the health of global populations. Research focused on more recent years has found that health contributed almost as much to income growth as education (Remes, et al., 2020). Despite the progress of the past century, in 2020 poor health and death due to COVID-19 will limit greatly economic prosperity in the future. This plays out in two ways. First, premature deaths limit growth by reducing the size of the potential labor force. Second, poor health or morbidity makes it hard for those suffering from health conditions to be economically active and realize their full productive potential.

Figure 3. Assessment of the state of national health care systems of Top 10 in the GHS Index by the following indicators: (1) prevention of the emergence or release of pathogens; (2) early detection & reporting for epidemics of potential international concern; (3) rapid response to and mitigation of the spread of an epidemic; (4) sufficient & robust health system to treat the sick & protect health workers; (5) sufficient & robust health system to treat the sick & protect health workers; (6) overall risk environment and country vulnerability to biological threats.

Notes: All data are normalized to a scale of 0 to 100, where 100 = best health security conditions.

Source: Global Health Security Index. (2019). Building Collective Action and Accountability. The Economist Intelligence Unit. Johns Hopkins Center for Health Security. October 24

OVERALL SCORE

Rank		Score
1	United States	83.5
2	United Kingdom	77.9
3	Netherlands	75.6
4	Australia	75.5
5	Canada	75.3
6	Thailand	73.2
7	Sweden	72.1
8	Denmark	70.4
9	South Korea	70.2
10	Finland	68.7

1. PREVENTION OF THE EMERGENCE OR RELEASE OF PATHOGENS

Rank		Score
1	United States	83.1
2	Sweden	81.1
3	Thailand	75.7
4	Netherlands	73.7
5	Denmark	72.9
6	France	71.2
7	Canada	70.0
8	Australia	68.9
9	Finland	68.5
10	United Kingdom	68.3

2. EARLY DETECTION & REPORTING FOR EPIDEMICS OF POTENTIAL INTERNATIONAL CONCERN

Rank		Score
1	United States	98.2
2	Australia	97.3
2	Latvia	97.3
4	Canada	96.4
5	South Korea	92.1
6	United Kingdom	87.3
7	Denmark	86.0
7	Netherlands	86.0
7	Sweden	86.0
10	Germany	84.6

3. RAPID RESPONSE TO AND MITIGATION OF THE SPREAD OF AN EPIDEMIC

Rank		Score
1	United Kingdom	91.9
2	United States	79.7
3	Switzerland	79.3
4	Netherlands	79.1
5	Thailand	78.6
6	South Korea	71.5
7	Finland	69.2
8	Portugal	67.7
9	Brazil	67.1
10	Australia	65.9

4. SUFFICIENT & ROBUST HEALTH SYSTEM TO TREAT THE SICK & PROTECT HEALTH WORKERS

Rank		Score
1	United States	73.8
2	Thailand	70.5
3	Netherlands	70.2
4	Canada	67.7
5	Denmark	63.8
6	Australia	63.5
7	Switzerland	62.5
8	France	60.9
9	Finland	60.8
10	Belgium	60.5

5. COMMITMENTS TO IMPROVING NATIONAL CAPACITY, FINANCING AND ADHERENCE TO NORMS

Rank		Score
1	United States	85.3
2	United Kingdom	81.2
3	Australia	77.0
4	Finland	75.4
5	Canada	74.7
6	Mexico	73.9
7	Indonesia	72.5
8	Lithuania	72.1
8	Slovenia	72.1
10	Liberia	71.5

6. OVERALL RISK ENVIRONMENT AND COUNTRY VULNERABILITY TO BIOLOGICAL THREATS

Rank		Score
1	Liechtenstein	87.9
2	Norway	87.1
3	Switzerland	86.2
4	Luxembourg	84.7
5	Austria	84.6
6	Sweden	84.5
7	Andorra	83.5
8	Monaco	83.1
9	France	83.0
10	Canada	82.7

Most prepared | More prepared | Least prepared

Figure 4. Global live expectancy at birth for the period of 1800-2000 (in years)
Source: Remes, Jaana, Katherine Linzer, Shubham Singhal, Martin Dewhurst, Penelope Dash, Jonathan Woetzel, Sven Smit, Matthias Evers, Matt Wilson, Dr. Kristin-Anne Rutter, and Aditi Ramdorai. (2020). Prioritizing Health: A Prescription for Prosperity. Executive summary. Ed. By Anna Bernasek. McKinsey Global Institute Report. July 8. McKinsey.com

Overall, according to estimations of the McKinsey Global Institute' experts the cost of ill health was more than $12 trillion in 2017, about 15 percent of global real GDP. Health shocks such as the COVID-19 pandemic, H1N1 influenza, and SARS can result in additional humanitarian and economic costs. The COVID-19 pandemic and its repercussions, such as the shelter in place measures to control the spread of the virus, are forecast to reduce global GDP by 3 to 8 percent in 2020 (Remes, et al., 2020).

Health has not typically been part of economic-growth discussions, but a number of trends suggest that health may well matter more for growth in coming decades. First, improving health can counter the drag on growth that result from slowing population growth. Labor force growth globally is expected to slow from an annual rate of 1.8 percent over the past 50 years to 0.3 percent in the next 50 years. Improved health can help extend healthy lifespan for workers of prime working age and older, and develop the physical and cognitive ability of children as the future labor force of the world. Second, persistent and in many cases growing health inequity creates a gap in health outcomes between rich and poor within societies. Third, healthier populations are more resilient in the face of new infectious diseases, like COVID-19, that can often present higher risks to people with existing health conditions.

From the point of view of the McKinsey Global Institute' experts the global disease burden could be reduced by about 40 percent by applying known interventions in broader segments of populations and with closer adherence to the most effective tools available. Over 40 percent of health improvements can be achieved at a net cost of less than $100 for every additional healthy life year. The economic benefits from the health improvements could be substantial enough to add $12 trillion or 8 percent to global GDP in 2040 that translates into 0.4 percent faster growth every year (Fig. 5). These benefits arise through the labor market, both by expanding future employment through fewer early deaths, fewer health conditions, and higher labor-force participation of healthier people and through the productivity gains achievable by workers who are physically and cognitively healthier.

Figure 5. The increase of global GDP from fewer health conditions and expanded participation in the labor force

Notes: [1]Includes on older adults (only high- and upper-middle-income countries), informal caregivers (only in OECD), and people with disabilities (global)

Source: Remes, Jaana, Katherine Linzer, Shubham Singhal, Martin Dewhurst, Penelope Dash, Jonathan Woetzel, Sven Smit, Matthias Evers, Matt Wilson, Dr. Kristin-Anne Rutter, and Aditi Ramdorai (2020). Prioritizing Health: A Prescription for Prosperity. Executive summary. Ed. by Anna Bernasek. McKinsey Global Institute Report. July 8. McKinsey.com

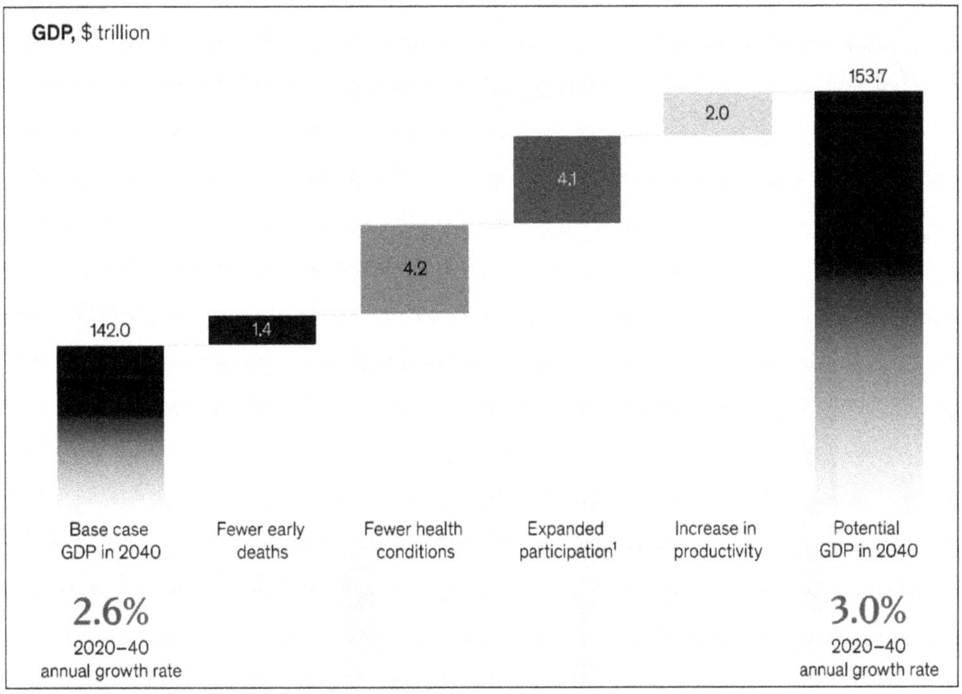

According to Fig. 5 by 2040, 245 million more people could be employed. About 60 million of them would have avoided early death from cardiovascular disease, cancers, malaria, and other causes, adding $1.4 trillion to 2040 GDP. Addressing mental health disorders, diabetes, or other conditions would no longer be a barrier to joining the labor force for an equivalent of about 120 million full-time workers, contributing an additional $4.2 trillion. Another $4.1 trillion could be unlocked by expanding labor-force participation among three groups: older populations for whom better health can be an opportunity to work longer (about 40 million people), informal caregivers who no longer need to care for loved ones (12 million people), and people with disabilities who can go to work because workplaces adapted to accommodate their needs (eight million people).

Lastly, improving health could drive up productivity and lift GDP by as much as $2.0 trillion by reducing presenteeism from chronic conditions such as low back pain, but also through investing in childhood nutrition, which improves the cognitive and physical health of the future workforce. Just addressing adolescents' mental and behavioral health issues, which affect about 60 million young people globally, could unlock $600 billion by 2040 through raising their educational attainment and earnings potential. As to the social benefits from improved health the total combined value of deaths averted and reduced ill health could be approximately $100 trillion without adjustments for income levels—eight times the estimated GDP benefits. Improving health could also help narrow health disparities within countries.

This in turn could also contribute to reducing income inequality within countries and strengthen the social contract. The best part is that focusing on known health improvements could deliver an incremental economic benefit of $2 to $4 for each $1 invested (Fig. 6).

Figure 6. Impact of improved health on incremental economic benefit
Notes: Snapshot view of the healthy growth scenario in 2040. Additional healthcare spending, GDP impact, and welfare gains directly attributable to better health only (excluding expanded participation)
Source: Remes, Jaana, Katherine Linzer, Shubham Singhal, Martin Dewhurst, Penelope Dash, Jonathan Woetzel, Sven Smit, Matthias Evers, Matt Wilson, Dr. Kristin-Anne Rutter, and Aditi Ramdorai. (2020). Prioritizing Health: A Prescription for Prosperity. McKinsey Global Institute Report. July 8. McKinsey.com

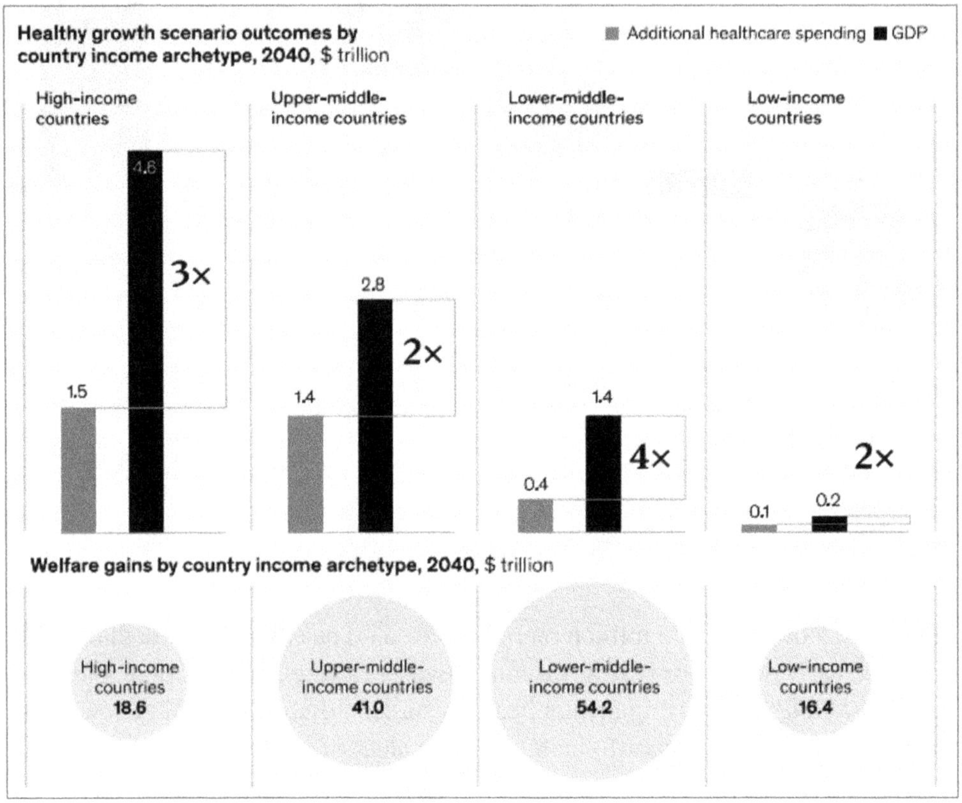

Realizing the benefits would mean shifting spending to prevention of diseases. And it is typically less expensive than treatment and reduces the need for more expensive treatment later on, contributing to a high economic return. Shifting incremental spending to prevention would not be simple, however, because it requires substantial changes in where and how healthcare is delivered, as well as changes to communities that would help individuals grow up, work, and age in healthy ways. That means it would necessitate change by governments and regional authorities, companies, innovators, and communities to shape environments and societies in ways that promote healthy lives and capture the societal and economic benefits. The COVID-19 pandemic provides a unique moment to engage governments, companies, and communities around the world in this endeavor. The pandemic has exposed deep vulnerabilities in healthcare systems, supply chains, and social structures, and vast inequities that need to be addressed.

The McKinsey Global Institute Report shows that investing in health can be a critical lever for future growth and an important part of the economic policy debate. Instead of thinking of health as a cost to society, focusing on health as an investment can deliver significant social and economic returns.

All of the data above allows the authors to estimate the scale of the humanitarian and economic disaster caused by the COVID-19 pandemic. However, this is only an external manifestation of the crisis consequences. In fact, any extreme situation such as the modern coronavirus pandemic that threatens human lives generates appropriate mechanisms to combat it. And if society and the economic system are interconnected dialectically, then the combined efforts of the state and citizens give a quick and effective result. However, the current course of events in almost all countries of the world, with a few exceptions, demonstrates the opposite. This is especially evident in the case of the United States, which consistently were the first in the top 10 of the rating of the Global Health Security Index (2019) by indicators such as (1) prevention of the emergence or release of pathogens; (2) early detection & reporting for epidemics of potential international concern; (3) rapid response to and mitigation of the spread of an epidemic; (4) sufficient & robust health system to treat the sick & protect health workers; (5) sufficient & robust health system to treat the sick & protect health workers; (6) overall risk environment and country vulnerability to biological threats. In other words, the United States had the greatest potential to withstand extreme life-threatening events such as the current COVID-19 pandemic. However, the government was unable to effectively take advantage of these opportunities in the context of a split in the social cohesion of society, in which the government is trying to limit the spread of infection in the country by introducing an emergency regime of restricting social communication, the mandatory wearing of masks, blocking the entertainment segment, public catering, and the population is opposing the actions of the federal government and regional administrations. And this is typical for almost all countries in the world. This is the essence of the problem of the destroyed dialectics of society and economy. Many ordinary citizens often perceive everything as a terrible social tragedy, which can be expressed as follows: “it doesn’t matter what to die of: from coronavirus or from hunger”. In other words, today, in the extreme conditions of the COVID-19 pandemic, the governments of the countries of the world must implement the most difficult imperative: how to save the lives of citizens and prevent them from starving to death after recovery.

8.2. COVID-19 Pandemic Shock: Safeguarding Lives and Ensuring Livelihoods of People as the Contemporary Imperative

The COVID-19 pandemic has put a strategic imperative for society on how the state can harmonize efforts to save lives and provide people with livelihoods. Saving people’ lives means the following: (1a) to suppress the virus as fast as possible; (1b) to expand testing, quarantining and treatment capacity; (1c) to find “cures”, treatment, drugs, vaccines. Safeguarding people’ livelihoods include the following: (2a) to support people and businesses affected by lockdowns; (2b) to prepare to get back to work safely when the virus abates; (2c) to prepare to scale the recovery away from a (-8) – (-13)% trough (Fig. 7).

Judging by Fig. 7 - 8, the most difficult situation arises in conditions when there is an exponential increase in the number of cases, and the state is fighting the infection by introducing emergency lockdown regimes. Business stops, people lose money for livelihoods, and a deadly virus threatens their lives.

The length of this period depends on many factors, including, first and foremost, the ability of the national health system to function effectively in the emergency conditions of exponential growth in morbidity and increase in the number of deaths, and, second, on the willingness of governments to provide instant, targeted support to those who have lost funds for livelihoods. As a result virus and the economy remains the central frame of reference.

Moreover, there can be many options for combining these two imperatives. In Fig. 9 only a few such alternatives are proposed. The vertical axis is denoted virus health impact и public health response, i.e. it is about effectiveness of public health response to virus health impact as to public controlling the health impact of COVID-19. The horizontal axis is knock-on effects in connection with economic policy response. It is about speed and strength of recovery that depends on whether policy moves can mitigate self-reinforcing recessionary dynamics (e.g., corporate defaults, credit crunch, etc.).

Figure 7. Two strategic imperatives caused by the COVID-19 pandemic shock on 01.11.2020
Source: COVID-19: Briefing materials. (2020). Global Health and Crisis Response. Update: October 30. McKinsey & Company. McKinsey.com

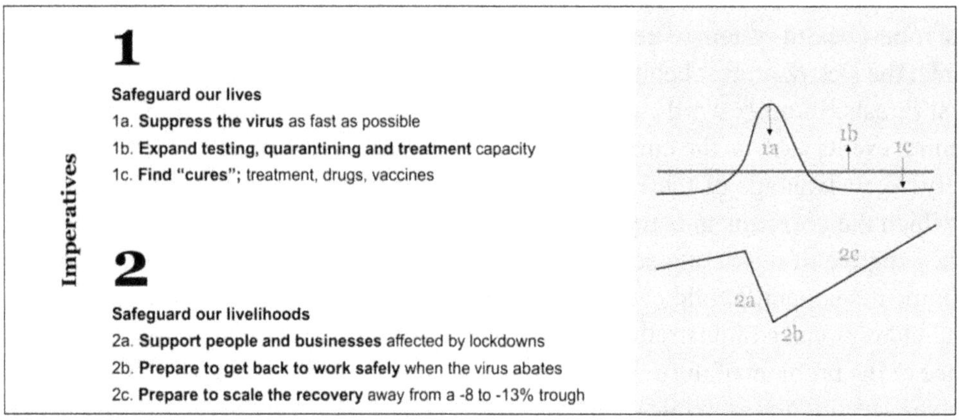

Figure 8. The illustration of the content of Fig. 7
Source: McKinsey&Company. (2020). Crushing Coronavirus Uncertainty: The big 'unlock' for our economies. Strategy & Corporate Finance Practice. May. McKinsey.com

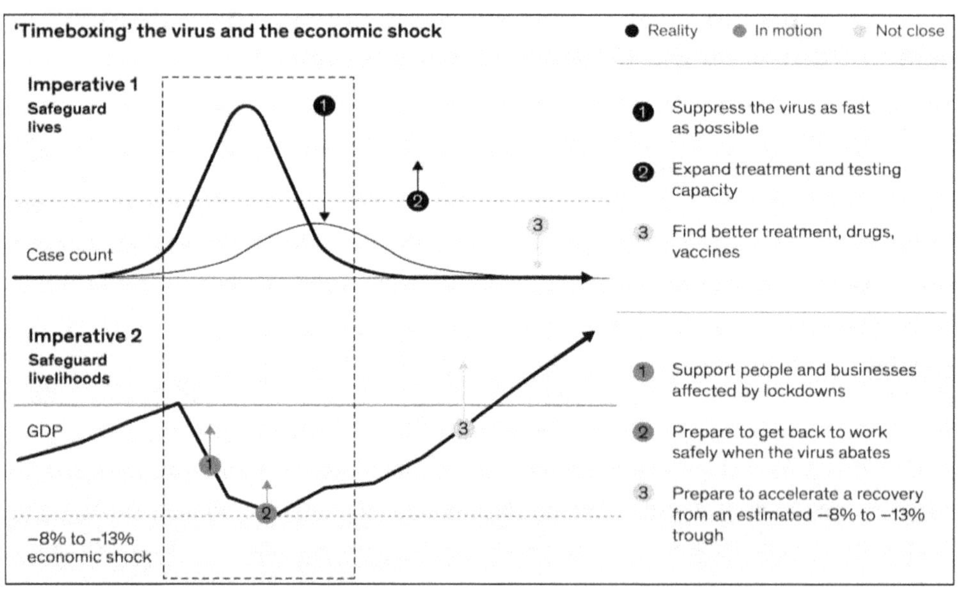

Figure 9. GDP scenarios for the economic impact of the COVID-19 pandemic shock, October 2020
Source: COVID-19: Briefing materials. (2020). Global Health and Crisis Response. Update: October 30. McKinsey & Company. McKinsey.com

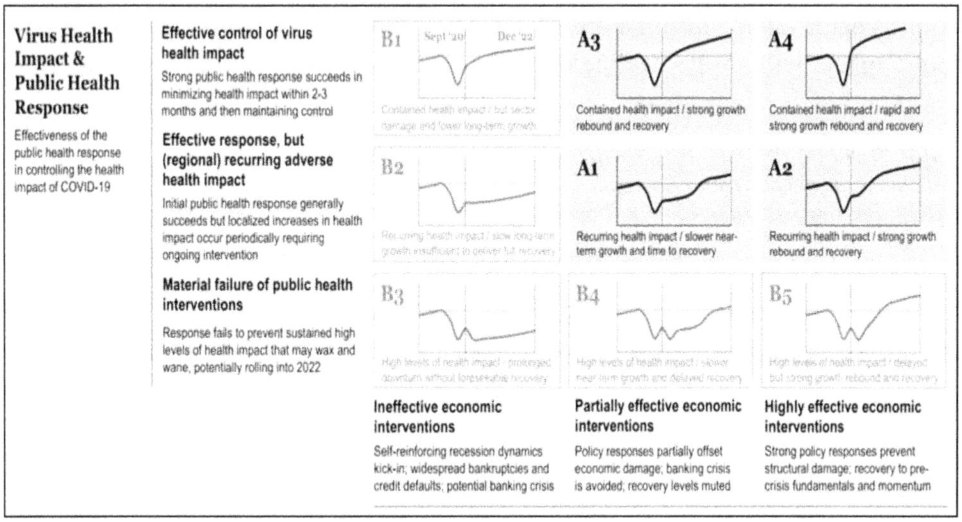

Considering GDP scenarios for the economic impact of the COVID-19 pandemic shock, presented by B_1, A_3 and A_4, then all these cases are distinguished by effective control of virus health impact. It means that strong public health response succeeds in minimizing health impact within 2-3 months and then maintaining control. But as to economic interventions than in B_1 scenario they are ineffective because of self-reinforcing recession dynamics kick-in, widespread bankruptcies and credit crunches, potentially possible banking crisis. In A_3 scenario economic interventions is partially effective. It means that policy responses partially offset economic damage; banking crisis is avoided, recovery levels muted. And A_4 scenario differs in highly effective economic interventions, because strong responses prevent structural damage; recovery to pre-crisis fundamentals and momentum. Provided the change sequence is maintained economic interventions from effective to partially effective and highly effective ones scenarios B_2, A_1 and A_2 differ effective response, but (regional) recurring adverse health impact. It these scenarios initial public health response generally succeeds, but localized increases in health impact take place periodically requiring ongoing intervention. And at last scenarios B_3, B_4 and B_5 differ in material failure of public health interventions. Response fails to prevent sustained high levels of health impact that may wax and wane, potentially rolling into 2022.

Experts of the McKinsey & Company tend to expect the positive tailwind continue if COVID-19 is not going to create further tailwind (Fig. 10-11)

Regardless of which scenario for the development of COVID-19 will be implemented, by the end of 2020, the decline in GDP is estimated from (-5.9) in the case of the dominance of scenario B5' (Fig. 10) to (-3) under scenario A3' (Fig. 11). However, already in 2021, the most effective scenario will be A3' (Fig. 12), which can provide up to + 8.2% growth in global GDP in real terms. For this it is necessary that effective control of virus health impacts is achieved across most large economies. Jump in Q3 2020 growth signals strong economic momentum that naturally continues. The B2' scenario will be the most ineffective, since the real growth of global GDP will not exceed (+1.5%). It takes place if structural damage has been done as business failures, personal bankruptcies and long-term unemployment take hold even as virus health impacts are largely controlled. In other words, the significance of the human factor is clearly manifested in the implementation of any scenario that combines imperatives of the safeguarding lives and livelihoods of people. Moreover, in the absence of a solution to the health crisis the extremeness of the situation is aggravated, since the effectiveness of public activities of the national governments in the economic sphere will always decline if citizens do not harmonize their behavior with the state.

Figure 10. Global economy tracking towards "A_3 scenario" in Q3
Note: [1]Reported data through Q2. Oxford Economics estimate for Q3.
Source: COVID-19: Briefing materials. (2020). Global Health and Crisis Response. Update: October 30. McKinsey & Company. McKinsey.com

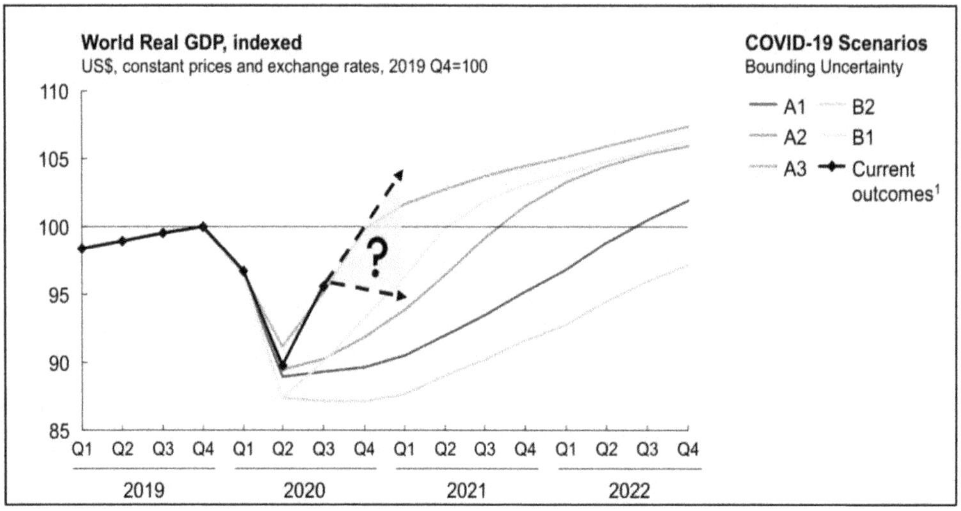

Figure 11. COVID-19 scenario pathways, October 2020
Source: COVID-19: Briefing materials (2020). Global health and crisis response. Update: October 30. McKinsey & Company. McKinsey.com

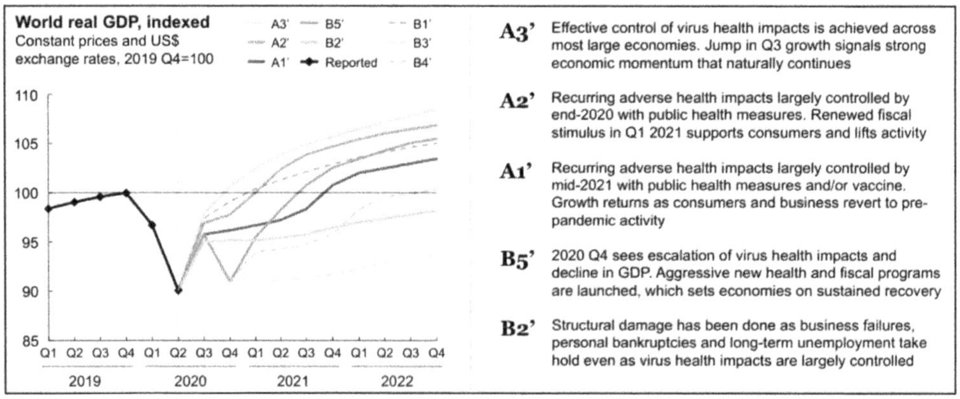

Figure 12. Changes in global GDP in real terms if realized COVID-19 scenario pathways, October 2020
Source: COVID-19: Briefing materials. (2020). Global Health and Crisis Response. Update: October 30. McKinsey & Company. McKinsey.com

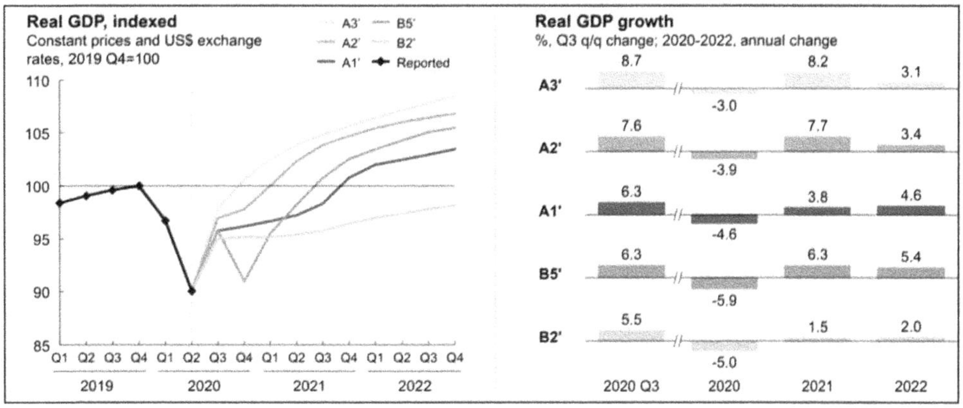

In other words, in the extreme conditions of a pandemic, lack of integrity of society predetermines absolute uncertainty about the path of economic recovery. So do the need for increasing fiscal action. The top priority is still public health. Policies that attenuate health risks contribute substantially to the restoration of confidence and trust, thereby helping economic activity and employment and reducing strains on public finances. And going forward, early and targeted containment procedures will have much more limited economic and fiscal costs, as compared to a general lockdown. Once effective vaccine and therapeutics against COVID-19 are widely available, it will be possible to enter a post-COVID world and truly escape the Great Lockdown. Until then, the governments of the countries of the world are completely dependent on the trust of their citizens in their actions.

The continuing spread of the coronavirus makes people fear for their health and their lives which exacerbate their sense of uncertainty about the future. As to their livelihoods people become cautious about spending in the face of uncertainty. High uncertainty makes business leaders find it impossible to make reliable plans for investment. So the uncertainty is toxic for national economic recovery (McKinsey & Company, May 2020). At the same time, it should be emphasized that the feeling of uncertainty has adjusted the assessments of individuals who have social grounds and predetermine their actions and behavior, formalized in the form of social institutions and informal institutions in the economy. In modern conditions, the main strategic goal of national governments must be to crush uncertainty as soon as possible. In essence, it is about restoring the unity of citizens and the state in understanding the specifics of the current extreme situation and the need for joint efforts in the fight against universal evil.

The validity of this conclusion is proved by the experience of exiting the previous crises, when uncertainty subsides, confidence returns and economic recovery unlocks—and the COVID-19 crisis has created the highest level of uncertainty in 35 years (Fig. 13).

On the example of the economic dynamics of the United States, there is a steady tendency of interaction of US Economic Policy Uncertainty Index and monthly year-over-year real GDP growth (Fig. 13): the more the Economic Policy Uncertainty Index falls, the more significant monthly year-over-year real GDP growth.

Figure 13. An illustration of the dialectics of society and the economic system interaction by the example of reducing uncertainty and resuming economic growth returns
Note: Policy-uncertainty index available through April 2020; April–June year-over-year real GDP growth estimated based on −10.3% contraction in McKinsey A1 scenario projections.
Source: Scott R. Baker, Nicholas Bloom, and Steven J. Davis. (2020). Measuring economic policy uncertainty. Economic Policy Uncertainty. Policyuncertainty.com; IHS Markit/Macroeconomic Advisors; McKinsey analysis in partnership with Oxford Economics

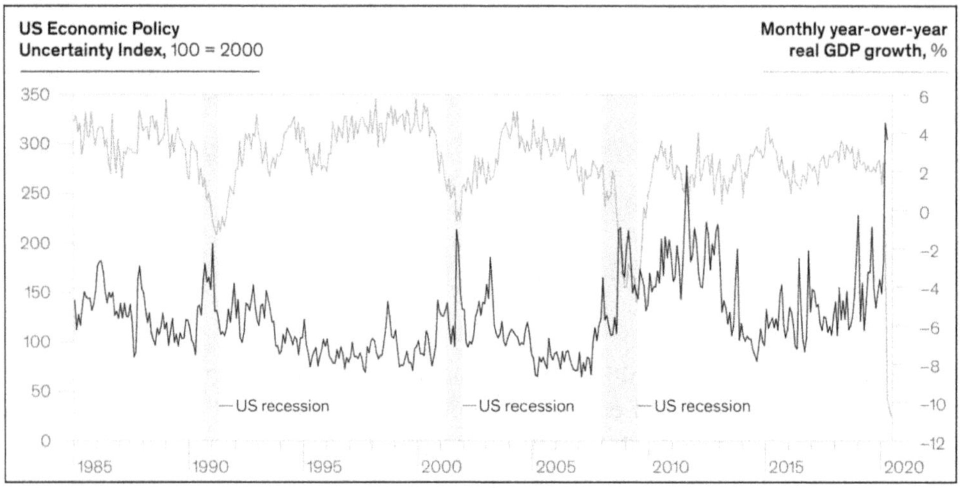

The path societies choose to control the virus spread and they have to prefer hard imperatives of the safeguarding lives and livelihoods of people and the stakes are high. From 2020 to the end of 2023, the difference — in lost global GDP — between economic scenarios with only partial virus-spread control and those in "near-zero virus" situations will be as much as $15 trillion (McKinsey & Company, May 2020).

The national governments all over the world explore the following three typical paths forward:

(1) The first imperative is called "balancing act". It is aimed at lifting lockdowns gradually while keeping the number of patients with COVID-19 within the capacity of their healthcare systems. This path proves to be effective if the public-health system supports the release of the lockdowns and becomes sufficient to keep the virus spread. But if a specific version of the balancing-act path becomes to be successful, uncertainty and risk will remain high for an extended period. This means that citizens become completely confident in their safety, seeing solid evidence that there will be no recurrence of the virus. And confidence in this does not arise immediately, but only after some time.

(2) The second strategy is called "near-zero virus". It means opening the economy imposing virus-control measures that stop short of a lockdown. It becomes effective in preventing virus spread. When releasing lockdowns on this path, the main goal becomes to crush uncertainty by implementing a collection of measures aiming at controlling the virus. They include the following: banning large-scale public events ("superspreading"); using masks; testing; tracking and tracing; quarantining infected individuals and their contacts; physical distancing; controlling borders; implementing work protocols; modifying public-transportation framework. This imperative is connected with effectively communicating the 'near-zero virus' package and presenting a clear road map to economic recovery. In this case uncertainty would be crushed for sure. The recovery process would accelerate with the

restoration of the confidence of consumers and of business leaders. Once a government achieves a stable near-zero-virus situation because of near-zero-virus package effectiveness, some of these measures could be gradually eased. But in any case uncertainty about a government's ability to implement such protocols will vary among countries.

(3) The third strategy is called "transition act". It involves switching from a balancing-act path to a near-zero-virus path by implementing elements of near-zero-virus packages as soon as they are ready (Fig. 14).

Figure 14. Three typical paths towards the imperatives of the safeguarding lives and livelihoods of people
Source: McKinsey & Company. (2020). Crushing coronavirus uncertainty: The big 'unlock' for our economies. Strategy & Corporate Finance Practice. May. McKinsey.com

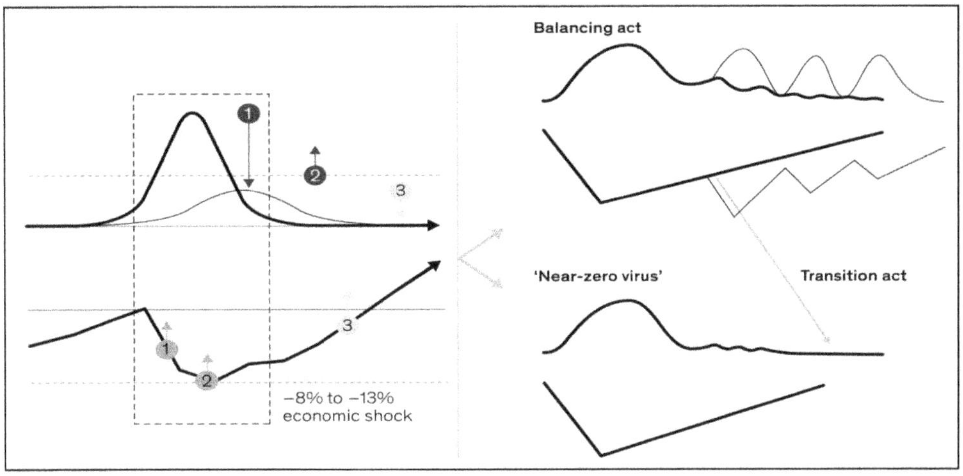

The imperative chosen by governments may likewise be to reach near-zero-virus status, but much later. It depends on the time required to put the right package of measures in place. There could be the obstacles connected with the lack of testing capacity, of personal protective equipment (PPE), or of "intelligent border controls". Overcoming these obstacles will make the future more and uncertainty would be reduced. The transition to the near-zero-virus path would crush uncertainty. But for many emerging markets, a near-zero-virus imperative may not be realistic because of financial and other reasons. As to many developed countries, some measures may be socially or politically unacceptable. But given the benefits of paths that drastically reduce uncertainty, even countries facing significant obstacles would benefit from exploring the viability of such imperatives.

Each imperative implies very different outcomes for lives and livelihoods. Crushing uncertainty each imperative determines the spread of the virus, the pace of economic recovery, and the speed. Most countries having used lockdowns to suppress the initial spread of COVID-19, are now exploring one of the three possible imperatives above mentioned (McKinsey & Company, May 2020). No matter which imperative is chosen, the economic cost of the coronavirus crisis will be unprecedented.

In Fig. 9 there are nine potential economic outcomes of the COVID-19 pandemic based on healthcare systems' and policy makers' responses. A moderately favorable scenario (A_3) could result in a global GDP decline from 2019 of $4 trillion to $5 trillion (McKinsey & Company, May 2020). The toll on individuals, in lost jobs and income, will be equally grave. In scenario A_1, the result would be a deeper drop in GDP and a different recovery trajectory. Imperative scenario A_3 would generate a recovery to pre-crisis level in late 2020 or early 2021 (Fig. 15).

Figure 15. The economic cost opportunities to eliminate uncertainty in the minds of citizens in imperative scenarios A_1 and A_3
Source: McKinsey & Company. (2020). Crushing coronavirus uncertainty: The big 'unlock' for our economies. Strategy & Corporate Finance Practice. May. McKinsey.com

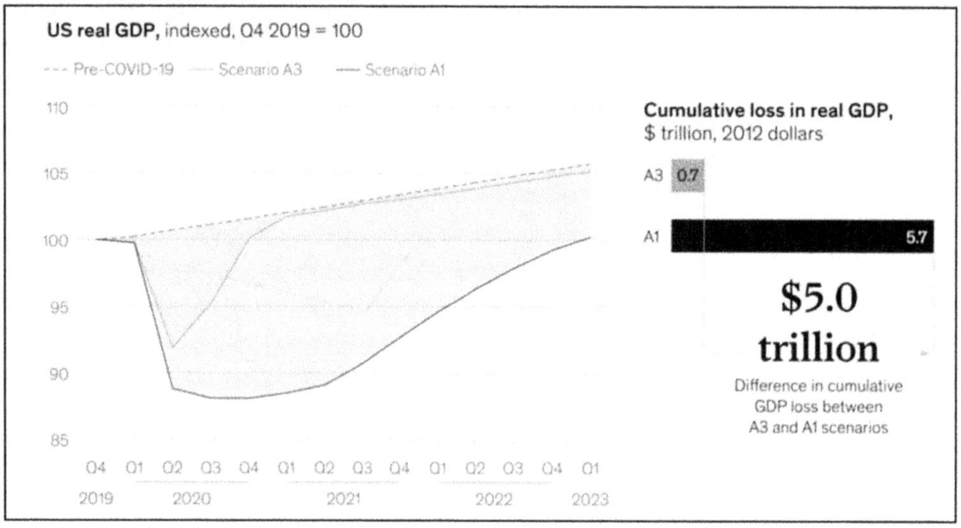

As to imperative scenario A_1 it would produce a muted recovery only after two to three years. The cumulative difference in lost global GDP between scenarios A_1 and A_3 could be as high as $15 trillion to $20 trillion. As to unemployment than scenario A_1 could generate about 10-15 million more unemployed people in the United States and 7-10 million jobs lost in Europe throughout the period of economic recovery in comparison with scenario A_3 (Fig. 15).

With controlling virus spread, life can come back. There remain clear rules but just thinking about the possibility of returning to normal life makes people be sure of uncertainty having been crushed. That is exactly how confidence returns. But people will only resume their lives when they *believe* in their safety, not when they merely hope so. Similarly, the economy cannot be forced to return to normal. That is why people concerned about their safety will protest demanding PPE before employees would return to their jobs.

But in any case lower virus levels are good for protecting lives and for protecting livelihoods, as it is easier to feel safe "returning to normal." The greatest difference achieving a near-zero-virus condition makes, relative to scenarios in which the virus is not fully under control, is that uncertainty is drastically lowered. Near-zero-virus packages and clear communication about the restrictions they require, along with fact-based justifications for them, encourage citizens and leaders alike to make decisions with more confidence. This, in turn, helps unlock economic recovery. The stakes are high and speed is of the essence. To safeguard lives and livelihoods, the national governments must restore confidence.

In other words, all of the above material indicates that the economy is predetermined by the state of society, i.e. the importance of trust, mutual understanding, and citizens' loyalty to the actions of the authorities. However, national governments have clearly demonstrated their ineffectiveness in combating the COVID-19 pandemic and in preventing its exponential spread across countries. The second wave of COVID-19 at the end of 2020 further undermined public confidence in the government's ability to create an effective health care system focused on rapid response in the face of a humanitarian disaster posed by mortal danger. And this was the first major argument in favor of distrust of the government, of the society, which empowered it to provide all citizens with public health services. It is the inability of such a system to provide the necessary assistance that predetermined the growth of uncertainty in the minds of citizens regarding their future.

The second no less significant circumstance that split the integrity of national communities was the problem of safeguarding livelihoods. On the eve of the COVID-19 pandemic, the situation of increasing polarization of society in income and wealth, a shrinking middle class, inequality in the growth of incomes of working citizens and prices for real estate, education and health, as well as inequality of opportunities led to the phenomenon of survival of working citizens and their families. In other words, we are not talking about a brilliant education and excellent health, but about the ability to survive in conditions when technological progress requires a new quality of personalities associated with intellectual autonomousness.

And the COVID-19 pandemic is exacerbating the current situation due to the decline in economic growth and the need to rebuild the business, bring the healthcare system into proper condition, taking into account the lessons of COVID-19. A paradoxical situation may arise: on the one hand, the technological revolution offers fantastic opportunities for transforming the person himself, and society, and society, and billions of dollars in assets have been accumulated in the hands of their holders, and the need for fundamental changes in society is urgent, and on the other hand, only a person is missing, or rather a critical mass of people, with a unique quality of intellectual autonomousness. And it does not exist today, and the current generation is considered lost, largely due to the COVID-19 pandemic, but, in fact, due to a violation of the dialectics of society and the economic system. A person is capable of doing the impossible, but he must realize that he wants to serve the society in which he is socialized. The existence of this phenomenon proves the fact that without eliminating the uncertainty of citizens regarding the future, i.e. trust in society and the state, quickly get out of the crisis caused by the COVID-19 pandemic is problematic.

8.3. COVID-19 Shock and Societal Crisis: Restoration of Citizens' Trust in the State as the Basis of the Dialectic of Society and Economy Interrelations

The extraordinary conditions of the exponential growth of the deadly infection in which the countries of the world find themselves allow the authors to make some generalizations. National health systems, which are supposed to protect the health of their citizens, have proven completely unable to do so in the face of the coronavirus pandemic. In this regard, it is logical to state the fact of the inefficiency of the modern state, which, in an effort to ensure macroeconomic equilibrium and financial stability, abstracted from the fact that its main function is to maximize human utility in various forms of its manifestation. Moreover, as it turned out, the state represented this goal mainly in the categories of material income or wealth, which were distributed exclusively "unfairly", which increased the differentiation of the population in terms of income and wealth and led to the erosion of the integrity of the national society. One of the forms of manifestation of this result has become a steady downward trend in the middle class. Only one aspect of the state's activity on the eve of the pandemic, mentioned above, which destroyed the consolidation of society, makes it possible to explain the introduction of economic and social lockdown regimes, which were resorted to by the states of the countries of the world for the most part. Why can this step by the state be attributed to a phenomenal event? It is because the state intentionally destroyed by its own efforts what it had strengthened during all the previous time.

The originality of the shock caused by the COVID-19 pandemic was due to the actions of states that failed to quickly identify the "zero" patient and introduced lockdown regimes that destroyed the structural integrity of national societies and the economics. Thus, the coronavirus exposed the main "fault line" (Rajan, 2010) of modern societies, which was unable to dampen the consequences of an unexpected infection, dangerous to human life, and contributed to the development of a societal crisis as a demonstration of national societies' structural disunity. It is in this context the Boston Consulting Group' experts (Boston Consulting Group Perspectives, April 2020) have treated the COVID-19 outbreak as the first and foremost a societal crisis. In the opinion of Daniel Susskind, the current situation should be associated with "…a self-inflicted economic catastrophe as a necessary policy response to contain its (COVID-19) spread" (Susskind, 2020).

In other words, the state with its own hands destroyed the structural ties in the economy, blocking business both in the economic and in the financial spheres. From a theoretical point of view, the shock rupture of both vertical and horizontal structural ties of the economic system was mediated by the actions of the state aimed at stopping the rapid spread of coronavirus infection. However, the rupture of structural ties and the blocking of all types of business, with the exception of those associated with the epidemiological situation and the provision of vital activity of citizens, demonstrated rather the action of the dialectical law of denial of denial rather than the transition of quantitative changes into qualitative ones. Of fundamental importance is the concretization of the law, in the implementation of which, without knowing it, the state took part, blocking structural ties in the economy in a shock manner. If it is about a turning point in the operation of the law of transition of quantitative changes into qualitative ones, then the restoration of the integrity of the economy and society will become a function of the state, which will do this in the image and likeness of what it was before COVID-19. Figuratively speaking, national societies will have to return into Groundhog Days and everything will continue as before. However, there are circumstances that suggest that the current shock and its mediation by the actions of states that have blocked the economy and society, implements the dialectical law of denial of negation. Then, denying both the structural level-effect and the structural level-cause the shock predetermines the crisis as a period of the leap of static economy into its dynamic state. And in this case, there can be no question of returning the "Groundhog Days", since the processes have become irreversible. It is this phenomenon that is associated with "New Normal" in many publications.

What indicates the scenario of dynamic changes in future economic system? First, the speed with which everything was destroyed suggests that the objective conditions for a shock discontinuity in the self-organization of static economies have long been ripe. The first evidence of imminent qualitative changes in a static economy was brought by the shock of 2007 and the following global financial crisis of 2008-2009, which for the first time did not lead to an automatic restoration of macroeconomic equilibrium, the market mechanism failed. In other words, the rapid restoration of structural ties along the vertical did not occur. As a result, the integrity of the economic system suffered and the restored structure could no longer fully strengthen the equilibrium of the system. The shock caused by the COVID-19 pandemic only occurred in objectively ripe conditions for the system prepared to jump from static state to the stage of self-development.

Second, the "ratchet effect" was formed, as it were, specifically in order to exclude the desire of society and the state to return everything back. It was associated with the destruction of the integrity of the social system in the face of a growing threat to the lives and health of people, the loss of material living conditions for them and their households, which set a strategic imperative for the state – "safeguarding people' lives and their livelihoods". The discussion of the latter problem has shifted from the sphere of theoretical justification and analysis to the practical plane of actions of national governments. It turned out that both the lost lives and the lost health of citizens have a phenomenally high economic assessment, the more it became possible to assess the actions of the state that allowed these losses in terms of Global Health Security Index (2019). And survivors of the COVID-19 pandemic began to associate their unsecured health and low level of material support with ineffective government actions. It instantly became obvious to the whole society that the overwhelming majority of citizens are rapidly becoming poorer, therefore they could not create a financial safety cushion during the period of work, and, having lost their jobs, they were on the verge of poverty, but the state was not able to fulfill the function of last resort and help them to survive. It is in the opposition of the interests and actions of citizens and the state, which is a form of manifestation of the essential problem of the absence of dialectical interaction between society and the state that the ratchet effect arose. And this should prevent society from returning to its previous state, which was distinguished by numerous manifestations of the separation of interests between citizens and society, since citizens do not want this. The problem was compounded by the shock and crisis caused by the COVID-19 pandemic. Perhaps for the first time it became obvious to the state that the restoration of citizens' confidence is a fundamental condition for further progress of both the economy and society.

Third, the problems of impoverishment of the population, which have been accumulating since the end of the last century and exacerbated in connection with the COVID-19 pandemic, have become a priority for society. To change something, the society needs people who will implement these changes. The analysis of statistic data and researches of practitioners on the issue made the following truth obvious: all the trends in the formation of human capital have a negative vector of changes. As for the Human Capital Index (HCI) it consists of three components: survival as component 1; school - component 2; and health - component 3. High qualitative human capital adds up to large benefits for national economies because they become richer accumulating more human capital. As a result, between 10 and 30 percent of per capita gross domestic product (GDP) differences is attributable to cross-country differences in human capital (Hsieh, et al., 2010). This percentage could be even higher when considering the quality of education or the interactions between workers with different skills. For the purpose of this chapter it is important to estimate the contribution of education to worker productivity of the country (Table 1).

The Human Capital Project's team (World Bank, 2018) measures the HCI in terms of the productivity of the next generation of workers relative to the benchmark of complete education and full health. According to their methodology the units of the index have a natural interpretation: a value of x for a country means that the productivity as a future worker of a child born in a given year in that country is only a fraction x of what it could be under the benchmark (Table 1). Usually, survival, education and health are considered to be the most important components of the HCI, based on their contribution to worker productivity (World Bank, 2018). A country in which a child born today can expect to achieve both full health (no stunting and 100 percent adult survival) and full education potential (14 years of high-quality school by age 18) will score a value of 1 on the HCI (it ranges between 0 and 1 (García, et al., 2016). Therefore, for example, a score of 0.70 signals that the productivity as a future worker for a child born today is 30 percent below what could have been achieved with complete education and full health. If a country has a score of 0.50, then the gross domestic product (GDP) per worker could be twice as high if the country reached the benchmark of potentially complete education and full health (Table 1). The most important in this regard is due to the fact that this HCI is measured in terms of the productivity of the next generation of workers. In this case, modern education is an essential part of shaping the human capital of the future, since it will have a serious impact on the labor effectiveness of the next generation of workers. In a country at around the 25th percentile of the distribution of each of the human capital' components, a child born in 2018 will be only 43 percent as productive as that child would be under the benchmark of complete education and full health (World Bank, 2018).

Education should be considered critical to ensuring that people are able to fully realize their human capital potential (Altinok, et al., 2018). This is due to the fact that of the three analyzed components of HCI, only education can increase the "leverage" of impact on economic development. The latter is explained by the fact that education can increase the economic potential of a society, provided there are constant survival rates and health care. It becomes possible on the basis of high quality education, which is associated with the ability of the individuals to generate and master innovations of the technological revolution 4.0.

Table 1. Measuring the productivity as a future worker of a child born in 2018. Maximum productivity = 1

		A country in the		
		25th percentile	**50th percentile**	**75th percentile**
	Component	***For component X has a value of...***		
	Component 1: survival			
1	Probability of survival to age 5	0.95	0.98	0.99
A	*Contribution to productivity*	*0.95*	*0.98*	*0.99*
	Component 2: school			
	Expected years of school	9.5	11.8	13.1
	Test score (out of approx. 600)	375	424	503
2	Quality-adjusted years of school	5.7	8.0	10.5
B	*Contribution to productivity*	*0.51*	*0.62*	*0.76*
	Component 3: health			
3	Fraction of children not stunted	0.68	0.78	0.89
4	Adult survival rate	0.79	0.86	0.91
C	*Contribution to productivity**	*0.88*	*0.92*	0.95
	Overall Human Capital Index [b]	**0.43**	**0.56**	**0.72**

Source: WDR 2019 team (World Bank, 2018, WDR, 2019).

Note: "Contribution to productivity" measures how much each component of the index, as well as the overall index, contributes to the expected future productivity as a worker of a child born in 2018 relative to the benchmark of a complete education and full health. A value of x means that productivity is only a fraction x of what it would be under the benchmark of a complete education and full health. Estimates of productivity contributions are anchored in microeconometric evidence on the returns to education and health. "Quality-adjusted years of school" equals the country's test score relative to the global best test score multiplied by the country's expected years of school. a. C is calculated as the geometric average of the contributions of numbers 3 and 4 to productivity. b. A × B × C.

Judging by Table 2, no country in the world reaches 1 - the maximum value of HCI. At the same time, there is a significant discrepancy in the labor force structure between what the modern labor market requires and what the modern education system can offer. Human capital is important because there is now a higher premium on adaptability (World Bank, 2019). To thrive in today's innovation-driven economy workers need much more different mix of skills than in the past. In addition to foundational skills like literacy and numeracy, they need competencies like collaboration, creativity and problem-solving and character qualities like persistence, curiosity and initiative.

The shift in skill demand has exposed a problem in skill supply: more than a third of global companies reported difficulties filling open positions in 2014, owing to shortages of people with key skills (Manpower Group, 2014). On the eve of the COVID-19 pandemic The World Development Report, 2018 [WDR, 2018] determined the current position of the education system in the world as the real learning crisis. This is reflected in the fact that learning outcomes are poor because of low levels, high inequality, slow progress (Pritchett, 2013). On the whole children learn very little in many education systems and after several years in school, millions of students lack basic literacy and numeracy skills. Many high-performing students in middle-income countries who have risen to the top quarter of their cohorts—would rank in the bottom quarter in a wealthier country. Although some countries are making progress on learning, their progress is typically slow. Besides, the foundational cognitive skills are essential, and educational systems cannot bypass the challenges of developing them as they target higher-order skills.

The COVID-19 pandemic has added to the education crisis the quality of the inadequacy of national health systems. In the current conditions of an increase in the level of poverty in the countries of the world and, of course, a decrease in the birth rate, it becomes obvious that society should become a priority area of activity if it adequately takes into account the prevailing circumstances associated with priority factors of economic self-development. An individual with the qualities of intellectual autonomousness becomes the main driver of a dynamic economy. But to realize its potential, it is necessary to restore the integrity of society in order to create conditions for a citizen with such a quality of human capital to adequately integrate into society. Here it is about adequate education, health care and welfare, as well as restoring trust in the state as priority conditions for the self-development of the economy, society as well as the technology.

Moreover, the trust of the population in the state is largely determined not only by the quality of health care and education, but also by the subjective assessment of the prevailing social justice in society. And in this context, citizens' assessment of justice is predetermined by the presence of three types of inequality: inequality of wealth, inequality of income, and inequality of consumption. This raises the fundamental question of economic opportunities. Economic inequality can be viewed as part of a dynamic system, in which an individual's endowments and opportunities lead to differences in economic outcomes (Fig. 16).

The picture above is a broad one, and the economic situation in individual G-7 countries in inequalities of income, wealth, and consumption, as well as other economic indicators, can vary considerably (Fig. 17). Some countries perform strongly on growth or employment but with higher levels of inequality or post-tax poverty, and vice versa. In the case of inequalities of opportunity, the percentage difference in median earnings by gender covers a range from 6 to 25 percent across G-7 economies. Variations in measures of social mobility are less pronounced, with managers being 2.2 times more likely to come from a family of managers in one country versus 1.8 times more likely in another. Citizens' beliefs are not correlated with specific economic outcomes across G-7 countries. It is not the case that citizens in the most equal or unequal economies, or those with the highest or lowest levels of growth and employment, are the most or least satisfied. This suggests that citizen discontent

Table 2. The Human Capital Index (HCI), 2018

Rank	Economy	Lower bound	Value	Upper bound
157	Chad	0.28	0.29	0.37
156	South Sudan	0.27	0.30	0.33
155	Niger	0.30	0.32	0.33
154	Mali	0.29	0.32	0.34
153	Liberia	0.31	0.32	0.33
152	Nigeria	0.32	0.34	0.36
151	Sierra Leone	0.33	0.35	0.37
150	Mauritania	0.32	0.35	0.38
149	Cote d'Ivoire	0.33	0.35	0.37
148	Mozambique	0.34	0.36	0.38
147	Angola	0.33	0.36	0.39
146	Congo. Dem. Rep.	0.35	0.37	0.39
145	Yemen. Rep.	0.35	0.37	0.39
144	Burkina Faso	0.35	0.37	0.38
143	Lesotho	0.35	0.37	0.39
142	Rwanda	0.36	0.37	0.39
141	Guinea	0.35	0.37	0.39
140	Madagascar	0.35	0.37	0.39
139	Sudan	0.37	0.38	0.39
138	Burundi	0.36	0.38	0.40
137	Uganda	0.37	0.38	0.39
136	Papua New Guinea	0.36	0.38	0.40
135	Ethiopia	0.37	0.38	0.40
134	Pakistan	0.37	0.39	0.40
133	Afghanistan	0.38	0.39	0.40
132	Cameroon	0.37	0.39	0.42
131	Zambia	0.37	0.40	0.42
130	Gambia. The	0.37	0.40	0.42
129	Iraq	0.38	0.40	0.41
128	Tanzania	0.39	0.40	0.41
127	Benin	0.38	0.41	0.43
126	South Africa	0.40	0.41	0.42
12S	Malawi	0.39	0.41	0.42
124	eSwatini	0.38	0.41	0.43
123	Comoros	0.36	0.41	0.44
122	Togo	0.39	0.41	0.43
121	Senegal	0.40	0.42	0.43
120	Congo. Rep.	0.39	0.42	0.44
119	Botswana	0.40	0.42	0.44
118	Timor-Leste	0.41	0.43	0.45
117	Namibia	0.41	0.43	0.45
116	Ghana	0.42	0.44	0.45
115	India	0.43	0.44	0.45
114	Zimbabwe	0.42	0.44	0.46
113	Solomon Islands	0.43	0.44	0.45
112	Haiti	0.42	0.45	0.47
111	Lao PDR	0.43	0.45	0.47
110	Gabon	0.43	0.45	0.48
109	Guatemala	0.44	0.46	0.47
108	Vanuatu	0.45	0.47	0.48
107	Myanmar	0.46	0.47	0.49
106	Bangladesh	0.47	0.48	0.49
105	Kiribati	0.45	0.48	0.50
104	Egypt. Arab Rep.	0.47	0.49	0.50
103	Honduras	0.47	0.49	0.50
102	Nepal	0.48	0.49	0.50
101	Dominican Republic	0.48	0.49	0.51
100	Cambodia	0.47	0.49	0.51
99	Guyana	0.48	0.49	0.51
98	Morocco	0.49	0.50	0.51
97	El Salvador	0.49	0.50	0.51
96	Tunisia	0.50	0.51	0.52
95	Tonga	0.50	0.51	0.53
94	Kenya	0.50	0.52	0.53
93	Algeria	0.51	0.52	0.53
92	Nicaragua	0.51	0.53	0.54
91	Panama	0.52	0.53	0.54
90	Paraguay	0.51	0.53	0.55
89	Tajikistan	0.51	0.53	0.55
88	Macedonia, FYR	0.53	0.53	0.54
87	Indonesia	0.52	0.53	0.55
86	Lebanon	0.52	0.54	0.55
85	Jamaica	0.53	0.54	0.56
84	Philippines	0.53	0.55	0.56
83	Tuvalu	0.53	0.55	0.57
82	West Bank & Gaza	0.54	0.55	0.56
81	Brazil	0.55	0.56	0.57
80	Kosovo	0.55	0.56	0.57
79	Jordan	0.54	0.56	0.58
78	Armenia	0.56	0.57	0.58
77	Kuwait	0.56	0.58	0.59
76	Kyrgyz Republic	0.57	0.58	0.59
75	Moldova	0.57	0.58	0.59
74	Sri Lanka	0.57	0.58	0.59

continues on following page

Table 2. Continued

Rank	Economy	Lower bound	Value	Upper bound
73	Saudi Arabia	*0.57*	0.58	*0.60*
72	Peru	*0.57*	0.59	*0.60*
71	Iran. Islamic Rep.	*0.57*	0.59	*0.61*
70	Colombia	*0.58*	0.59	*0.61*
69	Azerbaijan	*0.58*	0.60	*0.62*
68	Uruguay	*0.59*	0.60	*0.61*
67	Romania	*0.59*	0.60	*0.62*
66	Ecuador	*0.59*	0.60	*0.61*
65	Thailand	*0.59*	0.60	*0.62*
64	Mexico	*0.60*	0.61	*0.61*
63	Argentina	*0.60*	0.61	*0.62*
62	Trinidad & Tobago	*0.59*	0.61	*0.63*
61	Georgia	*0.60*	0.61	*0.63*
60	Qatar	*0.60*	0.61	*0.63*
59	Montenegro	*0.61*	0.62	*0.62*
58	Bosnia & Herzegovina	*0.61*	0.62	*0.63*
57	Costa Rica	*0.61*	0.62	*0.63*
56	Albania	*0.61*	0.62	*0.63*
55	Malaysia	*0.61*	0.62	*0.63*
54	Oman	*0.61*	0.62	*0.63*
S3	Turkey	*0.61*	0.63	*0.64*
52	Mauritius	*0.60*	0.63	*0.65*
51	Mongolia	*0.60*	0.63	*0.65*
50	Ukraine	*0.67*	0.65	*0.68*
49	United Arab Emirates	*0.64*	0.66	*0.67*
48	Vietnam	*0.65*	0.67	*0.68*
47	Bahrain	*0.65*	0.67	*0.68*
46	China	*0.66*	0.67	*0.68*
45	Chile	*0.66*	0.67	*0.69*
44	Bulgaria	*0.65*	0.68	*0.70*
43	Seychelles	*0.65*	0.68	*0.71*
42	Greece	*0.67*	0.68	*0.69*
41	Luxembourg	*0.68*	0.69	*0.70*
40	Slovak Republic	*0.68*	0.69	*0.71*
39	Malta	*0.69*	0.70	*0.71*
38	Hungary	*0.69*	0.70	*0.72*
37	Lithuania	*0.70*	0.71	*0.73*
36	Croatia	*0.71*	0.72	*0.74*
35	Latvia	*0.71*	0.72	*0.74*
34	Russian Federation	*0.68*	0.73	*0.77*
32	Spain	*0.74*	0.74	*0.75*
31	Kazakhstan	*0.72*	0.75	*0.77*

Rank	Economy	Lower bound	Value	Upper bound
30	Poland	*0.73*	0.75	*0.76*
29	Estonia	*0.73*	0.75	*0.76*
28	Cyprus	*0.74*	0.75	*0.76*
33	Iceland	*0.73*	0.74	*0.75*
27	Serbia	*0.74*	0.76	*0.77*
26	Belgium	*0.75*	0.76	*0.77*
25	Macao SAR, China	*0.75*	0.76	*0.76*
24	United States	*0.75*	0.76	*0.77*
23	Israel	*0.75*	0.76	*0.78*
22	France	*0.76*	0.76	*0.77*
21	New Zealand	*0.76*	0.77	*0.78*
20	Switzerland	*0.75*	0.77	*0.78*
19	Italy	*0.76*	0.77	*0.78*
18	Norway	*0.76*	0.77	*0.78*
17	Denmark	*0.76*	0.77	*0.79*
16	Portugal	*0.77*	0.78	*0.79*
15	United Kingdom	*0.77*	0.78	*0.79*
14	Czech Republic	*0.77*	0.78	*0 79*
13	Slovenia	*0.78*	0.79	*0.80*
12	Austria	*0.78*	0.79	*0.80*
11	Germany	*0.78*	0.79	*0.81*
10	Canada	*0.79*	0.80	*0.81*
9	Netherlands	*0.79*	0.80	*0.81*
8	Sweden	*0.79*	0.80	*0.81*
7	Australia	*0.79*	0.80	*0.81*
6	Ireland	*0.79*	081	*0.82*
5	Finland	*0.80*	0.81	*0.82*
4	Hong Kong SAR, China	*0.81*	0.82	*0.83*
3	Japan	*0.83*	0.84	*0.85*
2	Korea. Rep.	*0.83*	0.84	*0.86*
1	Singapore	*0.87*	0.88	*0.90*

Source: World Bank, (2018). The Human Capital Project. Washington D.C.: The World Bank Group

Note: The Human Capital Index ranges between 0 and 1. The index is measured in terms of the productivity of the next generation of workers relative to the benchmark of complete education and full health. An economy in which a child born today can expect to achieve complete education and full health will score a value of 1 on the index. Lower and upper bounds indicate the range of uncertainty around the value of the HCI for each economy.

HCI < 0.40 0.40 ≤ HCI < 0.50 0.50 ≤ HCI < 0.60 0.60 ≤ HCI < 0.7 0.70 ≤ HCI < 0.80 0.80 ≤ HCI is influenced by a range of economic and noneconomic factors (Lange, et al., 2019; McKinsey Global Institute, June 2019).

As a result individuals in developed countries are exhibiting significant discontent (Krugman, 1997; Case, et al., 2015). On average, 63 percent of residents of OECD countries say they believe their country is on the "wrong track," according to a 2018 survey, while just 37 percent say it is heading in the "right direction" (What worries the world, 2018) (Fig. 18). Forty-three percent of individuals in advanced economies believe the average person today is worse off than 20 years ago (Global attitudes survey, 2018). They are also pessimistic about the future: 45 percent of respondents in a poll of residents of G-7 nations say their country will be "worse" or "much worse" for future generations, compared with only 27 percent saying it would be "better" or "much better." Those in disadvantaged economic positions are the most pessimistic. Individuals who say their own financial position is not advancing are three times more likely to agree with the statement "I expect the next generation to advance more slowly in the future" than those who believe their position is advancing or neutral (McKinsey Citizen Development and Confidence Research, 2018; McKinsey Global Institute, July 2016).

Figure 16. Economic inequality can be viewed as part of a dynamic system, where endowments and opportunities lead to differences in economic outcomes.
Source: McKinsey Global Institute. (2019). Inequality: A persisting challenge and its implications. Discussion Paper. June. McKinsey.com

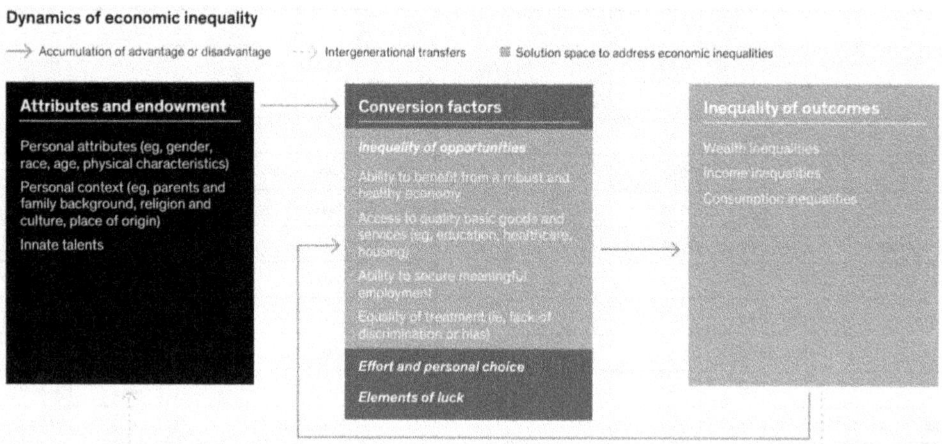

So, all the above data indicate that the state must still earn the trust of individuals who will possess the qualities of intellectually autonomous individuals. And in order to achieve this, society and the economy must offer appropriate forms of organization of human activity. And this concerns the fundamental transformations that accompany a dynamic economy at the stage of its self-development. Everything that the economy and society achieved by the beginning of the COVID-19 pandemic, unfortunately, has been connected with negative trends in relation to self-organization (education, health care and survival) of the human, and even more so, his socialization (self-development) with unequal opportunities, inequalities of income, wealth, and consumption, as well as other economic indicators that divide citizens and destroy the integrity of society. It is about the system that was based on the capital-centric form of organization of economic activity. The future of a dynamic system is associated with human-centric forms of organization of all spheres in technology, society as well as in economy.

And in this regard, the authors saw the presence of those structures that represent a dialectically complex structure and are able to structure both their internal environment and the external sphere of their functioning under the new human-centric principles of organization. It is about large and largest private companies with a mechanism of downwards and upwards causation. And these mechanisms implement their self-organization and self-development, respectively. In these processes, entrepreneurs, or rather CEOs of large and largest companies are able to nullify the uncertainty of future post-covid dynamic reality.

Figure 17. Dynamics of economic inequality in G-7 countries
Source: International Monetary Fund; OECD; World Economic Forum; World Inequality Database; Allianz; Pew Research Center; McKinsey Citizen Development and Confidence Research Survey; McKinsey Global Institute analysis, 2020. McKinsey.com

Worse than the G-7 average — Better than the G-7 average

			Median	Canada	France	Germany	Italy	Japan	United Kingdom	United States
Growth and participation	Economic indicators	Average GDP growth, 2010–18, %	1.9	2.3	1.3	2.1	0.3	1.6	1.9	2.3
		Median equivalized net income, 2016, $ thousand	24	34	24	24	18	N/A	23	36
	Employment	Employment rate, 2017, %	73	73	65	75	58	75	75	70
		Unemployment rate, 2017, %	4.5	6.4	9.2	3.8	11.4	3	4.5	4.4
	Economic fragility	Pretax relative poverty rate, %, 2016 or most recent	33	25	37	34	34	33	30	27
		Post-tax relative poverty rate, %, 2016 or most recent	12	12	8	10	14	16	11	18
	Wage stagnation	Number of income deciles showing falling real income, 2005–16	N/A	0	0	1	10	N/A	10	0
Inequality of outcome	Income	Income Gini, 2017 or most recent	0.33	0.31	0.29	0.29	0.33	0.34	0.35	0.39
		Top 1% income share, 2016, %	13	14	11	13	9	10	14	20
	Wealth	Wealth Gini, 2017	0.66	0.65	0.66	0.73	0.58	0.55	0.74	0.81
		Bottom 40% wealth share, 2016, %	3.4	3.4	2.7	0.5	4.5	5.3	3.4	-0.1
	Consumption	Share of household budgets spent on healthcare and education, 2016, %	5.9	5.9	5	6.2	4.2	5.9	3.1	10.1
Inequality of opportunity	Gender	Difference in median earnings by gender, 2014, %	17	18	10	16	8	25	17	18
	Parental occupation	Difference in likelihood that managers had parents that were managers vs laborers, 2002–14	1.92	1.94	1.93	1.88	2.22	N/A	1.81	1.9
Perceptions	Citizens' beliefs	Share of citizens who believe the average person is worse off than 20 years ago, 2018, %	48	48	56	46	72	41	53	45
		Share of citizens who believe that their country is on the wrong track, 2018, %	60	51	76	69	57	60	70	59
		Share of citizens who believe their country will be worse for future generations, 2018, %	47	33	47	48	44	50	51	42

CONCLUSION

The rapid spread of COVID-19, deadly dangerous for human life, served as stability test for the existing social foundations of national systems, as well as for the depth of mutual trust between people and society, citizens and the state. The originality of the crisis caused by the COVID-19 pandemic was due to the actions of states that failed to quickly identify the "zero" patient and introduced lockdown regimes that destroyed the structural integrity of national societies and the economics. The severity of such a test, which fell on the shoulders of individuals as their well-being and established way of living was destroyed, turned into an overestimation of the role of state and society in ensuring the stability of households. The most striking demonstration of such individual reassessments was the compliance or non-compliance by citizens with self-isolation regimes, since they became a function of the degree of their trust in the actions of their state and of individual desire to follow the extraordinary norms of behavior imposed in society in connection with the COVID-19 pandemic. Thus, the coronavirus has revealed the main "fault line" of modern societies, because of which the consequences of an unexpected infection, dangerous to human life, have become so devastating. As a result, the shock of the coronavirus pandemic highlighted the deepening societal crisis as a demonstration of the structural disunity of national societies. It is in this context the Boston Consulting Group' experts (Boston Consulting Group Perspectives, 2020) treated the COVID-19 outbreak as the first and foremost a societal crisis.

Figure 18. Answer to question "Do you believe your country is heading in the right direction, or on the wrong track?"([1] % of respondents by country)
Note: [1] Representative sample of 20,787 adults aged 16–64 in 28 participating countries, surveyed between August 24 and September 7, 2018; simple averages used for G-7, OECD, and world averages.
Source: What worries the world, Ipsos Public Affairs, September 2018; McKinsey Global Institute analysis

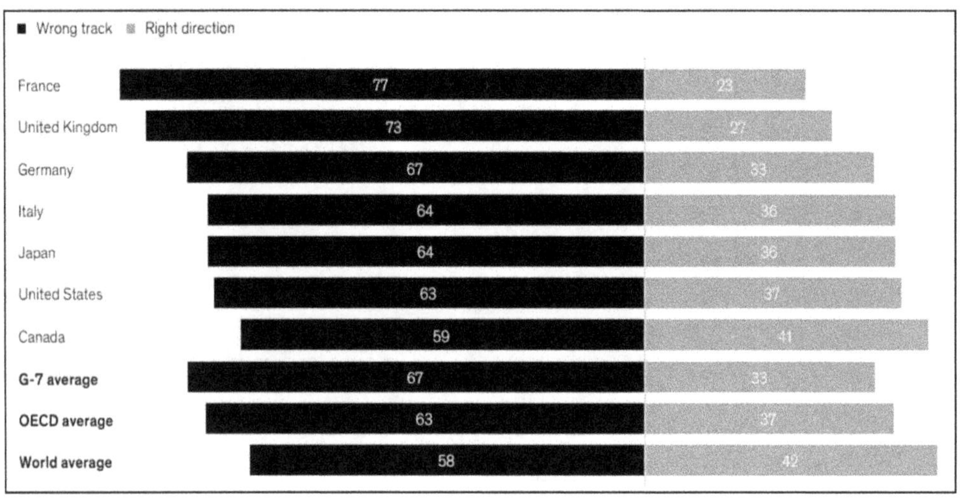

Really social and economic lockdowns aimed at halting the exponential growth of coronavirus cases in countries around the world caused unprecedented losses in both human life and national welfare. At the same time, COVID-19 proved the priority of social problems, which, moreover, were aggravated by the absolute drop in the volume of material production in the world. The pandemic dictated the uncontested subordination of the functions of the state: first, to stabilize the epidemiological situation in the country and only then to waste time for timely re-opening economics after lockdown. Moreover, the specificity of the first problem is related to the fact that, together with the physical health of citizens in the context of levelling the epidemiological situation in the country, perhaps the most important thing for states becomes to eliminate the negative consequences of the societal crisis. In the latter case, it is about the mechanisms of socialization of individuals in the structure of society.

From the viewpoint of the strategic goals of the social communities' progress in the post-coronavirus future, the most important becomes the restoration of their societal integrity as an objective condition for the rapid economic reopening after the lockdown and for the adequate acceptable scenario of the events in a case of the second and the third waves of the coronavirus pandemic. Actually, the following conclusion of World Health Organisation (WHO) Strategy Update of 14 April 2020 testifies to this: "Governments must also repurpose and engage all available public, community and private sector capacity to rapidly scale up the public health system." It is about restoring the sphere of intersection of the values of society as the integrity of citizens and public choice aggregated by the state.

Almost all experts admit that after the COVID-19 pandemic, the global world will become different, but it will retain both citizens and society and a societal crisis, which must be eliminated by the state as an indispensable condition for further socio-economic progress. In this regard, it should be emphasized that the institutional aspect of the mechanism of public intervention in society and the economy becomes of particular importance. This is due to the fact that it is the formal institutions in the hands of the state that can become an effective tool for restoring the societal integrity of national communities. And in this case, it is about the priority of the mechanism of institutionalizing socially significant norms of behavior of citizens in society. And the latter is impossible without restoring the societal integrity of society, and the trust of individuals in their state.

The social crisis predetermined the "new normal", which at its core contains the question of the society that was built and which will be constructed after COVID-19. Within the framework of the theory of shocks, the contours of the uncertain post-COVID-19 future include the restoration of the integrity of society and, on its basis, of the economy, the replacement of capital-centric principles of organization in the economy with human-centric ones, the formation of a new technological paradigm by individuals with the qualities of intellectual autonomousness as the basis for self-development of the socio-economic system.

REFERENCES

Acemoglu & Autor. (2012). What does human capital do? A review of Goldin and Katz's *The Race between Education and Technology. Journal of Economic Literature, 50*(2), 426–463.

Acemoglu, D. (1998). Why do new technologies complement skills? Directed technical change and wage inequality. *Quarterly Journal of Economics, 113*(4), 1055–89.

Altinok, N., Angrist, N., & Patrinos, H. A. (2018). *Global data set on education quality (1965–2015).* Policy Research Working Paper, 8314. Washington, DC: The World Bank Group.

Boston Consulting Group. (2020). *COVID-19: Win the Fight, Win the Future*. Featured Insights. April. BCG.

Boston Consulting Group Perspectives. (2020). *COVID-19: Facts, scenarios, and actions for leaders.* Version 2.2. BCG.

Case, A., & Deaton, A. (2015). Rising morbidity and mortality in midlife among white non-Hispanic Americans in the 21st century. *Proceedings of the National Academy of Sciences*, 112(49), 15078–83. 10.1073/pnas.1518393112

Cheng, Dua, Jacobs, Kerlin, Law, Safran, Schubert, Wang, Xu, & Zegeye. (2020). *Reimagining the postpandemic economic future*. McKinsey & Company.

García, J. L., Heckman, J. J., Leaf, D. E., & Prados, M. J. (2016). *The Life-Cycle Benefits of an Influential Early Childhood Program.* NBER Working Paper 22993, National Bureau of Economic Research.

Global attitudes survey. (2018). Pew Research Center.

Global Health Security Index. (2019). *Building Collective Action and Accountability*. The Economist Intelligence Unit. Johns Hopkins Center for Health Security.

Goldin, C., & Katz, L. (2008). The Race between Education and Technology. Belknap Press for Harvard University Press.

Hsieh, C.-T., & Klenow, P. J. (2010). Development accounting. *American Economic Journal. Macroeconomics*, *2*(1), 207–223. doi:10.1257/mac.2.1.207

Krugman, P. (1997). *The Age of Diminished Expectations. U.S. Economic Policy in the 1990s* (3rd ed.). MIT Press.

Lange, G. M., Wodon, Q., & Carey, K. (Eds.). (2019). *The Changing Wealth of Nations 2018: Building a Sustainable Future*. World Bank.

Manpower Group. (2014). *The Talent Shortage Continues: How the Ever Changing Role of HR Can Bridge the Gap*. Manpower Group.

McKinsey & Company. (2020). *Crushing coronavirus uncertainty: The big 'unlock' for our economies. Strategy & Corporate Finance Practice*. McKinsey.com.

McKinsey Citizen Development and Confidence Research. (2018). McKinsey & Company.

McKinsey Global Institute. (2016). *Poorer than their parents? Flat or falling incomes in advanced economies*. Mckinsey & Company.

McKinsey Global Institute. (2019). *Inequality: A persisting challenge and its implications*. Discussion Paper. McKinsey.com.

Okamoto, G. (2020). Knightmare Uncertainty. *IMF Finance & Development, 57*(3).

Pritchett, L. (2013). The Rebirth of Education: Schooling Ain't Learning. Washington, DC: Center for Global Development.

Rajan, R. G. (2010). *Fault Lines: How Hidden Fractures Still Threaten the World Economy*. Princeton University Press.

RBC. (2020). *The interview of the Dean of the Lomonosov's Moscow State University Professor A. Auzan to RBC*. Retrieved from: https://www.rbc.ru /society/10/04/2020/5e902e8b9a79479dc4a29234

Reinhart, C. V., & Rogoff, K. S. (2009). *This Time is Different: Eight Centuries of Financial Folly*. Princeton University Press.

Remes, J., Linzer, K., Singhal, S., Dewhurst, M., Dash, P., Woetzel, J., Smit, S., Evers, M., & Wilson, M. (2020). Prioritizing health: A prescription for prosperity. Executive summary. McKinsey Global Institute Report.

Susskind, D. (2020). How will the world be different after COVID-19? Finance & Development, 57(2), 26-27.

Taylor, L. H., Latham, S. M., & Woolhouse, M. E. (2001). Risk factors for human disease emergence. *Philosophical Transactions of the Royal Society of London. Series B, Biological Sciences*, *356*(1411), 983–989. doi:10.1098/rstb.2001.0888 PMID:11516376

WDR. (2018). *World Development Report 2018: Learning to Realize Education's Promise*. World Bank.

WDR. (2019). *World Bank. World Development Report 2019: The Changing Nature of Work*. World Bank.

What Worries the World. (2018). Ipsos Public Affairs.

World Bank. (2018). *The Human Capital Project*. The World Bank Group.

World Bank. (2019). *World Development Report 2019: The Changing Nature of Work*. World Bank.

Chapter 9
COVID-19 Shock and Schumpeterian "Creative Destruction": Self-Enforcing Companies and Self-Development of the Future Dynamic Economy

ABSTRACT

The COVID-19 pandemic shock pushed the objective processes of discontinuity in the evolution of a static economy. The new path of self-development of the economy in its dynamic state starts with transferring system to the basis of the Industrial Revolution 4.0. In this connection, the fundamental question arises related to what structure will be the main driver of the future dynamic processes. In this regard, the idea of J. Schumpeter about the entrepreneurs' ability to carry out "creative destruction" becomes highly relevant. It is about private business capable of self-regulation as well as building post-coronavirus systemic integrities both in the technological sphere, in society and economy. It is about their forced by COVID-19 understanding of the main factor of their success, associated with the employees and their potential which is largely formed in society and used in firms if they construct their internal organization on the principles of human centrism.

INTRODUCTION

The COVID-19 pandemic has become the greatest threat to business, which must reopen after the first and second waves of the COVID-19 pandemic, but cannot build long-term growth strategies in conditions of complete uncertainty and lack of understanding of the shocks' causes and their connection with the socio-economic systems' dynamics. In this situation, there are becoming more and more significant the expert developments of specialists in the field of adequate strategies of firms that re-build their busi-

DOI: 10.4018/978-1-7998-4309-2.ch009

ness after the pandemic. Indeed, it is difficult to reconstruct the future without a fundamental theoretical understanding of the phenomenon of shock and of the quality of uncertainty of the post-coronavirus reality. In such a situation, businesses are faced with the need for their companies' executive officers (CEOs) to re-think the quality of this uncertainty and the new factors of the business success in the emerging "New Normal".

The COVID-19 pandemic shock clearly laid bare a phenomenon that has become increasingly evident since the early 2000s. It is about the subjective component of all processes that took place in a self-organizing economy and in society. If abstracting from the essence of the phenomena of self-organization and self-development of economic systems (Chapters 2-5), then repeating financial bubbles remain on the surface; growing imbalances in national communities that divide citizens according to the degree of concentration of income and wealth; growing inequality in opportunities; inequality of access to education and health care, etc. A consequence of the growing contradictions between the interests of citizens and society, citizens and the state was the expansion of the area of shadow business, the reduction of the middle class, and, consequently, the prospects for households with lower middle income to raise their social status, not to mention the growing corruption in the higher echelons of power. The humanitarian disaster caused by the COVID-19 pandemic has made these problems obvious to everyone. The threat to life in connection with the coronavirus infection has affected everyone; the problem of deteriorating well-being or simply physical survival has spread to the most; the lost generation of young people has become a threat to the progress of all national communities.

COVID-19 shock has occurred in the modern capital-centric socio-economic system therefore it is objectively necessary to rethink its basic principles of functioning in the context of the devastating consequences that it caused. The same idea is discussed in several serious monographs published in 2019-2020. They substantiate the need to displace the capital-centric model of organizing socio-economic systems, since it has exhausted its potential (passed the optimum point). (Lonergan, and et al., 2020; Milanovic, 2011, 2019; Sandbu, 2020). Consequently, in the future, it will not be able to provide steadily growing rates of economics and of the welfare of citizens. These thoughts are shared by international expert communities studying the problems of private business development in the context of the COVID-19 pandemic and in the post-pandemic period, as well as developing specific strategic solutions for companies in conditions of complete uncertainty.

Arguing theoretically, the authors presented the structure of system categories and the mechanisms of their self-movement and, following dialectical logic, came to the conclusion that the functions of architecting structural bonds of a dynamic economy and the corresponding society can only be performed by companies. For this they must be viable, resilient, i.e. self-enforcing one. In this capacity, only large and largest companies act, which are dialectically complex organizational integrities that are capable to mediate downwards and upwards causation mechanisms. Downwards causation mechanism structures the individual behavior of employees as team members and institutionalizes its collective behavior. In the context of the COVID-19 pandemic, companies were the first to face a fundamental change in the principles of building a super-team of human potential and technological capabilities, which are increasingly focused on the motivational aspects of talents. It is in this context that categories such as trust, inclusiveness, openness, belonging, etc. are increasingly discussed in publications of international expert communities (Smit, et al. 2020; Davies, et al. 2019; Ghose, 2020; Dixon-Fyle, 2020]. The expansion by companies of the practice of using the "Inclusion & Diversity" ("I&D") strategy testifies to cardinal organizational changes in the internal structure based on the principles of human centricity (Boston Consulting Group, 2019).

As for the upwards causation mechanism, then self-enforcing companies are able to mediate it by structuring the external environment according to their requirements, which includes their interactions with numerous partners and with all stakeholders. It is by implementing the upwards causation mechanism that companies are able to re-architect the New Normal in society and economy. Moreover, they will do this by recreating (reproducing) in the external environment of their interactions human centric principals of organization, i.e. generating the process of self-organization of individuals with the qualities of intellectual autonomy and creating conditions for their self-development (socialization) as a growing middle class. And the latter is the structure-forming basic level of society, predetermining the integrity of society and realizing the boundless potential of its economic opportunities. All this allows the authors to single out large and largest self-enforcing companies, resilient in uncertain conditions of the COVID reality, as the main drivers mediating the mechanism of self-development of a dynamic economy, performing the main mission of transferring the entire human system to a new technological paradigm and introducing human-centric principles of organization of human activities. All this, with a reasonable approach of the state, will make it possible to realize in the future the limitless possibilities for social progress.

Based on the above, the chapter structure includes the sections devoted to the following issues: (1) the problems of self-enforcing (self-sufficient) companies and their ability to "creatively destroy" the structures of a static economy and to start building the new ones for its dynamic state beginning with the institutionalization of the downwards causation mechanism to reconcile collective routines and individual habits within firms; (2) the formation of strategies for self-sufficient companies, taking into account the main parameters of "Inclusive & Diverse", the adequate combination of which lets it possible to solve the fundamental puzzle of today associated with the introduction and institutionalization of human-centric principles of the internal organization of firms; (3 factors of the sustainability of self-sufficient companies in a dynamic economy associated with the dialectics of forming teams of intellectually autonomous individuals with the involvement of modern technologies with endless possibilities; (4) the role of self-sufficient companies in building new structural links of a dynamic economy through the mechanism of upwards causality and in institutionalizing the basic structural level of post-covid reality, represented by the middle class.

9.1. Self-Enforcing Companies and the "Creative Destruction" Effect for Dynamic Economy: Institutionalization of the Downwards Causation Mechanism for Reconciling Collective Routines and Individual Habits

The specificity of the shock of the COVID-19 pandemic manifested itself in an instant breakdown of vertical and horizontal structural ties in economic systems. In a matrix form, these issues are presented by Boston Consulting Group' (BCG) experts in Fig. 1. In their opinion, the COVID-19 shock uniquely raises liquidity and capital risks in both the financial system and the real economy simultaneously. Fundamental causal relationships mediating the self-movement of real markets disappeared due to shock and the economy was blocked. This means that the formal institutions that specified all relationships for the purpose of strengthening its integrity also ceased to function. As a result, the self-organization of the economic system was under threat, but this was only the "visible part of the iceberg".

The point is that the shock caused by the actions of national governments, which tore apart the object component of all structural interactions (market exchanges), was reflected in their subjective component. This is the main difference between the current situation and all previous shocks, since the form

Figure 1. BCG experts' views on the interrelation of structural problems of financial and real markets in a self-organizing economy
Source: BCG Center for Macroeconomics analysis

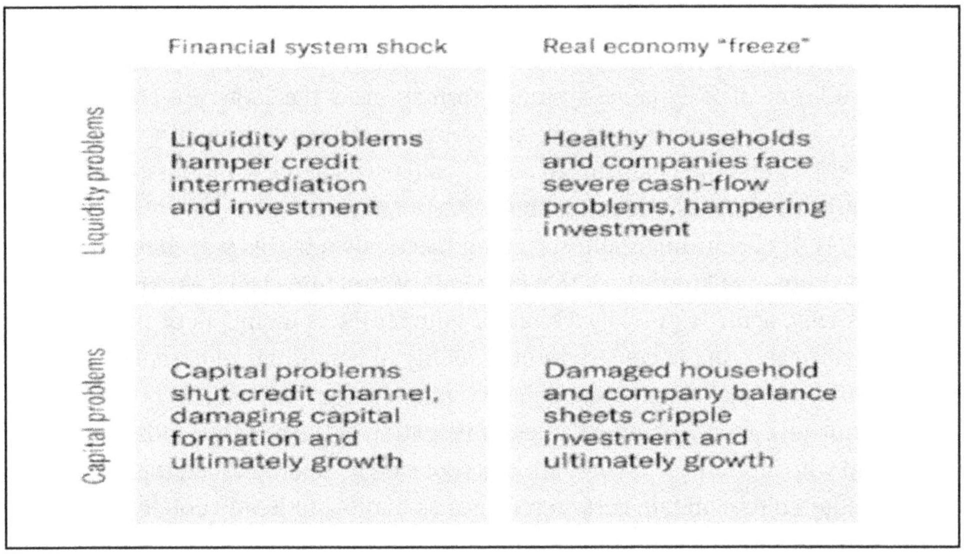

of its manifestation has ceased to be only price one and associated exclusively with a certain market of the traded asset. The shock of the COVID-19 pandemic not only broke the continuity of the process of self-organization of a static economy, but also outlined the main "fault line" of such an evolution - the lack of dialectical interaction between society and the economic system. Thus, the shock laid bare the limit in the complication of a static economy without taking into account the state of society and the characteristics of socialization of subjects of economic activity. Overcoming these limitations is associated with the operation of the law of denial of negation and the implementation of a dialectical leap into an indefinite post-covid future by a static economy, realizing its dynamic transformation. As for the interaction of statics and dynamics of economic systems and the dialectical laws that govern them, the authors theoretically put this puzzle together (Chapters 2 and 3). However, the question remains open as to who will perform the function of the self-development mechanism of a dynamic economy if the old structural ties of the self-organizing system are destroyed, and new ones have not yet appeared. In fact, this is related to the specific consequences of the shock implementation of the law of denial of negation in relation to the vertical and horizontal structures of a static economy.

Returning to the philosophical ideas about the system, elements and structure, the authors emphasize that in the conditions of the existing integrity of the system, the functions of the mechanism of its self-organization are successfully performed by the structure in its various modifications and complications. And in the conditions of its destruction, only its elements can fulfill the mission of ensuring self-propulsion of the system. To do this, they must participate in dialectically related processes of differentiation and integration of economic (as well as all human) activities, mediate the action of mechanisms of positive and negative selection, be able to divide into smaller elements and combine into more and more complex ones. This is on the one hand. On the other hand, they should be able to eliminate the main defect (fault line) of a static economy that emerged in connection with the shock of COVID-19 and restore the dialectical relationship between society and the economy. In this context, according to the authors, only the large and largest business can act as elements of dynamic systems in the economy, society, and, by the way, in technology, provided there are progressively thinking CEOs. Referring to the developments of J. Schumpeter, it can be argued that only they are capable of "creative destruction" and the construction of a new reality. Moreover, these firms as organizations are self-enforcing. And this becomes decisive argument in the theoretical justification by the authors of viable companies as organizations capable of realizing the self-development of dynamic systemic formations in the economy, society and technology.

A surprising fact was the coincidence of self-enforcing mechanisms regulating the self-movement of companies, in fact, with similar mechanisms of self-organization at the level of systemic integrity in the economy. It is about institutions as structures that determine the integrity of organizations in business (Hodgson, et al., 2004). By acquiring a self-enforcing mechanism in this way, large companies become organizations that have emergent properties that elementary structures lack (Argyris, et al., 1996; Levitt, et al., 1988). That is why, acting as the workforce of companies as members of their team, individuals acquire a priority significance in the construction of reality in conditions of complete uncertainty of the post-COVID-19 future. The fact is that companies as organizations in business provide a kind of social and physical environment, a space for action and manifestation of the habits of individuals as team members. If an individual who has left the organization is replaced by another, then the beginner has to learn the habits that are required to maintain certain routines as habits of already collective ones. As a result, the organization becomes self-enforcing, since it has internal structural links that ensure its integrity and implement the mechanism of self-movement. In the course of its functioning, the company implements its routines (as collective habits) through the object and subjective components (Blitz, 1992; Kontopoulos, 1993, Hodgson 2002, Weissman, 2000). In the process of its self-movement, the organization forms, reproduces and constructs new organizational routines, and, consequently, the individual habits of employees corresponding to them. Comprehension of the mutual influence of the theory of self-enforcing organization on the example of companies and the theory of a self-moving economic system (Aldrich, 1999) makes it possible to dialectically evaluate the downward and upward causation mechanisms in relation to social phenomena in their constancy and change. And this becomes especially important in the face of complete uncertainty of the future in connection with the shock of the COVID-19 pandemic. It is in this context that the authors identified the priority place of companies as organizations in business able to implement the mechanism of self-development of dynamic systems in all spheres of human activity. Moreover, business did not have such a unique chance in the context of the self-organization of the economy, since structural ties and corresponding formal institutions predetermined "meta-habits" as routines and their behavior.

In the context of constructing an uncertain reality after the end of the COVID-19 pandemic, it is firms that are able to structure the habits of individuals as members of their teams, as well as collective "meta-habits" as routines at the level of the entire organization. Mutually influencing each other in the course of intra-firm interaction of individuals, they structure the internal environment of the company. G.M. Hodgson (Hodgson, 2003) determined the fundamental role of habits in the reproduction of the rule-like behavior of individuals, which should be interpreted equally and as a consequence and as the reason for interaction with other individuals in their rule-like behavior. Then institutions should be understood as a relatively durable system of rules that can form habits and reproduce them in the actions of individuals through the mechanism of downwards causation. By structuring, limiting and directing individual behavior, institutions as social structures are able not only to shape the inclinations and behavior of individuals, but also to change their intentions. In fact, institutions depend on individuals for their existence, and individuals, in turn, can change them. In this interpretation, institutions are both objective "external" structures and subjective, "from the head of a person", products of human behavior (Hodgson, 2003). As for the individuals and the structure of the organization, they represent a typical dialectical pair that mediates the interaction of subjects, the stability of which predetermines individual habits and collective routines fixed by institutions (Archer, 1995). This is the meaning of "downward" and "upward" causality mediated by institutions (Hodgson, 2002, PP. 159-180).

The concept of "downwards causation" first appeared in psychology in the work of the Nobel Prize-winning psychologist and biologist Roger W. Sperry (Sperry, 1964; Sperry, 1969). Along with other scientists, K.R. Popper, and J.C. Eccles paid attention to this topic (Popper, et al., 1977) as well as others. By R.W. Sperry, any developing causes of the higher levels are due to the causal processes of the lower levels. Applied to organizations, institutions restrict individual behavior and develop the habits of individuals and the collective routines of the company's team to certain ones. G.M. Hodgson linked top-down causation to the ability of institutions to influence individual habits of thought and action (Hodgson, 2003).

Let us single out the feature of institutions that turns organizations, represented by modern companies, into the main actors in the self-development of a dynamic economy. It is about the hidden and very important ability of institutions to shape and change the individual dispositions and claims of individuals working in firms. It is in this that the function of institutions is manifested to mediate a stable process of "downward causation" in society. If it is possible to explain how institutional structures generate new or change existing habits, then the mechanism of causing downward causation becomes clear. According to G.M. Hodgson (Hodgson, 1988), it is institutions that have the property of transformative causation, affecting ingrained habits of a certain way of thinking and behavior. As a result of the repeated implementation of these actions, new habits of individuals and their individual behavior can arise, and habitual inclinations also change. Moreover, a significant part of the thought processes takes place within and taking into account public institutions. Habit is the key mechanism for this transformation. Institutions as social structures are associated with downward causation and reproduction of individual action. In part, the dependence of institutions on habits allows institutions to take root in the inclinations of individuals. Institutions are structures that individuals both encounter and give rise to. Institutions and their routines are used as templates in creating habits, forming intentions, making choices. As a result, transformative downward causation is an integral part of social life. These transformative causal processes are actually possible psychological processes of imitation, adaptation, conditioning and cognition.

The authors agree with the opinion of O.E. Williamson (Williamson, 1975) and R.N. Coase (Coase, 1937), who argued for the root rationale of the firm by assuming that transaction costs in viable firms are lower than they would be if production was coordinated through the market. Then, following G.M. Hodgson (Hodgson, 1997) individuals, as they form teams of companies, develop capabilities and enter into agreements that emerge from the firm's new institutional environment. As a result, the company will have a transformative effect on individuals (Hodgson, 1988). If habits are propensities or predispositions and behavior is action, then once habits are established, they become a potential basis for new intentions or beliefs, thus acting as a key hidden link in the causal chain. In this context, the transformative downward causation becomes understandable, which manifests itself in the form of creating and forming habits.

In other words, social institutions have structuring, changing and restrictive properties, causing new perceptions and new dispositions in individuals. Following the new habits that determine the thinking and behavior of individuals, their new preferences and intentions arise, not only within the firm, but outside it within the framework of society. A. Marshall associated with them "the development of new activities that generate new individual needs" (Marshall, 1949, P. 76). T.B. Veblen described this more specifically in connection with the psychological mechanisms involved in these processes. He was sure that today's situation shapes tomorrow's institutions through a process of coercion and selection, influencing the usual human vision of things (Veblen, 1899, P. 190). The individual is limited in his actions. In this regard, he acquires habits that are compatible with the restrictions both at the level of firms and the whole society.

As a result, acting indirectly on individual decisions, on habitual predispositions, social institutions, structured by companies, implement the action of a downward causal relationship, without reducing individual interactions to their results. Moreover, ascending causality from individuals to institutions is also possible without the assumption of a given or impeccably conceived individual (Chapter 10). However, in general, it should be emphasized that the above reasoning is not limited to either exclusively individuals or exclusively institutions. It is about a circular movement or mutual influence: a positive return from the institution to individuals, and from individuals to the institutions responsible for the integrity of the organization of the company, increases the stability of the self-enforcing company and its mechanism, represented by the institutional structure (Hodgson, 1998, PP. 166-192).

A theoretical understanding of the patterns of self-enforcement of companies is of great importance for determining the drivers in the modern economy, which, in the context of the COVID-19 pandemic and even more so in the post-coronavirus period, will structure "the New Normal" in the uncertain future. And this is very important because the coronavirus has created the great uncertainty, elevated stress and anxiety, and prompted tunnel vision, in which people focus only on the present rather than toward the future (Leonard, 2007). If the information is unavailable or inconsistent, and when people feel unsure about what they know (or anyone knows), individuals greatly desire for transparency, guidance, and making sense out of what has happened. While some may already be seeking meaning from the crisis and moving into the "next normal," others, feeling rising uncertainty and worried about the future, may not yet be ready for hope. And it becomes also true that crisis can produce great leaders and communicators, those whose words and actions comfort in the present, restore faith in the long term, and are remembered long after the crisis has finished. In this crisis the subjective factor connected with the leaders becomes of the great importance, because of their potential to build organizational resilience through an extended period of uncertainty, and even turn a crisis into a catalyst for positive change (Mendy, et al., 2020).

Every crisis has a life cycle, emotional states so it becomes possible to frame the COVID-19 crisis in five stages: resolve, resilience, return, re-imagination, and reform (David, 1994, PP. 297–316). These stages could lead the business to the next normal that will emerge after COVID-19 has been controlled. The duration of each stage depends on many factors including social institutions as well as on downward causal mechanism of the companies' structures (Fig. 2).

At a crisis's onset disruptive inputs overwhelm an individual ability to process the information. High levels of uncertainty, perceived threats, and fear can even lead to some kind of "cognitive freezing" (Edelman trust barometer, 2020). Employers often underestimate how much their employees depend on them as trusted sources (Clifford, 2020). As the COVID-19 health crisis turns into a lingering financial and economic crises, uncertainty and doubt will challenge efforts to restore business confidence. CEOs will face a critical period in which they will need to instill resilience in individuals as the members of their teams and tap sources of hope, trust, and optimism in order to unlock creativity and build momentum for the future. Channelling positive sentiments and encouraging a sense of broader community will be critical elements in building that momentum (Luthan, et al., 2007, PP. 774–800). This context makes it possible to understand the content of the institutionalization of new individual habits and collective routines that will shape the structure of the company and mediate its institutional downward causal mechanism in the new conditions caused by COVID-19. That is why, in the context of the introduction of the lockdown regime and blocking the activities of the majority of the company, the task of restoring the integrity of the company becomes unprecedentedly significant. It is about of rebuilding a common social identity and a sense of belonging based on shared values, norms, and habits.

Figure 2. Adjust your communication mix by your current crisis stage
Source: Mendy, Ana, Mary Lass Stewart, and Kate VanAkin (2020). A leader's guide: Communicating with teams, stakeholders, and communities during COVID-19. Organization Practice. McKinsey & Company. April. McKinsey.com

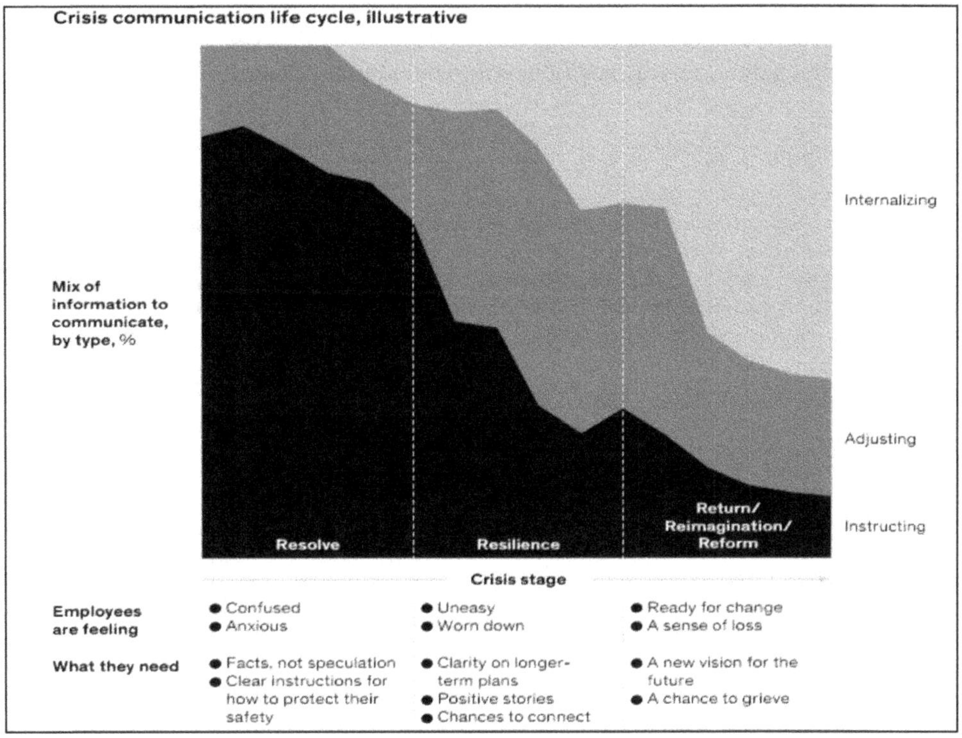

Many studies suggest that social bonds grow stronger during times of great uncertainty (Haslam, et al., 2010) (Fig. 3). Thus, the subjective aspect of organizational changes within the firm, including the institutionalization of the behavior of individuals and collective behavior, comes to the fore in comprehending the strategic actions of companies in the indefinite future of COVID and post-COVID reality. Companies weathered previous economic crises better by intervening early. Even more significantly, these resilient companies tend to outperform not just during the recovery but also for years to come. Thus, the construction of post-coronavirus reality is predetermined by the actions of resilient (self-enforcing) companies, which understand the importance of institutions that ensure their structural stability and correct the individual habits and behavior of individuals as their employees through the downward causal mechanism of their organization.

Let's make a reservation right away that the state will be ready only for "the Great Reset" (Patterson, 2020), since it will strive with all its might to restore what ensures the stability of the system in its previous state. Like the structure of the system, the state is intended to strengthen the stability of the socio-economic system in its previous state. Being empowered by the society, it cannot go beyond this fundamental mission: to keep the integrity of the system in a static state.

Following this logic, it can be assumed that "if the top (the state) cannot", then the mission of transferring the system to its dynamic state - as the realization of the moment of self-development - must be fulfilled by another structural level, which is represented by private business. And only indirectly through the upward causal mechanism of organizing companies resilient ones of them will be able to gradually form a basic structural level in society and in the economy (Chapter 9.4). And it is about the middle class, which is able to form the basic structural level of society, complementing the "creative destruction" implemented by resilient companies. Thus, understanding the "New Normal" of post-COVID-19 reality in the context of the formation of a dynamic economy at the stage of its self-development, then its main designer becomes undoubtedly resilient companies with self-enforcement quality.

Figure 3. Resilient (self-enforcing) companies did better at the outset of the downturn and afterward
Note: This analysis excludes financial companies.
[1]Calculated as average of subsector median performance of resilient and nonresilient companies; includes 1,140 companies.
[2] Resilient companies defined as top geometric mean TRS quantile by sector.
Source: CPAnalytics; McKinsey analysis; Smit, Sven, Martin Hirt, Ezra Greenberg, Hortense de la Boutetière, Bob Sternfels, and Daniel Pacthod. (2020). As you return from the summer break, can you lead toward a COVID-Exit? Strategy & Corporate Finance Practice. McKinsey&Company. McKinsey.com

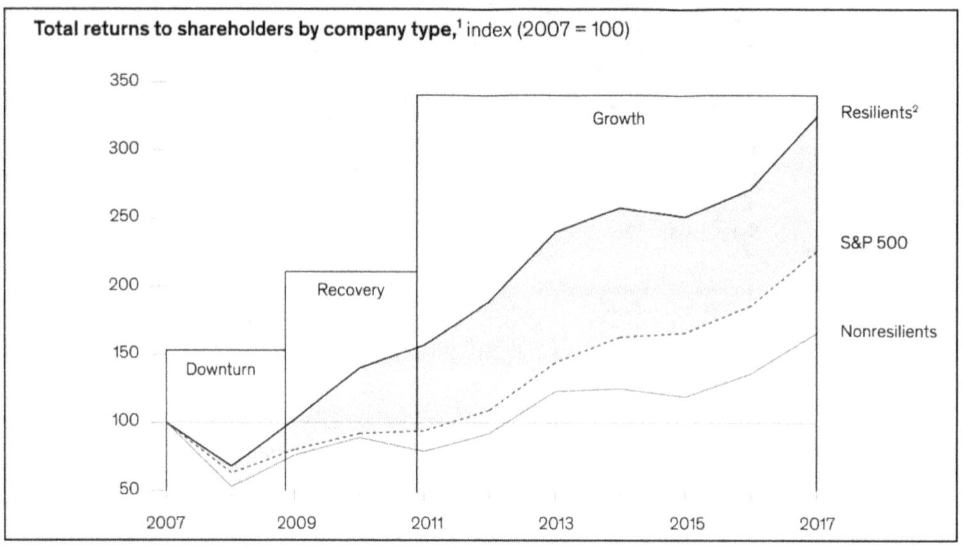

9.2. The "Inclusive & Diverse" Strategy of Self-Enforcing Companies: Institutionalization of Human-Centric Principles of Their Internal Organization

It is necessary to interpret the main feature of the human-centric socio-economic system from the point of view of the theory of shocks. All people-created systems - technological, economic, and social - are characterized by the fact that at a certain stage of their complication they acquire the ability to self-organize and self-development. This happens as the fundamental structural level is formed horizontally. It is represented by dialectically interacting pairs of participants of exchange operations. Moreover, all self-organization processes are based on the interaction of two dialectically related processes of disintegration and of integration of human activity. The meaning of their interaction is very simple: the more specialized types of activity can be combined into a cooperative system, the more the mutual benefits will be. A.A. Bogdanov (Bogdanov, 1934) paid great attention to these general organizational processes (Chapters 2, 3). A modern interpretation of these phenomena, adapted to the practice of contemporary companies, appeared in the interpretation of the experts from McKinsey & Company. So in 2015 there was a publication titled «Why diversity matters», in 2018 – «Delivering through diversity», and in 2020 – «Diversity wins: How inclusion matters». In other words, the phenomenon that A.A. Bogdanov defined as "specialization", "division", "disintegration" applied to the macro-level of the economics in the modern sense is adapted as diversity to the level of firms. In fact, the human-centric organization is the most important component of these fundamental transformations that the capital-centric system created by people came close to. COVID-19 pandemic proved that in the achieved form, it cannot progress, being dependent on capital and its investment preferences, which predetermine the division of society (disintegration, diversity) rather than its integration (inclusion). This predetermines the polarization of wealth and income, and the shrinking of the middle class and the growth of antagonism between different segments of the population, as well as between citizens and the state. The fundamental foundations of the post-COVID-19 reality should be based on the dialectical combination of the diversity (specialization/disintegration) and inclusion (cooperation /integration) of people of various specializations within the framework of a human-centric system with the priority of inclusion.

In this connection the experts of McKinsey & Company (Dixon-Fyle, et al., 2020) were among the first to adapt this idea to private business' practice in connection with post-COVID-19 future. Indeed, a successful (resilient, self-enforcing) companies should focus on building a team (the factor of including everyone in the success of the team) of people who have a highly professional specialization and who are united by a common goal. In this context, the essence of the processes of structuring the organizational integrity of the company should be emphasized. It is about the institutionalization of downward causal mechanism of structuring (coordination) of individual habits (and behavior) under the influence of the collective routines (and behavior) of the entire company. According to McKinsey & Company, as to the trajectories of hundreds of companies (more than 1,000 large companies from 15 countries) since 2014 the overall slow growth in diversity in fact masks a growing polarization among these organizations. These diversity winners are adopting systematic, business-led approaches to inclusion and diversity (I&D) as well as to create a long-lasting inclusive culture and to promote inclusive behavior. In fact, it is about the introduction of human-centric principles of the internal organization of companies. This conclusion is proved by specific data (Fig. 4).

Before COVID-19 pandemic this growing polarization between high and low performers was reflected in an increased likelihood of a performance penalty. In 2019, fourth-quartile companies for gender diversity on executive teams were 19 percent more likely than companies in the other three quartiles to underperform on profitability—up from 15 percent in 2017 and 9 percent in 2015. At companies in the fourth quartile for both gender and ethnic diversity, the penalty was even steeper in 2019: they were 27 percent more likely to underperform on profitability than all other companies in our data set. As a result the experts of McKinsey & Company suggest 2 fundamental factors of successful survival when fighting the coronavirus pandemic: a permanent business-led approach to inclusion and diversity organizational principals, and bold action on inclusion (Dixon-Fyle, et al., 2020). This is a specific manifestation of the downward causal mechanism in the context of the COVID-19 pandemic.

So, the actions of companies and their CEOs in the direction of optimizing the I&D approach as the basis for the successful use of digital and human capabilities is a decisive factor in building up a critical mass of companies in national economies as an indispensable condition for the formation of the human-centric socio-economic system. This is where the dialectic of self-development of people-created systems is realized. In this context, there is also a mechanism of shocks that destroy structural ties that have reached their ultimate state and require their replacement through the low of double negation, which will accelerate progress of the dynamic economic system in the post-COVID-19 future. Taking into account all of the above, it is necessary to highlight the fundamental processes that occur at the structural level of the business. It is about dialectically interconnected phenomena of "diversity" and "inclusion" (D&I), which are directly related to the transformation of the capital-centric system into a human-centric one. In the categories of shocks' theory, it is about the essence and forms of manifestation of an objectively operating mechanism of self-development of the dynamic economic system.

Figure 4. Financial outperformance of the business diversity in executive teams

Source: Dixon-Fyle, Sundiatu, Vivian Hunt, and Sara Prince (2020). Diversity wins: How inclusion matters. McKinsey & Company. May 19 Data Set

Notes: [1] Likelihood of financial outperformance vs the national industry median; p-value ˂0.05, except 2004 data where p-value ˂0.1, [2] n=383; Latin America, UK, and USA; earning before interest and taxes (EBIT) margin 2010-13. [3] n=991; Australia, Brazil, France, Germany, India, Japan, Mexico, Nigeria, Singapore, South Africa, UK, and US; EBIT margin 2011-15. [4] n=1,039; 2017 companies for which gender data available in 2019, plus Denmark, Norway, and Sweden; EBIT margin 20141-18. [5] n=364; Latin America, UK, and US; EBIT margin 2010-13. [6] n=589; Brazil, Mexico, Singapore, South Africa, UK, and US; EBIT margin 2011-15. [7] n=533; Brazil, Mexico, Nigeria, Singapore, South Africa, UK, and US, where ethical data available in 2019; EBIT margin 2014-18.

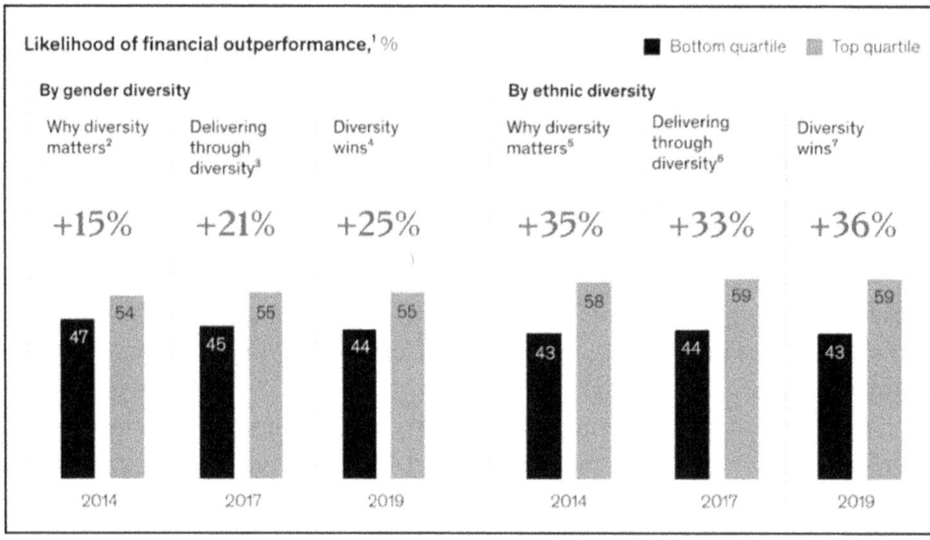

Almost a mirror image of the dialectic of specialization (separation) and cooperation (unification) processes occurring in the system at the macro level is the structural level represented by business. Only in modern publications on the organizational problems of firms in the before-coronavirus and post-coronavirus realities these processes are concretized as diversity (the result of specialization, division) and inclusion (for the purposes of unification, cooperation). In the capital-centric system before

COVID-19, with a dialectical combination of diversity and inclusion as organizational principles for structuring the organizational unity of firms, diversity dominated. The validity of these conclusions is proved by the results of CEOs' surveys conducted by the McKinsey & Company experts for the period from 2012 to 2019 (Fig. 5).

Figure 5. Overall sentiment on diversity was more positive than negative, but sentiment on inclusion was markedly worse
Source: McKinsey & Company data set. May 19, 2020

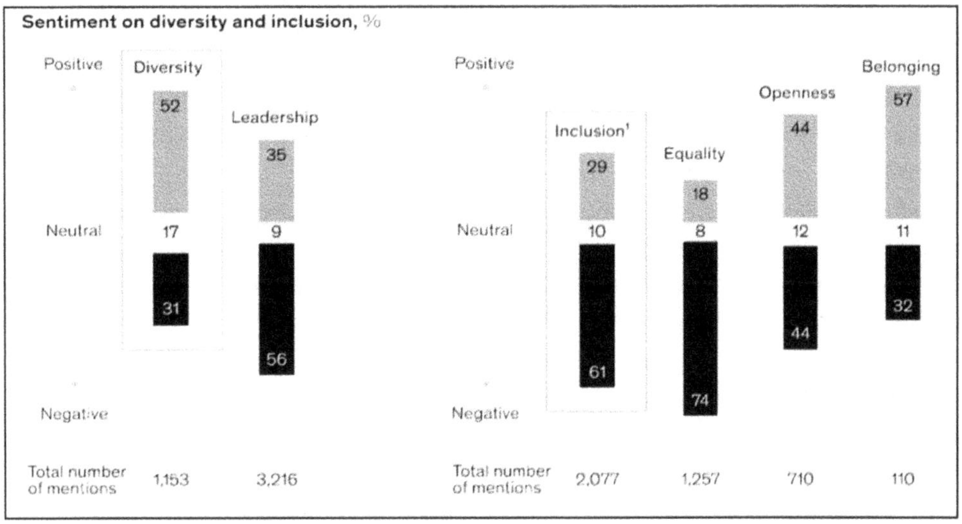

They encompassed 15 countries and more than 1,000 large companies. According to two indicators characterizing diversity - diverse representation and leadership accountability, a positive attitude towards this organizational principle steadily prevails (52% - positive and 31% - negative). This is a reflection of the dominance of the principle of diversity versus inclusion as the essence of the organizational principle of the capital-centrist system, which had already passed its optimum by the beginning of the COVID-19 pandemic. Actually, this is the main obstacle on the way of constructing post-coronavirus reality, which presupposes not so much equalizing the significance of the diversity (disintegration)-inclusion (integration) principles of constructing a new system, as raising the significance of unifying (inclusive) tendencies in its organization.

Not coincidentally, CEOs' polls on inclusion are counterproductive: 61% of the answers are negative, and 29% - positive. Moreover, of the three main indicators of inclusion - equality, openness, and belonging – the answers are differentiated as follows: as to equality 74% of answers – negative (only 18% - positive), openness has 44% positive and negative answers, but belonging are positively assessed by 57% of respondents (32% - negatively). On this basis, it could be concluded that the main problem of the capital-centric system is the dominance of the disintegration principle of organization at the macro level and of the diversity at the level of firms. And it is possible to remove this obstacle and radically transform organizational principles towards the dominance of unifying tendencies in comparison with separate ones at the macro level (and at the level of firms - increased inclusion versus diversity) only if the sentiment of CEOs changes to such a criterion of inclusion as equality. By the way, it is possible to achieve such fundamental changes as the basis for the formation of a human-centric system only by changing the ratio between the principle of D&I (diversity and inclusion) towards I&D (inclusion and diversity) at the business level. Only a critical mass of firms with inclusion priority will serve as a necessary condition for adjusting the disintegration-integration principles towards integration–disintegration ones.

From these positions, the relationship between the acceleration of digitalization at the firm level with the increase in the number of specialized activities and the deepening of specialization (as basis for differentiation) of employees of firms in the context of diversity of their skills becomes obvious. In fact, CEOs can only professionally use the organizational mechanism of including a growing number of professionally specialized employees in the team's activities. The more optimally the employees will be included, taking into account their differentiated abilities, the more successful the company will be. It is no coincidence that the McKinsey & Company experts emphasize, that the most diverse companies recognize I&D as more than a social-justice imperative; they also see it as a core enabler of growth and value creation. These diversity winners are pulling ahead of the rest. It is their critical mass that is capable of creating the foundation of a human-centric society.

It should be noted that the negative attitude of CEOs towards diversity and inclusion erects a few critical barriers in the way of the sustained change in company's culture, and the individual mindsets and behavior, that are needed to build a truly inclusive and diverse culture. The first barrier is a lack of purposeful follow through on diversity and inclusion pledges. It means that public commitments to build a diverse and inclusive company culture should be followed by systematic, business-led approach to I&D on the behalf of CEOs. The latter is necessary to translate these pledges into actual changes. HR director of one of the companies expressed this idea as follows: "A disconnect between what the company says and the progress it is making on the ground can seriously erode credibility both inside and outside of the organization, and further contribute to a lack of experienced inclusion" (Dixon-Fyle, et al., 2020). In other words, it is about the intentions of CEOs to implement the I&D strategy in their organizations and the absence of real steps to implement it in the activities of all departments and employees.

The second obstacle is more fundamental, and it largely explains the presence of the first one. The fact is that both inclusion and diversity imply the presence of certain parameters that determine them. Generally unaddressed misconceptions about fairness and meritocracy are one critical issue. The McKinsey & Company' experts (Dixon-Fyle, et al., 2020) quite rightly noted that, the logic behind prioritizing inclusion alongside diversity is coming more clearly into focus—but the full dynamics of the different aspects of inclusion, and their relative importance, are not yet fully understood.

So it becomes possible to highlight two indicators of a systematic approach to I&D, including diverse representation itself, and leadership accountability for I&D. As to core indicators of inclusion, its three core indicators are researched as follows (Dixon-Fyle, 2020): "equality" is defined as fairness and transparency in promotion, pay and recruitment, and equal access to sponsorship opportunities as well as other resources and retention support; "openness" is defined as an organizational culture where people treat each other with mutual respect, and where bias, bullying, discrimination and micro-aggressions are actively tackled; "belonging" is defined as an outcome resulting from the organization's demonstrating commitment to support the well-being and contributions of diverse and other employees. Leaders and managers foster connection with their diverse talent and between all employees, building a sense of community and encouraging them to contribute their diverse talents fully. The principal of inclusion is closely linked to employees' engagement, itself in turn a critical component of employees' retention, productivity and financial performance (Fig. 6).

Figure 6. Sentiments on inclusion are on average more negative than those on diversity (% of negative sentiments[1])

Source: Dixon-Fyle, Sundiatu, Vivian Hunt, Kevin Dolan, and Sara Prince (2020). Diversity wins. How inclusion matters. McKinsey&Company. May

Note: [1] Total number of mentions by theme: Diversity 1,153; Leadership 3,216; Inclusion 2, 077; Equality 1,257; Openness 710; Belonging 110.

[2] Weighted average of Equality, Openness and Belonging

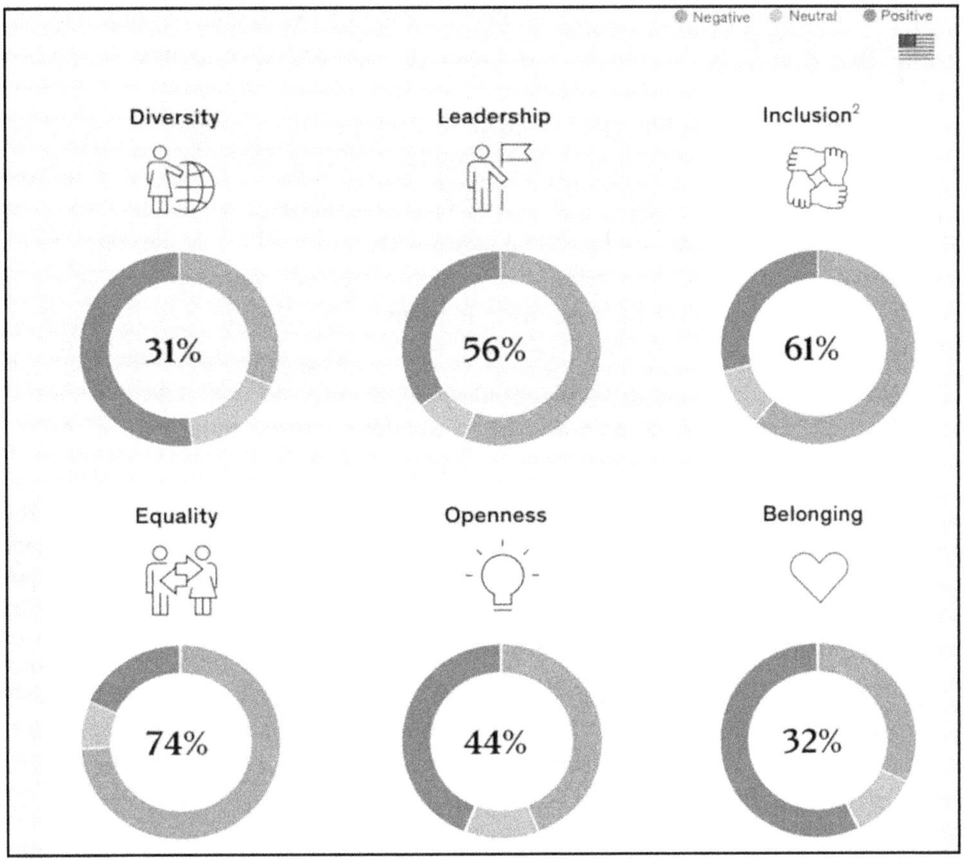

According to McKinsey & Company' research (Hunt, 2018; Dixon-Fyle, 2020), overall sentiment of CEOs on diversity is 5 2 percent positive and 31 percent negative. As to sentiment of CEOs on inclusion the results have become markedly worse at only 29 percent positive and 61 percent negative. Moreover, as far as "equality" is concerned, in the structure of assessments of CEOs who are inclined to implement the I&D strategy more broadly, 74% assess this position as negative. With regard to the 'openness' indicator, sentiments of 44% of respondent CEOs are negative, and together with the neutral assessments of the respondents, the negative attitude of CEOs to this indicator exceeds 50% of all respondents. These data indicate that CEOs themselves are not ready to create normal conditions for the socialization of gifted talented individuals capable of intellectual autonomy and realizing their potential for the benefit of rebuilding a stronger business in the face of uncertainty due to COVID-19.

The above conclusions lead to the question: if CEOs are forced to rebuild a stronger business in the face of uncertainty due to COVID-19 and realize that only people are the key factor in their success, then why do they have such a contradictory attitude towards the conditions of their socialization into the firm? The problem is that a firm is a structure that, on the one hand, socializes itself, i.e. is forced to integrate (be included) into the structural relationships of society, and on the other hand, it itself must socialize (include in the organization's team) individuals with different levels of education. So, when socializing into the structure of society, the company adapts to the environment in order to continue its activities in society. When it comes to socializing individuals into its structure, the firm must take into account the requirements of those individuals whose qualities meet the firm's top needs for employees. There are no questions about the growing demand for talented firms capable of adapting to their uncertain external environment. They must be able to tackle the non-trivial challenges faced by employers due to the COVID-19 pandemic.

The main problem is in the details. The point is that each of the components of the mechanisms of diversity and inclusion of talented employees in the firms' team, imply the introduction of certain behavioral norms that must be followed by all representatives of firms from lower to upper levels of management. For example, "gender" and "ethical" parameters, as well as "leadership" refer to the parameters of diversity, while "equality", "openness", "belonging" are characteristics of inclusion. As a result, among all firms that stepped up their efforts to implement the I&D strategy, financial performance improved among those that were able to more or less fully implement the conditions for the implementation of the processes of diversity and of inclusion in the teams of their organizations. And those firms that inconsistently implemented all these parameters either did not receive any return, or even worsened their financial performance.

The main problem of unsuccessful firms is connected with the negative attitudes of CEOs themselves towards certain I&D parameters, especially in terms of "leadership", "equality" and "openness". In fact, in this way, there appear the insurmountable PCBs of CEOs themselves, who formed as persons with qualities of intellectual autonomous in the capital-centric system. To rebuild a stronger business in the uncertain environment and achieve longer-term objectives, CEOs must learn to overcome their PCBs as to positive attitude to such parameters as "leadership" and "equality", as well as to "openness" and "belonging" to socialize talented employees for their organizations' success. By applying the lessons learned from implementations of the I&D strategy across businesses, CEOs can optimize these practices and enhance the efficiency, satisfaction, and engagement of the workforce over the long term. Satisfaction and engagement will also be crucial for retaining employees, especially as the market for talent heats up again during the recovery.

Organizations looking to institutionalize well-being of their employees into work should consider actions, policies, and mandates at the level of individuals, collective team, and organizational structure. The suggestions prepared by the experts of the "2021 Deloitte Global Human Capital Trends" offer the leaders changes they should make in five environments across the above mentioned five levels: (1) *Cultural* environment is connected with building well-being into social behaviors and norms; (2) *Relational* environment means fostering well-being in relationships among colleagues; (3) *Operational* environment aims at including well-being in management policies, processes, and programs; (4) *Physical* environment becomes obvious while designing the physical workspace to facilitate well-being; (5) *Virtual* environment means designing new technologies and virtual workspaces for well-being (Fig. 7).

As work itself changes at a rapid pace, the ways that an organization supports individual and team well-being must adapt in tandem. It's no longer about achieving work/life balance; the pandemic has shown that wellbeing is not about balancing work with life, but integrating them. When an organization is able to successfully design well-being into work, wellbeing becomes indistinguishable from work itself, embedded across all organizational levels and environments to not only drive and sustain human performance, but also human potential. Actually, this is the practical implementation of the process of institutionalization of individual habits and behavior for the purpose of their coordination within the framework of collective routines and behavior. In other words the above-described content of organizational changes that self-sufficient resilient companies must implement during and after the COVID-19 pandemic is associated with the results that the downward causation mechanism is guided by to strengthen the structural stability of the company.

Figure 7. Organizations can take a variety of actions to integrate well-being into work in order to optimally realize downwards causation mechanism
Source: 2021 Deloitte Global Human Capital Trends (2020). The social enterprise in a word disrupted: Leading the shift from survive to thrive. Deloitte. Insights

	Organizational	Team	Individual
Cultural *Building well-being into social behaviors and norms*		Model well-being behaviors such as taking micro-breaks or only making certain meetings video-focused	Be proactive and vocal about well-being needs
Relational *Fostering well-being in relationships among colleagues*	Form teams based on worker preferences, working styles, and personal needs		Check in frequently, proactively, and consistently with colleagues on their well-being needs and preferences
Operational *Including well-being in management policies, processes, and programs*	Embed well-being criteria in work scheduling, performance management processes, leadership evaluations, and rewards and recognition programs	Enable team agency and choice by allowing teams to adopt well-being practices best suited to them	
Physical *Designing the physical workspace to facilitate well-being*	Design work environments to support workers' physical, mental, and emotional health needs	Leverage physical workspaces that promote team collaboration and performance	
Virtual *Designing new technologies and virtual workspaces for well-being*		Use new technologies, like virtual reality, to train team members to navigate stressful situations (e.g., interacting with a frustrated customer)	Leverage wearable technologies and apps to help master distractions, increase mindfulness, and reduce anxiety

In other words companies resilient in the face of uncertainty accompanying the COVID-19 pandemic and even more so the post-coronavirus future, intuitively rather than theoretically determined the correct path for their adaptation to a rapidly changing reality. The most successful of them put the restoration and strengthening of the internal organizational structure in the first place on the agenda. They associate this goal with the introduction of human-centric principles of organization through the institutionalization of new habits and behavior of employees based on the optimization of processes of inclusion and diversity. In fact, it is about an adequate combination of certain behavioral norms that have a motivational coloration: "equality", "openness", "belonging". It is on them that individual rules and behavior are based, which are structured by collective routines and the behavior of the company as a whole. The complexity of institutionalizing structural ties within the company is associated with this emotional behavioral component, the maximum consideration of which makes the downwards causation mechanism successful. That is why the strategy of firms that optimally combine the principles of I&D will strengthen their positions in the uncertain situation of our time and successfully implement an upwards causation mechanism in the future. It is about expanding the practice of introducing human-centric principles of organization into the economy and society.

EMPIRICAL EVIDENCE

So, the authors' assessments based on the data of McKinsey & Company (Dixon-Fyle, 2020) showed the validity of the above conclusions that the I&D strategy serves as a form of implementation of the downwards causation mechanism for the purposes of introducing man-centric principles of organization into the activities of companies. In the context of the destruction of structural ties in the economy and society as a result of their emergency blocking to combat the COVID-19 pandemic, a fundamental restructuring of the internal organization of companies is the most important condition for their success in the face of dynamic changes in future reality. Moreover, the importance of the I&D strategy is growing at the firm level under conditions of uncertainty. The apparent simplicity of its implementation in the practice of firms becomes obvious when the subjective aspect in connection with the intentions of company leaders begins to seriously affect their financial results.

The authors took the approach of the McKinsey & Company' experts (Dixon-Fyle, 2020), who identified five groups of companies, that participated in the poll: (1) Diversity Leaders (5 percent of the data set); (2) Fast Movers (28 percent of the data set); (3) Resting on Laurels (29 percent of the data set); (4) Moderate Movers (10 percent of the data set); (5) Laggards (28 percent of the data set).

Diversity Leaders distinguishes a systematic, business-led approach to I&D for at least five years. For such companies the following is typical: a strong culture of accountability, deployment of innovative and ambitious interventions, and strong leadership commitment.

Fast Movers have strongly focused on I&D, including developing a bespoke business case with ambitious I&D targets, promotion of full transparency including talent processes, pay, and effective retention initiatives.

Resting on Laurels features a less systematic approach to I&D, including initiatives such as employee resource groups but with less emphatic efforts to tackle the barriers connected with other parameters of diversity.

For *Moderate Movers* it is typical to have failing commitments to I&D to translate them into tangible progress on representation, including workplace culture. This is largely due to the lack of a robust articulation of a "reason why" for diversity at all levels, and insufficient attention to inclusive mindsets and behaviour.

Laggards have typically not embarked on a purposeful I&D strategy. This is accompanied by lack of data and of insight into the I&D performance and by the fragmentation of the sparse efforts of fledgling employee resource groups. These companies typically have limited accountability for I&D at all levels, and significant challenges with inclusion.

The estimates below are based on data only for two parameters characterizing diversity: gender and ethnicity (Table 1).

Obviously, the distribution of such values as "Diversity leaders", "Fast movers", "Resting on laurels", "Moderate movers" and "Laggards" in a sample of 1000 firms is random. Analyzing this information, the authors introduced into the consideration generalized characteristics both according to gender and ethnic indicators:

weighted mathematical expectation $\mu = \sum_{i=1}^{5} p_i a_i$, (1)

weighted standard deviation $\sigma = \sqrt{\sum_{i=1}^{5} p_i (a_i - \mu)^2}$, (2)

coefficient of variation ! $V = \frac{\sigma}{\mu}$, (3)

where a_i – gender or ethnic data for the corresponding years.

In addition, it is interesting to estimate the value (***H***) entropy as an uncertainty measure of information:

$$H = \sum_{i=1}^{5} p_i \log_2 p_i. \quad (4)$$

For practical applications, it is convenient to express entropy in terms of binary logarithms In this case the unit of entropy has a special name of *bit*. Estimates obtained using formulas (1) – (4) make it possible to explore the statistical content of tabular data. In particular, based on, for example, an estimate of expectation $\boldsymbol{\mu} = 20.080$ it becomes possible to build a confidence interval [10.075; 30.085], into which the real value of this quantity will fall with the probability 0.68. On the other hand, coefficients of variation clearly demonstrate how much of the data spread $\boldsymbol{\sigma}$ falls on each unit $\boldsymbol{\mu}$.

It should be noted that in comparison with gender data the value of weighted standard deviation rises sharply for ethnic data. Thus for 2014 the weighted standard deviation $\boldsymbol{\mu} = 7.872$ is more than weighted mathematical expectation $\boldsymbol{\mu} = 7.360$. For 2019 these values are also very close: $\boldsymbol{\mu} = 12.860$ and $\boldsymbol{\sigma} = 7.872$. Moreover entropy as a measure of information uncertainty for ethnic data $\boldsymbol{H} = 2.25$ bit is more than $\boldsymbol{H} = 2.09$ bit - for gender data.

Table 1. Data describing the shares of companies implementing certain elements of the diversity strategy and their different results for the period from 2014 to 2019

	i	share of companies (p_i)	2014 Gender	2019 Gender	share of companies (p_i)	2014 Ethnicity	2019 Ethnicity
Diversity leaders	1	0.05	26	40	0.15	17	32
Fast movers	2	0.28	7	27	0.24	1	18
Resting on laurels	3	0.29	28	22	0.22	18	12
Moderate movers	4	0.10	12	19	0.11	3	10
Laggards	5	0.28	9	8	0.28	1	0
Weighted mathematical expectation (μ)			15.100	20.080		7.360	12.860
Weighted standard deviation (σ)			9.162	10.005		7.872	10.424
Coefficient of variation (CV)			0.607	0.498		1.070	0.811

Source: the authors' development on the base of the McKinsey & Company' research (Dixon-Fyle, 2020)

The above estimates confirm that the actions of companies in relation to the orientation towards diversity should be systematic. This means that the sustained change in company culture, and the individual mindsets and behavior are needed to build a truly diverse and inclusive culture. Inclusion is closely linked to employees' engagement, itself in turn a critical component of employees' retention, productivity and financial performance. According to the State of the Global Workplace report, (Gallup, 2017), business units successful in the I&D strategy are 17% more productive and 21% more profitable than those unsuccessful. They also have 20% higher sales, 10% higher customer metrics. Besides the above results show that even where companies are more diverse, many appear unable to cultivate inclusive work environments in an effective and consistent way. Such environments promote inclusive leadership and accountability among managers, equality and fairness of opportunity, and openness and freedom from bias and discrimination. More than that, fostering a diverse and inclusive culture is a critical success factor: it enables individuals both to shine in their own right and to pull together as a team.

9.3. Resilient Companies in Dynamic Economy: Dialectics of Intellectually Autonomous Individuals and of Modern Technological Systems

The above discussed "I&D" strategy could be treated in connection with the transferring all the company's operating activities to a new technological paradigm. In organizational psychology, what Scott Page calls a "diversity bonus" results from forming teams composed of different kinds of thinkers, meaning that heterogeneous teams outperform homogenous ones at solving problems, making predictions, and developing solutions. Research shows that organizations with above-average diversity produced a greater proportion of revenue from innovation (45% of total) than those with below-average diversity (26%), which translated into stronger overall financial performance (Levine, 2020; Lorenzo, et al., 2018). With AI bringing its own style of "thinking" to a team, the mix of human and machine intelligence can yield diversity bonuses that exceed those produced by teams composed of only humans, however diverse (Guszcza, et al., 2020).

As the world emerges from the pandemic, organizations have an opportunity to complicate their structures by forming *super-teams as* combinations of people and technology leveraging their complementary capabilities to pursue outcomes at a speed and scale not otherwise possible (Volini, et al., 2020). Superteams have yet to take hold as a widespread organizational strategy, in part because many companies still tend to view technology as a tool and enabler rather than as a team member and collaborator. The dialectics of technology and people is not an "either-or" choice but a "both-and" partnership. The top three above mentioned factors should be transformed to organizational culture, workforce capability, and technology (Fig. 8). All these factors must all work together for an organization to envision and assemble effective super-teams.

Figure 8. Both human capability and technological capability are critical to transforming work of the companies
Note: n=3,630 (executives).
Source: The 2021 Deloitte Global Human Capital Trends survey.

The experts of the "*The 2021 Deloitte Global Human Capital Trends survey*" put forward a hypothesis that is very consonant with the theory of organizations, according to which a self-enforcing company is able to optimize its structure effectively using the downwards causation mechanism. Today, companies are clearly undergoing changes that are adapting to the new conditions of a dynamic economy. By including people with intellectual autonomous qualities in the team, in-house institutions strengthen the structural ties of the company through the introduction of human-centric principles of structural organization. But the transfer of the activities of modern companies to a new technological base requires the leaders of the companies to adapt the I&D strategy to integrate the latest technologies into these teams. Moreover super-teams can give organizations the opportunity to re-architect work in more human ways, leveraging technology to elevate teams' ability to learn, create, and perform in new ways to achieve better outcomes. Superteams are most powerful when organizations use technology to empower teams in a way that makes work better for humans and makes humans better at work (Fig. 9). They hold the promise of helping organizations bring human and technological capabilities together to re-architect work and deliver new value to all stakeholders. When given the right environment to thrive, super-teams of humans and technology together can unlock organizational potential and achieve greater results together than either humans or machines could achieve on their own.

Figure 9. Both workforce capability and technological capability are critical to transforming work
Note: n=3,630 (executives).
Source: The 2021 Deloitte Global Human Capital Trends survey.

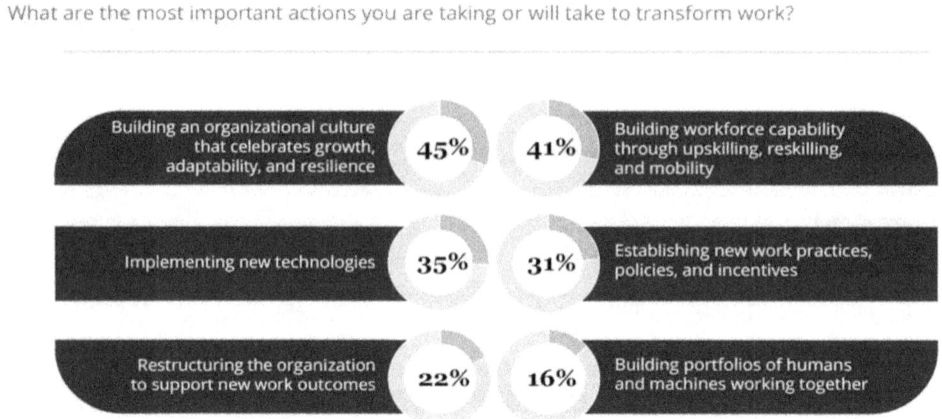

Superteams are most powerful when organizations use technology to empower teams in a way that makes work better for humans and makes humans better at work. In this connection it becomes of great importance to "reimagining" work. According to "The 2021 Deloitte Global Human Capital Trends survey", reimagining is the destination, re-architecting is the path to get there. Re-architecture makes it possible to put re-imagination into action as well as to unlock human potential. It could be the final step that empowers organizations to truly thrive. From theoretical point of view re-architecture shows how the downwards causation mechanism is realized. To be success the re-architecting work will require several changes in how both human resources (HR) and the organization approach work, teams, and capabilities (Fig. 10):

- Shifting the focus of work from outputs to outcomes. This change in mindset is critical for achieving results beyond doing what is done today cheaper and faster to doing what is needed to pursue new outcomes and better results;
- Looking at the re-architecture of work not as a one-time project or initiative, but as an ongoing capability that needs to be embedded into the organization's operations;
- Putting teams and super-teams at the center of how work gets done. This will be needed both within HR and across the broader enterprise to spark innovation;
- Approaching workforce development by identifying, cultivating, and capitalizing on workers' potential, with a focus on uniquely human capabilities such as analysis and synthesis, problem-solving, and social intelligence;
- Expanding the definition of capabilities to include the integration of both human and technological capabilities';
- Recognizing and proactively managing the leadership and cultural implications that come from embracing new ways of working.

Figure 10. From optimize to redesign to re-architect: HR's path to achieving new outcomes
Source: The 2021 Deloitte Global Human Capital Trends survey; BCG Mass uniqueness: a global challenge in the battle for talent

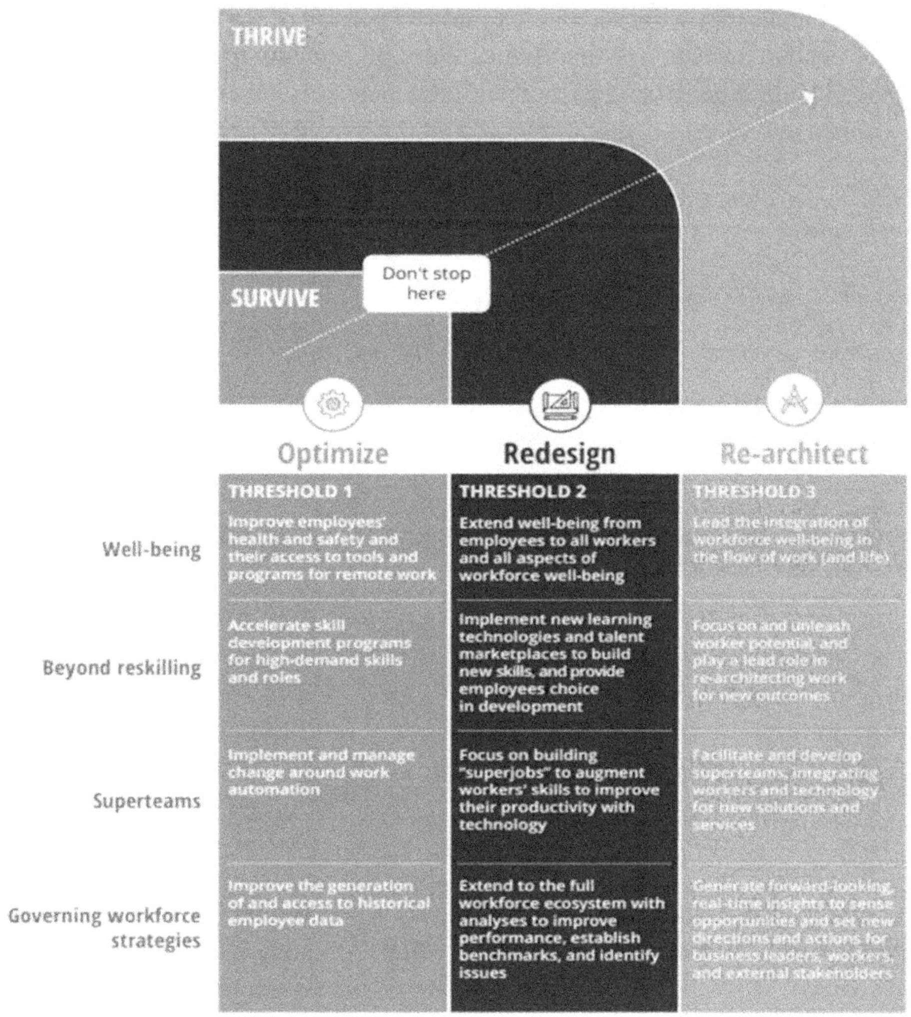

In fact, Fig. 10 shows an algorithm for the functioning of the downwards causation mechanism, as it is reflected in the heads of CEOs of companies. With an optimal combination of all re-architecting work steps, the structural integrity of the company will be strengthened and the institutionalization of collective routines and behavior will be carried out.

Bill McDermott (CEO) writes that the world now is all about people. It is a truly human moment where any connection that doesn't absolutely lean into people will go nowhere.... Clearly, companies need to update their talent strategy by identifying the types of skills needed and then mapping current employees' skills against their future needs (Fig. 11).

If over the future five years the skill gaps are not overcome, then the problems of self-development of a dynamic economy grow to extreme proportions (WEF, 2015, 2016, 2017, 2018; The business case for inclusive growth, 2018; Dixon-Fyle, et al., 2020). Back in 2019 according to the McKinsey&Company'

experts (Mckinsey&Company, September 2020), the resulting job displacement could be massive—think Industrial Revolution massive—affecting as many as 800 million people globally by 2030 and requiring up to 375 million of them to switch occupational categories and learn new skills. As a whole the companies lack the talents they will need in the future: 44 percent of respondents say their organizations will face skill gaps within the next five years, and another 43 percent report existing skill gaps (Agrawal, et al., 2020) (Fig. 11). In other words, 87 percent of respondents either are experiencing gaps now or expect them within a few years.

Figure 11. Respondents expect to see skill gaps as market and technology trends alter organizations' talent needs
Note: Figures may not sum to 100% due to rounding, n = 1,216.
Source: McKinsey Global Survey "Beyond hiring: How companies are reskilling to address talent gaps"; Survey conducted May 2019 and published February 2020

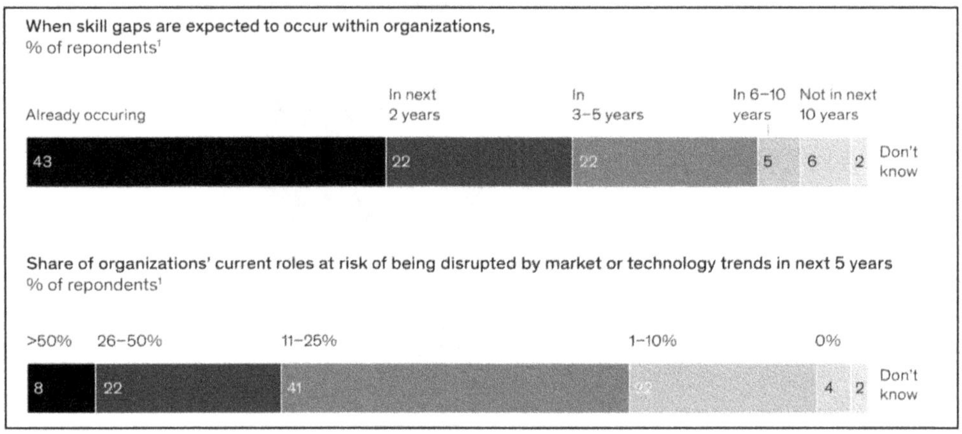

For CEOs today it becomes obvious that achieving strong performance in the new reality will require more than a rapid crisis response. Winning the fight will be a marathon and during this period, business continuity and competitive position will constantly be at risk and require active management. And, winning the future will demand making long-term, proactive moves even as the fight phase persists (Küpper, et al., 2020). To respond proactively, CEOs must focus on five priorities (Fig. 12). The framework provides the key activities that companies must pursue in five functional areas. And practically all of them are somehow connected with the socialization of talented individuals into the team of their organizations. And today the directions of the CEOs' policy aimed at solving the problems of the personnel gap are also known. It is about optimizing diversity and inclusion processes in the organizations through the development and implementation of the I&D strategy.

At the same time, the formatting super-teams of technology and employees depends on the quality of individuals. It is about the ability or inability of individuals to reflect, self-reflect and, most importantly, to transcend. Without going deep into the characteristics of the specific mechanism of institutionalization of individuals' behavior at the level of companies, it should be noted that it is largely due to the following experiences acquired by the individual at the end of the educational process. The acquisition by a student of a certain set of experiences as a result of education serves as the basis for diversity in society and predetermines the possibilities of his inclusion into the company's team. The latter is of decisive importance for understanding the situation that has developed due to COVID-19, in which companies and their CEOs are destined to form structural relationships of a new reality based on human-centrism including the formation of super-teams of humans and technology.

Figure 12. CEOs: framework for addressing five critical priorities
Source: Küpper, Daniel, Tom Reichert, Tom Reichert, Vaishali Rastogi, and Ryoji Kimura. (2020). How CEOs (chief executive officer) Can Win the Fight and Transform to Win the Future. BCG. June 8

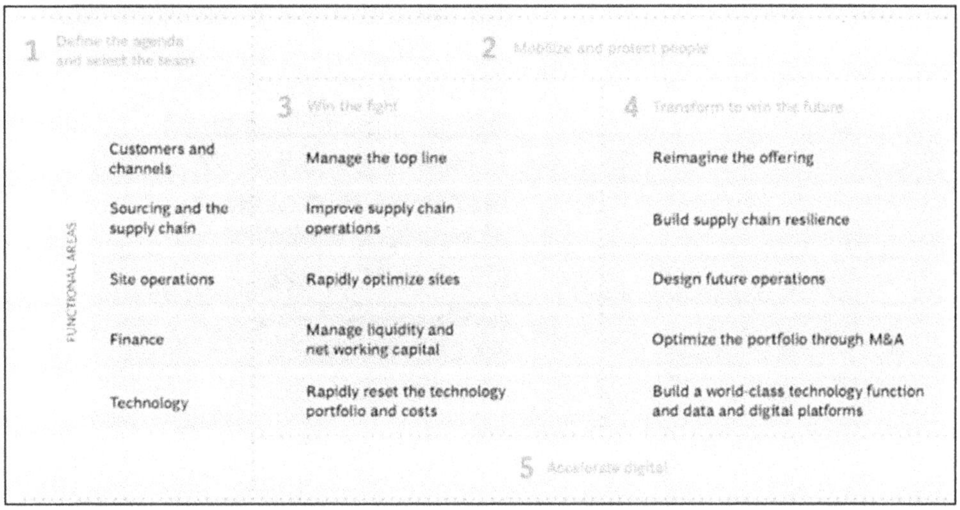

Technology leaders can take the imperative to design enabling technologies for well-being one step further by introducing new technologies to boost workers' health, performance, and quality of life. Such technologies could include "emo tech" to help people developing self-awareness and emotional regulation; "collaboration, presence, and trust tech" to help people build deeper group connections; and "well tech" that helps people maintain and optimize health and cognition to support general well-being (Wooll, et al., 2020). Technologies such as the above can improve well-being by allowing workers to better eliminate distractions, ease anxieties, connect with others, build presence and trust, and learn faster (2021 Deloitte Global Human Capital Trends, 2020).

Recent innovations in education, which have already begun to respond to the above-mentioned problems, are associated with the competence-based approach as a reaction to the widening gap between theoretical thinking (associated with education) and social practice (the mechanism of socialization). It is no coincidence that it was originally initiated by the Western business representing this social practice. On the one hand, CEOs needed graduates who would be ready to immediately get involved in work, and, on the other hand, firms were interested in young people being able to flexibly retrain and master new knowledge and technologies throughout their professional life. On the other hand, the competence-based approach to education assumes that educational competence should include both cognitive and operational-technological components, as well as motivational, ethical and social ones. In this case, educational competence must implement a predetermined social requirement (normal) for educational training. It is about a specific set of interrelated orientations, knowledge, abilities, skills, real experience of the student's activity in relation to a certain range of objects of reality, necessary for the implementation of personally and socially significant productive activity.

Figure 13. The companies' need of building employees' skills in critical thinking, leadership and management, and advanced data analysis

Source: Agrawal, Sapana, Aaron De Smet, Pawel Poplawski, and Angelika Reich (2020). Beyond hiring: How companies are reskilling to address talent gaps. Organization Practice and McKinsey Accelerate. January. McKinsey & Company

Note: [1]Out of 35 skills included in the Survey. Question was asked only of respondents who say their organizations have a re-skilling program currently under way or have already re-skilled ˃1 group, or class of employees; n= 394

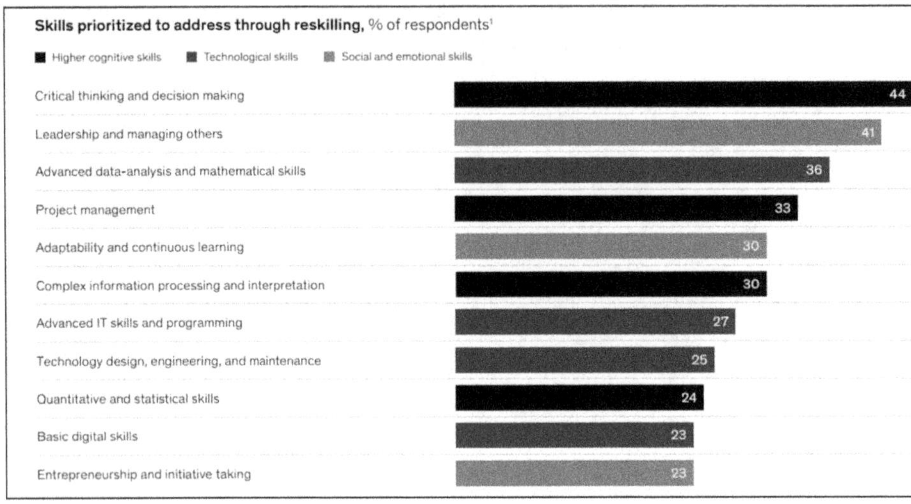

If self-sufficient companies recognize the need to fully integrate human potential for the success of the company, they will adapt their employees' education to these conditions. Moreover, the higher their intellectual potential, the more they claim to be an adequate internal organization of teamwork, focused on human-centrism. In this case, the education of employees is reoriented from exclusively meeting the needs of the company to the realization of the employee to learn in order to further develop his intellectual capital. This is the main difference between the mission of education in the human-centric systems and capital-centric one, the structure of which was destroyed by the first wave of the COVID-19 pandemic

The specificity of the situation that has developed as a result of the coronavirus, associated with the complete uncertainty of the future reality, is manifested in the fact that the structural level of firms is called upon to design it. It is they who, for objective reasons, cannot finish their activities as a result of an economic lockdown. Such a situation is predetermined by many essential features of entrepreneurs in the representatives of CEOs of modern companies, as well as their innovative function deeply described by J. Schumpeter (Schumpeter, 1949). As a result of the economic and social lockdowns, the business was forced to abandon its long-term development strategies due to the complete uncertainty of the future. But in the short run, CEOs are forced to take swift steps to minimize the negative impact of this uncertainty. According to figurative expression of the KPMG specialists self-enforcing resilient firms represented by their CEOs focus on finding opportunity in adversity (KPMG, 2020).

It was due to the coronavirus pandemic that CEOs began to rethink the uncertainty of the current situation and strengthen the structural integrity of the organization through the downwards causation mechanism and the institutionalization of new habits and behavior of individuals within the team. It is symptomatic that the adjustment of the institutionalization of the internal organizational structures is carried out, first of all, in connection with the attracting inclusion of talents as well as technological capabilities to form the super-team. It is with them that companies associate their accelerated digitalization and their future success in the new reality. This proves, in general, the validity of the above theoretical conclusions of the authors regarding the dialectics of the interaction of education and socialization of individuals and their place in the modern societal and economic crises. As for CEOs, in a crisis state of society, they come to the need to optimize the downwards and upwards causation mechanisms focusing on personnel with extraordinary abilities, which distinguishes intellectually autonomous individuals capable to cooperate with technologies (Fig. 13).

Figure 14. Top 10 ways employers can gain their employees' trust
Source: BCG (2020). Workforce Sentiment Survey. BCG.
Note: n=1002, Australia only

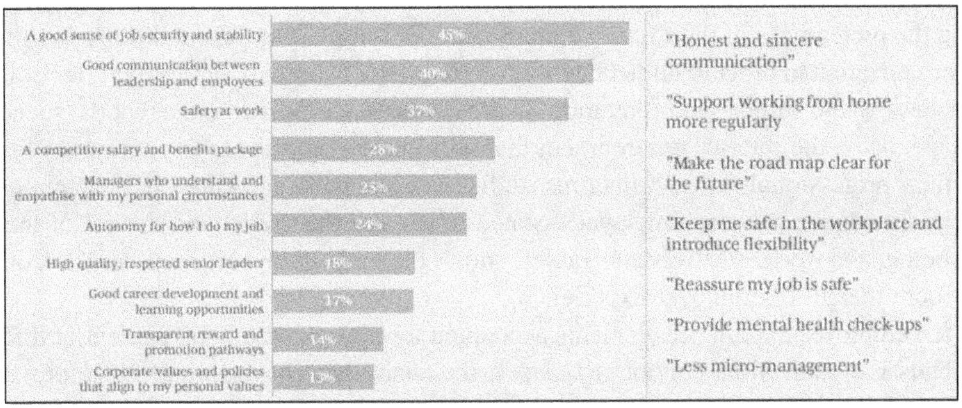

And if the future reality in the context of society or the environment of the firm's functioning is uncertain, therefore, the employee is needed in the totality of all his potential abilities, which predetermines his own socialization and success, as well as the successful socialization of the organizations in which he will work. In fact, CEOs evaluate and test a variety of mechanisms for socializing their firms into an uncertain future reality. As a result, theoretical conclusions and practical results are reduced to the same. The problem of talented employees (with the qualities of intellectual autonomousness) comes to the fore, since it is they who, adequately institutionalized through inclusion in companies' teams, mediate technologies for minimizing the uncertainty of future reality and simulate a variety of mechanisms for strengthening the position of business in the future post-coronavirus reality. Nearly all respondents classify closing potential skill gaps as a priority for their organizations, and about one-third put it among the top three priorities. Furthermore, organizations are acutely aware of the importance of learning in today's business environment. They also understand that the ability of the workforce to learn new skills, model new behavior, and adapt continuously is key to sustained success. And these requirements for the employee's abilities are obviously associated with the qualities of an intellectually autonomous personality capable of self-development. The experts express this idea as follows: "....only if the individual intentionally treat every moment as a learning opportunity, then everyday experiences and interactions could be accepted (treated) as tremendous learning opportunities" (Mattey, et al., 2020).

By prioritizing their requirements for the conditions of downwards causation institutionalization in the current uncertain environment due to COVID-19, CEOs understand the need to adapt to the priority preferences of talented employees. Being self-organizing, intellectually autonomous individuals will choose their future jobs and companies in accordance with their individual values. It is no coincidence that recently more and more organizations write about their aspiration to become an Employer of Choice in the new reality. It is about more holistic Employee Value Proposition (EVP) that matches their employees' needs and aspirations. A talented, happy and consistent workforce adds to an organization's overall competitive advantage.

Given COVID-19 is primarily a public health crisis, and the most common positive impact felt by people during this period was 'feeling safe', trust is increasingly important in times of uncertainty (Boston Consulting Group, 2020) (Fig. 14).

This is backed by 83% of employees stating that trust in their employer is important. While trust during COVID-19 restrictions is often linked to physical safety (e.g., hygiene protocols), it is also related to psychological factors such as job stability and security, as well as autonomy to get work done. Considering the preferences of their future employees, CEOs highlight the conditions that must be created in the organization in order to attract talented employees, i.e. possessing the qualities of intellectual autonomousness, in the author's interpretation. In other words, CEOs recognize that the success of their company depends on the internal environment that will initiate employees to continuous learning and improving their professional skills. Numerous studies of companies' practices in this area have shown a strong correspondence between employees' stated needs and the underlying drivers of their engagement, well-being, and work effectiveness. Table 2 shows the top employee's needs and outcome drivers, grouped by core themes of employee experience.

Jointly, ten employee experience elements accounted for approximately 60 percent of differences in outcomes. Thus as organizations continue to adapt to the crisis, they can meaningfully improve employee experience. Even if organizations may not be able to take compensate right now, they can achieve a 55 percent improvement in engagement by addressing employees' need for work recognition through non-financial means (Emmett, et al., 2020). To resume it should be noted that to address employees' needs and help them thrive during the return, organizations should focus on four areas: safety and security, relationships, culture, and purpose. It is because, according to the CEO of one organization, they are putting teams of their best people on the hardest problems – if they can't solve it no one can. CEOs of the most advanced organizations interpret this strategy as the art of the possible (COVID-19: Briefing materials, 2020).

Understanding the fundamental changes that COVID-19 has brought to the future of socio-economic systems is important for chief executive officers (CEOs) not so much from the standpoint of macroeconomics, but in the context of the need for a radical restructuring of intra-firm relations with personnel. Distant forms of work predetermined the need to increase the importance of horizontal structural ties in companies with an emphasis on the priority of the subject factor in all restored structural ties. In other words, to succeed, organizations must blend digital and human capabilities (Grasshoff, et al., 2020). In many ways, it is these new realities of the future practice of successful firms that predetermine uncertainty as the fundamental feature of the post-coronavirus future. Therefore, for firms, digitalization and the priority of the subjective component of horizontal and vertical structural ties in firms is an uncontested scenario of their successful future in an uncertain post-coronavirus reality. But many companies have not appeared to recognize the imperative of making long-term moves as they fight the pandemic.

In other words, in connection with employees with the qualities of intellectual autonomosness, it is the companies, represented by their CEOs, that must create the necessary conditions for their socialization (inclusion) taking into account those aspirations that will strengthen the integrity of the company and contribute to its rebuilding as a strong business in the conditions of uncertainty due to pandemic coronavirus. This approach differs significantly from the parameters of the capital-centric system, in which the parameters of success were set by capital owners and CEOs at the firm level, and by the state - at the level of society. They also dictated the basic conditions of socialization (inclusion), which were to be accepted by individuals unconditionally, as a given. The progress of the emerging reality with a self-developing person as a driver of the principles of its organization dictates new conditions for his socialization: the priority of individual requirements is gradually becoming unconditional both for the company and for society.

Table 2. Employees' engagement, well-being, and effectiveness, driven by a set of employee experience factors

Top employee needs and experience factors by core themes of employee experience			Improvement		
Theme	Need (rank)	Employee experience factors	Work effectiveness	Engagement	Well-being
Stable, secure work experience	Job security (1)	Organizational stability	+16.9%	+52.9%	+53.3%
	Financial stability (2)				
	Physical and mental health (6)	Compensation and benefits	+21.2%	+45.6%	+44.5%
	Being rewarded (8)				
Trusting relationships	Working with people I can trust (5)	Trust in leadership	+23.7%	+47.6%	+45.4%
		Relationship with company	+20.9%	+49.9%	+51.3%
	Being recognized for my work (10)	Nonfinancial recognition	+20-4%	+55.1%	+49.3%
Social cohesion and inclusion	Being treated fairly (4)	Fairness Involvement	+22.3%	+48.0%	+52.3%
			+14.8%	+32.4%	+51.1%
	Having supportive coworkers (9)	Respect Equality	+15.7%	+51.8%	+49.8%
			+16.2%	+50.8%	+50.9%
Individual purpose and contribution	Achieving work goals (7)	Alignment with organizational purpose and values	+20.3%	+49.0%	+49.3%
	Balance of work and private life (3)				
	Fulfilling my personal purpose at work (12)				

Source: Jonathan Emmett, Gunnar Schrah, Matt Schrimper, and Alexandra Wood (2020). COVID-19 and the employee experience: How leaders can seize the moment. Organization Practice. June. McKinsey & Company. McKinsey.com

9.4. Self-Enforcing Companies and Upwards Causation Mechanism in Middle-Class Revival: Institutionalization of Base Structural Level of the Post-COVID-19 Dynamic Economics

So, Chapter 9.1-9.3 was devoted to the drastic changes that took place within self-enforcing companies due to COVID-19 pandemic. From a theoretical point of view, these changes reflect the objective processes of restructuring the internal organization of companies under the influence of downwards causation mechanism. Institutionalization reinforced the result of this mechanism in the new habits and behavior of employees, which, in a pandemic, should increasingly acquire the quality of intellectually autonomous individuals, i.e. be talented, as experts call them. It is with such employees that CEOs associate the opportunity to create super-teams of intellectually advanced individuals on the new technological foundation. The participants of these new teams, with new habits and behaviors, are aligned in collective routines and in collective behavior, which strengthens the structural integrity of the company and makes it increasingly resilient in the face of the COVID-19 pandemic.

However, self-enforcing companies are able not only to reform (re-architecting) their internal organizational structure through a downwards causation mechanism, but also to structure the external environment of their functioning through an upwards causation mechanism. It is with this mechanism that the authors associate the formation of numerous ties by companies, which, upon completion of the stage of self-development of economic systems, will turn into structural interactions mediating the exchange of dialectical pairs in economy. However, in order for the economic system to successfully pass the stage of self-development and move on to the next stage of its self-organization, it is necessary first to restore the integrity of society. In modern conditions of the COVID-19 pandemic, it is about the need to eliminate the consequences of the societal crisis, to restore the critical mass of the middle class as the basic structural level of society. It is this function that self-enforcing companies can perform through an upwards causation mechanism.

In this context, a new trend is associated with the growing interest of CEOs of leading companies in strengthening the integrity of society and in the stability of social relationships at the national level. Thus, according to KPMG experts, the most CEOs have shifted their organizations' purpose from purely profit to its social valuation. As a result 54 percent of the respondents have taken a broader, purpose-driven approach aimed at multiple stakeholders' needs. And around 22 percent have connected their primary objective with improving society. Only less than a quarter (23 percent) of CEOs continued to view the overall purpose of the organization in the narrow sense of "governance for shareholder value". Thus more than 79 percent of CEOs had to re-evaluate their purpose as a result of COVID-19 (Fig. 15).

CEOs recognize that recovery from the pandemic does not mean a return to 'normal' of the past. We are talking about the formation of a new structure of relationships in the economy and society as an environment for the functioning of a firm in a dynamical economy on a new technological basis. COVID-19 has forced CEOs to radically adjust the goals of their organizations by increasing the importance of social aspects of activities. Already in 2020 CEOs become increasingly prepared to personally take part in tackling society's major challenges. According to 65 percent of the respondent CEOs, the importance of business in solving the societal crisis will increase as the trust of society and citizens in the state falls. Under these conditions, it becomes clear why 76 percent of the respondent CEOs mention their personal responsibility to be a 'leader for change on societal issues'. These results generally indicate the peculiarities of business socialization in the new conditions of the COVID-19 pandemic, which manifests itself both in the process of adapting it to new realities and of structuring it to fit new social requirements. In fact, this is how the dialectic of interaction of factors of self-organization and self-development of firms is realized in conditions when they are forced to turn into active participants in the processes of structuring a new reality. From the standpoint of shocks' theory, it is about the implementation by self-sufficient companies of their function of creative destruction in the context of participation in the formation of a new structure of a dynamic economy. Moreover, they are forced to do this, since the coronavirus shock either destroyed or changed the old rules of the game in the market (structural relationships). Thus, the trend towards the replacement of adaptive methods of doing business in society by creative actions that reconstruct reality at the request of practical organizations is gradually becoming more and more obvious.

The COVID-19 pandemic and the destruction of structural ties as a result of lockdown dictated new conditions for the subordination of these processes: companies, represented by their CEOs, become drivers of the processes of socialization (as a result of diversity and inclusion) of individuals. That is why it is they who are forced to be the first to structure organizational processes at the level of firms, rebuilding them on the human-centric principles (Küpper, et al., 2020). Gradually, they will predetermine the structuring of the future post-COVID-19 reality both in society and economy.

Figure 15. The impact of the pandemic: more powerful and relevant than ever purposes of CEOs
Source: KPMG. (2020). CEO Outlook: COVID-19. Special Edition. Executive summary. KPMG International

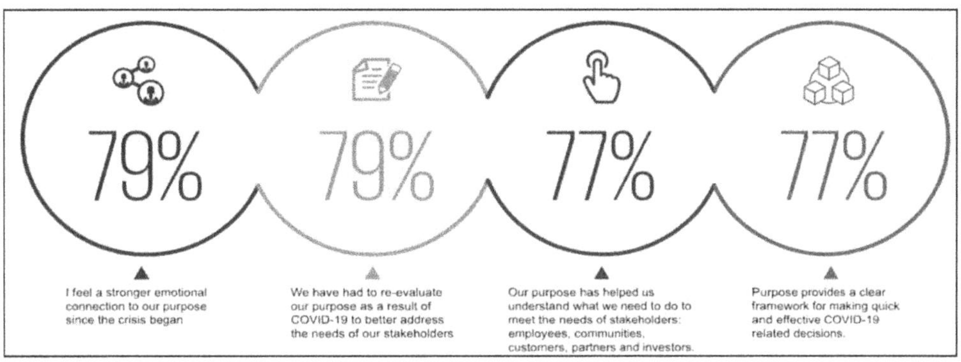

If companies use the downwards causation mechanism to structure the behavior of individuals at the firm level, then through the upwards causation mechanisms they participate in structuring the environment of their functioning at the macro level of the economy and society as a whole. Moreover, the change in priorities between I&D in the strategy of adaptation of self-enforcing companies to the new conditions of the post-covid crisis in favor of inclusion means a serious shift in dialectics of downwards and upwards causation mechanisms. Successful companies first institutionalize the internal environment of their organizations, strengthening their integrity on the basis of human-centricity. And by means of an upwards causation mechanism, they form, recreate the structure they need at the social level. It is in this context that self-enforcing companies are dialectically complex elements capable of realizing the mechanism of self-development of dynamic systems in the economy, society and technology, not to mention the system of social institutions. At the same time, the main principle of the restructuring of all structural ties is associated with their reorientation to human-centric forms of organization. And the quantitative and qualitative features of such forms of organization differ from capital-centric ones because in them the subjective component predetermines the self-movement of systemic integrities created by man in all spheres of his life. And in the interconnections between society and the economy of the society, or rather the quality of its integrity becomes decisive in the progressive complication of the economic system. And in the post-COVID-19 reality, it is the processes of self-organization and self-development of a person with the quality of intellectual autonomy that will predetermine the realization by society of the potential of the technological revolution 4.0, of economic opportunities and progressive changes in society.

All of the above allows the authors of the theory of shocks to substantiate the position that it is self-enforcing companies that are dialectically complex elements left over from a static economy. It is they who are able to mediate the action of the mechanisms of upwards and downwards causation, which in fact realize their own self-organization and self-development. So the self-organization of self-sufficient companies is manifested in the restructuring of their internal organization in accordance with the new realities of the time: the emergence of a critical mass of workers with the quality of intellectual autonomousness, of limitless potential predetermined by the technological revolution 4.0 and with human-centric principals of internal organization. These processes are realized through the mechanism of downwards causation. As for self-development, self-sufficient companies implement it as creators of a new structure of a dynamic economy, mediating the action of the mechanism of upwards causality.

As they plan their path to long-term growth, business leaders have to recognize that there occurring new challenges to contend with during the lockdown. The potential second and third waves of COVID-19 in key markets would likely deepen these concerns, with further adverse consequences in terms of retaining key employees, hiring talent and keeping their workforces productive and integrating the newest technological solutions. In January 2020, CEOs ranked talent risk behind 11 other risks to growth. However, since the start of the pandemic, talent risk has risen to be named as the most significant threat to their businesses ahead of supply chain, the threat of a return to territorialism and environmental risk (Fig. 16).

Figure 16. CEOs: Changing threats to growth
Source: KPMG 2020 CEO Outlook COVID-19 Special Edition

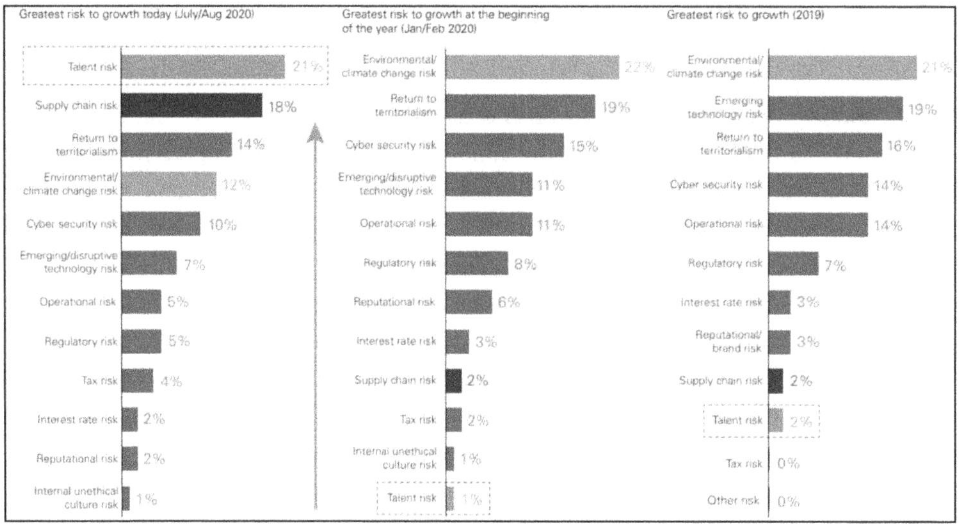

It is no coincidence that in 2019 BCG experts published the concept of human centricity in connection with the necessity of overcoming the skills mismatch (Boston Consulting Group, 2019). According to the BCG estimates, the growth of the world population from the current 7.6 billion to 8.6 billion by 2030 will be accompanied by changes in the age structure: by 2025, the world's workforce will consist of 26% Generation Z'ers, 37% millennials (Generation Y'ers), 28% Generation X'ers, and 9% baby-boomers. With the rapid development of the newest technological paradigm and the humanitarian catastrophe caused by COVID-19, economic and societal crises, a lost generation due to socio-economic problems and the transition to distance education, a human and the factors that predetermine his self-development in terms of becoming a person with the quality of intellectual autonomousness, become a priority in the construction of reality after COVID-19. Before the coronavirus pandemic the share of highly-skilled employees is highest in countries with high GDP per capita and in an innovative economy – 22% to 45% vs. the world average of 15% (Fig. 17). Already these data indicate that without the self-organization of a person, taking into account the quality of ensuring his health and the level of education, further technical progress, solving socio-demographic problems, and associated cultural transformations will be impossible.

In Chapter 5.1, the authors presented their point of view on the quality of the workforce, the demand for which began to form already in the early 2000s. Without repeating the essence of the authors' concept of self-organization of a person who, having learned to overcome the PCB, at the exit from the educational process acquires the quality of the intellectually autonomous personality, it should be emphasized that in this case it is this human that will be associated with the conclusions of BCG experts regarding high-skilled employee or talent. Although in reality everything is much more complicated, while checking the conclusions of the shocks' theory on the applied material of specialists, the authors were forced to look for certain associations. In this regard, the authors associate a personality with the qualities of intellectual autonomousness not only and not so much with factors of survival, ensuring health and a certain number of years spent in an educational institution. Trends on the eve of COVID-19, characterizing the labor force structure in Fig. 17, are impressive: high-skilled or "knowledge" labor force varies from 22% in innovative-driven economy in South Korea to 45% in the UK. Moreover aging of highly-educated population is 45 (median age) as well as tertiary education is 60%.

Figure 17. The increasing complexity of the economy is changing the requirements for human capital development

Notes: [1] Human development index, UNDP 2016; [2] E-Intensity digitalization index, BCG; [3] Based on Rasmussen's methodology: High-skilled – "knowledge" labor force that performs analytical, creative tasks under uncertainty. Medium-skilled – "rule" labor force that performs routine cognitive tasks. Low-skilled – "skill" labor force that performs repetitive primarily physical tasks. Source: Boston Consulting Group (2019). Mission Talent: Mass uniqueness: A global challenge for one billion workers. BCG August

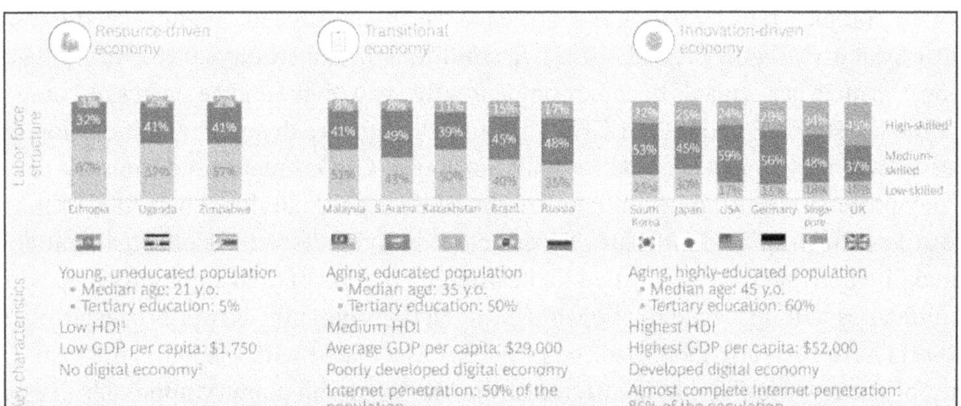

Wherein according to the BCG estimates, the skills mismatch in 2019 affects 1.3 billion people, and every year the global economy pays a 6% tax in the form of lost labor productivity (BCG estimate based on OECD data, 2016). And in connection with the COVID-19 pandemic and the accelerated processes of digitalization of the activities of companies, consumers, workers, etc. one can only agree with the opinion of practitioners that without the introduction of human-centric principles of organization in all spheres of human life in the foreseeable future it will be difficult to approach at least 50% of the share of talented employees in teams. That is why the authors insist that the problem of adequate education, necessary for the formation of the qualities of intellectual autonomousness in a graduate, is much more complicated than associating it with a simple accumulation of individual human capital.

Moreover, if BCG experts express the concept of human-centrism in society, then this already contradicts the interpretation of talents as capital or as a factor of production. Considering that health and education are necessary attributes of any creative worker, then human-centricity in the organization of all spheres of human activity means that without understanding the specifics of self-organization and self-development of a human as a person with the qualities of intellectual autonomousness, it is impossible to structure, project and implement self-developing processes in a dynamic economy and even more so to design the integrity of society.

At the same time, one should not forget that human capital represented by a person with special qualities of intellectual autonomousness is not just a factor, but a person with his own views, values, and desires. And his understanding of his importance aggravates the situation in society, since he will strengthen society with his behavior only if he shares its values and is convinced that they are fair and society is satisfied with such norms of behavior. That is why human-centrism as the dominant principle of future organization of any human systems presupposes a fundamental change in priorities: first, society demonstrates fair principles of collective living in society, and only then talented individuals choose for themselves the sphere in which they will serve society, working conditions for an employer and the priority of creativity in the form that suits him.

As for people with a high intellectual level, they, as a rule, are self-sufficient (self-enforcing). Therefore, they are able to share social preferences and follow the norms of behavior accepted in society only if they share them completely or at least partially. Therefore, the problem of socialization of highly intellectual individuals into the national community as the basis of its societal integrity is no less, and perhaps a more complex puzzle, which did not have much significance within the framework of the capital-centric system (Milanovic, 2011, 2019). In conditions of uncertain reality everything changes. In its structuring, the main participants become companies that can revive and be successful only if they take into account the latest trends and if their CEOs are able to optimize diversity and inclusion in organizational processes within firms. In accordance with the above, CEOs create conditions for creative work, adequately pay professionals, and institutionalize their habits and individual behavior so that collective routines are aligned with individual values. In this case, individuals with intellectual autonomoiusness will be financially motivated, creatively tied to the implementation of their capabilities. In addition, self-enforcing companies will influence relationships in society through the upwards causation mechanism.

BCG experts have correctly identified the problems associated with the skills mismatch, justifying the necessity of the new model that is different from the twentieth century approach. It is difficult to argue with the deep conclusion of the creators of the concept of human centricity that within a social framework it could be possible to involve unlocking one's personal and professional potential without harming others. However, from the point of view of the authors, the problem of human centricity is of a more fundamental nature and the problem cannot be solved only by the social environment of a talented person. If we consider the proposals of BCG specialists regarding the implementation of the concept of human centricity, they boil down to the following: development of a fundamental skill set, creation of an environment that enables lifelong employability, self-sustainability in choosing a career path, labor market transparency, skills liquidity, inclusiveness of the labor market, and value-driven employment (Boston Consulting Group, 2019).

The corrections introduced by the COVID-19 pandemic boil down to the fact that human-centrism, in order to be successful, must become a priority in terms of organizing all system structures in all spheres of human activity. First, it concerns the person himself. Before thinking about its inclusion in economic activity and its integration into the system of social relations, it is necessary to create an education system, not to mention health care, which would be able to prepare a graduate to realize his potential abilities, to form and use them by mastering the mechanism of overcoming psychological and cognitive barriers, and to the practical implementation of the knowledge gained. This is very important, but more important is that the education received should become the basis for the constant generation of knowledge by a person independently. This, perhaps, is the main distinguishing feature of a person with the quality of intellectual autonomousness and another person. In other words, a person receives an education that generates his ability to acquire new knowledge and form from it the structure of knowledge that makes him self-sufficient in any uncertain situation. This quality predetermines his ability to be creative, and it is for this human activity that the public education system should prepare.

Only by becoming self-sufficient in the acquisition of new knowledge, a person becomes able to acquire new opportunities for realizing his potential throughout his life. It is possible to force a person, but it is better to do this in the process of realizing by him that "freedom is a realized need". And in this context, a self-organizing person who has learned to serve society, to constantly generate new knowledge, being an intellectually autonomous person, will dictate the conditions for society to which he agrees to socialize. This is actually what human-centrism consists in: having received self-sufficiency from society during the period of self-organization, a creative person will regulate the structural ties of society, putting in the first place the human-centric principles of organizing all his activities. From the point of view of systemic categories, if a critical mass of persons acquires the quality of intellectually autonomous individuals, then they will build relationships in social and other types of communication based on their own ideas about norms, habits, behavior, etc. Only humans with such a quality become capable of constructing the post-coronavirus reality, which could dynamically make a tremendous leap forward in terms of technological and socio-economic progress.

So the COVID-19 pandemic has shown the increasing importance of self-sufficient individuals with the qualities of intellectual autonomousness and they should represent the critical mass of employees of the future because they will form the basic structural level of society, which is usually called the middle class. It becomes greatly necessary to have a large contingent of rich people who could save a greater proportion of their income than the poor and invest it in physical capital. This is the economic side of assessing the importance of the middle class, whose main representatives should become intellectually autonomous individuals in future. In addition, now that human capital is less than physical capital, quality education available to all is becoming the main factor in economic growth in the future. And broadly accessible education is difficult to achieve unless a society has a relatively even income distribution. Thus, the social side of the importance of the middle class comes to the fore. Really, widespread education not only demands relatively even income distribution but, spirally reproduces it as it reduces income gaps between skilled and unskilled labor.

The most significant social consequence of the expansion of the middle class to a critical size in society is advantages to reducing inequality. And they are both practical — facilitating economic growth — and ethical — reducing unwarranted income disparities between men and women, between people living in different regions of a country, or between citizens of different nations. The past quarter-century has seen contradictory changes: while many types of inequality have increased (particularly those within individual countries), others became less pronounced. A government's refusal to take steps to minimize inequality may reflect its view that redistribution is wasteful and hurts market incentives (endorsing the argument that there is a strong trade-off between equality and growth). However, one can look constructively at this problem through the prism of stimulating the education of intellectually autonomous individuals who, by self-development, will construct a social ladder that allows people to design their better future using the potential of education. Moreover, the coronavirus pandemic has shown that the state's stubbornness to fight inequality by improving the redistribution of income system in the context of COVID-19 has turned into a complete fiasco. Moreover, such methods of the state's struggle against inequality are also unpromising from the point of view of political reality: that the rich wield a disproportionate influence over policy because they are more politically active and contribute more to politicians than their less affluent counterparts.

A. Berg and his colleagues (Berg, et al., 2011a; Berg, et al., 2011b), discovered that equality appears to be an important ingredient in promoting and sustaining growth. The difference between countries that can sustain rapid growth for many years or even decades and the many others that see growth spurts fade quickly may be the level of inequality. Countries may find that improving equality may also improve efficiency, understood as more sustainable long-run growth. That is why the *igniting* growth is much less difficult than *sustaining* it (Hausmann, et al., 2005a, Hausmann, et al., 2005b). Even the poorest of countries have managed to get growth going for several years, only to see it peter out. This fact is extremely relevant in the context of constructing an uncertain post-coronavirus future.

However, current findings reveal that the top 10% in the income distribution holds almost half of the total wealth, while the bottom 40% accounts for only 3%. The OECD has also documented that economic insecurity concerns a large group of the population: more than one in three people are economically vulnerable, meaning they lack the liquid financial assets needed to maintain a living standard at the poverty level for at least three months (OECD, 2019). Moreover, children born to parents who did not complete secondary school have only a 15% chance of making it to university, compared to a 63% chance for children whose parents attended university. Health outcomes, and even life expectancy, are also heavily influenced by socio-economic background.

A strong and prosperous middle class is crucial for any successful economy and cohesive society. The middle class sustains consumption, it drives much of the investment in education, health and housing and it plays a key role in supporting social protection systems through its tax contributions. Societies with a strong middle class have lower crime rates they enjoy higher levels of trust and life satisfaction, as well as greater political stability and good governance.

Social class refers to a group of people who share the same socio-economic status. How this status is defined differs according to different academic traditions and the use to which the concept is being put OECD (OECD, 2016). There are very many definitions of "middle class" (Reeves, et al., 2018; Gornick, et al., 2013). Many economic analyses use income as key indicator to define middle class status. In the rest of the social sciences, most measures and indicators are based on occupation and employment status (Goldthorpe, 2016), although social, cultural and economic capital are also used (Savage et al., 2013; Savage, 2016). The middle class has also been defined using subjective measures such as social class identification (Bird, et al., 2017]. Authors use the middle class as the benchmark to highlight the role of the "middle class" in strengthening the integrity of society in the face of the humanitarian disaster caused by COVID-19. Moreover, undoubtedly, the "middle class" is defined as the population living in households with incomes ranging between 75% and 200% of the national median. The population in households with income below 75% of the median are the "lower-income class" and those with income above 200% of the median are the "upper-income class" (OECD, 2019).

World Economic Forum experts linked inequality with social immobility. In fact, decades of maximizing profits and economic growth are not correlated with the issue of equity and inclusion (WEF, 2020). In the context of the COVID-19 pandemic and in the post-coronavirus reality, it is obvious that to architecture "The New Normal" is impossible without solving the problem of equity and inclusion in the context of restoring the integrity of society after a societal crisis. At the same time, it is difficult to agree with the WEF experts that increasing social mobility implies levelling the playing field for individuals throughout life, from birth to adulthood (World Economic Forum, 2019).

So the shock of COVID-19 has posed challenges that address both the past and the future. The need to understand the patterns of development of events in the modern history of human society is due to the threat of a repetition of the scenario of exponential growth of an infection that is deadly for mankind and testing in an emergency mode of measures for safeguarding people's lives and livelihoods. As for the future, the question of "the New Normal" arises with inevitable necessity, which, in the opinion of almost all experts, will be radically different from the existing one, but today it is shrouded in an impenetrable veil of uncertainty. And at the same time, in reality, there are dialectically complex structures represented by companies that are forced to be the first to implement the "creative destruction" of a static economy and to begin to form the foundations of a future dynamic reality, gradually minimizing its uncertainty.

CONCLUSION

So, the COVID-19 pandemic brought to life a humanitarian catastrophe that objectively put a person at the crossroads of all modern problems. The coronavirus shock only pushed the objective processes of discontinuity in the evolution of a static economy and put it at the very beginning of its path of self-development (dynamics proper). For this path to be completed successfully, it is necessary not only to restructure the economic system and society with the help of the complex elements of the previous system, but to transfer system integrity to a new technological paradigm, realizing the potential of the industrial revolution 4.0. And on this path, a fundamental question arises related to who will be the main driver.

In the current situation of blocked business and social contacts, it is self-enforcing companies that are at the forefront of constructing this post-coronavirus future. The private business is faced with dramatic changes of the demand and supply of goods and services, as well as of the participants' behaviour in the market exchange. The uncertainty as the fundamental feature of the business environment caused by COVID-19 could become a major challenge for any business in shaping its growth strategy. Companies are unlikely to expand their economic activities in the long term if the environment has completely uncertain key parameters. In this situation, the success of the company depends on managers' understanding of the quality of this uncertainty and the development of an effective strategy for its growth, taking into account the main factors of the formation of the qualitatively new human-centric socio-economic system.

In this regard, the idea of J. Schumpeter about the ability of entrepreneurs to carry out "creative destruction" is absolutely relevant. According to the authors, it is the large and largest companies, since only they have their own self-propelled mechanism, capable of constructing the future post-coronavirus reality. It is about their understanding of the main factor of their success, associated with the individual, about the use of his potential as human and social capital, which is largely formed in society, in the practice of their internal organization on the principles of human centrism. At the same time, they definitely highly value the capabilities of workforce with the quality of intellectual autonomousness, as a priority in connection with the introduction of a new technological paradigm into the company's activities.

The rethinking of the role of companies in the future reality allowed the authors to single out them as drivers of future changes, since they are able to implement their internal mechanism of downwards causation, institutionalizing intra-firm structural ties with an orientation towards the primacy of a person with the qualities of intellectual autonomousness. And being capable of mediating the mechanism of upwards causation, the companies were the first to realize and began to replicate the human-centric principles of organization in all spheres of their interaction with all external stakeholders. By creating demand for high skilled workforce with the quality of intellectual autonomousness, resilient companies are able not only to revive full-fledged lifting in society thanks to the revival of the middle class, but also to form from it the basic structural level of post-coronavirus society. Providing high incomes to highly qualified employees, companies objectively participate in the formation and expansion of the middle class through the mechanism of upwards causation. It turned out that in modern conditions of the second wave of the COVID-19 pandemic, it is self-enforcing companies that are destined for the most important strategic mission of strengthening the unity of society. From the standpoint of restoring the integrity of society and structuring the economy, the activities of such advanced firms can hardly be overestimated. It is they who participate in the expansion of the middle class in society, which acts as the basic structural level of society, predetermining its integrity. By the way, this problem is becoming increasingly important by the end of 2020 in connection with the growing anti-government protests of citizens, terrorist acts and other anti-social phenomena in national societies.

So, based on the dialectical foundations of shocks theory, the authors substantiated the specifics of the situation that dominates the economy, society and technology today, and identified the driver on which the construction of the post-coved future depends. It is about self-sufficient companies that are distinguished by the qualities of self-enforcement and structural integrity. It is within the framework of their organization that social institutions are formed, and individual habits turn into collective behavior. And, most importantly, the social institutions created by the CEOs of these companies mediate the mechanisms of downwards and upwards causation. The latter pattern is, perhaps, of the greatest importance for understanding the essence of self-development of a dynamic economy and the role of self-enforcing companies in this process.

And finally, the most important thing is that private business was the first to realize the limits of the capital-centrist economic system, which has developed within national boundaries in a static economy. This is due to the fact that the capital-centric economic system, which dominates almost all countries of the world, demonstrated its extreme potential when the state, on its behalf, destroyed all structural ties in an attempt to stop or slow down the threat to human life that COVID-19 brought. Branco Milanivich (Milanovic, 2019) described this system as follows: "…the entire globe now operates according to the same economic principles – production organized for profit using legally free wage labour and mostly privately owned capital, with decentralized coordination." So, for the first time in the long years of triumphant march across the world capital-centric socio-economic system it demonstrated its inability to protect all social strata of society (ordinary people, asset owners, officials from the state, etc.) from the lethal effects of COVID-19. This situation is theoretically explained by the fact that the system, which is based on capital-centric principles of organization, has passed the marginal point (optimum) in its development. Under the new conditions, such a system is not capable of solving the problems of the post-COVID-19 uncertain future. In this situation, the success of the company depends on managers' understanding of the quality of this uncertainty and the development of an effective strategy for its growth, taking into account the main factors of the of the human-centric socio-economic system.

REFERENCES

2021Deloitte Global Human Capital Trends. (2020). *The social enterprise in a word disrupted: Leading the shift from survive to thrive*. Deloitte. Insights.

Agrawal, De Smet, Poplawski, & Reich. (2020). Beyond hiring: How companies are reskilling to address talent gaps. In *Organization Practice and McKinsey Accelerate*. McKinsey & Company.

Aldrich, H. E. (1999). *Organizations Evolving* (Vol. L). Sage.

Archer, M. S. (1995). *Realist Social Theory: The Morphogeneric Approach*. Cambridge University Press.

Argyris, C., & Schön, D. A. (1996). *Organizational learning II: Theory, method, and practice*. Addison-Wesley.

Berg, A., & Ostry, J. D. (2011b). *Inequality and Unsustainable Growth: Two Sides of the Same Coin?* IMF Staff.

Berg, A., & Zettelmeyer, J. (2011 a). What Makes Growth Sustained? *Journal of Development Economics*.

Bird, R., & Newport, F. (2017). What Determines How Americans Perceive Their Social Class? *Gallup, Polling Matters*. https://news.gallup.com/opinion/pollingmatters/204497/determines-americans-perceive-social-class.aspx

Blitz, D. (1992). *Emergent Evolution: Qualitative novelty and the level of reality*. Kluwer.

Bogdanov, A. A. (1934). *Tectology or General Organizational Science*. URSS.

Boston Consulting Group. (2019). *Mission Talent: Mass uniqueness: A global challenge for one billion workers*. BCG August.

Boston Consulting Group. (2020). *Workforce Sentiment Survey*. BCG.

Clifford, C. (2020). CEO of multibillion-dollar company Slack to employees amid coronavirus: 'Don't stress about work.' *CNBC*.

Coase, R. N. (1937). The nature of the firm. Economica, 4, 386-405.

COVID-19: Briefing materials. (2020). McKinsey & Company.

David, L. (1994). Sturges's seminal 1994 work on crisis communication. Communicating through crisis: A strategy for organizational survival. *Management Communication Quarterly*, *7*(3), 297–316.

Davies, Diemand-Yauman, & van Dam. (2019). Competitive advantage with a human dimension: From lifelong learning to lifelong employability. *McKinsey Quarterly*.

Dixon-Fyle, Hunt, & Prince. (2020). *Diversity wins: How inclusion matters*. Mckinsey & Company.

Edelman Trust Barometer. (2020). *Edelman trust barometer 2020 special report: Trust and the coronavirus*. Daniel J. Edelman Holdings.

Emmett, Schrah, Schrimper, & Wood. (2020). COVID-19 and the employee experience: How leaders can seize the moment. In *Organization Practice*. McKinsey & Company.

Gallup Report. (2017). *State of the Global Workplace*. New York: Gallup Press.

Ghose, B. (2020). *Why 2020 will see the birth of the 'trust economy'.* World Economic Forum.

Goldthorpe, J. (2016). Social class mobility in modern Britain: Changing structure, constant process. *Journal of the British Academy*, *4*, 89–111. https://dx.doi.org/10.5871/jba/004.089

Gornick, J., & Jäntii, M. (2013). *Income Inequality: Economic Disparities and the Middle Class in Affluent Countries*. Stanford University Press.

Grasshoff, G., Coppola, M., Pfuhler, T., Bochtler, S., Gittfried, N., Vogt, P., & Wiegand, C. (2020). *Global Risk 2020: It's Time for Banks to Self-Disrupt*. Boston Consulting Group.

Guszcza & Schwartz. (2020). Superminds, not substitutes: Designing human-machine collaboration for a better future of work. *Deloitte Review*, *27*.

Haslam, S. A., Platow, M. J., & Reicher, S. D. (2010). *The New Psychology of Leadership: Identity, Influence and Power*. Routledge.

Hausmann, R., Pritchett, L., & Rodrik, D. (2005a). Growth accelerations. *Journal of Economic Growth*, *10*, 303–329.

Hausmann, R., Rodrik, D., & Velasco, A. (2005b). *Growth Diagnostics. The John F. Kennedy School of Government*. Harvard University.

Hodgson G.M. (1988). Competence and control in the theory of the firm. *Journal of Economic Behavior and Organization*, *35*(2), 179-201.

Hodgson, G. M. (1988). *Economics and Institutions: A Manifesto or a Modern Institutional Economics*. Polity Press.

Hodgson G.M. (1997). The ubiquity of habits and rules. *Cambridge Journal of Economics*, *21*, 663-684.

Hodgson G.M. (1998). The approach of institutional economics. *Journal of Economic Literature*, *36*(1), 166-192.

Hodgson, G. M. (2002). Reconstitutive downward causation: social structure and the development of individual agency. In Intersubjectivity in Economics: Agents and Structures. Routledge.

Hodgson, G.M. (2003). The hidden persuaders: Institutions and individuals in economic theory. *Cambridge Journal of Economics*, *27*(2), 159-175.

Hodgson G.M., Knudsen, T. (2004). The firm as an interactor: Firms as vehicles for habits and routines. *Journal of Evolutionary Economics, 14*(3), 281-307.

Hunt, Prince, Dixon-Fyle, & Yee. (2018). Delivering through Diversity. Executive summary. *Mackinsey Quarterly*.

Kontopoulos, K. M. (1993). *The Logic of Social Structure*. Cambridge University Press.

KPMG. (2020). CEO Outlook: COVID-19. Special Edition. Executive summary. KPMG International.

Küpper, Reichert, Rastogi, & Kimura. (2020). *How CEOs (chief executive officer) Can Win the Fight and Transform to Win the Future*. BCG.

Leonard, H. B. (2007). Against desperate peril: High performance in emergency preparation and response. In D. E. Gibbons (Ed.), *Communicable Crises: Prevention, Response, and Recovery in the Global Arena*. Information Age Publishing.

Levine, S. R. (2020). Thought Leaders. Diversity confirmed to boost innovation and financial results. *Forbes*, (January), 15.

Levitt, B., & March, J.G. (1988). Organizational learning. *Annual Review of Sociology, 14,* 319-340.

Lonergan, E., & Blyth, M. (2020). *Angrynomics*. Columbia University Press.

Lorenzo, R., Voigt, N., Tsusaka, M., Krentz, M., & Abouzahr, K. (2018). *How diverse leadership teams boost innovation. BCG Henderson Institute*. The Boston Consulting Group, Inc.

Luthan & Youssef. (2007). Positive organizational behavior in the workplace: The impact of hope, optimism, and resilience. *Journal of Management, 33*(5), 774–800.

Marshall, A. (1949). The Principles of Economics (8th ed.). London: Macmillan.

Mattey, C., Hilberath, C., Sibilio, N., Aurora, J., & Ruiz, H. (2020). Personalisation for your people: How COVID-19 is reshaping the race for talent. McKinsey & Company.

McConnell, C., & Brue, S. (2008). *Economics* (17th ed.). McGraw-Hill.

McKinsey & Company. (2020). *From there to here: 50 years of thinking on the social responsibility of business*. McKinsey.com.

Mendy, Stewart, & VanAkin. (2020). A leader's guide: Communicating with teams, stakeholders, and communities during COVID-19. In *Organization Practice*. McKinsey & Company.

Milanovic, B. (2011). Income inequality has risen over the past quarter-century instead of falling as expected. *Finance & Development, 48*(3).

Milanovic, B. (2019). Capitalism, Alone: The Future of the System that Rules the World. Harvard University Press.

OECD. (2016). *Economic Policy Reforms 2016: Going for Growth Interim Report*. Paris: OECD Publishing. en doi:10.1787/growth-2016-

OECD. (2019). *Under Pressure: The Squeezed Middle Class*. Paris: OECD Publishing. doi:10.1787/689afed1-en

Patterson, G. (2020). *How to get your company strategy ready for the Great Reset*. Academic Press.

Popper, K. R., & Eccles, J. C. (1977). *The Self and Its Brain*. Springer International.

Reeves, R., Guyot, K., & Krause, E. (2018). *Defining the middle class: Cash, credentials, or culture*. Brookings. https://www.brookings.edu/research/defining-the-middle-classcash-credentials-or-culture/

Sandbu, M. (2020). *The Economics of Belonging*. Princeton University Press.

Savage, M. (2013). A New Model of Social Class? Findings from the BBC's Great British Class Survey Experiment. *Sociology*, *47*(2), 219-250. doi:10.1177/0038038513481128

Savage, M. (2016). *Poorest Made Poorer? Decomposing income losses at the bottom of the income distribution during the Great Recession*. Economic and Social Research Institute (ESRI). https://www.esri.ie/pubs/WP528.pdf

Schumpeter, J. A. (1949). The Theory of Economic Development: An Inquiry into Profits, Capital, Credit, Interest, and the Business Cycle. Harvard University Press.

Smit, Hirt, Dash, Lucas, Latkovic, Wilson, Greenberg, Buehler, & Hjartar. (2020). Crushing coronavirus uncertainty: The big 'unlock' for our economies. To safeguard lives and livelihoods, we must restore confidence. In *Strategy & Corporate Finance Practice*. McKinsey & Company.

Sperry, R. W. (1964). *Problems Outstanding in the Evolution of Brain Fuction*. American Museum of Natural History.

Sperry, R. W. (1969). A modified concept of consciousness. Psychological Review, 76(6), 532-536.

State of the Global Workplace report. (2017). Gallup.

The business case for inclusive growth. (2018). *Deloitte Global inclusive growth survey*. Retrieved from: www.deloitte.com

Trends, D. G. H. C. (2020). *The social enterprise in a word disrupted: Leading the shift from survive to thrive*. Deloitte. Insights.

Veblen, T. B. (1899). *The Theory of the Leisure Class: An Economic Study in the Evolution of Institutions*. Macmillan.

Volini, Denny, Schwartz, Mallon, Van Durme, Hauptmann, Yan, & Poynton. (2020, May 15). Superteams: Putting AI in the group. *Deloitte Insights*.

WEF. (2020). *The Global Social Mobility Report 2020. Equity, Opportunity and a New Economic Imperative*. Platform for Shaping the Future of the New Economy and Society Business Partners. January.

WEF. (2018). *The Global Competitiveness Report*. World Economic Forum.

Weissman, D. (2000). *A Social Ontology*. Yale University Press.

Williamson, O. E. (1975). *Markets and Hierarchies: Analysis and Ami-Trust Implications: A Study in the Economics and Organization*. Free Press.

Wooll, Hatfield, & Kulasooriya. (2020, Jan. 28). Technologies that touch you: How technology can help people bring their best selves to work. *Deloitte Insights*.

World Economic Forum. (2019). *Towards a Reskilling Revolution, 2019*. Author.

Chapter 10
Nation State and Fighting the COVID-19 Pandemic Shock
Who is Responsible?

ABSTRACT

Nation states have taken the brunt of the fight against the COVID-19 pandemic. The effectiveness of their actions was assessed by all the society in terms of growth rates of infected and deaths, of ability to quickly mobilize all medical services to work in extreme conditions, to increase the capacity of hospitals, of additional medical equipment, of laboratories' capacities and the availability of tests for COVID-19, not to mention the research the vaccine or effective means of treating the disease, etc. In addition, they introduced extreme regimes of lockdowns, having blocked the economy and social interconnections and given rise to an acute problem of the disadvantaged citizens' survival. The great question arose of who should have taken responsibility for missed opportunities. It is unreasonable to blame only the state because it has no alternative today. It is the weakest "link" in the structural "chain" of national societies, but by strengthening it, the entire chain becomes stronger to prevent future disasters.

INTRODUCTION

Increasing the effectiveness of the state remains the most burning issue for all countries in the world. All researchers of this problem are united in the opinion that the effective state formation is predetermined by the peculiarities of national economic systems and national communities (Pigou, 1924; Musgrave, 1959; Bator, 1960). However, the resolution of these particular problems must be preceded by an understanding of the fundamental problem related to the effective state functions and their positioning relative to the whole society preferences. The concept, proposed by authors, is based on the dialectical approach to the interpretation of the state as one of the components of its dialectical unity with society. In this interpretation, the state itself does not mean anything and is not able to create, provide or realize nothing. Being dialectically connected with society, the state assumes the existence of the latter and makes sense only if it exists. Such a dialectical unity can exist and develop only being dialectically contradictory, and all

DOI: 10.4018/978-1-7998-4309-2.ch010

the contradictions should be resolved dialectically, i.e. subject to the coordination of the interests of both the society itself and the state. Otherwise, this dialectic unity simply ceases to exist, and as a result, the very foundations of the institutional structure of the modern national community are destroyed.

As a result the state denial of the public opinion and the state behavior as the main partner in the dialectical unity is the main delusion of policy makers which violates the dialectical status of the interconnection of the society and of the state. And this hinders the dialectical resolution of contradictions, taking into account the dialectical laws unity and struggle of opposites, of the transition of quantity to quality; of negation of negations. In modern conditions, an example of the non-dialectical behavior of the state in relation to society is the implementation of pension reform in a number of countries with an emphasis on the retirement age and budgetary arithmetic with state funds. However, these issues are consistent with society under the new social contract. And it is between the future and current retirees, on the one hand, and the state, on the other. Only a preliminary public approval of government steps in relation to its interests will ensure the effectiveness of the state in this area as well as the dialectical social unity with the state. However, the theoretical interpretation of the interaction of the state and society as a dialectical unity, as well as the reasons for the ineffectiveness of the state defined on this theoretical platform has not yet been presented.

The theoretical emphasis on the state's ability to compensate for the market's "failures" has showed that in their majority they focus on the state' function related to the adequate allocation (allocation) of resources. However, the history of national economies development shows that the modern state fulfills significantly more obligations to society. J.M. Keynes (1936) substantiated that the state should implement stabilization policy in the national economy, ensuring the equilibrium of savings and investments in order to safeguard "full employment" in the economic system. That approach served as a theoretical basis for substantiating the state importance growth without focusing on the effectiveness of its activities. This apparently explains the fact that for a long time none of the known economic theories has considered the role of the state in reducing income inequality, in poverty combating or in protecting citizens from economic and financial risks. Today, with the growth of the importance of inclusive development factors of national societies, the social aspects of state activity could serve as adequate parameters for assessing the effectiveness of the government in the context of dialectical unity with society. It is not by chance that a number of philosophers and economists have seen great importance in the state's activities aimed at allocating budget expenditures for the purpose of implementing equity in the society income distribution (Hochman, and Rogers, 1969; Rawls, 1971; Sen, 1979).

R. Musgrave (1959) assigned an important role to the "redistributive function" of the state. He was sure that the redistribution of national incomes, allocation of resources and stabilization of the economy exhaustively determined all the key functions of the state. The national society redistributes part of GDP to the budget, and the state, in turn, spends it to financing its own functions. At the same time, there is no evaluation of the effectiveness of public spending, at least in the parameters of macroeconomic dynamics. This can explain a number of phenomena that arise with the mediation of the state as in the example of the Piketty's effect (Piketty, et al., 2016). Thus, there have been fundamental changes in the functions of modern national states, the quantitative and qualitative parameters of which are still not well understood (Ritter, 1996; Tanzi, and Schuknecht, 2000).

In the second half of the 20th century the state turned into a giant insurance company and an intermediary for all its citizens. Theoretically, this is due to the state functions expansion, which should be covered by increasing share of GDP redistributed through budgetary channels in favor of the state. It is during this period that phenomenal growth of public expenditures takes place all over the world. As a result the citizens are obliged to pay taxes (price), and in return receive public goods and services (benefits) (De Viti de Marko, 1936; Myrdal, 1954). For most citizens, the relationship between paid taxes and received benefits is not entirely obvious. This has led to the fact that in recent years the problems of fairness and efficiency have become a threat to the legitimacy of the dialectic integrity of the society and the state, which, apparently, underlies the non-effectiveness of the modern state (Solow, 1957; King, and Rebelo, 1993). As time passes the problem of the government activities effectiveness has only worsened. The fact of a significant proportion of GDP used by any national state makes it possible to assess negatively its impact on the economic development in its country. And this means inadequate performance by the state of its function to stabilize the economy. The results show the evidence that investigation of the state as a key element of the dialectical unity with the national society is very important for understanding the real causes of the state activities' inefficiency as to the contemporary national economic slowdown.

The international expert community publications are increasingly discussing categories such as trust, inclusion, openness, belonging, etc. (Smit, et al. 2020; Davies, et al. 2019; Ghose, 2020; Dixon-Fyle, 2020]. This is largely due to the fact that the public policy of economic lockdown and the regime of self-isolation of citizens undertaken by the national states as a reaction to the COVID-19 pandemic became a complete shock to all representatives of social system: for citizens, for business, for the state itself as well as for the whole society. Logically, the question arose about the inability of the capital-centric model of the economics organization to anticipate future shocks and solve the problems of the uncertain post-COVID-19 future.

All the problems posed by COVID-19 objectively predetermine the urgent necessity to rethink the following phenomena: (1) fundamental basis of the functioning of modern socio-economic systems and business with capital-centric principles of their organization; (2) the shock caused by the coronavirus pandemic, which revealed the marginal possibilities of the existing system of organizing economic activity; (3) patterns of structuring the future post-COVID-19 reality and the formation of business principles in the new human-centric socio-economic system; (4) conditions of shocks' ripening compared to that one occurred in early 2020s. It is about people-created systems in national economies and business, as well as about the behavior of the state and private investors, provided that they understand the patterns of self-organization and self-development of systemic integrity in the sphere of economic and social relations. As to the private business they are faced with dramatic changes of the demand and supply of goods and services, as well as the participants' behavior in the market exchange. The uncertainty as the fundamental feature of the business environment caused by COVID-19 could become a major challenge for any business in shaping its growth strategy. Companies are unlikely to expand their economic activities in the long term if the environment has completely uncertain key parameters. In this situation, the success of the company depends on managers' understanding of the quality of this uncertainty and the development of an effective strategy for its growth, taking into account the main factors of the formation of the qualitatively new human-centric socio-economic system.

This chapter provides a chronology of events in the spread of the COVID-19 pandemic across the countries of the world, which is accompanied by a list of responses by nation states that have turned out to be the main operating institution in the fight against a humanitarian disaster. The below material meets the following logic: (1) in paragraph 10.1, the authors structure the emergency actions of nation states, which were subordinated to the achievement of two main goals, summarized by experts in the framework of the "epinomic" policy, and give rough estimates of its economic and social effectiveness; (2) paragraph 10.2 substantiates the main negative consequence of the humanitarian catastrophe caused by the COVID-19 pandemic, which is associated with the destruction of the social integrity of society, which led to the loss of citizens' confidence in their states; and (3) paragraph 10.3 demonstrates the main vice of any state - its conservatism, which is predetermined by its fundamental purpose - to strengthen the structure of the current socio-economic system with all possible means at its disposal. As such, nation states widely used fiscal measures to support citizens, their households and businesses in the pandemic. However, this could not eliminate those deep fault lines in national systems that had developed even before the coronavirus pandemic. As a result, the question was posed as to whether the national societies should rely on the state in preventing possible disasters in the future. If so, what its actions should be today and in the near future.

10.1. Epinomic Policy of Nation States: Economic and Social Costs of Lockdowns

The originality of the crises caused by the COVID-19 pandemic was due to the fact that the national governments were forced to resort to emergency measures of fighting the COVID-19 pandemic by introducing a "self-isolation" regime for citizens and blocking the economic and financial systems at the national level. G. Gopinath, Economic Advisor and Director of the IMF Research Department, identified the 2020 global economic crisis as a global "lockdown" due to "great self-isolation" or "great quarantine" (IMF, 2020). In the opinion of Daniel Susskind, the current situation should be associated with "...a self-inflicted economic catastrophe as a necessary policy response to contain its (COVID-19) spread" (Susskind, 2020). Kristalina Georgieva, IMF Managing Director, associated the current period with 'the Great Lockdown' because to fight a health emergency the national governments have brought production and consumption to a standstill. This has never been done before (From great lockdown to great transformation 2020). Thus the originality of the crises caused by the COVID-19 pandemic was due to the actions of states that failed to quickly identify the "zero" patient and had to introduce economic and social lockdowns that destroyed the structural integrity of national societies and the economics. According to experts' estimates social and economic lockdowns aimed at halting the exponential growth of coronavirus cases caused unprecedented losses. As a result by the end of 2020, 170 countries – almost 90 percent of the world – are worse off with lower per capita income. In March 2020, more than a third of humanity was in lockdown, and by the end of April 2020, 1.6 billion workers stood in immediate danger of having their livelihoods destroyed. The public sector took fast action to protect their workers' health and safety, establish essential services, and deploy workforce strategies to support workers in real time. As of June 2020, governments and international organizations have invested close to $9 trillion to try to prevent the most immediate human and economic impacts. (WEF, 2020). But despite these efforts, the global economy is expected to contract by 3% in 2020, affecting the jobs and livelihoods of millions of people. Nature-related risks have precipitated a Great Deceleration and a structural socio-economic crisis.

In the face of a humanitarian catastrophe, nation states face a daunting mission of safeguarding lives and safeguarding livelihoods. As a result the pandemic dictated the uncontested reduction of state functions to the following two priorities: to stabilize the epidemiological situation in the country and to timely re-open economics after lockdown. The experts of the Boston Consulting Group (BCG) designated that newest dualism in government actions as "epinomics" (Gjaja, et al., 2020). Thus, the COVID-19 pandemic predetermined the sequence of goals of the epinomic policy: first, saving lives and ensuring the health of citizens, and then unblocking the economy.

Exponential growth of infections made national states independently develop their actions, implementing a certain set of means of combating coronavirus infection. The BCG experts divided the process of fighting the COVID-19 pandemic into three phases: flatten, fight, and future (Boston Consulting Group, 2020). On the first "flatten" phase national governments lock down to flatten the virus's exponential growth curve. The main goal is to urgently limit number of confirmed cases, especially critical care. Social distancing (lockdown) and partial business closures outside a few, lead to economic recession with large employment impact. The second "fight" phase is connected with finding paths to collectively fight the virus, restart the economy, and support society in safeguarding lives and livelihoods. Governments are aiming at moderate economic activity with recovering GDP, some business reopenings, and social distancing on sustainable level. A final "future" phase differs from the above phases with controlled disease through vaccine/cure/herd immunity, and treatment within sustainable medical capacities possible. Governments reactivate economy with strong business rebound and job growth, social restrictions become limited or completely suspended (Boston Consulting Group, 2020).

So the combination of the above two goals predetermines three main epinomic strategies of the state in fighting coronavirus infection: (1) crush and contain, (2) flatten and fight, and (3) sustain and support (Fig. 1). As a result, almost everywhere in the "flatten" and "fight" stages, national governments made choices in their politics between health outcomes and economic and societal costs. With confirmed cases of coronavirus and fatalities still rising fast, policymakers will have to keep the public health response their first priority. So the enduring lesson from the COVID-19 pandemic is that any lasting economic recovery will depend on resolving the health crisis. However, the latest World Economic Outlook (Grigoli, et al., 2020) shows that government lockdowns — while succeeding in their intended goal of lowering infections — contributed considerably to the recession and had disproportional effects on vulnerable groups, such as women and young people. It should be noted that the recession was also largely driven by people voluntarily refraining from social interactions as they feared contracting the virus. Therefore, lifting lockdowns is unlikely to lead to a decisive and sustained economic boost if infections are still elevated, as voluntary social distancing will likely persist. Yet the analysis finds that a balance can be achieved in protecting public health while preventing a protracted economic decline (International Monetary Fund, October 2020). Lockdowns impose short-term costs but may lead to a faster economic recovery as they lower infections and thus the extent of voluntary social distancing (Fig. 2).

The IMF experts analyze (Grigoli, et al., 2020) the economic effects of lockdowns and voluntary social distancing using two high-frequency proxies for economic activity: mobility data and job openings. So over the entire sample of 128 countries, lockdowns and voluntary social distancing contributed equally to the drop in mobility during the first 3 months of a country's epidemic. Fig. 3 shows that stay-at-home orders led to a sharper decline in the mobility of people aged 18 to 24 and 25 to 44 who tend to have younger children to care for when schools are closed and often have temporary job contracts that are more likely to be terminated during a crisis. The larger impact on these populations threatens to increase inter-generational inequality.

The effectiveness of lockdowns in reducing infections, coupled with the finding that infections can considerably harm economic activity because of voluntary social distancing, calls for re-considering the prevailing narrative about lockdowns involving a trade-off between saving lives and supporting the economy. This characterization of lives vs. livelihoods neglects that effective lockdown measures taken early during an epidemic may lead to a faster economic recovery by containing the virus and reducing voluntary social distancing. These medium-term gains may offset the short-term costs of lockdowns, possibly even leading to positive overall effects on the economy.

Figure 1. Three specific epinomic strategies of national governments in beating the coronavirus
Source: The World Bank, Oxford COVID-19 Government Tracker, Wordometer, BCG analysis.

	Crush and contain	Flatten and fight (MOST COMMON APPROACH)	Sustain and support
OBJECTIVE	**Full containment** to reduce the number of local coronavirus cases to close to zero through rapid, stringent lockdowns, combined with aggressive testing, tracking, contact tracing, quarantining, and isolating	**Attempted containment** with strong interventions to decrease the number of coronavirus cases and avoid overwhelming the health care system's capacity	**Open containment** with moderate interventions and primary reliance on voluntary restraint to limit the number of coronavirus cases until herd immunity is achieved or a vaccine or cure is developed
IMPLICATIONS FOR RESTART	**Opening the economy in a walled society,** focusing on strict border controls and testing to keep the number of new cases to an absolute minimum and restore economic vitality	**Progressively lifting restrictions and reopening the economy** without surpassing the health care system's limits	**Prolonged quarantining of the vulnerable population,** while the less vulnerable pursue economic activities with few constraints but continued health precautions
PREREQUISITES	• Early, stringent interventions and the acceptance of prolonged lockdowns, when necessary • Strict border control • High volumes of testing and contact tracing relative to the number of cases	• Resources to expand the health care system's capacity • Ability to increase coronavirus monitoring (testing, tracking, and contact tracing) • Adherence to safety protocols during the reopening	• Ability to isolate and support the socioeconomic well-being of the vulnerable • High trust in government translating into high compliance levels • Favorable demographics
EXAMPLES	China, New Zealand, South Korea, and Taiwan	Brazil, Germany, Italy, Nigeria, the UK, and the US	Sweden

Figure 2. Lockdowns reduced infections especially if adopted early (cumulated COVID-19 cases per thousand people)
Note: The lines denote cross-country averages. The shaded areas correspond to the inter quartile ranges
Source: Francesco Grigoli and Damiano Sandri. (2020). COVID-19's Impact in Real Time: Finding Balance Amid Crisis. Blog. October. IMF

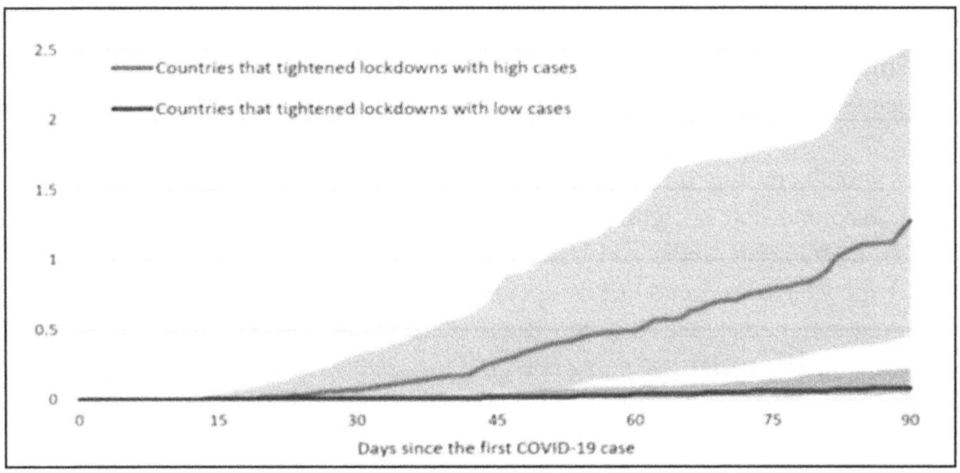

The contribution of voluntary social distancing was larger in advanced economies where people can work from home more easily or can even afford to stop working thanks to personal savings and social security benefits. Conversely, people in low-income countries are often unable to opt for voluntary social distancing as they do not have the financial means to cope with a temporary income loss. The analysis of job posting data provides similar insights, showing that both lockdowns and voluntary social distancing contributed substantially to the drop in labor demand.

Figure 3. The economic effects of lockdowns and voluntary social distancing on economic activity (percent decline in mobility)
Note: The chart displays the contributions of lockdowns and voluntary social distancing in reducing mobility during the first three months of each country's epidemic
Source: Francesco Grigoli, and Damiano Sandri. (2020). COVID-19's Impact in Real Time: Finding Balance Amid Crisis. Blog. October. IMF

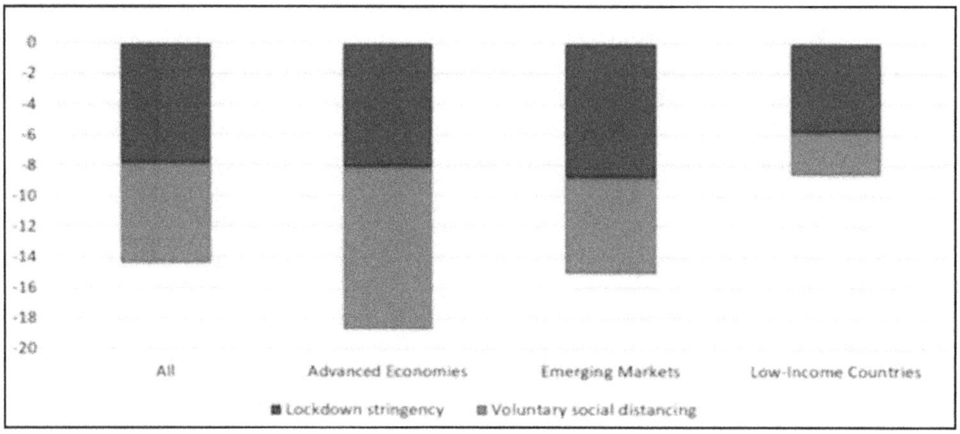

The specificity of the first problem is related to the fact that, together with the physical health of citizens in the context of levelling the epidemiological situation in the country, perhaps the most important thing for states becomes to eliminate the negative consequences of the societal crisis. In the latter case, it is about the mechanisms of socialization of individuals in the structure of society. But in any case the coronavirus is still out there, and unemployment and economic activity take huge hits. As a result, the societal crisis deepens and the uncertainties about which strategy to pursue are manifold (Gjaja, et al., 2020).

Nation states should consider different factors to decide on a choice or a combination of three main epinomic strategies of the state in fighting coronavirus infection (Fig. 4 and 5).

As for Fig. 6, then France, India and UK have extended the lockdowns starting week ending 18 April, whereas Turkey has a weekend lockdown. Denmark has allowed primary school to reopen, Spain has allowed non-essential businesses like construction and manufacturing workers to go back to work.

US has instituted stricter social distancing norms, Iran has allowed government offices and businesses outside Tehran to turn operational. China has lifted Hubei lockdown allowing people movement. Thus the shape of epinomic policy of different nation states may vary in depth and duration depending on country and sector composition of the economy.

Despite the absolute drop in the volume of material production in the world, social problems turned into much greater losses. Moreover, citizens make their main claims in connection with the coronavirus pandemic, the social and economic lockdown and its devastating consequences for individuals to the state. And it is the state who is accused of all coronavirus problems (Korchakova-Heeb, 2020, p. 12). And there is a lot of truth in this. It turned out that national systems for the supply of public goods such as health care and healthcare were completely unprepared to confront humanitarian disasters such as the COVID-19 pandemic.

Figure 4. Five different factors should inform the sequencing decision of the nation states' epinomic policy
Note: The virus resurgence risk factor takes into account frequency of contact, contact with external customers, physical proximity during interactions, likelihood of exposure to illness
Source: BCG (2020). COVID-19. BCG Perspective. Publication #2 with a focus on: Preparing for the restart. Version: 20 April 2020

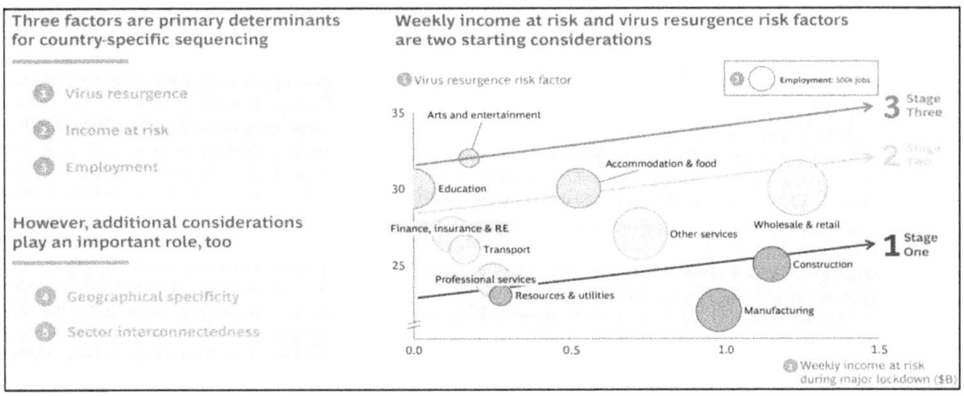

Figure 5. Scenarios and potential outcomes driven by five key questions as of 14 April 2020
Source: BCG (2020). COVID-19BCG Perspective. Publication #2 with a focus on: Preparing for the restart. Version: 20 April 2020

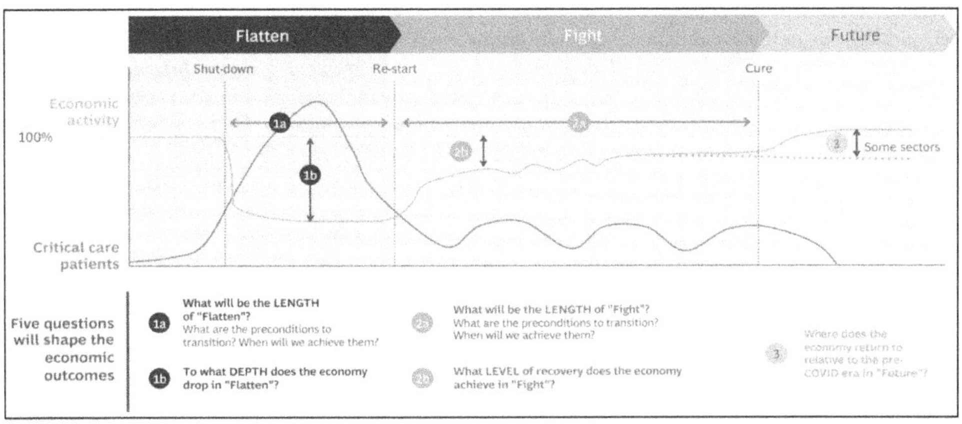

The case for strengthening the world's pandemic response capacity at the global, national, and local levels is compelling. The economic disruption caused by the COVID-19 pandemic could cost between $9 trillion and $33 trillion (McKinsey & Company, May 2020)—many times more than the projected cost of preventing future pandemics. The experts of McKinsey & Company, have estimated that spending $70 billion to $120 billion over the next two years and $20 billion to $40 billion annually after that could substantially reduce the likelihood of future pandemics (Craven, et al., 2020) (Fig. 7).

It is appropriate to emphasize that the main "failure" of the state in the socio-economic systems that have developed by 2020 is that economic goals are primary in its activity, and that ensuring the life and health of citizens plays a subordinate role. The extreme conditions of the deadly coronavirus pandemic have changed priorities, making the health of citizens an ongoing concern and the first paramount public goal. However, the growing number of infected and deaths from coronavirus, a social lockdown that has led to complete uncertainty about the future welfare of citizens, a radical change in their usual way of life have predetermined the societal crisis. It has manifested itself in the acute discontent of individuals with the state, in all-encompassing opportunism in relation to all of its anti-coronavirus actions. And this, undoubtedly, turns into the main obstacle to an effective strategy of the state aimed at the timely re-opening of the economy. Against this backdrop, rising unemployment and economic lockdown have become extremely expensive public strategy in the fighting COVID-19 pandemic. As a result, all these costs should be attributed to the losses of society due to the fact that the state was unable to build a public healthcare system capable of functioning in anticipation of the huge human and economic losses caused by COVID-19. In fact, they can be interpreted as the price of the fallacy of all the previous practice of national governments that provided rapid growth and optimizing economic output at the expense of underestimating the priority of creating a sustainable public health system. Such misunderstanding of the subordination of the goals of ensuring the health and well-being of citizens and economic growth rates at any cost largely predetermined the transcendental inefficiency of the state in the context of the COVID-19 pandemic, as well as in the implementation of the societal crisis. In practice, this turned into a catastrophic collapse of the global economy and the destruction of the societal integrity of national communities.

Figure 6. Government measures continue to be enforced US[1] gets stricter in hard-hit areas; China, Spain, Denmark, Iran selectively opening up

Source: BCG (2020). COVID-19BCG Perspective. Publication #2 with a focus on: Preparing for the restart. Version: 20 April 2020

Notes: [1] Includes nationwide actions and actions taken by major local or regional governments.

[2] Some German + US rail services are being reduced but not through government mandate International travel restrictions flagged if any bans put in place or limits in place; Internal travel restriction includes reductions in public transport, or restricted access; Non-essential businesses include at least restaurants, entertainment venues; School closures are any mandatory state closures; Assembly restrictions include mandatory and advised restrictions on large groups, restrictions on e.g. faith based gatherings; Non-essential local movement includes stated restrictions on being outside or curfews / Source: Government and media

The positive consequences of a successful epinomic policy of states in the categories of lost opportunities can be assessed using the results of the McKinsey Global Institute experts (McKinsey Global Institute, July 2020). Better health promotes economic growth by expanding the labor force and by boosting productivity as well as by delivering immense social benefits as a basis for eliminating the negative consequences of the societal crisis and restoring societal integrity of the society. Moreover in recent years, a focus on rising healthcare costs, especially in mature economies, has dominated the policy debate. But the health as an investment in national societies has largely been ignored (Vaslavskiy, et al., 2019). The COVID-19 pandemic, giving rise to a societal crisis, has put the health system first in the context of its priority for individuals, national societies and economics as well as for the global economic system. This approach makes it possible to assess the missed opportunities for individuals, societies, and economies in the case of effective state policy and prevention of the extreme human and economic losses.

Figure 7. Assuming a COVID-19-scale epidemic is a 50-year event, the return on preparedness investment is clear, even of it only partly mitigates the damage (estimated costs, $ billion)
Source: Matt Craven, Adam Sabow, Lieven Van der Veken, and Matt Wilson (2020). Not the last pandemic: Investing now to reimagine public-health systems. Healthcare Systems & Services, Public Sector, and Social Sector Practices. McKinsey & Company July

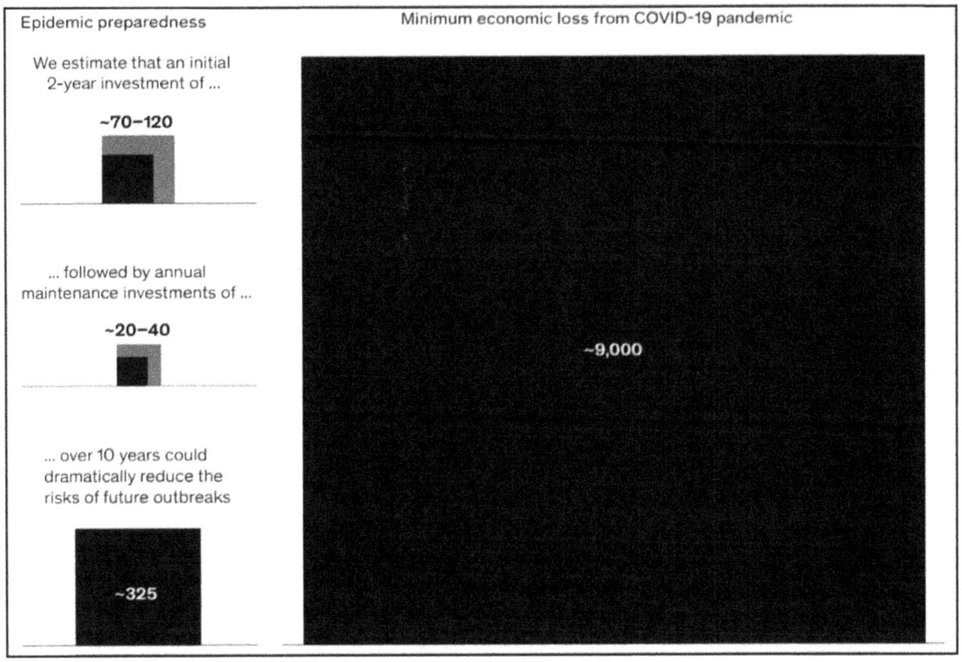

A well-functioning public healthcare system means that over 70% of the gains could be achieved from prevention by creating cleaner and safer environments, encouraging healthier behavior and addressing the social factors that lie behind these, as well as broadening access to vaccines and preventive medicine. As a result 230 million more people would be alive by 2040 and the welfare value of good health could be as high as $100 trillion. This is a rough estimate of the lost opportunities for society as a result of the failures of the state, which failed to form a highly effective national health system capable of preventing extreme conditions of the COVID-19 pandemic and societal crisis as a manifestation of citizens' distrust of the state. According to the McKinsey Global Institute evaluations, better health could add $12 trillion to global GDP in 2040, an 8 percent boost that translates into 0.4 percent faster growth every year (McKinsey Global Institute, July 2020). About half of these annual economic benefits come from a larger and healthier workforce. The remainder come from expanding the capacity of older people, people with disabilities, and informal caregivers to work as well as from productivity gains as the burden of chronic health conditions is reduced. The economic return could be $2 to $4 for each $1 invested in better health. In higher income countries, implementation costs could be more than offset by productivity gains in healthcare delivery (Fig. 8).

Figure 8. For each $1 invested in improving health, an economic return of $2 to $4 is possible.
Note: Note: Snapshot view of the healthy growth scenario in 2040. Additional healthcare spending, GDP impact, and welfare gains directly attributable to better health only (excluding expanded participation).
Source: McKinsey Global Institute (2020). Prioritizing Health: A Prescription for Prosperity. Executive Summary. July.

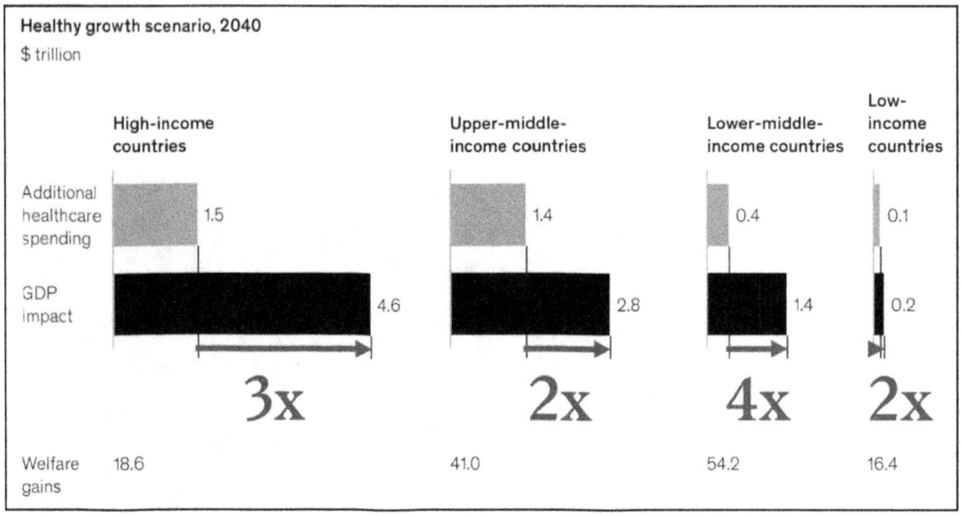

But as to the effective protection of those who are health vulnerable, the BCG experts would see lower infection rates among this population. Tragically, that is more the exception than the rule. A study of eight countries' long-term care facilities showed that these facilities accounted for anywhere from 19% (Hungary) to 62% (Canada) of COVID-19 deaths. In New Jersey, the second hardest hit state in the US, more than half of deaths occurred in long-term care facilities. Some estimates suggest that these facilities are home to more than 40% of US COVID-19-related fatalities, despite their residents accounting for about 0.5% of the overall population (Brimmer, et al., 2020). This would suggest that residents at these facilities are being infected at a rate that is at least three times that of the general population—and perhaps much more. That means capturing the health and economic benefits would not be easy. It requires reorienting thinking about and investing in health and healthcare delivery, as well as fostering healthier living conditions and changing behavior. It also requires changes in the workplace and economic policy to allow, among others, increased participation of older people in the workforce. But it's worth. According to early estimates of the McKinsey Global Institute, the pandemic and its repercussions could lead to a 3 to 8 percent drop in global GDP in 2020 (McKinsey Global Institute, July 2020). Moreover, each year, poor health reduces global GDP by 15 percent.

So as countries emerge from the COVID-19 crisis, they meet a once-in-a-generation opportunity to rethink the role of health in a post-pandemic future as well as the quality of the government that could be in a position to fulfil this historic mission. Making health a priority and shifting focus to areas with highest return can improve resilience, reduce health inequity, and promote greater individual, social, and economic well-being. Prevention of diseases is typically less expensive than treatment and reduces the need for more expensive treatment later on, contributing to a high economic return. Capturing the benefits would require dramatic changes that extend beyond what the state typically thinks of as healthcare. It requires substantial changes in where and how healthcare is delivered, as well as changes to communities that would help individuals grow up, work, and age in healthy ways. That means great changes in governments' and regional authorities' way of activities. As to companies, innovators, and communities they need to understand the necessity to shape environments and societies in ways that promote healthy lives and capture the societal and economic benefits. There could be a better moment to invest in global health to promote well-being and prosperity.

10.2. Social Impact of the Humanitarian Disaster Caused by the COVID-19 Pandemic: Undermining Trust of Citizens in Nation States

The coronavirus pandemic has put the state before the choice of safeguarding lives and safeguarding livelihoods of the citizens. The specificity of this dilemma lies in the fact that it has a pronounced fiscal form of manifestation, since it is associated with budget spending on health care and social security. At the same time, reopening business after economic and social lockdowns is a necessary condition for expanding tax revenues to budget revenues of nation states. In the context of the COVID-19 pandemic, the problem of balancing budgets has become threatening against the background of an absolute decline in global GDP. At the same time, against the background of growing budget spending associated with the fight against the COVID-19 pandemic, additional public debts and their servicing increased the budget deficits of the countries of the world (Chapter 10.3). It is these fiscal problems that today predetermine the choice by national governments of the prospects for structuring the post-coronavirus future.

From a theoretical point of view, there are two diametrically opposite alternatives: back to a static economy or forward to a dynamic reality. The question is whether the nation state is inclined to restructure the existing society and build a New Normal, changing only its form of manifestation, or to structure systemic integrity in the economy and in society, essentially changing the drivers of their self-movement and the principles of their organization. The speed of economic recovery after COVID-19, the main drivers, beneficiaries and mechanisms for transforming the economy and society, as well as scenarios for transforming the state itself and its fiscal functions will depend on the state's choice of the further path. What choice is progressive can already be judged today in connection with the growing phenomenon of citizens' loss of confidence in their nation states. Moreover, they had plenty of reasons for mistrust in the state even before the coronavirus pandemic. The humanitarian catastrophe that is developing today is largely predetermined by the failure of nation states to build highly effective health systems capable of protecting the lives and health of the population from pandemics in a preventive manner.

It should be emphasized that the state is not directly involved in the production of GDP in the country, and is only engaged in its redistribution (and partial distribution) in order to stimulate economic growth in the country and social security in terms of those public goods that the population needs (and, to varying degrees). In this case, the owners of the factors of production (land, capital, labor) produce GDP. At the same time, giving part of their revenues to the budget, taxpayers must be sure of the effectiveness of the state's actions, since in return it must create conditions, including spending budget revenues that stimulate economic growth and prosperity of societies. In this context, budgetary spending on health care of almost all nation states turned out to be ineffective. And this was manifested in the fact that national health systems were unable to prevent the growing number of deaths from coronavirus infection and ensure the health of all citizens in the face of the COVID-19 pandemic. As a result, the humanitarian catastrophe that unfolded all over the Globe proves the inefficiency of the state in its modern quality. The losses from the COVID-19 pandemic are huge and irreparable. Moreover, from the point of view of the authors, the most serious problem caused by the pandemic was the loss of citizens' confidence in their state. This is what turned into a societal crisis. In fact, it is about the destruction of the integrity of society, which is becoming the main obstacle to overcoming the consequences of the COVID-19 pandemic. If the state cannot return the trust of its citizens, then it is problematic to talk about an effective solution to the above problems.

However, the state today is far from choosing a strategy for future changes in society. Today it is trying to optimize budgetary spending to fight the pandemic and ensure livelihoods for those who survived. Nation governments face a more complex — and, in some respects, even more daunting – challenge: to begin relaxing physical-distancing guidelines in order to restart the economy and do so in a way that doesn't spark new outbreaks of infection. The stakes could not be higher. Making the right choices will allow economic and social activity to resume while keeping transmission at manageable levels (Keneally, et al., 2020). Making the wrong choices, however, could not only result in a renewed surge of cases and fatalities. Thus some state and regional governments around the world have already had to slow the reopening process or even institute new lockdowns in the face of spikes in the number of people infected (Table 1).

And in these conditions, the choice is usually determined by the fact how to use limited financial resources to maximize social and economic well-being. In other words, the fiscal budgeting process is the mechanism by which public officials assess the benefit-to-cost ratio of various spending choices and make critical spending decisions and tradeoffs. And this can be explained. As a whole during the COVID-19 pandemic spending on healthcare has been falling. Healthcare spending across the world's 60 biggest economies fell by 1.1% in US-dollar terms by the end of 2020 (Covid-19: the impact on healthcare expenditure, 2020). This forecast depends on the fact that 2020 year's economic downturn has been caused by a healthcare emergency the coronavirus pandemic as well as doctors' clinics have reported far fewer patients than normal.

It could be explained as follows. While governments and healthcare managers have poured resources and funding into combatting the virus, in many cases they have also cancelled or reduced non-urgent care for other conditions. Patients, meanwhile, are reluctant to go to hospitals or clinics, either because they fear contracting coronavirus, or because they worry about placing an additional burden on healthcare workers.

As to healthcare spending in local-currency terms in 2020 it decreased in the UK by 2.8% compared to the previous year, in Germany – by 1.6%, in the US – by 1% and in Japan – by 0.2% accordingly. Conversely, in India this indicator increased by 4.7%, and in China – by 8.5% compared with 2019. Over 2020 as a whole healthcare spending declines only slightly in nominal local currency terms in most developed countries.

Many countries will also need to spend heavily on the promised new treatments and vaccines for coronavirus as they seek a more permanent exit from quarantine. Meanwhile, the pandemic will have highlighted gaps in healthcare systems that governments will be under pressure to fill. To make decisions about relaxing physical-distancing guidelines, public officials should assess the benefits and costs of various types of social interactions to make informed tradeoffs that will allow more economic and social activity while also minimizing the risk of uncontrolled transmission. In other words, governments take part in preparing some sort of social interactions budget. If we return to the problem of citizens' trust in the state, which is subject to significant undermining, then the relationship between social contract and good quality of public services, on the one hand, and citizens trust in the government, on the other hand, proposed by the experts of the Act Church of Sweden deserves attention (Kidd, et al., 2020). The point is that it is advisable to assess low government revenues as the function of the declining citizens' trust in the government as the main challenges facing countries across the Globe. Really, governments build trust through the provision of universal public services for citizens in example of high quality health care and universal social security. Universal public services include schemes such as universal old age pensions, public health system, as well as the universal secondary education system. In a relatively short period of time all these universal public services built trust among their citizens, enabling governments to vastly increase levels of taxation. In fact, if social cohesion was strengthened, inequality was tackled, peace was maintained, economies grew, and prosperity was shared among the many, not the few, than government can count on an increase in budget revenues to over 50 per cent of GDP.

In this context, all the events that led to the humanitarian disaster as a result of COVID-19 pandemic contributed heavily to the undermining of trust in nation states. In effect, they are in danger of fanning the flames of an already dangerous fire. The COVID-19 crisis is an opportunity to re-think the paradigm of social security and learn the lessons of history. In theory, governments could gain the trust of their citizens by investing in universal health and education services. Yet, good quality health and education services take a long time to establish with citizens not noticing improvements for many years, resulting in them losing faith in governments. Building trust and a strong social contract is particularly important in dangerous times.

Trust in government is the basic building block of any successful nation state. It needs to be at the very top of the list of government priorities since, once trust is undermined, the state itself can be threatened. And as it turned out, it was not only the state.

The coronavirus pandemic showed that for many years until 2020, the disrupted dialectic of interaction between society and a static economy affected the gradual undermining of social integrity. And the shock of COVID-19 instantly reduced this problem to a loss of citizens' confidence in national governments, which significantly reduced the effectiveness of government actions in the fight against infection (IMF World Economic Outlook Databases). This was expressed both in the individual refusal of citizens of certain countries from the mask regime and social distancing, and in the hooligan actions of the population against certain branches of the official government in their countries during the fight against the pandemic. This form of manifestation of citizens' distrust of their government has a reason associated with the societal crisis. Ultimately, this is fraught with enormous problems for the state during the formation of conditions for the New Normal post-covid period.

According to the history a key factor in building trust in the nation states is the provision of universal public services, since they can be enjoyed by everyone on an equal and impartial basis. Despite the widespread belief that paying taxes is unpopular, the high-tax countries are ranked among the happiest countries in the world: Finland is ranked first, Denmark second, Norway third and Sweden seventh (Helliwell, et al., 2019). Indeed, the tax office in Sweden is one of the country's most trusted government agencies (Fouché, 2008; Fouché, 2009; Livingston, 2016; Jansson, 2018; Wiles, 2020). As a result, trust in government determines the extent to which governments are able to tax their citizens. Sweden's Ministry of Finance states: "If citizens do not trust that the resources they give up when they pay taxes or charges are used appropriately, there may be serious resistance to contributing to the common good" (Sweden Ministry of Finance, 2017). It is in this context that trust is at the heart of any relationship but especially within the national social contract. A further factor that builds trust in the state is governments acting impartially with their citizens and treating them fairly. As B. Rothstein (Rothstein, 2018) state: "The core idea of quality of government has been theorized to be that of impartiality in the exercise of power." Similarly, J. Jansson (2018) argues that: "Research has demonstrated that perceived fairness is decisive for tax compliance; if citizens perceive the tax system or the government's use of tax money

Table 1. Fiscal strategies during different phases of the pandemic

Fiscal Measures	1. Widespread Lockdowns	2. Gradual Reopening	3. Post–COVID-19 Recovery
Household Income Support			
Cash or in-kind transfers	Yes, they likely have the largest multipliers, particularly for basic necessities and public services	Transition and better target to those in need	Reconsider within the reforms to enhance social protection systems
Unemployment benefits	Expand coverage and extend duration	Refine the benefits to preserve work incentives as unemployment returns to normal levels	Key components when enhancing social protection systems
Employment Measures			
Short-term work-/ job-retention schemes	Yes, they can help preserve jobs and worker-firm relationships	Reduce use of these programs to encourage moving to new jobs if needed	Reduce access for prolonged cases
Temporary hiring subsidies	Not yet	Plan or initiate if supply disruptions have largely eased	Transition to active labor market policies (for example, retraining)
Active labor market policies	Not yet	Initiate with programs that improve labor skills (education, digitalization)	Yes, tailored to structural transformation in the post–COVID-19 economy
Public Investment			
	Planning for next phase	Could boost maintenance and public works; plan for next phase, emphasizing job creation and green recovery	Scale up quality investment with sustainable financing
Tax Measures			
Temporary deferral of taxes and social security payments	Yes, to protect cash flows for households and firms	Targeted deferrals, depending on taxpayers, pandemic developments, and strength of recovery	No, but could engage taxpayers as part of debt restructuring
General income tax cuts	No, because they largely benefit those not in need	No, because those benefiting are less likely to spend the additional income and because the cuts likely favor firms with profits	Consider as part of the stimulus package depending on fiscal space; could bring stronger effect if targeted to cash-constrained households
Accelerated depreciation or loss-carry backward	Not yet	Yes, to firms that resume activity	Yes
Progressive taxes	Consider, especially if financing is limited	Consider, especially if financing is limited	Yes, choice of instruments should conform to good tax law design; greater progressivity of taxes and ensuring highly profitable firms pay appropriate taxes helps finance other measures and may ease social tensions
Other Liquidity Support			
Loans, guarantees	Yes, could be partially conditional on preserving jobs, with restrictions on dividends/ executive pay	Refine with declining generosity	Tighten for a timely exit and manage fiscal risks
Solvency support (equity injections)	Yes, with dividend restrictions and imposing losses to shareholders	Interventions on systemic and strategic firms; restrictions on dividends/executive pay	Aim for a timely exit
Debt restructuring	No, possible debt moratorium	Prepare streamlined restructuring framework and mediation mechanism for a speedy workout	Yes, to facilitate reallocation and timely exit of nonviable firms

Note: Appropriate fiscal responses will be country-specific depending on the fiscal space, the development of the pandemic, and the strength of the recovery. Measures included here are not exhaustive and will need to be adapted to the specific tax and benefit systems of individual countries. For countries with less-developed social protection systems, other measures, such as in-kind provision of food and basic public services may be introduced. COVID-19 = coronavirus disease 2019.

Source: International Monetary Fund (IMF). 2020. Fiscal Monitor: Policies for the Recovery. Washington, October

as fair, it is more likely that they will comply." An important characteristic of universal public services is their impartiality and fairness: everyone is able to receive the same standard of service, irrespective of where they are placed in society. As B. Rothstein (2018) argues: "One of the most effective ways for decreasing economic inequality … is via universal or broad-based public services and benefits such as universal health care and pensions, childcare allowances and free higher education." Indeed, the provision of universal public services is at the heart of a virtuous circle that delivers decent societies through greater trust in government and higher government revenues (Fjeldstad, et al., 2014).

Unfortunately, it is common for the basic elements that build trust to be missing in the delivery of public services – including social security – in many countries in the period of the exponential increase of coronavirus infected. As a result, trust in government is undermined and the virtuous circle that generates high quality public services is absent, thereby contributing to a weakening of the national social integrity (Fig. 9). Not by chance, many low- and middle-income countries are currently experiencing the type of vicious circle that Europe faced prior to the Second World War. Governments provide poor quality services, which weakens citizens' trust in their governments, thereby undermining the social contract. As a result, citizens are discouraged from paying taxes, leading to low government revenues and, therefore, low investment in public services, which further undermines trust, and so it goes on. It is a vicious circle that countries need to break.

Trust in government is a precious resource. It is the basic building block of any successful nation-state. Once trust is undermined, the state itself can be threatened. According to the history a key factor in building trust is the provision of universal public services, which are given to everyone on an equal and impartial basis. In contrast, poverty-targeted schemes – such as the poor relief programs found across the Globe – are perceived as arbitrary and unfair and, therefore, actively undermine trust. It is unsurprising, therefore, that many countries that have used poor relief as the basis of the social security systems – and have purposively excluded the majority of the populations, in particular the 'missing middle,' from support – have weak social integrity and, as a consequence, low levels of government revenue.

The severity of such a test, which fell on the shoulders of individuals as their well-being and established way of living were destroyed, turned into an overestimation of the role of state and society in ensuring the stability of households. The most striking demonstration of such individual reassessments was the compliance or non-compliance by citizens with self-isolation regimes, since they became a function of the degree of their trust in the actions of their state and of individual desire to follow the extraordinary norms of behavior imposed in society in connection with the COVID-19 pandemic.

Thus, the coronavirus exposed the main "spring" of modern societies, which was unable to dampen the consequences of an unexpected infection, dangerous to human life, and contributed to the development of a societal crisis as a demonstration of national societies' structural disunity. It is in this context the Boston Consulting Group' experts (Boston Consulting Group Perspectives, 2020) have treated the COVID-19 outbreak as the first and foremost a societal crisis. Thus if trust is to be built quickly, the best means of doing so is through universal healthcare, education and social security. COVID-19 has created a major crisis across all countries and has highlighted the failings of the prevailing social and economic policies in most countries. A key problem is to use COVID-19 as the catalyst for the type of paradigm shift in social and economic policy of the nation states.

It is in this regard the most experts admit that after the COVID-19 pandemic the global world will become different, but both citizens and society will remain in it. At the same time, the consequences of the societal crisis should be eliminated by the state as an indispensable condition for further socio-economic progress. In this regard, it should be emphasized that the citizens' trust in the nation state becomes of particular importance. And the formal institutions in the hands of the state become an effective tool for restoring the societal integrity of national communities. In this context, it is about the behavior of the state, which must earn the trust of citizens by providing them with high-quality public goods of the first necessity - health care and education. After the deafening failure of nation states with the formation of a national health system that turned out to be unprepared for pandemics such as COVID-19, and with the crisis state of education manifested in the growing skills mismatch and skills gap, it will take a long time to consolidate national societies around governments. In other words, the emergency conditions caused by the coronavirus pandemic in 2020 made the national states is the weakest link on which the prospect of structuring the post-coronavirus future depends and which itself is limited in its actions by severe budgetary constraints.

Figure 9. The vicious circle of the cycle of undermining citizens' trust in the nation state
Source: Kidd, Stephen, Gunnel Axelsson Nycander, Anh Tran, and Madeleine Cretney. (2020). The social contract and the role of universal social security in building trust in government. Working Paper: November. Development Pathway. Sweden

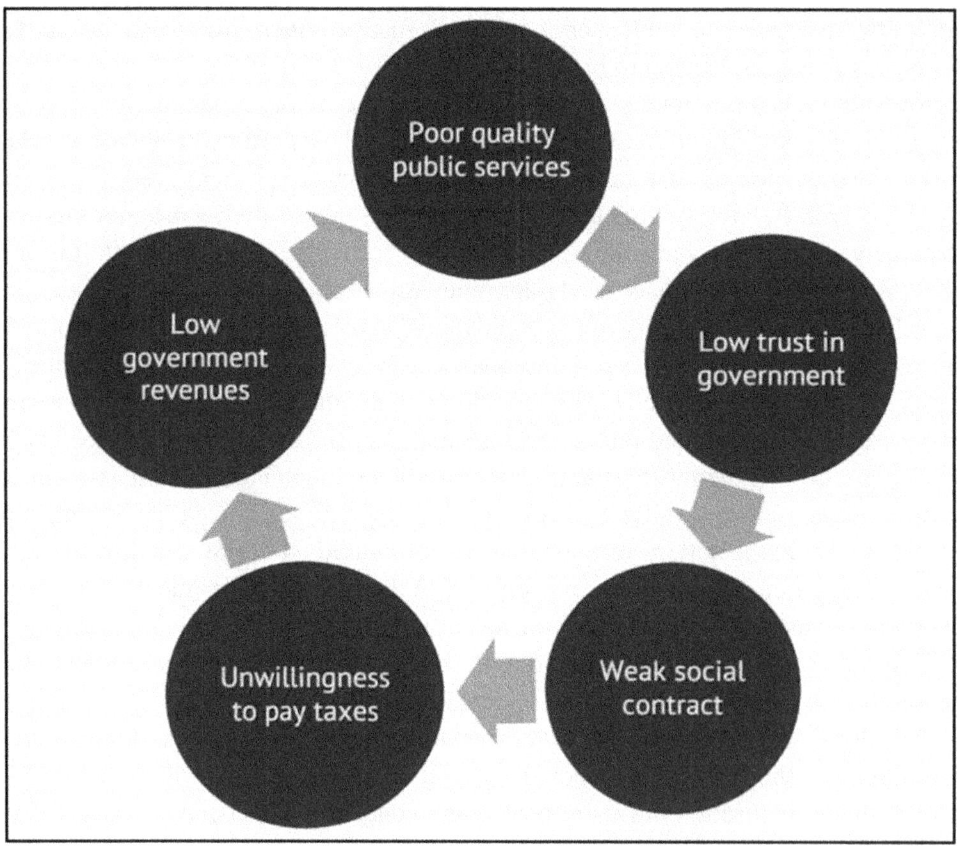

In the fight against coronavirus infection budgetary expenditures of national governments have reached a marginal level and budget revenues have been reduced to a minimum. As for entrepreneurs whose business has declined or completely closed, they have lost revenue and profits, the ability to pay salaries to employees, repay loans and pay taxes, and also build strategic development prospects (Keneally, et al., 2020). And given the significant financial resources redistributed by society to the state budget for the purpose of financing the production of socially significant goods, activities of the government must demonstrate a desire to become transparent, non-corrupt and subservient to the demands of citizens. In other words, the state, as the weakest link in the chain of interrelated problems of society, must be the first to demonstrate its adherence to socially significant norms of behavior. And this is a very difficult task, since the opportunistic behavior of the state itself is predetermined by the fact that the state is contradictory in essence, acting both as a subject and as an object of regulation (Pilipenko, et al., 2020).

Wherein, the state disposes of a significant part of the national income that is created in society and is redistributed by all representatives of society in the form of taxes and other contributions to the budget revenue. And by the way, the inefficiency of the state, and the implementation of its public activity are also carried out at the expense of society. With this approach, it becomes obvious that society has paid and is paying all the emergency expenses of national state in connection with the COVID-19 pandemic. Only as of September 11, 2020, governments and international organizations have invested more than $11 trillion to try to prevent the most immediate human and economic losses (World Economic Forum, 2020). But despite these efforts, the global economy is expected to contract by more than 4% in 2020, affecting the jobs and livelihoods of millions of people. Thus nature-related risks have precipitated a Great Deceleration and a structural economic crisis.

10.3. COVID-19 Shock and Government Inefficiency: From Fiscal Mechanisms of Fighting a Humanitarian Catastrophe Ex Post to the Priority of a Human-Centric Policy of Preventing It Ex Ante

Thus, the ineffectiveness of the state has received practical confirmation. It is connected with the growth of the already huge expenses of the state aimed at eliminating the consequences of its combating the exponential spread of the deadly coronavirus. At the same time, one should not forget that society paid and continues to pay for all ineffective actions of the state, or rather the results of its "opportunistic" behavior towards society. This interpretation is based on the fact that the state on behalf of society implements the functions of strengthening its integrity and stability of functioning. In other words, society not only made the nation state responsible for budget spending but also, most importantly, provided it with funds in the form of constantly growing tax revenues. Over the past decades, states in the developed countries of the world have shown an outstripping growth of budget expenditures in comparison with budget revenues. This is evidenced by data prepared by IMF experts (Table 2) (International Monetary Fund, October 2020).

Based on the data in Table 2, the general government fiscal balance was constantly negative, and the share of the average in advanced economies declined from (-5.5)% of GDP in 2012 г. to (-3,3) in 2019 accordingly. The US almost doubled this figure in 2019 (-6.3% of GDP), and the smallest indicator was in Canada with general government fiscal balance at (-0.3) % of GDP respectively. If we compare the average indicators of the general government fiscal balance in the countries of the world with the average annual growth rates of World Output in percent, it will become obvious that the latter indicator ranged from +3.5 in 2012 to + 2.8% in 2019 and average overall government fiscal balance across the world remained consistently negative: -3.8% of GDP in 2012 and -3.9% in 2019. In other words, the negative overall fiscal balance did not correlate with the growth rates of world output. So, when reducing the latter to +2.8% in 2019 compared with +3.8% in 2017, fiscal deficit widened to -3.9% of GDP in 2019 compared, for example, with -3.0% in 2017.

The opposite trend was observed in the dynamics of general government fiscal balance in emerging market and middle-income economies. For the period from 2012 to 2019 the national governments of these countries were intensively building up negative overall fiscal balance with -0.9% of GDP to -4.9% accordingly. Low-income developing countries showed an increase in overall fiscal balance of deficit: from -2.0% of GDP to -4.0% for a comparable period 2012-2019. As for 2020, the year of the coronavirus pandemic, all groups of countries showed almost the same growth in the negative overall fiscal balance, which differed only in its size. Thus, in 2020, compared to 2019, these world average indicators increased almost 3 times (from -3.9% of GDP to -12.7%), but in advanced economies – almost 4 times (-3.3% c -12.7% accordingly).

Table 2. General Government Fiscal Balance, 2012–2025: Overall Balance (Percent of GDP)

						Projections						
	2012	**2015**	**2016**	**2017**	**2018**	**2019**	**2020**	**2021**	**2022**	**2023**	**2024**	**2025**
World	**-3.8**	**-3.3**	**-3.5**	**-3.0**	**-3.1**	**-3.9**	**-12.7**	**-7.6**	**-5.9**	**-5.1**	**-4.8**	**-4.5**
Advanced Economies	**-5.5**	**-2.6**	**-2.7**	**-2.4**	**-2.7**	**-3.3**	**-12.7**	**-6.9**	**-4.6**	**-3.7**	**-3.4**	**-3.3**
United States	-8.0	-3.6	-4.4	-4.6	-5.8	-6.3	-18.7	-8.7	-6.5	-5.6	-5.4	-5.5
Euro Area	-3.7	-2.0	-1.5	-1.0	-0.5	-0.6	-10.1	-5.0	-2.7	-2.1	-1.8	-1.8
Japan	-8.6	-3.8	-3.7	-3.1	-2.5	-3.3	-14.2	-6.4	-3.2	-2.8	-2.6	-2.7
United Kingdom	-7.6	-4.6	-3.3	-2.5	-2.3	-2.2	-16.5	-9.2	-7.1	-5.8	-5.1	-4.4
Canada	-2.5	-0.1	-0.5	-0.1	-0.4	-0.3	-19.9	-8.7	-5.4	-3.0	-1.4	-0.3
Emerging Market and Middle-Income Economies	**-0.9**	**-4.3**	**-4.8**	**-4.2**	**-3.8**	**-4.9**	**-10.7**	**-9.2**	**-8.1**	**-7.5**	**-6.9**	**-6.3**
Low-Income Developing Countries	**-2.0**	**-3.7**	**-3.7**	**-3.6**	**-3.4**	**-4.0**	**-6.2**	**-5.1**	**-4.5**	**-4.1**	**-3.9**	**-3.7**
World Output (percent)	**3.5**	**3.4**	**3.3**	**3.8**	**3.5**	**2.8**	**-4.4**	**5.2**	**4.2**	**3.8**	**3.6**	**3.5**

Source: Composed by authors on the base of official data of IMF. International Monetary Fund (IMF). 2020. Fiscal Monitor: Policies for the Recovery. Washington, October.

Note: All country averages are weighted by nominal GDP converted to US dollars (adjusted by purchasing power parity only for world output) at average market exchange rates in the years indicated and based on data availability. Projections are based on IMF staff assessments of current policies. In many countries, 2020 data are still preliminary. For country-specific details, see "Data and Conventions" and Tables A, B, C, and D in the Methodological and Statistical Appendix. MENAP = Middle East, North Africa, and Pakistan.

1 For cross-country comparability, expenditure and fiscal balances of the United States are adjusted to exclude the imputed interest on unfunded pension liabilities and the imputed compensation of employees, which are counted as expenditures under the 2008 System of National Accounts (2008 SNA) adopted by the United States but not in countries that have not yet adopted the 2008 SNA. Data for the United States in this table may thus differ from data published by the US Bureau of Economic Analysis.

The above data of growth overall fiscal balance vary by country: in 2020 in comparison with 2019 г. In the USA this difference was about 300% (-6.3% of GDP and -18.7%), in Euro Area – negative fiscal balance increased 16.8 times (from (-0.6%) of GDP to (-18.7%); in the United Kingdom it increased 7.5 times (from (-2.2%) of GDP to -16.5%); in Canada – 66.3 times (from (-0.3%) of GDP to (- 19.9%) accordingly. Moreover, in 2020, world output decreased by 4.4% compared to 2019. According to the forecasts of IMF experts, all other things being equal, in 2021 the deficit of the general government fiscal balance should be approximately halved, and by 2025 r. it should return with greater or lesser variations to its original state in 2019 r. The consequences of such a stable budget deficit objectively caused an increase in the scale of general government debt (Fig. 10).

Figure 10. Historical patterns of general government debt (percent of GDP)
Notes: The aggregate public-debt-to-GDP series for advanced economies and emerging market economies is based on a constant sample of 25 and 27 countries, respectively, weighted by GDP in purchasing-power-parity terms. WWI =World War I; WWII =World War II
Source: International Monetary Fund (IMF). 2020. Fiscal Monitor: Policies for the Recovery. Washington, October.

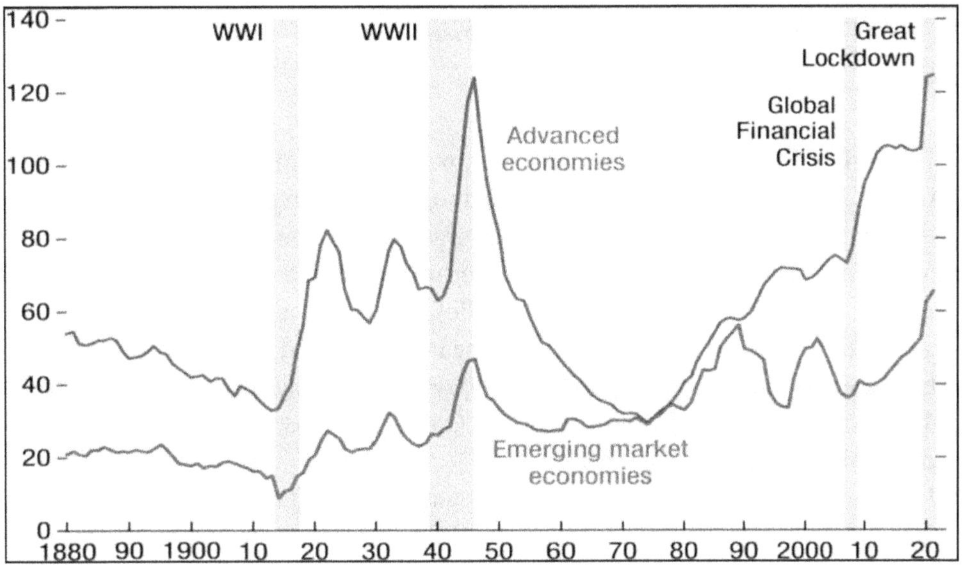

Sizable discretionary support, along with a sharp contraction in output and an ensuing fall in revenues, has led to a surge in government debt and deficits (Fig. 10). The fiscal support has been massive and swift, and much larger than the fiscal response to the global financial crisis. At the same time, it is phenomenon that in the developed countries the general government debt exceeds the annual volume of GDP. Even emerging market economies have reached general government debt levels that exceed 60% of their annual GDP. This means that future generations will pay interest on debts incurred by governments that have failed to perform their functions effectively in the past. The consequences of the crisis for public finances, combined with the revenue loss from the output contraction, have been great. In 2020, government deficits are set to surge by an average of 9 percent of GDP, and global public debt is projected to approach 100 percent of GDP, a record high (Fig. 11).

Under the baseline assumptions of a healthy rebound in economic activity and low, stable interest rates, the global public debt ratio is expected to stabilize in 2021, on average, except in China and the United States. Record-high public debt levels limit the room for further fiscal support, particularly in countries where borrowing costs or access to financing impose constraints. Official support to alleviate them has been overwhelmed by financing needs. Additional social assistance—supporting directly the poor and cushioning the recession—is expected to have a modest impact reflecting limited support and capacity constraints in some countries due to increase in poverty not less than to 90 million people.

Figure 11. Forecasts for general government gross debt and fiscal balance in 2020 (Percent of GDP)
Note: Data are as of July 24, 2020. Country groups are weighted by GDP in current US dollars adjusted for purchasing power parity. FM = Fiscal Monitor, WEO = World Economic Outlook
Source: International Monetary Fund (IMF). 2020. Fiscal Monitor: Policies for the Recovery. Washington, October

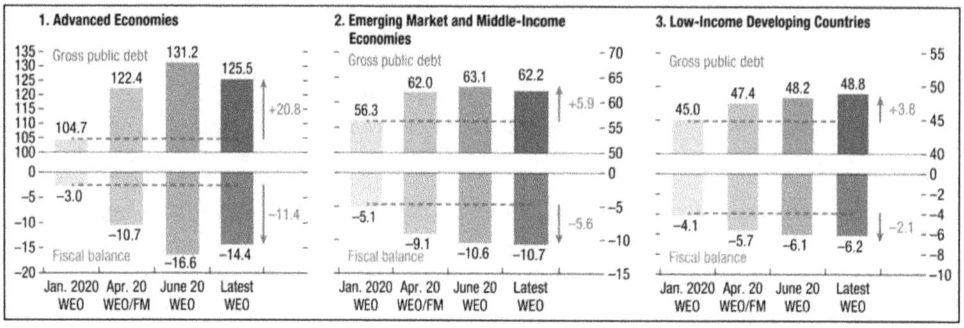

Fiscal policy will have to deliver more with less, putting a premium on careful design and implementation. At the same time, governments will need to be innovative and flexible, as many will have to address the deep scars from the crisis, including large rises in unemployment, public and corporate debt, and bankruptcies. The immediate focus of governments during the COVID-19 crisis thus far has been to address the health emergency and provide lifelines for vulnerable households and businesses. However, more needs to be done to prevent a large rise in poverty and income inequality, and promote a strong recovery amid heightened uncertainty. Overall, the fiscal measures deployed so far have helped mitigate the health and economic fallout from the COVID-19 crisis, more so in advanced economies where average fiscal support has been larger.

Nevertheless, the inefficiency of the state to adequately fulfill its functions, especially in terms of social ones, was most clearly demonstrated by the COVID-19 pandemic and by the measures taken to combat it. According to IMF experts, the coronavirus pandemic and associated lockdowns have prompted unprecedented fiscal actions that amounted to $11.7 trillion, or close to 12 percent of global GDP, as of September 11, 2020 (International Monetary Fund, October 2020). Half of the fiscal actions consisted of additional spending or forgone revenue, including temporary tax cuts, and the other half liquidity support, including loans, guarantees, and capital injections by the public sector. Although there is high uncertainty, based on the projected decline in per capita incomes, 100 million to 110 million people globally would be expected to enter extreme poverty relative to the pre-COVID projection, reversing the decades-long declining trend. Additional social assistance—supporting directly the poor and helping limit the recession—is expected to have a modest impact, containing the increase to 80 million to 90 million (Figure 12).

Figures 13-14 concretize measures of fiscal support of states in the countries of the world. Policies will need first to respond to the immediate health crisis, but over time foster the economic recovery and address the long-term challenges of the post-pandemic economy. Where lockdowns are extensive, fiscal policy has appropriately sought to do whatever it takes to save lives and livelihoods. Where lockdowns are eased, public health remains the number one priority, but policymakers have also begun to face the question of the appropriate pace of reducing lifelines to avoid an excessive increase in debt. When the health crisis is contained, the emphasis will shift to exiting from exceptional government interventions and to ensuring the sustainability of public finances while building resilience against future shocks and addressing pre-existing challenges such as inequalities and global warming.

Figure 12. Global extreme poverty rate (percent of total population)
Note: COVID-19 = coronavirus disease 2019
Source: International Monetary Fund (IMF). 2020. Fiscal Monitor: Policies for the Recovery. Washington, October

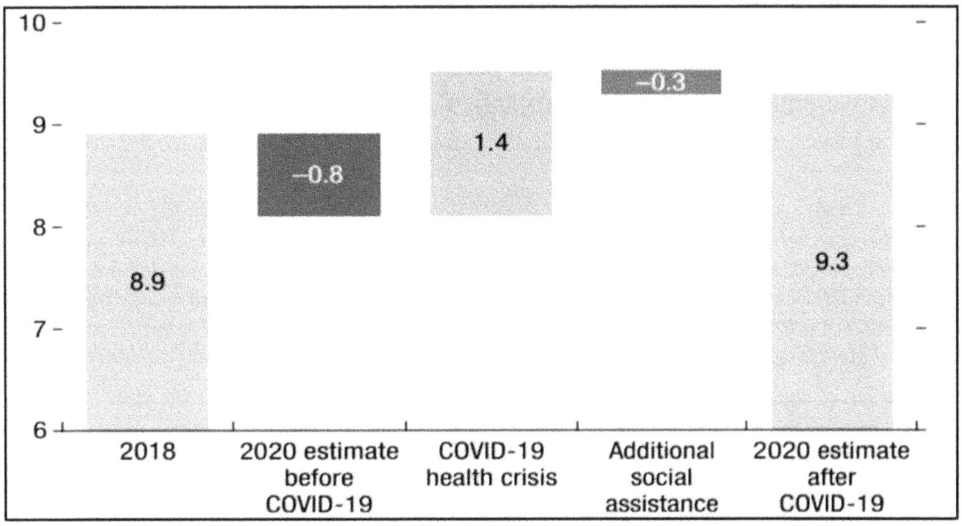

Figure 13. Breakdown of fiscal support by type (as of September 11, 2020; percent of GDP)
Note: Country group averages are weighted by GDP in current US dollars adjusted for purchasing power parity. AEs = advanced economies; COVID-19 = coronavirus disease 2019; EMMIEs = emerging market and middle-income economies; G20 = Group of Twenty; LIDCs = low-income developing countries; SMEs = small and medium enterprises
Source: International Monetary Fund (IMF). 2020. Fiscal Monitor: Policies for the Recovery. Washington, October

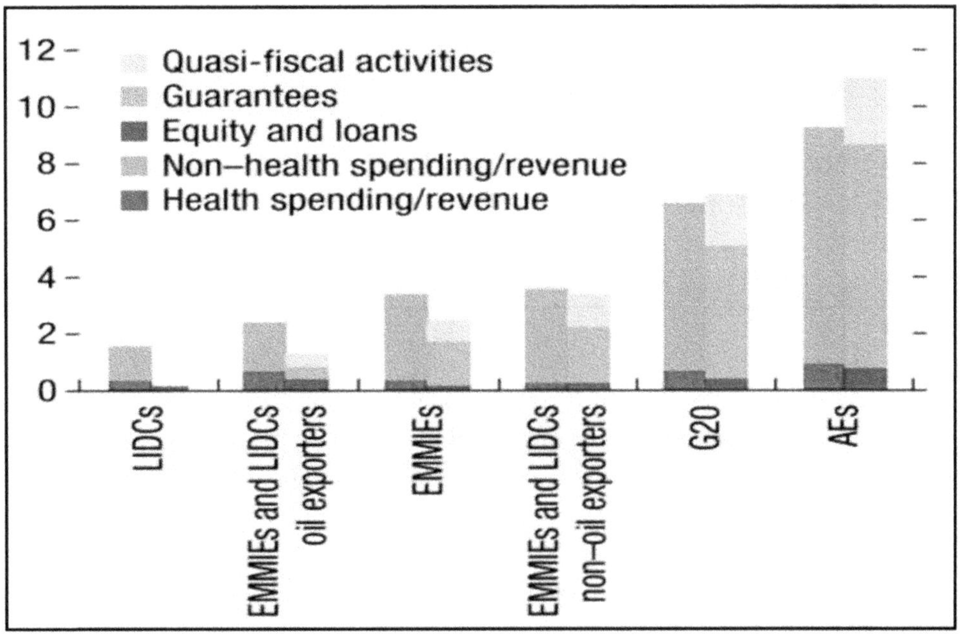

The nation state in the new post-pandemic economy should focus on tackling poverty and inequality to ensure restoration of citizens' confidence in the state, social integrity and sustainable growth, and on building resilience against future epidemics and other shocks. This includes policies to ensure that all people have access to basic goods (for example, food) and services (for example, health and education). Given the need for reducing emissions in the new post-pandemic economy, huge financial costs should also be predicted to eliminate a core long-term challenge after the pandemic. This will call for policies to increase carbon prices and catalyze investment in low-carbon technologies.

Figure 14. Distribution of fiscal support by beneficiary (as of September 11, 2020; percent of total)
Note: Country group averages are weighted by GDP in current US dollars adjusted for purchasing power parity. AEs = advanced economies; COVID-19 = coronavirus disease 2019; EMMIEs = emerging market and middle-income economies;G20 = Group of Twenty; LIDCs = low-income developing countries; SMEs = small and medium enterprises
Source: International Monetary Fund (IMF). 2020. Fiscal Monitor: Policies for the Recovery. Washington, October

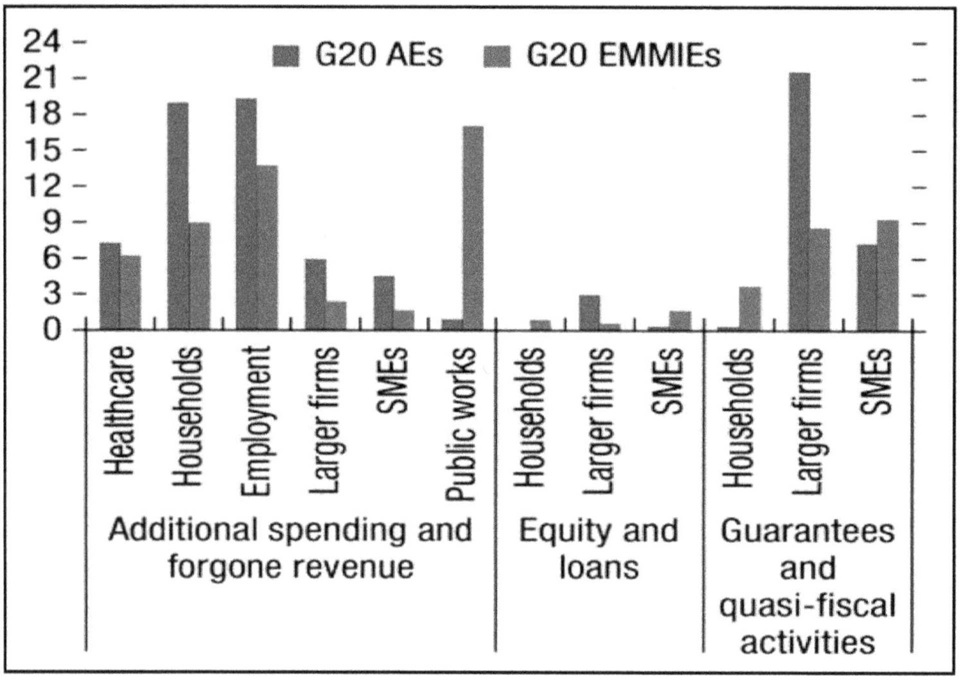

When health risks diminish and a durable recovery is foreseeable, support should shift from protecting employee-firm relationships to helping workers find new jobs, helping viable but still-vulnerable firms reopen, and supporting structural transformation toward the post-pandemic economy. Spending on digital infrastructure will be essential to support social distancing and to narrow the digital gap that exacerbates disparities in access to information, education, and work opportunities. At the same time, it should be noted that before the coronavirus pandemic, the states of the countries of the world increased their budget spending, increased budget deficits and credited them, increasing public debts, and at the same time achieved a phenomenal increase in social inequality in national communities. And it is this that robbed nation states of the confidence of their citizens in a humanitarian disaster.

In the pandemic the forceful response by governments has saved lives, supported vulnerable people and firms, and mitigated the fallout on economic activity. But after the coronavirus crisis ends, inequality issues won't go away: yet more needs to be done to address rising poverty, unemployment, and inequality and to foster the economic recovery. And this is not because economic inequality is only inefficient and unfair. All these manifestations of the societal crisis may have indirect effects on economic performance, since it is also associated with higher levels of terrorism, political instability, crime and lower levels of trust (Wilkinson, 2009). Research by the International Monetary Fund (IMF) has shown that high levels of inequality make it less likely for a country to sustain economic growth over the long term (Berg, et al., 2011) and that redistribution is largely benign for growth (Ostry, 2014). A recent IMF study (Grigoli, et al., 2017) concluded that the relationship between redistribution and economic growth is not linear. Below a Gini coefficient of 0.27, redistribution harms growth. However, above that low level of inequality, redistribution is good for economic growth (Grigoli, et al., 2017). Only 11countries have a Gini coefficient below 0.27.127 in 2014 (the most recent year that includes a large pool of countries: Belarus, Belgium, Czech Republic, Denmark, Finland, Iceland, the Netherlands, Norway, Slovenia, Sweden and Ukraine (Solt, 2017).

Actually, all these aspects of the interdependence of economic inequality and economic growth were widely discussed, evaluated and modeled before the COVID-19 pandemic. The highest relevance of these problems in the context of the coronavirus pandemic, according to the authors, is due to the fact that it fell into the crosshairs of the strategic question of the future New Normal. The point is that economic inequality, inadequate health care, a crisis in education, a shrinking middle class, etc. - these are links in one chain, in which the authors of this book have identified two main "rusted" links represented by society and the economy. It is about the broken dialectic of interaction between society - as a consolidated unity of citizens as subjects with their own ideas about justice and norms of behavior; and the economy in which the same citizens act as economic agents. The COVID-19 pandemic and lockdowns have destroyed material well-being and endangered the health and lives of citizens and their families. And as the main culprit, the citizens identified the state, to whose budget they constantly paid taxes and therefore hoped that it could be the guarantee of their safeguarding their lives and safeguarding their livelihoods. And the state turned out to be ineffective in the fight against coronavirus infection and lost the trust of its population. Thus, the return of citizens' confidence is the basis for restoring the integrity of society, eliminating the societal crisis and the possibility of further socio-economic progress in the post-covid future. In theoretical terms, the restoration of the dialectic of society and economy is the creation of conditions for self-organization and self-development of the subjects in this new social reality. All these transformations unambiguously predetermine the importance of the role of human as a driver of all future transformations.

This is one group of problems that must be recognized and resolved by the state. And the second group of problems is even more complex, since it is associated with the transfer of socio-economic systems from a static state to a dynamic one, and the state's best practices in such transformations are absent. And there are two extreme options: (1) well-known and understandable to the state experience of the past on returning to a static economy; (2) development of the latest strategy for transferring society and economy into a dynamic state. And in the latter case, human-centrism at the forefront of all government actions is indispensable. However, the forecasts made by the IMF regarding changes in the budgets of the balance sheets of the most nation states after 2020 can be regarded as the dominance of the first scenario.

Thus, the unprecedented spending of national governments in the fight against infection, for safeguarding citizens' lives and safeguarding their livelihoods, practically not only did not change the situation with the poor and poorest segments of the population of the world, but even worsened it (Fig. 12). Despite the absolutely correct words about the trust of citizens, the elimination of imbalances, of unemployment and poverty in 2020, already in 2021, according to the IMF, the deficits of the general government fiscal balances of the most nation states are predicted to halve relative to GDP (in percent of GDP) (Table 2). By 2025, these indicators are projected at approximately the level of 2017. It turns out that there will be no changes in the health care system due to its reorientation to preventive measures to combat pandemics. The economists of McKinsey Global Institute estimate that about one-third of economic growth in advanced economies in the past century could be attributed to improvements in the health of global populations. Research focused on more recent years has found that health contributed almost as much to income growth as education (McKinsey Global Institute, July 2020) (Fig. 15).

Figure 15. Economic losses of poor health
Source: McKinsey Global Institute. (2020). Prioritizing health: A prescription for prosperity. Report. July. McKinsey & Company.

If there are no changes, i.e. a person, his health care and education will not be defined as national priorities, and human-centrism will not become the basis for assessing the effectiveness of government decisions in society, economy and technology, then there will be no socio-economic progress, and there will be no technological revolution in society. At best, this will be a regression, a decline in growth rates and a loss of 2/3 of them due to poor health care and crisis education. Over time, society's needs for public goods and services have grown, and it is difficult to argue with this. GDP grew and budget revenues also increased, but budget expenditures grew faster. Let us single out only one group of expenditures related to social security for the most vulnerable segments of the population, pension provision, unemployment, etc. No one will deny the fact that society must implement the continuity of generations and not leave the disadvantaged to the mercy of fate. But the question of another plan should be asked. Why, during all these decades of more or less economic growth, this share of the underprivileged has not decreased. This is directly related to the social spending of the state budget. If the material security of citizens increased, their social status would rise, i.e. If a social escalator works, then the question of the lack of budgetary funds for the fiscal support of representatives of the social "bottom" would hardly be so acute. Why does the state stubbornly abstract itself from the fundamental reasons for the existence of disadvantaged strata of the population, which is multiplied by new generations of the same disadvantaged? This issue is raised in different interpretations by research centers, for example the

EBRD, which investigate this problem in the context of creating equal opportunities for all members of the population. However, these equal opportunities are interpreted to a greater extent in connection with the institutional changes that the state should make to solve the phenomenon of socially disadvantaged in the highly developed countries of the world.

It is of this quality that the fiscal policy of the state turns it into the weakest link, on which the strength of the entire chain of strategic relationships of healthy subjects with the qualities of intellectual autonomy, self-enforcing companies, capable of realizing an upwards causation mechanism and structuring the basic level of the middle class, which will strengthen societal integrity, depends. In this context the governments should also take into account new development priorities stemming from the COVID-19 crisis and start planning accordingly for projects that will accompany the likely social and economic transformations as economies recover from the crisis. Fiscal policy of the nation states should give prominence to spending and investments that reduce the likelihood or impact of future crises, including pandemics and climate change, and foster accelerated digitalization. In his annual Nelson Mandela lecture, António Guterres warned that the world is a "breaking point" and concluded that now is the ideal moment to promote a "new social contract for a new era". The countries that grasp the opportunity by re-construct solid social integrity are likely to be the winners from the COVID-19 crisis. Those that refuse to change and continue on the same path as before will likely continue to stumble from crisis to crisis: it is a future that their citizens are unlikely to welcome. The COVID-19 crisis is an opportunity to re-think the paradigm of dialectics of society and economics, of the essence of human-centric principal of organization, of the mechanisms of self-organization and self-development of the young generations as well as of the government steps to convert "how it was" in "how it will be".

Now is the time to look at this problem through the lens of stakeholders. They can be divided into two antagonistic groups. The first group is represented by citizens from the social "lower classes", their families, the older and younger generations, including, by the way, the now significant Z-ers. What is an effective way to remove them from the "balance sheet" of the state and turn them from recipients of social subsidies into effective tax-payers. This method is associated with the elimination of the crisis in the educational sphere and with the transformation of education into the form of the existence of a new generation. The transformation of young people from the poorest and poorest strata of the population into high-class specialists implementing modern technological progress will largely solve the problems of budget deficits, expand opportunities for social lifting, and, most importantly, eliminate the high skills mismatch as the main obstacle to economic and social dynamics after coronavirus. Naturally, this should not discount the huge budgetary costs of creating high-quality education and health care systems.

In this case, the state, representing the second group of interests, in one or two decades it will not have to solve the fundamental problem of smoothing out social inequality in society, debugging the police mechanism for suppressing asocial phenomena in society, limiting shadow business, etc. However, in the new conditions, the state in the long term may lose its current functions of last resort in an emergency and lose the current huge fiscal opportunities. But the game is worth the candle. Decades of ineffective use by the state of huge funds that society earned, and which turned into the loss of human lives in the coronavirus pandemic and fantastic economic losses, are finally coming to an end. And the state, expressing the interests of society, is forced to embark on the path of eliminating the very causes of all currently existing social ills, thereby depriving itself of the function of resolving them by fiscal methods **ex post**. If this happens, then this epoch-making event in the evolution of mankind can be defined with the words of Arthur C. Clarke "Childhood's End". Under the new conditions, the state, represented by policy-makers, will stop "plugging" the growing problem of social ailments with money (since the growth of budgets is beneficial to the authorities) and will eliminate it in its very inception **ex ante**. This phenomenon adequately corresponds to humanity at the stage of its maturation, i.e. construction of the latest post-coronavirus reality, which is still characterized by complete uncertainty.

CONCLUSION

The shock of the COVID-19 pandemic revealed the limiting state of society and the economy, which predetermined the deepening of the societal crisis and the destruction of the economic potential. The above has become the main obstacles in the fight against the coronavirus pandemic and on the way to transform a static economy into a dynamic one by implementing the achievements of the technological revolution 4.0. Nation states were the first to fight with the humanitarian catastrophe caused by the exponential spread of a life-threatening virus. The states of the countries of the world were forced in extreme conditions to solve the problems of an increase in the number of people infected with coronavirus infection, and deaths; blocking the economy and society; of massive increase in the number of poor and unemployed, and of loss by them a means of livelihood. In this situation, society recognized the inefficiency of the state in the fight against the COVID-19 pandemic. Meanwhile, the COVID-19 pandemic shock forced the state to act contrary to its fundamental mission to strengthen the structural integrity of the socio-economic system in any case. Lockdown regimes, introduced by the state as an emergency measure, tested the extreme tendency of national systemic entities to collapse. It turned out that all budgetary expenditures of the state, which traditionally exceeded the volume of incoming taxes, instead of strengthening the economy and society, gradually pushed them to the limit. Moreover, the COVID-19 pandemic shock instantly destroyed the social integrity of national communities. This was manifested in the fact that the ineffectiveness of fiscal decisions immediately became obvious to citizens, and they immediately began to "vote" with their growing distrust to the state. Their opportunism became obvious with their demonstrative speeches against the government's anti-coronavirus actions, against social distancing regimes, etc.

The great question arose of who should be held accountable for all the losses and missed opportunities due to the COVID-19 pandemic. It makes no sense to blame only the state for everything, because, firstly, there is no alternative to it today, and secondly, it made extreme efforts to bring down the wave of the coronavirus pandemic. The unique nature of the actions of national governments became evident when they blocked the the structural bonds in the economy and society contrary to their fundamental task of strengthening those structural ties. In other words, the modern nation states were focused on ensuring the structural integrity of a static economy during the period of its self-organization, in which a capital-centric system of organization was typical, social integrity was assessed by indicators of economic growth, and social integrity played a subordinate character. In that coordinate system, the main balancing mechanism in the economy and society was the fiscal and monetary policy of the state. That is why the states of the countries of the world have resorted to fiscal instruments for the redistribution of GDP in order to minimize the negative consequences of the economic blocking for households and private business.

However, the COVID-19 pandemic marked the leap of a static system into its dynamic state: out of the stage of self-organization into a completely unknown (uncertain) stage of self-development. And the state simply due to objective circumstances could not correspond to this new quality of the economy and society. That was why it acted the way it acted. In this situation, one can agree that today the state is the weakest "link" in the structural "chain" of national socio-economic systems. And the most reasonable thing for the near future, according to the authors, should be the need to strengthen the "weakest link" (nation states) in order to strengthen the entire "chain" (structure) of the national communities to prevent future disasters.

In the current conditions, one cannot abstract from the objective logic of irreversible processes of self-movement of systemic integrity, from the unlimited possibilities of the latest technological revolution and from the unknown and unrealized abilities of a person as a thinking being. The state is left with the least and most important thing - to launch these irreversible processes of self-movement of human wholes, abandoning their solution ex post and starting their solution ex ante (Chapter 11).

REFERENCES

Bator, F. M. (1960). *The Question of Government Spending: Public Needs and Private Wants*. Harper and Brothers.

Berg, A., & Ostry, J. (2011). *Inequality and Unsustainable Growth: Two Sides of the Same Coin?* https://www.imf.org/external/pubs/ft/sdn/2011/sdn1108.pdf

Boston Consulting Group. (2020). *COVID-19. BCG Perspective. Publication #2 with a focus on: Preparing for the restart.* Author.

Boston Consulting Group Perspectives. (2020). *COVID-19: Facts, scenarios, and actions for leaders.* Version 2.2. Boston Consulting Group.

Brimmer, A., Chin, V., Gjaja, M., Haslehner, R., Hutchinson, R., Kahn, D., & Lesser, R. (2020). *Protect the Vulnerable–Protect Us All.* Boston Consulting Group.

Covid-19: the impact on healthcare expenditure. (2020). A Report by The Economist Intelligence Unit. The Economist Intelligence Unit Limited.

Craven, Van der Veken, & Wilson. (2020). Not the last pandemic: Investing now to reimagine public-health systems. In *Healthcare Systems & Services, Public Sector, and Social Sector Practices*. McKinsey & Company.

Davies, Diemand-Yauman, & van Dam. (2019). Competitive advantage with a human dimension: From lifelong learning to lifelong employability. *McKinsey Quarterly*.

De Viti de Marko, A. (1936). First Principles of Public Finance. London: Jonathan Cape.

Dixon-Fyle, Hunt, & Prince. (2020). *Diversity wins: How inclusion matters*. McKinsey & Company.

Fjeldstad. (2014). *Local government taxation in SubSaharan Africa: A review and an agenda for research* (CMI Working Paper 2014: 2). Retrieved from: https://www.cmi.no/publications/file/5098-local-governmenttaxation-in-sub-saharan-africa.pdf

Fouché, G. (2008). Where tax goes up to 60 per cent, and everybody's happy paying it. *The Guardian, News*. Retrieved from: https://www.theguardian.com/money/2008/nov/16/sweden-tax-burden-welfare

Fouché, G. (2009). Why Scandinavia can teach us a thing or two about surviving a recession. *The Guardian, News*. Retrieved from: https://www.theguardian.com/society /joepublic /2009/aug /05/ scandinaviarecession-welfare-state

Georgieva, K. (2020). From great lockdown to great transformation. IMF Managing Director's Opening Remarks US Chamber of Commerce. June 9

Ghose, B. (2020). *Why 2020 will see the birth of the 'trust economy'*. World Economic Forum.

Gjaja, Hutchinson, Farber, Brimmer, & Kahn. (2020). *Three Paths to the Future.* Boston Consulting Group Analysis.

Gopinath, G. (2020). *World Economic Outlook*. IMF.

Grigoli, F., & Robles, A. (2017). *Inequality Overhang*. IMF Working Paper WP/17/76. https://www.imf.org/en/Publications/WP/Issues/2017/03/28/Inequality-Overhang-44774

Grigoli, F., & Sandri, D. (2020). *COVID-19's Impact in Real Time: Finding Balance Amid Crisis*. Blog. October. IMF.

Helliwell, J. F., Layard, R., & Sachs, J. D. (2019). *World Happiness Report 2019*. New York: Sustainable Development Solutions Network. Retrieved from: https://worldhappiness.report/ed/2019/#read

Hochman & Rodgers. (1969). Pareto optimal redistribution. *American Economic Review, 59*, 542-557.

IMF. (2020). *The Great Lockdown*. World Economic Outlook. April.

IMF. (2020). *World Economic Outlook Databases*. Retrieved from: https://www.imf.org/en/Publications/SPROLLs/world-economic-outlookdatabases#sort=%40imfdate%20descending

International Monetary Fund. (2020a). *Fiscal Monitor: Policies for the Recovery*. IMF.

International Monetary Fund. (2020b). *World Economic Outlook: A Long and Difficult Ascent*. IMF.

Jansson, J. (2018). Creating Tax-Compliant Citizens in Sweden. In S. H. Steinmo (Ed.), *The Leap of Faith: The Fiscal Foundations of Successful Government in Europe and America*. Oxford University Press.

Keneally, Brimmer, & Gjaja. (2020). *To Restart Economies, Governments Need a Social Interactions Budget*. BCG.

Kidd, S., Nycander, G. A., Tran, A., & Cretney, M. (2020). *The social contract and the role of universal social security in building trust in government.* Working Paper: November. Development Pathway.

King & Rebelo. (1993). Transitional dynamics and economic growth in the neoclassical model. *American Economic Review, 83*, 908-931.

Korchakova-Heeb, N. (2020). *We Are Building An Airplane While Flying It*. BCG.

Kristalina. (2020). *From great lockdown to great transformation.* IMF Managing Director's Opening Remarks US Chamber of Commerce.

Livingston, M. A. (2016). The Nordic model of taxation and its influence in North America: Image and Reality. *Nordic Tax Journal, 2016*(2), 77–86. doi:10.1515/ntaxj-2016-0008

McKinsey & Company. (2020). *Crushing coronavirus uncertainty: The big 'unlock' for our economies.* McKinsey.com.

McKinsey Global Institute. (2020). *Prioritizing health: A prescription for prosperity*. Executive summary. McKinsey.com.

Musgrave, R. (1959). *The Theory of Public Finance*. McGrow-Hill.

Myrdal, G. (1954). *The Political Element in the Development of Economic Theory*. Cambridge Mass., Harvard University Press.

Ostry, J., Berg, A., & Charalambos, T. (2014). *Redistribution, Inequality, and Growth*. https://www.imf.org/external/pubs/ft/sdn/2014/sdn1402.pdf

Pigou, A. (1924). *The Economics of Welfare* (2nd ed.). McMillan.

Piketty, T., Saez, E., & Zucman, G. (2016). *Distributional national accounts: methods and estimates for the United States.* NBER Working Paper Series, No. 22945.

Pilipenko, O. I., & Pilipenko, A. I. (2020). Mysteries of unsustainable public finance and of low economic growth. In M. Ziolo (Ed.), *Social, Economic, and Environmental Impacts Between Sustainable Financial Systems and Financial Markets*. IGI Global. doi:10.4018/978-1-7998-1033-9.ch009

Rawls, J. (1971). *A Theory of Justice*. Belknap Press of Harvard University Press.

Ritter, G. (1996). Storia dello Stato Sociale. Rome: Laterza.

Rothstein, B. (2018). *How the Trust Trap Perpetuates Inequality. Scientific American, Behaviour and Society.* Retrieved from: https://www.scientificamerican.com/article/how-the-trust-trap-perpetuatesinequality

Sen, A. (1979). Personal utilities and public judgments; or what is wrong with welfare economics? *Economic Journal*, *89*, 537-589.

Smit, Hirt, Dash, Lucas, Latkovic, Wilson, Greenberg, Buehler, & Hjartar. (2020). Crushing coronavirus uncertainty: The big 'unlock' for our economies. To safeguard lives and livelihoods, we must restore confidence. In *Strategy & Corporate Finance Practice.* McKinsey & Company.

Solow, R. M. (1957). Technical change and the aggregate production function. *Review of Economics and Statistics, 39*, 312-320.

Solt, F. (2017). Using the Standardized World Income Inequality Database. University of Iowa.

Susskind, D. (2020). How will the world be different after COVID-19? Finance & Development, 57(2), 26-27.

Sweden Ministry of Finance. (2017). *The Swedish Model. Information Material from the Ministry of Finance.* Retrieved from: https://www.government.se/informationmaterial/2017/06/the-swedish-model/

Vaslavsky, Y., & Vaslavskaya, I. (2019). Infrastructure public-private partnership projects: budget consolidation policy in Russia and government expenditures' efficiency increase. In B. S. Sergi (Ed.), *Modeling Economic Growth in Contemporary Russia* (pp. 199–228). Emerald Publishing. doi:10.1108/978-1-78973-265-820191007

WEF. (2020) *The Future of Nature and Business*. New Nature Economy Report II. World Economic Forum.

Wiles, D. (2020). *Why Swedes are OK with Paying Taxes*. The Official Site of Sweden. Retrieved from: https://sweden.se/society/why-swedes-are-okay-with-payingtaxes/#

Wilkinson, R., & Picketty, K. (2009). *The Spirit Level: Why Greater Equality Makes Societies Stronger*. Bloomsbury Press.

World Economic Forum. (2020). *The Global Social Mobility Report 2020. Equity, Opportunity and a New Economic Imperative. Platform for Shaping the Future of the New Economy and Society Business Partners*. WEF.

Chapter 11
The State and the Construction of the Post-COVID-19 Future:
What to Do?

ABSTRACT

The final chapter is the normative part of the shocks' theory, which defines the functions of the state in a dynamic economy. The process and object components of systemic integrity in economy are quite objectively regulated by the mechanisms of positive and negative selection of organizational forms and by three dialectical laws with shocks at their turning points. The subjective component of self-movement processes is governed by the state and its functions. If the structures of a static economy have been destroyed, the dynamic system's new structures must be created. The institutionalization of structures creation for dynamic systems is imputed to the state. It is about education and health of the critical mass of people as creators, about their adequate socialization in the society where people are "free, since they realize the need for it," about the institutionalization of self-sufficient companies' activities capable to form human-centric organizations through upwards and downwards causation mechanisms.

INTRODUCTION

The uniqueness of the situation that has arisen as a result of the COVID-19 pandemic is determined by the fact that many economic and social problems have been brewing for decades, and became obvious all of a sudden as a result of shock. At the same time, the humanitarian catastrophe, the blocking of the economy, the social crisis and the technological revolution 4.0 predetermined the main driver of all problematic decisions of the future. It is about a person with the quality of intellectual autonomousness and about self-enforcing companies capable of generating an adequate form of organization of human professional activity. The dialectical approach used by the authors in the formation of the foundations of the theory of shocks made it possible to solve the riddle of many of the above problems, substantiating the subordination of economic and social systems and highlighting a person with certain qualities who is able to find non-trivial solutions to the most complex problems of dynamic systems' self-development.

DOI: 10.4018/978-1-7998-4309-2.ch011

It is in this capacity that human connects both the economy, and society, and technology. According to the authors, the uniqueness of the moment caused by the COVID-19 pandemic lies in the fact that the static economy has gone to the end of its path of self-organization, and the shock blocking of structural ties by the state has put the system to the threshold of a completely new stage – self-development as a dynamic economy. And this perspective is characterized by complete uncertainty and requires not only non-trivial solutions, but also a complete rethinking of theoretical ideas about the economy, society, human, and state.

In the same vein, President of the European Central Bank Christine Lagarde said at the Davos Forum (WEF, January 2021) that 2021 will be accompanied by a very high level of uncertainty – until the moment when there will be a transition to a "new economy". And in this uncertainty, according to the WEF debates, another specificity of the future reality has appeared. The latter is due to the fact that, despite all previous experiences of post-shock recovery of countries of the world, each country will have to get out of the current global crisis individually, based only on national capabilities. This confirms the authors' idea that the irreversible process of self-development of the economy begins with the formation of its new structure, and it should be formed by national dialectically complex structures – companies that will assemble a new systemic integrity in the economy on a new technological foundation. And the main resource that each country can count on is associated with its own labor force and its level of education. In modern conditions, this workforce must have the quality of intellectual autonomousness in order to be able to "launch" a new "technological platform" and construct a dynamic economy on its basis. This actually confirms the validity of the conclusions of the debates at the WEF about the slowing down of globalization processes until the contours of the "new economy" appear in the countries of the world. In other words, the destruction of structural ties in national economies entails a negative impact on the processes of globalization. In this regard, it can be assumed that the hierarchy of structural ties within national borders, which has exhausted its potential, has objectively destroyed the established interdependencies of countries built over national borders. And, being at the beginning of its path of generating a new structure, a dynamic economy simply lost the ability to maintain transnational contacts with other countries in the global space, since old ties are dying out, and new ones have not yet been formed.

Based on the foundations of the theory of shocks, the following conclusion follows: if shocks destroy structural connections at the stage of self-organization of systemic integrity, then during the crisis the structures are restored and self-organization continues. If shocks are the starting point of entry of a static economy into its dynamic state as a result of the law of negation of negation, then the entire structural hierarchy becomes unviable and must be replaced by a completely different one, which will be generated on the newest technological base. Consequently, the global ties of economic systems that have embarked on the path of self-development are being built anew in parallel with the destruction of both national and global structures of static economies. At the same time, following dialectical logic, building a new mechanism of self-movement of the system can be carried out only through the structure-forming activity of the dialectically complex structures remaining from the previous system in the face of modern companies, which will act as elements of a new self-developing system.

It is self-enforcing companies that are dialectically complex elements left over from a static economy. It is they who are able to mediate the action of the mechanisms of upwards and downwards causation, which in fact realize their own self-organization and self-development. So the self-organization of self-sufficient companies is manifested in the restructuring of their internal organization in accordance with the new realities of the time: the emergence of a critical mass of workers with the quality of intellectual autonomousness, of limitless potential predetermined by the technological revolution 4.0 and with human-centric principals of internal organization. These processes are realized through the mechanism of downwards causation. As for self-development, self-sufficient companies implement it as creators of a new structure of a dynamic economy, mediating the action of the mechanism of upwards causality.

Only when the national systemic integrity is formed to the horizontal level of interaction of dialectical pairs, it will be able to be included in the global division of labor, integrating into dialectical ties at the transnational level. At the same time, the obtained theoretical interpretations of shocks allow the authors to assert with confidence that the progress of future global interactions will be much more diverse and difficult to predict today. This is due to the fact that the formation of self-developing national systemic integrities will lead to a significantly greater variety of forms of their organizations, which will be regulated by a completely unique variety of embodiment of the capabilities of the technological revolution 4.0 in combination with a national workforce with the qualities of intellectual autonomousness. In other words, each country will go its own way in this process. And already at the global level, integration alliances of differentiated types of national activities will give unimaginable combinations of them and provide tremendous socio-economic progress.

As a result, on the one hand, a significant number of fundamental questions were formed, united by one – "what to do?", and on the other, a set of necessary elements was formed, which makes it possible to solve the whole puzzle (Mazzukato, 2018, 2013). Indeed, the structures of both the economy and society are destroyed under the influence of the law of denial of denial, the systems are based on the structure of formal institutions that are provided by the state, people are not inclined to consolidate and become in opposition to all actions of the state in the fight against the COVID-19 pandemic. This is on the one hand. On the other hand, industrial revolution 4.0 rapidly spreads new technological solutions and gradually covers all spheres of human activity (Schwab, 2016; Schwab, 2018; Schwab, et al., 2020a, 202b, 2021). And in the first and second waves of the COVID-19 pandemic, self-sufficient companies are demonstrating the capabilities of the latest technological revolution and its economic results. In addition, it was the CEOs of these companies who were the first to raise the issue of talents, without which new technological projects cannot be introduced, new structural ties in the economy cannot be built, a new social reality cannot be constructed, and the collapsing relationships of human systems with nature cannot be harmonized. Thus, the humanitarian catastrophe caused by the COVID pandemic overnight reduced the human-created structural ties to ruins and at the same time gave humanity a chance to solve the riddle of a new post-covid reality, putting a person with the quality of intellectual autonomousness and the human-centric principles of organizing his activities in the basis of the systemic integrity (Chardin, 1987).

Realization of this chance will make it possible to shorten the time frame for the implementation of the results of the 4th technological revolution, to combine its potential opportunities and real socio-economic results by means of a fantastic transformation of human society from a "kingdom of necessity" into a "kingdom of freedom" (Marx, 1995). However, this image of the "City of the Sun" by Tommaso Campanella must be anticipated by no less fundamental transformations, the protagonist of which is a human (Berger, et al., 1966). It is the person, as the main subject of goal-setting in society and the main beneficiary of all the results obtained, who must become the main actor, embodying the technological and socio-economic reality of the future. A person with the qualities of intellectual autonomousness is able to understand the principles of interaction of material innovations introduced by various technologies, to combine digital production technologies with the biological world. Already today, designers and architects have managed to combine computer-aided design, additive technologies, materials engineering and synthetic biology for innovative development of systems for the interaction of microorganisms, human organisms and the products they consume (WEF. 2018). However, these fantastic plots can only be realized by a person with the qualities of intellectual autonomousness, capable of solving the most complex problems, both in theory and in practice. Given the rapid spread of new technologies and the breadth of their coverage of the spheres of human activity, the requirements for highly qualified specialists and their education are radically changing in connection with the enormous opportunities of the industrial revolution 4.0 (Cook, (ed.), 2019).

As a result, the role of education in the formation of the human with qualities of intellectual autonomousness changes (Becker, 1985a, 1985b; Schultz, 1960; Schultz, 1961; Mincer, et al, 1995). To understand the deep psychological patterns of changes in the essence of education, the authors were forced to delve into the theoretical aspects of human psychology and the psychology of education (Slobodchicov, et al., 1995; Slobodchicov, et al., 2000; Slobodchicov, et al., 2013). At the same time, the interpretation of the human phenomenon by the authors is consistent with the opinion of the great humanists (Vernadsky, 1960; Vernadsky, 2018; Gumilev, 2012a; Gumilev, 2012b), who associated it with a variety of known and unknown properties and qualities that, under certain conditions, can manifest themselves in society and be used for the benefit of social progress. In human psychology, the processes of self-organization and self-development interact dialectically, which predetermine its properties to reflection and to transcendence. In the conditions of the formation of a new technological paradigm, the most important property of a person is his ability to transcendence. This is due to the fact that an intellectually autonomous person is capable of self-development, easily adapts to a rapidly changing external environment, and copes with non-trivial problems due to the growing uncertainty of future transformations in all spheres of human activity. However, the emergence of the ability to transcend should be preceded by self-organization of a person in the process of education and the generation of his ability for intellectual autonomy.

Further research of the authors led them to the conclusion that technological and socio-economic transformations in an uncertain future are undoubtedly fundamental, which can only be achieved by an intellectually autonomous self-developing personality. And it is these constructions that will become the foundation of the human-centric socio-economic systems in the future. However, in order for the latter to become a reality, a person with the ability to transcendence must make the most important transformation, without which the human-centric system cannot function. It is about social construction of institutional reality (Berger, 1966). Institutional change and economic performance were asked by D. North (North, 1996; North, 2005). From his point of view, the primary for the realization of the potential of socio-economic progress and the creation of a human-centric system is their adequate institutional provision by the state. And in this regard, the change in the dialectic of the relationship between society and the individual as a self-developing personality predetermines the essence of cardinal transformations in the institutional structure of the human-centric system. Realizing the potential of the latest technological paradigm with adequate institutional provision of it by the state will gradually restore the relationship between man and nature (Nordhaus 1994). The novelty of these relations lies in the fact that a self-developing personality is armed with the latest technological capabilities to achieve material and non-material goals and is able to assess the priority of the natural system as a dominant of further irreversible progress of the human-centric socio-economic system (Malone, 2018).

The presentation of the material reproduces the logic of the problems discussed above. Paragraph 11.1 defines the role of health and education in a human-centric system, aimed at realizing the basic human abilities – for reflection and for transcendence. As for healthcare, its quality level is a prerequisite for the realization of human potential. A philosophical explanation of the importance of a person's abilities for self-organization and self-development is given. It is these qualities that characterize intellectually autonomous individuals who are called upon to play a key role in the formation of a new technological base for a dynamic economy and the spread of new technological solutions in all spheres of human activity. The substantiation of the economic effect that can be predetermined by high-quality health care and a high level of education is given. According to experts, the contribution of these two factors in the formation of an intellectually autonomous personality can provide 2/3 of the GDP growth of the global economy in the post-COVID-19 future.

The second group of questions (paragraph 11.2) is related to the definition of the role of self-enforcing companies in the formation of the structure of system integrity at the stage of their self-development. The specificity of their position in the processes of system formation is determined by the fact that they are dialectically complex elements left over from the previous static economy, which are capable of both self-organization due to the downwards causation mechanism, and of self-development through the implementation of the upwards causation mechanism. These companies mediate the process of socialization of people, first by integrating them into their internal teams, and then, through the development of collective routines and collective behavior, and into the structure of society. As a result, such self-enforcing companies will have to implement the "creative destruction" of outdated structural ties and build in their place new ones that meet the reality of a dynamic future. As such, these companies are able to form a new technological base that meets the requirements of the technological revolution 4.0, generate processes for eliminating the skills mismatch and the skills gap, and implement human-centric principles of organization in all spheres of human activity.

Paragraph 11.3 concludes the picture of structuring post-covid reality by considering the experience of the largest companies in mediating the mechanism of upwards causation. It is their growing interest in solving the problems of restoring the integrity of society that will allow a priori to solve urgent social problems, providing highly qualified workers (talents) with significant material rewards, the social standard of the middle class, the prospects for creativity and significant professional and social success throughout their lives. Thus, companies will be able to gradually minimize all problems of social injustice and the state will not have to humiliate the needy and vagrants with the social insurance system. The state will only need to prevent people from sliding "to the social bottom". In this context, health and education become paramount factors. Then the state with its social welfare system will be replaced by wealthy families who, in the words of Antoine de Saint-Exupery from "Le Petit Prince", will «**become responsible, forever, for what they have tamed**». A critical mass of nontrivially thinking self-developing individuals within the framework of companies capable of "creative destruction" will be able to realize unlimited prospects for the self-development of human-centric socio-economic systems only if the state is aware of such cardinal changes and the corresponding orientation of the economic and social institutions it creates.

11.1. The State and the Provision of a High Level of Healthcare and Education as Necessary Conditions for the Self-Organization of Individuals with the Quality of Intellectual Autonomousness

The COVID-19 societal and economic crises bring devastation, but it also brings an opportunity to re-evaluate what kind of a society should be created for future generations. So the society severely needs deep socio-economic rebuilding on the base clearly expressed the individuals' values. It is about the human-centric system and the state with the health and education priorities compared to economic benefits. In conditions when the COVID-19 pandemic has not yet ended, it is the state that should evaluate its actions in connection with the stabilization of the epidemiological situation in the country as a serious step towards its rehabilitation in the eyes of society and the return of public trust. According to the Boston Consulting Group experts, "those, that do will navigate more effectively through the current crisis, – will be ready for the next one" (Carrasco, et al., 2020). For these purposes, it is necessary to prioritize the need to develop policy solutions in connection with the societal crisis due to the COVID-19 pandemic. The state needs to recognize the priority of social integrity as a key moment in the combating any emergencies like the COVID-19 pandemic. Thus, the COVID-19 crisis has generated an increased focus on structural and subjective issues that go beyond political ones. Many of these problems could have been solved long ago, and tools and methods for their solution could have been found to become suitable for the current situation. But the COVID-19 pandemic has become the turning point to begin the hard work of rebuilding national societies and economies in the post-COVID future. So the epinomics could be "fit for purpose" only if oriented towards meeting of "people-first" needs.

Once governments did mobilize, some nations struggled to ramp up public communications, testing, contact tracing, critical-care capacity, and other systems for containing infectious diseases. While delayed governments countermoves worsened the death toll and economic damage (Craven, et al., 2020). Nevertheless, now is the moment to act. The world has seen repeated instances of what former World Bank president Jim Kim has called a cycle of "panic, neglect, panic, neglect," "whereby the terror created by a disease outbreak recedes, attention shifts, and we let our vital outbreak-fighting mechanisms atrophy" (Edwards, 2017). And while some are calling the COVID-19 crisis a 100-year event, it becomes possible to come to see the current pandemic as a test run for a pandemic that arrives soon, with even more serious consequences. The overall message is clear: infectious diseases will continue to emerge, and a vigorous program of capacity building will prepare the world to respond better than so far to the COVID-19 pandemic.

On the eve of the coronavirus pandemic, Global Health Security (GHS) Index experts assessed the state of national health systems in 195 countries. And the unsatisfactory result they received was confirmed during the struggle of national governments against the COVID-19 pandemic. The 140 GHS Index questions are organized across six categories (Global Health Security Index, 2019): 1. **Prevention** of the emergence or release of pathogens; 2. Early **detection and reporting** for epidemics of potential international concern; 3. **Rapid response** to and mitigation of the spread of an epidemic; 4. Sufficient and robust **health system** to treat the sick and protect health workers; 5. **Compliance** to improving national capacity, financing plans to address gaps, and adhering commitments to **international norms**; 6. **Overall risk environment** and country vulnerability to biological threats. The final expert opinion of the GHS Index was disappointing right on the eve of the COVID-19 pandemic. According to the results of the study, it turned out that national health security was fundamentally weak around the world. No country was fully prepared for epidemics or pandemics, and every country has important gaps to address (Global Health Security Index, 2019) (Table 1).

Thus the average overall GHS Index score among all 195 countries assessed is 40.2 of a possible score of 100. Among the 60 high-income countries, the average GHS Index score is 51.9. In addition, 116 high- and middle-income countries do not score above 50. Overall, the GHS Index finds severe weaknesses in country abilities to prevent, detect, and respond to health emergencies; severe gaps in health systems; vulnerabilities to political, socioeconomic, and environmental risks that can confound outbreak preparedness and response; and a lack of adherence to international norms.

Table 1. Results obtained by experts of the GHS Index

FINDINGS	DATA HIGHLIGHTS
OVERALL FINDING: National health security is fundamentally weak around the world. No country is fully prepared for epidemics or pandemics, and every country has important gaps to address.	• The average overall Global Health Security Index score totals 40.2 out of a possible score of 100 • 116 high- and middle-income countries do not score above 50
Countries are not prepared for a globally catastrophic biological event, including those that could be caused by the international spread of a new or emerging pathogen or by the deliberate or accidental release of a dangerous or engineered agent or organism. Biosecurity and biosafety are under-prioritized areas of health security, and the connections between health and security-sector actors for outbreak response are weak.	• 81% of countries score in the bottom tier for indicators related to deliberate risks (biosecurity) • 66% score in the bottom tier for indicators related to accidental risks (biosafety) • Fewer than 5% of countries provide oversight for dual-use research • No countries have legislation or regulations in place that require companies to screen DNA synthesis • 92% of countries do not show evidence of requiring security checks for personnel with access to dangerous biological materials or toxins
There is little evidence that most countries have tested important health security capacities or shown that they would be functional in a crisis.	• 85% show no evidence of having completed a biological threat-focused International Health Regulations (IHR) simulation exercise with the World Health Organization (WHO) in the past year • Fewer than 5% show a requirement to test their emergency operations center at least annually • 77% do not demonstrate a capability to collect ongoing or real-time laboratory data • 24% show evidence of a nationwide specimen transport system • 89% do not demonstrate a system for dispensing medical countermeasures during a public health emergency • 19% demonstrate at least one trained field epidemiologist per 200,000 people

Source: Global Health Security Index (2019). Building Collective Action and accountability. Johns Hopkins Center for Health Security. October

Specific scores for the GHS Index categories are as follows:

1. **Prevention:** Fewer than 7% of countries score in the highest tier for the ability to prevent the emergence or release of pathogens. The GHS Index scoring system includes three tiers. Countries that score between 0 and 33.3 are in the bottom tier (also called "low scores"), countries that score between 33.4 and 66.6 are in the middle tier (also called "moderate scores"), and countries that score between 66.7 and 100 are in the upper or "top" tier (also called "high scores").
2. **Detection and reporting:** Only 19% of countries receive top marks for detection and reporting.
3. **Rapid response:** Fewer than 5% of countries scored in the highest tier for their ability to rapidly respond to and mitigate the spread of an epidemic.
4. **Sufficient and robust health system:** The average score for health system indicators is 26.4 of 100, making it the lowest-scoring category

5. **Risk environment:** Only 23% of countries score in the top tier for indicators related to their political system and government effectiveness.

Knowing the risks and identifying the gaps, however, is not enough. Political will of the nation states is needed to save lives and build a safer and more secure world. The GHS Index will help decision makers in individual countries, regional and international organizations, and philanthropies to more effectively identify and provide resources to fill capability gaps. Because measuring risk is difficult and states will not be held accountable without regular assessments, the GHS Index over time will measure progress against benchmarks, promote mutual accountability, encourage transparency, and spur incentives for improvements.

It is in this regard that the number of questions to the state is increasing, which will have to structure the health care system capable of effectively repelling any emergency infections that are potentially possible in the future. Experts from McKinsey & Company identify five areas of nation states activity, which should be institutionalized in the form of the following government programs: building "always on" response systems, strengthening mechanisms for detecting infectious diseases, integrating efforts to prevent outbreaks, developing healthcare systems that can handle surges while maintaining the provision of essential services, and accelerating R&D for diagnostics, therapeutics, and vaccines (Craven, et al., 2020) (Fig.1)

While it cannot be possible to prevent all epidemics, the nation states can use all the tools in the current arsenal to prevent those they can. Three approaches to doing so stand out: reducing the risk of zoonotic events, limiting antimicrobial resistance (AMR), and administering vaccines more widely (Fig.2). Zoonotic events, in which infectious diseases make the jump from an animal to a human, touched off some of the most dangerous recent epidemics, including of COVID-19, Ebola, MERS, and SARS. Zoonosis can't be eliminated, but its occurrence can be reduced. Scientists have estimated that a large portion of zoonotic-disease outbreaks can be linked to changes in agriculture, land use, and wildlife hunting over the past 80 years. Economic incentives, legal changes, and public education can lessen contact between humans and wildlife and help protect forests and wilderness areas, thereby decreasing the likelihood of zoonosis.

There is also much more to learn about the threats through wider mapping of the viruses that exist in animal populations. To respond to the COVID-19 pandemic, nation states should make deliberate investments to reduce the chance of such a crisis happening again.

According to McKinsey & Company experts' estimates an initial global investment of $70 billion to $120 billion over the next two years ($35 billion to $60 billion per year), followed by an investment of $20 billion to $40 billion per year to maintain always-on systems, would significantly reduce the chance of a future pandemic (Craven, et al., 2020). The above figures, totalling $230 billion to $425 billion over the next decade, include spending at the global, country, and subnational levels (Fig. 3).

The playwright Edward Albee once said, "I find most people spend too much time living as if they're never going to die" (Richards, 1991). Adapting his words to the current state of health care in the countries of the world, it seems that nation states have spent too much time acting as if another deadly pathogen will never appear. Outbreaks of SARS, MERS, Ebola, and Zika led to some investments in pandemic preparedness over the past 20 years, but few of them are the lasting, systemic changes needed to detect, prevent, and treat emerging infectious diseases. And now, even with all of humanity's knowledge and resources, millions of people have been killed by a disease that was only identified a year ago.

Figure 1. Five shifts in healthcare systems to help reduce the chance of future pandemics
Source: Matt Craven, Adam Sabow, Lieven Van der Veken, and Matt Wilson (2020). Not the last pandemic: Investing now to reimagine public-health systems. Healthcare Systems & Services, Public Sector, and Social Sector Practices. McKinsey & Company July

From	To	Rationale
"Break glass in case of emergency" response systems	"Always on" systems and partnerships that can scale rapidly during epidemics	Outbreak response is most effective when it uses mechanisms that we apply regularly
Uneven disease surveillance	Strengthened global, national, and local mechanisms to detect infectious diseases	Effective detection capacity is needed at all levels
Waiting for outbreaks	An integrated epidemic-prevention agenda	Targeted interventions can reduce pandemic risk
A scramble for healthcare capacity	Systems ready to surge while maintaining essential services	Epidemics require the ability to divert healthcare capacity quickly, without lessening core services
Underinvestment in R&D for emerging infectious diseases	A renaissance in infectious disease R&D	COVID-19 has shown how fast we can move against infectious diseases when we are motivated

The COVID-19 pandemic won't be the last epidemic to threaten the world. The COVID-19 pandemic and its repercussions, such as the shelter in place measures to control the spread of the virus, are forecast to reduce global GDP by 3 to 8 percent in 2020. By taking action and funding changes now, the nation states can better withstand the next one (Fig. 4).

By 2040, as a result of the efforts of the expert community and national states to improve the reliability of the healthcare system, Global GDP may increase by $ 11,583B, of which 12% will be provided by fewer early deaths; 36% – by fewer health conditions; 34% – by expanded participation and 17% – by increase in labor productivity. The COVID-19 pandemic and its repercussions, such as the shelter in place measures to control the spread of the virus, are forecast to reduce global GDP by 3 to 8 percent in 2020. As countries grew richer, they invested in better food and safer environments, creating a virtuous cycle of improved health and higher incomes. Economists estimate that about one-third of economic growth in advanced economies in the past century could be attributed to improvements in the health of global populations (McKinsey Global Institute, 2020).

So, the coronavirus pandemic has raised the problem of ensuring public health as the most significant. And the peculiarity of the moment of transformation of a static economy into a dynamic one, which was announced by the shock of the COVID-19 pandemic, made the problem of education of citizens in connection with the younger generation paramount. This is due to the fact that it is young people who will have to form a new technological base, using the capabilities of the technological revolution 4.0, and structure the post-COVID-19 economy and society. Moreover research focused on more recent years has found that health contributed almost as much to income growth as education. In this context, generalizations can be made regarding the potential of only health and education factors, which, according to experts, form human capital. If to use the estimates of experts from the McKinsey Global Institute, then the economic benefits from the health improvements assessed to add $12 trillion or 8 percent to global GDP in 2040 that translates into 0.4 percent faster growth every year (McKinsey Global Institute, 2020).

Figure 2. Outbreak prevention: new approaches to zoonosis, antimicrobial resistance, and immunization (Summary of estimated epidemic-preparedness initiatives and investments in $ billion)
Source: Matt Craven, Adam Sabow, Lieven Van der Veken, and Matt Wilson (2020). Not the last pandemic: Investing now to reimagine public-health systems. Healthcare Systems & Services, Public Sector, and Social Sector Practices. McKinsey & Company July

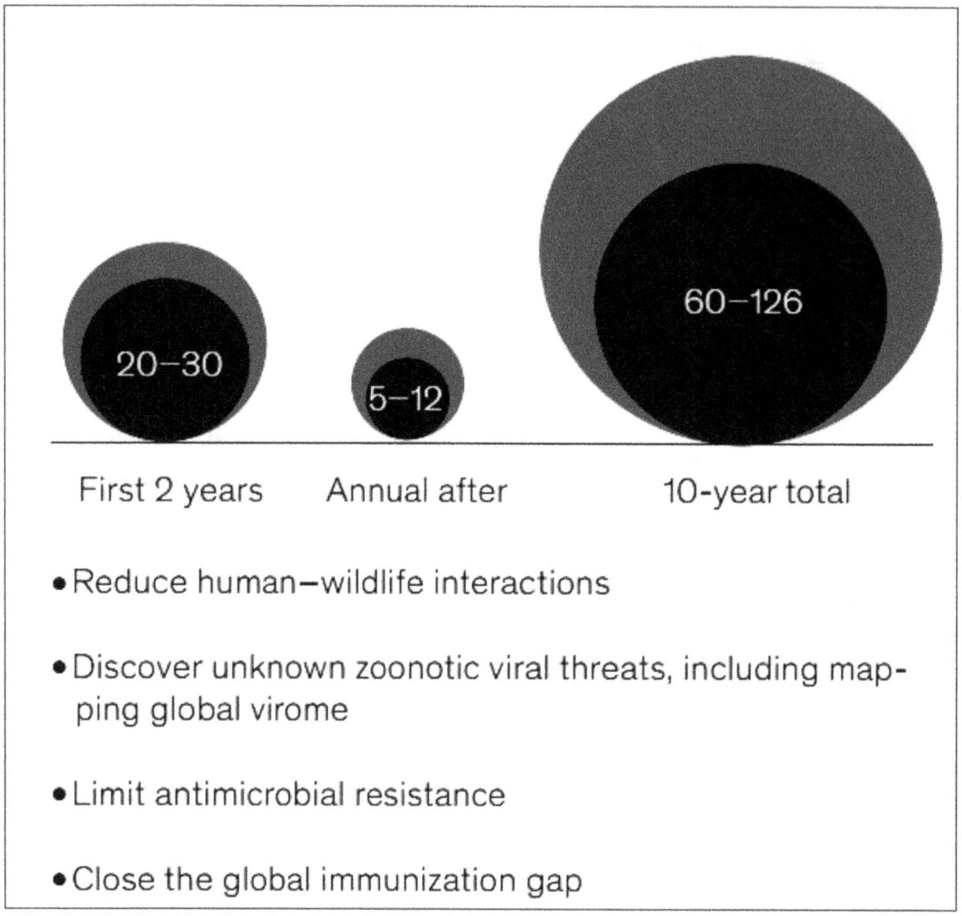

Relying on the fairness of the conclusion of the McKinsey Global Institute experts that the economic contribution to global GDP from the health and education improvements is approximately equal, it becomes possible to resume, that overall impact could be assessed to add $24 trillion or 16 percent to global GDP in 2040, that translates into 0.8 percent faster growth every year. The estimates of BCG experts make it possible to improve greatly the above mentioned estimates. In their opinion, solving the skills mismatch problem with the help of the qualitative education will allow accelerate GDP growth by 0.5-2% per year (Boston Consulting Group, 2019) (Fig .5). In other words, as a result of the creation of high-quality health care and education systems, the state can ensure GDP growth of the country by 0.9-2.4% per year only due to two factors related to the person.

Considering all of the above, it becomes possible to talk about an objective tendency towards the elevation of the principle of human-centrism in all processes accompanying the changes caused by the COVID-19 pandemic. Despite the unconditional importance of healthcare, education, nevertheless, predetermines the essence of the fundamental transformations of our time. And the phenomenon of deepening skills gap as well as skills mismatch directly proves this. According to the OECD, with the current global workforce of 3.5 billion, more than one billion workers on the labor market have competencies that either exceed or are not sufficient for the activities they perform. According to various estimates, in OECD countries 17% to 52% of the workforce, or, on average, two out of five employees, are affected by the skills mismatch problem. BCG estimates that 1.3 billion people are affected by the skill hole in this situation, costing the global economy 6% hidden tax in lost productivity [BCG estimates based on OECD data, 2016.] Moreover, if earlier technical skills became obsolete within 15–20 years, then recently - every 2–5 years (IEEE Spectrum, 2013). By 2022, the share of new activities will be 27% (WEF, 2018). Most workers today see the changes taking place in the labor market, but do not understand what professions and skills will be in demand in the future. Today's child will be able to change jobs at least seven times in his lifetime, and five of these jobs do not yet exist (Esteban Bullrich, Argentinian Minister of Education).

Figure 3. Funding for epidemic preparedness requires an up-front investment to close current gaps (Illustrative funding needed to invest in epidemic preparedness, $ billion)
Source: Matt Craven, Adam Sabow, Lieven Van der Veken, and Matt Wilson (2020). Not the last pandemic: Investing now to reimagine public-health systems. Healthcare Systems & Services, Public Sector, and Social Sector Practices. McKinsey & Company July

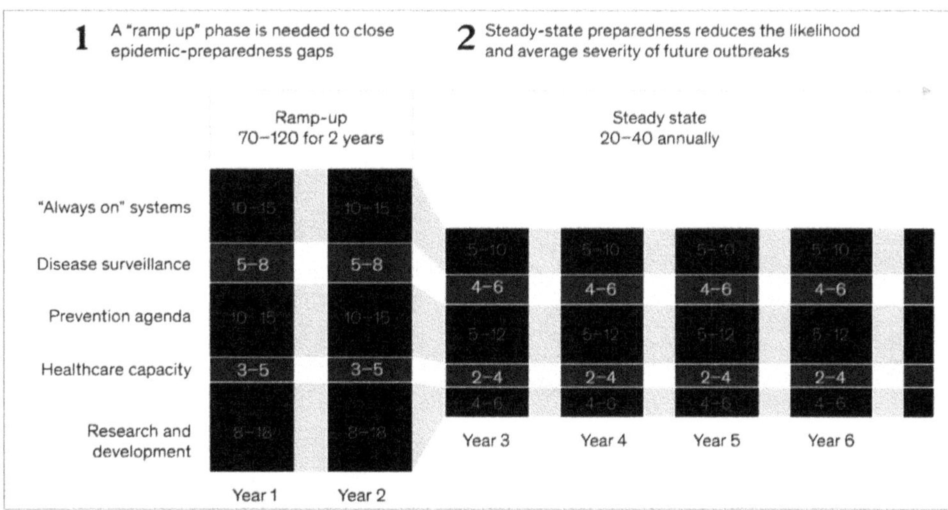

The authors associate mainly with the formation of the beginning of human-centrism in all the transformations that predetermined the coronavirus pandemic. This is manifested in the fact that the coming reality is fundamentally different from the before-covid reality, in which everything was predetermined by structural changes mediated by the objects' component, starting with goods and services and ending with financial assets. On the eve of the exponential spread of COVID-19 infection, this static system reached marginal changes in its self-organization. The law of denial of denial is at work and the reality after COVID-19 appears in complete uncertainty, both in terms of organizational foundations and in the context of those transformations that should be caused by the new technological revolution. At the same time, coronavirus infection has demonstrated the importance of a person as a worker, and as a consumer, as well as a saver.

Figure 4. Opportunities missed by the failure of most nation states to build robust health care systems
Source: Source: McKinsey Global Institute (2020). Prioritizing Health: A Prescription for Prosperity. Executive Summary. July.

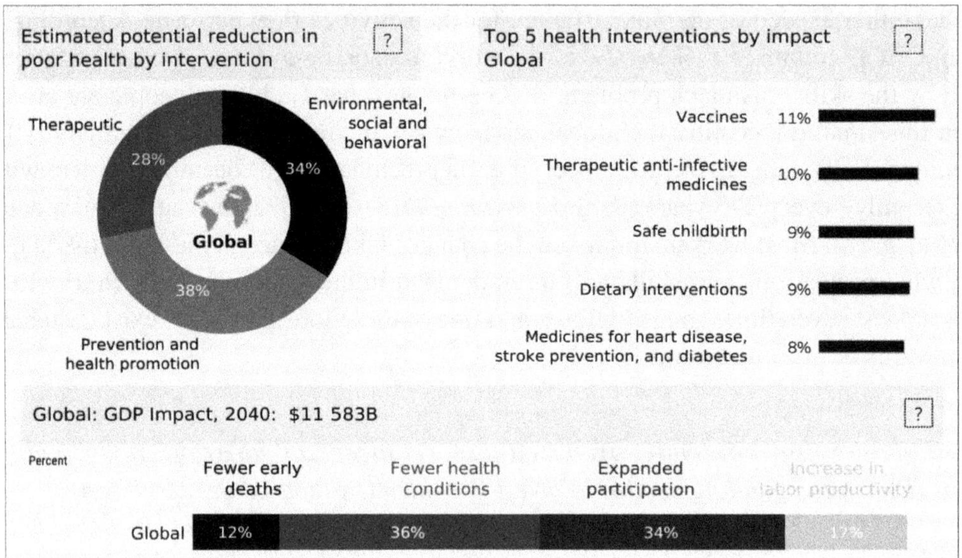

Figure 5. GDP growth potential with transition to a talent development system based on human centricity principles
Source: BCG. (2019). Mission Talent. Mass Uniqueness: A global challenge for one billion workers. August

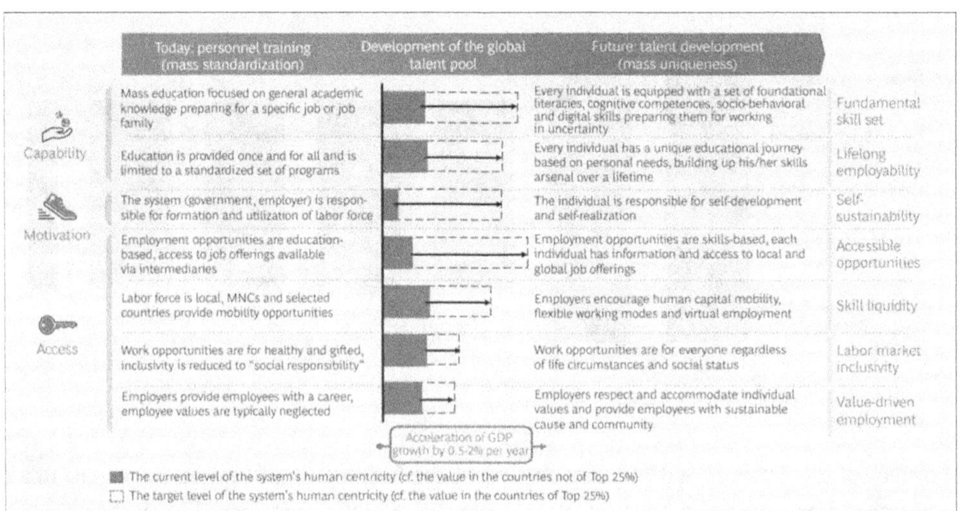

Moreover, as far as future reality is concerned, only an educated person with the quality of intellectual autonomousness is able to structure it. And this is largely predetermined by the fact that the complete uncertainty of the post-covid reality will require individuals who are able to make non-trivial decisions, generate new knowledge about the unknown reality and structure it for the benefit of the future progress of mankind. Actually, these arguments underlie the justification of human-centrism as the basic principle of organization, which should replace capital-centrism. And everything should start with the formation of such a person who will have an endogenously inherent mechanism of self-propulsion, which determines his self-sufficiency. The formation of such a personality should be subordinated to the education of the younger generation.

The problem is more than complicated, and it is accompanied by a number of questions that, in one way or another, relate to human-centrism and education. As interpreted by Justin W. Cook (Cook, (Ed.), 2019) they sound like this: "This volatile and uncertain moment raises questions of purpose for society's constitutional institutions—even and perhaps especially, education. What is the purpose of education? Should education systems be burdened with sustainability? And how should we determine its purpose? To what end do we learn?" At the same time, the key to understanding the essence of education in the process of becoming a person with the qualities of intellectual autonomousness lies in understanding the characteristics of his self-development. (Ananiev, 1977; Ushinsky, 2005; Elkonin, 1989; Piaget, 2008; Vygotsky, 1960; Slobodchicov, et al., 2013). In other words, human-centrism is possible only in the case of the formation of a critical mass of intellectually autonomous personalities capable of structuring an uncertain reality. In this capacity, they must have the ability to reflect, and the ability to transcend. If the first ability is generated in education, which accompanies the student's self-organization, then the ability to transcend is realized during the socialization of the subject, i.e. in the process of its integration into society at the stage of its self-development (Chapter 11.2).

The reflexive ability of a person is expressed in his reflection of the external world in internal subjectivity. Based on the author's concept of psychological and cognitive barriers (PCB) (Pilipenko, 1997; Pilipenko, et al., 2015; Pilipenko, et al., 2019), a person's ability to reflect (self-reflection) accompanies the processes of self-organization of his inner subjectivity. Education is destined to bring a person's abilities to the possibility of external realization of his subjectivity in society. If a person fails to learn to overcome PCB in education, then the level of his education does not provide him with the quality of intellectual autonomousness. As a result, not having learned how to overcome the PCB in education, a graduate will not be able to overcome the diverse PCB as a specialist in the latest technological and socio-economic environment. Actually, the crisis of modern education is manifested precisely in the fact that it exacerbated the gap between a person's ability to self-reflection and his ability to transcend, between the self-organization of his inner subjectivity and his self-development as a manifestation of self outside in the form of intellectual autonomousness.

The authors tried to identify the main problems of modern education, which call into question the time limits for the implementation of the 4th technological revolution. So, the content of education includes (1) the experience of cognitive activity, recorded in the form of its results - knowledge (cognitive component) and (2) the experience of implementing known methods of activity - in the form of the ability to act according to the sample. However, the content of education does not include (3) experience of creative activity - in the form of the ability to make effective decisions in problem situations (creative component) and (4) experience in the implementation of emotional-value relations - in the form of personal orientations (motivational-orientational component). So, in general, education in modern society should ensure the formation and implementation of diverse abilities and qualities of a person. At present, it is the cognitive and craft approach to the content of education that is most operationalized and technologically provided. Its educational result is famous Knowledge, Rules, and Skills. It is about the assimilation of practical skills and actions of a general cultural or industrial nature. These are the problems that theorists and practitioners in the field of education are concerned about both at the national and global levels. Thus, R. Winthrop and E. McGivney (2016, P. 14) believe that promoting a breadth of skills means "educating for a mastery of a wide range of competencies that will help mitigate the challenges posed by the changing world context".

The subject-disciplinary organization of the educational content and the craft type of training were attributes of the cognitive-craft approach. And its inconsistency began to be revealed more and more clearly when the graduate of the school entered an independent social life, the system of higher education, as well as practical activity, which were definitely not built on the subject-disciplinary principle. The cognitive-craft approach in its knowledge component has had and still has its undoubted achievements in terms of fundamental scientific education. However, when a graduate enters professional activity, school knowledge in most cases has been immediately devalued as untenable. This inconsistency takes the form of a completely practical problem associated with the need to transform school skill (the ability to solve school problems) into the ability to apply the knowledge gained in practice. Education built in a traditional way does not, in principle, solve this problem.

In the works of prominent Russian philosophers and methodologists (Davydov, 1996) it was determined that the ability to transform academic knowledge into smart action (skill) is associated with thinking. He was sure that the orientation of education to empirical thinking (to action according to a template and sample) is devoid of creative potential, does not allow a person to master the complex developing systems of the objective and social world, to create new forms of culture. As a result, the traditional educational practice that generates empirical thinking (technological style of thinking) does not develop the needs and ability to act independently, creatively, does not generate the ability for self-education and self-development.

G.P. Shchedrovitsky (1997) considered the activity approach in education, aimed at the formation and development of universal ways of thinking and acting. To do this, he constructed a hierarchy of three planes: on the first, he placed pure thinking or thinking in concepts, on the second - the transition from the theoretical level to the level of practices, and on the third – lower one - practical and effective action. So in the content of modern education there is no second - middle - level, which should carry out a consistent transition from theoretical thinking to practical actions. Meanwhile, it is this plane that should have special means, methods, techniques of work that allow combining mental and practical activities. In this context, it is about the formation of general abilities of thinking and activity, which constitute the main content of education and its main result.

The competence-based approach turned out to be an adequate means of understanding the phenomenon of the gap between theoretical thinking (associated with education) and social practice (OECD, 2016). It is no coincidence that it was initially initiated by representatives of practical organizations - Western companies. On the one hand, they needed graduates who were ready to immediately get involved in work, and, on the other hand, firms were interested in young people being able to flexibly retrain, master new knowledge and technologies.

From the point of view of the competence-based approach, educational competence includes both cognitive and operational-technological components, as well as motivational, ethical and social components. At the same time, educational competence is a predetermined social requirement (norm) for educational training. It is about a specific set of interrelated orientations, knowledge, abilities, skills, real experience of the student's activity in relation to a certain range of objects of reality, necessary for the implementation of personally and socially significant productive activity. The positive potential of the currently relevant competence-based approach is that it does not deny the importance of knowledge, but focuses on the ability to acquire, process and use the knowledge gained, including independently in practical life. And yet today the competence-based approach is not so much a concrete solution to social and educational problems in a fundamental formulation, but rather a successful form of their formulation. In other words, the competence-based approach took into account a sharp shift in the target emphasis in the content of education from educational knowledge and skills to competence as some actual and already formalized ability to act effectively in various social and practical situations.

A significant limitation of the competence-based approach is the derivation of the goals (and therefore the content) of education from the requirements of society (social order), first of all, from the needs of the state, and not from the goal of the forming a self-developing person. This social order is focused on identifying and transforming only individual, fragmentary human potentials into purely useful resources for their utilization in a particular social production. This specificity of the competence-based approach to the content of education can be clearly seen in the example of components of the OECD model of educational achievements (OECD, 2016) (Fig. 6).

Figure 6. OECD: model of educational achievements - 2030
Source: OECD, (2016). Schleicher A., Ramos G. Global competency for an inclusive world [online] Retrieved from: https://www.oecd.org/pisa/aboutpisa/Global-competency-for-an-inclusive-world.pdf

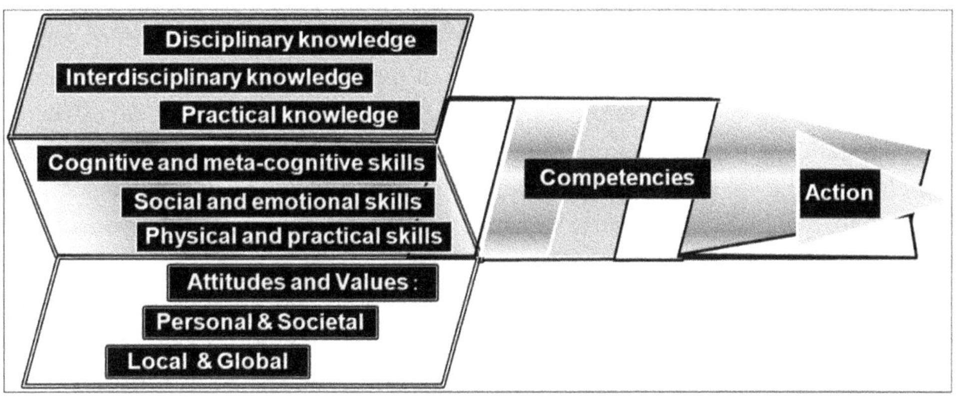

A competent person shows awareness of a specific issue and the success of action in a specific situation. This is the high pragmatic significance and social relevance of the competence-based approach in modern education. But utilitarianism and pragmatism cannot be absolute criteria for the universal education of a person, education - throughout life. Understanding development as the essence of man is presenting him as a natural-artificial or artificial-natural process at the same time, in which natural prerequisites and social conditions are transformed by man into means of his self-development. In this context, the education of a self-developing person must realize all types of development, the main of which is self-development. Self-development is the goal and value of anthropologically oriented education as a universal form of human self-development. This is the essence of education that generates a person with the qualities of intellectual autonomousness, the critical mass of which will predetermine the dominance of human-centrism in all social manifestations, and, first of all, in the dominance of "the human being in person". Only the latter turns a person into an intellectual driver of modern technological and socio-economic progress, the parameters of which today are absolutely unknown to either the state or society. Consequently, if the state is left with a mission to institutionally direct, regulate and motivate through the education of talented people, then an option can be realized, according to which they will "aim at what the state does not know and go where the state does not know".

Man as a natural social being appears in the aggregate of his essential forces, generic abilities, and the world as a unity of nature and society appears as a universe of objective forms of culture. These two poles - the objectivity of culture (in a broad sense) and the inner world, the essential forces of a person - are connected in education, are coupled in the content of education. Consequently, the graduates themselves with the qualities of intellectual autonomousness will have to determine what, how, with the help of what, etc. And the state with its attitudes and institutions can only slow down the creative and intellectual impulse of talented and highly qualified professionals. This, in fact, expresses the essence of human-centrism, which is generated in education as the student self-organizes and acquires the qualities of intellectually autonomous individuals who are able to overcome numerous existing and unknown PCBs in their future professional activities. Consequently, no one except the state will perform the functions of a smart mega-manager. But the state should start their implementation with a radical change in the understanding of the mission of education. It should generate (or awaken) in students the need for constant self-education, i.e. turn education into a way (form) of their existence. With such aspirations, unique individuals are able to solve a problem of any complexity.

In the conditions of the post-covid future, the intellectually autonomous personality, or rather their critical mass, which education should generate, is the main hope of the state as well as the society. However, this idea requires deep reflection on a theoretical and practical level. The modern state was formed to perform the function of ensuring structural integrity of the economy and society in their static states at the stage of self-organization. In other words, the state performed the function of a structure-forming principle in the capital-centric organization of the economy and society. Consequently, in the context of their dynamic changes, the state will need time and efforts of citizens, business and society to reorient towards institutionalizing the human-centric organization of a dynamic economy, consolidating society around a person with systems that ensure his health and education.

However, until now, all projects of international organizations and fiscal authorities in the countries of the world reproduce scenarios of changes that duplicate the past before-covid practice (Chapter 10). Even international analytical structures serving the interests of practical organizations, on the one hand, raise the fundamental problem of the inadequacy of the current education system, proving this fact with the growing skills mismatch (Boston Consulting Group, May 2020), on the other hand, they offer already known recipes that do not work within the framework of human-centric organizations that will dominate the future dynamic reality.

So, in Fig. 5 in a panel called «Future: talent development (mass uniqueness)» experts recognize that future professionals should have the following qualities: (1) every individual is equipped with a set of foundational literacies, cognitive competences, socio-behavioral and digital skills preparing them for working in uncertainty; (2) every individual has a unique educational journey based on personal needs, building up his/her skills arsenal over a lifetime; (3) the individual is responsible for self-development and self-realization; (4) employment opportunities are skills-based, each individual has information and access to local and global job offerings; (5) employers encourage human capital mobility, flexible working modes and virtual employment; (6) work opportunities are for everyone regardless of life circumstances and social status; (7) employers respect and accommodate individual values and provide employees with sustainable cause and community. In fact, the above qualities are inherent in intellectually autonomous individuals, the formation mechanism of which is described by the authors above in the framework of self-organization of students. At the same time, the authors highlighted the main feature that distinguishes such talented individuals as a result of education: the result of their self-organization is the awareness of the need to constantly reproduce their own education as a way of their existence. In other words, upon completion of learning, the student, in addition to a certain body of knowledge, must acquire a need for education as an inherent mechanism of his self-organization. But if this is so, then the unique individuals in their bulk will themselves determine in which area they need to improve their knowledge in order to realize their many abilities. On the one hand, this relieves society and the state of the burden of guessing fundamental changes in global reality and structuring them into the education system and models of the future labor market. But, on the other hand, they must quickly and efficiently respond to the ever-changing demands of intellectually autonomous individuals for educational services in new and emerging educational areas, professional segments and qualification niches.

In other words, the reduction of the skills mismatches as well as the skills gap, from the point of view of BCG experts, implies a modified deepening of the competence-based approach in education. For this, in their opinion, it is necessary that "each person receives a basic set of competencies necessary to work in conditions of uncertainty and of changes in the labor market". In other words, it is again about the goals of education proceeding from the needs of the state, acting on behalf of society. In this case, it is the state that should focus on identifying and transforming only individual, human capabilities into resources useful for society in the context of their use in the social production of the future post-covid reality. Thus, if proceeding from the needs of the state or the social production existing today or tomorrow or in the future, then it is the stakeholders mentioned above that must accurately imagine this specific future reality, to the needs of which they must adapt the education and qualifications of a particular professional, and at the same time try to realize his talents.

However, unfortunately, all and even the most enlightened policy-makers, the expert community of professionals in the field of education and the labor market, are representatives of the past generation, the past educational school, and due to their age they bear a certain amount of conservatism. In this context, it is advisable to recall the words of the famous United States Secretary of Defense Donald Rumsfeld, who made the following statement in February 2002: "There are known knowns; there are things we know we know. We also know there are known unknowns; that is to say we know there are some things we do not know. But there are also unknown unknowns – there are things we do not know we don't know." Today's critically-minded authorities representing nation-states should be aware that in an age of epic avalanche-like changes, there are fewer and fewer things they know that they know. At the same time, the number of things they don't know that they do not know. In other words, unknown unknowns increase exponentially in an indefinite post-covid reality. And it is this phenomenon that proves the correctness of the authors who associate human-centrism exclusively with the formation of a critical mass of self-organizing individuals. Society, represented by the state and companies, will only have to offer talents a variety of alternatives, from which they will choose those that best meet their potential for self-realization.

EMPIRICAL EVIDENCE

In September 2015, world leaders gathered to set ambitious goals for the global community future. Goal 4 of the Sustainable Development Goals (SDGs) seeks to ensure "inclusive and equitable quality education and promote lifelong learning opportunities for all" (UNESCO (United Nations Educational, Scientific, and Cultural Organization), 2016). As a result it becomes necessary to assess the level of educational failure, which prevents the formation of the necessary conditions for achieving a high level of learning in the country as well as of the inclusive growth.

Educational failure has certain economic evaluations. So, according to experts of the Centre for Strategic Research (Center for Strategic Research, 2018), the reduction of school unsuccessfulness twice (in our case up to 15% of all unsuccessful) corresponds to an increase in GDP growth by an additional 2% on a 10-year horizon (annual growth of 0.2%), by an additional 5-6% on a 20-year horizon (annual growth of 0.25%) and by an additional 10% on a 30-year horizon (annual growth of 0.3%). The correlation between educational and economic failure is high. The increase of students' economic success occurs in the process of modernization and of solution of the problem of the simultaneous rapid growth of the category "knowledge" and the reduction of the categories "rules" and "skill" in the preparation of schoolchildren. This effect, according to experts of Boston Consulting Group (Boston Consulting Group, 2017, PP. 56-57), is estimated at an additional 1.5% of annual GDP growth, which makes it possible to obtain a cumulative effect of 10 trillion rubles (Russia) (Table 2) in current prices by 2025. It means that the economic failure' level demonstrates the state of sufficient conditions, necessary for human capital formation as the main driver of national economic development (Pilipenko A.I., et al., 2019).

Table 2. Dynamics of the official annual exchange rate in Russia: Rubles / 1 US Dollar for the period 2001 – 2021

Jan.2001	Jan.2002	Jan.2003	Jan.2004	Jan.2005	Jan.2006	Jan.2007	Jan.2008	Jan.2009	Jan.2010
28.16	***30.13***	***31.78***	***29.45***	***27.74***	***28.78***	***26.33***	***24.54***	***29.39***	***30.18***
Jan.2011	Jan.2012	Jan.2013	Jan.2014	Jan.2015	Jan.2016	Jan.2017	Jan.2018	Jan.2019	Jan.2020
30.35	***32.19***	***30.37***	***32.65***	***56.23***	***72.92***	***60.65***	***57.60***	***69.47***	***61.90***

Source: cbr.ru

Below there are presented the calculations that evaluate the Russian educational system as an investment project.

1. The authors take half of the Russian graduates of the basic school (8-9 grades), who have only the basic level of education, i.e. they can use the knowledge acquired at school in simple familiar situations, at the same time, about one fifth of the graduates of the basic school do not reach the threshold level of formation of functional literacy in accordance with international requirements. Moreover, from the beginning it is taken for granted that the problem of eliminating school failure couldn't be immediately solved, therefore an additional 0.2% annual GDP growth rate due to the reorientation of the teaching technology and an increase in the level of learning can be observed only from 2022. And before this year, it would be ideal to get additional GDP growth of at least 0.1% per year. In order to compare the described estimates, the forecast data of GDP growth at current prices for the period 2000-2025 were constructed (Fig. 7).

To study and predict the dynamics of GDP_t, the authors use the capabilities of the adaptive Brown model (Brown, 1962).

The calculated value at time moment $\boldsymbol{t+\tau}$ is obtained according to the equation

$$\boldsymbol{Y}_{\boldsymbol{Br}}(\boldsymbol{t}-1+\tau)=\boldsymbol{a}_0(\boldsymbol{t}-1)+\tau\times\boldsymbol{a}_1(\boldsymbol{t}-1), \quad (1)$$

where τ – forecast horizon (lead interval or number of prediction steps).

If $\tau = 1$, then the formula (1) takes the form:

$$Y_{Br}(t) = a_0(t-1) + 1 \times a_1(t-1). \tag{2}$$

This value is compared with the actual level of the time series Y_t and resulting forecast error $e_t = Y_t - Y_{Br}(t)$ is used to adjust the model. Adjustment of parameters is carried out according to the formulas:

$$a_0(t) = a_0(t-1) + 1 \times a_1(t-1) + e_t(1-\beta^2) \tag{3}$$

$$a_1(t) = a_1(t-1) + e_t(1-\beta)^2, \tag{4}$$

where β – coefficient of data discount rate, reflecting a greater degree of confidence in earlier data. Its value varies from 0 to 1. In the calculations, the value is taken as $\beta = 0.8$.

Model modification process (t = 1, 2, ..., N), depending on current forecast qualities, ensures its adaptation to new patterns of development. The model obtained in the last step is used for forecasting (if $t = N$, where N – time series).

Figure 7. Dynamics of GDP of Russia in the scenarios: (1) forecast; (2) reduction the students' educational failure; (3) reduction of the students' economic failure for the period 2019-2025 (in billion rubles) (Dynamics of the official annual exchange rate in Russia: Rubles / 1 US Dollar for the period 2001 – 2021 in Table 2)

Sources: the authors' calculations based on the Rosstat' data

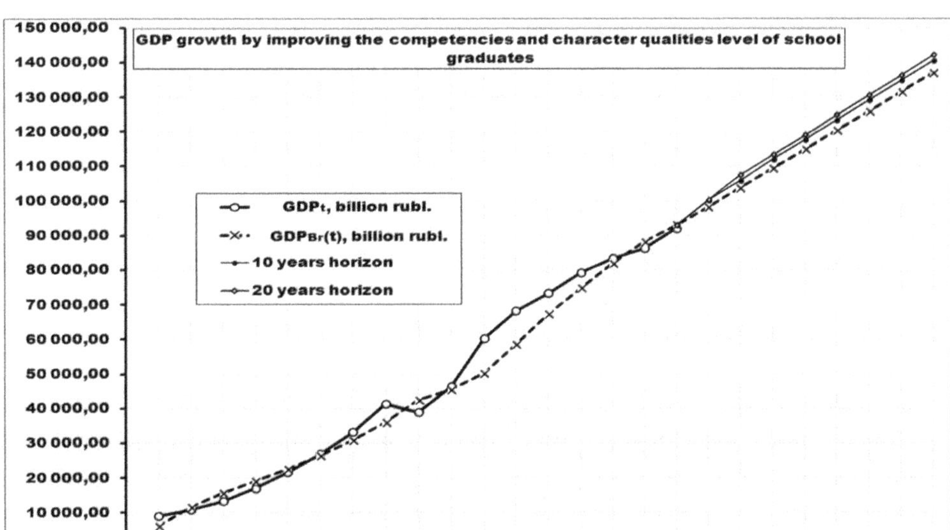

Figure 7 shows the dynamics of GDPt of Russia (*in billion rubles*): the corresponding adaptive Brown model of Russia $GDP_{BR}(t)$ *(in billion rubles*) and point forecast for this model (Table 2). In order not to overload the graph, the interval forecast is not given (Nf,kt).

The corresponding adaptive Brown model of Russia $GDP_{BR}(t)$ (*in billion rubles*) and point forecast for this model serves as a basis for comparing the dynamics of GDP, which is changing due to a factor of the school failure reduction: at first this growth is additional 0.1% per year, and after 2020 - additional 0.2%.

2. As noted above, the decrease of school failure of students results in a reduction in their economic failure. Economic assessments of the reducing economic failure' effect are also given by experts of Boston Consulting Group (2017). According to them, if you double the number of graduates from primary schools with a high level of learning, and consequently, with growing economic success, due to increasing competencies and character qualities, it could be possible to get additional annual GDP growth by a maximum of 1.5%.

At the same time, as in the case with school failure, the lag between the introduction of new learning technologies and returns in terms of economic effect has been taken into account. For this purpose, the problem of the economic return due to the reduction of the economic failure of general school graduates are differentiated as follows: in two years (2019-2020) the effect of improving preparedness is calculated only for 1/5 of the unsuccessful students because of the increase of the level of their competencies and character qualities. Then, since 2020, the economic effect is calculated as an additional 0.3% of annual GDP growth rate (+1.5% ВВП per year are divided into 5). In Fig. 7, this change is demonstrated by the GDP curve called 20 years horizon. It could be reasonable to add an extra 0.3% GDP growth each year, beginning from 2020. But the process of reducing school failure of the students and the following economic failure is a very long way, with a large number of problems and various obstacles. Fig. 7 demonstrates the conservative variant of the economic progress.

3. But the above assessments let us present the education system financing as the investment project. For this purpose the table is built (Table 3) to show the GDP of Russia (projected) in current prices, the net economic effect of reducing school unsuccessfulness of students (GDP of Russia, 10 years horizon) and of decreasing their economic unsuccessfulness (GDP of Russia, 20 years horizon) and education financing at the level of 2018 plans (3.6% of GDP) which is unchanged for the entire forecast period.

If considering education financing **(4)** as net costs, then GDP growth from the reduction of educational unsuccessfulness **(3)** and of economic unsuccessfulness **(2)** could be treated as net return on education investments. There have not been given the further authors' estimates of return on education investment from the view point of an investor, since the data obtained indicate unrealistically high (speculative) profits (significantly more than 100%).

In any case these calculations prove that even in conservative scenarios, Russian education can give a tremendous impetus to the growth of the national economy, but this will happen only if we take into account the many "BUTS". And the main "BUT" is connected with the implementation of the difficult reform of the teaching system in primary, secondary, secondary, tertiary education. The basic model of such a transformation is connected with the preparation of the teacher, who will be able to eliminate his own PCBs and the ones of his students (cited above). And this should be preceded by the same transformation of the consciousness of teachers and students of the universities, preparing the main "actors" of the educational system, and many others. Without such a serious transformation of the educational system, it hardly makes sense to wait for the economic effect of the growth of educational system' budget financing on the example of Russia.

Table 3. Evaluation of the financing of the Russian education system from the standpoint of an investment project for the period 2018-2025 (in billion rubles) ((Dynamics of the official annual exchange rate in Russia: Rubles / 1 US Dollar for the period 2001 – 2021 in Table 2)

Year	Forecasting horizon $GDP_{BR}(t)$, billion roubles (1)	Extra GDP growth due to the reduction of educational failure of schoolchildren (10 years horizon) (2)	Extra GDP growth due to the reduction of economic failure of schoolchildren (20 years horizon) (3)	Education system financing as planned for 2018 (3,6% GDP) (4)
2018	98 200.591	1 965.778	2 064.076	3 535.221
2019	103 740.937	2 071.683	3 547.639	3 734.674
2020	109 281.284	2 707.994	3 966.042	3 934.126
2021	114 821.630	2 852.321	4 192.293	4 133.579
2022	120 361.977	3 117.009	4 403.992	4 333.031
2023	125 902.323	3 272.902	4 615.690	4 532.484
2024	131 442.670	3 423.046	4 827.388	4 731.936
2025	136 983.016	3 573.190	5 039.087	4 931.389

Source: the authors' calculations based on the data of Fig. 7.

Today all over the Globe there are 264 million children and youth not going to school – this is a failure that must be tackled together, because education is a shared responsibility and progress that can only be sustainable through common efforts. This is essential to meet the ambitions of Sustainable Development Goal on education (SDG 4), part of the 2030 Agenda for Sustainable Development. Governments, schools and teachers have a frontline role to play here, hand-in-hand with students themselves and parents (UNESCO, (2017/8).

When public systems do not provide an education of sufficient quality, and for-profit actors fill the gap but operate without regulations, the marginalized lose out (United Nations, May 2012). So the education of insufficient quality strengthens social inequality and slows down economic growth. According to IMF estimates, with an increase in incomes of the richest individuals of the population by 1% of the national GDP for five years, it decreases by 0.08 p.p., and with an increase in incomes of the poorest, it increases by 0.38 p.p.

According to WEF experts (World Economic Forum, 2016), a moderate increase in inequality could stimulate the economic growth if social institutions work properly. In this case, the less affluent sections of society can increase their well-being. But this requires inclusive growth. Otherwise, the risks associated with inequality will only grow. The World Economic Forum (2018) created the most promising indicator called Inclusive Development Index (IDI). It relates to the evaluation of the intergenerational equity in a country in connection with national economic growth sustainability. It deals, in particular, with national existing pension system' quality, which directly links the elderly and young family members and predetermines informal institutions' quality, regulating the economic agents behavior in the society.

The OECD report (OECD, 2019) makes a key contribution to the OECD's Inclusive Growth initiative and its effort to develop a "people-centric inclusive growth model" in which well-being is the metric of success: where everyone has an equal opportunity to prosper; and where equity considerations are important in defining effective economic policies.

So, it is the person who created the entire systemic integrity who is called upon to construct the post-coronavirus reality and subordinate the principles of its functioning to his value ideas of justice and norms of behavior. However, he will be able to do this only if he can realize his limitless possibilities due to his own mechanisms of self-movement through due to self-organization (mainly due to education) and self-development (through adequate socialization into the structure of society). Psychological and cognitive barriers (PCB) stand in the way of the unhindered realization of human abilities. If in the process of education he learns to overcome them, then he will fully master the mechanisms of his self-movement. In this capacity, a person predetermines the imputation (endogeneity) of technological progress, of his own, as well as of other phenomena, into the self-movement of systemic integrities that it created. In other words, the embeddedness of the subjective factor into the mechanisms of self-organization and self-development of systems in different spheres of human activity makes it involved in all phenomena, since it is a person who mediates all the structural connections that accompany them. In other words, if you realize the endless possibilities of a person, packed into the mechanisms of his self-organization and self-development, then it is not difficult to solve the problems of structuring future reality. Moreover, the variety of forms of its implementation in each national community will be multivariate. And this shows the action of the universal mechanism of positive selection of differentiated types of human activity and forms of their organization in the global space. Moreover, the authors risk assuming that at this stage of post-covid self-development of national economic systems, new leaders may appear who will not be equal if they can initially identify the main driver of all transformations and form a critical mass of intellectually autonomous individuals. In this context, a highly effective health care system, a high-quality level of education for all citizens, as well as human-centricity as a fundamental principle of the organization of a post-COVID-19 society play a priority role.

11.2. The State and Self-Organization of Companies Through the Mechanism of Downwards Causation: Digitalization, Human-Centrism and Self-Development of High-Skilled Employees

The essence of human-centrism is manifested in the fact that a person moves to the center of the entire human-created "universe", which consists of a variety of systems for organizing his activities. To become the center of all processes of systemic structuring, the person himself must appear as a self-sufficient person, capable of both self-organization and self-development. Having acquired the qualities of an intellectually autonomous personality, a person is able to subordinate all processes and phenomena in the system integrities created by him to the goals of his own self-realization. In this context, the words of BCG experts are consonant, who wrote that «the depth of the required transformation of the educational system and the labor market will depend on the depth of penetration of human-centric tools and solutions, as well as on the context of each specific country" (BCG, 2019).

In the understanding of the authors, human-centrism originates in the education system, which should be subordinated to the formation of a personality capable of self-organization, overcoming the PCB in the learning process, which predetermines the quality of intellectual autonomousness. In other words, a person who is capable of transforming himself (his inner subjectivity) in the process of self-organization becomes able to transform society, transcending into it for the purposes of his own self-development.

Actually, the crisis of modern education is manifested precisely in the fact that education has aggravated the gap between a person's ability to self-reflection and his ability to transcend into society. Meanwhile, society acquires an endogenous mechanism of self-movement only if it becomes a structural integrity of intellectually autonomous individuals who have surpassed it, due to their ability to self-organization and self-development. In fact, in such a philosophical view, society repeats the model of self-organization and self-development of the economic system.

With the emergence of a critical mass of individuals with the quality of intellectual autonomy, society acquires an endogenous mechanism of self-movement, which is expressed in the man-centric principles of organizing all types of human activity. Gradually, human-centrism in the organization of society begins to multiply in structural ties in the economy and technology. At the same time, business plays the role of an intermediate link in the dialectic of interaction between society, economy and technology. This is due to the fact that companies are those dialectically complex elements that were generated by a static economy at the stage of its self-organization in the pre-coronavirus reality and which were not destroyed by the last shock. The fact is that the dialectical law of negation of negation destroyed both horizontal and vertical structural ties of the economic system and left intact dialectically complex elements of the economic system (Chapter 6.4). In this context, the elements of the system presented by companies capable of both self-organization and self-development, and will structure the new dynamic reality of the future. Moreover, the self-organization of dialectically complex companies is implemented by the mechanism of downwards causation, and their self-development – by the mechanism of upwards causation (Chapter 9). In this chapter, the mission of such self-enforcing companies is examined in the context of the implementation of the downwards causation mechanism that leads to internal restructuring of companies in the face of the crisis caused by the COVID-19 pandemic. Transforming from the inside under the influence of the laws of self-organization, they acquire the ability to creatively destroy the external environment, integrating into society, economy and technology for the purpose of realizing their own self-development (Chapter 11.3).

In the newest conditions, the winners will be those companies that have experienced the need to form human-centric organizations of their teams in a crisis situation, which will make it possible to attract highly qualified personnel and form new professional alliances – superteams, consisting of specialized groups of people and groups of specialized computers. Today it is difficult to even predict prospects for such fundamental transformations, but an indisputable fact is the priority importance of a self-developing human, whose intellectual asset will be the most valuable and expensive. In this regard, the words of the MIT Sloan Professor Thomas W. Malone (Malone, 2018) become extremely relevant: «instead of thinking in terms of a competition between humans and machines, let's instead choreograph a dance – a pas de deux – that involves people and machines and combines the wisdom of humans with the capabilities of technology for the greater good». In other words, a person who is intellectually autonomous, capable of independently solving non-trivial problems, overcoming PCB on this path, is able to create cyber-human systems in companies with human-centric principles of internal organization. Thus human and machine agents could work together on the same problem, using universal ways to solve it by differentiating and integrating joint activities. It is about integrating specialists into superteams of groups of people and of groups of computers in situations where that's helpful. In human-centric organizations of self-enforcing firms «people, in the opinion of Thomas W. Malone (Malone, 2018), should move from thinking about *putting humans in the loop* to *putting computers in the group*».

Indeed, during the crisis due to COVID-19 companies almost immediately faced one of the most difficult problems associated with organizational bottlenecks and the need to search for better balance between centralization and decentralization. It is in this context it is about an adequate model of the human-centric form of organizing teamwork in the company. Today's organizations are set up as traditional hierarchies or matrix organizations with roots stretching back to the industrial revolutions of the 18th, 19th, and 20th centuries. In theory, these structures provide clear lines of authority from frontline employees up through layers of management. In reality, matrix structures have only grown more complex as business has—to the extent that in some companies they are so cumbersome they hardly function. These old models cannot be fit for purpose in today's environment. Future-ready organizations structure themselves in ways that make them fitter, flatter, faster, and far better at unlocking value.

The CEOs are increasingly convinced that there is a simple, exciting, and executive structural model that can replace complex matrix structures and help leaders across industries and geographies who struggle with confused roles and labored decision-making processes, and who feel they are failing to move quickly enough to exploit new market opportunities (De Smet, et al., 2021). According to experts of McKinsey & Company, helix-like approaches could be defined of part and parcel of agile organizations (Fig.8).

Figure 8. Four interrelated trends are poised to unwind the old rules of management
Source: De Smet, Aaron, Chris Gagnon, and Elizabeth Mygatt (2021). Organizing for the future: Nine keys to becoming a future-ready company. McKinsey & Company. January. McKinsey.com

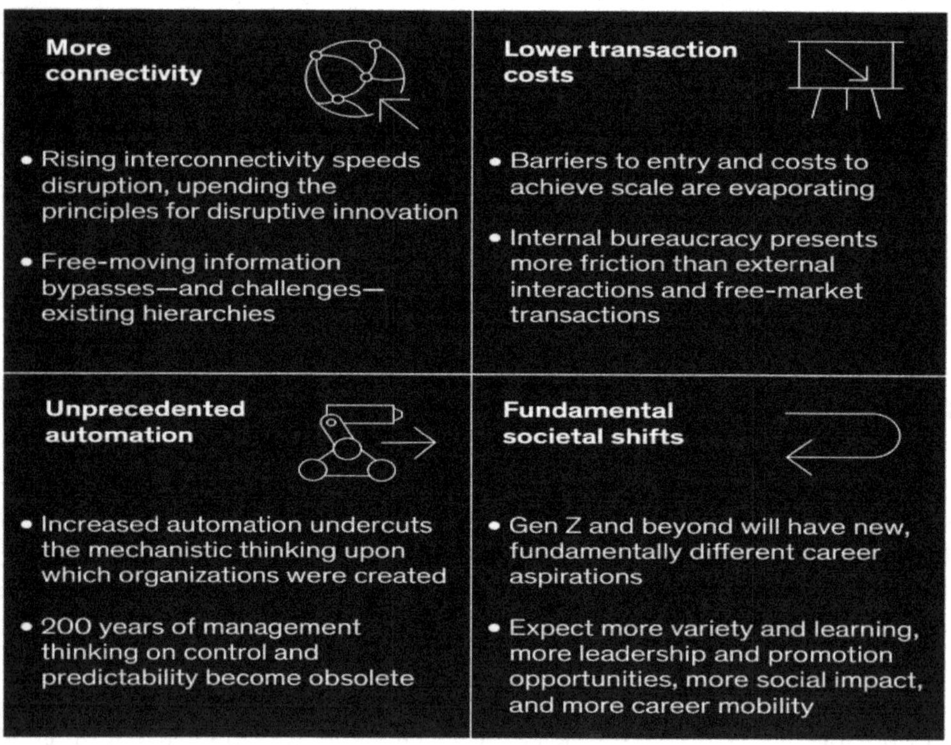

The helix type organization disaggregates the traditional management hierarchy into two separate, parallel lines of accountability, roughly equal in power and authority, from one hand, but fundamentally different, from another. One of the two lines helps develop people and capabilities, sets standards for how work is done, and drives functional excellence; the other focuses those people and capabilities on the priorities for the business (including overseeing their day-to-day work), creates value, and helps deliver a full and satisfying customer experience. The helix type organization decouples people-leadership tasks typically performed by one manager into two sets of tasks performed by two different managers, each of which is equally relevant. By decoupling these two lines of authority, the helix helps employees feel more empowered than in the traditional matrix, no longer in the crosshairs between two bosses, both of whom feel responsible for the same things and may give employees conflicting guidance. There are a few principal benefits of adopting a helix design (besides greater clarity and simplicity for the employee, which unlocks their productivity and performance). One of them is as follows: it alleviates tensions between centralized functions and decentralized business units, allowing entrepreneurship and flexible reactions in different business units without losing the positive scale effects of a global function.

The intensification of horizontal ties is already noticeable in the field of remote work due to some dispersion of the entire team, the absence of organizational structures familiar to the office. At a distance, communication along horizontal lines is activated due to the transfer of information and interaction outside the hierarchy – it simply cannot be organized at a remote location. In self-isolation, sane bosses must explicitly delegate some of their authority to the horizontal tier if they want the company to continue operating. And today it is primarily those teams that survive today, for which these horizontal connections are well developed, where there is no rigid centralization, where there is no super-competent leader. This trend, identified by the outbreak, can subsequently lead to more substantial changes in the logic of setting up workflows. And those companies that want to work more efficiently and flexibly will have to take these factors into account by expanding human-centrism.

Moreover, McKinsey & Company has already summarized the main considerations that have been formulated by CEOs of successful companies in the COVID-19 environment. Thus what many leaders feared, and the pandemic confirms, is that their companies were organized for a world that is disappearing – an era of standardization and predictability that's being overwritten by four big trends: a combination of heightened connectivity, lower transaction costs, unprecedented automation, and shifting demographics (Fig. 9) (De Smet, et al., 2021).

In fact, this confirms the authors' conclusion that with the COVID-19 pandemic crisis, the period of self-organization for systemic integrity in all spheres of human activity has ended, and a period of self-development has begun, which is characterized by uncertainty and their cardinal changes. Companies that are the basic forms of organizing the activities of future talents with the qualities of intellectual autonomousness cannot remain unchanged either.

It is reasonable to synthesize lessons to highlight how businesses can best organize for the future. The future-ready companies share three characteristics: they know who they are and what they stand for; they operate with a fixation on speed and simplicity; and they grow by scaling up their ability to learn, innovate, and seek good ideas regardless of their origin. After lockdowns companies can discover organizational "unlocks" and create new systems that are antifragile, more flexible, more organic, more interconnected, more purposeful – and simply more human (Katz, et al., 1978). According to Nassim Taleb's concept of antifragility, "the resilient resists shocks and stays the same; the antifragile gets better" (Taleb, 2012). For the helix to work, new processes and different mind-sets must be embedded to remove obstacles and overcome skepticism about the concept of antifragility. The smooth deployment of people will only happen if companies have, or are able to develop, a functioning internal talent market. A talent marketplace requires leaders to have a detailed understanding of available people – who they are, what they are doing, what skills and attributes they possess, and when they can be deployed from their current assignment.

In other words a few serious lessons can be learned today from the steps that organizations have already taken in response to the COVID-19 crisis. Thus, one lesson is that the crisis has brought about a sea change in executive mindsets on the role of technology in business (Fig. 10). As a result of the changes in executive mindsets on the role of technology in business remarkable changes take place in the speed with which companies have responded to a range of COVID-19-related changes especially as to digitalization (Fig. 11). When respondents were asked why their organizations didn't implement these changes *before* the crisis, just over half say that they weren't a top business priority.

Figure 9. The helix organization as a balance between flexibility and stability - hallmark of truly agile and human-centric approaches

Source: De Smet, Aaron, Sarah Kleinman, and Kirsten Weerda (2021). Beyond matrix organization, the helix organization. McKinsey Quarterly. 12.01. McKinsey & Company. Retrieved from: https://www.McKinsey.com/business-functions/organization/our-insights/the-helix-organization

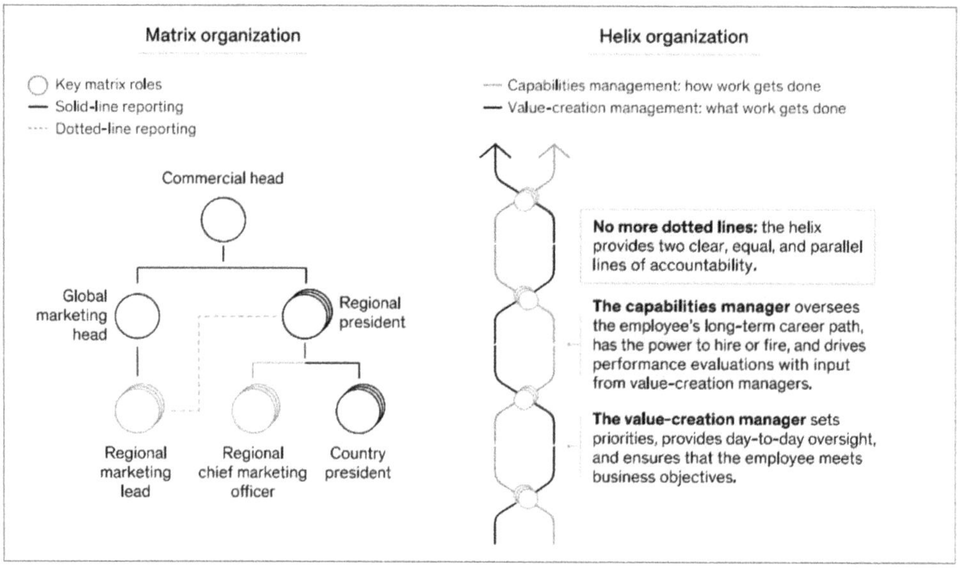

The second lesson is as follows. While the alignment on overall strategy and strong leadership have long been markers of success during disruptions or transformations the extent of technology's differentiating role in this crisis is stark. As a result in just a few months' time, the COVID-19 crisis has brought about years of change in the way companies in all sectors and regions do business.

This also applies to the digitization of their customer and supply-chain interactions and of their internal operations, which has been accelerated by three to four years. And the share of digital or digitally enabled products in companies' portfolios has accelerated by a shocking seven years (Fig. 12). Otherwise the COVID-19 crisis has made this imperative more urgent than ever. So most CEOs recognize technology's strategic importance as a critical component of the business, not just as a source of cost efficiencies.

Figure 10. Executive mindsets on technology's strategic importance have changed radically during the crisis

Source: LaBerge, Laura, Clayton O'Toole, Jeremy Schneider (2020). How COVID-19 has pushed companies over the technology tipping point—and transformed business forever. McKinsey & Company. October. McKinsey.com

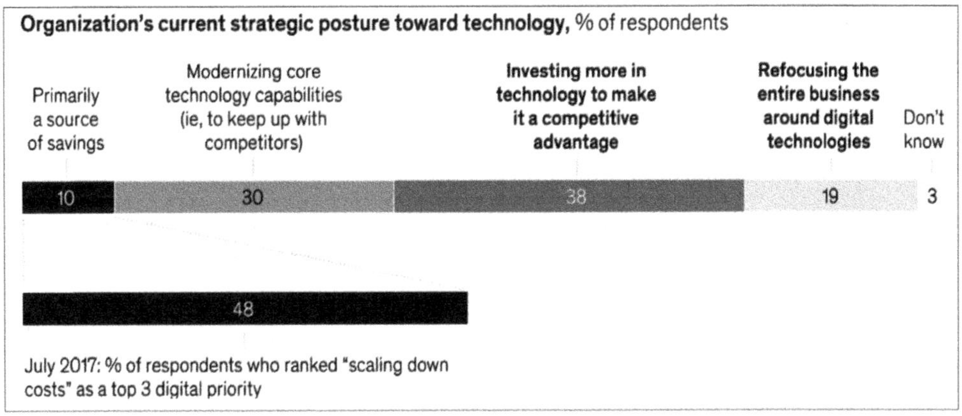

Figure 11. Executives say their companies responded to a range of COVID-19-related changes much more quickly than they thought possible before the crisis mindsets on technology's strategic importance have changed radically during the crisis

Notes: [1] Respondents who answered "entry of new competitors in company's market/value chain" or "exit of major competitors from company's market/value chain" are not shown; compared with the other 10 changes, respondents are much more likely to say their companies have not been able to respond

[2] For instance, increased focus on health/hygiene

Source: LaBerge, Laura, Clayton O'Toole, Jeremy Schneider (2020). How COVID-19 has pushed companies over the technology tipping point—and transformed business forever. McKinsey & Company. October. McKinsey.com

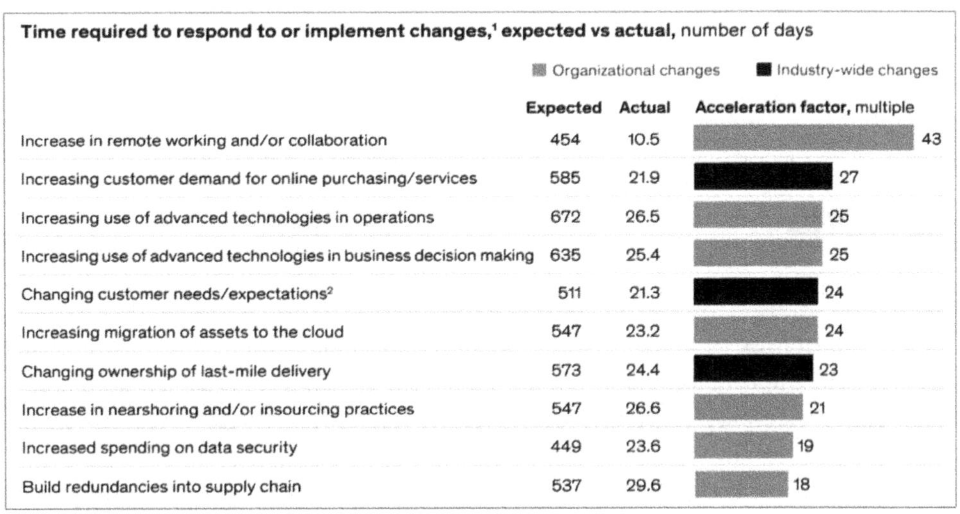

All of the above confirms the authors' idea that as a result of the self-organization of a static economic system, dialectically complex elements arose, represented by firms whose mission in a dynamic economy and post-crisis society is to restructure internal corporate interactions for the purpose of creative destruction of the external environment for them for the purposes of their successful self-development.

In this case, it is about the implementation of the mechanism of downwards causation, which, according to G.M. Hodgson (2002), changes the internal organization of the company.

In our case, it is about the formation of a new technological base for the activities of companies, which can be created only if CEOs of talents are attracted to their team. And for this, it is necessary to introduce the principles of human-centrism in the organization of internal interaction within companies. So along with the multiyear acceleration of digital, the COVID-19 crisis becomes a tipping point of historic proportions and will generate more changes as the human situation evolves.

Usually when CEOs identify the challenges resulting from their digital transformations, they most often cite human factor, especially the skill gaps (Fig.13). The next most-cited challenge is cultural differences between traditional IT and digital teams. To close the gap between current and future skill needs, the companies will have to replace or fundamentally retrain more than one-third of their IT employees over the next three years. And in this context, a problem arises related to human-centrism in the organization of teamwork in companies. It should be emphasized that any person, and especially one who has the quality of intellectual autonomousness, is self-sufficient. In other words, any employee has an internal mechanism of self-organization and self-development, and when he comes to the company, he independently coordinates the norms and values of the company with his internal subjective value ideas. If the individual values and the values of the company coincide, then the collective effect of teamwork in the company will be higher. And vice versa.

Figure 12. Experimentation with and investment in digital technologies have played a key role in helping companies navigate successfully through the crisis
Source: LaBerge, Laura, Clayton O'Toole, Jeremy Schneider (2020). How COVID-19 has pushed companies over the technology tipping point—and transformed business forever. McKinsey & Company. October. McKinsey.com

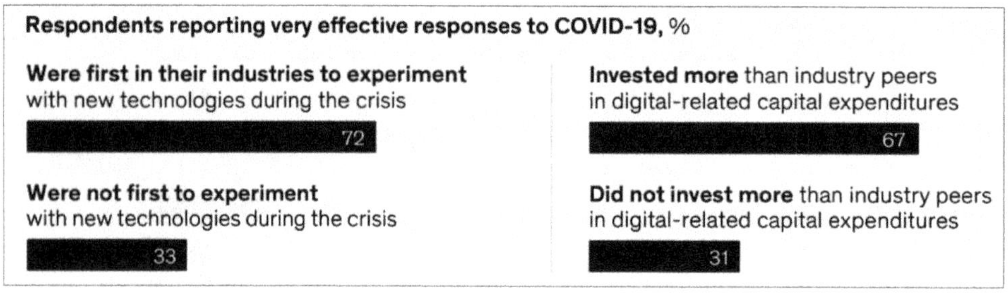

Human values are an important factor when defining individual purpose, as they help people determine what is personally important to pursue in life and work. Therefore, to better understand how people think about and experience purpose, it becomes necessary to map the type and intensity of a range of universally held human values including tradition, security, power, and achievement, among others (Schwartz, 2012; Schwartz, et al., 2012). Thus creating strong links to an individual purpose benefits individuals and companies alike—and could be vital in managing the post-pandemic uncertainties that lie ahead. Individual purpose benefits organizations because it can be an important contributor to employee experience, which in turn is linked to higher levels of employee engagement, stronger organizational commitment, and increased feelings of well-being (Schaefer et al., 2013).

Figure13. The most-cited obstacles encountered in digital transformations are talent and culture issues
Notes: [1] Question was asked only of respondents who said their organizations had pursued digitization in past 2 years. Respondents who said "none of the above" or "don't know" are not shown; n = 283
Source: Dhasarathy, Anusha, Ross Frazier, Naufal Khan, and Amit Rahul (2020) Managing the fallout from technology transformations. February. McKinsey.com

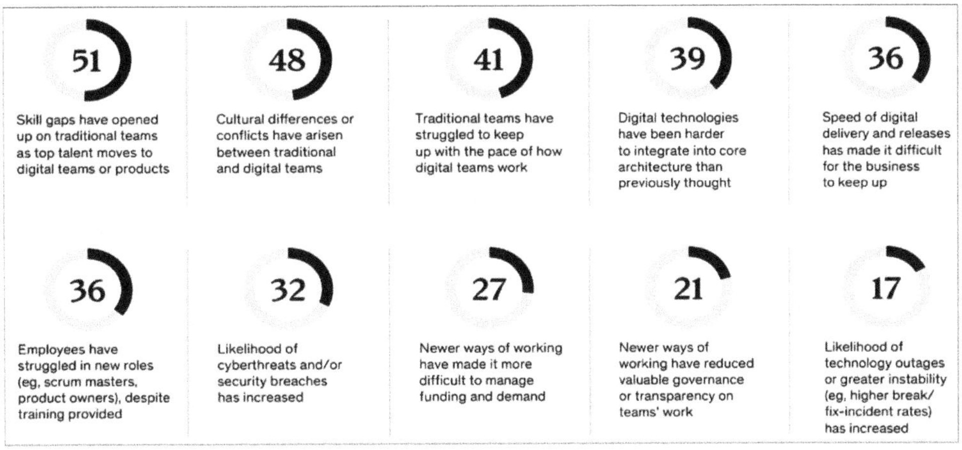

Experts of McKinsey & Company find a positive correlation between the purposefulness of employees and their company's EBITDA (earnings before interest, taxes, depreciation, and amortization) margin (Dhingra, et al., 2020). People seek psychological fulfillment from work, and, as the crisis recedes and companies ramp up new ways of working, some people will experience friction, and even dissonance, around issues of purpose. The intersection of organizational and individual goals is essential to the success of the company. This is because consolidated collective action of team partners multiplies company success and deepens employee experience. The essential part of CEOs job as organizational architect is to ensure that these two different forms of purpose – organizational and individual – are connected and mutually reinforcing. They should be ultimately a consideration in everything from hiring, feedback and incentives, and learning to matching individuals to jobs they will find most fulfilling.

So gradually, as the crisis progresses, more and more top managers and investors are beginning to realize that in the long term, their success depends primarily on their employees, as well as on customers, suppliers, and many stakeholders. It is in this connection that the concept of "shared value creation" should be mentioned, which was proposed in 2011 by Michael Porter and Mark Kramer (January-February 2011). Today, its fairness has been confirmed by the COVID-19 pandemic crisis, which, along with financial indicators, has prioritized goals related to the impact of companies on the environment, their social responsibility and the quality of corporate governance (environmental, social, governance – ESG). It is these concepts that develop the idea that a company capable of self-organization will seek to change the environment for the purpose of its successful self-development. In this context, we are talking about the implementation by the company of the mechanism of upwards causation (Chapter 9).

So, the participation of a person with an appropriate level of education in the processes of self-organization in the field of technology and economics testifies to the practically decisive role of the intellectually autonomous person in the self-organization and self-development of the entire society. If we move from the analysis of the patterns of self-organization in each individual sphere of human activity to synthesis, to the subordination of the stages of their complication, then we should note the priority role of a person and education in coordinating the thresholds of complexity that they achieve (Chapter 10). This is due to the fact that the significance of a person's influence on all processes of self-organization in all spheres with his participation is due to his integration into structural interactions either on the improvement of technologies or on the exchange of the results of economic activity. And, from a philosophical point of view, the structure is a way of internal interconnections of system elements. It is the structural relationships that preserve systemic integrity and determine how long the system will be qualitatively defined. The structure (structural connections) changes as the nature of the elements themselves (participants in structural connections) changes and exclusively under their influence. In other words, the structure of the new economy is largely determined by how quickly companies can adapt to new conditions of dynamic development through the upwards causation mechanism. Only then through the downwards causation mechanism they will begin to form new structural ties of the new dynamic economy as an entity.

Klaus Schwab (2018) wrote that a company is a social organism, in addition to striving economically to increase profits. And, according to J. Schumpeter (1949), only entrepreneurs are capable of "creative destruction" of their internal organization and external reality. All these aspects correspond to the quality of self-sufficient companies capable of self-organization (internal structuring) due to downwards causation mechanism and of self-development (to interact with similar business partners or any stakeholders in the external environment) through an upwards causation mechanism. So, COVID-19 outlined the main players in the field of constructing a new reality: a person with the qualities of intellectual autonomy, capable of self-organization and of self-development; self-sufficient companies capable of implementing mechanisms of downwards and of upwards causation, and a human-centric form of organizing their team activities on a new technological basis.

So, the shocks that mediated the operation of the law of denial of negation caused a landslide destruction of structural ties in national economic systems. This could not but affect the destruction of the global system of division of labor and international cooperation, which was discussed in January 2021 at the WEF forum in Davos. Now everything depends on the speed with which national systems will build the "new economy". The point is that as a result of the shock initiated by the COVID-19 pandemic, both the vertical and horizontal structural ties of static economies were destroyed and the problem of their rebuilding arose. In Chapter 11.1, as the main driver of all the transformations a person with the qualities of intellectual autonomousness was substantiated, which should be highly educated and adequately socialized into the structure of society. In this context, self-enforcing companies have a special role to play. After the destruction of the structural ties of the static economy, it also lost the mechanism of self-movement, since it was associated with its structure.

Consequently, new structures of an already dynamic economy will be constructed by dialectically complex elements that have formed in this capacity within the framework of a static economy, and which are able to form their internal structure through downwards causation processes, and external ones - through upwards causation processes. In fact, it is these complex structures of an already dynamic economy that are the intermediary link in the socialization of intellectually autonomous individuals. First, CEOs of companies will restructure their internal interactions according to their requirements, realizing their own self-organization, and second, after developing collective routines and collective behavior, they will build their external relations with their stakeholders, creating a new environment for the socialization of intellectually autonomous individuals into society. And in fact, in this way the self-development of the companies themselves occurs when they mediate the upwards causation process. In this process, companies adapt the latest achievements of the technological revolution with the help of high skilled work force, form superteams based on combining the capabilities of advanced specialists and the potential of new technological solutions. To implement these changes, companies are forced to change organizationally, increasingly resorting to the implementation of human-centric principles of organizing intra-team relationships. In fact, this is a scenario of self-movement of dialectically complex structural units of a self-developing economy, which has lost its own mechanism of self-movement and depends on its companies in building systemic integrity and a new mechanism for its own self-movement.

11.3. The State in the Dynamic "New Normal" of the Post-COVID-19 Reality: Companies' Upwards Causation Mechanism of Basic Structure Formation for Society Consolidation

Even before the coronavirus pandemic, corporate strategy researchers justified approaches to companies in terms of corporate social responsibility (CSR) (Beschorner, et al., 2013, PP. 285–298) and creating shared value (CSV) approaches (Porter, et al., 2011). Michael Porter, and Mark Kramer (2011) characterize CSR as essentially philanthropic, and as disconnected from a company's core businesses in the authors' words "separated from" versus "integral to profit maximization" (Porter, et al., 2011; Beschorner, January 2013). The concepts of CSR as well as of CSV were aimed at justifying the need for sustainable mediation by companies of the relationship between societal and economic progress. From the standpoint of Michael Porter and Mark Kramer (2011), there are three key ways that companies can create shared value opportunities: (1) by reconceiving products and markets; (2) by redefining productivity in the value chain; (3) by enabling local cluster development. In addition, they proved, that corporations should "utilize their skills, resources, and management capability to lead social progress". Stressing businesses as proactive societal actors is not a new proposal. This idea was discussed by L. Hartman, and P. Werhane (2013), D. Matten, and A. Crane (2005), by A. Scherer, and G. Palazzo (2007), S. Zadek (2001) and by many others. However, this was all before the COVID-19 pandemic.

The authors, following dialectical logic, came to the conclusion that the potential of leading companies in certain areas of their activities in a self-organizing economy was quite justifiably reduced to a purely economic mission, which began to complicate due to their increased contribution to the development of society. This happened as the importance of the subjective component in the mechanisms of self-organization of the economy increased while building its vertical structural hierarchy. However, the shock implementation of the law of denial of denial, accelerated by the COVID-19 pandemic, forced to rethink the fundamental ideas about the mechanisms of self-movement not only of systemic integrity in the economy, but in society and in the structural elements of the systems themselves. In the latter case, it is about large companies that themselves have acquired, within the framework of a self-organizing economic system, their own, endogenous mechanism of self-movement. According to the authors, the mechanism of self-organization (internal structuring) of companies as integrities is associated with the processes of downwards causation. As for the self-development mechanism of these companies, it is mediated by the processes of upwards causation (Chapter 9).

If we compare the periods of static complication of the economy at the stage of its self-organization and the dynamics of the economic system in the conditions of its self-development, then the mission of companies capable of self-moving changes significantly. In the conditions of the static economic system, the potential of companies was in demand depending on the needs of structuring relationships horizontally and vertically in the hierarchical chain in order to strengthen economic equilibrium and financial stability. It should be emphasized that the authors studied the problems of shocks, therefore, the problems falling into the sphere of their interests were analyzed more or less deeply, depending on the need to build the foundations of the theory of shocks. Therefore, the problems of the mission of companies in the conditions of self-development of economic systems are only outlined by the authors without disclosing the depth of the subject. The authors recognize that a fundamental approach to understanding the changing mission of companies will require significant research effort.

So, the self-development of economic systems is still presented only in theoretical construction. But already at this stage, the authors formulated their hypothesis, the validity of which has some practical confirmation (McKinsey Global Institute, (January 2021). The authors theoretically proceeded from the following. The shock destruction of vertical and horizontal structural links as load-bearing structures of systemic integrity in the economy meant the destruction of the mechanism of its self-organization. And this was confirmed by the logic of the functioning of the law of negation of negation. But, being capable of self-movement, the economic system must have such a mechanism both at the stage of its self-organization and at the stage of its self-development. The movement of system integrity is continuous in time. Having lost the ability to self-structure at the stage of self-organization, the economic system does not stop in its self-movement, realizing in dynamics its ability to self-development. But things get more complicated here. Having lost its structure, the economic system acquired the opportunity to realize the potential of the latest technological revolution 4.0, having its own dialectically complex structural units, represented by the self-sufficient large and largest companies (private business). It is they who act as an adequate form of organizing the activity of a new driver of technological, economic and social progress, which is represented by individuals with the qualities of intellectual autonomy (Chapter 11.1). In other words, a highly qualified talented professional and a company rebuilding its internal structure on the principles of human-centrism in order to adequately organize its activities are able to structure a new dynamic reality on a new technological platform, which is predetermined by the technological revolution 4.0.

At the same time, the state must take on a mission that companies cannot fulfill. It is about generating a critical mass of individuals with the quality of intellectual autonomousness. Considering the conclusions of P. L. Berger and T. Luckmann (1966) on the relationship between the sociology of knowledge and social construction, it should be emphasized that they are of fundamental importance in the current context of the COVID-19 pandemic. This is due to the fact that the man-centric organization of various human activities can become a new social reality. As an environment for the life of a self-developing personality, it will have to be distinguished by adequate institutional support for subject-subject relations both in society and in technological and economic systems. Based on the findings of D. North (1996; 2005), the authors associate the rate of human assimilation of the results of the 4th technological revolution and the introduction of new technological infrastructure in all spheres of human activity with the quality of the institutional environment. The adequacy of economic (formal institutions and informal restrictions) and social institutions to the mechanisms for making new technological decisions in the technological and economic spheres contributes to the acceleration of socio-economic progress in each national community. The concretization of this provision is the remark that the appropriate institutionalization of social relations is an unconditional priority for the full socialization of a critical mass of intellectually autonomous individuals. The resulting multiplier effect will be expressed in their active inclusion in the process of constructing social reality and realizing the potential of creative individuals in advanced companies as forms of organizing their professional activities.

P. L. Berger and T. Luckmann (1966) associated the difficulty of understanding this process with the specific nature of man, into which his sociality is intertwined in an unusually difficult way, since Homo Sapiens is always and to the same extent also Homo Socius (Durkheim, 1895). Fig. 14 presents in general all the variety of relationships in society, in which a person mediates them in different forms of their manifestation, which are objectively coordinated with each other. Judging by Fig. 14, any social order, especially in terms of the institutional environment, is a product of human activity as a result of its externalization. In its genesis, the social order is predetermined by past human activity. And in the present it exists, since a person continues to create it with his activity. Its instability as a fundamental property forces a person to ensure the stabilization of his behavior. It is institutions that make it possible to understand the causes of the emergence, maintenance and transmission of social order. It is in this context that the human-centric world is the result of the human construction of an institutional order that ensures both technological and socio-economic progress. Moreover, the connection between the individual and the human-centric system created by him is dialectical. The two aspects of the dialectic of this relationship are externalization and objectification. Externalization is expressed in the fact that society is a human product, and objectification turns society into an objective reality. At the same time, the third moment of this dialectic is internalization, which translates objectified social reality into the consciousness of the individual. Ultimately, internalization makes a person a social product. All these phenomena accompanying the processes of self-development of an intellectually autonomous personality predetermine the exceptional importance of companies as forms of organizing their professional activities. Moreover, the requirements for them are increasing as dialectically complex units of a new dynamic economy, which structures dialectical pairs not only in the economy, but also in society, strengthening their integrity. This happens when the company mediates the action of the mechanism of upwards causation.

Under the new conditions, companies are implementing Schumpeterian "creative destruction" as follows. They not only act as representatives of society, in conditions of a destroyed structure, only they are able to construct a new structural level in society, mediating the mechanism of upwards causation (Chapter 9.4). And in this case, they do not just carry out their own mission related to increasing profits and / or market share, and / or the value of the company's shares, and / or building up chains of value. In the context of self-development of systemic integrity, companies are called upon to fulfill a different fundamental mission. These companies solve the problems of the integrity of the future economic system and society by forming or generating mechanisms for creating a critical mass of highly qualified professionals or talents, as experts call them today.

(1) Their activities within companies will implement the capabilities of the 4.0 technological revolution, introducing new technological solutions into the practice of companies, which means the creation of a new technological base at the macro level as the foundation of a dynamic economy and the corresponding society.

(2) Receiving high material reward from their employers, intellectuals and talented workers solve the deepest social problems of the polarization of the population in terms of income and wealth, poverty and misery, pensions, etc. Macroeconomic and social benefits of companies' mediation of the mechanism of upwards causation will be expressed in the expansion of the size of the middle class and the restoration of the effect of social lifting. In other words, we are talking about the ability of companies to form the basic structure of society, which will predetermine its integrity.

Figure 14. The variety of forms of human manifestation in society as a worker, a consumer, and a saver in a system of exchange with institutions
Notes: [1] Individual inputs refer to commitments made by individuals in their roles as workers, consumers, and savers in the social contract. For example, workers commit their time and energy to an employer in return for paid employment. [2] Based on literature review; extent of expectations varies across countries and individuals. Individual level of satisfaction is influenced by which expectations are most important to them and the extent to which those expectations are being met. Our selection of indicators within each dimension is not exhaustive but illustrative, and based on data available for comparison across 22 countries between 2000 (or earliest) and 2018 (or latest). [3] Housing, healthcare, education, food, transportation, clothing, communications, recreation, and furnishings; other categories are restaurants and hotels, alcohol and tobacco, and miscellaneous goods and services.
Source: McKinsey & Company (2020). The social contract in the 21st century: Outcomes so far for workers, consumers, and savers in advanced economies. Executive summary. February. McKinsey.com

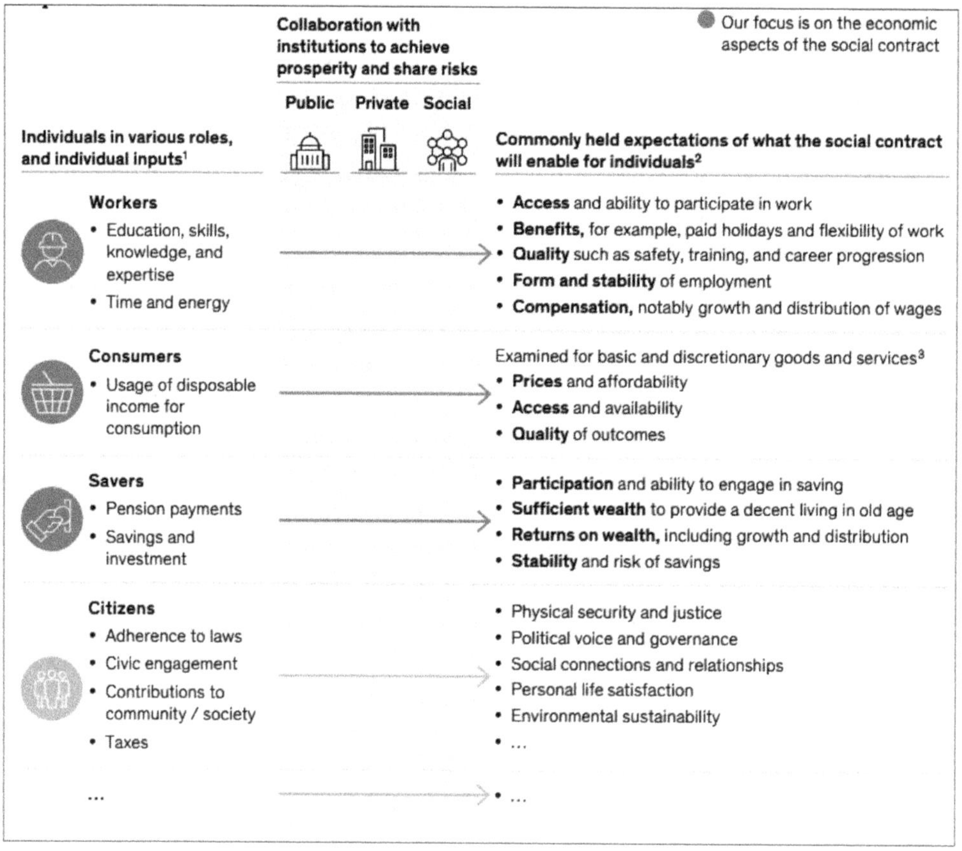

(3) Optimization of the interaction between companies and intellectually autonomous individuals will objectively bring to life the process of replacing the capital-centric principles of organizing systemic integrity with human-centric ones. First, this process will arise in intra-team interaction within companies, and then in structural ties in the economy and society as a result of the action of the mechanism of upwards causation.

So, the self-development of the economic system and its acquisition of the quality of structural integrity directly depend on the implementation of the fundamental mission by dialectically complex companies capable of both self-organization and self-development.

In this context, the most important social action of companies is to create new institutions and adjust the set of social institutions left over from the previous system to the requirements of the latest technological structures. C. Freeman and C. Perez (1988) wrote that the spread of new technologies in the world is possible only on the basis of many social and institutional changes that make it possible to generalize the entire intensive mass of production and the consumer paradigm. At the same time, C. Perez (2002) mentioned that the depletion of the old paradigm is accompanied by the inertia of the corresponding social and institutional mechanisms. It is they and the states that support them that could become an insurmountable barrier to the potential growth of a new technological paradigm (Arthur, 2009). As a result, it is outdated institutions and the state that supports them that can predetermine a structural crisis and become an obstacle to the rapid spread of new technological solutions.

Thus, at the stage of dynamics of systemic integrity in the economy and society, dialectically complex structural integrity of companies will fulfill the mission of forming their basic structural levels, which in the future will implement the mechanism of their self-movement. Until that moment, it is the companies that are the carrier structure of changes in technology, in the economy and in society, predetermining their self-development. In this context, the activities of companies act as a kind of tuning fork for the state, which must carefully monitor the results of their activities, providing it institutionally.

The example of China is a practical confirmation of the validity of the author's concept of the structure-forming function of large and largest companies at the stage of self-development of systemic integrity in technology, economy and society (McKinsey Global Institute, January 2021). The first thing to note is related to the place of education in China's transformation strategy until 2030. Thus, China's talent-development model is aimed at developing the skills needed in an innovative, digitized, economy according to the technological revolution 4.0 (Fig. 15). Representatives of the whole society (stakeholders) take part in it.

By 2030, up to 220 million Chinese workers, or 30 percent of the workforce, may need to transition between occupations due to automation. That's about one-third of global occupational and skills transitions. The perception among employers in China is that investing in training and skills development may not offer a worthwhile return, but this misses the broader point that skilled workers are more productive, drive faster revenue growth, and accelerate the creation of value. This exercise suggests that a company that invests more aggressively in reskilling could achieve a 5 percent increase in net present value of profit over the next ten years (Fig. 16). Investment in training can benefit the company in many different ways. Previous research has shown that the productivity premium for a trained worker is an estimated 23 percent, and that this premium leads to faster revenue growth and higher profit margins. By investing in training, a company also benefits from lower turnover. Research suggests that direct replacement costs can reach as high as 50 to 60 percent of an employee's annual salary, and total costs associated with turnover range from 90 to 200 percent of an annual salary.

These transitions will require transforming China's education and skills development system. It will be as follows. First, learning will need to be extended beyond schools to cover China's working adults (everyone); this implies tripling the scope of skills development. Second, content needs to evolve from basic to a broad range of skills (everything). The high cognitive, social and emotional, and technical skills that will be in demand could account for an additional 236 billion hours by 2030, or an average of about 40 days per worker. Third, education and skills development should be available to all throughout their lives (everywhere) to support all workers who need to undertake some reskilling every year.

Figure 15. Reskilling China—a potential institutional structure for implementation
Source: McKinsey Global Institute. (January 2021). Reskilling China: Transforming the World's Largest Workforce into Lifelong Learners. Executive Summary. www.McKinsey.com/mgi

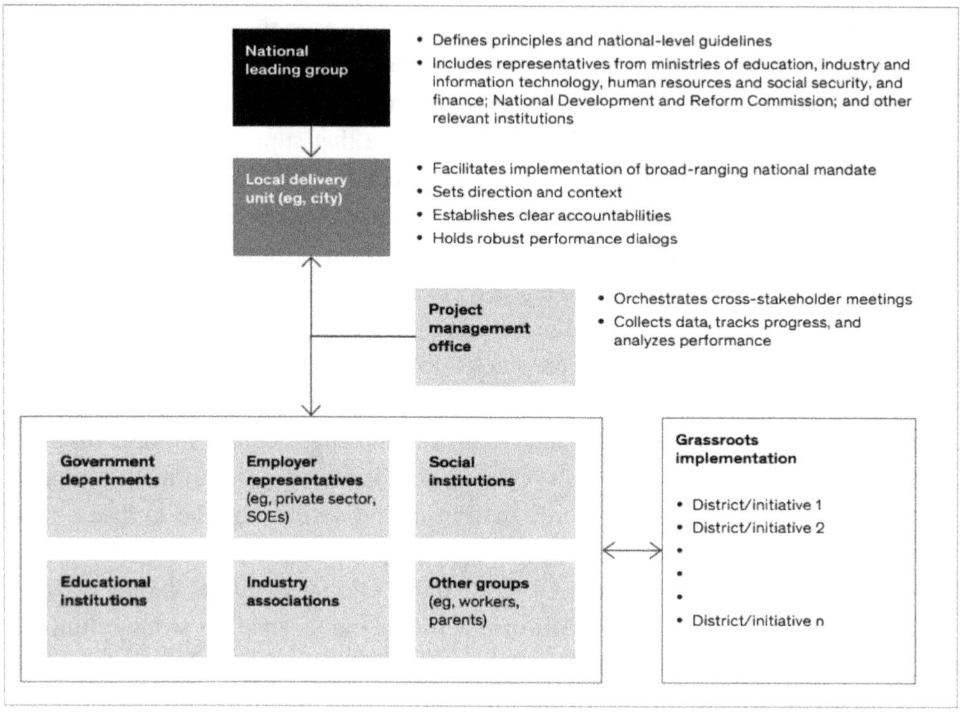

Figure 16. Mindset and incentives: simulation of the company perspective (illustrative case: manufacturing company)
Source: McKinsey Global Institute (January 2021). Reskilling China: Transforming the World's Largest Workforce into Lifelong Learners. Executive Summary. www.McKinsey.com/mgi

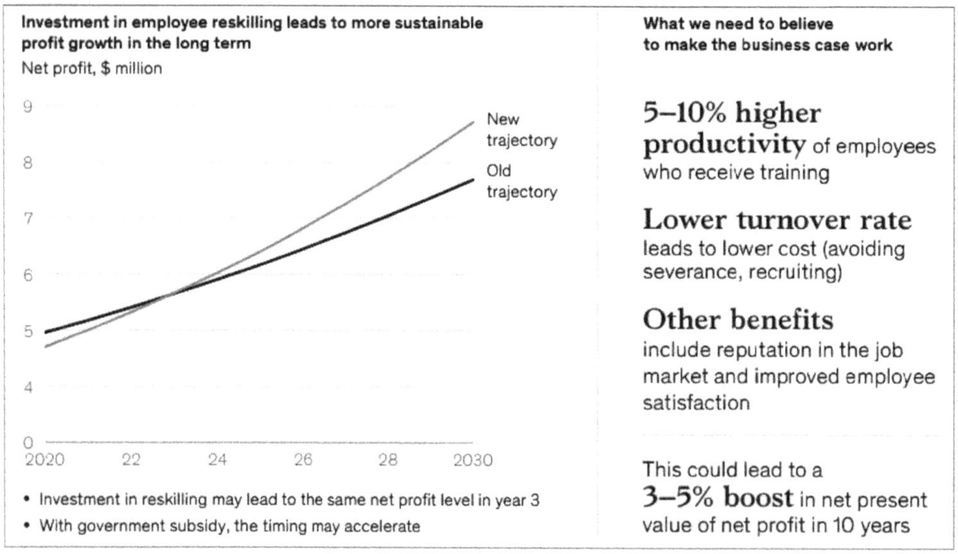

A talent revolution in China is aimed at enabling continuous improvement in living standards for all. Over the past three decades, China has achieved significant progress in incomes, labor productivity, and GDP growth. To continue to improve living standards, sustaining wage growth and productivity gains will be critical (Fig. 17). For China to achieve 70 percent of the average per capita GDP of high income economies by 2050, a long term goal as interpreted by Chinese think tanks, necessary per capita GDP growth of 4.7 percent and wage growth of 4.9 percent is implied. This requires a skills revolution in China's workforce.

Figure 17. Sustaining per capita GDP and wage growth is important for continuous improvement of living standards

Notes: 1.SomeChinesethinktanksdefinedalong-termscenarioinwhichChinaachieves70%oftheaverageofhigh-incomeeconomies'per capitaGDPby2050.TheWorldBankdefinesahigh-incomecountryasonewithgrosspercapitanationalincomeof$12,536ormorein2019. 2. Assuming labor share of income remains constant

Source: McKinsey Global Institute (January 2021). Reskilling China: Transforming the World's Largest Workforce into Lifelong Learners. Full Report. www.McKinsey.com/mgi

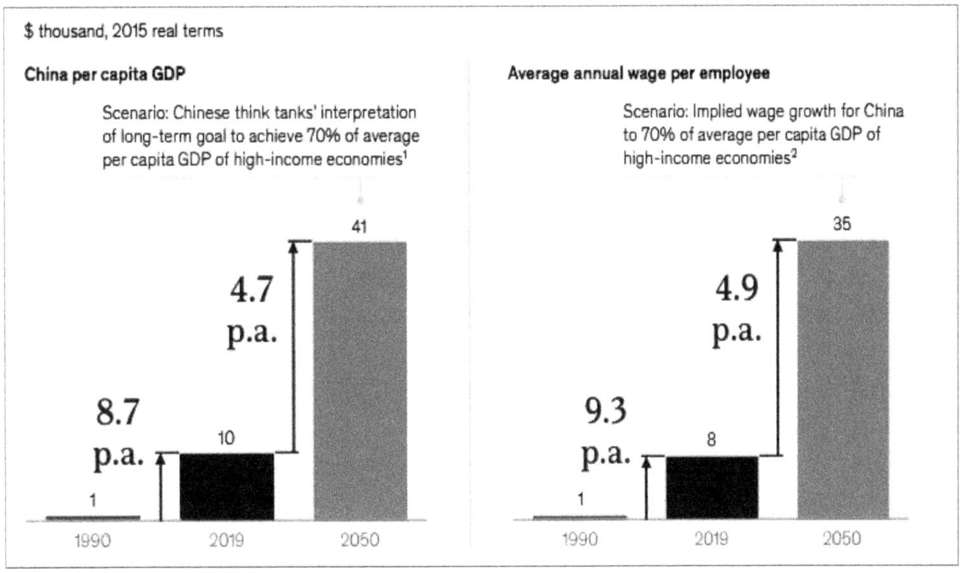

The government of China has already begun to explore the parameters of a new strategic direction, with new policies on vocational training and lifelong learning. At the heart of this effort will be collaboration between all the major players—government, companies, educators, social institutions, and students, whether in school or in vocational training.

The implementation of the national plan will happen at the local level; the question is what operating model is likely to be effective. The experts of this Report explore two ideas to develop a national strategy and translate it into execution at the local level: (1) setting up a national leading group focused on the future of work; and (2) forming delivery units at the local level (Fig.15). It is vital that employers, especially private sector players, become more engaged in this national effort, both as a source of market information for educational institutions so that they can match curricula and training to the jobs that are likely to be on offer to students, and as active participants in education and skills development.

So, the current situation in the world is different in that everything has changed and requires a change in the established structures in society. And this is natural, since over time, and even more so in a humanitarian catastrophe, obviously effective institutions at certain stages of self-movement of systemic integrity become unacceptable in the context of the COVID-19 pandemic and after it. Moreover, there can be no known universally effective formal institutions that are acceptable for any society in which the aggregation of individual values is realized. It turns out that each society represented by the state is forced to solve the problems of future self-development, proceeding from the national specifics, predetermined both by technological and economic circumstances, and by the state of the integrity of society. Nevertheless, intellectually autonomous individuals and the human-centric organization of their activities within the framework of companies capable of self-development objectively act as the main drivers of the future post-covid reality. Whether the state will be able to ensure their optimal functioning is a big question.

CONCLUSION

The last chapter of the book summarizes some of the results of the COVID-19 pandemic and substantiates the obstacles that the state will face, which was formed during the period of self-organization of economic systems, i.e. before humanitarian disaster. In this regard, the state can become the weakest link in the chain of all the transformations that national socio-economic systems will have to go through. In this regard, the chapter theoretically substantiates some of the practical steps that advanced companies are taking in the direction of constructing an uncertain post-covid future.

The main thing that needs to be rethought by the state is a change in the role of man in the processes of self-development of systemic integrity in technology, economy and society. Only human, having acquired the quality of intellectual autonomy will be able to form a new technological base of self-developing systems that meets all the latest achievements of the 4.0 technological revolution. It is these problems that should become a priority for the state in the context of preventing the threat of a humanitarian catastrophe in the future similar to coronavirus pandemic. Only the state, in partnership with all stakeholders, is able to form a high-quality healthcare and education system that meets all the requirements of modern self-development of a human.

The difficulties of the state in the implementation of human-centrism in education are associated with a change in its paradigm associated with the replacement of the competence-based approach with knowledge-based one, which should be aimed at the formation of a unique personality with an endogenously inherent ability to self-education as a way of its existence. Then the individual's own self-development becomes the goal of all his activities, regardless of the wishes of society or the state. Only such a person will be able to create something new in the uncertain environment of post-covid reality. Human-centrism at the stage of self-development of an intellectually autonomous personality is associated with the fact that its socialization into society and into the economic system should be carried out on his individual terms. And if the norms of behavior, values, and institutions established before the emergence of a new generation do not suit them, then either society or the state will correct them, or representatives of this generation will not integrate in the society in the name of universal prosperity. Naturally, the state will have the mission to institutionally cut off those manifestations of young talents who, by their opportunism, can destroy the integrity of the system, as well as in every possible way to encourage the progressive changes in the established foundations that they implement. The national society that will create the conditions adequate for young people to choose diverse spheres of manifestation of their creative principles will win.

In parallel, the state should think about the conditions for the self-development of a critical mass of such talented individuals. The main one will be organizational, associated with the domination of man-centric principles of organization in all spheres of human activity. Already at the stage of the COVID-19 pandemic, these problems were faced by large and largest companies capable of "creative destruction". They made the problem of skills mismatch and skills gap a priority. They were the first to adapt their internal organizational structures, implementing a downwards causation mechanism to implement human-centric principles of super-teams work.

The functioning of companies capable of being a driver of self-development of a dynamic economy will become another problem for the state. This is due to the fact that, on the one hand, such companies are an adequate form of organizing the activities of individuals with the quality of intellectual autonomousness. And in this the state should not interfere with them. But, on the other hand, the ability of companies to perform a structure-forming function in society, generating its basic structural level through their upwards causation mechanism, can cause significant problems for the state. And this is due to a significant share of the state's conservatism, which was formed and functioned under the conditions of the structural integrity of the system at the stage of their static changes. The state has yet adapted to the conditions of self-development and the formation of dynamic systems, and in practice it simply has no idea what needs to be done to support progressive changes.

And, meanwhile, by combining individuals capable of unlimited creativity and companies capable of creative destruction, it will be possible to successfully implement the mechanism of the human-centric internal organization of companies when they are transferred to a new technological level, as well as the mechanism of upwards causation mechanism for transforming external structural ties on the principles of human centrism. As a result, the dialectic of the interaction of these mechanisms in the behavior of intellectually autonomous individuals and creatively destructive companies will make it possible to form a new technological paradigm for post-image reality, to build new structural connections in society and the economy.

However, this path is thorny, since the current generations, due to their age, carry a significant charge of skepticism and conservatism. This means that before representatives of the new generation come to the government and governing bodies, more or less acute conflict situations may arise over new paradigms in the economy and society between the state, on the one hand, and, on the other hand, a critical mass of advanced individuals and firms speaking on their behalf in collaboration with their supportive stakeholders. Perhaps this gap in understanding the essence of the moment and future realities between young graduates with intellectual qualities and older generations who institutionalize current relations in society and the economy can be perceived as a socially determined obstacle to the further progress of society. How quickly it can be overcome, how successfully the national community will move along the path of self-development into the future. As for the state, then, on the one hand, it will not have to take upon itself the strategic determination of the prospects for moving forward and motivate citizens and firms to do so, since this will become the lot of self-sufficient individuals and companies, but, on the other hand, the importance of the state in terms of expert council, which will have to weed out the alternatives that have arisen that can destroy the integrity of the national society, and institutionally support those that will accelerate its progressive changes.

Considering all of the above, it can be argued that the path to a new post-coronavirus reality is long and thorny. Although today there is already a positive example of a country that demonstrates a model of adaptation of the state to new dynamic conditions by changing the model of education at the state level. It's about China.

REFERENCES

Ananiev, B. G. (1977). The Problems of Modern Human Science. Academic Press.

Arthur, W. B. (2009). *The Nature of Technology: What it Is and How it Evolves*. Free Press.

BCG. (2020). Governments Must Fix the Skills Mismatch. Boston Consulting Group.

Becker, G. (1985, January). Human capital, effort, and the sexual division of labor. *Journal of Labor Economics*, *3*(1), 33–58. doi:10.1086/298075

Berger, P. L., & Luckmann, T. (1966). *The Social Construction of Reality: a treatise on sociology of knowledge*. Penguin Book.

Beschorner, T. (2013, January). Creating shared value: The one-trick pony approach. *Business Ethics Journal Review*, *1*(17), 106–112. doi:10.12747/bejr2013.01.17

Beschorner, T., & Hajduk, T. (2013). From body of knowledge to ways of thinking: theoretical implications of sector-specific CR in Europe. In T. Beschorner, T. Hajduk, & S. Simeonov (Eds.), *Corporate Responsibility in Europe: Government Involvement in Sector specific Initiatives*. Bertelsmann.

Boston Consulting Group. (2017). Russia 2025: From Average Students to Talents. Moscow: Boston Consulting Group.

Boston Consulting Group. (2019). Mission Talent. Mass Uniqueness: A global challenge for one billion workers. Boston Consulting Group.

Brown, R. G. (1962). *Smoothing, Forecasting and Prediction of Discrete Time Series*. Prentice-Hall.

Carrasco, M., Chandran, P., Chin, V., Hayden, P., Hoteit, L., Subudhi, S., & Werfe, D. (2020). Start Reimaging Government Now. Boston Consulting Group.

Center for Strategic Research. (2018). Twelve Solutions for a New Education. Report of the Center for Strategic Research and High Economic School.

Clarke, A. C. (1954). *Childhood's End*. Sidgwick & Jackson Ltd.

Cook, J. W. (Ed.). (2019). Sustainability, Human Well-Being, and the Future of Education. Palgrave Macmillan. doi:10.1007/978-3-319-78580-6

Craven, M., Sabow, A., Van der Veken, L., & Wilson, M. (2020). *Not the last pandemic: investing now to reimagine public-health systems. In Healthcare Systems & Services, Public Sector, and Social Sector Practices*. McKinsey & Company.

Davydov, V. V. (1996). Developmental Learning Theory. Moscow: INTOR.

de Chardin, T. (1987). *Phenomenon of Human Being*. Russia: Science Publishers.

De Smet, A., Kleinman, S., & Weerda, K. (2021). Beyond matrix organization, the helix organization. *McKinsey Quarterly*. Retrieved from: https://www.McKinsey.com/business-functions/organization/our-insights/the-helix-organization

Dhingra, Emmett, Samo, & Schaninger. (2020). Igniting individual purpose in times of crisis. *McKinsey Quarterly*.

Durkheim, E. (1895). The Rules of Sociological Method. Beverly Hills, CA: Sage Publications.

Edwards, S. (2017). *Pandemic response a cycle of 'panic and neglect,' says World Bank President*. Devex.

Elkonin, D. B. (1989). *Selected Psychological Works*. Pedagogy Publisher.

Freeman, C., & Perez, C. (1988). Structural crisis of adjustment, business cycles and investment behavior. In G. Dosi (Ed.), *Technical Change and Economic Theory*. London: Frances Pinter.

Global Health Security Index. (2019). *Building Collective Action and Accountability*. Johns Hopkins Center for Health Security.

Gumilev, L. N. (2012a). Ethnosphere: History of People and History of Nature. Moscow: Eksmo Publishing House.

Gumilev, L. N. (2012b). Ethnogenesis and the Earth's Biosphere. Moscow: Eksmo Publishing House.

Hartman & Werhane. (2013). Proposition: Shared Value as an Incomplete Mental Model. *Bus Ethics J Rev*., *1*(6), 36–43. .01.06 doi:10.12747/bejr2013

Hodgson, G. M. (2002). Reconstitutive downward causation: social structure and the development of individual agency. In: Fullbrook, E. (Ed.) Intersubjectivity in Economics: Agents and Structures. L.; N.Y.: Routledge. PP. 159-180.

Katz, D., & Kahn, R. L. (1978). Evaluating the Application of Theories of Open Systems Thinking. McKinsey & Company. McKinsey.com

Malone, T. W. (2018). *Superminds. The Surprising Power of People and Computers Thinking Together*. London: Oneworld Publications.

Marx, K. (1995). *Capital: A New Abridgement*. Oxford University Press.

Matten, D. & Crane, A. (2005). Corporate Citizenship: Towards an Extended Theoretical Conceptualization. *Acad Mgmt Rev*., *30*(1), 166–179. .15281448 doi:10.5465/AMR.2005

Mazzucato, M. (2013). The Entrepreneurial State: Debunking Public vs. Private Sector Myths. London; New York: Anthem Press.

Mazzucato, M. (2018). *The Value of Everything: Making and Taking in the Global Economy*. UK. Allen Lane; Penguin Random House.

McKinsey Global Institute. (2020). *Prioritizing Health: A Prescription for Prosperity*. Special Report. Retrieved from: https://www.McKinsey.com/industries/healthcare-systems-and-services/ our-insights/ prioritizing-health-a-prescription-for-prosperity

McKinsey Global Institute. (2021). *Reskilling China: Transforming the World's Largest Workforce into Lifelong Learners*. Executive Summary. www.McKinsey.com/mgi

Mincer, J., & Polachek, S. (1995). Family investments in human capital: earnings of women (1974)'. In: Humphries, Jane (ed.), Gender and economics, Aldershot, England Brookfield, Vermont, USA: Edward Elgar. PP. 317–349.

Nordhaus, W. D. (1994). *Managing the Global Commons. The Economics of Climate Change*. The MIT Press.

North, D. (1996). *Institutions, Institutional Change and Economic Performance*. Cambridge University Press.

North, D. (2005). *Understanding the Process of Economic Change*. Princeton University Press. doi:10.1515/9781400829484

OECD. (2016). *Global Competency for an Inclusive World.* Retrieved from: https://www.oecd.org/pisa/aboutpisa/Global-competency-for-an-inclusive-world. pdf

OECD. (2019). Job polarization and the work profile of the middle class. *Cope Policy Brief.* Retrieved from: https://oe.cd/middle-class-2019

Perez, C. (2002). Technological Revolutions and Financial Capital. Cheltenham, UK: E. Elgar. doi:10.4337/9781781005323

Piaget, J. V. F. (2008). The Psychology of Intelligence. Moscow: Direct-Media.

Pilipenko, A. I. (1997). *Cognitive barriers in teaching physics and methodological principles for overcoming them.* The Dissertation Abstract for a Scientific Degree of Doctor of Pedagogics. Moscow: Russian Academy of Education Publisher.

Pilipenko, A. I. (2015). *Innovative Models of Education: The Aspect of Psychological and Cognitive Barriers*. http://ssrn.com/abstract=2597968

Pilipenko, A. I., Pilipenko, O. I., & Pilipenko, Z. A. (2019). Education and inclusive development: puzzle of low-learning equilibrium. In B. S. Sergi (Ed.), *Modeling Economic Growth in Contemporary Russia* (pp. 163–198). London: Emerald Publishing Limited. doi:10.1108/978-1-78973-265-820191006

Porter, M., & Kramer, M. (2011, January-February). Creating shared value. *Harvard Business Review*, *89*(1/2), 62–77. https://hbr.org/2011/01/the-big-ideacreating-shared-value

Richards, D. (1991, June 16). Edward Albee and the road not taken. *New York Times*.

Schaefer, S. M., Morozink Boylan, J., van Reekum, C. M., Lapate, R. C., Norris, C. J., Ryff, C. D., & Davidson, R. J. (2013). Purpose in life predicts better emotional recovery from negative stimuli. *PLoS One*, *8*(11), e80329. doi:10.1371/journal.pone.0080329 PMID:24236176

Scherer, A., & Palazzo, G. (2007). Toward a Political Conception of Corporate Responsibility: Business and Society Seen from a Habermasian Perspective. *Academy of Management Review*, *32*(4), 1096–1120. doi:10.5465/amr.2007.26585837

Schultz, T. W. (1960). Capital Formation by Education. *Journal of Political Economy*, *68*(6), 571–583. doi:10.1086/258393

Schultz, T. W. (1961). Investment in human capital. *The American Economic Review*, *51*(1), 1–17.

Schumpeter, J. A. (1949). The Theory of Economic Development: An Inquiry into Profits, Capital, Credit, Interest, and the Business Cycle. Harvard University Press.

Schwab, K. (2016). *The Fourth Industrial Revolution*. World Economic Forum.

Schwab, K. (2018). *Shaping the Future of the Fourth Industrial Revolution*. World Economic Forum.

Schwab, K., & Malleret, T. (2020). *COVID-19: The Great Resert*. World Economic Forum Publishing.

Schwab, K., & Malleret, T. (2020). *COVID-19's legacy: This is how to get the Great Reset right. In Sustainable Development Impact Summit.* WEF.

Schwartz, S. (2012). An overview of the Schwartz Theory of Basic Values. *Online Readings in Psychology and Culture*, *2*(1). doi:10.9707/2307-0919.1116

Schwartz, S. H., Cieciuch, J., Vecchione, M., Davidov, E., Fischer, R., Beierlein, C., Ramos, A., Verkasalo, M., Lönnqvist, J.-E., Demirutku, K., Dirilen-Gumus, O., & Konty, M. (2012). Refining the theory of basic individual values. *Journal of Personality and Social Psychology*, *103*(4), 663–688. doi:10.1037/a0029393 PMID:22823292

Shchedrovitsky, G. P. (1997). Philosophy. Science. Methodology. Moscow.

Slobodchicov, V. I., & Isaev, E. I. (1995). Human Psychology. Moscow: Academic Press.

Slobodchicov, V. I., & Isaev, E. I. (2000). Psychology of Human Development. Moscow: Academic Press.

Slobodchicov, V. I., & Isaev, E. I. (2013). Psychology of Human Education. Formation of Subjectivity in Educational Processes. Moscow: Academic Press.

Taleb, N. N. (2012). Antifragile: Things That Gain from Disorder. New York, NY: Random House.

UNESCO. (2016). *Global Education Monitoring Report, 2016. Education for People and Planet: Creating Sustainable Futures for All.* Paris: UNESCO. Retrieved from: http://unesdoc.unesco.org/ images/0024/002457/ 245752e.pdf

UNESCO. (2017). *Accountability in Education: Meeting our Commitments*. Global Education Monitoring Report. UNESCO Publishing.

United Nations. (2012). *Back to Our Common Future Sustainable Development in the 21st Century (SD21) Project.* Summary for policymakers.

Ushinsky, K. D. (2005). Selected Works (Vol. 4). Moscow: Academic Press.

Veber, M. (1947). *The Theory of Social and Economic Organization*. Oxford University Press.

Vernadsky, W. I. (1960). Biosphere. In Selected works. Moscow: Academic Press.

Vernadsky, W. I. (2018). Philosophy of Science. In Selected Works. Moscow: Youwright Publisher.

Vygotsky, L. S. (1960). Development of Higher Mental Functions. Moscow: Nauka Publisher.

WEF. (2018). *Towards a Reskilling Revolution: A Future of Jobs for All.* World Economic Forum.

Winthrop, R., & McGivney, E. (2016). Skills for a Changing World: Advancing Quality Learning for Vibrant Societies. Washington, DC: Center for Universal Education, Brookings Institution.

World Economic Forum. (2016). *Industry Agenda. New Vision for Education Unlocking the Potential of Technology*. World Economic Forum.

Zadek, S. (2001). *The Civil Corporation: The New Economy of Corporate Citizenship*. London: Routledge.

Conclusion

Fundamentals of the Theory of Shocks: The End of Humanity's Childhood and Reflections on the Future

The **first chapter** of the book outlined the steps required to establish the foundations of shocks' theory. They were implemented in subsequent **chapters**, and after the finishing **Chapter 11**, the authors tried to draw conclusions and outline further prospects for the development of shocks' theory.

First, it was necessary to define the concept of shocks: to find out the essence of the shock phenomenon and describe the forms of its manifestation. In fact, it was about turning the phenomenon of shock from the thing-in-itself, according to Immanuel Kant, into a category that everyone understands.

At this stage, it was necessary to build the logic of the study of shocks in such a sequence so that it becomes clear why they cause such devastating consequences for national economic systems. Following dialectical logic, the system as an integrity retains its stability, since it has structural connections that are designed to provide it with any changes in the system itself. Therefore, in order to violate its integrity, it is necessary to influence its structural connections (if we leave aside extraordinary phenomena such as man-made disasters and other similar destruction). And only in this way can you have a serious impact on the stability of the system.

A huge amount of historical material on shocks and crises has confirmed the validity of this assumption. On this basis, the authors formulated the first proposition related to shocks: their impact on the economic system is large, since shocks affect structural ties, breaking them. *So, it is advisable to consider* ***shocks*** *in connection with their destructive effect on the structural connections of the system.*

Those market ties that are characterized by constancy, repeatability, stability become structural. as such, they begin to mediate a certain order of exchange, which manifests itself as a pattern of their change (complication). It follows that *shocks*, in order to destroy the structural connections of the system and affect its integrity, must be internally embedded into the order of changes in the structural connections. In other words, *shocks* destroy the structural connections of the system, being built into the mechanism of self-movement of systems, which is predetermined by the ability of the structure, while changing, to ensure the stability and integrity of the system. So, *shocks*, in fact, are phenomena that can negatively affect the integrity (stability) of the system (economic), destroying its structural ties. *Shocks* have this ability only because they are objectively embeded into the self-propelled mechanism of the system, i.e. mediate a change in its structural ties and the operation of laws regulating the self-movement of systemic integrity.

If the essence of *shocks* is hidden from view, then the external manifestations of shocks are well understood by everyone. A shock is realized in the market of objects of exchange when market prices break away from their base level, overcome a certain marginal level, then structural ties are broken and do not return immediately to an equilibrium state. On this basis, the authors consider all shocks to be price in terms of their form of manifestation, although they are still tied to the object of exchange (oil shock, debt shock, credit shock, etc.).

Further logic of the study of shocks was dictated by their "multi-layered nature". As a mediator in the implementation of the dialectical laws of self-movement of systemic integrities, they are implemented in the object, subjective and process components.

Second, the study of the process component of the shock phenomenon turned out to be the most fruitful. The easiest way was to identify the form of self-movement of the economic system as an integrity that the existing economies have gone through due to the complication of their market exchange. With the emergence of stable dialectical pairs in exchange, structural ties began to be regulated by the law of unity and struggle of opposites, and shocks mediated their turning point - during the transition from unity to a struggle of opposites. The horizontal structures destroyed under the influence of shocks were restored rather quickly, since their stability was provided by cause-and-effect relationships, concluded within the framework of the dialectical pairs themselves.

Any shock was accompanied by a crisis, during which ineffective structural ties were replaced by new ones aimed at ensuring the integrity of the system. At this stage of the study of shocks, the authors formed an idea of a static economy, the self-movement of which was carried out due to the self-structuring of connections (in the process of self-organization of the system), when the horizontal structure was restored due to the shock "rejection" of non-working connections and their replacement with new ones that strengthen the system integrity.

Third, the analysis of structural changes at the stage of self-organization of economic systems under the influence of the law of transition of quantitative changes to qualitative ones made it possible to identify the specifics of self-structuring (complication) of the system in order to strengthen its integrity. Horizontal structures began to generate similar ones, but located vertically by implementing the principle of upwards causation. In other words, the process of self-organization of the system took place by building a vertical hierarchy of structural levels-causes and structural levels-effects. The authors have shown that as long as higher levels successfully solve problems of lower levels, the system is strengthened. But when the structural hierarchy becomes too cumbersome, jeopardizing the integrity of the system, shocks mediate a turning point in the law of transition from quantitative to qualitative changes. In this case, the vertical interdependence changes, and the structural levels-consequences turn into causes of destruction of the lower structural levels. Shocks generate crises, which in this case become more prolonged and cause more significant economic losses. The fragility of the system increases due to the rupture of causes and effects in the vertical relationships of dialectical pairs. In other words, the interconnections of horizontal dialectical pairs begin to be accompanied by additional vertically located cause-and-effect relationships.

This is how the potential for self-movement of systemic wholes is exhausted at the stage of their self-organization due to self-structuring (complication of the system structure).

Fourth, following dialectical logic, the authors understood that the self-movement of human-created systems is continuous in time. In other words, if the potential of one way of self-movement is exhausted, then another one comes to replace it. And it all starts all over again. So gradually, the authors began to take root the idea that the statics of systems, as a repetition of the past, the generation of similar structures, makes it possible to fully use the potential of the unlimited possibilities of the organization in the process of positive and negative selection of economic activities. But there is an end to everything, connected with the fact that a shock adjustment of certain segments of structural ties to strengthen the integrity of the system can bring it to the limit of maximum fragility. Then the entire structural basis of the integral system in the aggregate of its horizontal and vertical levels will collapse.

Fifth, in this case, the shock mechanism will mediate the action of the law of negation of negation, destroying both the vertical hierarchy (first negation) of structural levels and the horizontal level that gave rise to them (second negation). So, shocks realize the point of no return of a static system to its self-organization, this is how the continuity of the previous stage of self-organization of the system breaks and it is forced to make a "jump" into a new stage, indefinite, unknown, which in fact represents its dynamics at the stage of self-development.

Sixth, the study of the subjective component of shocks based on dialectical approaches allowed the authors to somewhat minimize the uncertainty of this stage of self-movement, in which national communities found themselves as a result of the shock caused by the COVID-19 pandemic. Thus, the study of the phenomenon of subjectivization of vertical structural ties in the context of the expansion of financial transactions and the generation of new and new segments of financial markets led to the conclusion that this is natural. As cardinal changes mature in the mechanisms of self-moving system integrity, the rise of the human factor becomes a necessary condition for structuring a new dynamic reality.

Seventh, this is due to many circumstances, the main of which are the following: (1) the stage of self-development of system integrity is accompanied by the formation of a qualitatively different technological base (today predetermined by the technological revolution 4.0) and only a critical mass of intellectually autonomous individuals can realize this epochal mission; (2) the peculiarity of such individuals is realized in their ability to self-organize (subject to high-quality education and health care) and to self-development for the purpose of realizing their creative abilities; (3) solving the problem (1) and (2) at the stage of self-development of systemic integrity in the economy can only be done by large and largest companies that are able to organize the activities of talented individuals within companies and, on the basis of the latest technology, create superteams of people and technology, (4) such companies are capable of self-organization, mediating the mechanism of downwards causation, and of self-development - mediating the mechanism of upwards causation; (5) At the same time, such fundamental changes in technology, in the economy, and in society will cause the displacement of capital-centrism as the dominant principle of self-organization (in a static economy) and its replacement by human-centrism in all spheres of human life at the stage of self-development of systems.

Eight, the main obstacle on the way of human movement towards dynamics, according to logic, can become the state, which was traditionally "sharpened" to ensure the equilibrium of the economic system and its financial stability by fiscal methods of influencing the representatives of society. It can only change in the future, when intellectually autonomous individuals become a critical mass of society. However, only the state can create it, only will it not "keep society in its usual childhood"? Although already today thoughts are being expressed that the future has already come, only the state and society have not yet realized this.

The **ninth direction** of further deepening the theory of shocks appeared after the authors familiarized themselves with the deep considerations expressed by the reviewer of this manuscript (Schoenman, 1966, Edmans, 2011). It seems very promising to consider the categories of "stocks" and "flows" in the context of the self-organization of systemic integrity in the economy and society and their self-development. Even a surface glance at these problems reveals certain associations of "flows" in connection with the complication of the structure of a static economy, and "stocks" in the context of the formation of a new structure of a dynamic economy at the stage of its self-development. In the latter case, it is about a fundamental restructuring of everything that society has: stocks of capital, labor, technological knowledge, etc.

The **tenth direction** of further research is inspired by the works of M. Mazzucato (2013, 2018), who raises the problem of "public values", the creation of which is of a collective nature. This acquires special significance in the context of the construction of post-covid reality, the need to restore societal integrity, return citizens' trust in the state and awareness of the new role of the state in society as objective conditions for structuring a dynamic socio-economic system.

What's next with shock theory? It is necessary to develop the applied part of the theory, to deepen its positive and normative parts, to develop the idea of shocks in the construction of a future dynamic reality. So, the short list of the research program is long. Only to be in time.

REFERENCES

Edmans, A. (2011). Short-term termination without deterring long-term investment: A theory of debt and buyout. *Journal of Financial Economics*. Retrieved from: www.elsevier.com/locate/jfec

Mazzucato, M. (2013). *The Entrepreneurial State: Debunking Public vs. Private Sector Myths*. Anthem Press.

Mazzucato, M. (2018). *The Value of Everything: Making and Taking in the Global Economy*. Penguin Random House.

Schoenman, J. C. (1966). An Analog of Short-term Economic Change. Stockholm Economic Studies.

About the Authors

Olga Ivanovna Pilipenko received her diploma of Higher Education from the Moscow State Institute for Foreign Relations (MGIMO University) in 1975. In 1981 she received her degree of Candidate of Science in Economics from the Institute of Latin America of the USSR' Academy of Science. In 1994 she received a degree of Doctor of Economics from Lomonosov's Moscow State University. She worked as a full Professor for many Russian Universities: All-Russian Correspondence Financial and Economic Institute (VSFEI), People's Friendship University of Russia (RUDN), Lomonosov's Moscow State University, Russian Presidential Academy of National Economy and Public Administration (RANERA) (last work). In the 1990s, under the interstate exchange program, she trained in Denmark (Hearning Institute of Technology, and Aarhus University). She has more than 130 publications, including ones indexed by RISC (RF), Scopus, Web of Science. Her scientific interests lie in the areas of bifurcation effects' modeling in global financial markets in connection with shocks, interaction of factors of global financial stability, of monetary circulation, of public finance, of monetary and fiscal policies interaction, of cyclical development of economic and financial systems in context with theory of shocks.

Zoya Andreevna Pilipenko received her Master's Degree in Economics from Lomonosov's Moscow State University in 2003. In 2004 she received her degree of Candidate of Science in World Economy, Finance, and Banking from Lomonosov's Moscow State University. In 2013 she received her degree of Doctor of Science in World Economy, Finance, and Banking from Lomonosov's Moscow State University. She worked as a financial analyst for the Insurance Company "Gefest" (Russia, Moscow), the Joint Stock Company "Sberbank" (Russia, Moscow). For the last 15 years she has been working for the Central Bank of Russia. She has teaching and research experience: more than 50 publications, indexed RISC (RF), Scopus, Web of Science. She has got certificates in Banking and Finance from practical seminars in Great Britain, Luxembourg, Austria, Italy, and France. She has got certificates in Banking and Finance from practical seminars in Great Britain, Luxembourg, Austria, Italy and France. Her research interests lie in the field of shocks theory and the implementation of dialectical laws in the processes of self-movement of systemic integrity in economics and finance, as well as the peculiarities of the formation and implementation of monetary and fiscal policy in relation to certain sectors of the financial market at the national and global levels.

Andrey Igorevich Pilipenko was graduated from the Leningrad State University (Faculty of Mathematics and Mechanics) in 1972. In 1984 he received his degree of Candidate of Science in Physics and Mathematics from the Institute of Physical Chemistry of the USSR' Academy of Science. In 1998 he received a degree of Doctor of Pedagogical Sciences from the Russian Academy of Education. For more than 40 years he worked as full Professor for many Russian Universities: All-Russian Correspondence Financial and Economic Institute (VSFEI), People's Friendship University of Russia (RUDN), Lomonosov's Moscow State University, Russian Presidential Academy of National Economy and Public Administration (RANERA) (last work). He was invited as a Professor by Gumilyov' Eurasian National University (Kazakhstan). He has more than 130 publications, including ones indexed by RISC (RF), Scopus, Web of Science. His scientific interests lie in the areas of mathematical modeling of processes of cyclical changes in economics and finance in terms of a synergistic approach to nonlinear fluctuations and waves; adaptation of the Heisenberg uncertainty principle in the choice of management decisions in public finance; stochastic processes in the context of shocks theory; the theory of psychological and cognitive barriers in education in the context of the mechanisms of self-organization (education) and self-development (socialization) of a person in post-coronavirus reality.

Index

C

cause-and-effect relationships 14, 58, 67, 72, 79, 82, 88, 95, 136-137, 146, 158, 180, 203
collective behavior 186, 273, 279, 300, 308, 349, 374
COVID-19 pandemic 24-25, 30, 32-33, 51, 55-56, 88, 96, 98, 102-103, 115, 127-129, 131, 134, 143, 147, 168-169, 191, 197, 203-204, 206-207, 210, 212-213, 217-218, 229, 233-234, 242-246, 248, 250-253, 257, 259-261, 263, 266-269, 272-276, 278, 281, 283, 286-288, 296, 299-301, 304-305, 307-308, 314, 316-318, 320-323, 325-327, 329, 331, 334, 337, 340, 345-347, 349-350, 352-354, 367, 369, 373-376, 382-383
creative destruction 193, 272, 274, 276, 280, 300, 307, 349, 371, 374, 377, 383
cyclical nature 154, 159

D

dialectical contradictions 62, 75, 80, 147, 150, 184
dialectical pairs 8, 18, 38-42, 51, 57-60, 64-67, 69-73, 75-77, 79-80, 82, 85-87, 94-96, 102, 106, 113-114, 117, 120, 136, 144-146, 169, 174, 177, 180-182, 187, 189, 193-195, 300, 347, 377
dialectical unity 13, 25, 61, 68, 116, 119, 129, 156, 171, 180, 235, 314-316
dialectically complex 101-102, 115-116, 124-125, 171, 174, 177, 189, 267, 273, 301-302, 307, 346, 349, 367, 371, 374-379

E

endogenous source 139, 142, 158

F

fault line 260, 268, 275

G

global financial crisis 1, 9, 14, 30, 32-35, 51, 59, 80, 82, 85, 88, 94-95, 152, 154, 184, 218-219, 228, 260, 333
Great Depression 30, 33, 51, 96, 160, 205, 242-243

H

harmonic oscillations 12, 21-22, 45, 122, 124
Homo Sapiens 168, 197, 377
human-centric principles 204, 232, 267, 274, 280-281, 288, 291, 301, 304-305, 308, 347, 349, 367, 375, 383
humanitarian catastrophe 213, 229-230, 243, 302, 307, 316-317, 325-326, 331, 340, 345, 347, 382

J

J.M. Keynes 137, 151, 158, 204, 315

L

linear oscillator 45-46, 122-123
loss-making position 89, 96

N

non-harmonic oscillator 90-91

P

post-coronavirus reality 242, 273, 279, 283, 297-298, 305, 307-308, 340, 366, 383
propagation problem 2-3, 5, 23, 25

Q

quantitative changes 13-14, 25, 30, 39, 42, 51, 57-59, 66, 71-77, 79-80, 86-88, 94-95, 101-102, 114,

116-119, 130, 136, 141, 145, 151-152, 154, 156-157, 167-168, 176, 180, 186-187, 189-190, 195, 202, 207, 228, 233, 260

R

Ragnar Frisch 1-2, 14, 17-20, 23-26

S

socio-economic system 55, 98, 103, 193, 223, 232-233, 235, 269, 273, 280, 282, 307-309, 316-317, 340, 348
structural interactions 40-41, 59, 66, 94-95, 115, 143-144, 146, 158, 181, 218, 274, 300, 374
systemic integrity 14, 25, 33-34, 36-40, 42, 51-52, 58-59, 65-66, 68-70, 73, 75, 89, 94-95, 100, 114-115, 117, 123, 125, 130, 135, 142, 144, 146, 168, 191, 197, 202-203, 207, 213, 217, 227, 229, 233, 235, 276, 316, 325, 341, 345-347, 366, 369, 374-379, 382

T

technological paradigm 100-103, 105, 107-109, 111, 113, 115-116, 118, 124-127, 130, 135, 139, 141-142, 157, 192, 204, 229-232, 242, 269, 274, 290, 302, 307-308, 348, 379, 383
technological progress 100, 104-107, 119, 124-126, 129-130, 137-143, 157-158, 167, 227, 230, 259, 339, 366
technological revolution 101-103, 108-111, 113, 115, 125-127, 129-130, 135, 139-141, 158, 189, 192, 197-198, 227, 232, 235, 259, 262, 301-302, 338, 340-341, 345-347, 349, 353, 355, 357, 374, 376-377, 379, 382

www.ingramcontent.com/pod-product-compliance
Lightning Source LLC
LaVergne TN
LVHW062116300926
849161LV00010B/2473